AF714623

Labour law in Nigeria

Malthouse law books

Adah C. E., *The Nigerian Law of Evidence*
Egweike, K., *Nigerian Commercial Law: Agency*
Egweike, K., *Nigerian Commercial Law: Hire Purchase*
Egweike, K., *Nigerian Commercial Law: Contract*
Sagay, I., *Family Law in Nigeria*
Sagay, I., *Law of Succession and Inheritance in Nigeria*
Shoyele O., *Principles and Practice of Administrative Law in Nigeria*
Shoyele O., *Succession: States and Governments*
Uvieghara E. E., *Sale of Goods (and Hire Purchase) Law in Nigeria*
Yakubu, J. A., *Press Law in Nigeria*
Yakubu J. A., *Limits to the Application of Foreign Laws*
Yakubu J. A., *International Contracts: Evolution and Theory*
Yakubu J. A.,(ed.) *Administration of Justice in Nigeria*
Yakubu J. A. & Oyewo, A. T., *Criminal Law & Procedure in Nigeria*

Labour law in Nigeria

Egerton E. Uvieghara

MALTHOUSE PRESS LTD

Malthouse Press Limited
8 Amore Street, Off Toyin Street,
PO Box 500, Ikeja, Lagos State, Nigeria

Lagos, Benin, Ibadan, Jos, Oxford, Port-Harcourt, Zaria

All rights reserved. No part of this publication may be reproduced, stored in a retrieval system, or transmitted, in any form or by any means, electronic, mechanical, photocopying, recording, or otherwise, without the prior permission in writing of Malthouse Press Limited.

This book is sold subject to the condition that it shall not, by way of trade or otherwise, be lent, re-sold, hired out, or otherwise circulated without the publisher's prior consent, in writing, in any form of binding or cover other than that in which it is published and without a similar condition including this condition being imposed on the subsequent purchaser.

© E. E. Uvieghara 2001
First Published 2001
ISBN 9-7826011-60

Dedication

To my late Father.

Servants, obey in all things your masters according to the flesh; not with eye services, as men pleasers; but in singleness of heart, fearing God:

Masters, give unto your servants that which is just and equal; knowing that ye, also have a master in heaven.

Colossians 3:22; 4:1

Preface

The writing of this book was undertaken during my sabbatical leave at the Nigerian Institute of Advanced Legal Studies, Lagos. Indeed the Institute accommodated me for the sole purpose of doing so. I am most grateful for the sponsorship. I am particularly grateful to the Chairman of the Council of the Institute, Dr. Adolphus Karibi-Whyte JSC, the first Director-General of the Institute, Dr. Akintola Aguda and his successor, Prof. A. Ajomo, the Secretary of the Institute, the staff of the Library and other staff of the Institute. I believe the book will meet the very high standards expected by the Institute.

The book is comprehensive enough in coverage and depth to meet the needs of law students, legal practitioners, trade union officials and members, and employers and their employees including personnel managers. For the benefit of law students and legal practitioners, I have indulged in fairly extensive quotations from several judgements. I believe in reading judgements first hand but unfortunately law reports are not readily available especially outside Lagos.

Lastly, I wish to express my profound gratitude to Mr. V. C. Richards of the Institute of Advanced Legal Studies and my Secretary Mrs. F. Oduguwa who, between them, typed the manuscript.

E. E. Uvieghara
Nigerian Institute of Advanced Legal Studies/Faculty of Law
University of Lagos
1 May, 1989

PS: The manuscript for this book had to be revised extensively owing to some delay in the publication of the book. My gratitude is due to Mr John Atuanya and Mrs Uddoh who, between them, typed the revised version.

E. E. Uvieghara
Nigerian Law Reform Commission
Federal Secretariat, Ikoyi, Lagos,
1 September, 2000

Contents

PART II: Collective Labour Relations

Table of cases

Ellis v *William Corry & Son Ltd* [1902] 1 KB 38, 188
Elufioye v *Halilu* [1993] 6 NWLR 570; 353, 375, 376, 377, 378
Emerald Construction Co Ltd v *Lowthian* [1966] 1 WLR 691; 475, 477
Emuakpor v *K. Chellaram & Sons (Nig) Ltd* unreported suit No. 5/2A/71, High Court Sapele; 78
Eperokun v *University of Lagos* [1986] 4 NWLR 162; 74, 88, 90
Esimaje Tsegbeyeri v *Glaxo Nig. Ltd* CCHCIJ/11/74, p. 1787; 57, 96
Essien v *University of Calaber* [1990] 3 NWLR 605; 85
Esso Petroleum Co Ltd v *Harpers's Garage (Stourport) Ltd* [1968] AC 269, 328; 24, 42
Estmaco (Kilner House) Ltd v *Greater London Counsel* [1982]1 All ER 437; 375, 376
Evans v *Bakare* (1974) 1 NMLR 78; 175
Evans v *National Union of Printing, Bookbinding & Paper Workers* [1938] 4 All ER 51; 371
Ewarami v *African Continental Bank* [1978] 4 SC 99; 82
Exchange Telegraph Co v *Gregory and Co* [1896]1 QB 147; 477
Express Newspapers Ltd v *Macshane* [1980] 1 All ER 65 78; 489
Eyutchae v *Nigerian Television Authority* [1986] 5 NWLR 395; 88
Facenda Chicken Ltd v *Fowler* [1983] IRLR 61; [1985] 1 All ER 724; 40
Fairman v *Oakford* (1860) 5 H & N, 635; 56
Fajemirokun v *Nigeria Airways Ltd* [1979] 3 LRN 238, [1979] 4-6 CCHCJ 198; 82
Fakuade v *OAUTH* [1993] 5 NWLR 47 57; 73, 83
Falomo v *Lagos State Public Service Commission* (1977) 5 SC 51; 90
Famuyiwa v *Folawiyo* [1972] 1 All NLR (Pt 2), 11; 302, 303
Faramus v *Film Artistes Association* [1964] AC 925; 344, 358, 362
Farquhar v *Chance Brothers Ltd* (1951) 2 TLR 666; 216
Farrow v *Wilson* (1869) LR 4 CP 744; 47
Fasesan v *NPA* Judgement of Federal Court of Appeal, Lagos (1984) p. 281; 95
Fastock Marketing Corporation Ltd v *Morgan* [1958] 1 All ER 646; 179, 182
Fawcett v *Cash* (1834) 10 ER 1026; 55
Federal Civil Service Commission v *Laoye* [1989] 2 NWLR 652; 90
Federal Ministry of Health v *National Association of Nigerian Nurses and Midwives* [1980-81] NICLR 18; 420
Federal Superphosphate Fertilizer Co Ltd v *Otaru* Federal Court of Appeal Judgments, Kaduna Div. July-Sept 1985 p.45; 153
Federal Supply & Cold Storage Company of South Africa v *Angehm* (1910) 103 LT 150; 67
Fenn v *Miller* (1900) 1 GB 788, 272
Fenton v *Owners of Ship Kelvin* [1925] 2 KB 473; 296
Fenton v *Thorley & Co Ltd* [1903] AC 443; 254
Ferguson v *O'Gorman* [1937] IR 620; 451, 485
Finch v *Telegraph Construction & Maintenance Co Ltd* [19491] 1 All ER 452; 233
Fitch v *Dewes* [1921] 2 AC 158; 43

Table of Statutes

Chapter references are to the Laws of the Federation of Nigeria, 1990 unless otherwise stated.

United Kingdom Statutes

States' Statutes

Part One

Individual employer-employee relation

Chapter 1

Introduction

The laws which govern employment occupy a position of considerable importance in any modern society. This is so because of the tremendous contribution which workers can make to national growth and development as well as the general well-being of the nation's citizenry. Issues of high unemployment, rampant strikes and other forms of industrial conflict, if not properly regulated and managed, may not only adversely affect the national economy but also its political stability. There is no doubt that an unstable political and economic climate discourages investment, especially foreign investment.

Labour law has a vital role to play in the mobilization of the work force for national growth and development. The Constitution itself seeks to ensure that the Nigerian worker is able to participate fully in the economic, social and political development of the nation. It provides that the state must direct its policy towards ensuring, *inter alia*, that:

(a) all citizens without discrimination on any ground whatsoever have the opportunity for securing adequate means of livelihood as well as adequate opportunities to secure suitable employment;
(b) conditions of work are just and humane;
(c) the health, safety and welfare of all persons in employment are safeguarded and not endangered or abused;
(d) there is equal pay for equal work without discrimination on account of sex or on any other ground whatsoever.[1]

It is the duty and responsibility of all organs of government and of all authorities and persons exercising legislative, executive or judicial powers to conform to, observe and apply these injunctions.[2] Although these rights, if they may be so-called, are not justiciable rights,[3] there can be no doubt that they provide a

---

[1] S. 17(3) Constitution of the Federal Republic of Nigeria, 1999. All references to the Constitution in this chapter are to this Constitution.

[2] S. 13

[3] S. 6(6) (c)

significant yardstick by which the reasonableness, if not the constitutionality, of our labour laws may be measured.

Sources of labour law

The sources of labour law include the Constitution, legislation and the common law. The common law includes the decisions of both the Nigerian and English courts.[4] However, the decisions of the English courts are merely persuasive, although in practice they are accorded the highest respect. Also decisions from other Commonwealth, even non-Commonwealth common law countries are found helpful. It does not appear that customary law has contributed in any way to our body of labour laws.

The power to legislate on labour is vested in the federal government exclusively.[5] Thus all labour statutes apply throughout the country unless a particular labour statute provides otherwise. Labour is defined as including trade unions, industrial relations, conditions, safety and welfare of labour; industrial disputes, prescribing a national minimum wage for the federation or any part of it, and industrial arbitrations.[6] It may be noted that item H 17(a) of the Concurrent List[7] also vests power in government for the Federation to make laws for the federation or any part of it with respect to the health, safety and welfare of persons employed to work in factories, offices, or other premises. This provision seems superfluous in view of the wide constitutional definition of labour and the exclusive power vested in the same government to legislate on the matters within the definition. There is no doubt that the health, safety and welfare of persons employed to work in factories, offices or other premises, fall within the definition of labour. Item H[8] also provides that the states are not precluded from enacting statutes with respect to the same matters. This again would appear to be in conflict with the exclusive power of the federal government to legislate on labour. However, when there is any inconsistency between any statutes enacted by the federal and any state government, the federal law prevails to the extent of the inconsistency.[9]

---

[4] For the reception of English law see S. 32 Interpretation Act, Cap 192 Laws of the Federation of Nigeria, 1990. A detailed consideration of the reception of English trade union laws is undertaken in E. E. Uvieghara, *Trade Union Law in Nigeria*, EPC Benin-City. For a detailed consideration of the reception of English law generally see Obilade, *Nigerian Legal System*, Sweet & Maxwell, London.

[5] S. 4(2) Constitution;

[6] Item 33 Exclusive legislative List, 2nd schedule of the Constitution.

[7] Part II 2nd Schedule of the Constitution.

[8] Paragraph 19

[9] S. 4(5) Constitution.

Who is an employee?

Employment may arise out of an agreement which is not enforceable in the law courts because it lacks consideration which is one of the essential ingredients of enforceability. For example, any one may offer his services or labour to another for no reward or payment. We are not here concerned with that type of employment which, in any case, is a rare phenomenon today and is more likely to be met with only within family arrangements. The typical employment today arises from a contract - an enforceable agreement between one person who offers his services or labour to another in return for payment.

Employment may, however, give rise to a number of different relationships. A person may be employed as an employee,[10] an independent contractor[11] or as an agent. Although, the relationship of employer and employee bears resemblance to those of both the principal and independent contractor, and the principal and agent relationship, there is no doubt that the former relationship is distinguishable from either of the two latter cognate relationships. Indeed there are some practical reasons why this distinction may sometimes have to be made. In the first place, the common law implies certain duties and rights in the relation of employer and employee which are not necessarily applicable in these other relationships.[12] Secondly, the common law doctrine of vicarious liability is confined to the relation of employer and employee.[13] An employer may be held vicariously liable for a tort committed by his employee in the course of the employee carrying out his duties under his contract of employment. Thirdly, the various labour statutes do not generally apply to those who are not employees at common law.

Where the well-known features of an employer-employee relationship are present, it is easy enough to identify the relationship. This is so in the vast majority of cases.

Among the common features of a service contract are an obligation by the employer to employ a man, and to pay him an agreed or proper wage, and a right to control his services and the manner in which he performs them, and to dismiss him if reasonable cause is shown; and, on the workman's side, he must obey all reasonable directions, present himself for work at an agreed hour, and continue

[10] In early law, and even quite often today, employee is referred to as a servant and the employer as a master; the relation is the same.
[11] The independent contractor is often referred to or described as a self-employed person.
[12] The implied terms are discussed fully below.
[13] But see below for vicarious liability in respect of an agent.

to work for the agreed period, and will be guilty of breach of contract if he refuses to perform these obligations.[14]

However, difficulties may arise in cases where some of these indices of the relationship are not present. As Denning LJ (as he then was) said in *Stevenson, Jordan and Harrison Ltd* v *MacDonald and Evans*,[15] "it is often easy to recognize a contract of service when you see it, but difficult to say wherein the difference lies."[16] The courts have therefore, over the years, put forward a number of tests for determining whether or not a particular relationship is that of employer-employee.

The control test

The earliest, and best known, if not the decisive, test employed by the courts is the "control" test. In the quotation above, the right of the employer to control an employee's service and the manner in which he performs his duties was mentioned as one of the indices of the employer and employee relationship. Anyone who may be told not only what to do but also how to do it is said to be an employee. Bramwell L. J. expressed this rule in 1880 as follows: A servant is a person subject to the command of his master as to the manner in which he shall do his work.[17] Quite recently the Court of Appeal said:[18] a servant may be defined as any person employed by another to do work for him on the terms that he, the servant, is to be subject to the control and directions of his employer in respect of the manner in which his work is to be done.

The essential factor which separates the employee from the independent contractor is control. As has been said, the employer can tell the employee not only what to do but also how to do it. But the independent contractor is only told what to do and left to carry on in his own way in achieving the agreed result. An independent contractor, therefore, is one who contracts to perform or provide services for another - he is said to be under a contract for services as distinguished from an employee who is under a contract of service. Applying this test, it is difficult to agree with the decision in *Nzenagu* v *Umuahia County Council*.[19] The plaintiff, a printer, won a contract award to supply market toll tickets to the defendant Council. Clause one of the contract spelt out the amount payable and "the contractor shall, to the satisfaction of the employer, execute

---

[14] Per Romer L.J. in *Denham* v *Midland Employers Mutual Assurance Ltd* [1955] 2 QB 437, 446.
[15] (1952) 1 TLR 101.
[16] Ibid:, 111.
[17] *Yewens* v *Noakes* (1880) 6 QBD 530,532-533.
[18] *Union Bank (Nig) Ltd.* v *Ajagu* [1990] 1 NWLR 328, 343
[19] (1965) NMLR 209

such work in all respects in accordance with the signed specification annexed hereto." No variation was to be carried out in the contract "without written authority from the Employer agreeing to the estimate." And Clause 6 provided that if "the contractor fails repeatedly to satisfy the Council...the Council shall be obliged to terminate the contract after three months notice in writing has been served on the contractor. The contract is also terminable by three months' notice served on the Employer by the Contractor." In an action for breach of contract, the court held that the contract was one that imported the relationship of master and servant between the parties and not the ordinary contractual relationship of supplier of goods.

In *Francis Dola* v *Cecilia John*,[20] the appellant, a licensed goldsmith, carried on business as a goldsmith. One Raimi, a trained but as yet unlicensed goldsmith, worked with him. An unlicensed goldsmith was, by law, not permitted to carry on business as a goldsmith on his own but must work under a licensed goldsmith. There was evidence that Raimi had no right to receive jobs from the public but could only get work from the appellant. He was not paid wages but was paid on piece-rate basis. Counsel submitted "that Raimi, being a trained goldsmith, exercised his own discretion as to the mode of doing any work given to him by the appellant and was therefore an independent contractor." The court held he was a servant of the appellant.

The relationship of employer and employee may also be distinguished from that of principal and agent using the control test. Whilst the employer has a right of control over his employee, the principal has no such right over his agent. Generally, an agent can bind his principal contractually to third parties, but an employee has no such power unless he is also appointed an agent or he occupies a position from which he derives the powers of an agent. One significant assimilation between the two relationships seems to have taken place. The employer or the principal may be held vicariously liable for the tort of his employee or "agent" respectively. In *Hans Schenhel* v *A. O. Nigeria Ltd and ATMN Ltd*,[21] the second defendants, who owned mining leases and property in Nigeria, gave a power of attorney to the first defendants to manage and run the mining leases and property. The first defendants employed all the expatriate staff while the second defendants employed all locally recruited staff. The plaintiff, a Swiss national, was employed by the first defendants as a motor mechanic in-charge of the motor repair and transport department at Barakin Ladi, owned by the second defendants. It was one of the duties of the plaintiff to give driving tests to prospective employees of the defendants before being engaged as vehicle

[20] 1973 NNLR, 14; 1973 (1) NMLR 58; 1974, 4, UILR 39; 3, ECSLR 302.
[21] 1967 (2) ALR Comm. 167

drivers. On 4 October, 1960 in the course of testing a driver the plaintiff, who was sitting beside the driver, was injured when their vehicle hit an obstruction. The plaintiff sued the two defendants for the negligence of the driver. The court held that the driver was not the employee of either the defendants at the time of the accident since both sides only contemplated a possible contractual relation in the future. But the court acceded to the submission of the counsel for the plaintiff that the driver was the agent of the second defendants. As the learned judge said, it is, of course, possible for the relationship of principal and agent to arise where the relationship of employer-employee does not. He relied on the decision in *Ormrod* v *Crossville Motor Services Ltd*,[22] in particular the statement of Denning L.J. (as he then was), where he said that:[23]

> It has often been supposed that the owner of a vehicle is only liable for the negligence of the driver if the driver is his servant acting in the course of his employment. That is not correct. The owner is also liable if the driver is his agent, that is to say, if the driver is with the owner's consent, driving the car on the owner's business or for the owner's business or for the owner's purposes.

The position of professionals

The emergence of a class of highly skilled and professional persons in modern times has, however, been seen as limiting the applicability of the control test. It is said that when one is dealing with a professional man, or a man of some particular skill and experience, the control test cannot be the decisive test. "In such cases there can be no question of the employer telling him how to do work; therefore, the absence of control and direction in that sense can be of little, if any, use as a test."[24] That is, of course, true. But it cannot be said to be limited to the employment of professionals or skilled persons. In any employment, it is obvious that there is hardly any room for control in the true sense of telling the employee how to actually carry out his duties. The employee may possess skill which is far in advance of or different from that of the employer or which the employer just does not possess. In such a situation there is clearly no room for control. The problem is further compounded by the impersonal relationships which usually exist in the big corporations of today. However, it is suggested that control is still quite useful as a test if "telling him how to do the work" is

---

[22] [1953] 2 All ER 753.

[23] Ibid., 754-755.

[24] Per Lord Parker C.J. in *Morren* v *Swinton & Pendlebury Borough Council*, [1965] 2 All ER 349, 351.

construed to mean the right to lay down guidelines and give instructions or directives as to how the work is to be carried out. No employer, either of an unskilled or professional man, tells the man how to do the work in the sense of directing him as to how to actually carry out his duties. The man is told what to do and directed as to where and when to do it and then left to get on with the job. As Lord Porter once said: "it is true that in most cases, no orders as to how a job should be done are given or required. The man is left to do his own work in his own way, but the ultimate question is not what specific orders, or whether any specific orders, were given, but who is entitled to give the orders as to how the work should be done."[25] The employer need not possess the relevant skill in order to lay down instructions and limits within which the work must be carried out. In practice the great majority of employers do not possess the relevant skills before laying down the limits within which professionals, who are admittedly employees, carry out their duties. In *Gold* v *Essex County Council*,[26] where nurses in a hospital were held to be employees, MacKinnon L.J. stressed that the principle of respondent superior is not ousted by the fact that a servant has to do work of a skilful or technical character for which the servant has special qualifications. With respect, that is valid.

The independent contractor or agent achieves the stipulated objective by his own devices free from directives from the principal once the work has been properly defined and agreed upon. In *Collins* v *Hertfordshire County Council*,[27] while the full-time house surgeon was held to be an employee the part-time surgeon was not. In *Cassidy* v *Minister of Health*,[28] there is no doubt that the court was influenced by the fact that both the assistant medical officer and the house surgeon were employed on full-time basis. As Somervell L.J. said, they "were employed like the nurses as part of the permanent staff of the hospital."[29]

No doubt, a full-time employment will invariably indicate an employer-employee relationship. Where employment is part-time it does not follow however that the relationship of employer-employee may not be created. It depends on the terms of the contract. The answer depends on a proper consideration of the contractual terms. How much freedom is allowed under the contract? It is suggested that this approach is not different from the multiple or

---

[25] *Mersey Docks & Harbour Board* v *Coggins & Griffiths (Liverpool) Ltd* [1947] AC 1, 17.
[26] [1942] 2 All ER 237.
[27] [1947] I All ER 633.
[28] [1951] 1 All ER 574.
[29] Ibid, 578.

organizational test or even from what Roskill J referred to as determination "by reference to what in modern parlance is called economic reality."[30]

Multiple test

One of the best known statements of this test is that of McCardie J in *Performing Right Society Ltd* v *Mitchell and Booker* where he said:[31]

> The nature of the task undertaken, the freedom of action given, the magnitude of the contract amount, the manner in which it is to be paid, the powers of dismissal and the circumstances under which payment of the reward may be withheld, all these bear on the solution of the question of who is a servant.

Lord Thankerton re-stated similar indicia of the employer-employee relationship in a more concise form in *Short* v *J. and W. Henderson Ltd*:[32] These are (a) the master's power of selection of his servant; (b) the payment of wages or other remuneration; and (c) the master's right of suspension or dismissal. But a contract of employment may exist even though some of these indicia are absent altogether or only present in an unusual form. For example, the master's power of selection or to pay wages or salary may be delegated to a third party. However, control seems to be crucial. It is certainly the one most relied upon by the courts. As McCardie J said in the *Performing Right Society* case, it seems "reasonably clear that the final test, and if there be a final test, and certainly the test to be generally applied, lies in the nature and degree of detailed control over the person alleged to be a servant"[33] and added that although this circumstance of control is one only of several to be considered, that it is usually of vital importance. Lord Thankerton made the same point in *Short's* case when he said:[34]

> The principal requirement of a contract of service is the right of the master in some reasonable sense to control the method of doing the work, and...this factor of superintendent and control has frequently been treated as critical and decisive of the legal quality of the relationship.

If control is viewed in the sense in which it has been suggested it should be, it is submitted that clearly, there was control by the Local Authority in *Morren* v

---

[30] *Argent* v *Minister of Social Security* [1968] 3 All ER 208.
[31] [1924] 1 KB 762, 767.
[32] (1946) 62 *TLR* 427, 429 these indicia were applied in *Thomas* v *Local Government Service Board*, unreported High Court of Western Region Suit No. (WN) 1/169/64.
[33] [1924] 1 KB 762, 767.
[34] (1946) 62 TLR 427, 429.

Swinton & Pendlebury Borough Council.[35] The Local Authority appointed the engineer, paid his salary, mileage and subsistence allowances and national insurance contributions. Above all, he was employed by the Authority to work with the consulting engineers who were under a contract to carry out some work for the Authority. In other words, the engineer worked within the general directive of the Local Authority. Indeed the issue was not whether the engineer was an employee. It was not in doubt that he was an employee and not an independent contractor or agent.

Organizational test

In *Stevenson, Jordan and Harrison Ltd* v *MacDonald and Evans*,[36] Denning LJ (as he then was) enunciated the test now commonly referred to as the organization or integration test as follows: "...under a contract of service, a man is employed as part of the business, and his work is done as an integral part of the business, whereas, under a contract for services, his work, although done for the business, is not integrated into it but is only accessory to it."[37] One year later, he re-stated the same test when he said that "the test of being a servant does not rest nowadays on submission to orders. It depends on whether the person is part and parcel of the organization."[38] This test does not seem to have received appreciable acceptance by the courts. This is perhaps unfortunate. The utility of the test lies in its application to the facts of each case. The term of the contract would determine whether or not a person is part and parcel of the organization. As has been said, once the facts are found, for, clearly the terms of a contract are questions of fact, it becomes a "pure question of law what is the reasonable inference based on the legal interpretation of the contract."[39] This, also, seems to be the basic principle of the so-called modern approach concept.

Modern approach

In *Ready Mixed Concrete (South East) Ltd* v *Minister of Pensions and National Insurance*,[40] Mackenna J, suggested[41] that a contract of service exists if the following three conditions are fulfilled:

---

[35] [1965] 2 All ER 349
[36] (1952) 1 TLR 101.
[37] Ibid., 111
[38] *Bank voor Handel en Scheepvaart N. V.* v *Slatford* [1953] 1 QB 248, 295.
[39] Per Lord Parker LCJ in *Morren* v *Swinton & Pendlebury Borough Council* [1965] 2 All ER 349, 352.
[40] [1968] 1 All ER 433.
[41] Ibid., 439-440.

i) the servant agrees that in consideration of a wage or other remuneration he will provide his own work and skill in the performance of some service for his master;
ii) he agrees, expressly or impliedly, that in the performance of that service he will be subject to the other's control in a sufficient degree to make that other master; and
iii) the other provisions of the contract are consistent with its being a contract of service.

This statement does not appear to vary or add to the solution provided by the control test in the enlarged sense already advocated. Condition (i) is usually part of (ii) and condition (iii) merely begs the question. Thus, we are left with the question whether a person agrees, expressly or impliedly, that in the performance of his service he will be subject to the other's control in a sufficient degree to make that other master. Cooke J's exposition in *Market Investigations Ltd* v *Minister of Social Security*,[42] is to the same effect. He said:[43]

> The fundamental test to be applied is this: 'Is the person who has engaged himself to perform these services performing them as a person in business on his own account?' If the answer to that question is 'yes' then the contract is a contract for services. If the answer is 'no' then the contract is a contract of service. No exhaustive list has been compiled and perhaps no exhaustive list can be compiled of considerations which are relevant in determining that question, nor can strict rules be laid down as to the relative weight which the various considerations should carry in particular cases. The most that can be said is that control will no doubt always have to be considered, although it can no longer be regarded as the sole determining factor; and that factors, which may be of importance, are such matters as whether the man performing the services provides his own equipment, whether he hires his own helpers, what degree of financial risk he takes, what degree or responsibility for investment and management he has, and whether and how far he has an opportunity of profiting from sound management in the performance of his task.

The English Court of Appeal has endorsed this approach. It said a court must "consider all aspects of the relationship, no single factor being in itself decisive and each of which may vary in weight and direction, and having given such balance to the factors as seems appropriate, to determine whether the person was

---

[42] [1968] 3 All ER 732; see also *Construction Industry Training Board* v *Labour Force* [1970] 3 All ER 220; *Global Plant Ltd* v *Secretary of State for Health and Social Security* [1971] 3 All ER 385.

[43] Ibid., 737-738.

carrying on business on his own account."[44] If he was carrying on business on his own account then, of course, he is an independent contractor; if not he is an employee.

Labour statutes and employees

Generally only those who are employed as employees at common law come within the coverage or application of the various labour statutes although a particular labour statute may not apply to all employees. Each labour statute stipulates the category or type of employees to whom its provisions apply. This is done by providing a definition and by express exclusion.

Thus, although statutory regulation also applies within the common law relationship of employer and employee, it does not follow that a particular labour statute applies to every employee at common law. Each statute determines those employees to whom it would apply. An employee who does not fall within a given definition in a statute or who is expressly excluded by a statute cannot claim a benefit under the statute nor can he be made liable under it. In *Union of P & T Workers of Nigeria* v *Attorney General of the Federation*,[45] the plaintiff union sued on behalf of its members, who had staged a 48-hour demonstration, for a declaration that the deductions representing 48-hour wage made from the members' wages were illegal being in contravention of Section 19 and 21 of the Labour Code Act.[46] The court held that it would be improper to make such a declaration in respect of some of the members of the union as it was clear they were not workers within the definition of the term in the Act.

---

[44] *O'Kelly* v *Trusthouse Forte* [1983] 1 *RLR* 369, 382.

[45] Unreported High Court of Lagos Suit No. LD/142/58.

[46] The Labour Code Act was repealed by the Labour Act 1974 which contains provisions similar to Sections 19 and 21. For a review of the Labour Act see also E. E. Uvieghara, 'The Labour Decree 1974: A Review,' *Nigerian Law Journal*, Vol. 9, 1975.

Chapter 2

The contract of employment

The basis of modern employment is the contract of employment. The contract of employment is a species of contracts and is therefore governed by the general principles of the law of contract: there must be *offer* and *acceptance*, a definite agreement between the parties; this being often expressed in the maxim *consensus ad idem* - that is, the meeting of minds. However, there was no contract where an acceptance was of an offer of employment made by the chairman of the council instead of by the secretary of the council who had the duty, under the constitution of the council, to communicate decisions of the council.[1] Although, the common law requirement of consideration is as vital for the validity of a contract of employment as for any other type of contract, the issue has not presented much difficulty in employment as, in practice, it is usually part of the agreement between the parties. The question whether a statement of either party to a contract of employment is a representation which induced the other party to enter into the contract or whether it is a term of the contract is answered by a consideration of the relevant general principles of the law of contract. The same principles govern the issue whether a misrepresentation is an innocent or fraudulent one and the consequences which follow upon such a misrepresentation. However, the contract of employment is not one *uberrima fidei*. A prospective employee or an employee is under no obligation to volunteer any fact or information including where, if such information were made known, it would affect him adversely.[2] The effect of vitiating factors such as mistake, coercion or duress on a contract of employment is the same as upon any other type of contract.

But the contract of employment has some peculiar features of its own. It is still not quite settled whether a repudiatory act of one party to the contract of employment automatically brings it to an end or whether, in accordance with the general principles of the law of contract, the innocent party has an option either

---

[1] *Ajayi-Obe* v *Executive Secretary*, Family Planning Council of Nigeria (1975) 3 SC1.

[2] *Oransaye* v *ECN* 1969 NCLR 93; *Hunter Huble* v *Nigerian Maritime Services* (1971) 1 UILR 231. The view of the majority of the Federal Court of Appeal in *Gwawoh* v *Bendel State Hospital Management Board*, Federal Court of Appeal, Benin, Judgements Mar-Dec 1980, p. 84 is wrong. The dissenting view of Okagbue J.C.A., with respect, represents the law.

to accept the breach or waive it.[3] Also, the remedy of specific performance is not readily available for a breach of a contract of employment.[4] It may also be noted that the relationship which arises out of a contract of employment is very largely affected by statutory provisions but it is unnecessary to make a comparison with other types of contracts on this ground.

Form of contract

There is no general law which stipulates the form which a contract of employment must take. It is governed by the common law. Thus, a contract of employment may be in writing and, if in writing, under seal, or it may be verbal or partly in writing and partly orally. It may be by conduct. An oral contract, no matter the status of the person so employed, is as valid as a written contract, but there is no doubt that an oral contract presents greater problems of proof both of its existence and of its terms. "The general principles of contract apply to the creation of the contract of service, and an agreement of service is equally enforceable... Whether it be expressed in writing, in deed, by word of mouth, or by conduct, though a case of a contract of service arising from conduct is not easily imagined."[4]

However, two classes of contracts of employment must be in writing. The contract of employment of seamen must, of necessity, be in writing.[5] A seaman is any person (except a master, pilot or apprentice or a person temporarily employed on the ship while in port) employed or engaged in any capacity on board a ship.[6] Also, the contract of apprenticeship and every assignment of it must be in writing.[7]

---

[3] See full discussion below: During the Second Republic, Oct. 1979 - Dec. 1983, many State governments failed to pay wages and salaries for several months; although this certainly was a breach, none of the civil servants and teachers concerned left their employment on this ground. Indeed, many were happy to survive the massive retrenchment which also took place.

[4] Per Kolawole J in *Adetoba* v *Godwin World-wide Ltd* (1982) *OGSLR* 160-161.

[5] S.21 (1) Merchant Shipping Act; seamen employed in certain ships are excepted; the agreement must contain certain terms listed in s. 22(2); the Act contains 433 sections under 100 chapters; some of the chapters deal with the discharge of seamen, distressed seamen, seamen left behind abroad, payment of wages, advance and allotment of wages, mode of recovery of wages and provisions of health and accommodation.

[6] S. 2 Merchant Shipping Act; this section defines a master as any person, except a pilot, having command or charge of any ship and defines a pilot as any person not belonging to the ship who has the conduct thereof; apprentice means a person duly indentured as an apprentice to the sea service s. 18, ibid.

[7] S. 53(1) Labour Act, cap. 198 Laws of the Federation of Nigeria, 1990; for the contract of apprenticeship see below.

Any contract, including a contract of employment, made on behalf of a company registered under the Companies and Allied Matters Act may be made in the form in which an individual may enter into any contract.[8]

Capacity to contract: *Infants*

The common law protects infants, i.e., those under twenty-one years of age, against disadvantageous contracts. In so far as contracts of employment are concerned the common law position is that such contracts are, *prima facie*, binding on the infant.[9] However, a contract of employment of an infant, when looked at as a whole, must be for the infant's benefit if he is not to be free to repudiate it. But the fact that one or more of the terms of the contract are disadvantageous to the infant is not conclusive. The total benefits must be weighed against the onerous ones. In *De Francesco* v *Barnum*,[10] Fry LJ stated the approach as follows:

> Now I approach this subject with the observation that it appears to me that the question is this, is the contract for the benefit of the infant? Not, is any one particular stipulation for the benefit of the infant? Because it is obvious that the contract of...labour must, like any other contract, contain some stipulations for the benefit of the one contracting party, and some for the benefit of the other. It is not because you can lay your hand on a particular stipulation which you may say is against the infant's benefit, that therefore the whole contract is not for the benefit of the infant.[11]

In *Doyle* v *White City Stadium Ltd*,[12] the plaintiff, a boxer, was granted a licence as a boxer by the Board of Control. A copy of the rules supplied with the licence contained a provision for forfeiture of any sum that would have been due to a boxer where he is disqualified. The plaintiff was disqualified and the board withheld the sum which would have been due to him. In his action claiming the money, he contended that as an infant the contract with the Board was not binding on him. The court held the contract was a binding one. Indeed where the

[8] S. 71 Companies and Allied Matters Act cap. 59 Laws of the Federation of Nigeria, 1990.

[9] *De Francesco* v *Barnum* (1890) 45 Ch. D. 430; this position is left untouched by statute unless where the employment comes within the Labour Act as to which see below.

[10] (1890) 45 Ch. D. 430.

[11] Ibid., 439.

[12] [1935] 1 KB 110.

terms of the contract are the usual ones in the type of employment the infant cannot complain. As Lush J said in the early case of *Leslie* v *Fitzpatrick*,[13]

> if such provisions were at the time common to labour contracts, or were in the then condition of trade such as the master was reasonably justified in imposing as a just measure of protection to himself, and if the wages were a fair compensation for the services of the youth, the contract is binding, in as much as it was beneficial to him by securing to him permanent employment, and the means of maintaining himself. If on the other hand advantage was taken of him to exact conditions which were unusual and unreasonable, or to secure his services for wages which were unreasonably low and inadequate, the infant is not bound.

Thus the fact that the same terms as applied to an adult employee are applied to an infant does not necessarily make the contract not binding. The contention that that should be so was rejected by the court in *Young* v *Hoffman Manufacturing Co Ltd.*[14] Sir Gorell Barnes said: "If, however, the terms of the contract are of the common kind, and such as the master might reasonably impose for his own protection, and the wages are fair, there seems no reason for implying terms different in kind in the case of the infant from those implied in the contract of the adult."[15] The same principles apply where an infant is an employer.[16]

Aliens

Any person who is not a citizen of Nigeria is prohibited from accepting employment, except with the federal or a state government, without the consent in writing of the chief federal immigration officer. Nor can he, on his own account or in partnership with any other person, practice a profession or establish or take over any trade or business or register or take over any company with limited liability, for any such purpose without the consent of the Minister responsible for immigration which may be given on such conditions as to the locality of operation and persons to be employed by or on behalf of such person.[17] Any such person who desires to enter Nigeria for either of these two

[13] (1877) 3 QBD 229, 232.

[14] [1907] 2 KB 646.

[15] Ibid., 654.

[16] *R.* v *The Inhabitants of St. Petrox* (1791) 4 Term Rep. 196.

[17] S. 8(1) Immigration Act; these powers became vested in the Industrial Development Co-ordination Committee established by the Industrial Development Co-ordination Decree 1988 cap.

purposes must produce the consent to an immigration officer.[18] Failure to do so is an offence and the person is also liable, in addition, to deportation as a prohibited immigrant.[19] Where any person is exempted from any provision restricting his employment and the exemption ceases, he is deemed to be a person seeking to enter into Nigeria for the first time and must, therefore, comply with the above requirements for employment or for the practice of a profession or the carrying on of a trade.[20]

Where any person[21] in Nigeria desires to employ a person who is a national of any other country he must, unless exempted, make application to the chief federal immigration officer in the prescribed manner and must give such information as to the provision to be made for repatriation of that national and his dependants as the chief immigration officer may reasonably require. No such person must be employed without the permission of the chief federal immigration officer given on such terms as he thinks fit.[22] Where the officer is not satisfied he may require provision to be made for repatriation, either generally as to all persons so employed by a person in Nigeria and their dependants or with reference to any particular person, by payment into the Consolidated Revenue Fund by way of deposit of such amount as the Minister may prescribe for the repatriation, or by a bond in such form as the chief federal immigration officer may approve for such purpose.[23] The minister may by notice exempt any person from the above requirements of section 34 on such conditions as he thinks fit but, subject to such exemption, any person who is employed under the section but ceases for any reason to be so employed, is deemed to be a prohibited immigrant as from the date of his entry into Nigeria.[24] The person who employed him is liable to pay all costs of and incidental to deportation of the prohibited immigrant and of his dependants.[25] The failure to comply with the

178. This Decree is now repealed by the Nigerian Investment Promotion Commission Act No.16 of 1995. While the Act does not seem to affect the provision for obtaining employment by aliens it does affect the establishment or take over of an enterprise; see Ss 19 and 32 of the Act.

[18] S. 8(2), ibid.

[19] S. 8(2), ibid., on conviction for an offence the penalty is a fine not exceeding ₦200 or imprisonment for a term not exceeding 6 months or to both; the court may, if it thinks fit, recommended the deportation of the offender; s. 47(1), ibid.

[20] S. 8(3) Immigration Act.

[21] Any person being a company or association is deemed to be in Nigeria if carrying out any work in Nigeria, S. 34(5), ibid.

[22] S. 34 ibid.

[23] S. 34(2), ibid.

[24] S. 34(3), ibid.

[25] S. 34(3), ibid.

provisions of section 34 is an offence[26] and on summary conviction the offender is liable to a fine not exceeding two hundred naira or to imprisonment for a term not exceeding six months or to both such fine and imprisonment and the court may, if it thinks fit, recommend the deportation of the offender.[27]

The State

At common law it was uncertain whether employees of the State were employed under contracts of employment.[28] However, the better view was that servants of the State (or Crown) were employed under contract but that the Crown could put an end to the contract at any time and for no reason and without compensation for loss of job. As it was stated by the English Court of Appeal in *Dunn* v *the Queen*,[29] there must be imported into the contract for the employment of the petitioners the term which is applicable to civil servants in general, namely that the Crown may put an end to the employment at its pleasure.[30] This common law principle was later underscored in the Pensions Act[31] which provided that nothing in the Act shall affect the right of the Crown to dismiss any officer at any time and without compensation.[32]

But even at common law it was established that the State's power to dismiss at its pleasure could be negatived by law.[33] Today the various civil service regulations or rules under which civil servants are employed are made by virtue of power conferred by the constitution. These rules prescribe the procedure for the removal of civil servants. As Wheeler J said in *Michael Oguche* v *Kano State Public Service Commission*:[34]

> Now it is common ground, in the present case, that the Public Service Regulations made under the now repealed Nigerian (Constitution) Order in Council 1954, originally published as *NRLN* 80 of 1960 and now published in vol. iv of the Laws of Northern Nigeria, still regulate the procedure of the

---

[26] S. 34(4), ibid.
[27] Ibid., s. 48(1).
[28] See e.g., *Reilly* v *The King* [1934] AC 176; *Okonkwo* v *P. S. C. Anambra State* [1981] 2 PLR 359.
[29] [1896] 1 QB 116
[30] Ibid;
[31] Cap. 147 Laws of the Federation of Nigeria and Lagos, 1958.
[32] Ibid; S. 6(1).
[33] *Gould* v *Stuart* [1896] AC 575.
[34] 1974 (1) NMLR 128.

> Public Service Commission of Kano State...Reading these regulations, I am satisfied that they fetter the right of the State to dismiss its servants at will.[35]

The Supreme Court held similarly in *Shitta-Bey* v *Federal Public Service Commission.*[36] As the court said: "these rules...have constitutional force and they invest the public servant over whom they prevail, a legal status; a status which makes his relationship with the respondent and the government although one of master and servant certainly beyond the ordinary or mere master and servant relationship."[37] Thus, it is now well-settled that civil servants are not only employed under contracts but also that the state is bound by the contractual terms embodied in the civil service rules.

It also seems now that an action whether in contract[38] or in tort[39] is maintainable against the government or government department. At common law the state (Crown) enjoyed immunity from court actions based on the ancient doctrine that the Crown could not be sued in his own courts. The immunity was not enforced with as much vigour in the law of contract as it was in the law of tort. In contract, an action by way of petition of right, that is a request to the Crown to do right in the matter, was developed and later formalised by statute.[40] This required the consent, usually referred to as "fiat", of the Crown to proceed with an action for breach of contract. The immunity from tort was applied with full vigour.[41] The remedy by way of petition of right was not applied to tort actions on the ground that the Crown could do no wrong. The Crown could also not authorise a wrong.

Now section 6(6) (b) of the Constitution of the Federal Republic of Nigeria 1999, provides that the judicial powers vested in the courts by the constitution[42] "shall extend to all matters between persons, or between government[43] or authority and any person in Nigeria, and to all actions and proceedings relating

---

[35] Ibid; 135.

[36] (1981) 1 SC 40.

[37] Ibid; 56

[38] E.g. action for wrongful dismissal.

[39] E.g. action for injury suffered at work; such an action may be framed in either contract or tort; *Matthews* v *Kuwait Buchtel Corporation* (1959) 2 QB 57.

[40] Petition of Right Act, Cap. 149 Laws of the Federation of Nigeria and Lagos, 1958. The States have identical statutes. The Petitions of Right Act is omitted in the Laws of the Federation of Nigeria 1990 on the ground that it is impliedly repealed by the Constitution.

[41] See *Ransome Kuti* v *A.G. for the Federation* (1985) 2 NWLR 211; *Adigun* v *Ayinde* [1993] 8 NWLR 516.

[42] S. 6(1), (2) and (5) Constitution.

[43] Government includes the Government of the Federation, or any State, or a local government council or any person who exercises power or authority on its behalf; s. 318 Constitution.

thereto, for the determination of any question as to the civil rights and obligations of that person." In the *Government of Imo State* v *Greeco Construction and Engineering Association Ltd*,[44] the Court of Appeal held that s. 6(6) (b) of the Constitution had impliedly repealed the Petitions of Right Act.[38] But the court did not say and it does not follow that a repeal of the Petitions of Right Act by the constitutional provision means an abrogation of the state's immunity in an action for breach of contract. In fact, it restores it in full vigour. In *Ransome Kuti* v *Attorney General of the Federation*,[45] Eso JSC who gave the leading judgment of the Supreme Court said[46] "Section 6 of the 1979 Constitution which vests the judicial powers of the country in the courts has to my mind removed this anachronism." This was a reference to the state's immunity in tort actions. But clearly, this was an *obiter dictum*.[47] Indeed, Oputa JSC in the same case only said section 6 (6) (b) may provide the answer to the problem of state immunity from tortious claims.[48] He added: "I say `may' because the court is not here called upon to decide that issue and without the aid of legal arguments on both sides, it is safer to use the word `may'."[49]

However, S. 6(6) (b) of the constitution has been held to expressly give access to the courts for the determination of any question as to the civil rights and obligations of any one.[49a]

Persons of unsound mind

A contract of employment entered into by a person who claims to be insane is nevertheless binding on him unless he can prove that he did not know what he was doing at the time he entered into the contract and further that the other party knew he was so insane as to have been incapable to understand what he was doing. Such proof will render the contract violable at the option of the insane

[44] (1985) 3 NWLR 71.
[45] [1985] 2 NWLR 211, 237; See also per Karibi-Whyte and Oputa J.J.S.C. at 252 and 259-260 respectively; See also the Court of Appeal in *Governor of Bendel State* v *Obayuwana* [1982] 3 NCLR 206.
[46] Ibid; 237.
[47] The court upheld a claim of state immunity in tort action.
[48] (1985) 2 NWLR 211, 259.
[49] Ibid; 259 - 260.
[49a] *Adediran* v *Interland Transport Ltd.* [1992] 8 NWLR 641. *A-G Kaduna State* v *Hassan* [1985]2 NWLR (pt.8)483 S.C., *Jallo* v *Military Governor of Kano State* [1991]5 NWLR 754; *Gunman* v *Bukar* [1991]1 NWLR (pt.168) 439.

person.[50] In *Hart* v *O'Connor*,[51] Lord Brightman, who delivered the judgement of the Privy Council, said that:

> the validity of a contract entered into by a lunatic who is ostensibly sane is to be judged by the same standards as a contract by a person of sound mind, and is not violable by the lunatic or his representative by reason of 'unfairness' unless such unfairness amounts to equitable fraud which would have enabled the complaining party to avoid the contract even if he had been sane.[52]

Corporations

A corporation established by statute such as the Nigeria Railway Corporation, the Nigerian Television Authority and the University of Lagos, etc., must act within the powers conferred on it by the statute establishing it.

Before 1990 the capacity of companies was governed entirely by the common law. Under the common law doctrine of *ultra vires*, a registered company could not lawfully act outside the powers or objects provided for either expressly or by necessary implication, in its memorandum of association. Any contract which it entered into outside those powers was void.[53] In *Continental Chemists Ltd* v *Ifeakandu*,[54] the company entered into contracts to train the defendant as a doctor and later to run a hospital at which he was required to practice. The Supreme Court dismissed an appeal against a decision which held these contracts *ultra vires* and therefore void. No clause of the memorandum enabled the company to do either. The Companies and Allied Matters Act[55] has modified the common law position. Now, broadly, no act of a company is invalid merely because it is *ultra vires* but a member of the company may apply to the court for an injunction to prohibit any *ultra vires* act.[56]

Legality of contract

Any contract, including a contract of employment, which has any object which is contrary to a statute or the common law or even public policy is illegal and may

---

[50] *Imperial Loan Co Ltd* v *Stone* [1892] QB 599; *Hart* v *O'Connor* [1985] 2 All ER 880.
[51] [1985]2 All ER 880.
[52] Ibid., 894.
[53] *Ashbury Railway Carriage & Iron Co.* v *Riche* (1875) LR 7 HL 653.
[54] [1966] 1 All NLR 1.
[55] Decree No. 1 of 1990; now Cap. 59.
[56] S. 39 Ibid.

be void and normally the courts will not assist in enforcing such a contract.[57] In *Lavabre* v *Excelsior Hotel Ltd*,[58] where a foreigner was only authorized to practice as an architect under a construction company, in accordance with the requirement of the Immigration Act, but he practised on his own instead, the court held that a contract he entered into was illegal. He was, therefore, not entitled to sue and recover money for services rendered under the contract; not even on the basis of *quantum meruit*. Similarly, in *Chivers* v *Davis of America*,[59] where an alien took up employment in defiance of the provisions of the Immigration Act, the court refused to lend its assistance in enforcing his action for damages for wrongful termination of employment.

Terms of the contract

The regulation of the relationship between an employer and an employee derives from two primary sources, *statute* and the *contract of employment* itself. The various labour statutes impose numerous duties and obligations on both parties to a contract of employment. It is not clear, however, and there are no judicial decisions, on whether statutory provisions are to be regarded as express or implied terms or indeed whether they are terms of the contract at all.[60] What is clear beyond doubt is that statutory obligations cannot be excluded by terms of the contract of employment, except where and to the extent that a statute itself so permits.

In any dispute as to the rights and obligations of the parties arising out of the contract of employment it is vital that the contractual terms be proved. The contract of employment must, therefore, be pleaded. As Uwais JSC said in *Morohunfola* v *Kwara State College of Technology*,[61] in an action for wrongful dismissal it is necessary, therefore, to plead to the contract of employment, which is the foundation of the action, and not to leave its terms to speculation by the defendant and the trial judge. Without the contract and its particulars being pleaded by the plaintiff, no evidence of the terms of the contract which has been

---

[57] Any detailed discussion of illegality of contracts is unnecessary; for a detailed discussion see Cooper's *Outlines of Industrial Law*, 6th edn. by J.C. Wood, (Butterworths) pp. 45-53. Contracts of employment and the doctrine of restraint of trade are considered below.

[58] (1967) LLR 141.

[59] 1971 (2) NCLR 89; CCHCJ/1/72, p. 121.

[60] However a statute may provide that certain provisions be deemed to be implied into the contract of employment; See, e.g., Trade Dispute Act. 47(2).

[61] (1990)4 NWLR 506; see also *Amodu* v *Amode & Kwara State College of Technology* (1990) 5 NWLR 356.

breached would be admitted at the trial; and this will be fatal to the action since it will lack foundation.[62]

The terms of the contract of employment are either *express terms*, that is those terms agreed or presumed to be agreed upon by the two parties at the time of entering into the contract, or *implied terms*. And as will be seen, collective agreement which, nowadays, plays a very significant role in settling the terms and conditions of employment has the force of law usually via the contract of employment either as express terms or implied terms.

Express terms

The express terms of a contract of employment are those terms which the parties themselves formulated before or at the time of concluding the contract. Where the contract is an oral one, it is a matter of oral evidence to prove what the terms agreed are. Many contracts are, however, partly in writing and partly by word of mouth, so that both oral evidence and a proper construction of the written terms will be necessary to show the express terms of the contract.[63]

Where, as often happens, a document which may have such a title as Conditions of Employment or Regulations and Conditions of Employment or Works Rules or Administrative Manual or simply a copy of a collective agreement is given to an employee, such a document can be regarded as containing express terms of the contract, strictly, only where it was issued to the employee before or at the time of the making of the contract or where reference to it is made at such a time.[64] Thus, in *Akpabot* v *College of Education, Uyo,*[65] where the letter of appointment had attached to it a memorandum setting out the terms and conditions of appointment, the Court of Appeal held that the memorandum formed part of the contract of employment. In *National Coal Board* v *Galley*,[66] where the contract of employment of the defendant who was employed as a deputy by the Coal Board provided that his "contract of service shall be subject" to certain collective agreement as varied from time to time, the English Court of Appeal held that his employment was governed by the terms of collective agreement as agreed from time to time between his union and the

[62] Ibid., 519.

[63] It seems that the parol evidence rule applies only to contracts which are intended to be exclusively in writing.

[64] *Olley* v *Marlborough Court Ltd* [1949] 1 KB 532.

[65] Court of Appeal Judgements 1985, p. 270, Jan Dec.

[66] [1958] 1 All ER 91.

employer. In practice, however, many such documents are given to employees after they have entered into the contract and even commenced work. Although, it is clear that in such cases under the general principles of contract law that the employer cannot unilaterally vary the terms of the contract,[67] but since invariably the employee continues in his work after receipt of such a document, he will be held to be bound by its terms.[68] In *Baba* v *Nigerian Civil Aviation Training Centre*,[69] the plaintiff was employed by letter and after assuming work he was given a copy of the Staff Regulations. The Court of Appeal held the Regulations were binding on the plaintiff. In *Ajayi* v *Texaco Nigeria Ltd*,[70] the parties entered into a contract of employment in December 1969. Over four years after, on 30 September 1975, the employer issued an Employee's Handbook which the employee signed for and received. The Supreme Court held that the handbook was binding on him when he tried to argue the contrary one and half years later. Oputa JSC said:

> The important thing is that the Appellant signed for Ex. D.1 and remained in the employment of the 1st Respondent's Company from 30 September 1975 until 26 of March 1977... He (the appellant) was thus not only by his admission in cross-examination but also by his conduct justified the 1st respondent/Company in believing that he (the Appellant) has accepted to be bound by all the terms and conditions contained in Ex. D.1. By his failure to question any part of Ex. D.1. or to repudiate same for a period of almost one and half years the Appellant is now estopped by his conduct from denying that he is bound by the employee's Handbook, Ex. D.1.[71]

A collective agreement concluded between an employer or a trade union to which the employer belongs and an employee's trade union stands on the same footing. At common law, a collective agreement is not regarded as contractually binding on the parties that concluded the agreement[72] although, as will be seen, the terms of a collective agreement may acquire contractual force by way of the implied term doctrine or by express provision.

---

[67] See *Cowey* v *Liberian Operations Ltd* [1966] 2 Lloyds Rep. 215.

[68] See e.g., *Aduke Watkinson* v *Pan American World Airways Inc.* (1967) FNLR 100; *Koleoso* v *Chellarams & Sons (Nig.) Ltd.* CCHCJ/1/73, p. 46; *Adekoya* v *Pan Electric Ltd.* (1974) 4 UILR 56; CCHCJ/2/73, p. 54.

[69] [1986] 5 NWLR 514.

[70] [1987] 3 NWLR 577; (1987), 910, SCNJ 1.

[71] Ibid., 596.

[72] *Ford Motor Co Ltd* v *Amalgamated Union of Engineering & Foundry Workers* [1969] 2 QB, 303.

In the great majority of cases of employment it is the employer who imposes the terms and conditions of employment upon the employee. Nevertheless, the common law has always taken the position, arising from its fundamental assumption of the equality of the parties, that by taking up employment with the employer he has agreed to those terms.[73] This position is, of course, wholly unrealistic but it has persisted. Thus, the common law does not generally concern itself with issues of whether the contractual terms are reasonable or unreasonable. The doctrine of restraint of trade does not apply, at least, during the continuance of the employment relationship. In *Warner Brothers Pictures Inc.* v *Nelson*,[74] Branson J said:[75]

> where as in the present contract the covenants are all concerned with what is to happen whilst the defendant is employed by the plaintiffs and not thereafter, there is no room for the application of the doctrine of restraint of trade.

And quite recently Lord Pearce affirmed that position:

> When a contract only ties the parties during the continuance of the contract, and the negative ties are only those which are incidental and normal to the positive commercial arrangement at which the contract aims, even though those ties exclude all dealings with other, there is no restrain of trade within the meaning of the doctrines and no question of reasonableness arises.[76]

However, the fact that the law will generally not be concerned with the reasonableness or otherwise of contractual terms is subject to the rule that the employer is not allowed to impose servile incidents on an employee. Any contract which tend to impose servile obligation upon any person is void and unenforceable in the court.[77] As Bowen LJ said in *Davies* v *Davies*:[78]

> The law...allows a man to contract for his labour, or allows him to place himself in the service of a master, but it does not allow him to attach to his contract of service any servile incidents.

---

[73] *Warner Brother Pictures Inc.* v *Nelson* [1936] 3 All ER 160; See also *Gaumont Corporation* v *Alexander* [1936] 2 All ER 1686.

[74] [1937] 1 KB 209.

[75] Ibid., 214

[76] *Esso Petroleum Co Ltd.* v *Harper's Garage (Stourport) Ltd* [1968] AC 269, 328; See also per Lord Wilberforce at 332.

[77] Per Warrington L.J. in *Horwood* v *Millar's Timber & Trading Co. Ltd.* [1917] 1 KB 305, 314.

[78] (1887) 36 Ch. D. 359, 393.

It is difficult, however, to categorically state what would amount to a servile obligation. A contract under which a person agrees to serve for life is not necessarily against public policy. Thus, in the leading case of *Wallis* v *Day*,[79] a contract to serve for life at a weekly salary was held not to be illegal. Also the assignment of the salary of a chaplain was held not to be against public policy.[80] In other words, moneys due under a contract of personal service can be assigned.[81] But where, by assigning his salary, an employee was deprived of the means of support of himself and his family the assignment was held to be contrary to public policy and unenforceable.[82] In *Coker* v *CFAO*,[83] a clause of the contract of employment which provided that the employer may retain all or any part of the deposit paid by the employee as security for damage or loss or shortages of goods entrusted to the employee as a storekeeper and "the employers' certificate in writing that the same or any given part thereof stated in such certificate are to be retained and of the cause of such retention shall be binding and conclusive evidence between the parties in all courts of justice" was held illegal and void as being against public policy.

Implied terms

Terms or a term may be implied into a contract of employment which would impose rights and obligations on the parties to the contract although they have not expressly provided for them. Implied terms may arise in a number of ways. Terms may be implied into a contract of employment by statute. The provisions of section 47(2) of the Trade Disputes Act amount to such an implication. By the sub-section where an award or terms of a settlement, at arbitration, become binding on the employers and employees to whom the award or settlement relate,[84] then, as from the date of the award or settlement, or any earlier or later date specified in it, the contract between the employers and employees must be deemed to include a provision that the rate of wages to be paid and the conditions of employment to be observed under the contract must be in accordance with the award or terms of settlement until varied by a subsequent

---

[79] (1837) 2 M & W, 273.
[80] *In re Mirans* [1891] 1 QB 594.
[81] *Russel & Co. Ltd.* v *Austin Fryers* (1909) 25 TLR 414.
[82] *King* v *Michael Faraday & Partners Ltd.* [1939] 2 All ER 478.
[83] 1967 NCLR 1.
[84] See below for arbitration settlements and awards and when they become binding.

agreement, settlement or award. The sub-section provides further that accordingly the provisions of the contract must be read subject to the award or terms of settlement and any failure to given effect to them constitutes a breach of contract.

Custom or practice may be implied into a contract of employment.[85] It would seem, however, that for a custom to be implied it must not only be notorious but its existence must also be known to the employee whose contract is in issue. In *Foxall* v *The International Land Credit Company*[86] Byles J said that a custom to be implied must be "a general custom of some reasonable antiquity and standing, uniform, and sufficiently notorious and well understood that people would make their contracts on the supposition that it exists."[87]

In *Luxor (Eastbourne) Ltd* v *Cooper*,[88] Lord Wright wrote of two types of implied terms as follows:

> The expression "implied term" is used in different senses. Sometimes it denotes some term which does not depend on the actual intention of the parties but on a rule of law...But a case like the present is different because what it sought to imply is based on an intention imputed to the parties from their actual circumstances.[89]

The terms which are implied into a contract of employment as a matter of law are discussed below under the two headings of *duties of the employer* and *duties of the employee*. These are rights and obligations of an employer or employee which have crystallized over the years in court decisions and are held to apply to the parties to a contract of employment unless excluded by the express terms of the contract or by statute. But the principle that an express term prevails over an implied term which, certainly is orthodox and seemingly well-established, received a vigorous but significant knock recently in *Johnstone* v *Bloomsbury Health Authority*.[90] Under the contract of employment the employer had power, by express provision, to require the employee to work a certain number of basic hours per week and additional hours of so many hours per week on average. The plaintiff, a medical doctor, claimed that by requiring him to work intolerable

---

[85] *Marshall* v *English Electric Co. Ltd.* [1945] 1 All ER 653.

[86] (1867) 16 LT 637.

[87] Ibid; 639; see also *Oke* v *Great Nigeria Insurance Co. Ltd.* CCHCJ/12/72 p.62; and for implied term to suspend an employee see below.

[88] [1941] AC 108, 137; See also *Lord Reid in Stirling Engineering Co. Ltd.* v *Patchett* [1955] AC 534, 547.

[89] Ibid; 137.

[90] [1991] 2 All ER 293

hours which deprived him of sleep and damaged his health as well as put at risk the safety of his patients, the employers were in breach of their implied duty to take reasonable care for his safety. Counsel contended that the express contractual power must prevail over the implied duty of care. But Smart-Smith LJ rejected the contention. He held, in effect, that a term implied as a rule of law, as in the instant case, is not inferior to an express term of the contract. Both are equally binding on the employer. However, the orthodox view prevailed, at least, for now. Leggatt LJ held that those bound by current contracts (cannot) be enabled by the ingenuity of their lawyers to derogate from obligations freely assumed.[91] And Sir Nicolas Browne-Wilinson VC agreed with him on the point.

It is now well accepted that there may be cases where it is obvious that a term must be implied if the presumed contractual intention of the parties is not to be defeated. To put it in other words, where it is inevitable to imply a term so as to give effect to the presumed intention of the parties, a term would be implied. However, whether a term may be implied or not is a question of law - it is for the courts to decide - but the exact term or terms which may be implied will depend on the circumstances of a particular case.

One test for determining whether a term may be implied or not is that laid down by Scrutton LJ in *Reigate* v *Union Manufacturing Co (Ramsbottom) Ltd*:[92]

> A term can only be implied if it is necessary in the business sense to give efficacy to the contract; that is, if it is such a term that it can confidently be said that if at the time the contract was being negotiated someone had said to the parties "what will happen in such a case" they would both have replied, "of course, so and so will happen; we did not trouble to say that; it is so clear." Unless the court comes to some such conclusion as that, it ought not to imply a term which the parties have not expressed.

A similar test was put by McKinnon LJ in *Shirlaw* v *Southern Foundries (1926) Ltd*,[93] where he said:[94]

> *Prima facie* that which in any contract is left to be implied and need not be expressed is something so obvious that it goes without saying; so that if while the parties were making their bargain an officious bystander were to suggest some express provision for it in their agreement they would testily suppress him with a common: "oh, of course."

---

[91] Ibid; 303
[92] [1918] 1 KB 592, 605
[93] [1939] 2 KB, 206; See also Bowen L.J. in *The Moorcock* (1889), 14 P.D. 64 at 68.
[94] Ibid; 227

In *Spring* v *National Amalgamated Stevedore & Dockers Society*,[95] the court seemed to have applied this test in a subjective rather than an objective manner. Sir Leonard Stone was, it seems, influenced by the fact that one of the parties had no knowledge of the fact that was sought to be implied. The test, clearly, is an objective one and it is for the court to determine whether a term would be implied. As Lord Tucker said these are cases "in which from their particular circumstances, it is necessary to imply in such manner as the parties would clearly have done if they had applied their minds to the contingency which has arisen."[96] In *Lister* v *Romford Ice & Cold Storage Co Ltd*,[97] the House of Lords was invited to imply a term into an employment contract. The employee was a driver and through his negligent driving which caused injury to his fellow employee who happened to be his father, the employers were rendered liable in damages for breach of their common law duty, to take reasonable care of the safety of the employee. The employers brought an action for damages for breach of the employee's implied duty to exercise reasonable care in the performance of his duties. The employee pleaded a number of implied terms in his defence. The House held that the suggested terms were not necessary to give business efficacy to the contract and that they were imprecise. Viscount Simonds said[98] that "the variety and multiplicity of the suggested terms were naturally contrasted with the general principle that an implication must be precise and obvious." Similarly in *O'Brien* v *Associated Fire Alarms Ltd*,[99] where, as Salmon LJ said,[100] there were "so many possibilities" the Court of Appeal declined to imply a term. In *Stevenson* v *Tees Side Bridge and Engineering Ltd*,[101] there was no express term in the contract that the employee would be required to go from site to site, but the employee had stated he was prepared to work away from home before he was employed and during employment he had in fact worked at various sites away from home and his contract made provision for travelling and subsistence allowances. The court held there was an implied term that the employee could be required to go from site to site.

[95] [1961] 2 All ER 211; [1956] 1 WLR 585.
[96] *Lister* v *Romford Ice and Cold Storage Co. Ltd.* [1959] 1 WLR 555, 594.
[97] *Supra.*
[98] Ibid., 574.
[99] [1969] 1 All ER 93.
[100] Ibid., 97.
[101] [1971] 1 All ER 296.

Collective agreements

Collective agreements constitute a very important source of the terms and conditions of employment. Many important terms and conditions of employment are today determined by collective bargaining and reflected in collective agreements. These terms include matters such as pension, redundancy,[102] medical care, transport and housing allowances, wages and salaries, and many more. Fresh employees normally have the terms of collective agreements applied to them while existing employees have their employment conditions improved upon by the collective bargaining process. It may, therefore, seem paradoxical to state that the law does not regard a collective agreement as a contract between an employer or employers' trade union[103] and an employees' trade union that concluded the agreement. Nor can an individual employee, whether or not a member of the union which is a party to a collective agreement, normally be able legally to enforce it.

The first case in which it was held that a collective agreement is not a contract is *Ford Motors Co Ltd* v *Amalgamated Union of Engineering and Foundry Workers*.[104] The decision was influenced by what Geoffrey Lane J regarded as the climate of opinion in England among trade union leaders, academicians and others as well as the view of the Donovan Commission on trade unions and employers associations[105] that parties to collective agreements do not always intend to enter into legal relations. The decision appears, however, to run contrary to the presumption of the law of contract that parties to a commercial or business transaction intend to enter into a legally enforceable relationship unlike in a social or domestic arrangement where the presumption is that there is no intention to create a legal relationship. The view of Megaw J in *Edwards* v *Skyways Ltd*,[106] which was cited in argument before Geoffrey Lane J accords with the contractual presumption. The learned judge said:

> In the present case the subject-matter of the agreement is business relations, not social or domestic matters...I accept the prepositions of counsel for the plaintiff that in a case of this nature the onus is on the party who asserts that no legal effect was intended, and the onus is a heavy one.[107]

---

[102] The existing statutory provision on redundancy applies only to a defined class of employees and is in fact limited in scope; see chapter 3

[103] Many employers are now members of registered trade unions of employers.

[104] [1969] 2 QB 303

[105] Cmnd 3623

[106] [1964] 1 All ER 494

[107] Ibid; 500

The Court of Appeal has held that a collective agreement is not a legally enforceable contract.[108] The court said,[109] "when, however, it comes to the hard reality of the law, the collective agreement becomes nothing more than a manifesto for labour relations."

It must not, however, be understood that the parties to a collective agreement approach the matter with the law at the back of their minds. Collective agreements are entered into with utmost seriousness and in a business-like manner and with a genuine intention to implement them. They are not entered into in the hope or expectation that they would not be enforced. Collective agreements are, in practice, invariably observed even though the parties may know they are only bound in honour to do so. Uwaifo JSC was right when he said of these agreements that "there can be no doubt that these formulations are intended to secure the best possible conditions through trade unionism efforts for the employees concerned if that would ensure industrial harmony."[110]

However, there are at least two ways by which a collective agreement may be made legally binding. The first is as provided by statute.[111] At least three copies of any collective agreement must be deposited by the parties to it with the Minister of Labour and Productivity within 14 days of its execution. It is an offence punishable with a fine of ₦100 to fail to do so. The minister may make an order specifying that the terms of an agreement or any part of them be binding on the employers and employees to whom they relate. Where this is done, any person who fails to comply with the terms of the order is guilty of an offence and liable, on conviction, to a fine of ₦100 or to imprisonment for six months.

Secondly, the parties to a collective agreement may, if they so wish, provide in the agreement that it shall have legally binding effect. And effect would be given to it as an agreed term of the contract. However, the ensuing contract would be between the parties to it and an individual employee may be unable to enforce its terms because of the doctrine of privity of contract. In *Holland* v *London Society of Compositors*,[112] a union member claimed that an agreement entered into between his union and another union was made for and on behalf of himself (like other members of the union) and that he was intended to be a beneficiary under the agreement and to be able to sue for breach of the agreement. The court held that it could not accept that contention and that the

[108] *Union Bank of Nigeria Ltd.* v *Edet* [1993] 4 NWLR 288
[109] Ibid; 299
[110] Ibid.
[111] S. 2 Trade Disputes Act, Cap. 432.
[112] (1924) 40 TLR 440.

agreement was made by the unions for their own purposes. The member, not being directly or indirectly a party to the agreement could not sue on it. Similarly, in *Union Bank of Nigeria Ltd* v *Edet*[113] a claim by a union member that his contract of employment was constituted by a collective agreement entered into between his union and a trade union of his employer was rejected by the Court of Appeal. The court said:[114]

> it is a collective agreement between employers and employees in their capacities as bodies of certain institutions. Such collective agreements are not intended or capable to give individual employees a right to litigate over an alleged breach of their terms as may be conceived by them to have affected their interest, nor are they meant to supplant or even supplement their contract of service.

However, there are a number of ways by which an employee may be able to enforce a collective agreement. As we have seen, one way of doing this is by express provision in the contract of employment of an employee or employees that their employment would be subject to or governed by either a specified collective agreement or any collective agreement entered into from time to time by the employer. In such a case, the terms of the relevant collective agreement would be regarded as express terms of the contract of employment.

A second way is by the implied term process. It would seem that the terms of a collective agreement would be implied into contracts of employment where the employer has, in fact, observed its terms in relation to its employees. Although this principle was not accepted by the Judicial Committee of the Privy Council in

---

[113] [1993]4 NWLR 288. See also *Nigeria - Arab Bank Ltd.* v *Shuaibu* [1991]4 NWLR 450, 469 per Noma - Egba JCA; *ACB Plc* v *Nbisike* [1995]8 NWLR 725, 741 per Edozie JCA. In *ACB Plc* v *Nwodika* [1996]4 NWLR 470, Ubawzonu JCA, in the leading judgment, cited *UBA* v *Edet, supra*, and *Chukwumah* v *Shell Petroleum Development Co. of Nigeria Ltd.* [1993]4 NWLR 512, for saying- "From the above set of authorities it may be said that Collective Agreement (as Exh E) are not by themselves binding on the individual employees and the employer unless such a Collective Agreement is incorporated into the contract of service or adopted as part of the contract or condition of service." P. 484 but he went on to, as he put it, to "examine another set of authorities." Ibid. These were the decisions of the Court of Appeal in *Shuaibu* v *UBN Plc* [1995]4 NWLR 173 and of the Supreme Court in *Nwobosi* v *ACB Ltd.* [1995]6 NWLR 658. He then concluded that whether collective agreements are binding on the individual employee and employer depends on a number of factors such as their incorporation into the contract of service if one exists, the state of the pleadings, the evidence before the court, and perhaps, the conduct of the parties; 484 ibid. But in both the Shuaibu and Nwobosi cases the point was not argued; the court simply accepted the collective agreement as the contract between the parties.

[114] Ibid., 298.

its decision in *Young* v *Canadian Northern Railway Co*,[115] it would appear, however, to be the basis upon which the decisions in a number of cases were given. In the *Young* v *Canadian Northern Railway Co* case an agreement between the employer and a union was applied by the employer to all employees, including the plaintiff in a particular department. The Judicial Committee held, nonetheless, that that did not establish contractual liability of the employer to the plaintiff. In *Union Bank of Nigeria Ltd* v *Edet*,[116] already mentioned, the Court of Appeal relied on this decision but the facts appear different. In Young's case the employer had, in fact, applied the terms of the collective agreement, a factor which was absent in Edet's case. Nevertheless the decision in Edet's case that the plaintiff's employment was not governed by the collective agreement was correct. There was no contention nor could there have been that its terms had become implied into the contract of employment of the plaintiff and there was no express provision constituting the collective agreement into the contract of employment of the plaintiff. As Akintan JCA said in the case:

> The learned trial judge was also in error to have applied the provisions of the booklet (Exh.13) titled Recognition and Procedural Agreement and main Collective Agreement between the Nigeria Employer's Association of Banks, Insurance and Allied Institutions and the Association of Senior Staff of Banks, Insurance and Financial Institutions. This is because he failed to advert his mind to the fact that both the plaintiff and the defendant in the case before him have not adopted the contents of the document as forming part of the respondent's term of employment. It is definitely necessary to expressly adopt the provisions of the document either in the letter of appointment or in a subsequent communication varying the terms of employment before the respondent could enforce its contents against the appellant.[117]

In *Maclean* v *Essex Line Ltd*,[118] the court held that the observance of a term contained in certain rules was cogent evidence that the rules were binding. In *Tomlinson* v *London, Midland & Scottish Railway Co*,[119] a "machinery of negotiation" agreed to between a railway company and the plaintiff's trade union was treated as incorporated in the contracts of service between the company and its employees on the ground that it was not disputed that it was to be so treated. Lord Greene, the Master of the Rolls, said "therefore, it forms one of the terms

---

115 [1931] AC 83
116 [1993] 4 NWLR 288.
117 Ibid., 305.
118 (1933) 45 LL. L. Rep. 254.
119 [1944] 1 All ER 537.

of that contractual relationship."[120] Similarly in *Rookes* v *Barnard*,[121] the House of Lords accepted the concession made by counsel that a term in a collective agreement had become incorporated in the contracts of employment.

Another way possibly by which an employee may enforce a collective agreement entered into by his employer and his trade union is provided by the law of agency. The law of agency is one way of getting around the doctrine of privity of contract. It is accepted that union officials or representatives at collective bargaining act as agents and the ensuing collective agreement is regarded as between their principal and the other party. If the trade union itself, which has all the attributes of a legal person, or the members collectively, is not to be regarded as the principal then each individual member would be a principal. This is bound to lead to difficulties given the fluctuating nature of their membership. Difficulties may also arise as to the authority given to the agents by each member, especially where it is sought to hold union members to the terms of a collective agreement. In *Edwards* v *Skyways Ltd*[122] the plaintiff was able to enforce payment to him, by his employer, of a certain fund based on an agreement reached at a meeting between his employer and his trade association. The plaintiff succeeded because the association's representatives were held to be the agents of the plaintiff. Megaw J said it was "not in dispute that the representative of the association were the duly authorized agents of the plain tiff, and that the representatives of the defendant company had full authority from that company in respect of all that was done and agreed at that meeting affecting the plaintiff."[123] The situation in this case may not occur too often. Those involved in the claim were a small group. But if a similar situation does occur, there is no reason why the same principle cannot apply although it must be remembered that in the case the court held that the presumption to create legal relations was not rebutted. To overcome this difficulty, the parties would have to provide expressly for contractual effect.

---

[120] Ibid., 539; and also per Goddard L.J. at 541.

[121] (1964) AC, 1129; an employee who has resigned as at the time an agreement becomes incorporated cannot enforce it; his contract was not in existence at the time; *Adegboyega* v *Barclays Bank of Nigeria Ltd.* 1977 NCLR 150.

[122] [1964] 1 All ER 494.

[123] Ibid.; 496.

Duties of the employer

Duty to pay wages

There is no doubt that the wages or salary which an employer is obliged to pay will normally be the subject-matter of an express term of the contract. Indeed, where an agreement for employment leaves out the matter of payment there might arise the question whether there is a contract of employment. However, at common law, a contract may be implied from the conduct of the parties. Where one party does work on the order of another under such circumstances as that it must be presumed that he looks to be paid as a matter of right, then a contract would be implied.[124] A term to pay will be implied in circumstances which clearly indicate that employment was not to be gratuitous.[125] Where there is an implied contract or term of a contract to pay, payment is *quantum meruit.*[126] In certain circumstances nothing less than the national minimum wage may be payable.[127]

An employee who takes part in a strike is not legally entitled to any wages or salary or any other remuneration for the period of the strike but, where there is a lock-out by an employer, the employees are entitled to be paid their wages or salary for the period of the lock out.[128]

Duty to provide work

This duty may more accurately be expressed in the negative. Generally, an employer is not under a duty to provide work for his employees to do; he fulfils his duty by paying wages.[129] "It is true," said Asquith J in *Collier* v *Sunday Referee Publishing Co*,[130] "that a contract of employment does not necessarily, or perhaps normally, oblige the master to provide the servant with work. Provided I pay my cook her wages regularly she cannot complain if I choose to take any or all of my meals out." Thus, an employee cannot complain of breach of contract where an employer keeps him idle but pays him the agreed wages or salary.

[124] Parke B in *Higgins* v *Hopkins* (1848) 3 Exch. 163, 166.
[125] Per Lord Atkin in *Way* v *Latilla* [1937] 3 All ER 759, 763.
[126] *Bryant* v *Flight* (1839) 5 M & W 114; *Peters of Oron* v *Symmonds* (1924) NLR 79.
[127] Under the National Minimum Wage Act, Cap 267; for which see below.
[128] S. 42 Trade Disputes Act Cap.432.
[129] *Turner* v *Sawdon & Co.* [1901] 2 KB 653.
[130] [1940] 2 KB 647, 650.

However, the suggestion has been made by the English Court of Appeal that this common law rule should be reversed in these modern times.[131] One of their Lordships, Lord Denning, the Master of Rolls, said: "To my mind, therefore, it is arguable that in these days a man has, by reason of an implication in the contract, a right to work. That is, he has a right to have the opportunity of doing his work when it is there to be done."[132]

Even at common law there are exceptions to the general rule. In certain contracts of employment the mere payment of wages or salary is not a discharge of the employer's duty under the contract; he must provide work. There are three categories of such contracts. In the contract of employment of actors and actress the need to gain publicity and enhance reputation requires that work be provided.[133] Similarly, in contract of employment in which work done is necessary and essential for the determination of wages payable, the employer is obliged to provide work. These include a contract of employment on a piece-rate or commission basis.[134] At common law an apprentice must also he provided with work to do in order that he may be able to learn his trade and acquire the necessary skills. Section 49(1) of the Labour Act now provides that a person may be apprenticed to an employer to train him or have him trained systematically for a trade or employment in which art or skill is required.[135]

Testimonial or reference

This duty may also more correctly be stated in the negative. There is no legal duty on an employer to provide an employee with a testimonial or character or to answer questions from interested parties concerning an employee's character.[136] However, nothing precludes an employer from doing so, and in practice many employers give references and testimonials. But an employer who opts to give a reference may be exposed to any of three possible actions for damages. An action for deceit will lie where an employer makes a statement or representation which he knows to be false or which he makes recklessly not caring whether or not it is true and from which loss has resulted to the party to whom it was made

---

[131] *Langton* v *Amalgamated Union of Engineering Workers* [1974] 1 All ER 980.
[132] Ibid; 987.
[133] *Clayton* v *Oliver* [1930] AC 209.
[134] *Devonald* v *Rosser & Son* [1906] 2 KB 728; *Rubel Bronze & Metal Co Ltd.* [1918] 1 KB 315; *Bauman* v *Hilton Press Ltd.* [1952] 2 ALL ER 1121.
[135] For the statutory regulation of contracts of apprenticeship see below.
[136] *Carrol* v *Bird* (1801) 3 Esp. 201.

and who acted upon it as was intended.[137] In *Wilkin* v *Reed*,[138] where the employee was dismissed owing to decrease in business and that was asserted to the plaintiff who employed him, the plaintiff's action based on the ground that the defendant employer knew that the employee had been dishonest while in his employment failed.

After the House of Lord's decision in *Hedley Byrne & Co Ltd* v *Heller & Partners Ltd*,[139] it has become possible for an action for negligent mis-statement which causes or results in financial loss to lie. In *Mutual Life & Citizens' Assurance Co Ltd*,[140] the Judicial Committee of the Privy Council held, by majority, that the necessary duty of care required to sustain such an action arises only where the maker of the statement carries on a business or profession which involves the giving of advice which calls for special skill and competence or where a person let it be known that he possesses skill and competence in the subject-matter of the inquiry. The House of Lords has now held that an employer possesses special knowledge derived from his experience of an employee's character and as such he owes a duty of care in the preparation of a reference under the Hedley Byrne principle.[141]

An action for defamation lies against an employer where he makes a statement to another which statement holds an employee to ridicule or contempt by reasonable persons or makes such persons shun him. However, truth, or justification as it is usually called is a defence to an action for defamation. Thus, an action will fail where an employer gives a true but damaging reference. It is submitted that it is not justification to state that an employee has stolen merely because he was suspected of stealing. A conviction by the courts is necessary.[142] But it is unclear whether it is justification to state that he is or was under suspicion. Newspaper disclaimers which merely state that the named ex-employee is no longer in the employer's employment are probably safe. An employer may also rely on the defence of qualified privilege being a person who is making a communication in discharge of a moral duty.[143] However, proof by the employee of malice in the employer destroys the defence. Malice may be proved by a number of ways, including proof of the fact that the employer knew the statement was false.[144]

---

137 *Foster* v *Charles* (1830) 7 Bing 105.
138 (1854) 15 CB 192.
139 (1964) AC 465.
140 (1971) AC 793.
141 *Spring* v *Guardian Assurance Plc.*, *Times Law Report*, 8 July, 1994.
142 Under the Constitution a person is presumed innocent until proved guilty
143 *Stuart* v *Bell* [1891] 2 QB 341.
144 For a fuller account, See Street On Torts 8th ed; Margaret Brazier, ed. Pp 411-413.

Duties of the employee

Duty to obey

The rule at common law is that an employee is under a duty to obey the orders of his employer.[145] "It has long been part of our law that a servant repudiates the contract of service if he wilfully disobeys the lawful and reasonable orders of his master."[146] Wilful disobedience is sufficient ground for summary dismissal of an employee.[147] But an order must be lawful and proper for it to be obeyed. An employee is not under a duty to obey an order which is against any statute or even the common law. Such an order is unlawful. Nor is an employee under an obligation to obey an order which will expose him to danger, either to his life or health. In *Turner* v *Mason*[148] although a domestic servant's request for permission to go and visit her sick mother was refused by her employer, she nonetheless did so and her disobedience was held to be a sufficient ground for her dismissal. But Alderson B. said that there "may undoubtedly be cases justifying a wilful disobedience of such an order; as where the servant apprehends danger to her life."[149] Rolfe B. added: "it is an unlawful order to direct a servant to continue where she is in danger of violence to her person, or of infectious disease."[150] In *Palace Shipping Company Ltd* v *Caine*[151] seamen, who were engaged for an ordinary commercial voyage of a peaceful nature, were held justified in refusing to obey an order to proceed to a port at a risk to their lives.

An order must not only be lawful but must also be proper and within the terms of the contractual duties of the employee. This includes the nature of the duties, and the time and place where these duties are to be carried out. Thus, in *Price* v *Mouat*[152] the court upheld the refusal of a lace buying employee to fold lace on cards. In *Briggs* v *Imperial Chemical Industries Ltd*[153] when a process

---

145 *Limland* v *Stephens* (1810) 3 Esp. 269; *Spain* v *Arnott* (1817) 2 Stark 256.
146 Per Karminski J in *Pepper* v *Webb* [1969] 2 ALL ER 216, 218.
147 *Turner* v *Mason* (1845) 13 M & W 112; *Callo* v *Brouncker* 172 ER 807.
148 *Supra*; see also *Ottoman Bank* v *Chakarian* [1930] A.C. 277 and *Bouzourou* v *Ottoman Bank* [1930] A.C. 271.
149 (1845) 13 M & W 112, 117-118
150 Ibid; 118.
151 [1907] AC 386; See also *Robson* v *Sykes* [1938] 2 KB 612.
152 (1862) 11 CBN 508.
153 (1968) 4 KIR 492

worker's plant was closed down he was asked to transfer to another plant within the employer's industrial complex. His refusal to do so was held to be a breach of contract. But Lord Parker CJ, commenting on clause 17 of the contract which provided that he must accept the employer's right to transfer him "to another job with a higher or lower rate of pay, whether day work, night work or shift work," said: "It is quite idle...to suggest that rule 17 would enable the employers to transfer a man from Billingham to some factory miles away, or, to take an absurd example, to transfer a carpenter to a plumber's job."[154] Similarly, in *O'Brien* v *Associated Fire Alarms Ltd*[155] the plaintiffs were held entitled to refuse their transfer. The plaintiffs worked for their employer for years in and around Liverpool where they lived. The employer's business fell in volume around Liverpool and the plaintiffs were asked to resume work at a place some 150 miles away. There were no evidence of the express terms of their oral employment. It was held that the circumstances of their employment indicated that what they had been doing during the years of their employment was all they could be required to do.

Faithful service

An employee is under a duty to serve his employer with good faith and fidelity.[156] As Greer J said in *Wessex Dairies Ltd* v *Smith*,[157] during the continuance of his employment, the employee must act in his employer's interests. During the employer's time he has to look after, not his own interests, but those of his employer. In *Sinclair* v *Neighbour*[158] an employee engaged as manager of a pool betting shop, took some money from the till to place on a bet elsewhere without the knowledge or consent of his employer. The court held his conduct was incompatible with his employment.

Spare-time work or moonlighting will normally not, in the absence of a contractual prohibition, express or implied, be in breach of faithful service. An employee is free to use his spare time as he wishes provided this does not interfere with his duties to his employer. Employees who worked in their spare time for a rival company of their employer were held to be in breach of faithful service on the ground that "if those employees continue to work for the defen-

[154] Ibid; 495
[155] [1969] 1 All ER 93
[156] *Robb* v *Green* [1895] 2 QB 315.
[157] [1935] 2 KB 80, 84
[158] [1967] 2 QB 279.

dants, they will put at the disposal of the defendants any confidential information which, in the course of their work for the plaintiffs, they may obtain."[159] In other words, there was danger of the employer's secret being divulged. An employee must not make or accept secret profits or bribe or use his position to obtain a reward.[160] An employer can, in an action for money had and received, obtain such profit or bribe from the employee.[161]

In the public sector of employment, the acceptance of bribes and secret profits, as well as the use of spare time, are also regulated by statute.[162] The code of conduct for public officers contained in the fifth schedule of the Constitution provides, *inter alia*, that a public officer must not put himself in a position where his personal interest conflicts with his duties and responsibilities. He must not receive or be paid the emoluments of any public office at the same time as he receives or is paid the emoluments of any other public office or engage or participate in the management or running of any private business, profession or trade. A public officer must not ask for or accept any property or benefits of any kind for himself or any other person on account of anything done or omitted to be done by him in the discharge of his duties. The Constitution established both a Code of Conduct Bureau and a Code of Conduct Tribunal to administer the code of conduct.[163]

There is implied in the contract of employment of every employee a term that he will not disclose the trade secrets and confidential information of his employer.[164] As Lynskey J put it,[165] "it is quite clear that an employee is under an obligation to his employers not to disclose confidential information obtained by him in the course of and as a result of his employment." In *Robb* v *Green*[166] the employee copied a list of his employer's customers and their addresses with the intention of using the list after leaving the employer's service and setting up on his own. This was held to be a breach of fidelity. The English Court of Appeal similarly held in *Wessex Dairies Ltd* v *Smith*[167] where, during the last week of his service, a milk roundsman while delivering milk to the employer's customers,

---

[159] Lord Greene M.R. in *Hivac Ltd.* v *Park Royal Scientific Instruments Ltd.* [1946] Ch. 169, 173.

[160] *Boston Deep Fishing & Ice Company* v *Ansell* (1888) 39 Ch. D. 339.

[161] *Reading* v *Attorney General* [1951] AC 507.

[162] The Regulated and Other Professions (Private Practice Prohibition) Decree 34 of 1984 which prohibited private practice within the public sector has been repealed by the Constitution of the Federal Republic of Nigeria (Certain Consequential Repeals) Act No. 63 of 1999

[163] See also Code of Conduct Bureau & Tribunal Act, cap. 56.

[164] *Robb* v *Green* [1895] 2 QB 315: *Alperton Rubber* v *Manning* (1917) 85 LJ Ch 377.

[165] *Bents Brewery* v *Hogan* [1945] 2 All ER 570, 576.

[166] *Supra.*

[167] [1935] 2 KB 80.

tried to induce them to give him their custom after he would have left the employer's service.

The duty not to disclose an employer's trade secret or confidential information continues even after the employment has ceased. In *Alperton Rubber* v *Manning*,[168] Peterson J said:[169]

> it is, to my mind, equally clear that it is a dishonest act on the part of a person in a confidential position, who, by virtue of the trust which is reposed in him, becomes acquainted with his employers' secret formulae, to disclose them either during or after his employment. Such conduct is a breach of trust or confidence, and is, in my view, a breach of the implied provisions in all contracts of service that the employee will observe the rules of honesty.

In *Facenda Chicken Ltd v Fowler*,[170] Goulding J, considered the duty of the employee not to disclose his employer's trade secrets in this way:[171]

> First there is information which, because of its trivial character or its easy accessibility from public sources of information, cannot be regarded by reasonable persons or by the law as confidential at all. The servant is at liberty to impart it during his service or afterwards to anyone he pleases, even his master's competitor.
>
> Second, there is information which the servant must treat as confidential (either because he is expressly told it is confidential, or because from its character it obviously is so) but which once learned necessarily remains in the servant's head and becomes part of his own skill and knowledge applied in the course of his master's business. So long as the employment continues, he cannot otherwise use or disclose such information without infidelity and therefore breach of contract. But when he is no longer in the same service, the law allows him to use his full skill and knowledge for his own benefit in competition with his former master; and...there seems to be no established distinction between the use of such information where its possessor trades as a principal, and where he enters the employment of a new master, even though the latter case involves disclosure and not mere personal use of the information. If an employer wants to protect information of this kind, he can do so by an express stipulation restraining the servant from competing with him (within reasonable limits of time and space) after the termination of his employment.

---

[168] 1917 86 LJ Ch. 377.

[169] Ibid., 379.

[170] (1983) IRLR 61; [1985] 1 All ER 724.

[171] Ibid., 65-66; 731-732.

> Third, however, there are, to my mind, specific trade secrets so confidential that, even though they may necessarily have been learned by head and even though the servant may have left the service, they cannot lawfully be used for anyone's benefit but the master's. An example is the secret process which was the subject-matter of *Amber Size & Chemical Co* v *Menzel.*[172]

In the Amber Size case the employer manufactured what was called amber size by a secret process comprising a secret mixture added to resin size at the critical moment. The employee acquired a material part of this secret process which he sought to make available to a competitor of his former employer. The court held he could be restrained by injunction from doing so although there was no express contractual term restraining him from doing so. However, an employer may seek to protect himself by express provision. And the law allows him to do so. In *Herbert Morris Ltd* v *Saxelby*,[173] Lord Atkinson, said an employer:

> is undoubtedly entitled to have his interest in his trade secrets protected, such as secret processes of manufacture which may be of vast value. And that protection may be secured by restraining the employee from divulging these secrets or putting them to his own use. He is also entitled not to have his old customers by solicitations or such other means enticed away from him.[174]

So an employer can, by introducing suitable and appropriate clause in the contract, protect only his trade secret; he is not allowed to prevent competition from the former employee. The passage from Lord Atkinson continued thus:

> But freedom from all competition *per se* apart from both these things, however lucrative it might be to him, he is not entitled to be protected against. He must be prepared to encounter that even at the hand of a former employee.[175]

In the same case Lord Parker said:[176]

> In fact, the reason, and the only reason, for upholding such a restraint on the part of an employee is that the employer has some proprietary right, whether in the nature of trade secrets, for the protection of which such a restraint is having regard to the duties of the employee reasonably necessary. Such a

---

172 [1913] 2 Ch. 239.
173 [1916] 1 AC 688.
174 Ibid. 702.
175 [1916] 1 AC 688,702.
176 Ibid; 710; See also per Farewell L.J. in *Sir W.C. Leng Co. Ltd.* v *Andrew* [1909] 1 Ch. 768; 773.

> restraint has, so far as I know, never been upheld, if directed only to the prevention of competition or against the use of the personal skill and knowledge acquired by the employee in his employer's business.

A contract in restraint of trade is *prima facie* void and unenforceable as being against public policy.[177] However, where a restraint is reasonable, that is reasonable in the interest of both parties and the public, it will be enforced against the employee. In resolving the issue of reasonableness, it may be said that the law is concerned, on the one hand, to give protection to the business secret of the employer and, on the other, to ensure that an employee is able to use whatever additional skill and experience he may have gained or acquired in his employment, for his own benefit and the benefit of the general public. As Pearson LJ said:[178]

> It is clear from the authorities that the plaintiffs were not entitled to impose a restriction which would prevent the defendant from using in competition with the plaintiffs the skill and aptitude and general technical knowledge acquired by him in his employment by the plaintiffs.

So that only trade secrets and confidential information may be protected. In *Commercial Plastics Ltd* v *Vincent*,[179] it was with difficulty that the court agreed there was confidential information. In *Koumoulis* v *Leventis Motors Ltd*[180] a spare parts specialist who, on behalf of his employer, dealt directly with the employer's customers both in Nigeria and overseas was held by the Supreme Court to be in possession of trade secrets. In *CFAO* v *George Leuba*,[181] the defendant employee entered into a written contract of employment which contained a restraint covenant. In an action for breach of covenant it was held to be unreasonable and therefore unenforceable. Webber J said:

> As to the nature of the covenantor's employment there is absolutely no evidence. The agreement does not disclose his duties, nor does the evidence, and I have been unable to find anything which may lead me to suppose that opportunities were afforded to the defendant to acquire trade secrets and

---

[177] *Nordenfelt* v *Maxim Nordenfelt Guns & Ammunition Co. Ltd.* [1894] AC 535; *Koumoulous* v *Leventis Motors* [1973] 1 All NLR 140; *Esso Petroleum Co. Ltd.* v *Harper's Garage* [1967] 2 WLR 811.

[178] *Commercial Plastics Ltd.* v *Vincent* [1965] 1 QB 623, 640.

[179] *Supra.*

[180] [1973] 1 All NLR (part 2) 140.

[181] (1918) 2 NLR 67.

> influence with customers or any special knowledge which may be used to the plaintiff's prejudice.[182]

The same point was made by Jackson, Assistant Judge, in *Anglo-African Supply Co Ltd* v *Benvie.*[183] He said: "In regard to the position held by Mr Benvie, I have looked in vain to Mr Haddow's evidence for any indication as to what were the precise duties of Mr Benvie, or as to how these duties did or might be held reasonable to protect."[184]

Other factors which the courts take into consideration in determining whether a restraint clause is unreasonable and so void are the scope of the restraint, relative to the employer's business or trade, the period of time it covers and the geographical area over which it extends. A restraint clause which seeks to give protection to the employer's business beyond the actual scope of the business may well render the contract void and unenforceable.[185] A covenant which restrains an employee from a type of work other than that upon which he was engaged will render the contract void.[186] Thus, where the plaintiff's activity was that of general medical practitioner and the covenant provided that the defendant after leaving the service, may not practice in any department of medicine, surgery, or midwifery, it was held that the restriction was wider than was necessary for the protection of the plaintiff's business.[187]

The duty of faithful service does not include a general duty to report a fellow servant's misconduct or breach of contract; whether there is such a duty depends on the contract and the terms of employment of the particular employee.[188] In *Asaolu* v *Olaiya Fagbamigbe,*[189] Ayoola J stated the rule, perhaps too broadly, when he said that an employee's duty of fidelity entails, amongst other things, his reporting to his employer or bringing to his notice whatever he finds out in the course of his duty, which might be harmful to his employer.[190] At any rate, this statement was only an *obiter dictum*.

---

182 Ibid., 77.
183 [1937] 13 NLR 158.
184 Ibid., 161.
185 *Commercial Plastic Ltd.* v *Vincent* [1965] 1 QB, 623.
186 *Routh* v *Jones* [1947]1 All ER 758.
187 Compare *Fitch* v *Dewes* [1921] 2 AC 158 with *Anglo African Supply Co. Ltd.* v *Benvie*, supra.
188 *Swain* v *West (Butchers)Ltd.* [1936] 3 All ER 261; *Sybron Corp.* v *Rochem Ltd.* [1983] 2 All ER 707.
189 [1982] 1 FNR 88.
190 Ibid., 93.

Termination of employment

The terms of a contract of employment, express or implied, may determine its duration. As we have seen, a contract to serve for life at a weekly salary was held to be perfectly legal.[191] In *Salt* v *Power Plant Co*[192] the employer had a right to terminate an employment within a period of three years "by giving 6 months notice in writing prior to the ensuing December 31, and in the absence of such notice the engagement to remain in force as a permanent one." Notice was not given within the three years and the court held that the employment was then for life.

However, the fact that the employment offered and accepted is described as permanent or pensionable does not necessarily mean an appointment up to retiring age. Such an appointment

> means no more than that the employer cannot, in the absence of agreement to that effect, tell the employee to stop work forthwith at will and without notice or compensation in lieu of notice. But does not mean, without more, that the employer is bound to retain the employee in employment for life.[193]

As Adefarasin J said: "The general principle is that the fact that the employment offered and accepted is described as permanent employment does not in itself normally create a promise of life employment or disentitle the employer from terminating the employee's contract of service on reasonable notice."[194] Lord Goddard is even more explicit:

> That an advertisement offers permanent employment does not...mean thereby that employment for life is offered. It is an offer...of general as distinct from merely temporary employment, that is that the person employed would be on the general staff with an expectation that, apart from misconduct or inability to perform the duties of his office, the employment would continue for an indefinite period. But apart from a special condition, in my opinion a general employment is always liable to be determined by reasonable notice. Nor do I think that, because a person is offered pensionable employment, the employer

---

191 *Wallis* v *Day* (1873) 2 M & W 273.

192 [1936] 3 All ER 322; the correctness of this decision was severely doubted in *McClelland* v *N. Ireland Health Board* [1957] 2 All ER 129 by the House of Lords but it was not overruled; see also *Ward* v *Barclay Parkins & Co. Ltd.* [1939]1 All ER 287.

193 Per Ekeruche J in *Abukogbo* v *AT & P Ltd.* [1966] 2 ALL NLR 89, 90,

194 *Porter* v *Nestle Products (Nigeria) Ltd.* [1968] NMLR 459, 461.

> thereby necessarily engages to retain the employee in his service long enough to enable him to earn a pension.[195]

It seems, however, that where a contract for a permanent and pensionable employment sets out the powers of the employer to terminate the employment in an exhaustive manner that the employment will continue until retirement, where the employer is unable to terminate it in any of the ways spelt out in the contract. The difficulty, however, is how to determine whether the rights set out are exhaustive or not - a matter which the courts have not examined in principle. In *McClelland* v *N. Ireland Health Board*[196] the House of Lords decided by a majority of three to two that a clause of the contract entitled "Dismissal and reduction in rank, and termination of employment otherwise" was intended to be comprehensive. In *Uwagbanebi* v *Nigerian Palm Produce Board*[197] the conditions of service provided, under "Termination", that "a staff of the Board may have his appointment terminated on any of the following grounds" and then listed eleven grounds. The plaintiff was given notice of termination not based on any of the enumerated grounds. The Court of Appeal held that the employer had not reserved to itself the right to terminate the plaintiff's employment for any other reason than those listed and accordingly he was entitled to stay in his employment until the retiring age provided there was no breach of any of the listed grounds.

The fact that a probationary period is expressed to be for a definite period after which the employment may be confirmed does not mean that the employment cannot be terminated within the probationary period. In *Ihezukwu* v *University of Jos*[198] the contract of employment provided that the appointment will be for a period of two years in the first instance after which it will be to the retiring age of 60 if it is confirmed. The Supreme Court held that this provision did not disentitle the employer from terminating the employment within the two years probationary period. Also, where an employee who contends that his employment has been wrongfully terminated nevertheless accepts the terminal benefits he would be entitled to upon lawful termination the employment would be held to have been properly and validly terminated. His reinstatement wou'd not be ordered as there would be no contract to enforce.[199]

---

[195] *McClelland* v *N. Ireland Health Board* [1957] 2 All ER 129, 133 - 134

[196] *Supra.*

[197] [1996] 3 NWLR 489.

[198] [1990] 4 NWLR 598; the decision in *Olukoya* v *Intercotra Ltd.* 1969 NCLR 357 to the contrary must be seen as wrong.

[199] *Onalaja* v *African Petroleum Ltd.* [1991]7 NWLR 691; *Guinness (Nig.) Ltd.* v *Agoma* [1992] 7 NWLR 728.

It must also be noted that the common law presumption of yearly hiring and its attendant consequence on termination no longer exist.[200] In *Ahuronye* v *University College, Ibadan*[201] the court doubted the continued existence of the presumption and in *Richardson* v *Koefod*[202] the English Court of Appeal held it no longer exists. Lord Denning MR said the time has now come to state explicitly that there is no presumption of a yearly living.[203]

An employment for a fixed term or period, e.g. five years, or for a specific job,[204] will, of course, come to an end at the expiration of the stipulated term or upon the contractual completion of the job unless it is earlier brought to an end.[205] However, the great majority of employment's are of indefinite duration. At common law such an employment may be brought to an end by performance, agreement of the parties, frustration, the giving of notice or summary dismissal.

Performance

There is no doubt whatsoever that the majority of employments only come to an end upon retirement.

Agreement

The parties to an employment contract can, at any time, by mutual agreement, either in accordance with the terms of the contract or otherwise, bring the employment to an end. And this is true whether the contract is of a definite or an indefinite duration.

---

200 For the presumption and its consequences see below.

201 [1959] WRNLR 232.

202 [1969] WLR 1812

203 Ibid; 1816. But in *International Drilling Co. (Nig) Ltd.* v *Ajijola* (1976) 2 SC 115; (1976) 1 NMLR 52 the Supreme Court held merely that a presumption of yearly hiring did not arise as the contract provided for its termination by the giving of two weeks notice or payment in lieu of notice. This principle had long been established, see e.g. *Mulholland* v *Bexwell Estates Co. Ltd.* [1950] 66 TLR (Pt. 2) 764; *Ahuronye* v *University College, Ibadan* [1959] WRNLR 232.

204 *In Sadler* v *Hendock* (1855) 4 E & B, 570 a man who was employed for a job, i.e., to clean out a drain was held to be an employee; Crompton J said at p. 578; No distinction can be drawn from the circumstance of the man being employed at so much a day or by the job.

205 Such earlier termination could be by breach, agreement, frustration or under the terms of the contract, if any such provision.

Frustration

Any contract of employment may be brought to an end by frustration.[206] When frustration occurs it "kills the contract itself and discharges both parties automatically."[207]

A contract of employment will be brought to an end by frustration where changes in the circumstances of the employment either render further performance of the contract impossible or where the obligations undertaken by the parties under the contract have become radically different. Quite recently Lord Brandon stated, with admirable lucidity, the requirements for the application of the doctrine of frustration. As he said:

> there are two essential factors which must be present in order to frustrate a contract. The first essential factor is that there must be some outside event or extraneous change of situation, not foreseen or provided by the parties at the time of contracting, which either makes it impossible for the contract to be performed at all, or at least renders its performance something radically different from what the parties contemplated when they entered into it. The second essential factor is that the outside event or extraneous change of situation concerned, and the consequences of either in relation to the performance of the contract, must have occurred without the fault or the default of either party to the contract.[208]

Events such as the death of either party to a contract, illness of an employee, outbreak of war, change in the law or even imprisonment of an employee may bring about frustration. In *Farrow* v *Wilson*[209] the plaintiff entered service as a farm bailiff and served the employer until the employer's death, when he was dismissed. In holding that the personal representative of the deceased employer was not bound to continue the plaintiff in employment Wills J held:[210]

> Generally speaking, contracts bind the executor or administrator, though not named. Where, however, personal considerations are of the foundation of the contract, as in cases of principal and agent and master and servant, the death

---

206 *Notcutt* v *Universal Equipment,Ltd.* [1986] 3 All ER 582.

207 Per Viscount Simon L.C. in *Joseph Constantine Steamship Ltd.* v *Imperial Smelting Corporation Ltd.* [1942] AC 154, 163. see also *Bank Line Ltd.* v *Arthur Capel & Co.* [1919] AC 435.

208 *Paul Wilson & Co.* v *Partenreederei Hannah Blumenthal* [1980] 1 AC 854, 909.

209 (1869) LR 4 CP 744; see also *Graves* v *Cohen* (1939) 46 TLR 21

210 The quotation is the judgement in full.

> of either party puts an end to the relation; and, in respect of service after the death, the contract is dissolved, unless there is a stipulation express or implied to the contrary. It is obvious that, in this case, if the servant had died, his master could not have compelled his representatives to perform the service in his stead, or pay damages, and equally by the death of the master the servant is discharged of his service, not in breach of the contract, but by implied condition.

In so far as companies are concerned it has long been established that an order for winding up a company is notice of discharge to all persons in the employment of the company.[211] A voluntary winding up seems to have the same effect. In *Fowler* v *Commercial Timber Co Ltd*[212] the English Court of Appeal refused to imply a term in the contract of employment of a managing director that if the company, his employer, was voluntarily wound up his right to employment should cease. Rather, to voluntarily wind up a company amounts to breach of contract of employment and the employee is entitled to damages.

The sale of a company has the effect of determining the employment of all employees who are employed in the company.[213] Where a receiver is appointed by the court on behalf of debenture holders the result of such appointment is to discharge the employees of the company and entitle then to sue for damages for wrongful dismissal.[214] It seems, however, that the appointment of a receiver out of court and as an agent of the company does not determine contracts of employment.[215]

The effect of the dissolution of a partnership is not quite clear. It will seem that an employment contract does not continue after the death of a partner in a firm.[216] In *Brace* v *Calder*[217] the retirement of two out of the four partners was held to dissolve the firm and operate as a dismissal of the plaintiff who was employed by the partnership as a manager. However as the business was carried on by the remaining partners who offered to continue the plaintiff in the employment on the old terms, an offer which he declined, he was held entitled only to nominal damages. But in *Phillips* v *Alhambra Palace Co*[218] the English

---

[211] *Re: General Rolling Stock company, Chapman's Case* (1866) LR 1Eq 346; *Re Oriental Bank Corporation* v *MacDowall's Case* [1886] 32 Ch. D. 366.

[212] [1930] 2 KB 1.

[213] *Re: Foster Clark Indenture Trusts* [1966] 1 All ER 43.

[214] *Reid* v *Explosives Company Ltd.* (1887) 19 QBD 364.

[215] *Re: Foster Clark Indenture Trust supra*; *Re Mack Trucks (Britain) Ltd.* [1967] 1 All ER 977.

[216] *Tasker* v *Shepherd* (1861) 6 H & N 575.

[217] [1895] 2 QB 253.

[218] [1910] 1 KB 39.

Court of Appeal held that the death of a partner puts an end to a contract of employment only where the contract has some relation to the personal conduct of the deceased partner. Presumably the retirement of a partner from a partnership is to be similarly interpreted so that both death and retirement do not automatically discharge a contract of employment.

It has long been settled that illness of an employee does not necessarily bring his contract of employment to an end. In *Cuckson* v *Stones*[219] the plaintiff was employed as a brewer for a term of years. Some years after commencing employment he fell ill and when he recovered and resumed work the employer refused to pay him for the period of the illness. He brought an action to recover the wages and the court held he could recover Lord Campbell CJ said, "he could not be considered incompetent by illness of a temporary nature; but, if he had been struck with disease so that he could never be expected to return to his work, we think the defendant ought to have dismissed him and employed another brewer in his stead."[220] In *Carr* v *Hadrill*[221] the workman, a biscuit marker, was employed on terms that his contract could be terminated by a week's notice. He took ill and was absent from work for five weeks. The employer refused to allow him resume work. The court upheld the workman's contention that he had a right to consider himself in service until the employer gave him a proper notice of dismissal. In other words the temporary illness did not bring the contract to an end and the employer was at liberty to give notice to terminate it. In *Warburton* v *Co-operative Wholesale Society Ltd*[222] the employee met with an accident and had to be away from work for three months. The English Court of Appeal held that his contract of employment was not frustrated. The Master of the Rolls, Lord Cozens-Hardy, said,[223] "it has been long settled that a contract of service is not terminated by incapacity to work by reason of temporary illness, and that on return to work the man can recover his wages during the period of his absence." Scrutton LJ added, "under decided cases a servant incapacitated by illness and in the absence of notice under the contract does not cease to be employed unless the illness is such as seriously to interfere with or frustrate the business purpose of the contract."[224]

However an employee has no automatic right to recover wages or salary for the period of absence owing to illness although it has not brought the

---

[219] (1858) 1 E & E 248.
[220] Ibid., 257.
[221] (1875) 39 JP 246.
[222] [1917] 1 KB 663.
[223] Ibid., 665.
[224] [1917] I KB 663, 668.

employment to an end by the doctrine of frustration. It depends on the terms of the contract, express or implied, whether or not wages or salary are payable during such illness. In *O'Grady* v *M. Saper Ltd*[225] Mackinnon LJ said in a judgement with which the other two members of the English Court of Appeal agreed, that: The whole question in such a case as this is: What were the terms of the contract between the employer and the servant and what did those terms provide in regard to payment of wages to him during his absence from the service by reason of illness?[226] In the contract in this case there was no express term regarding payment during illness but there was evidence before the court that the plaintiff had been away sick on three occasions without asking for or receiving payment. It was, therefore, easy for the court to imply a term into the contract that he was not entitled to wages during absence from work due to illness. The court approved this judgement in the subsequent case of *Mears* v *Safecar Security Ltd*[227] and disapproved the decision of Pilcher J in *Orman* v *Saville Sportswear Ltd*[228] which sought to establish a presumption in favour of payment of wages during absence through illness unless rebutted by a term of the contract, express or implied. In place of such a presumption the court substituted "an approach to the facts and evidence in each case with an open mind unprejudiced by any preconception, presumption or assumption."[229] In following this approach, where there is no express term on the issue, the court held that a court could properly have regard to the conduct of the parties in ascertaining whether the implied term of the contract is whether wages are payable during illness or not.

Illness may, however, bring a contract of employment to an end by frustration. Where frustration occurs the contract is automatically brought to an end and both parties are discharged from further performance of any obligations under the contract. A frustrated contract ceases to bind the parties. Whether a contract is frustrated by illness is a question of the facts of each case. The question to ask is: is the employee's incapacity, brought about by illness or injury, of such a nature, or did it appear likely to continue for such a period, that further performance of his obligations in the future would either be impossible or would be a thing radically different from that undertaken by him and agreed to

---

225 [1940] 2 KB 496.

226 Ibid., 473.

227 [1982] 2 ALL ER 865.

228 [1960] 3 All ER 105; the decision in *Okudolo* v *Nigeria Airways Ltd.* [1977] NCLR 493, based on Orman's Case may, therefore, now not be good law.

229 [1982] 2 All ER 865, 876

be accepted by the employer under the agreed terms of his employment?[230] Sir John Donaldson has suggested that in considering the answer to this question the following should be taken into account:

(a) the terms of the contract, including the provisions as to sick pay;
(b) how long the employment is likely to last in the absence of sickness;
(c) the nature of the employment;
(d) the nature of the illness or injury and how long it has already continued and the prospects of recovery; and (e) the period of past employment.[231]

As Sir John adds these factors are interrelated and cumulative but are not necessarily exhaustive of those which have to be taken into account. Any other factors which bear on the issue must also be considered.[232]

The outbreak of a war can also bring about the frustration of a contract of employment. As McCardie J said in *Marshall* v *Glanvill*,[233] "a state of war is presumed to be of such prolonged duration as *prima facie* to put an end to contracts which are conditional upon the continuance of a particular state of things which is only consistent with peace."[234] Thus the judge held that as the employee, a sales representative, having been interned, could not fulfil any of his duties and the employer could not accept any of the services under the contract, the contract came to an end. However, the decision of the same judge in the earlier case of *Nordman* v *Rayner & Sturges*[235] shows that where internment is merely of a temporary nature there is no frustration. In *Unger* v *Preston Corporation*[236] the court found that the internment was more than a temporary interruption and held that the contract was frustrated in that "it interfered with and frustrated the business purpose of the contract."[237] A number of court cases arose out of the civil war of 1967 to 1970 especially as a result of the blockade of the then Eastern Region which sought to break away from the country to form Biafra. In *Brown* v *Haco Ltd*[238] the employee, a clerk with the company, was stationed in a branch of the company in Port Harcourt in the former Eastern Region of Nigeria. When the civil war broke out he was cut off by the blockade

---

[230] See per Sir John Donaldson in *Marshall* v *Harland & Wolf* [1972] 2 All ER 715.
[231] [1972] 2 All ER 715, 718-719.
[232] Ibid., 719.
[233] [1917] 2 KB 87.
[234] Ibid., 91.
[235] [1916] 33 TLR 87.
[236] [1942] 1 All ER 200
[237] Ibid., 91.
[238] [1970] 2 All NLR 47.

and his employers did not hear from him until over fifteen months after when he reported in Lagos at the company headquarters to claim his salary for the period he was cut off. The court agreed with the employer that the occurrence was such a change of circumstances as to frustrate the contract. The same conclusion was reached in *Johnson* v *UAC* where the employee who was away on leave was unable to return to Lagos on the outbreak of the war.[239]

In *Hare* v *Murphy Brothers Ltd*[240] the English Court of Appeal had to decide, in essence, whether a contract of employment is frustrated by the imprisonment of an employee. An employee had been involved in a brawl as a result of which he was imprisoned. The court held, unanimously, that the contract came to an end but while Lord Denning MR based his decision firmly on frustration Stephenson LJ said it did not matter how the termination was labelled "whether as by a frustrating event or by repudiatory conduct or by a breach going to the root of his contract of employment or by impossibility of performance."[241] Lawson LJ did not say whether it was frustration or repudiation. In *London Transport Executive* v *Clarke*[242] the same court said that imprisonment could not bring about frustration since frustration can only be brought about where the supervening event is not the fault or default of either party to the contract. The court held that imprisonment of an employee is a repudiatory act of the employee. Similarly, in *Norris* v *Southampton City Council*[243] Kilner Brown J said where, however, there is fault as in the case of deliberate conduct which leads to impossibility of performance, then it is not a case of frustration but of repudiatory conduct.[244]

It is clear, as Lord Brandon said, that one essential factor necessary to frustrate a contract is the absence of fault in either party in bringing about the supervening event. This point was emphasised by Lord Summer in *Bank Line Ltd* v *Arthur Capel & Co*[245] when he said: "I think it is now well settled that the principle of frustration of an adventure assumes that the frustration arises without blame or fault on either side."[246] What has remained uncertain is the meaning of "fault". As was said in *Paul Wilson & Co* v *Partenreederei Hannal Blumenthal*, the courts have not defined with precision the meaning of the expression

239 [1975] NCLR 87.
240 [1974] 3 All ER 940.
241 Ibid; 943
242 [1981] ICR. 355.
243 [1982] ICR. 177.
244 Ibid., 179.
245 [1919] AC 435.
246 Ibid., 452.

"default" in this context. In *Poussard* v *Spiers* Viscount Simon raised the problem rather than supply an answer.[247] He said:[248]

> Some day it may have to be finally determined whether a *prima donna* is excused by complete loss of voice from an executory contract to sing if it is proved that her condition was caused by her carelessness in not changing her wet clothes after being out in the rain. The implied term in such a case may turn out to be that the fact of supervening physical incapacity dissolves the contract without inquiring further into its cause, provided, of course, that it has not been deliberately induced in order to get out of the employment.

The recent decision of the English Court of Appeal in *F.C. Shepherd & Co Ltd* v *Jerrom*[249] seems still to leave the issue of fault in a state of flux. An apprentice took part in an affray and was sentenced to borstal training. The employer contended that this frustrated the contract while the apprentice's contention was that it constituted a repudiatory conduct. Of course, where it is a repudiatory conduct the contract is not, at least, in law automatically brought to an end. All the three members of the court held that the contract was frustrated. But only Lawton LJ dealt with the issue of absence of fault clearly. He said:[250]

> The apprentice's criminal conduct was deliberate but it did not by itself have any consequences on the performance of his contract. What affected performance was his sentence of borstal training, which was the act of the judge and which he would have avoided if he could have done so. It cannot be said, I think, that the concept of "self-induced frustration" can be applied to this case.

Mustill LJ's ground of decision seems to be that the party not in default can rely on frustration brought about by the act or default of the other party. As he said he is disentitled to treat himself as discharged if the frustrating event is self-induced; but this will not affect the position of the other party, for whom the event is not self-induced.[251] Balcombe LJ simply said it was not a case of repudiation.

---

[247] [1942] AC 154
[248] Ibid., 166.
[249] [1986] 3 All ER 589.
[250] Ibid., 596.
[251] Ibid., 602.

Notice

There is no doubt that either party to a contract of employment has a common law right to bring the contract to an end by giving notice of this intention to the other party. This rule developed over a long period of time and it was not always clear this principle would be the outcome of the development. The uncertainties arose out of the early common law presumption of yearly or general hiring. Where employment was of an indefinite duration it was held to mean that such a contract could not be brought to an end before the end of the current year of the employment. Thus *R.* v *The Inhabitants of Birdbrooke*[252] a contract to serve a farmer at so much per week and with liberty to depart from the employment on a fortnight's notice was held to be a hiring for a year. Lord Kenyon said:[253]

> But it is said, that this cannot be considered to be a hiring for a year, because there was a reservation of weekly wages, and because each party was to be at liberty to put an end to the agreement on giving a fortnight's notice; but whether the wages are to be paid by the week or the year cannot make any alteration in the duration of the service, if the contract were for a year. This therefore was a contract for a year, at so much a week, with liberty to quit at any time...on giving a fortnight's notice; but the power of giving notice makes no difference, for it has been held, that an agreement to leave the service on giving a month's warning, did not defeat the settlement.

In *R.* v *The Inhabitants of Hampreston*[254] there was an agreement to serve a miller at an agreed wages per week, and the parties had liberty of parting on a month's notice on either side but there was no mention of time or for how long the servant would serve. The servant worked under the contract for about two and a half years. It was held to be a yearly hiring. Buller J said:[255]

> This is either a definite or an indefinite hiring: if the latter, the law says it is a hiring for a year. Then it was incumbent on the counsel, who contended that it was a definite contract, to define its duration: but nothing has been stated to show that it was a definite hiring. It could not be merely a hiring for a week,

[252] (1719) 4 Term Rep. 245.

[253] Ibid., 246; this statement was in fact, *obiter*, as Lord Kenyon held that the contract expressly provided that it was a contract for a year.

[254] (1793) 5 Term Rep. 205; see also *R* v *The Inhabitants of Lyth*; *R.* v *The Inhabitants of Long Whatton* (1993) 5 Term Rep. 327, 447 respectively and *R.* v *The Inhabitants of Hanbury* [1802] 2 East 423 and compare *R* v *The Inhabitants of Newton Toney* 2 Term Rep. 453.

[255] (1793) 5 Term Rep. 205, 208

> because the contract was only to be determined by giving a months notice: nor for a month only, as one of the counsel admitted. It must then be taken to be a general hiring; and the condition of being at liberty to part on a month's notice will not defeat the settlement.

In *Robinson* v *Hindman*[256] in 1800 Lord Kenyon gave an early hint of the possibility of termination by notice at any time. As he said, if a master turned away his servant without warning, or previous notice, and there was no fault or misconduct in the servant to warrant it, he ought to have the allowance claimed, of a month's wages.[257] The action was brought to recover a month's wages on the ground of a discharge without notice. In *Beeston* v *Collyer*,[258] where the plaintiff was employed as a clerk, the yearly hiring doctrine was re-emphasised although the case also showed that the contract of service of a domestic servant was always treated apart.[259] Gaselee J said:[260]

> There can be no doubt that a general hiring is a hiring for a year. In domestic service there is a common understanding that such a contract may be dissolved on reasonable notice; as a month's warning or a month's wages. There does not appear to be any such practice with respect to servants in husbandry, and we have no evidence what is the custom with clerks. We must, therefore, decide this case according to the general rule, and hold the contract between the parties to be a hiring for a year.

Similarly, in *Fawcett* v *Cash*,[261] where the employee was a warehouseman, the court held that since it was not the case of a domestic servant, where the contract might have been put an end to by paying a month's wages or giving a month's notice, there was clearly a contract for a year. But evidence of custom was allowed to show that a yearly hiring could be terminated by notice. In *Metzner* v *Bolton*[262] a contract to serve for a year as a commercial traveller was held determinable by three month's notice on proof of trade usage.

Similarly in *Foxall* v *International Land Credit Company*[263] the employers led evidence to prove a custom in their type of employment of giving three

---

[256] (1800) 3 Esp. 235
[257] Ibid.
[258] (1827) 4 Bing 309
[259] See *George* v *Davies* [1911] 2 KB 445
[260] (1827) 4 Bing 309, 313
[261] (1834) 10 ER 1026
[262] (1854) 9 Ex 518
[263] (1867) 16 TLR 637

months' notice to terminate the employment. In *Fairman* v *Oakford*[264] the plaintiff had worked on a previous occasion for the defendant and had then been removed by payment of a month's salary in lieu of notice. When a subsequent employment with the defendant as a clerk for one year was terminated before the end of the year by one month's notice the court held that the jury were right in holding the second employment to be on the same terms as the first. Pollock CB said:[265] "From much experience of juries, I have come to the conclusion that, usually, the indefinite hiring of a clerk is not a hiring for a year, but rather one determinable by three months' notice."

Indeed only seven years after this decision, Byles J said in *Hilcox* v *Batchellor*[266] that, as there was no stipulation in the contract as to the notice to be given by either side, all that could be said was that the notice must be a reasonable one. In *Creen* v *Wright*[267] Lord Coleridge CJ relied on both these judgements when he said there "is some authority for saying that as a proposition of general law reasonable notice is to be implied as a term of such a contract of hiring as this."[268]

At the beginning of the last century the law was already well settled. In *African Association Ltd and Allen*[269] the court said it must be taken to be the law that a contract of employment confers no right on the employer, in the absence of misconduct, to terminate the engagement without reasonable notice, unless the agreement contained clear words indicating a contrary intention. Eight years later *Payzu* v *Hannaford*[270] held the same view and in *De Stempel* v *Dunkels*[271] the English Court of Appeal confirmed the rule as a rule of law. Greer LJ said[272]

> ...I think that there must be implied in the contract...a term to the effect that the plaintiff's employment should be determined only by a reasonable notice.

Where a contract of employment provides expressly for the length of notice which may be given to terminate it that length of notice will be regarded as reasonable notice. And where the stipulated notice is given the party given the

---

[264] (1860) 5 H & N 635
[265] Ibid.; 636
[266] (1867) 15 L.T. 543
[267] (1876) 35 L.T. 339
[268] Ibid.; 340
[269] [1910] 1 KB 396
[270] [1918] 2 KB 349
[271] [1938] 1 All ER 238
[272] Ibid.; 247

notice cannot be heard to complain. In *Chioze* v *United Africa Company Ltd*[273] the contract provided for one month's notice on either side to terminate it and also that where an employee was suspected of serious misconduct he could be suspended pending the completion of investigation. When the plaintiff was arrested and charged with stealing from his employer he was given one month's salary in lieu of notice. His contention that he ought not to have been removed before the conclusion of the criminal charge was held to be baseless. In *Ikekhide* v *Lagos University Teaching Hospital Management Board*[274] where the contract provided for the giving of one month's notice and the plaintiff was given one month's notice he failed in his action for damages for wrongful termination of appointment. In *Maiza* v *Taylor Woodrow of Nigeria Ltd*[275] although the employee had been with the employers for about twenty years his employment was held to have been validly terminated when he was given one month's notice as provided in his contract.

However difficulties may arise where an employee has been promoted and he assumes greater responsibilities as well as earn higher pay and enhanced status but nothing is said about an initial stipulation of period of notice in the contract of employment. In *Esimaje Tsegbeyeri* v *Glaxo Nig. Ltd*[276] the plaintiff was employed by letter which provided that his appointment could be terminated by either side giving one month's notice. Many years after his appointment he was promoted senior manager by another letter which, however, was silent as to period of notice for termination. The court said the two letters must be read together and having so read them held that the length of notice was as provided in the first letter. The Supreme Court decided similarly in *Olaniyonu* v *British American Insurance Co Ltd.*[277] The plaintiff who had been promoted contended that the new memoranda which affected the manner of calculating his salary had altered the written contract of employment under which he was employed. The court held that the contract still subsisted and that the two week's notice or payment in lieu there provided was still valid.

Both decisions would seem to support the rule that an original contract of employment subsists upon promotion subject to any express or implied variation of its terms. There are dicta in the cases which support such a rule. In *Adams* v *Union Cinemas Ltd*,[278] Stable J said:

---

[273] [1956] 1 ERLR 28
[274] CCHCJ/6/74 page 715
[275] CCHCJ/12/72 page 52; see also *Mamah* v *Standard Bank (Nig) Ltd* 6 ECSLR 199; *Adeyemi* v *P.Z.* CCHCJ/8/74 page 1141.
[276] CCHCJ/11/74 page 1787
[277] [1974] (1) NMLR 64.
[278] [1939] 1 All ER 169

> The question as to when the variation of the terms of a contract constitutes a fresh contract and cases in which it is a mere modification of an existing contract are really cases which involve the splitting of hairs, and are a mere question of words. Here the relationship of master and servant which subsisted was a continuous relationship, although the obligations on either side, as happens every day in the case of master and servant, from time to time, varied. I think that everyone would be astonished if they were told that, when an employee is put to more responsible work, or given a rise of salary, that constitutes an entirely new contract, and constitutes an entirely new relationship, and that the law, whatever that may mean, presumes that, whenever something of that sort takes place, there is a new hiring, it may be for a year or for some other period.[279]

Similarly, in a more recent case, *Re Mack Trucks (Britain) Ltd*[280] Pennycuick J said:

> It must frequently happen in the case of a long period of service with a single employer that employer and employee enter into a whole succession of new contracts, e.g. upon promotion or for other reasons. But in ordinary speech one would in such circumstances treat the period of employment as dating from the commencement of the first of these contracts and not from the commencement of the contract currently in force at the date of it's termination.[281]

In *Meek* v *Port of London Authority*[282] the English Court of Appeal approached the issue purely on contractual principles. The plaintiffs were promoted to different grades on increased wages. The court held that on promotion there was in each case a fresh contract of employment. The difficulty which arises from such an approach is that, on every promotion, there is an ending of continuity of employment and consequently an earlier period of employment cannot count for pension and other purposes, including, indeed, period of notice, which normally may increase with both status and length of employment. Clearly the better view is that there is only the initial contract although its terms may change from time to time, expressly or impliedly, by mutual agreement.

---

[279] Ibid., 171.
[280] [1967] 1 All ER 977
[281] Ibid., 983.
[282] [1918] 2 Ch. 96.

Where a contract of employment is silent as to the length of notice required to terminate it the principle of law is that reasonable notice is required.[283] The sole question is, in such cases, what is reasonable notice? This is a question of fact and the answer depends on the circumstances of each case.[284] As Adio JCA said in *Honika Sawmill (Nig.) Ltd* v *Hoff*[285] All the circumstances of the case, such as the type of employment, the intervals at which the remuneration is paid or the period in relation to which the remuneration is stated, have to be considered. Previous decisions can only be used as a guide as each case depends on its own circumstances.[286] In *Ogunsanmi* v *C.F. Furniture (WA) Ltd*[287] the court took the following factors into consideration in determining reasonable notice: (i) the nature of the employment; (ii) the length of the employee's service with the employer and (iii) the fact that the employee was paid by the month. In *PZ & Co Ltd* v *Ogedengbe*[288] Madarikan JSC, who delivered the judgement of the Supreme Court, said:

> upon the uncontroverted facts of this case, especially having regard to the status of the plaintiff in the employment of the defendants and the length of service already put in by her, we fail to see how the decision of the learned trial judge that three months' notice was reasonable could be successfully challenged.[289]

In *Jimoh* v *Northern States Marketing Board*[290] the plaintiff was employed as a senior accountant and the employer gave evidence that the practice of the Board was to give employees of the status of the plaintiff one month's notice and that the plaintiff was aware of this practice. Nonetheless the court held that reasonable notice was six months but it failed to state the ground for this conclusion. The courts have said, in a number of cases, that it is not enough for an employee merely to contend that the notice given to him is not reasonable but

---

283 *PZ & Co. Ltd.* v *Ogedengbe* [1972] 1 All NLR 202; *Honika Sawmill (Nig.) Ltd.* v *Hoff* [1992] 4 NWLR 673.

284 *Aduke Watkinson* v *Pan American World Airways Inc* [1967] FNLR 120; *Sole* v *Mobil Oil Nig. Ltd.* [1968] NCLR 191; *Oke* v *Great Nigerian Insurance Co. Ltd.* CCHCJ/12/72p.62; *Alraine (Nig.) Ltd.* v *Eshiett* [1977] 1 SC 89.

285 *Supra.*

286 Ibid., 682.

287 [1961] All NLR 862.

288 [1972] 1 All NLR (pt.1) 202

289 Ibid., 204.

290 1971 (2) NCLR 311.

that it is desirable and prudent for him to adduce evidence of what he considers to be reasonable.[291]

In terminating employment by notice the law does not require that any reason or reasons for so doing be stated.[292] The reason or motive for giving notice to terminate is absolutely irrelevant for any consideration of the wrongness or otherwise of a termination. The crucial consideration is whether the required notice has been given. As Obaseki JSC said for the Supreme Court *in Ajayi* v *Texaco Nigeria Ltd*:[293]

> Where in a contract of employment there exists a right to terminate the contract given to either party, the validity of the exercise of that right cannot be vitiated by the existence of malice or improper motive. It is not the law that motive vitiates the validity of the exercise of a right to terminate validly an employment of the employee. There must be other considerations. The exercise is totally independent of the motive that prompted the exercise.

The Court of Appeal has held similarly. In the leading judgement of the court in *Calabar Cement Co Ltd* v *Daniel*[294] Katsina-Ala JCA said, "so long as the termination is lawful the motive therefore is not relevant." The party seeking to determine the contract by giving adequate notice as prescribed under the contract does not have to justify his action because he is not guilty of breach of contract.[295]

There is also no general rule of law that notice must be given at the end of the month so that it can take effect from the 1st of the next month.[296] However once notice is given it cannot be unilaterally withdrawn except there is an express provision for such a withdrawal.[297] As Diplock J said, in *Riordan* v *War Office*,[298] "the giving of a notice terminating a contractual employment, whether

---

[291] See e.g. *Gaiser* v *Cole* (1958) LLR 83; *Daniels* v *Shell BP Petroleum Company of Nigeria Ltd.* (1962) I All NLR 19; *Aduke Watkinson* v *Pan American World Airways Inc.* (1967) FNLR 100.

[292] *Gilbert Grunitzky* v *ITT* (Nig.) Ltd (1981) 2 PLR 25.

[293] [1987] 3 NWLR 577, 593; see also *Chukwumah* v *Shell Petroleum Development Company of Nigeria* [1993] 5 KLR; *Nfor* v *Ashaka Cement Co. Ltd.* [1994] 1 NWLR 222; *Taiwo* v *Kingsway Stores Ltd.* [1950] 19 NLR 122; *Nwaokolo* v *Sapele Urban District Council* [1965] I All NLR 224; *Sogbetun* v *Stirling Products (Nig.) Ltd* 1973 NCLR 323.

[294] [1991] 4 NWLR 750.

[295] Ibid., 758.

[296] *Appiarr* v *Esso West Africa Inc.* (1968) NCLR 32.

[297] *Mitchell* v *De Facto Works Ltd.* (1966) LLR 212.

[298] [1959] I WLR 1046.

by employer or employee, is...a unilateral act requiring no acceptance by the other party and...once given it cannot...be withdrawn save by mutual consent."[299]

It seems quite settled that any employment may be brought to an immediate end by the payment of wages or salary in lieu of the requisite notice which would normally be worked out. Where the contract provides for termination either by notice or payment in lieu or by payment in lieu of notice there is, of course, no difficulty as termination will be in accordance with the contractual terms. Thus in *Mamah* v *Standard Bank Nigeria Ltd.*[300] Ogbobine J said the true position is that the bank has fallen on its right under the agreement of service to terminate the contract on payment of a month's salary in lieu of notice, and having agreed to be bound by the terms of the contract, it is not open to plaintiff to complain nor can the court question the right of the bank to do so.[301] But even where there was no express provision in the contract for termination by payment in lieu of notice the courts have held that such termination was not wrongful.[302] It is suggested, therefore, that the decision of the Court of Appeal in *British Airways* v *Makanjuola*[303] must be seen as unhelpful. There the contract provided for termination by "two month notice in writing" but the plaintiff was given two months' salary in lieu of notice in writing. This was held to be a wrongful termination. Ubaezonu JCA, who gave the leading judgement, said. "This is not however what the contract says. The contract of service...provides for 'two month notice in writing' NOT two months' salary in lieu of notice...In nowhere does the contract of service provide for payment of salary in lieu of notice. This particular contract of service however is silent on payment of salary in lieu of notice."[304]

It is suggested that there are at least two reasons for supporting the principle of law that wages or salary can always be paid in lieu of notice. The first is based on the normal quantum of damages recoverable for a breach of a contract of employment. Since the damages recoverable for wrongful termination is normally the wages or salary payable for the period of notice required to lawfully terminate a contract of employment there cannot be any complaint where such

---

[299] Ibid., 1054.
[300] 6 ECSLR 199.
[301] Ibid., 206.
[302] *Porter* v *Nestle Products (Nig.) Ltd.* [1968] NMLR 459; *Salako* v *Foremost Dairies (Nig.) Ltd.* CCHCJ/6/74p.719; even the decision of the Court of Appeal in *International Paints (WA) Ltd.* v *Ogwi*, Court of Appeal Judgements Jan - Dec. [1985] p. 1087 would appear to be based on this principle.
[303] [1993] 8 NWLR 276.
[304] Ibid., 286.

wages or salary are paid forthwith.[305] As Ayoola J said in *Shokoya* v *Nigeria Tobacco Co Ltd*[306] if, they failed, as in this case to give a month's notice, the plaintiff would be entitled to one month's salary in lieu of notice as liquidated damages.[307] It may be noted that in the British Airways case Ubaezonu JCA said that the measure of damages for failure to give two months' written notice "may be the appellants two months' salary in lieu of notice or something within that range."[308] The second reason in favour of the principle can be based on the rule at common law that an employer generally fulfils his duty under a contract of employment by paying wages or salary and need not provide an employee with work to do.[309]

Where termination is by payment in lieu of notice such payment must actually be made at the time of the termination.[310] Where payment was made three months after a letter of termination was given to an employee the Supreme Court held that the termination was wrongful.[311] The only effect of this is, probably, that the date of the wrongful termination is altered.[311a]

Summary dismissal

In 1817 in *Spain* v *Arnott*[312] Lord Ellenborough agreed that where an employee persists in refusing to obey his master's orders the master will be justified in dismissing him. As he said, after a refusal on the part of the servant to perform his work, the master is not bound to keep him on as a burdensome and useless servant to the end of the year.[313] Similarly in *Callo* v *Brouncher*[314] Parker J said if there was any moral misconduct, either pecuniary or otherwise, wilful disobedience, or habitual neglect, the defendant should be at liberty to part with the plaintiff.[315] Incompetence was relied upon in *Searle* v *Ridley*[316] where the

---

305 *French* v *Brookes* (1830) 6 Bing 354 can be so explained; see also *Baker* v *The Denkera Ashanti Mining Corp. Ltd.* (1903) 20 TLR 37.
306 (1970) NCLR 343.
307 Ibid., 345.
308 [1993] 8 NWLR 276, 288.
309 *Konski* v *Peet* [1915] 1 Ch. 530.
310 *Chukwumah* v *Shell Petroleum Development Company of Nigeria Ltd.* [1993] 5 KLR 93; [1993] 4 NWLR (pt. 289) 512.
311 Ibid.
311a See *NNPC* v *Idoniboye-Obu* [1996] 1 NWLR 655.
312 (1817) 2 Starke 256.
313 Ibid.; 258
314 (1831) ER 807
315 Ibid.
316 (1873) 28 LT 411

court said that an employer had a common law right to dismiss an employee for incompetence to do the work for which he contracted.

In the well-known case of *Harmer* v *Cornelius*[317] the plaintiff was employed as a scene-painter having responded to a newspaper advertisement for "two first-rate panorama and scene-painters." On the second day of his employment he was dismissed for incompetence. The court held that his dismissal was justified as it would be unreasonable to compel an employer to go on employing a person who, having presented himself as competent, turns out to be incompetent. Willes J laid it down that when a skilled labourer, artisan, or artist is employed, there is on his part an implied warranty that he is of skill reasonably competent to the task he undertakes.[318] But even unskilled employees owe a duty to exercise reasonable care in the performance of their contractual duties. In *Lister* v *Romford Ice & Cold Storage Co Ltd*[319] the House of Lords held that it was an implied term of the contract of employment of a driver that he would perform his duties with proper care. Viscount Simonds said that "even in so-called unskilled operations an exercise of care is necessary to the proper performance of duty."[320]

However, strictly, it is unnecessary to categorise or label misconduct which may justify summary dismissal. The point was made by Bramwell B in *Horten* v *McMurtry*[321] when he said:[322]

> Cases may be cited in which the courts have laid down certain criteria as to when a master is justified in discharging his servant; but if these decisions are examined it will be evident that they do not afford an exhaustive set of cases, but only a certain number.

It is not even necessary that misconduct should include moral turpitude.[323] As Dickson J has said: "The sole question is whether there is justification for dismissal."[324]

Under the general law of contract only conduct or breach which amounts to a repudiation of a contract will justify the innocent party in opting to bring the

---

317 (1858) 141 ER 94.
318 Ibid.; 98
319 [1959] 1 WLR 555
320 Ibid.; 573
321 (1860) 5 H & N 667
322 676
323 Ibid.
324 *Nunnick* v *Costain-Blaneevoort Dredging Ltd* (1960) LLR 90, 94

contract to an end. In *Freeth* v *Burr*[325] which involved a contract of sale of iron to be delivered in instalments, Lord Coleridge CJ said that "in cases of this sort, where the question is whether the one party is set free by the action of the other, the real matter for consideration is whether the acts or conduct of the one do or do not amount to an intimation of an intention to abandon and altogether to refuse performance of the contract."[326] Lord Coleridge added that "the true question is whether the acts and conduct of the party evince an intention no longer to be bound by the contract."[327] This was termed a test by Lord Collins in *General Billposting Company Ltd* v *Atkinson*[328] in which the House of Lords approved it. The test is applicable to contracts of employment. As Lord Evershed, MR, said in the interesting case of *Laws* v *London Chronicle Ltd*[329] "since a contract of service is but an example of contracts in general, so that the general law of contract will be applicable, it follows that, if summary dismissal is claimed to be justifiable, the question must be whether the conduct complained of is such as to show the servant to have disregarded the essential conditions of the contract of service."[330] However the test needs to be modified in the light of the decision in *Laws* v *London Chronicle Ltd*[331] The test is not whether conduct evinces an intention no longer to be bound by the contract or that it shows a disregard of all the essential conditions of the contract but rather, whether it demonstrates a disregard of "one of its essential conditions." As we have seen, breach of an employee's duty to obey a lawful and proper order of his employer or to exercise reasonable skill or care in the discharge of his duties has been held to justify summary dismissal. In *Laws* v *London Chronicle Ltd*[332] Lord Evershed MR said:[333]

> It is, no doubt, therefore, generally true that wilful disobedience of an order will justify summary dismissal, since wilful disobedience of a lawful and reasonable order shows a disregard - a complete disregard - of a condition essential to the contract of service, namely, the condition that the servant must obey the proper orders of the master and that, unless he does so, the relationship is, so to speak, struck at fundamentally.

---

[325] (1874) LR 9 CP 208
[326] Ibid.; 213
[327] Ibid.
[328] [1909] AC 118, 122
[329] [1959] 2 All ER 285
[330] Ibid.; 287
[331] *Supra*
[332] *Supra*
[333] Ibid.

Similarly, in *Pepper* v *Webb*[334] Karminski LJ said that it has long been part of our law that a servant repudiates the contract of service if he wilfully disobeyed the lawful and reasonable orders of his master.[335] Lord Dunpark makes the same point generally in these words:

> There are any number of cases in which one party has fulfilled, or been willing to fulfil, all his contractual obligations except one, and that one failure has been held to be a material breach of contract.[336]

And a single act of misconduct may justify summary dismissal.[337] Misconduct, whether cumulative or single, is viewed in the same way. The real difficulty is in determining whether misconduct evinces an intention to disregard an essential condition of the employment. Not every misconduct amounts to a repudiatory misconduct although there is no fixed rule of law which defines the degree of misconduct which amounts to a repudiation. In *Okoye* v *Nigeria Airways*[338] Desalu J said, "misconduct inconsistent with the due and faithful discharge by the servant of the duties for which he was engaged is good cause for the dismissal but there is no fixed rule of law defining the degree of misconduct which will justify dismissal."[339]

The issue of what degree of misconduct will justify a dismissal is different and separate from the question of a definition of misconduct. Thus the statement of the Court of Appeal in *Oyedele* v *Ife University Teaching Hospital Complex Management Board*[340] that "under our law there is no definition of what is misconduct anywhere. A misconduct is what the employer considers to be misconduct. In the instant case the employers of the appellant considered the two allegations made against him to amount to "misconduct" and so they retired him"[341] is misleading and not to the point.

---

[334] [1969] 2 All ER 216

[335] Ibid.; 218

[336] *Blyth* v *The Scottish Liberal Club* [1983] 1 RLR 245 251

[337] *Boston Deep Sea Fishing & Ice Co Ltd.* v *Ansell* (1888) 39 Ch. D 339; *Laws* v *London Chronicle Ltd.* [1959] 2 ALL ER 285; *Oyedeji* v *Fasheun* (1976) 6 UILR 134, *Adiatu* v *Polythene Enterprises (Nig.) Ltd.* (1978) 5 CCHCJ 884; *Abati* v *Tourist corporation of Nigeria* (1980) 1 PLR 437. The statement of Adesanya J in *Chamma* v *Five Star Industries Ltd.* 1974 NCLN 138, 144, in this regard, probably accords with the law.

[338] [1979] 3 LRN 82; (1979)1-3 CCHCJ 339; see also *Akinbule* v *UBA Ltd.* [1980] 1-3 CCHCJ 363; and per Lord James in *Clouston & Co. Ltd.* v *Corry* [1909] AC 122, 122. 129.

[339] Ibid.; 96.

[340] [1990] 6 NWLR 194.

[341] Ibid.; 199; see also the same court in *Anakism* v *Union Bank of Nigeria Ltd* [1994] 1 NWLR 557

What has to be decided, and it is the courts which are the final arbiters, is whether misconduct is sufficient to justify a dismissal. In *British-American Insurance Company (Nig) Ltd* v *Omolaya*[341a] the Court of Appeal itself held that absence from work was gross misconduct which entitled the employer to dismiss summarily. In *Usen* v *Bank of West Africa*[342] the Supreme Court upheld the summary dismissal of an employee who had issued a false teller in spite of his pleas that he had served the bank for 14 years without blemish. In *New Nigeria Bank Ltd* v *Obevudiri*[343] an accountant who verified forged signatures on forged bank drafts and certified them as genuine was held by the Court of Appeal to have committed "misconduct, gross enough to justify" summary dismissal. In *Co-operative & Commerce Bank (Nig) Ltd* v *Nwankwo*[344] the allegations against a bank employee were that he cashed crossed cheques across the counter, overlent money and engaged in private practice. The Court of Appeal held that these acts, which were proved, justified his dismissal as they undermined the confidence which should exist between a bank manager and his employer.

In *Chamma* v *Five Star Industries Ltd,*[345] the plaintiff was dismissed on the ground that he called the managing director "a thief, cheat, rogue." In an action for wrongful dismissal Adesanya J agreed that it is not enough to allege gross insubordination and rudeness but that particulars as to the precise form of misconduct must be given. He said: "Insubordination, insolence, rudeness, derogating language these are vague terms which in my view can disguise a multitude of types of misconduct. Some of them may properly justify such a drastic step as summary dismissal. Many of them may not justify summary action."[346] In *Oyekunle* v *Prestrest (Nig.) Ltd*[347] the plaintiff's duty included the checking of the pay roll and the certification of its correctness. It was found that for over a period of 80 weeks the weekly figures were inflated. When the plaintiff was issued with a query he refused to accept it but instead slammed the door in the MD's face. The court held his dismissal was justified. In *Nwobosi* v *ACB Ltd*[347a] the Supreme Court affirmed the judgement of the Court of Appeal which held that the employee who had, in complete defiance, granted loans and overdrafts in disregard of express instructions committed misconduct which justified summary dismissal. It was also held that a clause of the contract of

---

[341a] [1991] 2 NWLR 721.
[342] [1965] 1 ALL NLR 244.
[343] [1986] 3 NWLR 387.
[344] [1993] 4 NWLR 159
[345] (1975) NCLR 138.
[346] Ibid.; 142.
[347] (1979) OGSLR 69; see also *Asaolu* v *Olaiya Fagbamigbe* [1982]1 FNR 88
[347a] [1995] 6 NWLR 658.

employment which provided that staff may be dismissed for certain offences, including certain listed ones, was not exhaustive and did not preclude the application of the general common law.

Where incompetence is alleged the onus is on the employer not only to prove the incompetence but also that is justifies summary dismissal.[348] Thus where an employer alleged incompetence but he was unable to prove it the dismissal was held to be wrongful.[349]

Where misconduct is committed outside working hours it will justify summary dismissal only when it is proved to be harmful to the employer's business or that it reflects on the employee's capacity to perform his duties in accordance with the contractual terms, express or implied.[350]

Even when summary dismissal is held justified it cannot be made to take retrospective effect from the date of the misconduct held to justify the dismissal.[351] However no reason need be given at the time of dismissal and a dismissal may be justified by facts or misconduct not known at the time of dismissal but which have only subsequently become known.[352] In *W. Devis & Sons Ltd* v *Atkins*[353] Lord Dilhorne said that in an action for damages for wrongful dismissal an employer can rely as justifying the dismissal an information only acquired after the dismissal.[354] Where, however, an employer who has full knowledge of a misconduct which would justify summary dismissal chooses to continue the employee in his service he cannot thereafter rely on the same facts to justify a dismissal.[355] He would be held to have waived or condoned the misconduct.[356] However the doctrine of waiver or condonation applies only where the employer was in possession of or had full knowledge of the facts of the misconduct. In *Federal Supply & Cold Storage Company of*

---

348 *AT & P (Nig.) Ltd* v *Gbagu* [1966] NCLR 56; *Akinbule* v *UBA Ltd* (1980) 1 - 3 CCHCJ 363.

349 *Nunnick* v *Costain Blaneevoort Dredging Ltd* (1960) LLR 90; *Garabed* v *Asaad Jamakani* [1961] 1 All NLR 177.

350 *Clouston & Co Ltd* v *Corry* [1909] AC 122; *Thomson* v *Alloa Motor Company Ltd* [1983] 1 RLR 403 Cf. *Werner Moeller* v *Monier Construction Co Ltd* [1961] 1 All NLR 167.

351 *Healey* v *Societe Anonyme Francaise Rubastic* [1917] 1 KB 946; *Odugbemi* v *NBC* [1974] NCLR 452; *New Nigeria Bank Ltd* v *Obevudiri* [1986] 3 NWLR 387.

352 *Ridgway* v *Hungerford Market Company* [1835] 3 Ad & Eb 71; *Boston Deep Sea Fishing & Ice Co* v *Ansell* (1888) 39 Ch D 399; per Sacks LJ in *Cyril Leonard* v *Simo Securities* [1972] 1 WLR 80, 87; *Onifade* v *K. Chellaram & Sons (Nig.)Ltd* (1974) NCLR 230; *Ishola* v *North Brewery Ltd* [1974] 4 UILR 72.

353 [1977] AC 931.

354 Ibid.; 950.

355 Per Bramwell, B, in *Horton* v *Mc Murtry* (1860) 5 H & N 667, 675

356 *Electricity Corporation of Nigeria v Nicol* [1968] 1 All NLR 201; *Onifade* v *K. Chellaram & Sons (Nig.) Ltd* (1974) NCLR 230.

South Africa v *Angehm*[357] the employer accepted the employee's denial of misconduct and continued him in employment. The subsequent dismissal of the employee on the same misconduct when it became fully known to the employer was held justified by the Judicial Committee of the Privy Council. Lord Atkinson, who delivered the judgement of the Committee, said:[358]

> If the master accepts the servant's denial of quilt, and honestly comes to the conclusion that the servant is innocent, then, whatever the master's credulity, the case does not come within these authorities, since no man can condone a wrong which he does not believe was committed upon him.

Criminal misconduct

It seems that two decisions of the Supreme Court have been accepted as establishing a principle of law that, by virtue of the constitutional provision on fair hearing in criminal cases, an employee can be lawfully dismissed for misconduct which also constitutes a criminal offence, only after he has been tried in the courts and conviction obtained.[359] The earlier of the two decisions was given in *Denloye* v *Medical And Dental Practitioners Disciplinary Committee.*[360] It seems clear, however, that the decision in this case was reached entirely by applying the provisions of a particular statute. Also, strictly, it was not a case of removal from employment. And the Supreme Court expressly declined to consider the effect of the constitutional provision on fair hearing. The second decision was in *Sofekun* v *Akinyemi.*[361] In giving the judgement of the court Fatai-Williams, CJN, said:

> it seems to me that once a person is accused of a criminal offence, he must be tried in a "court of law" where the complaints of his accusers can be ventilated in public and where he would be sure of getting a fair hearing as set out in subsection (4) to (10) of section 22 of the Constitution of the Federal Republic of Nigeria.[362]

---

[357] [1910] 103 LT 150.

[358] Ibid.; 152.

[359] E.g. *Akinwale v Ondo State Housing Corporation* (1992)Vol. 11 ODSLR 210; *Anakism* v *Union Bank of Nigeria Ltd* [1994]1 NWLR 557.

[360] [1968] NSCC 260.

[361] [1980] NSCC 175.

[362] Ibid., 184. Section 22 of the 1963 Constitution became s. 33 of the 1979 Constitution and is now s. 36 of the present constitution.

There is no doubt that the decision was correct on its facts. The Regulations under which the plaintiff was purportedly dismissed provided for dismissal where "an offence against any enactment (being a criminal offence as defined for the purposes of these Regulations) may have been committed by a public officer." The plaintiff, a medical doctor and an employee in the public service, was accused of, *inter alia*, attempting to have carnal knowledge of and unlawful and indecent assault on a female patient, both being within the definition of a criminal offence in the Regulations and the Criminal Code. The Supreme Court was, therefore, justified in insisting that the plaintiff should have, first, been found guilty of committing the offences. He had been charged or accused of committing criminal offences under an enactment and, the constitutional provision requires that a person charged with a criminal offence be given a fair hearing by a court or tribunal.

It is submitted, however, that, in the absence of a provision such as was contained in the regulations, it cannot be said that an employee alleged to have committed a misconduct which also amounts to a crime, is necessarily charged or accused of the crime. It is true, of course, that the same misconduct may give rise to both a breach of contract and a criminal offence just as it can be tortuous and also criminal. But it does not follow that to allege a contractual misconduct means also a charge of a crime. Therefore, in such cases, the constitutional provision need not be applied. An employee who is dismissed for a misconduct would not be held to have been convicted for any crime which the misconduct may constitute. The consequences which follow such a dismissal are not those which attend a criminal conviction. To charge is generally understood to mean charged for the purpose of prosecution for a crime. This view is shared by the House of Lords. In *Stirland* v *DPO*[363] the accused, who was on trial for forgery, asserted in examination- in-chief that he had never been "charged" with any offence. He was then asked questions suggesting he had been "questioned about a suggested forgery" sometime by his former employer. In construing the word "charged" in a section of a statute which read in part "every person charged with an offence..." Viscount Simon L. C. said:[364]

> It is necessary, however, to guard against a possible confusion in the use of the word "charged"...It is plain that its meaning in the section is "accused before a court" and not merely suspected or accused without prosecution. When the appellant denied that he had ever been "charged" he may fairly be

[363] [1944] AC 315.
[364] Ibid., 323 - 324.

> understood to use the word in the sense it bears in the statute and to mean that he had never previously been brought before a criminal court.

In practice some employers prefer, because it may be in the best interest of the business, to dismiss rather than report a criminal misconduct to the police. However employers may, and many in fact, dismiss for such misconduct and in addition report the matter to the police. There is no doubt that the application of the constitutional provision has put employers in a quandary. What does an employer do when, for a number of reasons, including tardiness, police investigation drags on and on or is inconclusive or even abandoned? What is a employer expected to do when prosecution is not recommended for any of several reasons, some propitious and others not so? In *Biishi* v *Judicial Service Committee,*[365] the appellant, an area court judge, grade II, was alleged to have demanded and received ₦20 from a litigant in order to relist a case which had been struck out. He was suspended and, after police investigation, he was compulsorily retired with full benefits. Although the DPP thought the police investigation showed that the appellant conspired with others to receive the gratification, the Attorney General was "of the view that having regard to the smallness of the amount involved public time should not be wasted in pursuing the prosecution." But the Court of Appeal held that the offence was a serious criminal offence and the appellant should have first been prosecuted! And in some cases, because of the desire to avoid the undesirable consequences of applying the constitutional provision, both employers and the courts have had to resort to some amount of subtlety in their conduct or judgement. In *Gukas* v *Jos International Breweries Ltd,*[366] the plaintiff, a warehouse supervisor, took delivery of a quantity of cartons of beer but was unable to account for the loss of some of them. After being issued with a query he was suspended form work and later dismissed. The plaintiff contended that the dismissal was invalid on the ground that since the allegation amounted to an offence under the Penal Code the failure to first try him to conviction before dismissal was a denial of fair hearing under s. 36(4) of the Constitution. The Court of Appeal held that since there was no allegation in the query or the letters of suspension and dismissal that he committed any crime there was no breach of the constitutional provision. Mukhtar, JCA, said: "As can be understood from all the...evidence it is clear that the appellant was dismissed, not for any criminal allegation, but for gross negligence and misconduct."[366a] Fortuitousness also determined the outcome of

[365] [1991] 6 NWLR (pt.197) 331.
[366] [1991] 6 NWLR 614.
[366a] Ibid. 621.

the appeal in *Okosun* v *Central Bank of Nigeria*[366b] Following an allegation of crime the appellant was queried and handed over to the police for criminal investigation. He was subsequently suspended from duty and then had his employment terminated by payment in lieu of notice. The appellant contended that the termination of his employment was wrongful being based on an allegation of a crime for which he had not been charged to court and found guilty. In the leading judgement Okunola JAC said:[366c]

> The earlier queries which charged the plaintiff with fraud were not pursued as they were abandoned and no issue arose on them. Neither did the trial court make a finding of fact to the effect that the termination was based on an allegation of crime as the court held that no reason was given. It must be observed that this finding was unchallenged and must form the basis of the determination of this appeal and any such argument contrary to it deserves to be discountenanced and I so hold.

It is suggested that the ends of justice would be better met without applying section 36(4) of the Constitution to employment cases.[366d] It seems that all that is required under section 36 of the Constitution is that no one be condemned to any sanction, civil or criminal, without a fair hearing before an impartial court or tribunal established by law. There is no doubt that any employee has a right to challenge his dismissal or removal from employment where he believes it is wrongful or otherwise unlawful. And a dismissal or removal, whether for criminal misconduct or otherwise, being, as we have argued, a civil rather than a criminal matter, the right to fair hearing is guaranteed not by subsection 36(4) but by subsection 36(1). Where the removal or dismissal is on the ground of criminal misconduct section 137 of the Evidence Act would, probably, be applicable and the employer obliged to prove the criminal misconduct beyond reasonable doubt.[366e] Failure to do so would sound in damages only as in all cases of wrongful removal from employment.[366f] But insistence on the application of s. 36(4) means that an employer may have to pay either benefits or

---

[366b] [1996] 2 NWLR 77; for other similar cases see below.

[366c] Ibid., 86.

[366d] Or to the universities as was done in *Garba* v *University of Maiduguri* [1986] 1 NWLR (pt.18) 550.

[366e] Even in such cases it seems that, at common law, the standard of proof required is as for civil cases and not beyond reasonable doubt; *Bater* v *Bater* [1950] 2 ALL ER 458; *Hornal* v *Neuberger Products, Ltd* [1956] 3 All ER 970 especially per Morries LJ at 978; the common law position seems preferable since such a case is essentially a civil case.

[366f] *Shuaibu* v *Union Bank of Nigeria Plc* [1995] 4 NWLR 173. Excluding cases with statutory flavour, of course.

damages to an employee who would otherwise forfeit his benefits. Any employer who may want to avoid such payment or otherwise wishes to comply with the subsection will, as we have shown, face grave uncertainties. And it may be bad for industrial relations.

However, there is every indication that the Supreme Court would re-examine the issue. In *Yusuf* v *Union Bank of Nigeria* Ltd[366g] in the leading judgement, with which all the Justices agreed, Wali JSC said:[366h]

> It is not necessary, nor is it a requirement under s.33 of the 1979 Constitution that before an employer summarily dismisses his employee from his services under the common law, the employee must be tried before a court of law where the accusation against the employee is for gross misconduct involving or bordering on criminality.

But this statement was an *obiter dictum.*[366j] It is suggested that when the opportunity truly presents itself the court should have no difficulty in distinguishing *Sofekun*'s case where, as has been pointed out, the provision of the statute in issue could justify the decision given.

Where an employer has alleged misconduct, whether criminal or otherwise, can he, instead of summary dismissal, terminate the employment by giving notice? It seems clear that, at common law, this option is always available to an employer.[367] In *Sule* v *Nigerian Cotton Board*[368] the Supreme Court held that the employee could not be heard to complain having been retired on full benefits instead of dismissal for which the employer had good cause.[369] The court wished that it had the power to replace the retirement with summary dismissal. In *Fakuade* v *OAUTH*[370] the plaintiff was issued with a query over a missing stainless steel bowl and asked to say all she knew about it. Shortly after this and without reference to the missing bowl her appointment was terminated by notice. Her claim for wrongful termination was rejected and both the Court of Appeal and the Supreme Court upheld the rejection. But the employer had said in evidence that the termination did not arise from the query or any other misconduct but as a result of a retrenchment exercise evidence of which was

---

[366g] [1996] 6 NWLR 632

[366h] Ibid., 644

[366j] In *Arinze* v *First Bank (Nig) Ltd* [2000] 1 NWLR 78 the Court of Appeal missed the point, holding, in effect, that the employee was given a fair hearing before his dismissal.

[367] See e.g. *Chioze* v *United Africa Company Ltd* (1956) 1 ERLR 28.

[368] [1985] 2 NWLR 17.

[369] In *NEPA* v *El-Fandi* [1986] 3 NWLR 884 a dismissal was subsequently converted to a termination with benefits and the Court of Appeal held the employer was competent to do so.

[370] [1993] 5 NWLR 47.

given. In *Calabar Cement Co Ltd* v *Daniel*[371] the contract of employment provided for both dismissal and termination by notice. There was evidence that the employee came under suspicion of theft and, indeed, that he was invited to appear before an administrative enquiry concerning the theft but which he failed to attend. The Court of Appeal held that the trial court was in error in holding that the employer should have first proceeded under the provision for dismissal. Katsina-Ala, JCA, who gave the leading judgement, said: "It is settled practice that the two provisions, i.e. for dismissal and termination of a contract of employment, operate independent of each other."[372] Similarly the contract of employment in the case of *Union Bank of Nigeria Ltd* v *Edet*[373] provided for termination by notice and summary dismissal for misconduct. The plaintiff was queried over irregular foreign exchange transactions and asked to make an explanation which she did. But without further reference to the foreign exchange matter her employment was terminated by payment in lieu of notice. The Court of Appeal held that the termination was not wrongful. Uwaifo JCA with whose judgement the other judges of the court agreed, said:[374]

> It seems to me that the 1st defendant relied on the condition in paragraph 5 of the Agreement of service (Exh.21) to determine the employment of the plaintiff, by the payment to her of one month's salary in lieu of notice. It did not seem to have taken into account then of any wrongdoing on her part which might have called paragraph 7 of the Agreement into play, that is to say, determination of the employment without notice.

However the Court of Appeal has also decided somewhat differently in two subsequent cases. In *British Airways* v *Makanjuola*[375] there were provisions made in the contract for both termination by notice and dismissal for misconduct. The employee was accused of ticket malpractice and an inquiry carried out after which he was advised to retire or resign. Upon his refusal to do either he was given a letter of termination of appointment and offered two months' salary in lieu of notice. The plaintiff employee brought an action for damages for wrongful termination on the ground that the reason for the termination was the accusation of misconduct. The court held that by its failure to deny that contention the employer was deemed to have admitted that the termination was as a result of the accusation of ticket malpractice and having

---

[371] [1991] 4 NWLR 750.
[372] Ibid., 759.
[373] [1993] 4 NWLR 288.
[374] Ibid., 297.
[375] [1993] 8 NWLR 276.

failed to follow the procedure for dismissal for misconduct the termination was wrongful. In *Nfor* v *Ashaka Cement Co Ltd*,[376] the plaintiff alleged that the main reason his employment was terminated by being given proper notice was his failure to appear and testify before a committee set up by the employer to investigate workers conflict in the company. Although the termination was upheld as not wrongful the court said: "There was no finding of misconduct and a conclusion that the removal was a consequence of misconduct."[377]

The better view is the one that accords with the common law. Even in *British Airways* v *Makanjuola*[378] where the court said the employer should have exercised the power to dismiss for misconduct since there was misconduct, the court, nonetheless, held that the appointment came to an end, albeit, wrongfully, and the plaintiff entitled to damages.[379] The rule at common law is that, normally, neither the employer nor the employee will be compelled to continue the employment relationship. One reason given in the early cases for this rule is that the courts are unable to compel the performance of the duties under the contract.[380]

Where there is statutory intervention the picture becomes somewhat different. Where statute provides directly the procedure for removal for misconduct and there is power to terminate by notice given under regulations made under statutory power must the procedure for removal for misconduct be embarked upon whenever there is misconduct or can termination by notice be resorted to instead? In spite of counsel's strong argument on this important question in the cases of *Olaniyan* v *University of Lagos*[381] and *Eperokun* v *University of Lagos*[382] the Supreme Court failed to address the issue squarely although it presented itself. In each of the two cases the ratio seems to be that once misconduct is alleged the laid down procedure must be followed and where not followed the removal is null and void. In *Eperokun*'s case, Irikefe CJN in his judgement with which all the other members of the court agreed, said that "it was argued with some force that if the respondent has evidence of misconduct it can, at will, waive it and proceed to act on clause 7 of the memorandum of

376 [1994] 1 NWLR 222.

377 Ibid., 233

378 [1992] 8 NWLR 276

379 Both the statement on and the amount of damages awarded were wrong; indeed, the whole decision in the case is easily one of the most unsatisfactory decisions of the Court of Appeal in the area of labour law.

380 See e.g. *Clarke* v *Price* 37 ER 270, *Baldwin* v *Society for the Diffusion of Useful Knowledge* (1838) 9 Simons 893.

381 [1985] 2 NWLR 599.

382 [1986] 4 NWLR 162.

agreement. This indeed it can do, provided the appointee has no knowledge of such allegation of misconduct.[383]

It would seem, therefore, that once an allegation of misconduct is made the power to terminate by notice is lost. The procedure for removal for misconduct must then be followed. It, probably, also follows that where there is evidence of misconduct but an allegation is not made termination by the giving of notice will be proper. In *Ajolore* v *Kwara State College of Technology*[384] the Court of Appeal held that the appointment of a lecturer was properly terminated when he was given three months' salary in lieu of notice although it said the position was "odd and illogical" in that the college could always side-track the misconduct procedure by giving notice. However there was no allegation of misconduct in the case. Similarly, although Shaw LJ in *Gunton* v *London Borough of Richmond upon Thames*[385] felt such a situation "would produce a grotesque result, for it would mean that the council could without assigning any reason terminate the plaintiff's employment by a month's notice, but could not, if it complained of misconduct on his part, determine that employment save by what might prove a long and protracted process,"[386] he said the disciplinary procedure for misconduct did not deprive the Council of its contractual power to determine the contract by serving of notice.

It would seem quite unobjectionable for an employee who has been accused of misconduct to be afforded the opportunity not only to vindicate his name but also to enjoy the statutory protection offered. As Ademola CJN said:[387]

> A dismissal from the service carries such infamy that a termination does not carry. One finds, as in the present case, that the appellant was entitled to certain benefits like gratuity, etc., which under pain of dismissal he would not be entitled to.

There have been conflicting decisions and *dicta* as to the effect which a wrongful dismissal has on the contract of employment. In some of the cases it has been held that a contract of employment, like any other contract, subsists despite a wrongful dismissal except where the dismissal, being a repudiatory act, is accepted by the other party while in others there are dicta to the effect that a

---

383 Ibid., 173.

384 Unreported suit No. FCA/K/63/81; see also *Morohunfola* v *Kwara State College of Technology* [1986] 4 NWLR 732.

385 [1980] 3 All ER 577

386 Ibid. 580-581; see also per Buckley and Brightman LJJ at 584 and 593 respectively.

387 *Irem* v *Obubra District Council* [1960] 5 FSC 24, 27

contract of employment is, in this regard, *sui generis*, in that a repudiation brings the contract to an end automatically.

There is no doubt of the general contractual position. It is well-established that where one party to a contract repudiates it the other party has a right either to accept the repudiation thus bringing the contract to an end or waive or refuse to accept it and thereby keep the contract on foot. In *Heyman* v *Darwins Ltd* [388] Viscount Simon L.C. said "repudiation by one party standing alone does not terminate the contract. It takes two to end it, by repudiation, on the one side, and acceptance of the repudiation, on the other."[389] Similarly in *White and Carter (Councils) Ltd* v *McGregor*[390] Lord Reid said:

> If one party to a contract repudiates it in the sense of making it clear to the other party that he refuses or will refuse to carry out his part of the contract, the other party, the innocent party, has an option. He may accept that repudiation and sue for damages for breach of contract, whether or not the time for performance has come; or he may if he chooses disregard or refuse to accept it and then the contract remains in full effect.[391]

Lord Hodson stated simply that "it is settled as a fundamental rule of the law of contract that repudiation by one of the parties to a contract does not itself discharge it."[392] In *Howard* v *Pickford Tool Co Ltd,*[393] Asquith LJ in the English Court of Appeal, was more graphic. He said, "an unaccepted repudiation is a thing writ in water and of no value to anybody."[394]

In *Denmark Productions Ltd* v *Boscobel Productions Ltd*[395] the majority of the court, Salmon and Winn LJ, thought the contract of employment is governed by these same rules. Indeed, Winn, LJ, said: "For my part, I do not regard a contract of employment as *sui generis*, but as a type of bilateral contract to which the same principles apply."[396] But Harman LJ said an employee dismissed in breach of his contract of employment cannot choose to treat the contract as subsisting.[397] In *Decro Wall International S.A.* v *Practitioners in Marketing*

---

[388] [1942] AC 356
[389] Ibid. 361
[390] [1962] AC 413
[391] Ibid.; 427
[392] Ibid.; 444
[393] [1951] 1 KB 417
[394] Ibid.; 421
[395] [1969] 1 QB 699
[396] Ibid; 732
[397] Ibid; 737

Ltd,[398] Salmon LJ affirmed his earlier view and Sach LJ can be said to support him although he said it was unnecessary to determine whether on a true analysis contracts of personal service do in strict law form an exception to the rule that an innocent party has an option when faced with a repudiation. Both judges, however, acknowledged the fact that in practical terms repudiation brings such a contract to an end. In *Sanders* v *Neale*[399] Sir John Donaldson said: "The appellants' case does not come within any exception to the general rule relating to contracts of employment, namely, that they are terminated by notice whether or not that notice is given in breach of contract and whether or not the employee accepts the notice as having that effect."[400] In *Gunton* v *London Borough of Richmond upon Thames*[401] only Shaw L. J said clearly that the general common law rules do not apply to a contract of service. In *R* v *East Berkshire Health Authority, ex parte* Walsh,[402] the majority, which included Sir John Donaldson, later the Master of the Rolls, agreed that a contract of employment is unilaterally terminated by a repudiation of the contract.[403] But in *Olaniyan* v *University of Lagos,*[404] in the Supreme Court, Karibi-Whyte, JSC, observed that "the contract of service comes to an end after the unilateral repudiation only if the employee accepts the repudiation expressly or by implication."[405]

On the whole it would seem that the weight of opinion is that in strict law a contract of employment is not brought to an automatic end by a repudiatory conduct. However, there is no doubt that in practice a repudiatory misconduct does bring a contract of employment to an end and the law has had to accommodate this practical effect. As Sach LJ said in *Decro-Wall International S.A.* v *Practitioners in Marketing Ltd,* [406]

> The truth of the matter is that there are a great many cases in which it is of no benefit to the innocent party to keep the contract alive (for the simple reason that, in the long run, unless the repudiating party can be persuaded or impelled to change his mind and withdraw his repudiation, the only remedy available to the innocent party will lie in damages.) So there are vast numbers of cases where the innocent party can in one sense be said to be forced to

[398] [1971] 1 WLR 361
[399] [1974] 3 All ER 327
[400] Ibid; 334
[401] [1980] 3 All ER 577
[402] [1984] 3 All ER 425.
[403] May LJ said he preferred the unilateral approach; ibid; 434
[404] [1985] 2 NWLR 599
[405] Ibid; 683; for acceptance by implication see *Morohunfola* v *Kwara State College of Technology* [1986] CA 6 (Part II) 187.
[406] [1971] 1 WLR 361

adopt the only practicable course because any other would be useless. In such cases it is the range of remedies that is limited, not the right to elect.[407]

Suspension

It is convenient here to discuss an employer's power or right to suspend an employee as a disciplinary measure, although, as will be seen, it seems settled that suspension does not bring a contract of employment to an end.

There is no common law right to suspend an employee as a disciplinary measure, that is, with loss of pay. As we have seen the general rule is that an employer may suspend an employee from work with full pay but where suspension from work is to carry with it loss of earnings an employer must act by virtue of a right or power to do so. Where there is no such right a suspension is wrongful and the employee is entitled to his wages or salary for the period of the wrongful suspension.[408] Also where there is a right to suspend the terms of the right must be complied with in carrying out a suspension otherwise the suspension is wrongful. In *Osu* v *Nigerian Railway Corporation*[409] a clause of the conditions of service left the issue as to the payment of wages either in full or in part for the period of any suspension to the discretion of the employer. Ajose-Adeogun J said the discretion must be exercised judiciously. He held it was unreasonable to withhold the wages of an employee who had been suspended but had earned increase in wages and granted leave after his suspension.

A right to suspend may be acquired by the terms of the contract, express,[410] or implied, or by statute.[411] Express provision of a power to suspend is not uncommon nowadays in employer's conditions of service handbooks. The acquisition of a right to suspend may also be by way of an implied term. In *Marshall* v *English Electric Co Ltd,*[412] the English Court of Appeal held that a practice of such suspension which had existed for quite some time had become implied into contracts of employment but the court differed a great deal in its

---

[407] Ibid; 375; the words in bracket may not apply where it is the employee's misconduct which constitutes repudiation.

[408] *Alamu* v *Afrotec Technical Services (Nig.) Ltd* [1986] 2 QLRN 126; *Adekunle* v *Western Region Finance Corporation* (1963) WNLR 5; *Emuakpor* v *K. Chellaram & Sons (Nig)Ltd* unreported suit No.5/2A/71, High Court, Sapele; *Abidoye* v *Wema Bank Ltd* CCHCJ/9/74 p.1343; *Aghwe* v *Zapata Marine Service (Nig)Ltd* 6ECSLR 268; *Oyelude* v *Central Bank of Nigeria* [1977] NCLR 368.

[409] [1978] 10-12/CCHCJ 326.

[410] See *Peter Abalaka* v *Igboeli* [1988] 1 QLRN 103.

[411] For an example of a statutory power of suspension see S.19(2) Nigerian Dock Labour Act, 1999 .

[412] [1945] 1 All ER 653.

reasoning. In *Okunoren* v *UAC Ltd*,[413] there was evidence that the employer enforced a rule whereby any employee charged with a criminal offence was suspended without pay and dismissed with retrospective effect if and when adjudged guilty of the charge. The court found that the plaintiff knew of this rule and, therefore, held that he was bound by it. De Comarmond Ag CJ said: "My reason for so doing is that the plaintiff kept away from work from the date he was charged until...when he went to prison and did not claim payment of salary."[414] In *Aghwe* v *Zapata Marine Service (Nig.) Ltd*,[415] Omo J said:[416] "Once the practice is established, it becomes incorporated into the workman's contract of service and becomes binding on him even if he is ignorant of it *vide Sagar* v *Ridehalph & Sons Ltd*."[417] This statement was an *obiter dictum* as the learned judge had held there was no power, express or implied, to suspend. However, although it is true that the practice of deduction from the wages of workers for bad work was incorporated into the workman's contract even upon the claim of ignorance of the practice by the workman it is suggested that the authority of that decision is considerably weakened by the fact that the practice was very well known in the area. Evidence showed that it prevailed in over 85 per cent of the mills in the whole country.[418] Furthermore the Master of the Rolls said clearly that he, like the trial judge, did not believe the plaintiff was not aware of the practice. It would seem, therefore, that for a right of suspension to be implied into the contract of employment of an employee it must be shown that the employee knew or, given the notoriety of the practice, he ought, reasonably, to have known about it.

The exact effect which a suspension has on a contract of employment has been the subject of differing opinions. It has been said that, in truth, suspension is dismissal with an intimation to re-employ if the employee chooses to apply for reinstatement.[419] This view, if accepted, will have an adverse effect on any right of an employee, such as pension, which depends on continuity and length of employment. The view which is, perhaps, more realistic and practical, is that an employee is able

> when the suspension ended, to claim as of right to continue in his old job. The clause operates in accordance with its terms; the whole contract is

---

413 (1951) 20 NLR 25.
414 Ibid., 26.
415 6 ECSLR 268.
416 Ibid., 272.
417 [1931] 1 Ch 310.
418 See per Lawrence L J at 339 and ibid.
419 Per Goddard LJ in *Marshall* v *English Electric Co Ltd* [1945] 1 All ER 653, 655.

> suspended, in the sense that the operation of the mutual obligations of both parties is suspended, the workman ceases to be under any present duty to work, and the employer ceases to be under any consequential duty to pay. That is the natural meaning of the word "suspend" when applied to a contract of employment, and...it is also its legal meaning.[420]

In *Nigeria Airways Corporation* v *Nwaka*,[421] at the Court of Appeal, Pepple JCA put it this way: "By that suspension, his duty to serve and obey the appellant, and the appellant's duty to pay for his services and provide him with other perquisites of his office were put in abeyance."[422] It follows, upon this view, that when an employee is suspended his contract of employment remains subsisting and unbroken. There are authoritative support for this view. In *Warburton* v *Taff Vale Railway Company*[423] Lord Alverstone thought the employee was in the employer's service during the period of his suspension.[424] In *Adekunle* v *Western Region Finance Corporation*[425] Fatayi-Williams J said:

> By merely suspending him from performing his duties, the defendant corporation has allowed the contract of employment to subsist during the relevant period and it is not open to them to put an end to it retrospectively...They cannot, in my view, escape liability for paying the plaintiff's salary during this period by dismissing him retrospectively.[426]

It has similarly been held that, where an employer subsequently dismisses an employee who has been on suspension, he must be paid his wages or salary for the period of the suspension.[427]

Remedies

The remedy which an employee, who considers that his employment has been wrongfully terminated either because he was given insufficient notice or by

---

[420] Per Scott LJ in *Bird* v *British Celanese Ltd* [1945] 1 KB 336,341.
[421] Federal Court of Appeal, Benin, Judgements Jan-Dec., [1983] p.463.
[422] Ibid., 473-474.
[423] (1902) 18 TLR 420.
[424] Ibid
[425] [1963] WNLR 5.
[426] Ibid., 10.
[427] *Nicol* v *ECN* [1965] LLR 261; appeal dismissed in *ECN* v *Nicol* [1968] All NLR 201; *Onioshun* v *Oshogbo District Council* [1972] NMLR 22; see also Lord Alverstone in *Warburton* v *Taff Vale Railway Company* (1902) 18 TLR 420.

failure to justify his dismissal, may seek, is any one of the remedies normally available for breach of contract.

Specific performance

The courts took an early stand that the equitable remedy of specific performance would not be decreed in the case of contracts of service. This included any remedy the effect of which would lead to the specific performance of such a contract.[428] This principle was based on a variety of reasons. In *Clarke* v *Price*[429] Lord Chancellor Eldon refused to make an order compelling an employee to continue to carry out his duties on the ground that the court had no means of compelling him to do so. He also advanced an absence of mutuality as a basis for the refusal.[430] Lord Eldon said: "If there be any remedy in this case, it is at law."[431] In other words the common law remedy of damages was the one available to the plaintiff.

This decision was followed in *Baldwin* v *Society for the Diffusion of Useful Knowledge*[432] where the court refused to grant an injunction on the ground that the court would be unable to compel specific performance of the contract. In *Johnson* v *The Shrewsbury and Birmingham Railway Co*[433] an injunction was refused on the ground that damages would be a sufficient remedy. Later in the same century the courts founded their refusal on public policy - the need not to decree servitude. Thus in *De Francisco* v *Barnum*[434] Fry L. J said:[435]

> For my own part, I should be very unwilling to extend decisions the effect of which is to compel persons who are not desirous of maintaining continuous personal relations with one another to continue those personal relations. I have a strong impression and a strong feeling that it is not in the interest of

[428] *Whitwood Chemical Company* v *Hardman* [1891] 2 Ch. 416.

[429] 37 ER 270.

[430] See also *Flight* v *Bollard* (1828) 4 Russ. 298 and *Pickering* v *The Bishop of Ely* (1843) 2Y & C 249. In the former case, where an infant filed a bill for the specific performance of a contract, the Master of the Rolls said at p. 301 that - It is not disputed that it is a general principle of courts of equity to interpose only where the remedy is mutual. See also *Page One Records* v *Britton* [1967] 3 All ER 822.

[431] 37 ER 270, 273.

[432] (1838) 9 Simons 393

[433] (1853) De MG & G 914

[434] (1890) 45 Ch D 430; see also Lindley MR in *William Robinson & Co Ltd* v *Hever* [1898] 2 Ch 451, 455 - 456

[435] Ibid; 438

> mankind that the rule of specific performance should be extended to such cases. I think the courts are bound to be jealous, lest they should turn contracts of service into contracts of slavery; and therefore, speaking for myself, I should lean against the extension of the doctrine of specific performance and injunction in such a manner.

The decision in *Lumley* v *Wagner*[436] was, however, an early exception to the rule. But, even there, the injunction was granted to restrain the breach of a negative stipulation in the contract of service. The employee had agreed not to serve any other employer nor perform at any other place. The court granted an injunction restraining the employee from breaching this negative covenant. As Branson J put it in *Warner Brothers Pictures Inc.* v *Nelson*:[437]

> Where a contract of personal service contains negative covenants the enforcement of which will not amount either to a decree of specific performance of the positive covenants of the contract or to the giving of a decree under which the defendant must either remain idle or perform those positive covenants, the court will enforce those negative covenants.

This exception does not depend on the form of the stipulation but upon its substance.[438] Thus a term under which an employer agreed with his employee that "he will not, except in the case of misconduct or a breach of this agreement, require the manager to leave his employ" was held to be positive in substance although negative in form.[439] As the judge said, it was distinctly equivalent to a stipulation by the employer that he would retain the manager in his employment.[440]

A more recent decision in which an injunction was granted is *Hill* v *C.A. Parsons Ltd.*[441] But both Lord Denning MR and Sach LJ, in granting the injunctions, based their decision on the ground that the case was, in the words of Sach LJ "indeed an exceptional case."[442] The third member of the English Court of Appeal, Stamp LJ who dissented, supported the rule that an injunction will not be granted to decree specific performance of a contract of employment. Also a

---

[436] (1852) 1 DE GM & G 623

[437] [1937] 1 KB 209, 217

[438] *Davis* v *Foreman* [1894] 3 Ch. 654

[439] Ibid.

[440] Ibid.; 658

[441] [1972] 1 Ch 305

[442] Ibid; 320; see also Salvage J in *Aigoro* v *University of Lagos* (1979) 10-12 CCHCJ 9 where, at p. 40, the learned judge said the case of *Hill* v *Parsons* is one in which the circumstances were exceptional.

declaration has been refused on the ground that its effect would be that the wrongfully terminated contract was still subsisting.[443] Thus, in *Thomas* v *Local Government Service Board*[444] Ademola J said:

> Where there has been a purported termination of a contract of service a declaration to the effect that the contract of service still subsisted would rarely be made and would not be made in the absence of special circumstances, because of the principle that the courts will not grant specific performance of contracts of service.

Thus only when special circumstances exist would a declaratory judgement be given. An order of *certiorari*[445] or even mandamus[446] may also become available although its effect will be to enforce specific performance.

What circumstances amount to special circumstances? The Supreme Court has said: "Such special circumstances have been held to arise where the contract of employment has a legal or statutory flavour thus putting it over and above the ordinary master and servant relationship."[447] This is so where the procedure for the determination of the employment is regulated either directly by statute or by rules or regulations made by virtue of statutory power. "It is now well established," said Uwaifo JCA, "that when an office or employment has a statutory flavour in the sense that its conditions of service are provided for by statute or regulations made thereunder, any person in that office or employment enjoys a special status over and above the ordinary master and servant relationship."[448]

---

[443] *Sofola* v *Mbadiwe, Sodipo & WAAC Ltd* unreported suit No. LD/115/64 High Court of Lagos; *Bankole* v *NBC* [1968] 2 All NLR 327, appeal held statute barred, *NBC* v *Bankole* [1972] 4 SC 94; [1972] 2 All NLR 327; *Fajemirokun* v *Nigeria Airways* Ltd [1979] 3 LRN 238; [1979] 4-6 CCHCJ198; *Iserhierhien* v *Public Service Commission, Bendel State* [1981] 2 PLR 661; *Odemwingie* v *New Nigeria Bank Ltd*; Federal Court of Appeal Judgements, Benin, Mar - Dec. [1980] p.417; *Barber* v *Machester Regional Hospital Board* [1958] 1 All ER 633. In *Ewarami* v *African Continental Bank* [1978] 4 SC 99, Irikefe, JSC, delivering the judgment of the Supreme Court said, *obiter*, at page 103 - as the lower court did not rule that a case for unlawful dismissal had been made out, we would refrain from expressing an opinion on whether at common law only an action for damages would lie.

[444] Unreported Suit No. (WN) 1/169/64; reversed on other grounds in *Thomas* v *Local Government Service Board* [1965] NMLR 310; *NNPC* v *Idoniboye-Obu* [1996] 1 NWLR 665.

[445] *Adedeji* v *Police Service Commission* [1967] 1 All NLR 67.

[446] *Shitta-Bey* v *Federal Civil Service Commission* [1981] 1 SC 40.

[447] *Chukwuma* v *Shell Petroleum Development Company of Nigeria Ltd* [1993] 5 KLR 93, 111.

[448] *University of Nigeria Teaching Hospital Management Board* v *Nnoli* [1992] 6 NWLR 752, 768; affirmed by the Supreme Court [1994] 8 NWLR 376.

However it is not enough merely that the employer is a statutory body. The fact that the employer is a statutory body does not mean that the conditions of service of its employees must be of a special character ruling out the relationship of mere master and servant.[449] As Uwaifo JCA has said:

> it is untenable to conclude that simply because the defendant is a statutory body the conditions of service of its employees must be presumed to be of a special character making it necessary to rule out the relationship of mere master and servant between the defendant and its employees. It must be ascertained, that is to say, through evidence adduced, that there are rules and regulations which govern the employment to give it a status of a particular tenure.[450]

Similarly, in *R* v *East Berkshire Health Authority*, *Ex parte* Walsh,[451] the English Court of Appeal said that whether a dismissal from employment is subject to public or administrative law remedies or only to the common law remedies for breach of contract depends, not merely, on employment by a public authority but on whether there are statutory restrictions on the power to dismiss. The Master of the Rolls, Sir John Donaldson said:[452] "Parliament can underpin the position of public authority employees by directly restricting the freedom of the public authority to dismiss, thus giving the employee *public law* rights and at least making him a potential candidate for administrative law remedies."

The onus of establishing that his employment is regulated by statute or by rules or regulations made under and by virtue of a statute lies on the employee.[453] But it is not enough to show that the rules and regulations were made under or by virtue of statutory power. They must be shown to offer protection. As the Court of Appeal has said "where the conditions for appointment or the determination of a contract of service are governed by the preconditions of an enabling statute, so that a valid determination or appointment is predicated on satisfying such statutory provisions such contract is one with statutory flavour. The contract is determinable not by parties, but only by statutory pre-conditions governing its

---

[449] Per Kutigi, JSC, in the leading judgement of the Supreme Court in *Fakuade* v *OAUTH* [1993] 5 NWLR 47, 57

[450] *Udemah* v *Nigeria Coal Corporation* [1991] 3 NWLR 477, 489

[451] [1984] 3 All ER 425; see. also *R.* v *Crown Prosecution Service, Exparte Hogg*, The Times Law Report, April 14 [1994], where the English Court of Appeal held that the appointment of a Crown Prosecutor under statute was not underpinned by the statute as it did not impose a code or restrictions on his dismissal.

[452] Ibid; 431.

[453] *Imoloame* v *WAEC* [1992] 9 NWLR 303; *David-Osuagwu* v *A-G Anambra State* [1993] 4 NWLR 13; *Pillai* v *Singapore City Council* [1968] 1 WLR 1278

determinable not by parties, but only by statutory pre-conditions governing its determination."[453a] In *Sule* v *Nigerian Cotton Board*[454] the Supreme Court held that the onus was on the employee of the statutory body to show that his contract of service included the civil service rules made under constitutional power. In *Oguike* v *Nigerian Steel Development Authority*[455] the plaintiff was removed from his employment by the payment of one month's salary in lieu of notice. He contended that the removal was wrongful as being in breach of the rules of natural justice.[456] Wheeler CJ said although the plaintiff was employed by a statutory body he must, nevertheless, show that he was removable only for cause. And,

> this, of course, turns on an examination of the plaintiff's conditions of service where the plaintiff is at once faced with the provisions of clause A205 which the defendants invoked in his own case, and which, on their face, contemplate the Authority being entitled to terminate the employment of a permanent and confirmed member of staff on notice or with salary in lieu of notice.[457]

Where there is statutory intervention or restriction a failure to follow the laid down procedure amounts to wrongful removal which could be declared null and void.[458] And, as the Court of Appeal has said: "It is settled law that once the removal of a public servant is declared null and void, the effect of such pronouncement is that such public servant was always and still is a public servant."[459] In *Adedeji* v *Police Service Commission*[460] the plaintiff asked for an order of *certiorari* to quash the deeision of the Police Service Commission to dismiss him from the police service for misconduct. It was alleged he took a bribe in order to issue certificates of road worthiness in respect of a motor cycle and a car. He contended that the dismissal was wrongful in that the Commission did not comply with certain of the rules in the General Orders which required that he be given a full opportunity to exculpate himself and also that no

---

[453a] *Okosun* v *Central Bank of Nigeria* [1996] 2 NWLR 77, 84, see also *NITEL* v *Jattau* [1996] NWLR 392.

[454] [1985] 2 NWLR 17; (1986)2 QLRN 102.

[455] [1976] NWLR 125.

[456] For natural justice see below; see also *Conley* v *Folawiyo & Sons Ltd.* (1980) 1-3 CCHCJ 66

[457] Ibid; 127.

[458] *Obot* v *Central Bank of Nigeria* [1993] 9 SCNJ 268; *Essien* v *University of Calabar* [1990] 3 NWLR 605; *Adewuyi* v *Kaduna Local Authority* [1971] (2) NCLR 279.

[459] *University of Calabar* v *Inyang* [1993] 5 NWLR 100, 118.

[460] [1967] 1 All NLR 67; [1968] MNLR 102; see also *Roberts* v *Attorney General of the Federation*, Suit No. LD/375.65 at *Nigeria Lawyers' Quarterly* [1968] Vol. III Nos. 1 and 2, p.113.

documentary evidence be used against him unless he had previously been supplied with a copy of it or given access to it. The Supreme Court found there were, in fact, breaches of these rules and accordingly declared the dismissal "inoperative, void and of not effect." The court also held that an accused person must know the name of his accuser and all what he said about him before it could be said he was given a full opportunity of exculpating himself. In *Bendel State Civil Service Commission* v *Buzube*[461] the plaintiff was reduced in rank without following the civil service regulations. The Supreme Court affirmed the judgement of the Court of Appeal and not only said the reduction in rank was null and void but also that "is deemed not to have occurred."[461a] In *Michael Oguche* v *Kano State Public Service Commission*[462] Wheeler J said:[463]

> Now it is common ground in the present case that the Public Service Commission Regulations made under the now repealed Nigerian (Constitution) Order in Council 1954 originally published as *NRLR* 80 of 1960 and now published in vol. IV of the Laws of Northern Nigeria, still regulate the procedure of the Public Service Commission of Kano State...Reading these regulations, I am satisfied that they fetter the right of the State to dismiss its servants at will.
>
> In the ordinary case of master and servant the general rule is that a declaration that the servant's dismissal was null and void will not be made by the courts as that would be indirectly granting specific performance of a contract for personal services. The law is otherwise, however, in the case of the holder of an office which is the position of the plaintiff here.

Similarly in *Adeyemo* v *Oyo State Public Service Commission*[464] Fakayode CJ in giving a declaratory judgment to the effect that the termination of employment of the plaintiff civil servant was null and void said:[465]

> This country has a great reputation that its civil servants can enjoy a tenure of office to their retiring age from their probationary period if they are efficient and have good character and are not incapacitated to discharge the functions of their office by any physical or mental infirmity. It is sheer administrative

---

[461] [1984] NSCC 505, see also *Head of the Federal Military Government, etc., The Public Service Commission of Mid-West State; in Re Maclean Okoro Kubeyinje* [1974] 1 All NLR (Part II) 269; *Thomas* v *Local Government Service Board* [1965] NMLR 310; (1965) WNLR 58.

[461a] Ibid; 516.

[462] [1974] 1 NMLR 128.

[463] Ibid; 135.

[464] [1979] 1 FNR 28; but see per Ovie-Whiskey CJ in *Iserhierhien* v *Public Service Commission, Bendel State* [1981] 2 PLR 661.

[465] Ibid; 38.

> lawlessness for a Public Service Commission to terminate the appointment of a civil servant - probationary or pensionable - without any just cause and without complying with the relevant provisions of the General Orders and Regulations.

This liberal approach[466] further received the approval of the Supreme Court in *Bashir Alade Shitta-Bey* v *The Federal Public Service Commission.*[467] Shitta-Bey, a civil servant, was legal adviser in the Federal Ministry of Justice. His name became connected with the trial of a Nigerian lady in the United Kingdom for alleged importation of seven cases of Indian hemp. The Public Service Commission directed that he be retired from the service after his representations on the matter had been examined and rejected. The High Court declared that the purported retirement was irregular, illegal, null and void on the ground that the proper procedure had not been followed in retiring him. But his attempt to resume work was rebuffed. He went back to the High Court for an order of mandamus but, this time, his request was refused on the ground of "the well settled principle of common law not to force a master to accept the services of a servant which he has determined, even unlawfully." For the same person the Court of Appeal dismissed his appeal. The Supreme Court, however, unanimously granted an order of mandamus. Idigbe, JSC, who delivered a judgement with which the other four members of the court agreed, said:

> The Civil Service Rules of the Federal Public Service govern conditions of service of Federal Public Servant and they are made pursuant to the powers conferred on the respondent by virtue of the Constitutional provisions in the 1963 Constitution; and the rules relevant to these proceedings were made in 1974, pursuant to the provisions of section 160(1) of the 1963 Constitution, Act No. 20 of 1963. These Rules, therefore, in my view, have *constitutional force* and they invest the public servant over whom they prevail, a *legal status;* a status which makes his relationship with the respondent and the government although one of master and servant certainly beyond the ordinary or mere master and servant relationship. Under these Rules (i.e. The 1974 Civil Service Rules which, as I have already pointed out, have statutory force and, therefore, ought to be "judicially noticed"), paragraphs 04121 provide the procedure which *must* be adopted in the removal or retirement from service, as well as the general disciplining, of public servants in the

---

[466] Some periods of military government have, however, been quite different; massive retrenchments were carried out and statutes enacted to oust the jurisdiction of the courts. See the Public Offices (Special Provisions) Decree enacted in 1984 and the Supreme Court in *Garba* v *Federal Public Service Commission* [1988] 1 NWLR 449.

[467] [1981)] 1 SC 40; [1981] 2 PLR 202.

> established pensionable cadre...There exists, therefore, a declaratory judgement in a suit to which the respondent was a *party* and before whom a court of competent jurisdiction duly exercising its supervisory powers, had made a pronouncement declaring its action invalid; and the effect of which pronouncement is that the appellant was always, at all times material to the proceedings...and *still is*, an officer in the Federal Public Service.[468]

The Supreme Court has held, similarly, in two decisions involving some professors and a registrar of the University of Lagos, that their purported removal from employment for alleged misconduct without following the statutory procedure for such removal was null and void.[469]

Where, however, the laid down procedure is utilised in removing an employee he cannot be heard to complain about his removal.[470] It also does not follow that a reinstated employee cannot subsequently be removed by due process or, it is submitted, by proper notice. There are no rules on job security. In *Eyutchae* v *Nigerian Television Authority*[471] the plaintiff's appointment was terminated by a letter of August 1 1979. In an action in the High Court of Anambra State the termination was held to be wrongful and his reinstatement was ordered. He was duly reinstated and he worked and was paid his salaries up to May 1984 when another letter of termination was given to him. In dismissing an appeal by the employer against the order of reinstatement the Court of Appeal said the appeal had nothing to do with the second letter of termination:

> This court cannot now affirm the spent declarations made in the judgement of 17 June 1981 or the order of injunction therein which in effect was an order to reinstate the respondent whose services were in obedience to order of the court reinstated until his second termination on 24 May 1984. As this appeal was no longer a live issue up to the time of respondent's second termination of appointment we cannot now affirm the order of injunction to reinstate the respondent as the court cannot make an order in vain.[472]

---

[468] Ibid; 55 - 57; 211 - 212

[469] *Olaniyan* v *University of Lagos* [1985] 2 NWLR 599; *Eperokun* v *University of Lagos* [1986] 4 NWLR 162. See also *Federal Polytechnic, Mubi* v *Yusuf* [1991]1 NWLR 81.

[470] *Nwagbara* v *Nigeria Produce Marketing Co Ltd* [1966] NCLR 196; *Sobowale* v *Statutory Corporations Service Commission* CCHCJ/9/74 p.1449; [1974] NCLR 221.

[471] [1986] 5 NWLR 395.

[472] Ibid., 406.

Fair hearing

Some employees who contest their removal from employment have sometimes prayed in aid the common law rules of natural justice in their attempt to have the removal nullified. Natural justice is made up of two main rules. In employment reliance has more often been placed on the rule that no one may be condemned without being given a reasonable opportunity to answer any case or charge made against him. This is the rule expressed in the maxim *audi alteran partem*. The second rule finds expression in the maxim *nemo judex in causa sua* which means simply that no one who has direct interest in a matter or in its result is qualified to take part in its resolution.

It is well-settled that the relationship of employer and employee does not give rise, at common law, to the application of the rules of natural justice.[473] There is no principle of the common law that an employee must be afforded an opportunity to answer to an allegation of misconduct before he is summarily dismissed. As we have seen all that is required is justification whenever the employer is called upon to do so. And, even if wrongful, a dismissal brings a contract to an end, at least, in practical terms, and the employee is only entitled to damages for wrongful dismissal. Reinstatement is not normally available at common law. As Lord Reid said:[474]

> There cannot be specific performance of a contract of service, and the master can terminate the contract with his servant at any time and for any reason or for none. But if he does so in a manner not warranted by the contract he must pay damages for breach of contract.

In *Udemah* v *Nigeria Coal Corporation*[475] the Court of Appeal made quite a picturesque statement of the non-applicability of the rules of natural justice to contracts of employment:[476]

> Natural justice of *audi alteram partem* is not a sleepless and restless ombudsman or an ever weeping Jeremiah prying into or pleading over every private arrangement between parties for it to be modified in its implementation in order to achieve a particular result. When a valid and lawful contract has been entered between two parties, there can be no room

---

[473] *Pillai* v *Singapore City Council* [1968] 1 WLR 1278.
[474] *Ridge* v *Baldwin* [1964] AC 40,62.
[475] [1991] 3 NWLR 477.
[476] Ibid., 490.

> for invoking or inviting natural justice to intervene if there are no particular rules and regulations in support of that course; or if there are no special occasions making a hearing or, indeed, that observance of the rules of natural justice imperative. The performance and obedience of such contract may well depend entirely on its terms and conditions, not on the intervention of natural justice, as some hope, descended in white robes through the clouds as an arbiter.

In those employment's with the so-called statutory flavour, i.e. where statute or rules or regulations made under statute has provided a code or procedure for removal and thus putting restrictions on the power of the employer to remove his employee, the statutory provisions usually encapsulate the rules of natural justice.[477] In such cases it is advisable for the courts to apply and be seen to apply the statutory provisions rather than embark upon an unnecessary, sometimes irrelevant, and, always fruitless, excursion into the niceties of the common law principles of natural justice.

In *Aiyetan* v *NIFOR*,[478] which appeared to be a straightforward case of an ordinary master and servant relationship and without statutory flavour, the Supreme Court applied the rules of natural justice. The plaintiff was initially employed as a daily paid employee but had his employment confirmed as a permanent and pensionable employee. He was dismissed for causing a huge financial loss to his employer after a departmental inquiry so found. The employer was a creature of statute which statute also empowered it to make disciplinary regulations for its staff but which regulations were not made. The Supreme Court said, "in such circumstances...recourse must be had to the rules of the common law and equity and of course to section 33 (I) of our constitution."[479] But, surprisingly, the court proceeded to apply the *audi alteram partern* rule. Although Nnamani JSC said "it is correct, ...that the principles of natural justice ought to be considered in the circumstances of each case."[480] the court failed to consider whether the principles were, in fact, applicable in the

[477] See *Adedeji* v *Police Service Commission* [1968] NMLR 102; *Falomo* v *Lagos State Public Service Commission* [1977] 5 SC 51, *Shitta-Bey* v *Federal Public Service Commission* [1981] 1 SC 40; *Bendel State Civil Service Commission* v *Buzugbe* [1984] 7 SC 19; *Olaniyan* v *University of Lagos* [1985] 2 NWLR 599; *Eperokun* v *University of Lagos* [1986] 4 NWLR 162, *Federal Civil Service Commission* v *Laoye* [1989] 2 NWLR 652; *Bakare* v *Lagos State Civil Service Commission* [1992] 8 NWLR 641; and *Adeniyi* v *Governing Council of Yaba College of Technology* [1993] 6 NWLR 426 are some of the remarkable decisions of the Supreme Court in this area. The central issue in all of these cases was constitutional or statutory underpining,

[478] [1987] 3 NWLR 48; see also *Awobokun* v *Sketch Publishing Company* [1973] 3 UILR 502.

[479] Ibid, 64, 68, 81.

[480] Ibid, 64.

case. In *Olatunbosun* v *NISER*[481] the basis for the application of natural justice in an employment which the Supreme Court itself held was governed purely by contract may also be questioned. But, having found that the employer failed to observe natural justice by not affording a hearing, the court awarded 6 months' salary (presumably as damages) which was the amount the employer had paid in lieu of noticê in accordance with the contract and which both the trail court and the Court of Appeal had held was a valid termination. Clearly there was no room for natural justice. Of course, damages may be awarded in such cases, if suffered, but in addition to reinstatement. Reinstatement means putting an employee back into employment as far as possible in the same position as he occupied before the termination of his employment.[482] Failure to apply natural justice where applicable renders a removal void. It is as if there never was a removal. In *Vine* v *National Dock Labour Board*[483] where a dock worker's removal was held to be illegal, the House of Lords upheld a declaratory judgment to that effect. Viscount Kilmiur LC said:[484]

> This is an entirely different situation from the ordinary master and servant case; there, if the master wrongfully dismissing the servant, either summarily or by giving insufficient notice, the employment is effectively terminated, albeit in breach of contract. Here, the removal of the plaintiff's name from the register being, in law, a nullity, he continued to have the right to be treated as a registered dock worker with all the benefits which, by statute, that status conferred on him.

Lord Morton of Henryton added that "to give an award of money, as the learned judge did, for the damages he suffered up to the date of the judgment is only to give him part of the relief which he ought to have."[485]

In some of the cases that have been before the Supreme Court,[486] it was also said that a failure to afford a hearing was a breach not only of the *audi alteram partern* rule but also of s. 33 (1) of the 1979 Constitution.[487] But in none of

---

[481] [1988] 3 NWLR 25.

[482] Per Taylor C.J in *Ejegi* v *Agip (Nig.) Ltd* [1968] 2 All NR 151

[483] [1957] AC 488

[484] Ibid.; 500

[485] Ibid.; 504

[486] See f.n 477 ante.

[487] See e.g. per Uwais JSC in *Aiyetan* v *NIFOR* [1987] 3 NWLR 48, 70; per Craig JSC in *Olatunbosun* v *NISER* [1988] 3 NWLR 25, 65; per Wali JSC in *Adeniyi* v *Governing Council of Yaba College of Technology* [1993] 6 NWLR 426, 465. Section 33 is now s.36 of the 1999 Constitution.

them was it ever considered whether the subsection may be applied. Its application was assumed. The sub-section is as follows:

> In the determination of his civil rights and obligations, including any question or determination by or against any government or authority, a person shall be entitled to a fair hearing within a reasonable time by a court or other tribunal established by law and constituted in such manner as to secure its independence and impartiality.

It has been said in the Supreme Court that this subsection of the Constitution is an embodiment of the rules of natural justice. According to Obaseki JSC in *Aiyetan* v *NIFOR*[488] Section 33(1) of our Constitution is an omnibus provision the compliance with which automatically ensures compliance with the rules of natural justice.[489] Similarly, in *Bakare v Lagos State Civil Service Commission*[490] Ogundare, JSC, who delivered the leading judgment with which the other members of the court agreed, said: "In my view both sections 22(1) of the 1963 Constitution and s. 33(1) of the 1979 Constitution are a re-statement of the age long legal maxim that a man be not condemned unheard by an unbiased arbiter. This legal maxim either under the English common law or under our Constitution means one and the same thing."[491] This, probably, means that the same considerations apply to any determination of whether there has been compliance with either the rule or the subsection. Does it also mean that s. 33(1) only applies where natural justice applies, and that the same consequences follow from non-compliance with either? Or does s. 33(1) have a wider or no application at all to employment?

It seems clear enough, by interpretation, that the subsection guarantees fair hearing, or, if preferred, the application of natural justice, in the determination of the rights and obligations of any person by a court or tribunal established by law. Courts are those established by the Constitution or by statute by virtue of constitutional power. With respect to tribunals, Bello, CJN, has rightly said that the tribunal envisaged by the subsection is a tribunal established by law and charged with the duty to determine the civil rights of any person.[492] It would appear, therefore, that, like natural justice, s. 33(1) has no application to an ordinary or pure master and servant relationship. In *Union Bank of Nigeria Ltd* v

---

[488] *Supra.*
[489] Ibid; 68
[490] [1992] 8 NWLR 641
[491] Ibid; 674
[492] *Baba* v *Nigeria Civil Aviation Training Centre* [1991] 4 LRCN 1234, 1261; see also *Legal Practitioners Disciplinary Committee* v *Fawehinmi* [1985] 2 NWLR 300

Ogboh[493] the collective agreement, which the court held was the contract between the parties[494] provided for a hearing before dismissal for misconduct. The plaintiff was issued a query over what was described as suppression of cheques and was later dismissed without a hearing. The plaintiff claimed a declaration that his dismissal was unlawful, *ultra vires* and of no effect as being against the principles of natural justice. The Court of Appeal held that there was a violation of s. 33(1). Ogundare JCA who gave the leading judgement said:[495]

> Section 33 of the 1979 Constitution on fair hearing was therefore violated. A plea of unlawful dismissal raises the issue of a dispute, in the resolution of which the rule of natural justice as enshrined in Section 33 of the Constitution comes into play whether so pleaded or not.

Mohammed, JCA, "entirely agree(d)" and Aikawa JCA, "agree(d) entirely" with the leading judgment. Indeed Mohammed JCA added: "I agree also that the appellants have violated the provisions of s. 33 of the 1979 Constitution, on fair hearing, in handling the case of the respondent."[496] Yet the court set aside the order of reinstatement made by the trial court. Surely where there is a breach of a fundamental right the High Court has the constitutional power to make such orders as it considers appropriate for enforcing any right to which a person is entitled. Surely reinstatement which is the normal consequence of non-observance of natural justice should be available for breach of s. 36(1)? However it seems clear that the case was really no more than a case of breach of contract and consequential damages. The court itself held there was no statutory flavour so there could have been no tribunal established by law.

Even the application of s. 36(1) to an employment held to be of statutory flavour may prove superfluous except, perhaps, to any extent that, being a fundamental right, it offers protection over and above the statutory underpinning or it offers some other advantage such as the procedure for a claim for breach of a fundamental right or the order which the court has power to make for any such breach. Statutory underpinning may itself satisfy the constitutional requirement of fair hearing. Section 36(2) of the Constitution may be noted in this regard. Where a law confers on any government or authority power to determine questions arising in the administration of a law that affects or may affect the civil rights and obligations of any person such a law is not invalidated

---

493 [1991] 1 NWLR 369.

494 See *Union Bank of Nigeria Ltd* v *Edet* [1993] 4 NWLR 288 for a contrary view which, it is submitted; is the better view; see p.25 *et seq*.

495 [1991] 1 NWLR 369, 386.

496 Ibid; 392

(unconstitutional), if it provides for the person to present his case before a decision is reached and the decision is not made final and conclusive. Such a person should still be entitled to fair hearing before a court or tribunal under s. 36(1).

Damages

Where an employee is wrongfully removed, either by a summary dismissal which has not been justified or by the giving of insufficient notice, the normal remedy to which he is entitled is damages. As we have seen his reinstatement will not normally be ordered:

> Put in another way, the remedy for breach of contract of personal service, save in exceptional circumstances...is damages. It is not open to the respondent to proceed on the basis that his contract of employment was still subsisting and a claim for loss of salary and other perquisites of his employment for the period he did not work. This is in consequence of the general principle of law that the court will not grant specific performance of contracts of service.[497]

As a general rule the measure of damages is the amount the employee would have earned under the contract for the period until the employer could validly have terminated it, less the amount the employee could reasonably be expected to earn in other suitable employment, because the dismissed employee, like any innocent party following a breach of contract by the other party, must take reasonable steps to minimise his loss.[498] This is in consonance with another rule of the common law that, where a party sustains a loss by reason of a breach of contract, he is, so far as money can do it, to be placed in the same situation, with respect to damages, as if the contract had been performed.[499] Damages are, therefore, awarded to compensate the employee for the actual pecuniary loss he has suffered as a result of the loss of job.

The main head of damages is the salary or wages which the wrongfully removed employee would have earned up to the earliest time at which the

---

[497] Onu JCA in *Cooperative & Commerce Bank (Nig) Ltd* v *Nwankwo* [1993] 4 NWLR 159, 174.

[498] Per Udo Udoma JSC in giving the judgment of the Supreme Court in *NBC* v *Adeyemi*, Ureported Appeal No. SC/45/1969.

[499] See Parke B. in *Robinson* v *Harman* (1848) 1 Exch. 850, 855.

employer could validly have terminated the employment contract.[500] This principle has long been established. In *French* v *Brookes*[501] the plaintiff was employed in England to go to Buenos Aires to supervise mines and his contract could be terminated by twelve months' notice in writing or twelve months' salary in lieu of notice. He was also entitled to a reasonable sum towards defraying his expenses from South America to England. In an action for damages for wrongful dismissal the court held that the jury were right in awarding him twelve months' salary in addition to the expenses for travelling. Tridal CJ said:[502] "The jury, therefore, have not erred if they have put the plaintiff in the same situation as if the directors, upon dismissing him, had paid at the time twelve months' salary, and a reasonable sum towards defraying his expenses from South America to England." In *Hartley* v *Harman*[503] the plaintiff was employed as superintendent of works and under a contract which gave either party an 'option of terminating it by one month's notice. Plaintiff was dismissed without notice. Lord Denman CJ said on such a dismissal a month's wages must be looked upon as stipulated damages.[504] And all of Coleridge J's judgment reads as follows: The breach of contract stated is dismissal without notice. All the damages consequent upon that is the loss of a month's wages.[505] Similarly in *Gordon* v *Potter*[506] where the plaintiff, a cook and housekeeper, brought an action to recover damages for wrongful dismissal, Justice Hill, in summing up to the jury, said the jury could award as damages "a calendar month's wages...as a master had a right to discharge a servant simply by payment of a month's wages, in addition to the accruing wages up to the time of the discharge." In *Baker* v *Denkera Ashanti Mining Corporation Ltd*[507] the plaintiff was employed to work in the Gold Coast, now Ghana, as a miner. The contract provided that the employers could terminate the employment by giving two months' notice in writing or two months' salary in lieu of such notice. He was dismissed without notice or salary in lieu. In an action to recover damages Granthan J held that the defendants were not liable for more than two months' salary. As he said,[508] the defendants could

---

[500] Per Ajegbo JSC in the judgment of the Supreme Court in *Western Nigeria Development Corporation* v *Abimbola* [1961] 1 All ER 159, 161; see also *Beredugo* v *College of Science & Technology* [1991] 4 NWLR 651, C.A.

[501] (1830) 6 Bing 354.

[502] Ibid; 360

[503] (1840) 11 A&E 798

[504] Ibid; 801

[505] Ibid; 802

[506] 175 ER 888

[507] (1903) 20 TLR 37

[508] Ibid; 38

not be made liable for more damages simply because they had not a good reason for dismissing the plaintiff.

Thus, where a contract provides expressly that it is terminable by the giving of a stipulated period of notice the damages recoverable for a wrongful termination or dismissal will be the amount of wages or salary the employee would have earned during the stipulated period.[509] If, for example, a contract provides for one month's notice then damages will ordinarily be one month's salary or wages. In *Western Nigeria Development Corporation* v *Abimbola*[510] the contract provided for its termination by either the employer or the employee by giving one month's notice in writing. The employee was not given notice. The Supreme Court held, on appeal, that all the employee could get as damages was one month's salary.

Where there is no provision made in a contract for the length of notice required to terminate it the question of damages is determined by a consideration of the length of notice that would have been reasonable to terminate it.[511] In *Onalaja* v *African Petroleum Ltd*[512] Akpabio JCA summed up the law on notice and damages as follows:[513]

> I think the most important thing to emphasise in this judgment is that in cases of wrongful dismissal, the amount of damages recoverable by a plaintiff must be geared to the period of notice given by the employer as stipulated in the contract of employment. If it is six months' notice, then six months' salaries must be paid; if it is one month's notice, then one month's salary must be paid. If no period of notice was prescribed, then the common law rule will apply, namely that a reasonable period would be given, usually one month or three months, depending on the category of staff being dismissed.

---

[509] *Mandridas* v *Tangalakis* [1932] 11 NLR 62; *Nigerian Produce Marketing Board* v *Adewunmi* [1972] 1 All NLR (pt.2) 433; [1972] 11 SC 111; *International Drilling Co (Nig) Ltd* v *Ajijola* [1976] 2 SC 115; [1976] 1 MNLR 52; *Adiatu* v *Polythene Enterprises (Nig.) Ltd* [1978] 5/CCHCJ 884; *Soyemi* v *Federal Housing Authority* [1982] CCHCJI; *Temola* v *Barclays Bank of Nigeria*, Federal Court of Appeal, Ibadan, Judgements, Jan-July [1983] p.421; *Fasesan* v *NPA*, Judgment of the Federal Court of Appeal, Lagos, 1984, p. 281.

[510] [1966] 1 All NLR 159; 1966 *NCLR* 157; 1966 NMLR 381; see also *Chukwumah* v *Shell BP* (1993) 5 KLR 93; *Obot* v *Central Bank of Nigeria* (1993) 9 SCNJ 368. In *Abdallah* v *Achou* 1978 NCLR 226 the Supreme Court held that wages or salary which have accrued due but unpaid at dismissal cannot be claimed as damages but as a debt.

[511] *Addis* v *Gramophone Co Ltd* [1909] AC 488; *PZ & Co Ltd* v *Ogedengbe* [1972] All NLR (pt.1) 202; *David Olaja* v *Kaduna Textiles Ltd* 1970 NNLR 42.

[512] [1991] 7 NWLR 691.

[513] Ibid., 698

However it appears that where an employer's right to terminate an employment by notice is excluded by the terms of the contract a wrongfully dismissed employee will be entitled to damages calculated on the basis of the salary he would have earned up to his retirement. Thus, in *NBC* v *Adeyemi*,[514] under a clause of the contract only the plaintiff had the power to give notice to terminate once he attained age 45 years. He was wrongfully removed at 51. The trial court awarded damages made up of his salary until 55 his retiring age. The Supreme Court affirmed the award.[515]

Where employment is for a fixed period and it is wrongfully terminated before the end of the fixed term of employment the salary or wages for the unexpired period of employment are recoverable as damages.[516] Akintan JCA explains the principle this way:[517]

> The position in law is that where a contract of employment is for a specific period and the employee was wrongfully dismissed or removed from office, then an award of damages in the full amount of salary, allowances and other entitlements which the employee would have earned, if the contract of service had run up full course, is the maximum amount that is recoverable except that the amount may be reduced slightly in respect of being payable immediately instead of the due dates.

---

[514] 1969 (1) ALR Comm 107.

[515] Unreported Appeal No. SC/45/1969. A similar award in *National Bank of Nigeria* v *Ilaka*, suit No.SC/18/70, by the Supreme Court was clearly wrong. Adefarasin C.J said of Ilaka's case in *Esimaje Tsegbeyeri* v *Glaxo Nig. Ltd* CCHJ/11/74 P. 1787 at 1791 that it "presents great difficulty to our courts and it is very hard to follow." Similarly the Supreme Court allowed damages which appeared to have been calculated on wrong principles in *G.B. Ollivant* (Nig.) *Ltd* v *Agbabiaka* (1972) 2 SC 137; the case was rightly distinguished by the Federal Court of Appeal in *Nigeria Airways Ltd v Adewunmi*, Federal Court of Appeal Judgments, Lagos Div, 1981 page 119. Compare also the Court of Appeal and the Supreme Court in *Union Beverages Ltd* v *Owolabi*, Court of Appeal Judgments, Ibadan, Jan-Feb. 1985, p. 130 and (1988) 1 NWLR 128 respectively. In *Oyediran* v *Lagos City Council Caretaker Committee* (CCHJ/9/72 p. 57) and *Ogunlana* v *Statutory Corporations Service Commission* (CCHCJ/10/72 p.44) both decisions of the High Court of Lagos State, damages were awarded, wrongly, it is submitted, to cover the period from dismissal to retirement age. In Oyediran's case the court relied both on *NBC* v *Adeyemi*, supra, and *Ilaka* v *NBN*, supra. But, as we have seen, Adeyemi's case can only be justified on its peculiar facts. Dosunmu J, himself, probably thought his decision was odd as he lamented his lack of power to order reinstatement rather than giving an "unearned income, so to say, covering a period of ten years." See p.67 ibid.

[516] *Mandridas* v *Tangalakis* (1932) 11 All NLR 62; *Oransaye* v *ECN* [1969] NCLR 93.

[517] *David - Osuagwu* v *A-G Anambra State* [1993] 4 NWLR 13, 45.

In *Afrotec Technical Service Ltd* v *Hunt*[518] the plaintiff was employed as a sales and organisation manager for two terms certain but renewable by mutual consent. There was no provision for terminating the contract before the expiration of the two years term. The defendants conceded they wrongfully terminated the contract after only six months and the sole question before the court was the measure of damages. The court held the plaintiff was entitled to damages made up of his salary for the eighteen months which the contract had to run. The Court of Appeal affirmed that decision.

Other heads of damages include all monetary losses consequent upon the wrongful ending of the employment. These include any entitlement under a pension or gratuity scheme,[519] commission where payable under the contract,[520] leave allowance where leave is already earned, house or quarters allowance,[521] and even tips where receivable by an express or implied term of the contract.[522]

But there is no basis for an award of general damages being a breach of contract,[523] or for injured or ruffled feelings as a result of the loss of job,[524] or for any difficulty in finding another employment.[525] Also the courts take into consideration the legal obligation to mitigate loss arising from a breach of contract. A wrongfully removed employee is expected to take reasonable steps to obtain another suitable employment and if he does whatever he earns at that employment will be deducted from the damages otherwise recoverable. However the onus is on the employer to prove that the employee has or ought reasonably

---

518 [1981] 4 CA 222.

519 *ECN* v *Nicol* [1968] 1 All NLR 201; *NBC* v *Adeyemi, Supra*; *Obot* v *Central Bank of Nigeria* [1993] 9 SCNJ 268.

520 *Bold* v *Brough, Nicholson & Hall Ltd* [1964] 1 WLR 201.

521 *Mandridas* v *Tangalakis* [1932] 11 NLR 62; *G.B. Olivant* v *Agbabiaka* [1972] 2 SC 137.

522 *Manupens* v *Leon* [1918] 1 KB 208.

523 *Western Nigeria Development Corporation* v *Abimbola* [1966] 1 All NLR 159; *NBC* v *Adeyemi*, Supra; *PZ & Co Ltd* v *Ogedengbe* [1973] 3 UILR 288; *International Drilling Company (Nig.) Ltd* v *Ajijola* [1976] 1 NMLR 52. In view of these Supreme Court decisions it is surprising that the same court said in *NRC* v *Odemuyiwa* [1974] 1 NMLR 115, 118 that the issue is an open one. See also *Alraine (Nig.) Ltd* v *Eshiett* (1977) 1 SC 89. *Onaja* v *Micho & Co.* [1961] 1 All NLR 324; *Ighile* v *Shell Petroleum Development Co of Nigeria Ltd.* unreported suit No.W/19/71; *Bello* v *NEPA* [1978] 1 LRN 200. *Stocco* v *Maja* [1968] NMLR 372.

524 *Addis* v *Gramophone Co.* [1909] AC 488; *Shove* v *Downs Surgical Plc.* [1984] 1 All ER 7; *Baba* v *Nigerian Civil Aviation Training Centre* [1986] 5 NWLR 514; *Nigeria-Arab Bank Ltd* v *Shuaib* [1991] 4 NWLR 450.

525 *Addis* v *Gramophone Co Supra*; *Lawal* v *Christlieb* (Nig.) Ltd CCHCJ/9/73, p 139.

to have obtained an alternative employment.[526] In the Supreme Court decision in *Okongwu* v *NNPC*[527] Nnaemeka-Agu, JSC, stated the law as follows:[528]

> The duty to mitigate "is one imposed by law on a plaintiff to take all reasonable steps to mitigate the loss caused by the breach of contract. I must, however, emphasise that that duty imposed upon the plaintiff is to act reasonably. Whether or not the plaintiff has failed to take a reasonable opportunity of mitigation of his loss is a question of fact depending upon the particular circumstances of each case. The burden of proving that the plaintiff has failed to take such an opportunity is always on the defendant and is a very heavy one."

In *Walter Loeb* v *Solomon Nasser* [529] the plaintiff was wrongfully dismissed by the defendant and was awarded damages by the lower court. On appeal the defendant contended that the damages should have been nominal because a few days after the dismissal the defendant offered to re-employ the plaintiff, an offer which he refused. It was held that the refusal was not unreasonable as the parties had quarrelled and the defendant had been guilty of not a mere technical breach but of an actual breach of contract. In *Yetton* v *Eastwoods Froy Ltd*[530] a joint managing director was offered continued employment as assistant managing director with other terms and conditions as before. It was held that his refusal of the offer was not unreasonable as it was a step down or reduction in status. Blain J said:[531]

> As I see the matter, it is a plain question of fact for the court in any particular case, whether any particular refusal to accept alternative employment which would reduce a plaintiff's loss is a reasonable or an unreasonable refusal, and factually, even if not as a strict matter of law, personal factors clearly are more likely to be of weight or are likely to be of greater weight in cases of personal services than in what I call (for want of a better word) soulless cases of sale of goods contracts where money may often be the only important factor.

---

[526] *Oransaye* v *ECN* [1969] NCLR 93; *Afrotec Technical Service (Nig.) Ltd* v *Hunt* [1981] 4 CA 222; *Okongwu v NNPC* [1989] 4 NWLR 296.
[527] [1989] 4 NWLR 296.
[528] Ibid., 305.
[529] (1937) 3 WACA 227.
[530] [1966] 3 ALL ER 353; see also *Shindler* v *Northern Raincoat Co Ltd* [1960] 1 WLR 1038.
[531] [1966] 3 All ER 353, 365.

In *Okongwu* v *NNPC*[532] the plaintiff resigned his job by payment in lieu of notice to go and assume another job which, however, was withdrawn. One of the three offers made to him was that he could go back to his old job but with loss of pay for the period of the break in that employment. His rejection of that offer was held not to be unreasonable. But in *Paul Wenegiene* v *Roofco (Nig.) Ltd*[533] the converse was the case. The plaintiff was offered appointment but when he reported for duty he was told the position had been filled and that a letter to that effect and including a cheque for compensation had already been sent to him. However the employer arranged an interview for appointment with another employer for him. He was to be the only candidate at the interview and there was every likelihood he would be employed but the plaintiff failed to attend the interview. The court held he had failed to take reasonable steps to mitigate his loss and the salary he would have earned for one month at the likely employment was deducted from the damages of three months salary.

It is established that damages may be reduced by a small sum in order to take account of the advantage of immediate payment as against payment in the future on due dates.[534] It is equally established that the tax liability of the employee may be deducted from the damages.[535]

---

[532] [1989] 4 NWLR 296.

[533] [1976] NNLR 160.

[534] *Angello Cattaneo* v *Candido Da Rocha* [1932] 11 NLR 57; *Garabedian* v *Jamakani* [1961] All NLR 177; *David Osuagwu* v *A-G. Anambra State* [1993] 4 NWLR 13,45.

[535] *Nunnick* v *Costain - Blaneevoort Dredging Ltd* (1960) LLR 90; *British Transport Corporation* v *Gourley* [1956] AC 185.

Chapter 3

The Labour Act

The Labour Act may, properly, be described as a workers' charter. It provides greater protection in certain areas of employment to certain classes of employees than the common law does. This is a long-established policy which has its origin in the first labour statute, the Master and Servant Ordinance of the Gold Coast.[1] The most significant feature of this statute, with the long title, "An ordinance for regulating the relations between employers and employed under contracts," was that it applied only to the contracts of employment of certain classes of employees. The Ordinance was amended in 1895[2] and after the creation of both the Northern and Southern Protectorates in 1900 similar legislation was enacted for each Protectorate. The Master and Servant Proclamation[3] for the Southern Protectorate was repealed in 1908 after the merger of the Colony of Lagos with the Southern Protectorate in 1906.

After the amalgamation of the two Protectorates in 1914 the Master and Servant Ordinance No. 16 of 1917 was enacted for the whole country. This Ordinance, just like the earlier ones, applied only to certain classes of employees. It provided that a contract of service means any contract, whether in writing or oral, to employ or to serve as a servant for any period of time or to execute any work, and includes an indenture or contract of apprenticeship, and servant means any artificer, journeyman, handicraftman, canoeman, hammockman, carrier, messenger, labourer, domestic servant or apprentice.[4] The 1917 Ordinance was repealed by the Labour Ordinance, 1929, which was itself later repealed by the Labour Code Ordinance, 1945, which was described as an Ordinance to amend and consolidate the law relating to labour and constitute the labour code for Nigeria. The Labour Code did not apply to all who were

---

[1] No. 16 of 1877. It applied in the colony of Lagos which was administered as part of the Gold Coast Colony between 1974 and 1886.

[2] By the Master and Servant Ordinance No. 1 of 1895.

[3] No.3 of 1901.

[4] S.2. Maste. and Servant Ordinance, 1917, No. 16 of 1917.

employees at common law. It was in force until 1974 when it was repealed and replaced by the Labour Act[5] which is still in force.[6]

The Labour Act is divided into four parts. The provisions of part one apply only to an employee who is a worker as defined by the Act. Part two deals with the recruitment of labour, while part three covers a miscellany of matters including the employment of apprentices, aspects of the employment of women, the employment of young persons and domestic servants. Part three also makes provisions for labour health areas, employment exchanges and forced labour.[7] Part four provides for the administration of the Act including the settlement of disputes between employers and workers.

Who is a worker?

Part one of the Act refers throughout its sections to the term "worker" and this term has a restricted meaning by definition in the Act. It will be seen that not every employee at common law is a worker under the Act. Thus part one of the Act may not necessarily apply to everyone who is an employee at common law. Such an employee must also fall within the definition of the term worker for a provision of part one to apply to him.

The Act defines a worker as any person who has entered into or works under a contract with an employer, whether the contract is for manual or clerical work or is expressed or implied or oral or written and whether it is a contract of service or a contract personally to execute any work or labour, but does not include:

(a) any person employed otherwise than for the purposes of the employer's business; or
(b) persons exercising administrative, executive, technical or professional functions as public officers or otherwise; or
(c) members of the employer's family; or
(d) representatives, agents and commercial travellers in so far as their work is carried on outside the permanent work place of the employer's establishment; or
(e) any person to whom articles or materials are given out to be made up, cleaned, washed, altered, ornamented, finished, repaired or adopted for sale

[5] Decree No. 21 of 1974; now cap. 198 Laws of the Federation of Nigeria, 1990.
[6] It is deemed to have come into force on 1 August, 1971.
[7] The provisions on labour health areas and employment exchanges are omitted in this book.

in his own home or on other premises not under the control or management of the person who gave out the articles or the material; or

(f) any person employed in a vessel or aircraft to which the laws regulating merchant shipping or civil aviation apply.[8]

There is no doubt that this definition is extremely complex and confusing but it is clear that an employee must come within it for the provisions of part one of the Act to be applied to him.[9] The point must also be made that where an employee is a worker within the definition then any relevant provision must be applied to him. Although the common law continues to apply to a worker the rule of law is that where a common law principle is at variance with a statutory provision the latter prevails. But there is no reason why a worker may not take advantage of a common law rule where it is more favourable to him than a provision of the Act. It seems clear that in such a case there can be no contravention of the statutory provision. Generally the statutory provisions are merely minima and in practice workers enjoy far greater benefits, via collective agreements and their contracts of employment, than the Act stipulates.

Under the main body of the definition a worker is a person who has entered into or works under a contract with an employer. The contract of employment may be (i) either for manual labour or clerical work; (ii) express or implied; (iii) oral or written; and (iv) a contract of service or a contract personally to execute any work or labour. There is no difficulty with an express contract nor should there be with an implied contract. A contract of employment can be inferred from the conduct of the parties. The contract, whether express or implied, may be oral or be in writing. In these respects the contract of employment of a worker is not different from a contract of an employee at common law. However, a worker for the purposes of the Act need not be an employee at common law. A worker's contract of employment may be either a contract of service, making him an employee at common law, or "a contract personally to execute any work or labour." This latter phase is generally understood to refer to self employed persons also usually referred to as independent contractors.[10] Thus it has been said that the phrase contemplates a contract whose dominant purpose is that the party contracting to provide services under the contract performs

[8] S. 91 Labour Act which is the definition section of the Act. All references to sections in this chapter are to the Labour Act unless otherwise stated.

[9] *David Olaja* v. *Kaduna Textiles Ltd.* 1974 (2) NCLR 431; *NTC Ltd.* v. *David O. William* 1975 NNLR 204; *Ikozuonu* v. *Julius Berger Nigeria Ltd.* (1979) 7-9 CCHCJ Vol. 4. 56.

[10] *Westall Richardson Ltd.* v. *Roulson* [1954] 2 All ER 448.

personally the work or labour which forms the subject-matter of the contract.[11] It seems, however, that the crucial consideration in determining whether an employee or an independent contractor is a worker is the nature of the work he is employed to do. He must be employed under his contract either for manual labour or clerical work. The Act defines neither manual labour nor clerical work. At common law manual labour involves the use of the hands in carrying out the real and substantive work employed to be done and not merely the use of the hands in matters incidental to the work.[12] Clerical work is work such as book-keeping, copying, transcribing, letter writing, tabulating or stenography.[13] *The Shorter Oxford English Dictionary*, 3rd edition, defines a clerk as a subordinate employed to make written entries or keep accounts.

As we have seen certain persons employed either as employees or independent contractors are excluded from the definition of a worker even if they are employed for manual labour or clerical work. The first exception is determined by the purpose of the employment. A person employed otherwise than for the purpose of employer's business is not a worker. The facts have to be examined. For example, while it may be said that a domestic servant or a driver employed by a managing director of a company is not employed for the purposes of the business of the company, can the same be said where the servant or driver is employed by the company to serve its managing director? The exception in (b) presents little or no difficulty. Although there are no definitions of the terms administrative, executive, technical or professional functions, there seems no doubt that these functions do not embrace manual labour or clerical work. Such functions will appear to mean not only possession of skill but also the power of supervising, managing, controlling or directing others. The exclusion of persons who exercise these functions may, therefore, be said to be superfluous. Also a member of the employer's family is not a worker. Family, as defined,[14] is confined to blood-relation so that employers such as a government or government ministry or department, corporations, registered companies can have no family for this purpose. A partnership or firm is, probably, in the same position. The wording of the exceptions contained in (d) suggests that such persons are not workers only in so far as their work is carried on outside the permanent work place of the employer. Does it mean that when carrying on their

---

[11] *Gunning* v. *Mirror Group of Newspapers Ltd.* [1986]1 All ER 385, 393, per Balcombe L. J.; *Quinnen* v. *Howells* [1984] ICR 525.

[12] See *Bound* v. *Lawrence* [1892] 1 QB 226.

[13] *Black's Law Dictionary*, 6th ed.

[14] S.14 and 1st Schedule Workmen's Compensation Act Cap 470 Laws of the Federation of Nigeria, 1990; see s. 91 and also below.

work within the employer's permanent work place they are workers? Such a conclusion will not only be ridiculous but also not sustainable. It does not appear such persons perform manual labour or clerical work. Those excluded under (e) as well, indeed, as under (d), appear to be independent contractors. Their exclusion accords with the purport of part one of the Act. The provisions of this part do not seem appropriate for application to independent contractors. It may, indeed, be suggested that it was never intended to apply to independent contractors. An amendment of the definition of a worker is necessary to achieve that intention.

Seamen are also not workers within part one of the Act nor are the crew of an aircraft.[15] Both these categories are excluded under paragraph (f). The Act, as a whole, does not apply to serving members of the armed forces or to the Nigeria Police Force.[16]

Terms of employment

An employer must give to a worker, not later than three months after the worker has commenced his employment, a written statement specifying the following:[17]

(a) the name of the employer or group or employers and, where appropriate, of the undertaking by which the worker is employed;
(b) the name and address of the worker and the place and date of his engagement;
(c)the nature of the employment;
(d) if the contract is for a fixed term, the date when the contract expires;
(e) the appropriate period of notice to be given by the party wishing to terminate the contract;[18]
(f) the rates of wages and method of calculation and the manner and periodicity of payment of wages;[19]

---

[15] For who is a seaman see ante; crew means every person employed or engaged in an aircraft in flight on the business of the aircraft; see Civil Aviation (Aviation Navigation) Regulations, 1965.
[16] S. 88(2)
[17] S. 7(1).
[18] It is provided that due regard must be had to S.11 in fixing period of notice. The section lays down the period of notice either party must give if he wishes to terminate the employment by notice. The length of notice stipulated varies with the length of actual employment. Since it is impossible to know at the commencement of an employment for how long the employment would be it is difficult to know what to do. To state a longer or shorter period than provided can, possibly, be an infringement. The safest thing to do is to adhere to the statutory provision.

(g) any terms and conditions relating to (i) hours of work, or (ii) holidays and holiday pay, or (iii) incapacity for work due to sickness or injury, including any provisions for sick pay;[20] and
(h) any special conditions of the contract.

Where a worker's employment is terminated but he commences another employment with the same employer, on the old terms, not more than six months after the termination, no further statement need be given by the employer.[21]

Where there is a change in any of the terms required to be contained in a statement after the date of the statement the employer must inform the worker of the nature of the change by a written statement not more than one month after the change. The employer may do so by leaving the statement of the change with the worker or by preserving it and ensuring that the worker has reasonable opportunity of reading it in the course of his employment or by making it reasonably accessible to him in some other way.[22]

However, a statement of the terms required to be given or of a change in any of those terms may, for all or any of the terms, refer the worker to some other document, e.g., a collective agreement, which the worker has reasonable opportunities of reading in the course of his employment or which is made reasonably accessible to him in some other way.[23] Also where an employer indicates to a worker in a statement referring him to a document containing the terms otherwise required to be given in a statement that future changes in the terms will be entered in the document or recorded by some other means the employer need not inform the worker of any change which is duly entered or recorded not more than one month after the change is made.[24]

It is important to stress that a written statement given in accordance with the statutory obligation is not necessarily the contract between the employer and the worker. It has been said that it is not even conclusive evidence of the terms of

---

[19] By S. 14 wages become due and payable at the end of the period for which the contract is expressed to subsist, i.e. whether daily, weekly or any other agreed period but where the period is more than one month the wages become due and payable at a period not exceeding one month. This later provision will apply to indefinite contracts, i.e. those not expressed to subsist for a specified period. Indeed s. 9(4) provides that no contract must provide for the payment of wages at intervals exceeding one month unless the written consent of the Governor of the State has been previously obtained.

[20] For statutory provision for sick pay see below.

[21] S. 7(5).

[22] S. 7(2)

[23] S. 7(3)

[24] S. 7(4)

the contract.[25] As an English Court said with respect to a similar provision, "in general the status of the statutory statement is this: it provides very strong *prima facie* evidence of what were the terms of the contract between the parties, but does not constitute a written contract between the parties. Nor are the statements of the terms finally conclusive."[26]

Where a worker enters into a written contract of employment which covers each of the particulars required to be contained in a written statement and he has a copy of the contract all the statutory provisions as to a written statement do not apply.[27] This is an encouragement to employers to enter into written contracts when employing workers. It may not only save administrative costs but may also eliminate disputes.

Any employer who contravenes any of these provisions is guilty of an offence and liable, on conviction, to a fine not exceeding ₦800 or, for a second or subsequent offence, a fine not exceeding ₦1,500.[28] Clearly where a statement should be given it would be an offence not to do so. Perhaps it is also an offence to give an inaccurate statement.

Medical examination

Every worker who enters into a contract must be medically examined by a registered medical practitioner at the expense of the employer.[29] The Governor of a State may, by order, exempt workers from the requirement of medical examination where they are entering into contracts for (a) employment in agricultural undertakings not employing more than a limited number of workers as specified in the order or (b) employment in the vicinity of the workers' homes in agricultural work or in non agricultural work which the Governor is satisfied is not of a dangerous character or likely to be injurious to the health of the workers.[30]

---

[25] *Robertson* v. *British Gas Corporation* (1983) ICR 351; *Turriff Construction Ltd.* v. *Bryant* (1967) 2 KIR 659.
[26] *System Floors (U.K) Ltd.* v. *Daniel* (1982) ICR 54, 58.
[27] S. 7(6).
[28] S. 21(1)(c)
[29] S. 8(1)
[30] S. 8(2)

Freedom of contract

A contract cannot be deemed to be binding on the family or dependants of a worker unless it contains an express provision to that effect.[31] Every employer is responsible for the performance of any contract made by any person acting on his behalf.[32] No worker shall be bound by virtue of any contract under the Act to answer for the debt, default or miscarriage of any other person.[33]

The transfer of any contract from one employer to another is subject to the consent of the worker and the endorsement of the transfer on the contract by an authorised labour officer.[34] However before endorsing a transfer the officer must ascertain that the worker has freely consented to the transfer and that his consent has not been obtained by coercion or undue influence or as a result of misrepresentation or mistake.[35] If, by the transfer, a worker will change his employment from one which is the subject of an exemption from medical examination or be subject to such a change of conditions as, in the opinion of the labour officer, renders such a course advisable, the officer may require the worker to be medically examined or re-examined as the case may be.[36]

Capacity of worker

A person under the age of sixteen years is prohibited from entering into a contract as a worker but he may enter into a contract of apprenticeship.[37] However this prohibition does not affect the capacity of an infant, whether below or above sixteen years old, to enter into a contract of employment at common law. Such an infant may, for example, and if found expedient, be employed to perform administrative, professional, technical or executive functions.

Hours of work

Section 13(1) provides that normal hours of work in any undertaking are those fixed (a) by mutual agreement, or (b) by collective bargaining within the organisation or industry concerned or (c) by an industrial wages board where

---

[31] S. 9(1).
[32] S. 8 (2).
[33] S. 9 (5).
[34] S. 10(1).
[35] S. 10(2)(a).
[36] S. 10(2)(b).
[37] S. 9(3)

there is no machinery for collective bargaining. The subsection is quite confusing and unhelpful. Does mutual agreement mean an agreement between an employer and an individual worker? It probably does but it is difficult to see how they can fix normal hours of work for an undertaking. In any event the subsection hardly offers any benefit to a worker over and above the common law since it permits the fixing of hours of work of an individual worker by agreement with him. Even where hours of work have been fixed by collective agreement there is no legal compulsion on an employer to employ upon the terms of an agreement. And although industrial wages boards recommendations on working conditions may be made legally binding there are, in fact, no functioning industrial wages boards.

Any hours which a worker is required to work in excess of the normal hours of work constitute overtime.[38]

Rest intervals

A rest interval means an interruption of work the length of which is fixed beforehand and during which a worker is free to dispose of his time and is not required to remain at the place of work.[39] Where a worker is at work for six hours or more a day his work must be interrupted to the extent which is necessary having regard to its character and duration and to working conditions generally, by allowing one or more suitably spaced rest-intervals of not less than one hour on the aggregate. However exceptions may be made where unforeseen circumstances render them necessary and where it is found unavoidable in view of the nature of the work and the working conditions in general. In such a case time off for a meal at the work-site or in the immediate vicinity may be substituted for the rest-interval.[40]

Breaks

Where, by reason of its connection with a mechanical process or as a result of other circumstances, the work involves continuous strain or is particularly trying in other ways, a worker must be allowed the requisite number of suitably

---

[38] S.13(2)
[39] S. 13(4)
[40] S. 13(3)

adjusted and spaced breaks in the work.[41] A break in the work means a short intermission in the work fixed beforehand which is ordered with a view to allowing the worker to detach himself from his work and which is not to be counted as a rest-interval.[42]

Rest day

In every period of seven days a worker is entitled to one day of rest which must not be less than twenty four consecutive hours.[43] However, if any reduction is made in the weekly rest period corresponding time off work must be allowed as soon as possible and in any case not later than fourteen days after or wages at overtime rates must be paid in lieu.[44]

Provision of transport

Where a worker is required to travel sixteen kilometres or more from his normal place of work to another work-site he is entitled to free transport or an allowance in lieu.[45] Where transport is provided the vehicle or vessel must be suitable, in good sanitary condition and not over crowded.[45]

Any employer who contravenes the provision on rest-interval, breaks, rest day or transport is guilty of an offence and liable, on conviction, to a fine not exceeding ₦800 or, for a second or subsequent offence, a fine not exceeding ₦1,500.[46]

Sick leave

A worker is entitled to be paid his wages for up to twelve working days in any one calendar year during absence from work caused by temporary illness certified by a registered medical practitioner.[47] Certification by a herbalist or

[41] S. 13(5)
[42] S. 13(6)
[43] S. 13(7)
[44] S. 14(1)
[45] S. 14(2)
[46] S. 21(l)(c).
[47] S.16

witch doctor will not do. However a worker is not so entitled unless the contract remains in existence during the period of absence[48] and the worker is ready and willing to perform his part of the contract save for the incapacity produced by the illness and, the worker, if so requested by the employer, consents to be examined by a qualified medical practitioner nominated by the employer.[49] The entitlement is also subject to whatever compensation, if any, the worker may have received under the workmen's compensation scheme.[50] In the calculation of sickness benefit only that part of his wages which a worker receives in money, excluding overtime and other allowances, are to be taken into account.[51]

Provision of work

Except where a collective agreement provides otherwise, every employer must, unless a worker has broken his contract, provide work suitable to the worker's capacity on every day, except rest days,[52] and public holidays,[53] on which the worker presents himself and is fit for work.[54] If an employer fails to so provide work he must pay to the worker, in respect of each day on which he has so failed, wages at the same rate as would be payable if the worker had performed a day's work.[55] This does not apply where a worker is suspended from work as a punishment for a breach of discipline or any other offence.[56] The practical effect of these provisions is that an employer discharges his statutory obligation to a worker by the payment of the appropriate wages unless when he is on suspension. However, where, owing to a temporary emergency or other circumstances beyond the employer's control, the period of which does not exceed one week or such longer period as an authorised labour officer may allow in any particular case, the employer is unable to provide work, the worker is entitled to wages only on the first day of the emergency or other circumstance.[57]

---

[48] For example, the illness may frustrate the contract, as to which see ante. It may also be terminated, rightly or wrongfully, before the twelve working days are exhausted.

[49] S. 16 proviso.

[50] S.19

[51] S. 16.

[52] For rest days see ante.

[53] For public holidays see Public Holidays Act Cap. 378 as amended by the Public Holidays (Amendment) Decree No. 26 of 1984.

[54] S. 17(1).

[55] S. 17(1).

[56] S. 17(1) proviso (b); it is submitted that the subsection does not confer a power to suspend; for power to suspend see *ante*.

[57] S. 17(1) proviso (a).

It seems to follow that where an emergency or other circumstance lasts for more than a week where no authorisation is obtained or where an authorised period has expired that the duty of the employer to provide work or pay the appropriate wages must be resumed. Presumably the employer can stop payment of wages by terminating the contract or if it is brought to an end by frustration.

Where a worker is employed in any agricultural undertaking on a plantation on a contract of service under which he earns wages calculated by reference to the number of days' work performed in each month of his service, the employer must provide the worker with work suitable to his capacity on not less than twenty four days in each month during the whole of which he is so employed. If an employer fails to provide work on any of those twenty four days on which the worker presents himself, and is fit for work, he must pay to the worker in respect of each such day wages at the same rate as would be payable if the worker had performed a day's work.[58] In computing twenty four days account must not be taken of more than six days in any one week.[59]

Any dispute between an employer and a worker as to a worker's fitness for work my be referred to an authorised labour officer who may take such medical or other advice as he thinks appropriate and whose decision is final.[60] The finality of the decision is doubtful, however, in view of the constitutional provisions on access to the courts, especially section 6(6) (b) of the 1999 Constitution which provides that the judicial powers of the courts extend to all matters between government or authority and any person for the determination of any question as to the civil rights and obligations of any person.

Annual holidays

Every worker is entitled, after twelve months continuous service, to a holiday, with full pay, of at least six working days.[61] Apprentices and other persons below the age of sixteen years are entitled to, at least, twelve working days as holiday also within twelve months of continuous service.[62] A holiday may be deferred by agreement between an employer and a worker.[63] The proviso which follows that upon deferment "the holiday-earning period shall not thereby be increased

[58] S. 17 (2).
[59] S. 17 (2) proviso.
[60] S. 17 (3).
[61] S.18 (1) (a).
[62] S.18 (1) (b).
[63] S.18 (2).

beyond twenty-four months continuous service" is absurd. The holiday earning period is twelve months continuous service. It is suggested that what is meant by the proviso is that deferment may not be for a period longer than twelve months after a holiday earning period of twelve months continuous service. In other words a worker or an apprentice or other young person must take a holiday within twelve months after he has earned his holiday. Where deferment is for twelve months a worker will, of course, earn a further holiday. It is unlawful for an employer to pay wages in lieu of a holiday to a worker whose contract has not terminated.[64] To do so is an offence and the employer is liable, on conviction, to a fine not exceeding ₦800 or for a second or subsequent offence, a fine not exceeding ₦1,500.[65] A person who ceases to be employed after having completed less than twelve but not less than six months in the continuous employment of an employer since he last qualified for a holiday must be paid, with respect to that period of employment, an amount bearing the same proportion to full pay for one week at his normal rate as that period bears to twelve months.[66]

In the calculation of leave pay only that part of his wages which a worker receives in money, excluding overtime and other allowances, are to be taken into account.[67]

Redundancy

Section 20 makes some provisions for the redundancy of workers. It defines redundancy to mean an involuntary and permanent loss of employment caused by an excess of manpower.[68] In the event of redundancy the employer must inform the trade union or workers' representative concerned of the reasons for and the extent of the anticipated redundancy.[69] However, since redundancy is not tied up with termination of employment generally and there is no job security employers may be tempted to terminate by notice rather than acknowledge redundancy wherever it will benefit them to do so. In *Obaleye* v. *Dunlop Nigerian Industries Ltd*[70] the plaintiff was dismissed without reason assigned. He

---

[64] S.18 (3).
[65] S. 21 (2) (c).
[66] S.18(4)
[67] S.19.
[68] S.20 (3).
[69] S.20 (1)(a).
[70] 1975 NNLR 220; 5 ECSLR 445.

claimed that where an employee[71] is terminated and no reason is assigned and with his character and efficiency unimpugned, be must be regarded as having been made redundant. Bate SPJ said - the mere fact that the defendants politely refrained from expressing their reason for dispensing with the plaintiff's services would not justify the presumption that the plaintiff was made redundant in the true sense of that word.[72] It is suggested that it would be in line with the objective of the section to require an employer to show that the removal of a worker is not on the ground of redundancy. Such a requirement will not put a burden on an employer over and above the requirements of the section nor will it affect his common law right not to give any reason for his intention to bring a contract to an end by notice. In this regard the decision, at arbitration, in *Food, Beverages and Tobacco Staff Association* v. *Premier Brewery Ltd*[73] is more realistic. The employers terminated the employment of thirty three senior employees by offering each one month's salary in lieu of notice. An arbitration tribunal found that the termination was occasioned by the scaling down of the production lines from three to one due to lack of essential raw materials. The tribunal held that the termination was on the ground of redundancy. The National Industrial Court upheld that decision.[74]

Where an employer has informed the trade union or workers' representative concerned of the reasons and extent of an anticipated redundancy he is required, in discharging the workers affected, to adopt the principle of "last in, first out."[75] However he can also have regard "to all factors of relative merit, including skill, ability and reliability." Other indicia of merit which may be suggested are productivity, diligence, efficiency and even experience which may not necessarily coincide with seniority. In *Guinness (Nig.) Ltd.* v. *Agoma*,[76] the plaintiff, who was employed as a staff nurse, was retrenched some five years after her appointment. Ejiwunmi, JCA, in the leading judgment of the Court of Appeal said:[77]

---

71 There was, however, no consideration or finding as to whether the employee was a worker; however, the contract itself contained a definition of redundancy identical with the statutory definition.

72 1975 NNLR 220,222.

73 Unreported Suit No NIC/1/89.

74 It does not seem that the employees came within the definition of the term worker so as to justify the application of the section on redundancy which the court held was breached by the employers. However there were two collective agreements which dealt with redundancy and the employers were in breach of these.

75 S.20(1) (b).

76 [1992] 7 NWLR 728.

77 Ibid., 741.

> It is however clear from that section that the application of the principle of LIFO was made subject to factors of relative merit, including skill, ability and reliability. In my view while that section seems to preserve the rights of an employee who had been long in the employment of an employer to remain in his employment in a general retrenchment exercise by his employer, it could appear that he can only escape being retrenched if he has shown that he is relatively better in merit, skill, ability than the other workers who are in the same category with him.

This statement, useful as it is, was a mere *obiter*. This is so for many reasons including the reason that the employee, a nurse, was not a worker. However, although it is quite clear that an efficient worker may not be retrenched before an indolent one who has been in employment before him, it is equally clear that an employer must act in good faith and with honesty if harmonious industrial relations is to be maintained.

The Minister is empowered to make regulations providing, either generally or in particular cases, for the compulsory payment of redundancy allowances.[78] No such regulations have, as yet, been made. In the mean time the requirement that an employer "use his best endeavours to negotiate redundancy payments" has to apply.[79] Where the workers are not sufficiently organised it is doubtful if an employer's best endeavours will ever be good enough.

Termination of employment

Section 9 (7) provides for the termination of the contract of employment of a worker. It provides that a contract is terminated by the expiry of the period for which it is made or by the death[80] of the worker before the expiry of the period for which it is made or by notice in accordance with section 11 of the Act or in any other way in which a contract is legally terminable or held to be terminated. The phrase "in any other way in which a contract is legally terminable or held to be terminated" obviously embraces all the common law modes of termination of a contract of employment. It follows that the contract of employment of a worker may be terminated or held terminated in the same way as that of an employee at common law. As we have seen, at common law, a contract of employment may

---

[78] S.20 (2).

[79] S.20 (1)(c).

[80] The termination of a contract by death of a worker is without prejudice to the legal claims of his personal representatives or dependants; S.9 (8).

be brought to an end by agreement of the parties, by performance, frustration, the giving of notice and summary dismissal.[81]

In so far as notice is concerned the period of notice required to be given by either party is laid down in section 11 which also provides that either party to a contract of employment may terminate the contract on the expiration of notice given by him to the other party of his intention to do so.[82] The period of notice is one day where the contract has continued for a period of three months or less, one week where the contract has continued for more than three months but less than two years, two weeks where it has continued for two years but less than five years and one month where it has continued for five years or more.[83] A period of notice does not include the day on which notice is given[84] and any notice for one week or more must be in writing.[85] Either party may waive his right to notice and he may accept a payment in lieu of notice.[86] In the calculation of a payment in lieu of notice only that part of the wages which a worker receives in money, exclusive of overtime and other allowances are to be taken into account.[87] All wages payable in money must be paid on or before the expiry of a period of notice.[88]

Where an employer gives notice to terminate the contract of employment of a worker who has been continuously employed for three months or more, the employer is not liable to make any payment in respect of a period during which the worker is absent from work with the leave of the employer granted at the request of the worker.[89]

The decision in *Wenegiene* v. *Roofco (Nig.) Ltd*[90] shows that there is some amount of haziness in the courts as to the application of the provisions of the Labour Act. The plaintiff was, by letter which he accepted, appointed a personnel supervisor with the defendant company. When he attended to resume work he was told the position had been filled and that a letter, containing a

---

[81] S. 11(5) is, thus, superfluous.

[82] Hence the power to terminate by notice may be said to be statutory.

[83] S. 11 (2) ; it must be noted that the period of notice has nothing to do with the period for which a contract is expressed to subsist; the sole question is for how long the worker has worked with the employer. Thus a daily worker who has worked with the same employer for e.g. three years is entitled to two weeks notice; see *Ikezuonu* v. *Julius Berger Nigeria Ltd.* (1979)7-9 CCHCJ(Vol.4) 56.

[84] S. 11 (4).

[85] S. 11 (3).

[86] S. 11 (6).

[87] S. 11 (9).

[88] S. 11 (7).

[89] S. 11 (8).

[90] 1976 NNLR 160.

cheque for ₦800 as compensation, had been sent to him to inform him of that position. In an action for damages for breach of contract the court sought to apply section 11 in determining the measure of damages but declined to do so on the ground that the Act could not apply. The court said:[91]

> *Prima facie* by the provision of s.11 of the Labour Decree, the plaintiff who had not even assumed duty for one day would be entitled to a day's notice. However I do not think that will be the right construction to be given to the section because it is too narrow in context. The intention in the promulgation of the Labour Decree it seems is to make provisions governing the relationship between the employer and the employed following the assumption of the employment by the employed. So that in my view, the provisions of the Decree do not apply to the situation where the employed has not started working as in this case.

The court was, probably, correct in deciding that the Act did not apply. The plaintiff, who was a personnel supervisor, would not seem to be a worker within the Act. However, the reason given for that decision can be faulted. The Act applies, generally, to persons who have a contract of employment with an employer. Specifically, section 11 , with the marginal note, Termination of contracts by notice, gives either party to "a contract of employment" the right to terminate it by notice given in accordance with the section. There was no doubt that the plaintiff had a contract of employment with the employer. It's breach by the employer was, therefore, an excellent example of an anticipatory breach of contract.[92]

Protection of wages

The wages of a worker are offered protection by the Act with respect to the manner and mode of payment, advances to workers, deductions and the opening of shops for the sale of provisions to workers. The provisions are inherited from Great Britain where statutes were enacted as early as the fifteenth century in an attempt to curb a number of abuses associated with the wages of workers.[93]

---

[91] Ibid., 163.

[92] For an example of anticipatory breach of contract of employment see *Ukpong* v. *Incar (Nig.)Ltd.* CCHCJ/8/74 p 1147 and for measure of damages for anticipatory breach of contract of employment see E. E. Uvieghara, Measure of Damages for Anticipatory Breach of Contract, *Sekoni* v. *Shell B.P. I CCHCJ/93, Nigerian Journal of Contemporary Law* 1975.

[93] The earliest statute was in 1464 but the basis of the modern law is the Truck Act 1831; deductions were dealt with in the Truck Act 1896.

Examples of such abuses included the payment of wages in kind, usually inferior goods which could not compete favourably with the employer's goods in the open market, the imposition of fines and penalties for bad or poor workmanship and deductions from wages on account of such and other fines, payment of wages in drinking places and the opening of shops, referred to as Tommy shops, by employers at which workers were compelled to buy usually at inflated prices dictated by the employer.

Manner of payment

The wages of a worker must, in all contracts, be made payable in legal tender and not otherwise and if in any contract the whole or any part of the wages are made payable in any other manner the contract is illegal, null and void.[94] However an employer may provide food, a dwelling place or any other allowance or privilege as a part of a worker's remuneration where the food, dwelling place, allowance or privilege is prescribed by law, a collective agreement or is an arbitration award because it is customary or desirable in view of the nature of the industry or occupation in which the worker is engaged.[95] But in no case must an employer give to a worker any intoxicating liquor or noxious drug by way of remuneration.[96] And, unless expressly permitted by the Act, wages payable in money must be paid in legal tender or, with the prior consent in writing of the worker concerned, by cheque or postal order.[97] Any payment or purported payment in any other form is illegal, null and void.[98]

No employer must impose, in any contract for the employment of any worker, any terms as to the place at which or the manner in which or the person with whom any wages paid to the worker are to be expended; any contract containing any such terms is illegal, null and void.[99] Also wages must not be paid to a worker in premises used for the sale of intoxicating liquor or for the retail sale of goods except in the case of a worker employed on the premises.[100]

---

[94] S.1(1); such a contract being void the worker would, presumably, be able to recover for any services rendered on a *quantum meruit*; a statutory right to claim was provided under the Labour Code Act repealed by the Act.

[95] S.1(2).

[96] Ibid.

[97] S.1(3).

[98] Ibid.; it probably follows that a worker can then get paid properly.

[99] S. 2.

[100] S. 3.

Advances

An employer may not make to a worker an advance of wages in excess of one month's wages.[101] Where such an advance is made the minimum period for its recovery must not be less than three months.[102] No advance of wages may be made to a worker who is still liable to repay any part of an earlier advance except in cases of necessity as so approved by the employer.[103] An employer must not make any deduction by way of discount, interest or any similar charge on account of any advance of wages paid to a worker in anticipation of the regular period of payment of the wages.[104]

The Governor of a State may, by order, declare that the provisions on advances may not apply to any particular kind of advance paid to any particular class of workers or to all workers.[105]

Deductions

Section 5(1) provides that, except where it is expressly permitted by the Act or any other law,[105a] no employer must make any deduction, or make any agreement or contract with a worker for any deduction, from the wages to be paid by the employer to the worker or for any payment to the employer by the worker for or in respect of any fines. Thus an employer cannot rely on an agreement or contract made with a worker for, e.g. a loan to the worker, as authority for any deduction from that worker's wages. Only deductions by virtue of the provisions of a law can be made. The same applies to a fine imposed by the employer on a worker; a contractual authority will not suffice. Fine has been defined as a financial loss agreed on in the case of the non-fulfilment of some contractual obligation.[106]

In *Sealand Petroleum Co.* v. *Barrat*[107] a clause of the contract of employment provided that, if the employer sustained any loss of cash, stock, tools or equipment as a result of the employee's breach of contractual or other duty, the

---

101 S. 4 (1).
102 S. 4 (2).
103 S. 4(3).
104 S. 4(4).
105 S. 4(5).
105a It is suggested that "law" means statutory law only; if it is otherwise, for example, if it includes the common law of contract, then the protection offered will be illusory.
106 *Bristow* v *City Petroleum Ltd.* Note: [1987] 2 All ER 45 House of Lords.
107 [1986] 2 All ER 360.

employer would hold the employee responsible for such loss and the employer reserved the right to deduct up to the amount of the loss from the employee's pay. Deductions were made, including the whole wages earned on one occasion, for shortages in the sale of petrol. The court held that the clause appeared, without any doubt, to provide for a financial penalty. Nolan J said the clause is "a clause providing for the deduction of a financial penalty and thus a fine from remuneration."[108]

The section itself provides for a number of deductions. With the prior consent in writing of an authorised labour officer a reasonable deduction may be made in respect of injury or loss caused to the employer by the wilful misconduct or neglect of the worker.[109] It is suggested that the word wilful governs both misconduct and neglect so that reasonable deduction may be made only in respect of injury or loss caused by an intentional act of the worker. Also an employer may, with the consent of a worker, make deductions from the wages of a worker and pay to the appropriate person, any contributions to provident or pension funds or other schemes agreed to by the worker and approved by the governor of a state.[110] Deductions may also be made from the wages of a worker in respect of an overpayment of wages but this can only be done in respect of any such overpayment made during the three months immediately preceding the month in which the overpayment was discovered.[111]

Subsection (3) of section 5 deals with trade unions' check-off system. Where an employer has recognised a registered trade union, and every employer is obliged to recognise a registered trade union of which his employees are members,[112] he must make deduction from the wages of every worker who is eligible to be a member of the union for the purpose of paying contributions to the trade union so recognised.[113] And he must pay any sum so deducted directly to the registered office of the trade union.[114] Eligibility must, of course, be determined by the registered rules of the union. When making a payment an employer must include with such payment a list of the "employees" from whose wages deductions were made.[115] The reference to employees must be in error; deductions are required to be made only from the wages of workers. Indeed sub-section 5(4) provides that no deductions must be made from the wages and

---

[108] Ibid., 365; the clause was held to fall foul of a provision of the Truck Act 1896 similar to S.5 (1).
[109] S. 5(1) proviso.
[110] S. 5(2).
[111] S. 5(5).
[112] See below as to recognition of trade unions by an employer.
[113] S. 5(3)(a)
[114] S. 5(3)(b)
[115] S. 5(6).

salaries of persons who are eligible members of any of the trade unions specified in part B of schedule 3 to the Trade Unions Act except the person concerned has accepted, in writing, to make voluntary contributions to the trade union. The trade unions specified in that part of the schedule are of senior staff and employers. Senior staff are not workers within the statutory definition of a worker. However a worker may contract out of the check-off system, in writing, and where he does so no deduction must be made from his wages.[116] Presumably such contracting out must be addressed to the employer to ensure its implementation.[116a]

In all the total amount of deduction which may made from the wages of a worker in any one month must not exceed one-third of his wages for that month.[117]

Opening of a shop

The Minister of Labour and Productivity may, after consultation with the governor of a state, give approval to an employer to establish a shop for the sale of provisions to his workers but no worker must be compelled by any contract or agreement, written or oral, to purchase provisions at any shop so established.[118] No employer may establish a shop for the sale of provisions to his workers or permit such a shop to be established or kept otherwise than in accordance with the above provision.[119] Any employer who contravenes the provision is guilty of an offence and liable, on conviction, to a fine not exceeding ₦800 and, for a second or subsequent offence, to a fine not exceeding ₦1,500.[120]

Any employer who enters into any agreement or contract or gives any remuneration for employment contrary to part one of the Act or which is declared by that part to be illegal or unlawful or makes any deduction from the wages of any worker or receives payment from any worker contrary to any

---

[116] S. 5 (3)

[116a] See p. 348 *et seq* for new provisions which probably render S.5(3) otiose.

[117] S. 5(7): Deductions permitted by other statutes must, of course, be taken into account. These include especially personal income tax which may be imposed only by the State in which the worker is resident; see S. 2(2) Personal Income Tax Act No. 104 of 1993. Note may also be taken of possible deduction under the Matrimonial Causes Act Cap. 220 Laws of the Federation of Nigeria, 1990. Unlike with the NPF before it the Nigeria Social Insurance Trust Fund Act 1993 No. 73 does not expressly authorise deduction.

[118] S. 6(1).

[119] S. 6 (2).

[120] S. 21(1)(c).

provision of part one is guilty of an offence and liable on conviction to a fine not exceeding ₦800 or, for a second or subsequent offence, to a fine not exceeding ₦1,500.[121]

Where an employer is charged with any offence, under part one, he is entitled, upon information duly laid by him, to have any other person whom he charges as the actual offender brought before the court at the time appointed for hearing the charge.[122] And, if, after the commission of the offence has been proved, the employer proves to the satisfaction of the court that he had used due diligence to enforce the provisions of part one, i.e. sections 1 to 20, and that the other person committed the offence without his knowledge, consent or connivance, the other person must be convicted of the offence and the employer must be exempted from any liability.[123] However where it is made to appear to the satisfaction of the minister at the time of the discovery of an offence that the employer used due diligence to enforce part one of the Act and by what person the offence was committed and that it was without the knowledge, consent or connivance of the employer, the Minister must proceed against the person whom he believes to be the actual offender without first proceeding against the employer.[124]

Nothing in part one of the Act is to apply to a worker who is the father, mother, husband, wife, son or daughter of the employer or to any body of persons working on any agreement of co-operation.[125]

Recruiting workers

Part 11 of the Act[126] deals with the recruiting[127] of any Nigerian citizen for employment as a worker either in Nigeria or elsewhere. No person or association may recruit any Nigerian citizen for employment as a worker in Nigeria or elsewhere except in pursuance of an employer's permit[128] or recruiter's

---

[121] S. 21 (1) (a) and (b)
[122] S. 21(2)(a)
[123] S. 21(2)(b).
[124] S. 21(3).
[125] S. 22.
[126] I.e. ss 23-48.
[127] Recruiting includes all operations undertaken with the object of obtaining or supplying the labour of persons who do not spontaneously offer their services at the place of employment, at a public emigration or employment office or at an office conducted by an employers'. association and supervised by the minister; s.91.
[128] Employer's permit means an employer's permit granted under s.24 of the Act; s.91

licence.[129] However, where a worker is employed by an undertaking for which it is proposed the worker would recruit other workers or is formally commissioned in writing by his employer to recruit other workers for the undertaking, or does not receive any remuneration or other advantage from the recruiting and does not make advances of wages to the workers he recruits, the Minister may waive the need for a permit or licence but issue to the worker a certificate to recruit for service in Nigeria subject to such conditions as he thinks fit.[130] Where any worker to whom a certificate has been issued is convicted of certain offences the minister may, forthwhth, cancel the certificate.[131] These provisions on recruiting do not apply to the recruiting of Nigerian citizens for service as workers in Nigeria if the recruiting is undertaken by or on behalf of an employer who does not employ more than twenty five workers or is undertaken within a radius of forty kilometres from the place of employment and is not undertaken by a professional recruiter, that is to say, a person who holds a recruiter's licence.[132]

The minister may make regulations, with such modifications, if any, as he thinks appropriate, applying the provisions of part two to labour contractors, that is to say, persons who undertake to provide another party with the services of workers while themselves remaining the employers of the workers in question.[133] The procedure for application for an employer's permit and the conditions for a grant of such a permit or a licence to recruit persons for employment either within or outside Nigeria are elaborate and complex. One condition for a grant of an employer's permit is that the employer must give security in any amount stipulated by the Minister either by way of a deposit or otherwise.[134] Certain other limitations on recruiting are also laid down.[135] Every recruited worker[136] must be medically examined and the recruiter or employer must provide transport to the place of employment[137] as well as be responsible for the expenses of the journey.[138] A recruited worker who becomes incapacitated by sickness or accident during the journey to the place of employment or is found medically unfit for employment or for any reason not his fault is not engaged

---

[129] S.23(l); recruiter's licence means a recruiter's licence granted under s.25 of the Act; s.91.
[130] S. 23(2).
[131] S. 23(3).
[132] S.48(1).
[133] S.48(2).
[134] S.24(7); see also ss.24, 25, 33 and 40.
[135] S.26.
[136] S.28.
[137] S.29.
[138] S.30.

after being recruited must be repatriated at the expense of the recruiter or employer.[139]

The personal effects and tools of workers or members of their family who are repatriated either by the employer or the government are exempt from custom duties.[140]

Section 40 lists thirteen terms relating to conditions of employment which must be included in every foreign contract, i.e. a contract to employ a worker outside Nigeria. Such a worker is also entitled, at the expense of the employer, to have his family - not more than two wives and such of his children under sixteen years of age as he desires to accompany him - to accompany him and remain with him for the full duration of the contract.[141] But where the contract is for less than one year the family may remain for less than the full duration of the contract.[142]

Any contract of a worker who is recruited to work either in Nigeria or outside Nigeria to which the worker is induced to enter by fraud, falsehood, intimidation, coercion or misrepresentation is void but the employer is liable to pay wages due under the contract and provide for the return of the worker and any members of his family who accompanied him.[143] Any employer who neglects or ill treats any worker is guilty of an offence and liable, on conviction, to a fine not exceeding ₦800 or to imprisonment for a period not exceeding one year or to both.[144] Section 47 also creates a number of offences including the offence of recruiting without a permit or licence.

Apprentices, women and young persons

In part three the Labour Act regulates the contract of employment of apprentices, certain aspects of the employment of women, and the employment of young persons and domestic servants. The part also deals with labour health areas, labour schemes, labour exchanges, registration of employers and forced labour.[145]

---

[139] S.31.
[140] S.43.
[141] S. 44.
[142] S.44 proviso.
[143] S.45.
[144] S.46.
[145] Part three includes sections 49 - 74; sections 65 - 66 on labour health areas, 67 on registration of employers, 68 on labour schemes, 69 - 70 on employment exchanges and 71 which creates offences with respect to labour schemes are not discussed.

The parent or, in the case of an orphan, the guardian,[146] of a person above the age of twelve years but under the age of sixteen years may, with the consent of such a person testified by his execution of a written contract of apprenticeship,[147] apprentice him to an employer to train him or have him trained systematically for a trade or employment in which art or skill is required, or as a domestic servant, for any term but not exceeding five years.[148] Where such a young person is without known parents or a guardian an authorised labour officer may authorise his apprenticeship and appoint some fit and proper person to execute the written contract of apprenticeship and act generally as his guardian.[149] Any young person who is sixteen years of age or above and who is not presently under any contract of apprenticeship may apprentice himself for any term not exceeding five years to any trade or employment in which art or skill is required.[150] Every contract of apprenticeship and every assignment of it must be in writing but no such writing is valid unless attested by and made with the approval of an authorised labour officer certified under his hand on the contract or assignment.[151]

However, before attesting any contract of apprenticeship the labour officer must ascertain that the apprentice consented to the contract and that his consent was not obtained by coercion or undue influence or as a result of misrepresentation or mistake.[152] He must also satisfy himself that

(i) the apprentice has been medically examined and certified by a qualified medical practitioner to be physically and mentally fit to be employed and trained in the employment specified in the contract;

---

[146] Guardian includes any person to whose care a young person has been committed, even temporarily, by a person having authority over the young person or any person lawfully having charge of a young person who has no parents or whose parents are unknown; young person means a person under the age of eighteen years. S. 91.

[147] S. 52(a) empowers the Minister to make regulations providing for, *inter alia*, the form of contracts of apprenticeship. Regulation 47 of the Regulations made under S. 62 Labour Ordinance No.1 of 1929 which have been kept alive require a deed. See S. 90(2) and paragraph 4 of the schedule; and also S. 20 Interpretation Ordinance cap. 89 Laws of the Federation 1958 and Labour Code Act cap. 91 Laws of the Federation of Nigeria and Lagos, 1958.

[148] S.49 (1).

[149] S.49 (2).

[150] S.49 (3).

[151] S.50(1); any contract of apprenticeship may, with the consent of the parties, be assigned by the employer; s. 49(5).

[152] S.50(2)(a); presumably, coercion, undue influence, misrepresentation or mistake apply as in the general law of contract.

(ii) the parties to the contract fully understood its terms before signing or otherwise indicating consent;

(iii) provision is made in the contract as to the manner in which any remuneration in cash or otherwise due to the apprentice is to be determined and as to the scale of increase in remuneration during the course of the apprenticeship;

(iv) provision is made in the contract for payment of remuneration to the apprentice during illness and during holidays, if any;[153]

(v) where the apprentice is unable, by reason of his apprenticeship, to return to his home at the end of each day, the contract contains adequate provision to ensure that he is supplied with food, clothing, accommodation and medical attention; and

(vi) the terms of the contract are in accordance with any regulations made by the minister. As we have seen, regulations provide that the contract of apprenticeship be in the form of a deed.[154]

The age of any person may, where no register of births is available, be enquired into and determined by the labour officer before whom a contract of apprenticeship is attested and the age so determined is conclusive for all purposes in relation to the contract of apprenticeship.[155]

If any person with whom an apprentice has been placed retains the apprentice in his service after the stipulated period of service has expired without any agreement between the parties for the payment of wages the apprentice is entitled to recover from the person wages at the ordinary current rate payable for service similar to that performed by the apprentice.[156]

Any person who removes or attempts to remove any apprentice who is above the age of twelve years but under sixteen years from Nigeria without the authority in writing of the Minister is guilty of an offence and liable, on conviction, to a fine not exceeding ₦800 or to imprisonment for a period not exceeding one year or to both such fine and imprisonment.[157] Also any person who employs an apprentice for more than six months on a contract which has not been attested or who induces or attempts to induce any apprentice to quit the service of his employer is guilty of an offence and liable, on conviction, to a fine

---

[153] An apprentice is entitled to a holiday with full pay of, at least, twelve working day after twelve months continuous service; s.18(1)(b).

[154] See note 147 *ante*.

[155] S. 49(4).

[156] S. 51.

[157] S.53(1).

not exceeding ₦800 or to imprisonment for a period not exceeding six months or to both.[158]

Any question arising out of a contract of apprenticeship or any dispute between any of the parties to such a contract whether arising from breach of the contract or otherwise is to be heard and determined by a magistrate's court or, where a magistrate's court has no civil jurisdiction, a district court, in accordance with the powers conferred on these courts under the Act.[159]

The Minister may make regulations providing for

(a) the form of contracts of apprenticeship, the terms and conditions upon which contracts of apprenticeship may be lawfully entered into and the duties and obligations of apprentices and their masters;
(b) the registration of contracts of apprenticeship with a specified officer;
(c) the number of apprentices who may be apprenticed during a specified period in any specified trade or employment;
(d) the technical and other qualifications of employers entitling them to take and train apprentices;
(e) the conditions governing the entry into apprenticeship;
(f) the mutual rights and obligations of employer and apprentice;
(g) the supervision to be established over apprenticeship with a view to ensuring in particular that the regulations governing apprenticeship and the terms of any contract of apprenticeship are observed, that the training is satisfactory and that there is reasonable uniformity in the conditions of apprenticeship; and
(h) the holding of examinations of apprentices on the expiry of the period of apprenticeship and, where necessary, in the course of apprenticeship, determining the methods of organising the examinations and the issue of certificates based on the results of the examinations.[160]

---

[158] S.53(2).

[159] S.49(6); for the powers of these courts see below; at common law, it was held that damages for breach of a contract of apprenticeship included long term loss, i.e., the better wages which would have been earned; at least for a year or two, if the apprentice had completed his apprenticeship; see *Dunk* v. *George Waller & Son Ltd* (1970) 2 All ER 630.

[160] S. 51 , Regulation 4 of the Labour Regulations which are extant. (see f.n. 147 *ante*), provides that an employer under a deed of apprenticeship must give to an apprentice who has served his apprenticeship, a certificate of proficiency according to the ability of the apprentice. If an employer refuses to do so the apprentice may appeal to the governor or the minister who, if he thinks fit, may cause the apprentice to be examined by a qualified person and issued with a certificate if found deserving of one. The employer is liable to the government for the expenses of and in connection with the examination.

Protection of women

Woman means any member of the female sex whatever her age or status.[161]

Maternity protection

In any public or private industrial or commercial undertaking or in any branch of such an undertaking or in any agricultural undertaking or in any branch of it a woman has the right to leave her work if she produces a medical certificate given by a registered medical practitioner stating that her confinement will probably take place within six weeks and she must not be permitted to work during the six weeks following her confinement.[162] If she had been continuously employed by her then employer for a period of six months or more immediately prior to her absence on confinement she must be paid not less than fifty per cent of the wages she would have earned if she had not been absent.[163] This provision is not

[161] S. 91.

[162] S. 54(1)(a) and (b). Agricultural undertaking means any undertaking in which a worker is employed under a contract of employment for the purpose of agriculture, fisheries, horticulture, silviculture, the tending of domestic animals and poultry or the collection of the produce of any plants or trees but does not include any such undertaking in which only members of the same family are employed; industrial undertaking includes mines, quarries and others works for the extraction of minerals from the earth, industries in which articles are manufactured, altered, cleaned, repaired, ornamented, finished, adapted for sale, broken up or demolished or in which materials are transformed, including shipbuilding and the generation and transformation of electricity or motive power of any kind, the construction, maintenance, repair, alteration or demolition of any building, railway, tramway, harbour, dock, canal, inland water way, road, tunnel, bridge, viaduct, sewer, drain, well, telegraph or telephonic installation, electrical undertaking, gasworks, water-works, or other works of construction, as well as the preparation for or the laying of the foundation of any such work or structure and transport of passengers or goods by road, rail, air, sea or inland waterways, including the handling of goods at docks, quays, wharves, warehouses and airports, and including the carrying of coal or other materials by hand to or from lighters or ships but does not include any commercial or agricultural under-taking, any undertaking in which only members of the same family are employed or any customary occupation of a kind normally carried on at home; mine includes any place, excavation or working whereon, wherein or whereby any operation in connection with mining is carried on; s.91, Commercial undertaking is not defined; if it is confined to commerce or trading then women in offices, especially in the Public Sector, may not be covered by the provision; I.L.O. Convention No.3 of 1919 on which this provision was based was revised in 1952 by Convention No. 103 which also covers now -"industrial occupations" which is widely defined.

[163] S. 54(1)(c)

affected by any fixation of a minimum wage;[164] the entitlement is to at least half the wages which she would have earned if she were at work.

Where a woman is nursing a child, whether legitimate or illegitimate, she must be allowed half an hour twice a day during her working hours for that purpose.[165] Even in 1974 when this provision and several others of the Labour Code Act[166] were re-enacted it was obvious that the provision was inadequate to achieve its objective. It does not even state for how long the privilege should be allowed. However, in practice employers allow nursing mothers to close from work an hour earlier, some for a period of three months and others for up to six months.

An employer is not liable, in his capacity as an employer, to pay any medical expenses incurred by a woman during or on account of her pregnancy or confinement.[167] The word "during" may mean that a woman may forfeit a right to medical treatment which she may otherwise have had when not pregnant or on confinement.

Where a woman is absent from her work during the twelve weeks of maternity leave or remains absent from her work for a longer period as a result of illness certified by a registered medical practitioner to arise out of her pregnancy or confinement and to render her unfit to work, "then, until her absence has exceeded such a period (if any) as may be prescribed, no employer shall give her notice of dismissal during her absence or notice of dismissal expiring during her absence."[168] In *Okunbowa* v. *Group Consultants Nigeria Project Advisers (Nigeria) Ltd.*[169] the defendants not only refused to pay the plaintiff her wages but also terminated her appointment while she was away on confinement having given the defendants a medical certificate. The court held that although her contract of employment did not provide for maternity leave she was entitled to such leave by virtue of sections 145 and 146 of the Labour Code Act[170] since the defendants were a commercial undertaking. She was held to be entitled to her salary for the whole period of maternity leave as well as damages

---

[164] S. 54(2).

[165] S. 54(1)(d) and (5).

[166] i.e. the Labour Code Ordinance 1945; I.L.O. Convention No. 103 which revised Convention No.3 of 1919 on which this provision is based now provides, by Article 5, that a nursing mother is entitled to interrupt her work for the purpose of nursing her child at a time or times prescribed by law.

[167] S.54(3).

[168] S.54(4); presumably the prescription is to be done by the Minister under his powers under s.88 (1)(e) to prescribe anything which is to be prescribed under the Act and is not otherwise provided for; no prescription has been done

[169] CCHCJ/2/74 page 159.

[170] Now S.54(1). and (4) respectively.

for wrongful termination. The damages were to cover the period of notice to terminate her appointment after the period, of her maternity leave.

Breach of any provision on maternity leave is, in addition to any civil liability, a criminal offence. Any person, who, being the proprietor, owner or manager of any industrial, commercial or agricultural undertaking, contravenes any provision on maternity protection is guilty of an offence and liable, on conviction, to a fine not exceeding ₦800 or to imprisonment for a period not exceeding three months or to both.[171]

Night work

Except as permitted below a woman must not be employed on night work in any private or public industrial undertaking or in any branch of it or in any agricultural undertaking or any branch of such an undertaking.[172] Night, for this purpose, means, as respects industrial undertakings, a period of at least eleven consecutive hours and including the interval between ten o'clock in the evening and five o'clock in the morning, and, as respects agricultural undertakings, a period of at least nine consecutive hours including the interval between nine o'clock in the evening and four o'clock in the morning.[173] However, in the case of industrial undertakings, the minister may, by order, permit the eleven hours period to be reduced to ten hours on not more than sixty days in any one year if he is satisfied that the undertaking is influenced by the seasons of the year or that the reduction is necessary because of special circumstances.[174] Any person who employs a woman in contravention of these provisions on night work is guilty of an offence and on conviction liable to a fine not exceeding ₦800 or to imprisonment for a period not exceeding one month or to both.[175]

The prohibition against night work for women does not apply to women employed as nurses in any public or private industrial undertaking or in any agricultural undertaking nor to women holding responsible positions of management who are not ordinarily engaged in manual labour.[176]

In any proceedings brought for a violation of the prohibition on night work, it is a good defence if it is shown to the satisfaction of the court trying the proceedings that the night work in question was due to an interruption of work

[171] S.58(1).
[172] S.55(1); for the definition of industrial or agricultural undertaking see note 162 ante.
[173] S.55(3).
[174] S.55(4).
[175] S.58(2).
[176] S.55(2).

which it was impossible to foresee and which is not of a recurring character or that the night work had to do with raw material or materials in course of treatment which are subject to rapid deterioration and it was necessary to preserve such materials from certain loss.[177]

The minister may, by order, exclude the prohibition on night work in respect to women covered by a collective agreement in force which permits night work for women but, before making such an order, he must satisfy himself that adequate provision exists for the transportation and protection of the women concerned.[178]

Underground work

A woman must not be employed on underground work in any mine.[179] But this does not apply to women holding positions of management who do not perform manual labour or women employed in health and welfare services or women who, in the course of their studies, spend a period of training in underground parts of a mine or any other women who may occasionally have to enter the underground parts of a mine for the purposes of a non manual occupation.[180]

Any person who employs a woman in underground work in contravention of the prohibition is guilty of an offence and on conviction liable to a fine not exceeding ₦100 or to imprisonment for a period not exceeding one month or to both.[181]

The minister may make regulations prohibiting or restricting, subject to such conditions as may be specified in the regulation, the employment of women in any particular type or types of industrial or other undertakings or in any process or work carried on by such undertakings.[182]

Employment of young persons

A young person is a person who is under the age of eighteen years.[183] It will be remembered that a person under the age of sixteen years is prohibited from

---

177 S.55(2).
178 S.55(5).
179 S.56(l).
180 S. 56(2).
181 S. 58(2).
182 S. 57.
183 S. 91

entering into a contract of employment except as an apprentice.[184] The Act, therefore, makes provisions for the employment of such persons and other young persons.

No young person must be employed in any employment which will be injurious to his health or which is dangerous or immoral.[185] Where an employer is notified in writing by the minister, either generally or in any particular case, that the kind of work upon which a young person is employed is injurious to his health or dangerous or immoral or otherwise unsuitable, the employer must discontinue the employment but without prejudice to the right of the young person to be paid such wages as he may have earned up to the date of discontinuance.[186]

No young person under the age of sixteen years must be employed in circumstances in which it is not reasonably possible for him to return each day to the place of residence of his parent or guardian except with the approval of an authorised labour officer and on a written contract which conforms with the contract of employment of a worker.[186a] Also a young person under sixteen years of age must not be employed to work underground or on machine work or on a public holiday.[186b] He must also not be required to work for a longer period than four consecutive hours nor permitted to work for more than eight working hours in any one day.[187] No person must continue to employ such a young person after receiving notice either orally or in writing from his parent or guardian that he is employed against the wishes of the parent or guardian.[188]

A young person under the age of fifteen years must not be employed nor work in any industrial undertaking but this does not apply to work done by young persons in technical schools or similar institutions if the work is approved and supervised by the ministry of education or a corresponding department of government of a state.[189]

A young person under the age of fourteen years may be employed only on a daily wage on a day to day basis and so long as he returns each night to the place

---

184 S. 9(3) and see ante.

185 S. 59(6).

186 S. 59(6).

186a S. 59(4); this provision does not apply to employment in a domestic service except where regulations on domestic service, which have not been made, provide otherwise.

186b S. 59(5).

187 S. 59(8) and see note 186a ante.

188 S. 59(7); this does not apply where the employment is under a written contract entered into with the approval of a labour officer; S.59(7) proviso.

189 S. 59(2).

of residence of his parents or guardian or a person approved by his parents or guardian.[190]

No child must be employed nor work in any capacity except where he is employed by a member of his family on light work of an agricultural, horticultural or domestic character approved by the minister.[191] He must not, in any case, be required to lift, carry or move anything so heavy as to be likely to injure his physical development.[192] Child means a young person under the age of twelve years.[193]

Night work

No young person must be employed during the night.[194] Night means a period of at least twelve consecutive hours including, in the case of young persons under the age of sixteen years, the interval between ten o'clock in the evening and seven o'clock in the morning and, in the case of young persons over the age of sixteen years a prescribed interval of at least seven consecutive hours falling between ten o'clock in the evening and seven o'clock in the morning.[195] In the case of young persons over sixteen years the minister may prescribe different intervals for different areas, industries, undertakings or branches of industries or undertakings but he must consult the employers' and workers' associations or organisations concerned before prescribing an interval beginning after eleven o'clock in the evening.[196]

However young persons over the age of sixteen years may be employed during the night in cases of emergency which could not have been controlled or foreseen and are not of a periodical character and which interfere with the normal working of an industrial undertaking.[197] Young persons under sixteen years may be employed during the night in the following industrial undertakings or activities which by reason of the nature of the process are required to be carried on continuously day and night - these include the manufacture of iron and steel, in processes in which reverberatory or regeneratory furnaces are used and

---

190 S.59(3).
191 S.59(1)(a).
192 S.59(1)(b)
193 S.91.
194 S.60(1).
195 S.60(4).
196 S.60(5).
197 S.60(3).

in the galvanising of sheet metal or wire, except the pickling process; glass works; manufacture of paper or raw sugar and gold mining reduction work.[198]

Young persons and shipping

No young person must be employed in a vessel[199] as a trimmer or stoker but where a trimmer or stoker is required in a place in which only young persons are available such persons of and over the age of sixteen years may be employed so however that two such young persons must be engaged and employed in the place of each trimmer or stoker required.[200] No young person must be employed in any vessel other than a vessel in which only persons of his family are employed unless he is in possession of a certificate signed by a registered medical practitioner to the effect that he is fit for the employment or work.[201] Where such a certificate is issued the certificate is valid for one year from the date of issue or, if it would otherwise expire in the course of a voyage, until the end of the voyage in question but it may at any time be revoked by a qualified medical practitioner if he is satisfied that the young person is no longer fit for the employment or work.[202]

No young person under the age of fifteen years must be employed in any vessel except where the vessel is a school or training vessel and the work on which the young person is employed is work of a kind approved by the minister and supervised by a public officer or by a public department or is work on which only members of the family of the young person are employed.[203]

There must be included in every agreement with the crew of a vessel a list of young persons who are members of the crew together with particulars of the dates of their births.[204] But in the case of a vessel in which there is no such agreement the master must keep a register, which must at all times be open to inspection by an authorised labour officer or customs officer, of such young persons as may be employed in the vessel with particulars of the dates of their births and the dates on which they became or ceased to be members of the crew.[205]

---

198 S.60(2).
199 Vessel includes floating craft of every description except ships of war; S.61(5).
200 S.61(2).
201 S.61(3).
202 S.61(3).
203 S.61(l)
204 S.61(4
205 Ibid; Custom Officer means any person employed in the Department of Customs & Excise or, for the time being performing duties in relation to customs and excise; s. 61(5).

Keeping of register

Every employer of young persons in an industrial undertaking must keep a register of all young persons in his employment with particulars of their ages, the date of employment and the conditions and nature of their employment and such other particulars as may be prescribed and must produce the register for inspection when required by an authorised labour officer.[206]

Where any person employs a young person in contravention of any of the provisions on the employment of young persons or of any regulations made by the minister with respect to such employment the proprietor, owner and manager of any undertaking in which a young person is so employed and any parent or guardian of a young person who permits the young person to be so employed is guilty of an offence and on conviction liable to a fine not exceeding ₦800.[207] If, in a charge for an offence, it is alleged by the person conducting the prosecution that the person in respect of whom the offence was committed was under the age of twelve, fourteen, fifteen, sixteen or eighteen years at the date of commission of the alleged offence, the magistrate or other person presiding at the hearing must, after such enquiry as he may think necessary and after hearing any evidence that may be tendered by any party to the proceedings, determine the age of the young person and any such determination is final.[208]

The minister may make regulations

(a) exempting any occupation which forms part of an industrial undertaking from all or any of the provisions on employment of young persons or from any regulations made by him under this section;
(b) providing for the registration and identification of young persons;
(c) prescribing the records to be kept and the returns to be made by employers of young persons;
(d) further restricting the employment of young persons in specified occupations;
(e) prescribing additional conditions upon which young persons may be engaged or employed; and
(f) making further provision for the care of young persons by employers.[209]

---

[206] S. 62.
[207] S.64(1).
[208] S.64(2)
[209] S.63.

Domestic service

The minister may make regulations providing for the engagement, repatriation or supervision of domestic servants, the employment of women and young persons as domestic servants, the housing, accommodation and sanitary arrangements of domestic servants and the conditions of domestic service generally.[210] Under the Act a domestic servant is any house, stable or garden servant employed in or in connection with the domestic services of any private dwelling house and includes a servant employed as the driver of a privately owned or privately used motor car.[211]

No regulations have been made and, as we have seen, a domestic servant is not a worker within the Act. Therefore the employment of a domestic servant and, indeed, for this purpose, the question, who is a domestic servant continue to be governed by the common law. At common law a domestic servant is entitled to one month's notice or one month's wages in lieu of such notice to terminate his employment.[212]

Forced labour

Under the fundamental rights provisions of the Constitution every individual is entitled to respect for the dignity of his person.[213] This includes, *inter alia*, that no person be required to perform forced or compulsory labour.[214]

By article 2(1) of the International Labour Organisation Convention concerning Forced or Compulsory Labour, 1930, which Nigeria has ratified, the terms forced or compulsory labour mean all work or service which is exacted from any person under the menace of any penalty and for which the said person has not offered himself voluntarily. However both the Convention and the Constitution contain exceptions which are similar. Under the Constitution forced or compulsory labour does not include

(a) any labour required in consequence of the sentence or order of a court;

---

[210] S.65.
[211] S.91.
[212] *Arewa Textiles Ltd.* v. *Ibrahim Biu* 1967 (1) ALR Comm 59; and see ante.
[213] S.34(1) Constitution of the Federal Republic of Nigeria, 1999.
[214] S. 34(1)(c) ibid.

(b) any labour required of members of the armed forces of the Federation or the Nigeria Police Force in pursuance of their duties as such or, in the case of persons who have conscientious objections to service in the armed forces of the Federation, any labour required instead of such service;

(c) any labour required which is reasonably necessary in the event of any emergency or calamity threatening the life or well-being of the community; or

(d) any labour or service which forms part of (i) normal communal or other civil obligations for the well-being of the community, (ii) such compulsory national service in the armed forces of the federation as may be prescribed by a Federal statute, or (iii) such compulsory national service which forms part of the education and training of citizens of Nigeria as may be prescribed by a federal statute.[215]

Under the Constitution any one who alleges that any of his fundamental rights, including the right not to be required to perform forced or compulsory labour, has been, is being or is likely to be contravened in any state may apply to a High Court in that state for redress.[216] The court has power to make such orders, issue such writs and give such directions as it may consider appropriate for the purpose of enforcing or securing the enforcement of any rights to which the person may be entitled.[217]

Also, under the Labour Act, certain conducts in relation to forced or compulsory labour amount to criminal offences. Any person who requires any other person, or permits any other person to be required, to perform forced labour contrary to the constitutional provision is guilty of an offence and, on conviction, liable to a fine not exceeding ₦1,000 or to imprisonment for a period not exceeding two years, or to both.[218] And any person who, being a public officer, puts any constraint upon the population under his charge or upon any members of such population to work for any private individual, association or company is guilty of an offence and, on conviction, liable to a fine not exceeding ₦200 or to imprisonment for a period not exceeding six months or to both.[219]

---

[215] S. 34(2), ibid.

[216] S.46 (1) ibid.

[217] S.46 (2) ibid.

[218] S.73 (1).

[219] S.73 (2); public officer means any person employed by a public authority and public authority means the federal government, a state government, a local government authority, a statutory corporation or a government controlled company, i.e., a limited liability company in which the federal or state government has a controlling interest; s.91.

However, the Labour Act also permits the requirement of certain labour. These, presumably, come within the constitutional exceptions. The inhabitants of any town or village[220] may be required by the prescribed authority to provide labour for any of the following purposes:

(a) the construction and maintenance of buildings used for communal purposes, including markets but excluding juju houses and places of worship;
(b) sanitary measures;
(c) the construction and maintenance of local roads and paths;
(d) the construction and maintenance of town or village fences;
(e) the construction and maintenance of communal wells, and
(f) other communal services of a similar kind in the direct interest of the inhabitants of the town or village.[221]

However no such labour must be required unless the inhabitants or their representatives have been previously consulted by the prescribed authority with regard to the need for the proposed service and a majority of them agreed to the requiring of the labour.[222]

And any person who does not wish to execute his share of any labour so required may be excused from doing so on payment to the prescribed authority of such sum per day, while the labour is being done, as represents the current daily wage for unskilled labour.[223] It is, however, not clear who or what the prescribed authority is. Presumably it is one of those things which the minister may make regulations to prescribe under his power to make regulations prescribing anything which is to be prescribed under the Act and is not otherwise provided for.[224]

The minister may make regulations regulating the requisition of any labour required in the event of any emergency or calamity threatening the life or well-being of the community or labour that forms part of normal communal or other civic obligations for the well-being of the community both of which are not forced or compulsory labour under the constitution.[225] Such regulations may specify for an offence under the regulations, including a failure or refusal,

---

[220] Town or village does not include a township but includes any area (other than a township) declared by the minister by order to be a town or village for the purposes of the section; s.74 (5).
[221] S.74 (3).
[222] S. 74(4)
[223] S. 74(6)
[224] See S. 88(l)(e)
[225] S. 74(1)

without reasonable cause, to render labour lawfully required under the regulations, a fine not exceeding ₦200 or imprisonment for a period not exceeding six months, or both and as a daily penalty a fine not exceeding ₦10 or imprisonment not exceeding seven days or both.[226] The regulations may also add to, amend or repeal the provisions under which the prescribed authority may require the inhabitants of a town or village to provide labour.[227] No work or service must be exacted from any person for which that person has not offered himself voluntarily and which, apart from the provisions of the Act, would have been illegal exaction.[228]

Settlement of disputes

The jurisdiction to hear complaints arising out of a contract of employment of a worker is vested in the magistrate court or, in a state where a magistrate's court has no civil jurisdiction, in a district court.[229] If the complainant claims an amount beyond the civil jurisdiction of the court, the court must forward the complaint to the nearest court having jurisdiction.[230] The court may exercise jurisdiction in the complaint if the respondent is in its area of jurisdiction at the time the complaint is made whether or not the grounds of the complaint arose within that area.[231]

If, at any time, after the laying of the complaint it appears to the court by information on oath that the respondent is about to abscond the court may cause him to be arrested and detained in custody unless he finds security to appear and answer the complaint and to abide by the decision of the court.[232] Where the court is of the opinion that the complaint could more properly or conveniently be dealt with by civil proceedings, it may, at any time before giving its final decision on the complaint, order that the remedy, if any, for the matters complained of be by an action brought in accordance with the law relating to civil proceedings and not by the proceedings here provided.[233]

---

[226] S. 74(2)(a)
[227] S. 74(2)(b)
[228] S. 74(7)
[229] S.80(1); the aggrieved party is the complainant and the party complained against is the respondent; s.81(1).
[230] S.81(2).
[231] S.81(3).
[232] S.81(4).
[233] S.81(5).

Where an employer or worker neglects or refuses to fulfil a contract or any question, difference or dispute arises as to the rights or liabilities of a party to a contract or touching any misconduct, neglect, ill-treatment or injury to the person or property of a party to a contract any party to the contract feeling himself aggrieved may make a complaint to the court and the court may then issue a summons to the respondent.[234] In dealing with the complaint the court

(a) may adjust and set off one against the other all such claims on the part of the complainant and the respondent arising out of or incidental to the relationship between them as the court may find to be subsisting, whether the claims are liquidated or unliquidated or for wages, damages or otherwise, and may direct the payment of such sum as it finds due by one party to the other;

(b) may direct fulfilment of the relevant contract and, in a case where damages might be awarded for any breach of contract, may in place of the whole or part of the damages which would otherwise have been awarded direct the party committing the breach to give security to the satisfaction of the court for the due performance of so much of the contract as remains unperformed; the security may be given, without prejudice to any other method of giving security which the court may consider appropriate in any particular case, by making in or under the direction of the court a written or oral acknowledgment, to be known as a recognizance, of the undertaking or condition by which and the sum in which the person making it is bound; any such recognisance must be made as nearly as possible in the same way as recognisances of bail and is liable to be forfeited and enforced in the same way as recognisances of bail;

(c)if the party directed to find security fails to find security and the court is satisfied that the failure is not due to the inability of the party to find it, may commit him to prison for a period not exceeding three months, until he finds the security;

(d) may rescind the contract upon such terms as to apportionment of wages or other sums due under it and as to the payment of wages or other sums due under it and as to the payment of wages or damages or other sums due, as it thinks just, and

---

[234] S. 81 (1) ; subsection 81 (6) provides that s. 81 does not apply to a trade dispute, that is to say, any dispute or difference between employers and workers (or between workers and other workers) connected with (a) the employment or non-employment; or (b) the terms of the employment; or (c) the conditions of labour of any person. For our opinion, see below on settlement of trade disputes.

(e) where the court has criminal jurisdiction and it appears to the court that an employer or worker has been guilty of an offence under the Act, may, in place of or in addition to exercising any of the powers conferred on it under paragraphs (a) to (d) above, pass on the offender any sentence which is authorised by the Act and is within its criminal jurisdiction.[235]

Where the court imposes any fine or directs security to be given by way of deposit or enforces payment of any sum secured by a recognisance, it may direct that the fine, deposit or sum when recovered, or such part of if as it thinks fit, must be applied to compensate any employer or worker for wrong or damage sustained by him by reason of the act or thing in respect of which the fine was imposed or by reason of the non-performance of the relevant contract.[236] Where it appears to the court that the complainant, where he is a worker, has not the means and is otherwise unable to obtain food for himself pending the determination of the complaint, it may cause the complainant to be supplied with necessary food at the expense of the federal government.[237] However the cost of the food is a debt due to the government from the complainant and may be deducted by the court from any moneys received by the court for or on behalf of the complainant or must otherwise be paid by the complainant.[238]

The process of the court for compelling the attendance of the respondent and all necessary witnesses can be instituted at the expense of the federal government and without any fees of court.[239] However, at the final determination of the complaint the court may make such order for the payment of costs by either party as it thinks proper in the circumstances.[240] And, if, at the hearing of the complaint, the court is of the opinion that the complaint is vexatious or frivolous, it may, there and then and without any fresh action or proceeding, order that the complainant pay a fine not exceeding ₦50 and defray the cost of the process and the witnesses and, in default of payment of the fine and costs, be liable to imprisonment for a period not exceeding one month.[241]

---

[235] S.82.
[236] S.84(1).
[237] S.84(2).
[238] S.84(3).
[239] S.85(1).
[240] S.85(2).
[241] S.85(3).

Court procedure

Section 83 provides that, subject to the section itself and all the above provisions on the settlement of disputes, the law regulating the procedure in criminal cases are to apply to a complaint and any orders for the payment of money made in consequence of a complaint. However the court may order that the law regulating civil proceedings be applied to a complaint and any such orders if, in any case, it considers that the interests of justice so require.[242] In any event the law regulating civil proceedings must be applied where the court has no criminal jurisdiction.[243]

Where, in consequence of a complaint, the court makes an order for the payment of any sum by a public authority, no execution must be issued but the court must forward a copy of the order to the minister for finance and economic development, if the public authority is the federal government, or to minister for finance of a state where the public authority is a state and, in any other case, to the public authority concerned.[244] It is then the duty of the minister or public authority to ensure that the amount in the order is paid by the officer or department.[245]

If, immediately before the hearing of a complaint the respondent was not in actual custody, he must not be compelled to enter the dock or other place usually assigned for persons under trial on a criminal charge or be otherwise treated as under arrest during the hearing of a complaint. But the court may cause a respondent to be arrested and detained in custody if it is satisfied that it is necessary to do so in order to secure his attendance.[246]

At the hearing of a complaint the respondent is a competent but not a compellable witness and an authorised labour officer may represent him at the hearing of the complaint at his request.[247]

Administration of the Act

The responsibility for administering the Act is vested in labour officers. The minister may, by writing under his hand, authorise any public officer serving in

---

242 S.83(1)(a).
243 S.83(1)(b).
244 S.83(2); for definition of public authority see ante.
245 S.83(2).
246 S.83(3).
247 S.83(4) and (5).

his ministry and, with the consent of a state governor, any officer in the public service of a state, to be an authorised labour officer for the purposes of the Act.[248] For the purpose of facilitating or ensuring the proper operation of the Act an authorised labour officer has the power to

(a) enter, inspect and examine, by day or night any labour encampment, farm, factory or other land or work place if he has reasonable cause to believe that any worker is employed there;

(b) enter, inspect and examine by day any premises provided by an employer in which he has reasonable cause to believe workers are living;

(c) enter, inspect and examine any hospital building, sanitary convenience, mess-room or water supply provided for or used by workers;

(d) take with him a police officer if he has reasonable cause to apprehend any serious obstruction in the execution of his functions;

(e) require the production of any registers, certificates, notices or other documents kept in pursuance of the Act and inspect, examine and copy any of them; and

(f) make such examination and enquiry as may be necessary to ascertain whether the provisions of the Act are being complied with.

Other powers of an authorised labour officer include the power to

(i) inspect and examine all food provided for the use of workers and take samples;

(ii) take or remove for the purpose of analysis samples of materials and substances used or handled by workers in premises not covered by factory legislation;

(iii) interrogate, either alone or in the presence of another, any person whom he finds in any work place with respect to any matter with which the Act relates;

(iv) direct any person who has in his opinion contravened any provision of the Act to remedy the contravention;

(v) direct the posting of a notice if he is satisfied it is necessary or expedient for the proper implementation of the Act; and

---

[248] S.77(1).

(vi) with the written consent of the minister, prosecute, conduct or defend any complaint or other proceeding arising under the Act or otherwise in the exercise of his functions as an authorised labour officer.[249]

Any person who obstructs an authorised labour officer in the exercise of his functions or fails to comply with his direction to remedy a contravention or his direction to post a notice is guilty of an offence and, on conviction, liable to a fine not exceeding ₦1,000 or to imprisonment for a period not exceeding two years or to both such fine and imprisonment.[250]

---

[249] S.78(1); the power to prosecute is subject to the Constitutional power of the Attorney-General.
[250] S.78(3).

Chapter Four

Injuries at work

An employee who suffers injury at work may either obtain damages at common law or claim compensation under the statutory scheme known as Workmen's Compensation. A common law action for damages is either an action for negligence, i.e. an action for breach by an employer of the duty of care he owes to his employee, which action is available to any employee, or an action for breach of statutory duty imposed by the factories or similar legislation. An action for breach of statutory duty is available only to those who are covered by the legislation. Factories legislation is discussed in the next chapter and workmen's compensation in the chapter after that.

Employer's duty of care - negligence

It is now well established that an employer is under a duty, at common law, to take reasonable care to ensure that his employee is not exposed to risk of injury at his work. To put it more factually, where an employee suffers injury at his work as a result of the neglect or default of his employer to take reasonable care for his safety, the employer is obliged to pay damages in respect of the injury to the injured employee.[1]

It seems that the earliest clear statement of this duty was in *Priestly* v. *Fowler*[2] although it was also in the same decision that the seed of the doctrine of common employment, which was later to impede the growth of the duty itself, was sown. These were the facts of the case. The defendant, a butcher, asked the plaintiff employee, to go in a van, conducted by another employee, with goods of the employer; the van was overloaded and it broke down throwing the plaintiff to

[1] Where an employee dies as a result of an employer's default the liability to pay damages is dealt with by the various fatal accidents statutes in the states.

[2] (1837) 3M&WI. see *Boson* v. *Sandford* (1690) 19 ER 382 where Holt CJ said, at p. 382, that a master is liable for the act of his servant "and undertakes for his care to all that make use of him;" for whoever employs another is answerable for him, which could include liability to a fellow employee; see also the same judge in *Middleton* v. *Fowler* 91 ER 247.

the ground as a result of which he suffered a thigh fracture. Lord Abinger held that the plaintiff could not recover damages from his employer. He said that:

> In fact, to allow this sort of action to prevail would be an encouragement to the servant to omit that diligence and caution which he is in duty bound to exercise on the behalf of his master, to protect him against the misconduct or negligence of others who serve him, and which diligence and caution while they protect the master, are a much better security against any injury the servant may sustain by the negligence of others engaged under the same master, than any recourse against his master for damages could possibly afford.[3]

But Lord Abinger had said that the master "is, no doubt, bound to provide for the safety of his servant in the course of his employment to the best of his judgment, information and belief."[4] Although this statement was rather vague and, perhaps, unhelpful there is no doubt that it was a recognition that an employer owed some duty to his employee for the employee's safety.

In *Hutchinson* v. *York, Newcastle and Berwick Railway Co*[5] where the doctrine of common employment blossomed, Alderson B. acknowledged that an employer owed a duty of care to his employee. He said:

> the master shall have taken due care not to expose his servant to unreasonable risks. The servant, when he engages to run the risks of his service, including those arising from the negligence of fellow-servants, has a right to understand that the master has taken reasonable care to protect him from such risks by associating him only with persons of ordinary skill and care.[6]

But the main preoccupation of the court in this case was with the doctrine of common employment. An employee was travelling on duty in his employer's train when the train collided with another train which also belonged to the employer. The employee suffered injury from which he died. In an action for damages by his administratrix it was held that the employer was not liable because the collision was caused by the negligence of a fellow employee. Alderson B said the case was indistinguishable from *Priestley* v. *Fowler*.[7] In laying down the doctrine of common employment he said:

---

[3] Ibid., 6.
[4] Ibid., 6.
[5] (1850) 5 Exch 343.
[6] Ibid., 353.
[7] *Supra.*

> The difficulty is as to the principle applicable to the case of several servants employed by the same master; and injury resulting to one of them from the negligence of another. In such a case, however, we are of opinion that the master is not in general responsible, when he has selected persons of competent care and skill. Put the case of a master employing A and B, two of his servants, to drive his cattle to the market. It is admitted, that if by the unskilfulness of A a stranger is injured, the master is responsible. Not so, if A by his unskilfulness hurts himself; he cannot treat that as the want of skill of his master. Suppose, then, that by the unskilfulness of A, B the other servant is injured while they are jointly engaged in the same service, there we think B has no claim against the master. They have both engaged in a common service, the duties of which impose a certain risk on each of them; and in case of negligence on the part of the other, the party injured knows that the negligence is that of his fellow-servant and not of his master. He knew, when he engaged in the service, that he was exposed to the risk of injury, not only from his own want of skill or care, but also from the want of it on the part of his fellow-servant; and he must be supposed to have contracted on the terms that, as between himself and his master, he would run this risk.[8]

He added that:[9]

> The principle is, that a servant, when he engages to serve a master, undertakes, as between him and his master, to run all the ordinary risks of the service, and this includes the risk of negligence on the part of a fellow-servant, whenever he is acting in discharge of his duty as servant of him who is the common master of both.

In *Tarrant* v. *Webb*[10] in 1856, Williams J, while agreeing that the cases had established that a master was not generally responsible for an injury to a servant from the negligence of a fellow servant, said "but that rule is subject to this qualification, that the master is guilty of no want of care in the selection of proper servants."[11] In 1868 in *Wilson* v. *Merry and Cunningham*[12] the House of Lords held that the employers, having provided a proper system of ventilation in

[8] Ibid., 350-351.

[9] Ibid., 352.

[10] (1856) 18CB 797.

[11] Ibid., 805; see also *Roberts* v. *Smith* 2 H&N 213.

[12] (1868) LR ISC & Div. 326; see also *Bartonshill Coal Co* v. *Reid* (1858) 3 Macq 266 and *Bartonshill Coal Co* v. *McGuire* (1858) 3 Macq 300.

their mine, were not liable for its temporary disruption by the negligence of an employee as a result of which another employee died. Lord Colonsay said:[13]

> there are duties incumbent on masters with reference to the safety of labourers in mines and factories, on the fulfilment of which the labourers are entitled to rely, and for the failure in which the master may be responsible. A total neglect to provide any system of ventilation for the mine may be of that character. Culpable negligence in supervision, if the master takes the supervision on himself; - or , where he devolves it on others, the heedless selection of unskilled or incompetent persons for the duty - or the failure to provide or supply the means of providing proper machinery or materials; - may furnish grounds of liability...

But

> There are perils...that may result from the carelessness or recklessness or other fault, of one or more of those persons composing the organised body engaged in working the mine. The master does not impliedly insure the workmen against such perils.

Put in simpler words the employer's duty was to provide a safe system of work, select skilled and competent employees and provide machinery or materials for the work. In *Smith* v. *Baker*[14] Lord Herschell expressed the duty thus:

> It is quite clear that the contract between employer and employed involves on the part of the former the duty of taking reasonable care to provide proper appliances, and to maintain them in a proper condition, and so to carry on his operations as not to subject those employed by him to unnecessary risk.[15]

An employer who satisfied these duties could not be held liable for injury caused to his employee by the negligence of his fellow employee. As we have seen, the doctrine was that an employee impliedly undertook, under his contract of employment, the risk of injury caused by the negligence of his fellow employee. There was, of course, the difficulty of determining whether an injury was caused by a failure of the employer to discharge his duty, say, the employment of an unskilled or incompetent employee, or whether it was caused by the negligence of a competent and skilled employee. That was only a problem of determining the facts; once determined the law was clear. In *Wilsons and Clyde Coal Co*

---

[13] Ibid., 344-345.
[14] [1891] AC 325.
[15] Ibid., 362.

Ltd v. *English*[16] the House of Lords reiterated the principle that common employment did not apply to the duty of the employer. The issue was whether the employer had provided a safe system of work. Lord Thankerton said:

> The workman, under his contract of employment, is not to be held impliedly to have taken the risk of want of due care in the provision of a reasonably safe system of working, and the master cannot transfer the duty on to the shoulders of a subordinate. If he appoints a servant to attend to the discharge of such duty, such servant, in this respect, is merely the agent or hand of the master, and the maxim *qui facit per alium facit per se* renders the master liable for such servant's negligence as being, in the view of the law, the master's own negligence. The same servant may have other duties relative to the working or operation of the mine, as to which the doctrine of common employment might apply; but that doctrine is not applicable to the provision of reasonably safe conditions under which the working or operation of the mine is to be carried on.[17]

Lord Wright, on his part, said:

> I think the whole course of authority consistently recognises a duty which rests on the employer and which is personal to the employer, whether the employer be an individual, a firm, or a company, and whether or not the employer takes any share in the conduct of the operations. The obligation is threefold, as I have explained.[18]

Earlier he had said that the employer's duty is to take reasonable care to select proper and competent persons to direct and superintend the work, to furnish them with adequate materials and resources for the work and to provide a proper system of working.[19] After the abolition of the doctrine of common employment[20] it became easier to state the employer's duty of care. In *Davie* v. *New Merton Board Mills Ltd.*[21] Viscount Simonds said the determination "to avert, or at least reduce, the consequences of that decision (*Priestley* v. *Fowler*) led to a great deal of artificiality and refinement which could have been unnecessary. The shadow of it is still upon us. But we can at least return to the

---

[16] [1938] AC 57.
[17] Ibid., 70.
[18] Ibid., 84.
[19] Ibid., 81; Lord Wright quoted Lord Colonsay in *Wilson* v. *Merry and Cunningham* (1868) LR I SC & Div 326.
[20] Law Reform (Personal Injuries) Act, 1948.
[21] [1959] AC 604.

simple question which is at the bottom of it all - "Has the employer taken reasonable care for the safety of the workman?" a question which can only be answered in each case by a consideration of all its circumstances.[22] And more recently Lord Keith said - The ruling principle is that an employer is bound to take reasonable care for the safety of his workman, and all other rules or formulas must be taken subject to this principle.[23] In *Buckingham* v. *Daily News Ltd*[24] Birkett LJ said:[25]

> But I think that it is always to be understood that the common law duty which is invoked, where it is said that the employers failed in their common law duty, is that the master must take reasonable care for his servant's safety. That is how it is simply expressed, and all that *Wilsons & Clyde Coal Co Ltd* v. *English* does is to enlarge upon the detail of that duty. In particular, Lord Wright said that it was a three-fold duty: the provision of a competent staff of men; adequate material, and a proper system of effective supervision. It is not an enlargement of the duty but an illustration of the nature of the common law duty which has always rested upon the employer: he must take reasonable steps for the safety of his workmen.

The words "reasonable care" govern and limit the scope of the employer's duty. The employer is not required to guarantee the safety of an employee but he fulfils his duty by exercising reasonable care in the provision of competent staff, materials and a safe system of working. In other words a plaintiff must prove negligence in the employer in order to succeed in a common law action for breach of an employer's duty to take reasonable care for his safety. What reasonable care demands naturally varies according to the circumstances of each case.

Breach of duty

An employer who fails to take such steps for the safety of an employee as a reasonable employee would take in the same circumstances will render himself liable in damages to an employee who has suffered injury as a result of the failure. But the onus is on an injured employee to prove such a failure or breach of duty. It must be shown that an employee employed by the employer is

---

[22] Ibid. 618-619.
[23] *Cavanagh* v. *Ulster Weaving Co Ltd* [1960] AC 145, 165.
[24] [1956] 2 QB 534.
[25] Ibid., 538.

incompetent and a source of danger to others or that he has failed to provide or maintain machinery, plant, equipment, tools premises, etc., which are reasonably safe or that he has failed to provide a safe system of work.

Not many actions have arisen out of the employer's duty to provide competent fellow employees. This may, probably, be because the abolition of common employment has made it possible for an employer to be held vicariously liable for the negligence of his employee which has caused injury to another employee. In *Hudson* v. *Ridge Manufacturing Co Ltd*,[26] Streatfield J said he had to decide the case on first principles. Over the course of some years while in employment, an employee was in the habit of tripping other employees up or otherwise engaging in horseplay and skylarking notwithstanding repeated reprimands. On one occasion he got hold of the plaintiff from behind and in trying to force him down the plaintiff put his hand out to help himself and fractured his right wrist. The learned judge held that the employee's non-removal was a breach of the duty which lay "fairly and squarely on the employer to remove that source of danger."[27]

Where an alleged breach of duty consists of an omission to provide safety machinery or equipment or premises, etc., or a safe system of work the courts have often relied on a statement of Lord Dunedin in the Scottish case of *Morton* v. *William Dixon Ltd*[28] that - where the negligence of the employer consists of what I may call a fault of omission, I think it is absolutely necessary that the proof of that fault of omission should be one of two kinds, either to show that the thing which he did not do was a thing which was commonly done by other persons in like circumstances, or - to show that it was a thing which was so obviously wanted that it would be folly in anyone to neglect to provide it. It is clear from this statement that evidence of existing practice is admissible to prove reasonableness only in cases of like circumstances.[29] Indeed, it has been said that the circumstances of the practice must be precisely similar to those in which an accident has happened.[30] But, no doubt, such situations will be rare. In *Cavanagh* v. *Ulster Weaving Co Ltd*,[31] the House of Lords held, for this reason, that evidence of practice is not necessarily conclusive but that it is only one factor to be used in consideration whether in all the circumstances of a case

---

26 [1957] 2 All ER 229.

27 Ibid., 230.

28 [1909] SC 807, 809; see also per Lord Normand in *Paris* v. *Stepney Borough Council* [1951] AC 367, 382.

29 See also *Morris* v. *West Hartlepool Steam Navigation Co Ltd* [1951] AC 552; *Paris* v. *Stepney Borough Council, Supra.*

30 Lord Somervell in *Cavanagh* v. *Ulster Weaving Co Ltd* [1960] AC 145, 167.

31 *Supra.*

reasonable care has been taken. Similarly it is a question of the facts of each case whether something or a precaution is so obviously wanted that it would be unreasonable to omit to provide it.

An employer who has to provide tools, machinery, etc., is not bound, at once, to adopt all the latest improvements and appliances.[32] It is a question of fact in each case whether it is a want of reasonable care not to have adopted the latest improvements or appliances.[33]

The question has often arisen whether an employer's duty to provide equipment, tools, protective appliances or clothing, etc., extends to a further duty to urge or supervise an employee or employees in the use or to use what has been provided. In the leading case of *Qualcast, Ltd* v. *Haynes*[34] the House of Lords said it is a question on the evidence in each case whether there is a duty to advise everyone whether experienced or inexperienced as to the use of an equipment provided. Lord Radcliffe cautioned that "though, indeed, there may be cases in which an employer does not discharge his duty of care towards his workmen merely by providing an article of safety equipment, the courts should be circumspect in filling out that duty with the much vaguer obligation of encouraging, exhorting or instructing workmen, or a particular workman, to make regular use of what is provided."[35] In *Bux* v. *Slough Metals Ltd*[36] Edmund Davies LJ, in the English Court of Appeal, said the question of whether instruction or persuasion or even insistence in using protective equipment should be resorted to is, therefore, at large, the answer depending on the facts of the particular case.[37] And he added that "one of the most important of these is the nature and degree of the risk of serious harm resulting if it is not worn."[38] This consideration had influenced Paul J in his judgment in *Nolan* v. *Dental Manufacturing Co Ltd*.[39] The plaintiff was a toolsetter. In the course of his work he had to sharpen his tools on a carborundum wheel usually two or three times a day. While using this wheel in a machine room a chip struck his left eye and he lost its use. The court held that the employer had a duty not only to provide goggles but also to give strict orders that they were to be used and to supervise their use. Paul J said although the risk of accident happening was not a very great one, that risk was a very serious one, since if an accident did happen, the

---

[32] Per Sir Arthur Channel in *Toronto Power Co Ltd* v. *Paskwan* [1951] AC 734, 738.
[33] Ibid.
[34] [1959] AC 743.
[35] Ibid., 753.
[36] [1973] 15 KIR 126.
[37] Ibid., p. 136.
[38] Ibid.
[39] [1958] 2 All ER 449.

consequences would in all probability be the loss of sight of one eye and a possibility of the loss of the sight of both eyes.[40]

Nolan's case was relied upon by Fatayi-Williams J in upholding the decision of the Chief Magistrate in *Western Nigeria Trading Co* v. *Ajao*;[41] the learned judge said "I entirely agree with the findings of the learned chief magistrate, based on the Nolan's case that the employers were under a common law duty not only to provide the plaintiff with goggles but also to see that they were used."[42]

Similarly in *Mensa Sosu* v. *Technoexportstroy*[43] where the plaintiff was engaged in drilling a hole in a metal the court held that the employer should not only have provided goggles but should also have ensured that they were used. In *Odhigbo* v. *Saipen SPA*[44] the employee, a welder, was supplied with goggles but he never wore them. A bit of metal went into his left eye and he became virtually blind. Akpata J held that the employer "must also establish a proper system by which the workmen use the equipment and take the necessary precautions.[45] The basis of the Court of Appeal's decision in *Federal Super phosphate Fertilizer Co Ltd* v. *Otaru*[46] is unclear. The plaintiff was eighteen years old when he was employed. He was taught the method of processing sulphuric acid for about two weeks before being put to work. About six weeks after employment he was assisting a Japanese worker in the sulphuric acid plant section when sulphuric acid splashed on them as the Japanese was unbolting a belt of the sulphuric acid line in order to change a viewing glass. In holding the employer negligent the Court of Appeal said:[47]

> In a case of this nature it is essential that the person who issued protective materials to the employee should testify or a record of the issuance be tendered in evidence. A general statement that all employees are issued with protective materials and that they are instructed of their use is not sufficient, particularly where the assertion is made not by the person who issued the protective materials or gave instruction as to their use. Even granted that the respondent was fully instructed as to the dangers of sulphuric acid and he was provided with suitable protective clothing and appliances, it was obligatory

---

[40] Ibid., 4S4.
[41] [1965] 2 All NLR 100.
[42] But the facts in the two cases were not quite the same; in Ajao's case a fellow employee was cutting steel with a sledge hammer when a splinter of steel flew into Ajao's eye; however Ajao was himself engaged in cutting steel with a cutting machine.
[43] (1977) II/CCHCJ 2647.
[44] 1979 NCLR 328.
[45] Ibid., 340.
[46] Federal Court of Appeal Judgments Kaduna Div.; July - Sept, 1985, p.45.
[47] Ibid., 55.

> on the appellant to give strict orders that they were to be used, compel the use of them and to supervise the respondent.

One arm of the employer's duty of reasonable care is the duty to provide a safe system of work. A system includes, "or may include, according to circumstances, such matters as the physical layout of the job - the setting of the stage, so to speak - the sequence in which the work is to be carried out, the provision in proper cases of warnings and notices and the issue of special instructions. A system may be adequate for the whole course of the job or it may have to be modified or improved to meet circumstances which arise: such modifications or improvements appear to me equally to fall under the head of system.[48] The underlying reason for system is safety. In providing a safe system of work the question is, again, whether a system, or any modification of it, dictated by the exigencies of the work, is reasonable given all the circumstances of the particular case. Such circumstances include the nature of the work and the circumstances of an individual employee including his experience, training, age, or disability. In *Paris* v. *Stepney Borough Council*[49] the House of Lords held that the fact that the plaintiff had only one good eye demanded consideration since it meant that there was a risk of a more serious or graver injury. But in *James* v. *Hepworth & Grandage Ltd*[50] the English Court of Appeal overruled the trial court which had held that the illiteracy of the employee which prevented him from reading safety notices was a relevant consideration in determining the reasonableness of the employer in not providing him with spats.

Where there is a foreseeable risk whether an employer will be in breach of duty in not taking, or in the remedial or prebautionary measures taken, depends on the circumstances of each case. As Lord Reid said, it is the duty of an employer, in considering whether some precaution should be taken against a foreseeable risk, to weigh, on the one hand, the magnitude of the risk, the likelihood of the accident happening and the possible seriousness of the consequences if an accident does happen, and, on the other hand, the difficulty and expense and any other disadvantage of taking the precaution.[51] In *Latimer* v. *AEC Ltd*,[52] as a result of an unusually heavy rainstorm, the floors of a large factory were flooded and an oily cooling mixture, normally contained in a channel in the floor, rose and mixed with the floodwater. When the water subsided the floors became slippery. The employer spread all the available

[48] Lord Greene MR in *Speed* v. *Thomas Swift & Co Ltd* [1943] 1 All ER 539, 542.
[49] [1951] AC 367.
[50] [1968] 1 QB 94.
[51] *Morris* v. *West Hartlepool Steam Navigation Co Ltd* [1956] AC 552,574.
[52] [1953] AC 643.

sawdust over the floors but some areas remained uncovered. An employee who was attempting to load a heavy barrel onto a trolley in the uncovered area slipped and injured his angle. In an action for damages it was held at first instance that the employer should have closed the factory until the remedial steps had completely removed the danger. The Court of Appeal reversed that judgment and the reversal was upheld by the House of Lords. Lord Porter said: "The probability of a workman slipping is one matter which must be borne in mind...The seriousness of shutting down the works and sending the night shift home and the importance of carrying on the work upon which the factory was engaged are all additional elements for consideration."[53] In *Okogele* v. *Associated Metal and Allied Works Ltd*[54] an employee was engaged as a machine operator. While working on a power pressing machine, used for the production of aluminium clothes hangers, the machine gave way and crushed his right hand index finger which had to be amputated. There was evidence that all the machines in the factory were usually tested each morning before work and that the machine used by the plaintiff was in fact tested on the morning of the accident. However there was also evidence that many other employees had had similar injuries on the machines and in particular that two employees had lost three fingers each and two two fingers each within a year. The court held the employer was in breach of duty to provide reasonable care. Oshodi J said: "In considering the system in the defendant's factory one has to consider the sequence in which the work is to be carried out, the provision in proper cases of warnings and notices and the issue of special instructions."[55] In *George Wimpey & Co (Nig.) Ltd* v. *Ezebuiro*[56] the plaintiff was asked to loosen four bolts holding the arm of a pail loader. After loosening two bolts and was in the process of loosening the third the arm fell on him and pressed him against the axle of the loader. He suffered severe injuries to his pelvis and other parts of his body. The Court of Appeal upheld the trial judge who held the employer negligent in not providing a proper system of work by providing proper support for the arm.

Where an employer knows or ought to know that safety equipment or machinery provided are defective and so constitute a source of danger he has a duty to remedy the defect. An employer is under a duty to maintain plant and equipment in proper working condition.[57] In *Taylor* v. *Rover Co Ltd*[58] the

---

[53] Ibid., 653.
[54] (1978) 7/CCHCJ 1269.
[55] Ibid., 1276.
[56] Federal Court of Appeal Judgments, Kaduna Division, 1980, p. 161.
[57] *Wilsons & Clyde Coal Co Ltd* v. *English* [1938] AC 57.
[58] [1966] 1 WLR 156.

plaintiff was using a cold chisel and hammer in knocking out washers when, owing to the excessive hardness of the top of the chisel, a piece of metal of it flew into his eye. About four weeks earlier a piece of the same chisel had struck another employee while using it. Baker J held that it was the keeping of the chisel in circulation with the knowledge that it was dangerous that caused the accident. Similarly in *Ikezuonu* v. *Julius Berger Ltd*[59] the court held that an employer was negligent as he "had caused or permitted the said machine to be in use continuously without servicing same, thus constituting it a danger to the plaintiff."[60] Here the employer had failed to service a machine for a period of one and a half years when it should have been serviced every six months.

The fact that an employer is not in control of the premises in which his employee is working is merely one of the ingredients in the consideration of the question of want of reasonable care.[61] As Lord Parker C J put it:

> Now at one time it was often thought that where a master sent his servant to work on somebody else's premises he owed no duty to the servant in regard to those premises. I think that that was a misunderstanding as to the true position and that, as has been indicated, a duty to take reasonable care is always there, but what will be a performance of it will vary according to all the circumstances, including whether the premises are the premises in the occupation and control of somebody else.[62]

In *Wilson* v. *Tyneside Window Cleaning Co*[63] the plaintiff, an experienced window cleaner, sent to clean windows in the premises of another, fell and was injured when a handle by which he was supporting himself gave way. It was contended that reasonable care necessitated a preliminary inspection to ascertain any danger and so provide for it. The English Court of Appeal held, however, that failure to inspect was not sufficient evidence of want of care. However, by the decision of the House of Lords in *General Cleaning Contractors Ltd* v. *Christmas*[64] an employer can escape liability in this way, even to an experienced employee, only where he shows that he has given adequate consideration to the problems of the work and devised a reasonable system of work with respect to the dangers commonly found in the work. Thus in *Smith* v. *Austin Lifts Ltd*[65]

---

[59] (1979) 7-9 CCHCJ (vol 4) 56; see also *Stokes* v. *Guest, Keen & Nettlefold (Bolts & Nuts) Ltd* (1968) 5 KIR 401.
[60] Ibid., 63.
[61] *Wilson* v. *Tyneside Window Cleaning Co* [1958] 2 All ER 265.
[62] *Mace* v. *R & H Green Silley Weir Ltd* [1959] 1 All ER 655, 657.
[63] *Supra.*
[64] [1958] AC 180
[65] (1959) I AII ER 81.

where an employee sent to work on another's premises reported defects in those premises to his employer and, apart from informing the owners of the premises of the defects, the employer did nothing to repair or have the premises repaired, the employer was held liable for the injury to the employee caused by the defect.

There is no doubt that employers may and that in fact they, in practice, use the instrumentality of others to discharge their duty of care. Where an employer obtains equipment or tools from independent contractors for the use of its employees whether he will be liable for any injury resulting from the use of such an equipment would seem to depend on whether he took reasonable care in the choice of the source of the supply. In *Davie* v. *New Merton Board Mills Ltd*[66] the House of Lords held that in all cases the question is whether the employer has taken reasonable care in all the circumstances. In *Mason* v. *Williams & Williams Ltd*[67] the employer supplied a chisel which he bought from the manufacturers. While being used a chip of it struck the employee using it in the eye and the eye had to be removed. The employer was held not to be liable for the injury. Finnemore J said that,

> although employers have to act as reasonable people and take reasonable care, but if they buy their tools from well known makers...they are entitled to assume that the tools will be proper for the purposes for which both sides intended them to be used, and not require daily, weekly or monthly inspection to see if in fact all is well.[68]

In Davies case both Viscount Simonds and Lord Tucker approved of the decision.[69] It would seem, therefore, that an employer who obtains supplies of equipment from a reputable manufacturer will invariably be held to have taken reasonable care.[70] Of course an employee who suffers injury from an accident which occurs while using such an equipment may have a cause of action against the manufacturer of the equipment based on the well known principle in *Donoghue* v. *Stevenson*.[71] But there are many obstacles. The manufacturer may be unknown and it must be noted that although the category of manufacturer has been somewhat extended to include repairers it does not seem to include mere

---

[66] [1959] AC 604.

[67] [1955] I WLR 549.

[68] Ibid., 551.

[69] [1959] AC 604, 626, 648 respectively.

[70] See also *Summer* v. *William Henderson & Sons* [1963] 1 All ER 408 which judgment was, however, set aside by the Court of Appeal [1963] 2 All ER 712n on the ground only that the procedure by special case was wrong.

[71] [1932] AC 562.

suppliers.[72] Even where the manufacturer is known he may not be in the country and that may necessitate a foreign action. The *Donoghue* v. *Stevenson* principle itself is not free from difficulties. In *Paine* v. *Colne Valley Electricity Supply Co Ltd*[73] where faulty premises were provided through a manufacturer and an employee, a fitter's mate, was electrocuted while working inside it, an action against the manufacturer was lost. The court held that as there was a reasonable probability that the premises would be examined by the employer the manufacturer owed no duty of care to the employee. In *Taylor* v. *Rover Co Ltd*[74] a chisel was supplied by manufacturers. The Plaintiff, who had been using the chisel for about six weeks, sustained injury when using it when a splinter of it flew into his left eye. About three weeks earlier a small piece had also flown off the same chisel and cut the foreman's cheek while using it. An action by the plaintiff against the manufacturers failed. Although the court held that there was no reasonable probability of examination by the employers, i.e. the manufacturers owed a duty of care to an employee who had to use the chisel, which duty they had broken, the court held, nonetheless that it was not the manufacturer's negligence that caused the injury. The court held that the employer, having known of the defect in the chisel, through the foreman, its failure to withdraw it from use was the cause of the injury.

However the employee succeeded against the manufacturer of the chisel he was using when he sustained injury in the case of *Mason* v. *Williams and Williams Ltd.*[75] The words of Finnemore J which seem to be a re-couching of the well known doctrine of *res ipsa loquitor* are worthy of note. He said:

> I appreciate that I am faced with another problem, as was indicated in *Donoghue* v. *Stevenson*, that *res ipsa loquitor* does not apply and the court has to be satisfied, and therefore the plaintiff has to prove, that there was negligence on the part of the manufacturers. Of course, that cannot normally be proved by being able to say that on such and such a date such and such a workman did this, that, or the other. I think that when one eliminates anything happening in the present case at the first defendant's factory, there remains the fact that when it came from the second defendants the head was too hard and that undue hardness could have been produced either carelessly or deliberately to make a harder and more durable head while it was being manufactured by them; and in my opinion that is really as far as any plaintiff can be expected to take his case. What the plaintiff says here is: "This is your

---

[72] *Haseldine* v. *C A Daw & Son Ltd* [1941] 2 KB 343.
[73] [1938] 4 All ER 803.
[74] [1966] 2 All ER 181.
[75] [1955] 1 WLR 549.

> chisel: you made it and I used it in the condition in which you made it, in the way you intended me to use it and you never relied on any intermediate examination; therefore, I have discharged the onus of proof by showing that this trouble must have happened through some act in the manufacture of this chisel in your factory, which was either careless or deliberate, and in either event it was a breach of duty towards me, a person who, you contemplated would use this article which you made, in the way you intended it to be used: If that is right he would be entitled to succeed against the second defendants.[76]

And he did although, as we have seen, he failed against his employers, the first defendants. Similarly in *Wright* v. *Dunlop Rubber Co Ltd*,[77] where employees of an employer who bought chemicals from manufacturers were exposed to danger in using the chemicals, the English Court of Appeal held that the manufacturers owed a duty to the employees to take reasonable steps to satisfy itself that the chemicals were safe and that what was reasonable steps depended on the knowledge of the manufacturers.

Causation

For an employee to succeed in an action for damages for injury suffered he must not only prove negligence, i.e. breach of duty by the employer, but must also show that such negligence caused or materially contributed to his injury.[78]

There must be proof to the satisfaction of the court that there is a causal connection between the employer's negligence and the injury suffered. The standard of proof is a balance of probabilities and not beyond reasonable doubt as in criminal cases. However, it is not necessary to prove that the employer's negligence was the sole cause of the injury; it is enough to show that the employer's breach of duty materially contributed to causing the injury. In *McGhee* v *National Coal Board*[79] an employee whose normal work for many years was to empty pipe kilns was asked to work on emptying brick kilns where the working conditions were hotter and dirtier than at the pipe kilns. Three days later he felt extensive skin irritation and was later found to be suffering from dermatitis. It was admitted that the dermatitis was attributable to the work at the brick kilns. In an action for damages for negligence in that the employer had

---

[76] Ibid., 551-552.
[77] (1973) 13 KIR 249.
[78] *Bonnington Castings Ltd* v. *Wardlaw* [1956] AC 613.
[79] (1972) 13 KIR 249

failed to provide adequate washing facilities including showers, soap and towels to enable the employee remove dust from his body the employer admitted this breach but contended that it was not proved that his failure caused the onset of the disease. The House of Lords held that, on the evidence, the employer's default contributed materially to the injury. Lord Simon said: "In my view, a failure to take steps which would bring about a material reduction of the risk involves, in this type of case, a substantial contribution to the injury."[80] And Lord Salmon said: "A factor, by itself, may not be sufficient to cause injury but if, with other factors, it materially contributes to causing injury, it is clearly a cause of injury."[81]

It is, of course, a question of the facts in each case whether an employer's negligence is the sole cause or whether it materially contributes to an injury. As Lord Reid has said, "one must discriminate between those faults which must be discarded as being two remote and those which must not. Sometimes it is proper to discard all but one and to regard that one as the sole cause, but in other cases it is proper to regard two or more causes as having jointly caused the accident."[82] In *Manwaring* v. *Bellington*[83] the employee was given instructions at the beginning of his employment to always ensure that his ladder was secured at the top and bottom before going up the ladder. On one occasion, although the employer made available to the plaintiff and his fellow employee lashings and sackings for securing their ladder, the plaintiff went up the ladder without securing it. As he was climbing up the ladder he slipped and was thrown against some fittings which caused him injury. He was held to be the sole cause of his injury. In *Ginty* v. *Belmont Building Supplies Ltd*[84] the employee, an experienced asbestos sheeter, had been instructed not to work on asbestos roofs without using boards and boards were provided for his use. Furthermore he knew there were statutory regulations on the use of boards. His failure to use boards when he went up a roof from where he fell and suffered serious injuries was held to be the sole cause of his injuries. Similarly in *Horne* v. *Lec Refrigeration Ltd*[85] where the employee consciously disregarded the prescribed safety procedure which he knew and understood and upon which he had been given adequate instructions the court held that the sole fault which caused his death was his conduct.

---

[80] Ibid., 479.
[81] Ibid., 483.
[82] *Stapley* v. *Gypsum Mines Ltd* [1953] AC 666, 681.
[83] (1952) 2 TLR 689.
[84] [1959] 1 All ER 414.
[85] [1965] 2 All ER 898.

But an employer cannot escape liability in this way unless he has discharged his responsibilities by giving proper instructions, supplying proper and adequate equipment for the work or laying down a proper system of work. In *Thompson* v. *National Coal Board*[86] the employee was employed as a pump attendant and tippler operator but on occasions when there was shortage of staff he worked as a wagon lowerer although he was not fully trained for that job. When he was lowering a set of wagons on his own volition and without supervision an accident occurred in which he died. The employer was held to be in breach of his duty to provide a safe system of work. "It was foreseeable that the deceased, although his primary work was that of tippler, would go to the assistance of the wagon lowerers and attempt to do their work without supervision, and there was no evidence of any sufficient warning that he was not to do so."[87] In *Ross* v. *Portland Cement Ltd*[88] the deceased and two others were simply given instructions to carry out repairs on a wire netting at some height from the ground and left to carry out the work in their own way. They chose to use a ladder which was the only equipment available and which evidence showed was obviously an unsafe way of doing the work. The deceased fell from the ladder and died. The House of Lords held that the employers could not wholly escape liability. Lord Reid said that an employer who has given proper instructions and has provided proper equipment cannot make provision against disobedience by his servant but "it is his responsibility to see that proper instructions are given and proper equipment is available."[89] But the employer failed to take steps to see that proper equipment was made available; furthermore there was no evidence that the deceased had done that type of work before and he was not instructed to discuss any problems he may encounter in the carrying out of the work.

The decision of the House of Lords in *Boyle* v. *Kodak Ltd*[90] has, perhaps, made the greatest inroad into the doctrine or defence of sole cause. And it will seem now, by the decision, that an employer who is in breach of a statutory duty cannot escape liability altogether where injury results. The plaintiff was to paint the outside of a large oil storage tank 30 feet high. The upper part of the tank had to be painted by standing on a ladder the top of which rested on a rail which ran round the roof of the tank. To ensure safety it was necessary to lash the top of the ladder to the rail to prevent it slipping sideways. The plaintiff was going up the ladder to lash it when he fell with the ladder from about 20 feet up. There

---

[86] [1982] I CR 15.
[87] Ibid., 21.
[88] [1964] I WLR 768.
[89] Ibid., 778.
[90] [1969] 2 ALL ER 439.

was a staircase running round the outside of the tank which the plaintiff could have used to get to the top of the tank and there lash the ladder before going up by it. There were statutory regulations requiring that every ladder must be securely fixed so far as practicable so that it can move neither from its top nor from its bottom points of rest. The House agreed that it is open to an employer to show that an employee is the sole cause of his injury. In the words of Lord Diplock "if the employer can prove that the only act or default of anyone which caused or contributed to the non-compliance was the act or default of the plaintiff himself, he establishes a good defence."[91] But that was not the case here. The House held that the employer's failure to take steps to ensure that the employee understood the regulations was a contributory factor. The main point of the decision appears to be the fact that since there was available a means of safely securing the ladder before use the regulations would not have been satisfied unless that means was used. And the injured workman may, quite understandably, not have realised that. He should have been told by the employer. As Lord Reid said:

> In a case where the regulations require no more to be done than any skilled man would know from his practical experience to be necessary, it may well be that the employer is under no duty to instruct the man as to his duty. But in the present case both the witness thought that the manner in which the work was being done was the correct manner, and there being nothing to suggest that any skilled man, going by his practical experience, would have thought otherwise.[92]

Hence, as Lord Reid also said: "Employers are bound to know their statutory duty and take all reasonable steps to prevent their men from committing breaches. If an employer does not do that he cannot take advantage of this defence."[93] That is, the defence of sole cause.

In *Richardson* v. *Stephenson Clarke Ltd*[94] where the employers had supplied safety equipment and the injured employee was an experienced person, the defence of sole cause was successful in a common law action for negligence. In the earlier case of *Woods* v. *Durable Suites Ltd*[95] the English Court of Appeal similarly gave judgment for the employer. The employer posted a notice at the place of work specifying the precautions to be taken to avoid dermatitis. He also

[91] Ibid., 446.
[92] Ibid., 442.
[93] Ibid., for statutory duties in factories see next chapter.
[94] [1969] 3 All ER 705.
[95] [1953] 2 All ER 391.

instructed the workmen in the protective steps required and provided the necessary barrier cream, soap and washing facilities. But unknown to the employer the plaintiff had failed to observe the precautions fully and as a result contacted dermatitis. The court held that the employer had taken reasonable steps to provide a safe system of work. Some words of Morris LJ in the case are particularly instructive. He said:

> If an employer allows safety precautions to lapse and to fade into desuetude, it may well be that, on the facts of a particular case, there may be proof that there has been a failure to exercise due care and skill and to provide a proper system of work, but each case must depend on its own exact facts. The duty to exercise due care to provide effective supervision does not involve that an employer must provide a corps of overseers to ensure that some process, in regard to which there has been faithful and ample coaching, is at all times properly carried out. If a time comes when there is knowledge of the neglect of, or the rejection of, safety precautions, then, on the facts of the particular case, it may be that it can be established that there has been a failure to take reasonable care to supervise the smooth working of a safe system.[96]

An employer who is in breach of duty is not precluded from asserting and proving that it was not his negligence that caused the injury.[97] No reason has ever been suggested," said Lord Reid, "why an employer should be barred from proving that his fault, whether common law negligence or breach of statutory duty, had nothing to do with the accident."[98] Lord Reid also said, "If I prove that my breach of duty in no way caused or contributed to the accident I cannot be liable in damages. And if the accident would have happened in just the same way whether or not I fulfil my duty, it is obvious that my failure to fulfil my duty cannot have caused or contributed to it."[99] In *McWilliams* v. *Sir William Arrol & Co Ltd*[100] the deceased was working at a height on a tower which his employer was engaged to construct. He was an experienced steel erector but fell from a height of about 70 feet and died. The employers were under a statutory :duty to provide a safety belt and there were safety belts available two or three days before the accident when they were taken away to another work site. In an action by the wife of the deceased the employers contended that if safety belts had been available the deceased would not have worn one and that, therefore, the

---

[96] Ibid., 396.
[97] *Bonnington Castings Ltd* v. *Wardlaw* [1956] AC 613.
[98] *McWilliams* v. *Sir William Arrol & Co Ltd* [1962] 1WLR 295, 306.
[99] Ibid., 305-306.
[100] *Supra*; see also *Nolan* v. *Dental Manufacturing Co Ltd* [1958] 2 ALLER 449.

failure to provide a belt was not the cause of his death. The House of Lords held that the evidence demonstrated to a high degree of probability that if safety belts had been made available the deceased would, in any event, not have worn one. The House disapproved of a dictum in *Roberts* v. *Dorman Long & Co Ltd*[101] that it is often said that a person who omits to do his duty "cannot be heard to say" that it would have made no difference even if he had done it. Lord Denning has also called the statement an overstatement.[102] He said a "judge may infer the omission to be a cause, but he is not bound to do so. If, at the end of the day, he thinks that, whether the duty was omitted or fulfilled, the result would have been the same, he is at liberty to say so."[103]

Action for breach of statutory duty

About the only legislation that has been enacted to deal with safety of work people, as well as their health and welfare, is factory legislation.[104] The first factory legislation was enacted in 1955 and was only replaced in 1987 by the Factories Act.[105] The sanctions provided for breach of the provisions of the statute are penal but the courts have had engrafted to factory legislation a common law action for breach of statutory duty. There is no doubt now that an action will lie at common law for breach by an employer of certain duties imposed upon him by the Factories Act. Such an action was established by the English Court of Appeal in its decision in 1898 in *Groves* v. *Wimborne.*[106] The employer was under a statutory duty not only to fence dangerous machinery but also to maintain the fence in an efficient state.[107] A fence which had been provided had been removed and a boy employed to work on the machinery suffered injury as a result. In an action for damages it was contended that the boy had no good cause of action in that the penalty of a fine provided by the statute was intended to be the only sanction for breach of its provisions. That contention was firmly rejected by the court and an action for breach of statutory

---

101 [1953] 2 ALLER 428.

102 *Qualcast* v. *Haynes* [1959] AC 743, 762

103 .Ibid.,

104 But see the Minerals (Safe Mining) Regulations made under section 118 of the repealed Minerals Act Cap 226 Laws of the Federation of Nigeria, 1990.

105 Act No.16 of 1987. Now Cap. 126 Laws of the Federation of Nigeria, 1990. The Act is dealt with fully in the next chapter.

106 [1898] 2 QB 402.

107 S.5(4) Factory & Workshop Act 1878.

duty has ever since been recognised by the courts.[108] As Somervell L.J. has said the courts clearly lean in favour of conferring on workmen a right to claim damages for breaches of statutory duty imposed on their employers or the occupiers of factories in which they work.[109]

In *Haigh* v. *Charles W. Ireland Ltd*[110] Lord Diplock explained the purpose of factory legislation and the nature of the action for breach of statutory duty arising from the statute as follows:[111]

> its purpose is to compel the taking of precautions in factories to secure the safety, health and welfare of those who work there. The primary duty is to ensure that the precaution for the safety of workers specified in the Act or in regulations made thereunder is imposed on the occupier of the factory. Failure on his part to do so is a criminal offence whether or not such failure results in any personal injury to anyone employed there. It is not the primary purpose of the Act to bestow a civil remedy in damages to employees who sustain personal injuries at their work in factories, though this is the incidental consequence of the legislation which brings it most frequently to the attention of the courts. In this respect the Act does no more than supplement the general law of negligence by imposing on the occupiers of factories in respect of the conditions of their premises, plant and equipment and the method in which certain specific processes are carried out, a more onerous duty to those who work in their premises to take precautions for their safety than that required by the common law duty to take reasonable care.

Nonetheless a statutory duty does not necessarily supersede an employer's[112] common law duty for the care of his employee. In *Bux* v. *Slough Metals Ltd*[113] the English Court of Appeal held that although the employers had satisfied their statutory duty to provide goggles they had failed in their common law duty to urge the employees to use the goggles. They had acquiesced "in the die-casters going on in their old illegal ways."[114] Stephenson LJ said there is

---

[108] *Groves* v. *Wimborne* was referred to with approval by the House of Lords in *Butler (or Black)* v. *Fife Coal Company Ltd* [1949] 1 All ER 544.

[109] *Solomons* v. *Gertzenstein Ltd* [1954] 1 All ER 625, 631.

[110] [1973] 3 All ER 1137.

[111] Ibid., 1147.

[112] *Franklin* v. *The Gramophone Co Ltd* [1948] 1 KB 542. See also per Lords Porter and Reid in *National Coal Board* v. *England* [1954] AC 403, 415, 425 respectively and per Lord Reid in *Gill* v. *Donald Humberson & Co* [1963] 3 All ER 180, 183.

[113] (1974) 15 KIR 126.

[114] Ibid., 141 per Stephenson L.J.

> no presumption that a statutory obligation abrogates or supersedes the employer's common law duty or that it defines or measures his common law duty either by clarifying it or by cutting it down - or indeed by extending it. It is not necessarily exhaustive of that duty or coextensive with it and I do not...think it is possible to lay down conditions in which it is exhaustive or to conclude that it is so in this case. The statutory obligation may exceed the duty at common law or it may fall short of it or it may equal it. The court has always to construe the statute or statutory instrument which imposes the obligation, consider the facts of the particular case and the allegations of negligence in fact made by the particular workman and then decide whether, if the statutory obligation has been performed, any negligence has been proved. In some cases such proof will be difficult or impossible; in others it may be easy.[115]

It is well settled that an injured factory employee can, in his action for damages, allege both a breach of statutory duty and of the common law duty of care and that he may succeed in one although failing in the other but where he succeeds in both he can only obtain one set of damages.[116] Again, Stephenson LJ made the point in the Bux case, that, in every case where a plaintiff has alleged a breach of statutory duty he is entitled to allege negligence at common law and to ask the court to answer the question whether he has proved negligence, irrespective of his having proved a breach of statutory duty.[117]

It is not a breach of every provision of the Factories Act that gives rise to an action for breach of statutory duty. The decision in *Groves* v. *Wimborne* was in respect of a safety provision and it has become settled that an action may lie for breach of a safety provision of a factory legislation. The cases are legion.[118]

Some health provisions have also given rise to a cause of action, although earlier cases created some doubt. In *Ebbs* v. *John Whitson & Co Ltd*[119] Denning LJ said he need not say whether a section on heath gave rise to a civil action for damages.[120] However the two other members of the court did not refer to the point which was, in fact, not in issue. In *Graham* v. *Cooperative Wholesale Ltd*[121] the court said it was unnecessary for it to decide whether s. 4(1) of the Factories Act 1937 gave a right to sue. But in *Carroll* v. *North British*

[115] Ibid., 139.
[116] *Western Nigeria Trading Co Ltd* v. *Ajao* [1965] 2 All NLR 100.
[117] (1974) 15 KIR 126, 140.
[118] See *Lochgelley Iron & Coal Co* v. *M'Mullan* [1934] AC 1 and the next chapter.
[119] [1952] 2 QB 877.
[120] Ibid., 885.
[121] [1957] 1 All ER 654.

Locomotive Co Ltd[122] it was held that an action lay for breach of a health provision. The workman complained of a breach, by his employer, of section 1 (I) (b) of the Factories Act 1937 - s. 7(1) (b) Factories Act - in that the employer had not cleaned the floor of his workroom for months as a result of which it was covered with several centimetres of foundry sand and dust and that his footwear and socks had become impregnated with the sand and dust resulting in his contracting dermatitis. The court rejected the contention that an action could not lie. The court said: "if the duty of keeping a factory clean is imposed to protect the health of workmen, as I think it clearly is, and if a workman's health is injured as a result of a failure in that duty, I can see no reason why, in appropriate circumstances, he should not recover damages."[123] In *Nicholson* v. *Atlas Steel Foundry and Engineering Co Ltd*[124] breach of a s. 4(1) of the Factories Act 1937 - s. 9(1) Factories Act - was admitted and the House of Lords, having found that the deceased workman suffered from *pneumocomiosis* as a result, awarded damages. In *Thornton* v. *Fisher & Ludlow Ltd*[125] in which damages were awarded for a breach of the equivalent to s. 10(1) Factories Act, there was not even a discussion as to whether an action could not be available.

Also an action for damages may be available for breach of a welfare provision although it is not possible to generalise. Breach of a welfare provision may or may not give rise to a right to civil action depending on whether it does or does not give protection respecting safety over and above purely welfare consideration. As Lord President Clyde said in the Scottish case of *Reid* v. *Westfield Paper Co Ltd*:[126]

> Some of the welfare provisions...which deal(s) with facilities for sitting seem to have a purely welfare outlook; others...which deal(s) with first aid, seem to impinge substantially on matters of health or safety. In the present case I find it unnecessary to decide whether a purely welfare provision could, if breached, involve a claim for damages by a person injured by its breach. In my opinion, s. 42 (1) [our s. 41 (1)] although primarily directed to protecting

---

[122] (1957) SLT (sh ct) 2.

[123] Ibid., 3.

[124] [1957] 1 All ER 776.

[125] [1968] 2 All ER 241; see also *Clarkson* v. *Modern Foundries Ltd* [1958] 1 All ER 33; *Lane* v. *Gloucester Engineering Co Ltd* [1967] 2 All ER 293.

[126] (1957)SC 218, 225. In *McCarthy* v. *Daily Mirror Newspapers Ltd* [1949] 1 All ER 801 two workmen whose clothing were stolen from pegs provided by their employer brought an action for damages for their loss and the English Court of Appeal said that risk of theft was a relevant consideration in determining whether adequate and suitable accommodation for clothing had been provided as required by a provision similar to s.42 of the Factories Act.

welfare, does also involve considerations of health and safety, which this Act is mainly devoted to protecting. If so, its breach could involve civil liability.

In an action for breach of statutory duty the onus is on the injured employee to prove not only a breach of a provision of the Act but also that such breach or fault caused or materially contributed to his suffering the injury. Breach of the provisions of the Factories Act is dealt with in the next chapter. With respect to causation the position is the same as in a common law action for negligence already discussed.

Defences

Three defences were developed at common law and were available to an employer in an action against him for breach of his duty of care. These were the defences of common employment, voluntary assumption of risk and contributory negligence. The defences also became available in an action for breach of statutory duty.

Common employment

We have seen how this doctrine developed. The defence was abolished in the former Eastern and Western Regions in 1962 and 1958 respectively.[127] It was abolished in the Federal Territory of Lagos in 1961.[128] Thus common employment was not available as a defence in any of the states created out of these regions and the Federal Territory of Lagos. However, it continued to apply in the states created out of the former Northern Region[129] until its abolition, apparently, for the whole country, in 1988.[130]

Volenti non fit injuria

The defence of voluntary assumption of risk usually expressed in the maxim *volenti non fit injuria* arose, like the defence of common employment, apparently, based on the notion that when an employee enters into a contract of employment he thereby impliedly agrees to take the risks of the employment upon himself. We may recall, for example, the words of Alderson B in

[127] S.4 Torts Law, Cap. 125 Laws of Eastern Nigeria, 1963; s.13 Torts Law Cap. 122 Laws of Western Region of Nigeria, 1959.

[128] S.3 Law Reform (Torts) Act 1961.

[129] *Hans Schenkel* v. *A.O. Nigeria & A.T.M.N. Ltd.*, 1967 (2) ALR Comm. 167; *Agunanne* v. *Nigeria Tobacco Co. Ltd.* [1979] 2 FNR 144.

[130] S.11 (A)(1) Labour (Amendment) Decree No.27 of 1988; now S.12 Labour Act Cap. 198 Laws of the Federation of Nigeria, 1990. For the constitutional position see *ante*.

Hutchinson v. *York, Newcastle and Berwick Railway Co*[131] where he said "the principle is, that a servant, when he engages to serve a master, undertakes, as between him and his master, to run all the ordinary risks of the service, and this includes the risk of negligence on the part of a fellow-servant, whenever he is acting in discharge of his duty as servant of him who is the common master of both."[132]

Many of the decisions on the defence were given within the last two decades of the 19th century. And they contain a variety and highly interesting conceptions of the defence. In *Clarke* v. *Holmes,*[133] although the Court of Exchequer Chamber held the employer liable for failure to repair defective fencing of machinery which had been brought to his knowledge by the employee who subsequently suffered injury resulting from the defective fencing, it is clear that the court was fully aware of the defence. In *Woodley* v. *Metropolitan District Co*[134] the employee worked at a place, a bend, where trains passed frequently. The place was without light and the space where the employee had to stand while working was just sufficient to allow him keep clear of a train if he knew it was approaching. No warning of an approaching train was ever given and it was not possible for him to realise the approach of a train until it was quite near his working place. He was struck by a train while so working. The Court of Appeal held, by a majority, that *volenti non fit injuria* applied. Cockburn C.J said that a man who enters on a necessarily dangerous employment with his eyes open takes it with its accompanying risks.[135] And added: "If a man chooses to accept the employment, or to continue in it with a knowledge of the danger, he must abide the consequences, so far as any claim to compensation against the employer is concerned."[136]

In 1887 two differing judgments were given. In *Thomas* v. *Quartermaine*[137] the employee was employed in a brewery. He worked in a cooling room where there were two vats, a boiling vat and a cooling vat, which, in spite of its description, contained hot liquid. The employee was pulling a board from under the boiling vat when, as the board came away suddenly, he fell back into the cooling vat and was scalded. The Court held that the defence of voluntary assumption of risk applied. Bowen LJ said: "For many months the plaintiff, a man of full intelligence, had seen this vat - known all about it - appreciated its

---

[131] (1850) 5 Exch 343.
[132] Ibid., 352.
[133] (1862) 7 H & N 937.
[134] (1877) 2 Ex D. 384.
[135] Ibid., 388.
[136] Ibid., 389.
[137] (1887) 18 QBD 685.

danger - elected to continue working near it. It seems to me that legal language has no meaning unless it were held that knowledge such as this amounts to a voluntary encountering of the risk.[138] This decision was the high-water mark of the defence. In *Yarmouth* v. *France*[139] the tide began to change. The plaintiff's duty, in this case, involved driving carts to load and unload goods. Among the horses owned by the employer was one known to be of a vicious nature. The plaintiff objected to using this horse but the foreman told him he must go on using it and that if any accident happened the employer would be responsible. While using the horse an accident did happen. The horse kicked him and his leg was broken. The Divisional Court distinguished *Thomas* v. *Quartermaine* and held that the circumstances did not conclusively show that the risk was voluntarily incurred by the plaintiff; a new trial was ordered. But what was of particular significance was that the Master of the Rolls, Lord Esher, said that mere knowledge of the danger will not do: there must be an assent on the part of the workman to accept the risk, with a full appreciation of its extent, to bring the workman within the maxim of *volenti non fit injuria*. If so, that is a question of fact.[140] Just one year after Hawkins J said the fact that an employee continues in his work does not mean he has consented to incur any risk which he may encounter in the course of such work and that he may have continued only because he does not want to lose his means of livelihood - "his poverty, not his will, consented to incur the danger."[141] But Lord Bramwell's opinion was diametrically opposed to these views. He posed a question which, clearly, contained its own answer:

> The master says here is the work, do it or let it alone. If you do it, I pay you; if not, I do not. If he has engaged him, he says, I discharge you if you do not do it; I think I am right; if wrong, I am liable to an action. The master says this, the servant does the work and earns his wages and is paid, but is hurt. On what principle of reason or justice should the master be liable to him in respect of that hurt?[142]

But, fortunately, Lord Herschell said he would reserve his opinion on that statement.[143] A more definite principle was, perhaps, finally laid down by the

---

[138] Ibid., 699

[139] (1887) 19 QBD 647

[140] Ibid., 657.

[141] *Thrussel* v. *Handyside* (1888) 20 QBD 359, 364.

[142] *Membery* v. *Great Western Railway Co* (1889) 14 App Cas 179, 188.

[143] Ibid., 192.

House of Lords in its decision in *Smith v. Baker*[144] in 1891. An employee was engaged at work at a drill. His duty was to hold a drill and keep it in position while two fellow employees hammered on it alternatively. Other employees were engaged in cutting stones which were then occasionally swung over the heads of the drillers by a crane. While stones were being so swung one of them slipped from the crane and fell on the plaintiff causing him serious injury. The House of Lords held that *volenti non fit injuria* did not apply. Lord Herschell said:

> Where, then, a risk to the employed, which may or may not result in injury, has been created or enhanced by the negligence of the employer, does the mere continuance in service, with knowledge of the risk, preclude the employed, if he suffers from such negligence, from recovering in respect of his employer's breach of duty? I cannot assent to the proposition that the maxim "*volenti non fit injuria*" applies to such a case and that the employer can invoke its aid to protect him from liability for his wrong.[145]

In *Bowater* v. *Borough of Rowley Regis*,[146] in the English Court of Appeal, Scott L.J doubted if the maxim can very often apply in circumstances of an injury to a servant by the negligence of his master.[147] The court held that for the defence to succeed an employer must show that the employee undertook that the risk of the employment should be on him and that this is not shown merely by proof that the employee continued in his work with full knowledge of the risk involved. The maxim is not *scienti non fit injuria* but *volenti non fit injuria.*

In *Baddeley* v. *Earl Glanville*[148] it was held that the defence has no application to cases where injury arises from a breach of a statutory duty on the part of an employer. This decision was later approved by the Court of Appeal.[149] The underlying reason would appear to be that it would be contrary to public policy to allow an employer to contract out of duties which statute has specifically imposed on him for the safety of his employee. However the House of Lords decision in *Imperial Chemical Industries Ltd* v. *Shatwell*[150] shows that the non-application of the defence in actions for breach of statutory duty is not without exceptions. The House of Lords held that where an employer is not

[144] [1891] AC 325.
[145] Ibid., 362.
[146] [1944] 1KB 465.
[147] Ibid., 465-466.
[148] (1887) QBD 423.
[149] *Wheeler* v. *New Merton Board Mills Ltd* [1933] KB 669.
[150] [1965] AC 656.

himself in breach of statutory duty but its liability is vicarious through a breach of an employee's statutory duty by the employee who is not superior to the injured employee the defence is available to an employer. The House otherwise agreed with the principle of non-applicability of the maxim in an action for breach of statutory duty. Lord Reid said: "I entirely agree that an employer who is himself at fault in persistently refusing to comply with a statutory rule could not possibly be allowed to escape liability because the injured workman had agreed to waive the breach."[151] The ICI principle succeeded in the common law negligence case of *Bolt* v. *William Moss & Sons, Ltd*[152] and in *O'Reilly* v. *National Rail and Tramway Appliances Ltd.*[153] Nield J said the defence was open to the employer although it was not, in fact, applied.

Contributory negligence

The defence of contributory negligence, like the defence of *volenti*, is not limited to the law of employment. One of the earliest cases in which the defence was applied is *Butterfield* v. *Forrester.*[154] The defendant's house was close to the road and he wished to carry out some repairs to the house. He put a pole across his side of the road and the plaintiff, who had just left a public house at 8 p.m, though not drunk, rode his horse violently and came against the pole and fell with his horse. The trial judge directed the jury that if they were satisfied that the plaintiff was riding along the street extremely hard and without care they should find for the defendant which they did. A motion for a new trial on the ground of misdirection was refused. Bayley J said: "If he had used ordinary care he must have seen the obstruction; so that the accident appeared to happen entirely from his own fault."[155] Lord Ellenborough CJ came to the same conclusion. He said: "Two things must concur to support this action, an obstruction in the road by the fault of the defendant, and no want of ordinary care to avoid it on the part of the plaintiff."[156] In *Caswell* v. *Worth*[157] contributory negligence was held to apply to a breach of statutory duty to fence machinery. "The plaintiff says that the defendants omitted a duty, viz., to fence their machinery, whereby the plaintiff was injured. The plea alleges that the plaintiff was not injured thereby, but by the

[151] Ibid., 674.
[152] (1966) 110 Sol. Jo 385.
[153] [1966] 1 ALL ER 499.
[154] (1809) 11 East 60.
[155] Ibid., 61.
[156] Ibid.
[157] (1856) 5 E & B 849.

plaintiff's own wilful act, in setting the machinery in motion. It is clear, both upon principle and authority, that this is a good defence."[158] The defence was a total defence; no account being taken of any fault on the part of the defendant. As Lord Campbell CJ said in *Butterfield* v. *Forrester* and several subsequent cases, it has been held that the want of ordinary care in avoiding an injury disentitles the party injured from suing.[159]

It is quite unnecessary to discuss to any greater extent the development of the defence of contributory negligible before the intervention of statute especially the devices adopted by the courts in their attempt to ameliorate the chances of success of injured workmen which had become quite slim because of the availability of the defence. One such device must, however, be mentioned as it has been held to survive statutory intervention. The courts introduced what may be regarded as an element of subjectivity into the determination of whether or not a workman had been contributorily negligent.[160] In *Caswell* v. *Powell Duffryn Associated Collieries Ltd*[161] the House of Lords approved of this approach which took into account the conditions of the work of the workman. Lord Wright said:

> What is all important is to adapt the standard of what is negligence to the facts, and to give due regard to the actual conditions under which men work in a factory or mine, to the long hours and the fatigue, to the slackening of attention which naturally comes from constant repetition of the same operation, to the noise and confusion in which the man works, to his preoccupation in what he is actually doing at the cost perhaps of some inattention to his own safety.[162]

This concession survives statutory intervention although the House of Lords has, itself, held that it may be applicable only in an action for breach of statutory duty.[163] With statutory intervention, contributory negligence is no longer a total defence. The courts are now empowered only to reduce the damages which an injured employee would have recovered if he were not contributorily negligent by "such extent as the court thinks just and equitable having regard to the claimant's share in the responsibility for the damage."[164] As we have seen in

---

[158] Ibid., 856 per Wightman J

[159] Ibid., 855.

[160] *Flower* v. *Ebb Vale Steel, Iron & Coal Co* [1934] 2 KB 132.

[161] (1939) 55 TLR 1004.

[162] Ibid., 1012.

[163] *Staveley Iron & Chemical Co Ltd* v. *Jones* [1956] AC 627.

[164] See e.g. S.16 Law Reform (Torts) Law Cap 115 Laws of Lagos State of Nigeria, 1994. There are identical statutory provisions applicable in all the States of the Federation and Abuja.

discussing the question of causation it is open to the courts, on the facts of each case, to determine whether an injury was caused solely by the negligence of the employer or of the employee or whether both of them have contributed in causing the injury. Lord Atkin has said: "the injury may be the result of two causes operating at the same time, a breach of duty by the defendant and the omission on the part of the plaintiff to use the ordinary care for the protection of himself...that is used by the ordinary reasonable man in those circumstances."[165]

In *Mullard* v. *Ben Line Steamers*[166] the plaintiff, an experienced riveter, who had worked in ships for thirty five years, was working on the repair of batch covers in a ship and had to go to another part of the ship to collect a tool. The part of the ship through which he had to pass was in total darkness and he fell down a hatch and sustained injuries. The employers were in breach of their statutory duty to fence the hatch. The trial judge found the plaintiff guilty of contributory negligence and apportioned the blame equally between him and his employers. But the Court of Appeal held that that was too hard on the plaintiff and put two-thirds of the blame on the employers. The court said, relying on earlier views,[167] that an employee is not to be judged too harshly in such circumstances in order not to defeat the objective of factory legislation which is to protect workmen. Indeed, it seems that where an employer is in breach of his statutory obligation and this breach has caused or contributed to an injury that the courts will be wary of apportioning blame to the injured workman. In *Hawkins* v. *Ian Ross (Castings) Ltd*[168] the court held that even if the employee's contributory negligence was in part a cause of his accident it was not just or equitable to reduce his damages given all the circumstances of the case. Fisher J said: "It seems to me that it is wrong to impute contributory negligence to a man in the position in which the plaintiff was when he is himself the sufferer from the failure of the defendants to carry out the duties which parliament has imposed on them."[169] In *McGuiness* v. *Key Markets Ltd*[170] the English Court of Appeal emphasised the point that the primary purpose of the statutory provision to fence dangerous machinery is to protect employees even against foolish acts. Therefore the courts must be careful not to emasculate the statutory provision by the side wind of apportionment. It.was said that where employers are in breach

[165] *Caswell* v. *Powell Duffryn Associated Collieries Ltd* (1939) 55 TLR 1004,1007; see also *Evans* v. *Bakare* (1974) 1 NMLR 78; *Appah* v. *Costain* (WA) Ltd [1974] 1 All NLR 235.

[166] [1971] 2 All ER 424.

[167] Lord Tucker in *Staveley Iron & Chemical Co Ltd* v. *Jones* (19561 AC 627,648 and Sellers L.J in *Quintas* v. *National Smelting Co Ltd* [1961] 1 WLR 401, 408.

[168] [1970] 1 All ER 180.

[169] Ibid., 188.

[170] (1973) 13 KIR 249.

of an absolute duty, e.g. s.17 of the Factories Act,[171] to which an injured employee is no party at all, the employer cannot wholly escape liability by establishing contributory negligence.

Vicarious liability

With the abolition of common employment an employer may now be held liable to his employee who has suffered injury caused by the tort, i.e. negligence, of another of his employees in the course of his duties. The doctrine of vicarious liability arises purely from the relationship of employer and employee[172] and an employer's liability is not depended upon his knowledge or consent to the commission of the tort. It is based only on the fact that it was committed by the employee in the course of carrying out his duties under his contract of employment.

A number of attempts have been made to either explain or justify the doctrine. In *Duncan* v. *Findlater*[173] Lord Brougham said:

> The rule of liability and its reason, I take to be this: I am liable for what is done for me and under my orders by the man I employ, for I may turn him off from that employ when I please; and the reason that I am liable is this, that by employing him I set the whole thing in motion; and what he does, being done for my benefit and under my direction, I am responsible for the consequences of doing it.[174]

Parke B said much the same thing in *Quarman* v. *Burnett.*[175] Upon the principle that *qui facit per alium facit per se*, the master is responsible for the acts of his servant; and that person is undoubtedly liable, who stood in the relation of master to the wrong-doer, he who had selected him as his servant, from the knowledge of or belief in his skill and care and who could remove him for misconduct, and whose orders he was bound to receive and obey;[176] and in *Swanson* v. *North-Eastern Railway Company*[177] Bramwell LJ said a master is liable for an injury done to a stranger by his servant within the scope of the

---

171 See Chapter IV.
172 Or the relationship of principal and agent; see ante.
173 (1839) 6 CL & F 894.
174 Ibid., 909-910.
175 (1840) 6 M & W 499.
176 Ibid., 509.
177 (1878)11 Ex D 341.

latter's authority "because the stranger has had no hand in the choice of the servant."[178] And Lord Reid has said of the maxims *respondent superior* and *qui facit per alium facit per se* with respect to the doctrine that the former merely states the rule baldly in two words and the latter merely gives a fictional explanation of it.[179] The doctrine can, perhaps, be best justified by its utility.[180] It enables the party better placed economically to bear the financial burden to be made to do so in a situation where, clearly, both parties have some share in creating the loss and it is difficult, if not, impossible to equitably apportion the blame.

An employer can be held vicariously liable only where the injury is caused by the tort of an employee when acting in the course of his duties. Whether an employee is acting in the course of his duties is a question of the facts and circumstances of each case[181] but the onus is on the injured employee to prove facts which would establish that the employer is vicariously liable.[182] A tanker driver who smoked while unloading petrol rendered his employer liable for the resulting explosion.[183] And a driver who was doing overtime and deviated from the proper route to go and eat was in the course of his duties.[184] Similarly a milkman who had been instructed never to employ children-to assist him in the distribution of milk but did so was acting in the course of his duty of distributing milk.[185] Thus an express prohibition does not necessarily take a conduct outside duty. An employee may carry out his duty in an unauthorised or otherwise wrongful manner. Also the fact that a conduct involves fraud may not necessarily take it out of course of performance of duty.[186] In *Oloko* v. *Slab Engineering Company Ltd*[187] an employee whose duty it was to receive goods recorded lorry loads of stones as having been received although the stones were no where to be found. It was held that the employer was liable to pay for the stones.

It sometimes happens that an employee is hired to another employer along with some equipment such as a tractor or crane. The problem may arise as to which of the two employers will be held vicariously liable for a tort, usually negligence, the employee may commit while carrying out duties for the

---

[178] Ibid., 348.
[179] *Staveley Iron & Chemical Co Ltd* v. *Jones* [1956] AC 627, 643.
[180] Liability is joint and several.
[181] *UAC Ltd* v. *Saka Owoade* 13 WACA 207; [1955] AC 130.
[182] *Chukwu* v. *Uhegbu* [1963] 2 All NLR 209.
[183] *Century Insurance Co* v. *N. Ireland Road Transport Board* [1942] AC 509.
[184] *Iko* v. *John Holt* (1957) 2 FSC 50.
[185] *Rose v. Plenty* [1976] 1 All ER 97.
[186] *UAC Ltd* v. *Saka Owoade* supra; *Lloyd* v. *Grace, Smith & Co* [1912] AC 716.
[187] 1977 NCLR 482.

temporary employer. In the Nigerian case of *A.H. Bull & Co* v. *West African Shipping Agency and Lighterage Co Ltd*[188] the two parties were shipowners and one party let a lighter to the other together with two lighter boys to man the lighter. While the lighter was tied up a strong ebb developed one night and the lighter parted its moorings, drifted with the current out of the Lagos harbour and broke up some distance away. It was a total loss. The question was - who was to be held responsible for the negligence of the two lighter boys? The Judicial Committee of the Privy Council held that the proper test to apply was that suggested by Bowen LJ in *Donovan* v. *Laing, Wharton & Down Construction Syndicate*[189] where he said that in such a case the liability will fall on "the person who has a right at the moment to control the doing of the act."[190] That is, at the time when the negligent act was carried out. But in *Mersey Docks & Harbour Board* v. *Coggins & Griffiths (Liverpool) Ltd*[191] the House of Lords, more or less, disapproved of Donovan's case. In the Mersey Docks' case, as in Donovan's case, the permanent employer let a crane and its driver. The driver set the crane in motion negligently and caused the plaintiff injury. The House of Lords held that in driving the crane the driver was acting as the employee of the permanent employer. Lord Macmillan said that although the temporary employer were entitled to tell him where to go, what parcels to lift, and where to take them, i.e., they could direct him as to what they wanted him to do, "but they had no authority to tell him how he was to handle the crane in doing his work."[192] The question to ask will seem to be - who is entitled to tell the hired employee the manner in which he is to do the work upon which he is engaged and not whether the hirer has control over the work to be performed. If the temporary employer is to be held vicariously liable he must be shown to also control the way in which the hired employee carries out the work given to him. It is a question of fact and, as the House held, the onus is on the permanent employer to prove the facts which will establish the liability of the temporary employer.

---

[188] 7 NLR 13. [1927] AC 686.
[189] [1893] 1 QB 629.
[190] Ibid., 634.
[191] [1947] AC 1.
[192] Ibid., 13.

Chapter Five

The Factories Act

Introduction

The first legislation on factories in Nigeria was the Factories Ordinance No. 33 of 1955. This was based on the British Factories Act 1937 which was an Act to consolidate the Factories and Workshop Acts 1901 to 1929 and other related enactments.

The earliest legislation which dealt with factories and mills in Great Britain and Ireland was the Health and Morals of Apprentices Act 1802. It provided that the walls and ceilings of all rooms in a factory or mill must, at least, twice a year, be well and sufficiently washed with quick lime and water and that sufficient number of windows and openings be provided to ensure a proper supply of fresh air. Apprentices working in the mills and factories were to be supplied with two suits a year and with suitable linen, hats, stockings and shoes; no apprentice was to work for more than 12 hours a day and apprentices were to be instructed in reading, writing and arithmetic during working hours. The Act also regulated night work of apprentices and also provided that male and female apprentices must not sleep in the same room and that for at least one hour every Sunday every apprentice must be instructed and examined in the principles of the Christian religion.

Justices of the peace were empowered to appoint two visitors - one a justice of the peace and the other a clergyman - with full power and authority from time to time and at any time of the day or during the hours of employment, to enter any factory. They were to report in writing on the state and condition of the mills and factories and the apprentices employed in them. Any one who obstructed a visitor was liable, for every such offence, to pay a sum not exceeding ₦20. Copies of the Act were required to be hung up in two or more conspicuous places in the mill or factory. Any master or mistress of a mill or factory who wilfully contravened any provision of the act was liable to a fine. One half of such a fine was to be paid to the informer by the justice who tried the offence. It may be that the purpose of the payment was to enforce compliance.

It will be seen that this Act laid down the basic pattern upon which present day factories legislation is based although the most significant provisions of today's legislation upon the welfare, health and especially the safety of those employed in factories were conspicuously absent. Similarly, the early provisions for instruction of apprentices in academic and religious education as well as the requirement for provision of clothing are not of great importance today. No factories legislation in Nigeria has ever dealt with hours of work.

Meaning of factory

It would seem obvious that ordinarily the provisions of the Factories Act will apply only to the factories and all such factories as come within the definition of factory given by the Act unless, of course, the Act itself provides otherwise.[1] Section 83 of the Act makes this clear. It provides that, except where the Act otherwise expressly provides, the provisions of the Act apply only to factories as defined by the Act and except where the contrary appears, they apply to all such factories.

The definition of factory is in two parts. The first arm of section 87(1) gives a general definition after which it goes on to list nine different types of premises in which various processes are carried on as factories. There may be some overlap. For instance it seems that premises in which newspapers are published come within the general definition and also paragraph (iv) of the sub-section.

Factory means any premises in which or within which or within the close or curtilage or precincts of which one person, or more persons are employed in any process for or incidental to any of the following purposes, namely:

(a) the making of any article [2] or of part of any article; or

---

[1] The law in force as from June 11, 1987, is the Factories Act No.16 of 1987, now cap. 126 of the Laws of the Federation of Nigeria 1990; it repealed the Factories Act. The Act applies to factories belonging to or in the occupation of the Government of the Federation or of a State; s. 84; however in the case of any public emergency the Head of State may, by order, to the extent and for the period stipulated in the order, provide that the Act shall not apply to factories generally or to any class or description of factory; s. 85; all section references in this chapter are to Cap. 126 unless otherwise stated.

[2] Article is defined by the Act to include any solid, liquid or gas or any combination of these; s. 88; in *Fatstock Marketing Corporation Ltd* v *Morgan* [1958] 1 All ER 646 the English Court of Appeal held that a live animal was not an article but in *Longhurst* v *Guildford, & District Water Board* [1963] AC 265, the House of Lords held that water was an article; there was no definition of article under the Factory and Workshop Act 1901 there under consideration in the former case or in the Factories Act 1937 in the later case.

(b) the altering, repairing, ornamenting, finishing, cleaning, or washing, or the breaking up or demolition of any article; or

(c) the adapting for sale of any article; being premises in which or within the close or curtilage or precincts of which the work is carried on by way of trade or for purposes of gain and or over which the employer of the person or persons employed therein has the right of access or control.

A number of the features of this general definition are significant and are the relevant factors that must be taken into consideration-in deciding whether premises are or are not a factory. First, the premises may be open air premises;[3] they need not be enclosed.

Also, it has been said that a close need not have any boundary wall or fence.[4]

Second, at least one person must be employed on the premises;[5] such employment must be for wages. The word employed does not mean merely busy, or engaged or occupied.[6] There must exist the relationship of master and servant and employment for wages.[7] Thus it was held in *Pullen* v. *Prison Commissioners*[8] that a prison is not a factory as there is no employment for wages in the case of prisoners. Similarly, a technical school owned by a public authority is not a factory in as much as those there are scholars and not employees.[9] It must be noted that an apprentice is deemed to be a person employed;[10] also a person who has not attained the age of eighteen years and works in a factory, whether for wages or not, in collecting, carrying or delivering goods, carrying messages or running errands is deemed to be employed in the factory "for the purposes of this Act or of any proceedings thereunder."[11]

Third, and this appears crucial, any one of the three purposes stated in the definition must be carried on the premises. The purposes include the processes of making any article or part of any article or the altering, repairing, ornamenting, finishing, cleaning, washing, breaking up or demolition of any article

---

[3] S. 87(6).

[4] *Barry* v *Cleveland Bridge Co.* [1963] 1 All ER 192, 195.

[5] Under the old statute, the Factories Act, Cap. 66 Laws of the Federation of Nigeria and Lagos, 1958, ten or more persons had to be employed and they had to be employed in manual labour; under the present statute it appears the crucial issue is the processes being carried out on or in the premises.

[6] See per Wrottesley J. In *Weston v London County Council* [1941] 1 All ER 555,558.

[7] Per Lord Goddard C.J. In *Pullen v Prison Commissioners* [1957] 3 All ER 470,471.

[8] [1957] 3 All ER 470

[9] *Weston v London Council* [1941] 1 All ER 555

[10] S. 88(4)

[11] S. 88(5)

or the adapting for sale of any article. There is no doubt that the question whether any of these processes is being carried on is one of fact. As Jenkins L.J. said in *Cockram* v *Tropical Preservation Co Ltd,*[12] the question whether a given operation amounts to the finishing of an article or the adapting of any article for sale is very much a question of fact and degree.

It seems that the mere purpose of cleaning or washing of an article would constitute a premises a factory. In *Jones* v. *Crosville Motor Services Ltd,*[13] a bus depot in which buses were washed and where a cleaner fell from a ladder he had placed against a bus he was to clean, it was argued strenuously by counsel that the premises were a factory. In rejecting this contention the court had to rely on the words "not being any premises used for the purpose of housing locomotives or vehicles where only cleaning, washing, running repairs or minor adjustments are carried out" as showing an intention to exclude premises in which only these purpose are carried out. These words which were in the earlier statute are not contained in the present statute.

With respect to the process of adapting for sale Viscount Dunedin has said that it "points clearly to something being done to the article in question which, in some way, makes it in itself a little different from what it was before."[14]

The learned law Lord has also suggested as a test that:

> you must look at what is the finished article to be turned out. If that finished article is only put into the condition of a finished article by the processes to which it has been subjected...then the purpose will fall within the expression 'altering or adapting for sale.'[15] But adapting an article for sale does not necessarily require alteration in the article. There is no reason for requiring alteration of substance to make adapting for sale in view of the fact that adapting for sale is a separate thing from altering. "If this were necessary, there would be no need to insert "adapting for sale." [16]

Interesting illustrations of processes that have been held to be or not to be adapting for sale abound. A few examples must be given. The composing, printing and publishing of a newspaper has been held to be the making of an article or the adapting for sale of an article.[17] Similarly, premises in which spare

---

[12] [1951] 2 KB 827, 839.

[13] [1956] 3 All ER 417

[14] *Groves v Lloyds British Testing Company Ltd* [1931] AC 446, 467

[15] *Kaye* v *Burrows* [1931] AC 446, 484.

[16] Per Scrutton L.J. in *Baily v Potteries Electric Traction Co Ltd* [1931] 1 KB 385, 495.

[17] *Revenue Officer* v *Cardiff (Borough) Assessment Committee and Western Mail Ltd* [1931] 1 KB 47.

parts were packed for export were a factory because the application of protective dressings and placing of the parts in waterproof containers or wrappings were a finishing or adapting of the parts.[18]

The process whereby already brewed beer [19] was matured, carbonated, filtered and bottled was adapting for sale;[20] so also where seeds in a rough, unclean and impure state were treated by machinery with the object of separating good seeds from weed seeds and dirt of various sorts;[21] it was also adapting for sale where mixed rags of wool, silk, jute, etc. and comprising old garments and tailors' new clapping were ripped, clipped, graded or blended and classified and all dirt and foreign matter removed before being sold to heavy woollen manufacturers.[22] Although, the slaughter of an animal may not be an adapting for sale the preparing of it for sale is adapting for sale.[23] On the other hand where manufactured cables had to be tested and the testing was done by sawing away three links which were subjected to a specific breaking strain it was held there was no adapting for sale; [24] the "testing does not in any way make the article different as an article from what it was before."[25] The answer seems different however where the testing is part of the manufacturing process of the article. Thus where manufacturers of propellers tested them in premises different from those in which they were manufactured, the former premises were held to be a factory as "the testing which was carried out at the propeller testing station was all part of the process of manufacture."[26] In *Moon* v *London Country Council*[27] it was held that a printing shop in which reels of ticket pulp were cut into sections, stained and printed after which they were cut and make up into bundles was a factory.[28]

Fourth, the work which is carried on on the premises must be carried on by way of trade or for purposes of gain. The Act expressly excludes from this requirement any premises owned by government. Any premises belonging to or in the occupation of the Government of the Federation, or of a State or Local Government Council or corporation constituted under any Act, or Law, shall not

---

[18] *Cockram* v *Tropical Preservation Co Ltd* [1951] 2 KB 827.
[19] The beer had been brewed in different premises.
[20] *Sedgwick* v *Watney, Combe, Reid & Co.* [1931] AC 446.
[21] *Hines* v *Eastern Counties Farmers Cooperative Assobiation Ltd*, ibid.
[22] *Kaye* v *Burrows* [1931] AC 446.
[23] *Fatstock Marketing Corporation Ltd* v *Morgan* [1958] 1 All ER 646.
[24] *Groves* v *Lloyds British Testing Coy Ltd* [1931] AC 446.
[25] Ibid. p. 467
[26] *Acton Borough Council* v *West Middlesex Assessment Committee* [1949] 2 KB 10, 13.
[27] [1931] 1 KB 385
[28] In any case any premises in which printing is carried out are factory under s. 87(l)(iv).

be deemed not to be a factory by reason only that the work carried on thereat is not carried on by way of trade or for purposes of gain.[29] So that in respect of premises not belonging to or occupied by government, unless trade or gain are the ends served by the work carried out on the premises, such premises would not be a factory. However, either trade or gain will suffice. If there is a trade there is no need to consider gain.[30] The "disjunctive or followed by the words for purposes of gain is put in for the express purpose of contrasting gain with trade."[31] Where articles are manufactured not for sale but, for producing goods or services to be sold or rendered, the work would be regarded as being carried on for purposes of trade.[32] Gain need not be direct gain; it may be indirect profit. In *Stranger* v *Hendon Borough Council*,[33] a consulting civil engineer carried on processes for testing of concrete for which he installed machinery in his premises in a residential area. He supplied information based on these tests to clients for reward. It was held that this was gain.

Specific factories

Unlike under the general definition where the employment of one person is sufficient to constitute the premises in which he is employed a factory, provided one of the enumerated process is there carried on, in the case of any of the nine specific premises mentioned, at least ten persons must be employed upon the premises and must be for wages. It must be noted that since these premises are factories all the provisions of the Act apply to them in the same way and to the same extent as they apply to premises which fall within the general definition of a factory.

Any yard or dry dock (including the precincts thereof) in which ships or vessels are constructed, reconstructed, repaired, refilled, finished or broken up is a factory. It would appear that although this definition certainly does not comprehend wet docks,[34] that is, "an enclosed area of water in which vessels may lie for loading or unloading or when laid up or waiting for their turn at the berth,"[35] that it may include not only a dry dock but also a wet dock or basin

[29] S. 87(7).
[30] Per Scrutton L.J. in *Baily* v *Potteries Electric Traction Co Ltd.* [1931] 1 KB 385, 575.
[31] Per Scott L.J. in *Stranger* v *Hendon Borough Council* [1948] 1 KB 571, 575
[32] *Baily* v *Potteries Electric Traction Col Ltd. supra.*
[33] [1948] 1 KB 571.
[34] For the provisions which apply to dock see s. 55 and below.
[35] Per Lord Wright in *Smith* v *Cammell Laird & Co* [1940] AC 242, 269

which forms part of a ship yard for the construction, reconstruction, repair, refitting, finishing or breaking up of a ship or vessel.[36]

Any premises in which the business of washing or filling bottles or containers or packing articles is carried on incidentally to the purpose of any factory.

Any premises in which the construction, reconstruction or repair of locomotives, vehicles or other plant for use for transport purposes is carried on as ancillary to a transport undertaking, or other industrial or commercial undertaking.[37]

Any premises in which printing by letterpress, lithography, photogravure or other similar process or book-binding is carried on by way of trade or for purposes of gain[38] or incidentally to another business so carried on.

Any premises in which mechanical power[39] is used in connection with the making or repair of articles of metal or wood incidentally to any business carried on by way of trade or for purposes of gain.

Any premises in which the articles are made or prepared incidentally to the carrying on of building operations or works of engineering construction not being premises in which such operations or works are being carried on. Thus the premises in which building operations or works of engineering construction are carried on are not themselves factories.[40] Building operation means the construction, structural alteration, repair or maintenance of a building (including re-painting, re-decoration and external cleaning of the structure), the demolition of a building, and the preparation for the laying of the foundation of an intended

---

[36] *Smith* v *Cammell Laird, supra.*

[37] Under the English Factories Acts of 1937 and 1961 and our repealed Factory Act, Cap. 66, of the Laws of the Federation of Nigerian and Lagos, 1958, any premises "used for the purpose of houshng locomotices or vehicles where only cleaning, washing, running repairs or minor adjustments are carried out" were excluded. There is no such exclusion under the Act. It is submitted that if the facts of *Griffin* v *London Transport* [1950] 1 All ER 716 came before our courts the decision would be the same even if the court were to hold that the repairs were only running repairs.

[38] See *supra,* for meaning of "by way of trade or for purposes of gain."

[39] Mechanical power is not defined; in *Willmott* v *Paton* [1902] 1 KB 237, the English Court of Appeal held that a crane put in motion by hand was not using mechanical power; however this was in interpreting the words "any premises in which, steam water or other mechanical power is used" under the Factory and Workshop Act 1878 and the court felt that the words "other mechanical power" was *ejusden generis* with steam and water power. The Act uses the words "mechanical power" alone; [note s. 88(3).]

[40] For the Minister's power to extend the application of all or any of the provisions of the Act to building operations and works of engineering construction see below.

building.[41] Work of engineering construction means the construction of any railway line or siding, and the construction, structural alteration or repair (including re-painting[42] and re-painting) or the demolition of any dock, harbour, inland navigation, tunnel, bridge, viaduct, waterworks, reservoir, pipeline, aqueduct, sewer, sewage work, or gas-holder.[43] Any premises in which ten or more persons are employed in or in connection with the generating of electrical energy for supply by way of trade or for supply of any industrial or commercial undertaking or of any public building or public institution[44] or for supply to streets or other public places.

Any premises in which mechanical power is used for the purposes of or in connection with a water supply being premises in which such person or persons are employed.

Any laundry carried on as ancillary to another business or incidentally to the purposes of any public institution.

Any line or siding (not being part of a railway)[45] which is used in connection with and for the purposes of a factory are deemed to be part of the factory but, if any such line or siding is used in connection with more than one factory belonging to different occupiers, the line or siding is deemed to be a separate factory and the provisions of the Act will then apply as if such different occupiers are jointly the occupiers of the line or siding so deemed to be a factory.[46]

Any work place in which, with the permission of or under agreement with the owner[47] or occupier, ten or more persons carry on any work which would constitute the work place a factory if the persons therein were in the employment of the owner or occupier, is deemed to be a factory and the provisions of the Act

---

[41] S. 88(1); the definition provides that building operation "does not include any operation which is a work of engineering constructions within the meaning of this Act." However such works, like building operations, are not a factory; for the meaning of engineering construction see text.

[42] The word is, most likely, "re-pointing."

[43] S. 88(1); it includes also "such other works as may be prescribed." No prescription has been made.

[44] Public institution is not defined; an institution which provided clothing, board and education for destitute orphans free of charge and depended on subscriptions from the public has been held to be a public institution; *Seal* v *British Orphan Asylum* (1911) 75 J.P. 152; similarly, a school maintained by Freemasons entirely for their own benefit was held a public institution; *Royal Masonic Institution for Boys* v *Parkes* (1912) 3 KB 212.

[45] Railway means any railway used for the purposes of public traffic, whether passenger, goods or other traffic and includes any works used in connection with and for such purposes; s.88(l)

[46] S.87(2)

[47] Owner means the person for the time being receiving the rents or profits of the premises whether on his own account or as the agent or trustee for any other person or who would so receive the same if the premises were leased; s.88(l); for the meaning of occupier see below.

apply to it as if the owner or occupier of the work place were the occupier of the factory and the persons working therein are persons employed in the factory.[48]

No premises in or adjacent to and belonging to a mine,[49] not being a quarry,[50] but being premises in which the only process carried on is a process ancillary to the getting, dressing or preparation for sale of minerals are to be deemed to be a factory.[51]

Where a place situate within the close, curtilage or precincts forming a factory is solely used for some purposes other than processes carried on in the factory, that place, is not to be deemed to form part of the factory but if it comes within the definition of a factory is deemed to be a separate factory.[52] A place situated within the close, curtilage or precincts forming a factory is not part of the factory only if the place is "solely used for some purposes other than processes carried on in the factory." In *Thorogood* v. *Van Den Berghs*,[53] the English Court of Appeal said these words "must be construed as if it read for some purpose other than the processes for or incidental to the main purpose of the factory."[54] The court held that a separate building within the curtilage of a factory for the manufacture of margarine was part of the factory as the testing, in that building, of machinery used in the manufacture of margarine was incidental to the manufacture of margarine. *Thorogood* was relied upon in *Powley* v. *Bristol Siddeley Engines*.[55] There, an administrative block of offices with its own entrance from the street but situated within the premises of a factory for the manufacture of aeroplane engines was held to be part of the factory in as much as the process of designing, and drawing of engines carried on in the block was a process incidental to the manufacture of aircraft engines.

In *London Co-operative Society Ltd* v. *Southern Essex Assessment* Committee,[56] a canteen used by persons employed in a laundry, which was a factory, was held not to be a place solely used for some purpose other than the process carried on in the laundry. Tucker J. said the "element which, to my mind, is decisive is that the facts stated show that the canteen was necessary and

[48] s.87(3).

[49] Mine includes any place, excavation or working whereon, wherein or whereby any operation in connection with mining is carried on; s.88(l) Factories Act and s.259 Minerals & Mining Act, 1999 No. 34.

[50] Quarry means any place, excavation or working, others than a mine, wherever, wherein or whereby any operation in connection with the extraction of sand, stone, laterite or any similar materials is carried on; s.88(l)

[51] S. 87(4)

[52] S. 87(5)

[53] [1951] 1 All ER 682

[54] See per Cohen L.J. at P. 686 ibid.; Lord Guest approvdd this approach in *Longhurst* v *Guildford, Godalming & District Water Board* [1963] AC 265 at 279

[55] [1965] 3 All ER 612.

[56] [1942] 1 KB 53

essential for the welfare and efficiency of the workers engaged,[57] in the factory. This decision was followed in *Luttman* v. *ICI Ltd*,[58] where a canteen, a new building within the precincts of a factory, was held to be part of the factory as the purposes of feeding and entertaining the people working in the factory was a purpose that was incidental to the processes of manufacture carried on at the factory. On the other hand, in *Longhurst* v. *Guildford, Godalming & District Water Board*,[59] where the premises consisted of two buildings one of which contained machinery and plant for filtering and chlorinating water and the other machinery for pumping the water for distribution after the purification, the House of Lords held that the pumping was not incidental to the filtering of the water.

The minister may, if in special circumstances he thinks it expedient so to do, at any time by order exempt any premises or part of any premises being a factory within the above definitions from the application of all or any of the provisions of the Factories Act.[60]

Special extensions

Part VII applies certain provisions of the Act to some premises which do not fall within either the general or specific definition of a factory and also confers power on the minister to apply all or any provisions of the Act to some other premises.

Any part of a building of which a part is let off as a separate factory.[61] Where part of a building is let off as a separate factory certain provisions of the Act apply to any part of the building used for the purposes of the factory though that part is not comprised in the factory. These provisions are those of part two with respect to cleanliness and lighting, of part three with respect to prime movers, transmission machinery, hoists and lifts, chains, ropes and lifting machines, safe means of access and safe place of employment, steam boilers, steam receivers and steam containers, and air receivers, and the power of an inspector to issue notices as to dangerous or unsafe conditions and practices and dangerous or unsafe factories.

The owner of such a building is responsible for any contravention of any of the above provisions. The owner, instead of the occupier of the factory, also has responsibility for any contravention, as respects the factory, of the provisions of

---

[57] Ibid. p. 60
[58] [1955] 3 All ER 481.
[59] [1963] AC 265.
[60] S. 87(7) proviso.
[61] S.54.

part two with respect to sanitary conveniences[62] and of part three with respect to hoists and lifts, prevention of fire and safety provisions in case of fire.[63] However, the responsibility of the owner of the building for the cleanliness of sanitary conveniences arises only when the conveniences are used in common by several tenants. Also, his responsibility for any contravention of any of the provisions of part three above arises only in so far as the provisions relate to matters within his control. In any case, the occupier of the factory has responsibility for any contravention of any of the above provisions of part three with respect to any machinery or plant belonging to him or supplied by him whether as respects the factory or otherwise. For the purposes of all the provisions applied to such a building the following, that is, lifting machines attached to the outside of the building and chains, ropes and lifting tackle used in connection with a lifting machine so used must be disregarded.

Docks, wharves and quays

Section 55 provides that certain provisions of the Act apply to every dock, wharf or quay as if it is a factory and to the process of loading, unloading or coaling of any ship in any dock or harbour and to all machinery or plant[64] used in those processes as if the processes are carried on in a factory and the machinery or plant were machinery or plant in a factory. The expression dock, it has been said,[65] means the solid structure and body of the dock and not the water space within its limits while a wharf[66] is a place contiguous to water which is used in loading and unloading goods. It has, however, been held that a structure moored in a river at some distance away from the shore was also a wharf since it performed the functions of a wharf.[67]

The responsibility for compliance with the provisions is put on the person who has actual use or occupation of the dock, wharf or quay or the person who carries on the processes of loading, unloading or coaling any ship in any dock or

[62] Sanitary conveniences include - urinals, waterclosets, earth-closets, privies, ashpits, and any similar conveniences; s.88(l).

[63] For the purposes of the provisions with respect to prevention of fire the factory is deemed to include any part of the building used for the purpose of the factory.

[64] Plant includes any gangway or ladder used by any persons employed to load and unload or coal a ship; s.55(3)

[65] Lord Macnghten in *Houlder Line Ltd* v *Griffin* [1905] AC 220, 224.

[66] *Haddock* v *Humphrey* [1900] 1 QB 609.

[67] *Ellis* v *William Corry & Son Ltd* [1902] 1 KB 38.

harbour as if the person is the occupier[68] of a factory. A shipowner does not have the actual use or occupation of a dock merely because the ship is afloat in the dock.[69] But a firm which contracted to do the painting and plumbing on a ship lying in a dock has actual use of the dock.[70] It seems that no one can carry on an operation on a ship floating in a dock without having the use of the dock, and that when you have persons who have taken such a contract and are engaged in carrying it out, they have the use of that area of the dock for the purpose of their work.[71]

The provisions of the Act which apply to docks, wharfs and quays and the processes of loading, unloading or coaling a ship in a dock or harbour and to all machinery or plant used in those processes are all the provisions of parts three and four on safety and welfare respectively,[72] the provision of part five with respect to the power of the minister to make regulations for health, safety and welfare, and of part six on the notification and investigation of accidents and industrial diseases. Other provisions are those of part eight with respect to the abstract of the Act, regulations and notices, general registers (as far as applicable) and preservation of registers and records, subject to such modifications as may be made by regulations by the minister, and the provisions with respect to duties of persons employed and the prohibition of deductions from wages. Lastly the provisions of part nine with respect to powers and duties of inspectors and to regulations and orders made under the Act and those of part ten on offences, penalties and legal proceedings are also applicable.

Premises in which steam boilers are used

Section 56(1) applies some provisions of the Act to any premises in which steam boiler[73] is used, other than, of course, premises which form part of a factory or premises to which the provisions of the Act have been applied by sections 54 and 55. The provisions apply as if such premises in which steam boiler is used

---

[68] Responsibility under the Act is generally placed on the occupier; for who is an occupier see below.

[69] *Houlder Line Ltd* v *Griffin* [1905] AC 220.

[70] *Bartel* v *W. Gray & Co* [1902] 1 KB 225.

[71] Per Collins M. R. Ibid. P. 229.

[72] These do not apply in relation to any machinery or plant used in any of the processes of loading, unloading or coaling which is on board a ship and is the property of the ship owner; s.55 (2) proviso.

[73] Steam boiler means any closed vessel in which for any purpose steam is generated under pressure greater than atmospheric pressure and includes any economizer used to heat water being fed to any such vessel and any superheater used for heating steam; s.88(1).

are a factory and as if the person having the actual use or occupation of the premises is the occupier of a factory.

The provisions which apply are the provisions of part three with respect to steam boilers and to steam receivers and steam containers (including the provisions as to exceptions as to steam boilers, steam receivers and steam containers) so, however, that the owner of the boiler, receiver or container shall, instead of the person deemed to be the occupier, be responsible for any contravention of these provisions in so far as they relate to matters within his control and with respect to the power of an inspector to issue notices as to dangerous or unsafe conditions and practices and as to dangerous or, unsafe factories, the provisions of part five with respect to regulations for health, safety and welfare, of part six with respect to notification of accidents and the power of the minister to extend the provisions as to notice of accidents to dangerous occurrences and of part eight with respect to general registers (so far as applicable) and preservation of registers and records, subject to such modifications as may be made by regulations made by the minister and the provisions with respect to duties of person employed; also applicable are the provisions of part nine with respect to the powers and duties of inspectors and to regulations and orders made under the Act; lastly, the provisions of part ten with respect to offences, penalties and legal proceedings.

If, in any premises, not being premises forming part of a factory, a steam boiler is newly taken into use, the occupier must send a written notice to the Director of Factories. The notice must contain the name of the occupier of the premises, the address and location of the premises and the nature of the work carried on in the premises. The following particulars in respect of each steam boiler in use must also be stated; type, description and distinctive number, country and year of manufacture, the date of the last thorough examination and name of the person by whom the examination was made[74] and the maximum permissible working pressure in kilogrammes per square centilitre.[75]

Extension to other premises

The minister may, by order and subject to such conditions as he may specify in the order, extend the application of all or any of the provisions of the Factories Act to any of the following classes of premises, processes or operations:[76]

---

[74] See above as to examination.

[75] S.56(2) and schedule 5 of the Act; a similar notice is required by the sub-section to be sent by the occupier of any such premises in which a steam boiler is used.

[76] S.57.

a) warehouses not forming part of any factory;
b) any premises, not being premises forming part of a factory, in which a hoist or lift is used;
c) any work carried out in a harbour or wet dock in constructing, reconstructing, repairing, refitting, painting, finishing or breaking up a ship or in scaling, scurfing or cleaning boilers (including combustion chambers and smoke boxes) in a ship, or in cleaning oil-field tanks or bilges in a ship or any tank in a ship last used for oil of any description carried as cargo;
d) building operations[77] undertaken by way of trade or business or for the purposes of any industrial or commercial undertaking, and any line or siding which is used in connection there with and for its purposes and is not part of a railway,[78] and
(e) works of engineering construction[79] undertaken by way of trade or business or for the purpose of any industrial or commercial undertaking, and any line or siding which is used in connection with and for the purposes of such works and is not part of a railway.[80]

Registration of factories

The provisions for the registration of factories are contained in part one of the Act. Before any person occupies or uses as a factory any premises which were not so occupied or used by him as at 11 June, 1987, he must apply for the registration of the premises to the Director of Factories;[81] the application must contain the particulars set out in schedule 2 of the Act[82] and must, in fact, have been filed with the Director at least six months before the commencement of actual construction of a building or structures intended to be used as a factory.[83]

---

[77] For definition of building operation see *supra.*
[78] For definition of railway, see *supra.*
[79] For definition of works of engineering construction see *supra.*
[80] See not 78 *supra.*
[81] S.3(l); in the case of a factory in occupation as at 11 June, 1987 the occupier ought to have applied for registration within one month of 11th June, 1987.
[82] S.3(l); if, at any time after an application has been sent to the Director, any change occurs with respect to the particulars set out in the application the occupier must forthwith inform the Director, in writing, of such change; failure to do so is an offence s.4; the offence is punishable on conviction to a fine not exceeding ₦500 or to imprisonment for a term not exceeding three months or to both such imprisonment and fine; if the contravention continues after conviction a further offence is committed which is punishable with a fine not exceeding ₦100 for each day on which the contravention is continued; S.70.
[83] S. 3(3).

Upon receipt of an application and on being satisfied that the premises are suitable for use as a factory of the nature stated in the application, the Director must cause the premises to be registered and he must issue to the applicant a certificate of registration.[84] Any person who has not been issued a certificate of registration but occupies or uses as a factory any premises which have not been registered as a factory or who has been issued a certificate of registration but occupies or uses as a factory any premises which have not been registered as a factory is guilty of an offence.[85] On conviction such a person is liable to a fine not exceeding N2,000 or to imprisonment for 12 months or to both such and imprisonment; if, after conviction, the contravention continues he is guilty of a further offence and liable on conviction to a fine not exceeding ₦100 or imprisonment not exceeding 14 days for each day on which the offence is so continued.[86]

Where the director refuses to issue a certificate of registration he must, if so requested by the applicant, state in writing the grounds of such refusal.[87] If any person is aggrieved by a decision of the Director he may, within 30 days from the date of such decision, send to the Chairman of the Factories Appeal Board[88] and to the Director of Factories written notice of his intention to appeal to the Board against the decision; the notice must state the grounds of appeal.[89] On receipt of the notice the chairman must appoint a day and place for the hearing of the appeal and must notify the parties in the appeal.[90] The Board, may, on hearing the appeal, confirm, vary or reverse the decision of the Director and its decision is final.[90a]

---

[84] By s.1 the Director of Factories must keep a register of factories in which he must cause to be entered such particulars in relation to every factory required to be registered as he may consider necessary or desirable.

[85] S. 3(4).

[86] S. 3(5).

[87] S. 3(6).

[88] The minister may, by notice in the Gazette, appoint such persons as he thinks fit to constitute Factories Appeal Board. If he deems it expedient to appoint a person holding office in the public service, he must inform the President Commander-in-Chief of the Armed Forces who may, if he thinks fit appoint such a person; the Board must consists of a Chairman who must be a legal practitioner of not less than 10 years standing and not less than four other members; s. 5.

[89] S. 6(1).

[90] S.6(2); s.6(3) provides that the Director is a party concerned in the appeal; he, as well as the appellant, are entitled to appeal and be heard and entitled to be represented by a legal practitioner if they so desire.

[90a] But there is a constitutional guarantee of access to the courts; see s. 6(6)(b) of the Constitution.

Health, safety and welfare in factories

The next four parts of the Act, that is parts II, III, IV and V deal respectively with general provisions on health, safety and welfare and special provisions on health, safety and welfare in factories.

We have seen that the common law developed a duty of care for the safety of an employee but it neglected, almost entirely, to provide for his health and welfare. This has been left to statute. The Factories Act now makes provisions for the health and welfare of persons employed in factories and, indeed, the provisions on safety are far more detailed than the common law requirements of care. Furthermore, while the role of the common law was, on the whole, chiefly compensatory, the provisions of the Act are directed primarily to the prevention of accidents and health hazards to those engaged in factories. However, as we have also seen, the common law has come to the aid of the factory employee by developing the action for breach of statutory duty.

General provisions on health

The general provisions on health are contained in part two of the Act.

Cleanliness

The health provisions start off with a general requirement that every factory must be kept in a clean state and free from effluvia arising from any drain, sanitary convenience or nuisance.[91] But, without prejudice to this general duty, a number of specific obligations are imposed.

Accumulations of dirt and refuse must be removed daily by a suitable method from the floors and benches of workrooms and from the stair case and passages.[92] The floor of every workroom must be cleaned at least once in every week by washing or, if it is effective and suitable, by sweeping or other method.[93] All inside walls and partitions and all ceilings or tops of rooms and all walls, sides and tops of passages and staircases must, where they have a smooth impervious surface, be washed with hot water and soap or cleaned by other suitable method at least once in every period of twelve months; and where they

---

[91] S.7(1)

[92] S.7(1)(a)

[93] S.7 (1)(b) for an action for breach of this subsection see below.

are kept painted with oil-paint or vanished, be repainted or revanished at least once in every five years but must, at least once in every twelve months, be washed with hot water and soap or cleaned by other suitable method. In any case they must be kept white-washed or colour-washed and the white-washing or colour-washing repeated at least once in every period of twelve months.[94]

Overcrowding

A factory must not, while work is carried on there, be so overcrowded as to cause risk of injury to the health of the persons employed in the factory.[95] However, and without prejudice to this general obligation, a factory is deemed to be so overcrowded if the number of persons employed at a time in any workroom is such that the amount of cubic space allowed for every person employed is less than four hundred cubic feet.[96] Every workroom must not be less than nine feet in height measured from the floor to the lowest point of the ceiling or, where there is no ceiling, to the lowest point of the roofing material.[97] However in calculating the amount of cubic space in any room no space more than four metres from the floor must be taken into account and, where a room contains a gallery, the gallery must be treated as if it is partitioned off from the remainder of the room and formed a separate room.[98]

If an inspector so requires there must be posted in the workroom a notice specifying the number of persons who, having regard to the above requirements, may be employed in that room and the minister may make regulations increasing the number of cubic metres which must be allowed for every person employed in a workroom.[99]

Ventilation, lighting, drainage and sanitary conveniences

Effective and suitable provision must be made for securing and maintaining, by the circulation of fresh air in each workroom, the adequate ventilation of the room.[100] Also effective provision must be made for securing and maintaining

---

[94] S.7 (1)(c) the Director of Factories may, by order, direct that any of these provisions be not applied to any class or description of factory in certain circumstances; S.7(2).

[95] S.8(1)

[96] S.8(2)

[97] S.8(3)

[98] S.8(6)

[99] S.8(5) and (7)

[100] S.9(1); in *Ebbs* v *John Whitson & Co. Ltd.* [1952] 2Q.B. 877, the English Court of Appeal held that S.4(1), i.e., our S.9(1), is only directed towards the provision of ventilation and this in spite

sufficient and suitable lighting, whether natural or artificial, in every part of a factory in which persons are working or passing.[101] All glazed windows and skylights used for the lighting of workrooms must, so far as practicable,[102] be kept clean on both the inner and outer surfaces and free from obstruction but windows and skylights may be white-washed or shaded to mitigate heat or glare.[103]

Where any process is carried on which renders the floor liable to wet to such an extent that the wet is capable of being removed by drainage effective means must be provided and maintained[104] for draining off the wet.[105]

Sufficient and suitable sanitary conveniences for the persons employed in the factory must be provided, maintained and kept clean, and effective provision must be made for lighting the conveniences.[106] Where male and female persons

---

of a second arm in S.4(1) which read "and for rendering harmless, so far as practicable, all such fumes, dust and other impurities generated in the course of any process or work carried on in the factory as may be injurious to health." The court held that the plaintiff, who was employed as a finisher by scraping and sand papering, could not recover when he contracted dermatitis as there was no breach of the subsection the employers having provided adequate ventilation. In *Graham* v *Co-operative Wholesale Society Ltd.* [1957] 1 All ER 654 Delvin J. followed *Ebb*'s case; he held that although S.4(1) appeared to be in two parts it was clear the subsection must be regarded as a whole and as dealing only with ventilation. It is submitted that this contention is much stronger under S.9(1) which does not contain a second arm. But it seems that where it can be shown that there is inadequate ventilation, i.e., a breach of S.9(1), and that this breach caused injury to health that the injured workman would be able to recover damages. In *Nicholson v. Atlas Steel Foundry and Engineering Co. Ltd.* [1957] 1 All ER 776, where damages were allowed by the House of Lords, a breach of S.4(1) was admitted and the house held, on a balance of probabilities, that the employer's breach caused the deceased's illness. By S.9(2) the minister may make regulations specifying a standard of adequate ventilation for all or any class or description of factory.

[101] S.10(1); effective means lighting which is functioning effectively; lighting is not effective when not turned on; per Danckwerts L.J. in *Thornton v. Fisher & Ludlow Ltd.* [1968] 2 All ER 241, 243. By S.10(3) the minister may make regulations specifying a standard of suitable and sufficient lighting for all or any class or description of factory.

[102] The phrase "so far as practicable" used to qualify the standard required to discharge some of the obligations imposed on the occupier of a factory necessarily involves some regard being had to existing practice or knowledge common at the relevant time; see *Adsett* v *Steelfounders and Engineers* [1953] 2 All ER 320.

[103] S.10(2)

[104] Maintained, wherever it occurs, means maintained in an efficient state, in efficient working order and in good repair; S.88(1). The standard of the duty to maintain "is clear. It...falls into a category long recognised and firmly established by authority; it is a strict or absolute duty and neither intention nor lack of care need be shown in order to prove a breach of it." Per Lord MacDermott in *Galashiels Gas Co. Ltd.* v *O' Donnell* [1949] AC 275, 286.

[105] S.11

[106] S. 12(2) For what are sanitary convenience see foot note 62; the minister may make regulations determining what is sufficient and suitable.

are employed[107] the conveniences must afford proper separate accommodation for persons of each sex.[108]

Where an inspector finds any act or default in relation to any drain, sanitary convenience or water supply or any nuisance or other matter in a factory which appears to him to be the concern of any local government under any law, he must give notice of it in writing to the local government council. If, after three months of the notice, the nuisance remains unabated the inspector must take such action as he deems necessary to abate it and the owner or occupier of the premises must bear the cost of abating it.[109]

General provisions on safety

These are contained in part three of the Act. Fencing of machinery is dealt with in three sections of this part. These machinery include prime movers,[110] transmission machinery[111] and every dangerous part of any machinery other than prime movers and transmission machinery.[112]

Every flywheel directly connected to any prime mover and every moving part of any prime mover must be securely fenced whether the flywheel or prime mover is situated in an engine house or not.[113] Also, every part of any electric generator, motor or rotary converter and every flywheel directly connected to it must be securely fenced unless where it is in such a position or of such construction as to be as safe to every person employed or working on the premises as it would be if securely fenced.[114] The head and tail race of every water wheel and of every water turbine must be securely fenced.[115]

---

[107] Except where the only persons employed are members of the same family.
[108] S. 13
[109] S.13
[110] S.14; prime mover means every engine, motor or other appliance which provides mechanical energy derived from steam, water, wind, electricity, the combustion of fuel or other sources; s.88(l).
[111] S.15; transmission machinery means every shaft, wheel, drum, pulley, system of fast and loose pulleys, coupling, clutch, driving belt or other device by which the motion of a prime mover is transmitted to or received by any machine or appliance; s.88(l).
[112] S.17; for meaning of "dangerous part of any machinery" see below.
[113] S.14(l); it must be noted that prime movers other than those mentioned in s.14(3) must be securely fenced whether hidden away in an engine house or not and whether they are safe by reason of some other position or by construction.
[114] S.14(3).
[115] S.14(2).

Every part of any transmission machinery must be securely fenced unless it is in such position or of such construction as to be as safe to every person employed or working on the premises as it would be if securely fenced.[116] Efficient devices or appliances must be provided and maintained in every room or place where work is carried on by which the power can promptly be cut off from the transmission machinery in that room or place.[117] No driving belt,[118] when not in use, must be allowed to rest or ride upon a revolving shaft which forms part of any transmission machinery.[119] Suitable striking gear or other efficient mechanical appliances must be provided and maintained and used to move driving belts to and from fast and loose pulleys which form part of the transmission machinery, and any such gear or appliance must be constructed, placed and maintained as to prevent the driving belt from creeping back on to the fast pulley.[120]

Every power driven machine having its individual source of power must be provided with an efficient starting and stopping appliance or control and every electrical equipment or appliance intended for use in a factory must be of such construction as to be safe for use by all persons required to use it or who come into contact with it and must be maintained at all times in a safe condition.[121]

Every dangerous part of any machinery, other than prime movers and transmission machinery, must be securely fenced unless it is in such a position or of such construction as to be as safe to every person employed or working on the premises[122] as it would be if securely fenced; provided that, in so far as the safety of a dangerous part of any machinery cannot, by reason of the nature of the operation be secured by means of a fixed guard, the requirement to securely fence is deemed to have been complied with if a device is provided which, in the opinion of the Director of Factories, satisfactorily protects the operator or other persons from coming into contact with that part.[123] Any part of a stock-bar which projects beyond the headstock of a lathe must be securely fenced unless it is in

---

[116] S.15(l).

[117] S.15(2).

[118] Driving belt includes any driving strap or rope; s.88(l).

[119] S.15(3).

[120] S.15(4); the Director of Factories may, be certificate in writing, grant exemption in respect of any of the requirements of s.15(2),(3) and (4) where he is satisfied that compliance is unnecessary or impracticable, but subject to any conditions he specifies, s.15(5).

[121] S.16.

[122] For interpretation of "person employed or working on the premises" see *Uddin* v *Associated Portland Cement Manufacturers Ltd*, [1965] 2 All ER 213.

[123] S.17(l).

such a position as to be as safe to every person employed or working on the premises as it would be if securely fenced.[124]

The words securely fenced in all three sections have been given the same meaning.[125] Fencing means the erection of a fence or guard. The duty to securely fence is an absolute one in the sense that a guard must be provided even if it will render the machinery in question commercially impracticable or mechanically impossible to use when fenced.[126] To put it differently, absoluteness means that, failure to fence for any reason whatever will amount to a breach of the duty to securely fence. As Salter J. said - If a machine cannot be securely fenced while remaining commercially practicable or mechanically useful the statute in effect prohibits its use.[127] The absoluteness of the duty is not to be cut down by reading in some such qualification as "so far as practicable" or "so far as reasonably practicable."[128] But does the absoluteness of the duty mean that the guard or fence must be such as would give protection against all dangers or is it only to give security against all foreseeable dangers?

In *Burns* v. *Joseph Terry & Sons Ltd*[129] the English Court of Appeal held, by a majority, that securely fenced must be considered with regard to circumstances which could be reasonably foreseen. The House of Lords approved this test in *John Summers & Sons Ltd* v. *Frost*.[130] This case involved injury to the thumb of a fitter who was grinding a piece of metal on a grinding wheel revolving at a very high speed. The back and top of the wheel were fenced by a guard in the shape of a hood but part of it remained unguarded. Lord Keith said:

> It must at least be fenced against the dangers that are reasonably foreseeable and for the reasons I have stated, these same dangers still remained, though in a reduced degree, when the machine here was being worked in its fenced condition. The grindstone, in my opinion, was not securely fenced.[131]

However, it is settled that the fencing need protect only against dangers which may arise as a result of the workman making physical contact with the machinery required to be securely fenced. "The fence is intended to keep the

---

124 S.17(2).

125 See *Carrol* v *Andrew Barclay & Sons Ltd* [1948] AC 477.

126 *John Summers & Sons Ltd* v *Frost* [1955] AC 740; *Davies* v *Thomas Owen & Co* [1919] 1 KB 39 *Miller* v *William Boothman & Sons Ltd*, [1944] 1 All ER 333.

127 *Davies* v *Thomas Owen & Co* [1919] 1 KB 39, 41.

128 *John Summers & Sons Ltd* v *Frost, supra.*

129 [1951] 1 KB 454.

130 [1955] AC 740

131 Ibid., 775.

worker out, not to keep the machine or its products in."[132] Thus where bits of the material on which the worker was working flew out and injured him, the House of Lords held he had no remedy under the fencing provision.[133] Similarly, the House held that fencing does not impose an obligation to guard against bits of machinery itself being ejected.[134] This restrictive interpretation of the fencing provisions was not without its critics and dissenters.[135] It has been criticized as being based on an illogicality. Commenting on one of the fencing sections Holroyd Pearce L.J. said.[136]

> The argument (of counsel for the plaintiff) has shown how technical and artificial the question of protection under s.14[137] has become and how illusory in certain respects the words...shall be securely fenced have become...There is no protection under S.14 against a class of obvious perils caused by dangerous machinery, namely perils which arise from a dangerous machinery ejecting at the worker pieces of the material or even pieces of the machinery itself. Thus there is now left a gap which neither logic nor common sense appears to justify.

Nonetheless, in *Close* v. *Steel Company of Wales*[138] the House of Lords affirmed the two previous decisions. In *Sparrow* v. *Fairy Aviation Co Ltd*[139] the House not only once again affirmed these decisions but also extended their application. It was held that the duty to fence does not involve fencing against the tool which the workman is using coming into contact with machinery required to be fenced. Lord Reid said he did not "think that it would accord with the decision in Close's case to say that there is a duty to fence against anything that a man might have to use in the course of his work."[140] The court agreed however, that there is hardly any difference between fencing against contact between a workman's body and machinery and between his clothing and machinery.[141]

---

[132] Per Lord Simonds in *Nicholls* v *F. Austin (Leyton) Ltd* [1946] AC 493, 505.
[133] *Nicholls* v *F. Austin (Leyton) Ltd* [1946] AC 493.
[134] *Carroll* v *Andrew Barclay & Sons Ltd* [1948] AC 477.
[135] See e.g. *Dickson* v *Flack* [1953] 2 All ER 840; *Rutherford* v *R.E. Glanville & Sons (Bovey Tracey) Ltd*, [1958] 1 All ER 532.
[136] *Eaves* v *Morris Motors Ltd*, [1961] 2 QB 385; 396 - 397.
[137] S.17.
[138] [1962] AC 357.
[139] [1964] AC 1019.
[140] [1964] AC 1019 at 1034.
[141] It might have been expected that the Factories Act, enacted over three decades after the first factory legislation and about two decades after the last of the House of Lords decisions, would have plugged the gap highlighted and decried in some of the decisions. In *Nicholls* case, the earliest of the House of Lords decisions, the House relied on two major grounds for its

Where an employer is in breach of his duty to fence and an accident results from that breach he will be liable even though the accident occurred in an unexpected way.[142]

The duty to securely fence is removed, as we have seen, in certain cases where the machinery "is in such position or of such construction as to be safe to every person employed or working on the premises as it would be if securely fenced."[143] Clearly, if machinery is to be regarded as safe by reason of position or construction as it would be if securely fenced, the position or construction of the machinery must afford the same protection or safety as would be given if the machinery were securely fenced. As we have seen securely fenced is meant only to afford protection against foreseeable risks. The same test should logically be applied in determining whether machinery is as safe as it would be if securely fenced.[144] In determining whether any part of any machinery is in such a position or of such construction as to be safe to every person employed or working on the premises as it would be if securely fenced, no account must be taken of any person carrying out, while the part of machinery is in motion, an examination or any lubrication or adjustment shown by such examination to be immediately necessary, being an examination, lubrication or adjustment which it is necessary to carry out while the part is in motion.[145]

In the case of any part of transmission machinery used in any process in any factory with respect to which the Director of Factories had declared, by certificate in writing, that he is satisfied that, owing to the continuous nature of such process, the stopping of that part would seriously interfere with the carrying on of the process in such factory, no account must be taken of any person carrying out in the factory by such methods and in such circumstances and subject to such conditions as may be specified in the certificate, any lubrication

---

interpretation - one, that the alternative to fencing provided is deemed to have been complied with if a device is provided which "automatically prevents the operator from coming into contact with that part,"; and two that the minister is given power to make regulations with respect to the fencing of materials or articles which are dangerous while in motion. Neither the repealed Factories Act nor the Act confers a similar power on the minister. As to ground one s.17 proviso is in similar terms. However the courts need not feel bound by the English decisions.

142 *Millard* v *Serck Tubes Ltd* [1969] 1 WLR 211; approved by the House of Lord in *Johnson* v *F.E. Callow Ltd* (1971) AC 335; see also *Allen* v *Aeroplane & Motor Aluminium Castings* [1965] 1 WLR 1244.

143 Ss.14(3),15(l),17(l) and (2), but "or of such construction" is omitted in s.17(2)

144 *Burns* v *Joseph Terry & Sons Ltd* [1951] IKB 454; and see per Lord Reid in *John Summers & Sons Ltd* v *Frost* [1955] AC 740; 769.

145 S. 18 (1) (a).

or any mounting or shipping of belts.[146] However, the provisions of s.18(1) apply only where the following provisions of s. 18(2) are satisfied:

(a) the examination, lubrication or other operation is carried out by a male person who has attained the apparent age of eighteen years and has been appointed by the occupier of the factory by certificate attached to the general register to carry out such examination, lubrication or other operation and has been furnished by the occupier with a copy of such certificate signed by him and has been sufficiently trained for the purposes of the work entailed by and is acquainted with the dangers of moving machinery arising in connection with such examination, lubrication or other operation and has also been provided by the occupier with and is wearing a close fitting single piece overall suit in good repair and fastened by means having no exposed loose ends and no external pockets other than a hip pocket; and
(b) another person, instructed as to the steps to be taken in case of emergency, is immediately available within sight or hearing of any person carrying out such examination, lubrication or other operation; and
(c) such steps as may be necessary, including where appropriate and reasonably practicable erection of a barrier, are taken to prevent any person, other than a person carrying out the operation, from being in a position where he is exposed to risk of injury from the machinery; and
(d) any ladder in use for the carrying out of such examination, lubrication or other operation is securely fixed or lashed or is firmly held by a person stationed at the foot of the ladder.[147]

Section 19 provides that all fencing or other safeguards provided in pursuance of the fencing provisions must be of substantial construction and constantly maintained and kept in position while the parts required to be fenced or safeguarded are in motion or in use. There are two exceptions in which, although, the parts are in motion or in use, they need not be fenced: i) when the parts are necessarily exposed for examination; and ii) when they are exposed for any lubrication or adjustment shown by such examination to be immediately necessary. In both cases the requirements of section 18(2) must be complied with. The general effect of s.19 as explained in *Smith* v. *Morris Motors Ltd,*[148] is

---

[146] S. 18 (1) (b).
[147] S. 18(2)
[148] [1949] 2 All ER 715

that it is to indicate how and when the duty imposed under sections 14, 15 and 17 is to be carried out:

> That duty is to be carried out, as far as the provision of fencing is concerned, by providing fencing of substantial construction, by constantly maintaining the fencing, which means keeping it in good and efficient working order and repair and also keeping the fencing in position while the parts required to be fenced or guarded are in motion or in use, with certain exceptions. The effect really is that s. 14[149] imposes the duty and s.16[150] defines its extent and introduces exceptions as to when it need not be carried out.[151]

The problem which the courts have had to face is over the meaning of the words in motion or in use. If machinery is not "in motion or in use" there is no obligation to keep the fencing or guard in position so that an employee who suffers injury then cannot allege breach of statutory duty by the employer - there is then no duty to fence. When, then, is machinery in motion or in use? *In Richard Thomas & Baldwins Ltd* v. *Cummings,*[152] a fitter was making adjustments in an electric-power driven machine but from which power had been cut off at the time. In order to rotate the face plate of the machine he pulled on one of the belts through which power was normally transmitted when on, and in so doing he crushed his finger between the belt and a pulley. The House of Lords held that the machinery was not in motion or in use at the time of the accident. But the reasoning was not unanimous. Lord Tucker's judgement is unhelpful. Lord Oaskey felt that machinery are not "in motion or in use" unless they are being used for the purpose for which they are intended to be used.[153] Lord Porter agreed that "in use" certainly meant doing the work it is meant to do and that "in motion" meant "running as it was meant to run but not doing the work it was meant to do."[154] Lord Reid in whose judgement Lord Keith concurred, said the phrase "in motion" appears to me to be more apt to describe a continuing state of motion lasting or intended to last for an appreciable time.[155] In *Irwin* v. *White, Thomkins & Courage Ltd,*[156] another House of Lords decision, Lord Pearce was, with respect, conect in his summary of the decision in Cummings' case. As he

---

[149] S. 17.
[150] S. 19.
[151] Per Lynskey J. in *Smith* v *Morris Motors Ltd,* [1949] 2 All ER 715, 718.
[152] [1955] AC 321.
[153] [1955] AC 321, 329.
[154] Ibid., 332.
[155] Ibid. 33; see also per Holroyd Pearce L.J. in *Knight* v *Leamington Spa Courier Ltd,* [1961] 2 QB 253, 262-263
[156] [1964] 1 All ER 545.

said - the views of Lord Porter and Lord Reid with which Lord Keith concurred "are inconsistent with the view that machinery...is not in motion or in use...when it is not actually engaged in commercial production."[157] In other words, one general principle that can be distilled from that judgement is that machinery may be in motion or in use even when it is not being run for the purpose of production. Within that principle the question whether a machine is in motion for the purposes of the Act is a matter which is largely one of fact and degree in every case. It is not possible to lay down any general principles to provide a solution to the problem.[158]

In *Knight* v. *Leamington Spa Courier Ltd*[159] the English Court of Appeal applied Cumming's decision. A printing machine had two buttons, one, an inching button, which caused the blanket rollers of the machine to revolve slowly and the other which caused the rollers to revolve at very high speed for normal printing operations. A press operator was injured while cleaning the rollers and using the inching button to rotate it. It was held that the machinery was not in motion or in use. The decision of the same court in *Mitchell* v. *W.S. Westin Ltd*[160] was the same. In order to rotate the collar of a lathe, a fitter switched it on and off quickly. It was held that the machinery was not in motion. In both cases the court seemed to have been influenced by the fact that the movements were not for any appreciable length of time. "The slow, sporadic rotation or intermittent movement of machinery intended to place it more advantageously for cleaning or repair is not normally motion or use within the section, whether it be produced by manpower or mechanical power."[161] In *Stanbrook* v. *Waterlow & Son Ltd,*[162] where the cylinder of a printing machine was being prepared for printing and in order to do so it was necessary to rotate it by an electric motor which brought it to a high speed within a matter of seconds and it was therefore necessary to switch the motor on and off very quickly, the same court held the machinery was in motion. Lord Denning M.R. drew a distinction between a thing which is being moved slowly and a thing which is in motion at a fast speed. Danckwerts L.J. decided on the broader base that there was no difference between the meaning of motion and movement. Diplock L.J. agreed with both of

[157] Ibid., p. 555.

[158] See per upjohn L.J. in *Knight* v *Leamington Spa Courier Ltd* [1961] 2 QB 253, 264. see also per Donovan L.J. at 265.

[159] [1961] 2 QB 253.

[160] [1965] 1 All ER 657.

[161] Per Holroyd Pearce L.J. in *Knight* v *Leamington Spa Courier Ltd* [1961] 2 QB 253, 263, see also per Sellers L.J. in *Mitchell* v *W.S. Westin Ltd,* [1965] 1 All ER 657, 662.

[162] [1964] 2 All ER 506.

them. In *Joy* v *News of the World,*[163] the court, ruled out slowness as the determining factor. There the proper movement of the machinery was a slow and continuous movement.

Dangerous part of machinery

Section 17, we have seen, applies in respect of every dangerous part of any machinery other than prime movers and transmission machinery. In applying the section the courts have had to determine the issues of what is dangerous part of machinery and, indeed, the meaning of machinery itself.

As long ago as 1897, Wills J. in *Hindle* v *Birtwistle*[164] formulated a test of what constitutes dangerous part of machinery and this test has been consistently applied ever since.[165] In the case, the occupier of a cotton factory was summoned for failure to fence the shuttles of his looms.[166] Shuttles occasionally flew out from the shuttle race in the process of weaving. The flying out of shuttles could be caused by the negligence of the weaver in charge of the machine or by reason of some foreign substance getting into the shuttle-race by accident or even by defect in the yarn. The recorder said that there could be liability only for machinery which was in itself dangerous in the ordinary course of careful working. In the Divisional Court, Wills J. disagreed with that interpretation and said such an interpretation would limit most materially the benefit of the statute. He said:[167]

> It seems to me that machinery or parts of machinery is and are dangerous if in the ordinary course of human affairs danger may be reasonably anticipated from the use of them without protection...In considering whether machinery is dangerous, the contingency of carelessness on the part of the workman in charge of it, and the frequency with which that contingency is likely to arise, are matters that must be taken into consideration. It is entirely a question of degree.

In *Walker* v. *Bletchley Flettons Ltd,*[168] Du Parcq J. said he entirely accepted the test thus formulated, which he explained, as meaning that in considering whether

[163] [1972] 13 KIR 57.
[164] [1897] 1 QB 192.
[165] Per Lord Edmund Davies in *Wearing* v. *Pirelli Ltd,* [1977] 1 All ER 339,344,345.
[166] S:5(3) Factory and Workshop Act 1878 as amended by S.6(2) Factory & Workshop Act, 1891.
[167] [1989] 1 QB 192,195-196.
[168] [1937] 1 ALL ER 170.

machinery is dangerous it must not be assumed that everybody will always be careful but rather, it must be assumed that somebody will sometimes be careless. In his own words he said; a part of machinery is dangerous if it is a possible cause of injury to anyone acting in a way in which a human being may be reasonably expected to act in circumstances which may be reasonably expected to occur.[169] The House of Lords endorsed this test of reasonable foresee ability in *Close* v. *Steel Co of Wales.*[170] Lord Guest, said machinery is dangerous if it is "a reasonably foreseeable cause of injury to anybody acting in a way in which a human being may be reasonably expected to act in circumstances which may be reasonably expected to occur."[171] It is clear that although the words are of Du Parcq. J. but the test is of Wills J. It is a question of fact in every case whether part of machinery is dangerous.[172]

However, in *Eaves* v. *Morris Motors Ltd,*[173] the English Court of Appeal, held that fencing is in respect of dangers arising in the course of the normal operation of the machinery and that it does not extend to dangers arising from abnormal or unusual behaviour of machinery. The reason for this seems to be that, as Wilmer L.J. said,[174] "no man could be expected to foresee and guard against the almost unlimited possibilities of danger that might arise from a machine going wrong or operating in a way that it was never designed to do." This view seems to have received the support of the House of Lords in *Midland & Low Moor Iron and Steel Co Ltd* v. *Cross.*[175] Lord Evershed said:[176]

> As it seems to me, the question whether it can properly be said that some parts of a piece of machinery is dangerous must depend upon considering whether such danger exists and arises from the normal operation of the machinery, that is, from the purposes of the mechanical work which the machine is specifically designed to achieve; and if a part of such machine becomes undoubtedly dangerous from such normal and projected operation, then it follows that, such part of the machine is a dangerous part within the meaning of section 14(1).

That is, our s.17(1).

---

[169] Ibid., 175.
[170] [1962] AC 367.
[171] Ibid., 412.
[172] *Carr* v. *Mercantile Produce Co Ltd* [1949] 2 KB 601.
[173] [1961] 2 QB 385.
[174] Ibid., 399.
[175] [1965] AC 343.
[176] Ibid., 367.

Lord Evershed approved the view of Holroyd Pearce in Eaves' case that where a moving part of machinery becomes dangerous from juxtaposition with its normal material, then it could be held to be dangerous part of machinery.[177] The House however, expressly reserved an opinion on whether danger arising from stationery part of a machine in juxtaposition with material or article is dangerous part of machinery.[178] In *F.E. Callow (Engineers) Ltd* v. *Johnson*,[179] the House decided affirmatively that juxtaposition of moving work-piece with a stationary machine could constitute dangerous part of machinery. Once it is accepted, said Lord Hailsham, that a nip is 'dangerous' within Section 14, it seems to be immaterial whether it is caused by two moving parts or by a moving part in juxtaposition with a stationary part.[180]

As to what machinery section 17 applies, the House of Lords has given two important decisions. In *Parvin* v. *Morton Machine Co Ltd*,[181] a dough-brake had been manufactured and assembled in the factory. An infant employee was asked to clean it and while doing so he was injured when his hand was dragged between the rollers of the machine. The House of Lords held that s.14(1) - that is our s.17(1) - does not apply to machines or machinery which are the products of the manufacturing processes carried on in the factory. Rather the section only applies to machinery which is part of the equipment of a factory. Lord Asquith said the "structure of sections 12, 13 and 14, to my mind, implies that their operation is wholly within the framework or ambit of machinery used as a productive agent, and does not extend to machinery emerging as a product."[182] However, in *Irwin* v. *White, Thomkins & Courage Ltd*[183] the House held that machinery which has been completely installed as part of factory equipment comes within the fencing provisions even though the machinery has not been put into use but provided it is intended to be so used. In *British Railways Board* v. *Liptrot*,[184] a more liberal interpretation was adopted by the House. The issue was whether a mobile crane is machinery. In *Cherry* v. *International Allys Ltd*,[185] the Court of Appeal had held that a Lister truck was not machinery partly on the ground that the section is not meant to deal with vehicles. The House held that

---

[177] And also the opinion of Lynskey J. in *Hoare* v. *M & W Grazebrook Ltd* [1957] 1 All ER 470.
[178] Lord Morris did not deal with this point.
[179] [1971] AC 335.
[180] Ibid., 351.
[181] [1952] AC 515.
[182] Ibid., 524-525; see SS 14,15, and 17 respectively; see also Lords Normand and Reid at 521, 523 respectively.
[183] [1964] 1 All ER 545.
[184] [1967] 2 All ER 1072.
[185] [1960] 3 All ER 264.

Cherry's case was wrongly decided and that the section applies to any dangerous part of machinery in any machine whether mobile or fixed provided it is part of the equipment of the factory. Viscount Dilhorne said:[186]

> While it would not be right to describe a vehicle as machinery, it may contain machinery, and if the vehicle forms part of the equipment of the factory, then, in my opinion, s.14 imposes an absolute obligation, subject to the proviso in that section, to fence securely every dangerous part of the machinery that it contains...I can see no valid reason for excluding any part of the equipment of a factory which contains machinery from the operation of the Act of 1961 on the ground that it is mobile or can be described as a vehicle.

Lord Hodson used much the same words and added that he found it difficult to see how a ropeway carrying buckets could be excluded from machinery as was done in *Quintas* v. *National Smelting Co Ltd.*[187] In that case the employer operated an overhead travelling cable-way, on each side of which ran a cable from which large buckets were suspended at intervals. The buckets carried ore or other materials from one end to the other and returned empty. The cable-way passed over the flat roof of a crushing plant building. The plaintiff an employee was standing on this roof close to an edge and directly under the cable-way when a bucket knocked him and he fell to the ground. The majority of the Court of Appeal held that the bucket and the rope-way were not one piece of machinery. But Wilmer L.J., dissenting, felt that rope-way, viewed as a whole could be properly described as machinery for use in the factory ancillary to the processes of manufacture. It should, therefore, have been securely fenced in accordance with section 17.

Construction and disposal of new machinery

In the case of any machinery in a factory, being a machine intended to be driven by mechanical power, every set-screw, bolt or key on any revolving shaft, spindle, wheel or pinion must be so sunk, encased or otherwise effectively guarded as to prevent danger and all spur and other toothed or friction gearing which does not require frequent adjustment while in motion must be completely encased unless it is so situated as to be safe as it would be if completely encased.[188] Any person who manufactures, assembles, sells or lets on hire, or

---

[186] [1967] 2 All ER 1072, 1078.
[187] [1960] 1 All ER 104.
[188] S.20(l).

who as an agent of the manufacturer, assembler, seller or hirer causes or procures to be sold or let on hire for use in a factory any machine intended to be driven by mechanical power which does not comply with these requirements commits an offence and is liable, on conviction, to a fine not exceeding five thousand naira.[189] The seller, however, does not owe a duty of care to the employees of the factory occupier who has bought a machine with an unencased gearing.[190] Thus an employee in the factory who is injured by such a machine as a result of the breach of these requirements cannot maintain a civil action against the seller.

The minister may by order published in the Gazette, extend these requirements to such other dangerous part of machinery or plant as may be specified in the order.[191]

Vessels containing dangerous liquids

Every fixed vessel, structure, sump or pit of which the edge is level with or less than ninety one centimetres above the adjoining ground or platform must, if it contains any scalding, corrosive or poisonous liquid, either be securely covered or be securely fenced to at least that height or where by reason of the nature of the work neither secure covering nor secure fencing to that height is practicable, all practicable steps must be taken by covering, fencing or other means to prevent any person from falling into the vessel, structure, sump or pit.[192] A warning notice in English and in such Nigerian languages as an inspector may direct, indicating the nature of the danger, must be marked on or attached to any of the plants or, if this is not reasonably practicable, be posted nearby.[193]

Self-acting machines

No traversing part of any self-acting machine and no material carried on it must, if the space over which it runs is a space over which any person is liable to pass, whether in the course of his employment or otherwise, be allowed on its outward or inward traverse to run within a distance of forty-six centimetres from any fixed structure not being part of the machine.[194] All practicable steps must be

189 S.20(2).
190 *Biddle* v. *Truvox Engineering Co Ltd & Greenwood & Batley Ltd* [1951] 2 ALL ER 835.
191 S.20(3).
192 S.21(l).
193 S.21(2).
194 S.22(1)

taken by instructions to the person in charge of the machine to ensure that no person employed shall be in the space between any traversing part of a self-acting spinning mule and any fixed part of the machine towards which the traversing part moves on the inward except when the machine is stopped with the traversing part on the outward run.[195]

Training and supervision of inexperienced workers

No person must be employed at any machine or in any process, being a machine or process liable to cause bodily injury, unless he has been fully instructed as to the dangers likely to arise in connection with it and the precautions to be observed and has received a sufficient training to work at the machine or in the process or is under adequate supervision by a person who has a thorough knowledge and experience of the machine or process.[196]

Hoists and lifts

Every hoist or lift must be of good mechanical construction, sound material and adequate strength, and be properly maintained.[197] The duty of the employer to ensure that every hoist or lift is of sound material is absolute.[198] In other words, there will be an infringement of the sub-section where a hoist or lift is not of sound material. In *Galashiels Gas Co Ltd* v. *O'Donnell,*[199] the House of Lords held that the duty imposed by the sub-section is an absolute and continuing one so that proof of any failure in the mechanism of a hoist or lift establishes a breach even though, it is impossible to anticipate the failure or to explain it afterwards and even though, all reasonable steps have been taken to provide a suitable hoist or lift and to maintain it properly. Similarly, the Court said in *Oldfield* v. *Reed & Smith Ltd,*[200] that it is no defence for an employer to prove either that there was no ascertainable cause for a failure in the working of the

---

[195] S.22(2).

[196] S.23.

[197] S.24(l); no lifting machine or appliance shall be deemed to be a hoist or lift unless it has a platform or cage the direction of movement of which is restricted by a guide or guides; s.24(9). A forklift truck is not a hoist or lift; *Oldfield* v. *Reed & Smith Ltd* [1972] 2 All ER 104; maintained means, maintained in an efficient state, in efficient working order, and in good repair; s.88 (1).

[198] *Whitehead* v. *James Scott & Co* [1949] 1 KB 358; see also *Payne* v. *Weldless Steel Tube Co Ltd* [1955] 3 All ER 297.

[199] [1949] AC 275.

[200] *Supra.*

machine or that the failure occurred despite an efficient system of routine inspection and maintenance.

Every hoist or lift must be thoroughly examined at least once in every period of six months by a person approved for the purpose by the Director of Factories by a certificate in writing; and a report of the result of every such examination in the prescribed form and containing the prescribed particulars must be signed by the person making the examination and must, within fourteen days, be filed with the Director of Factories and also be entered in or attached to the general register.[201]

Every hoistway or liftway must be efficiently protected by a substantial enclosure fitted with gates, being such an enclosure as to prevent, when the gates are shut, any person falling down the way or coming into contract with any moving part of the hoist or lift.[202] Any such gate must be fitted with efficient interlocking or other devices to secure that the gate cannot be opened except when the cage or platform is at the landing and that the cage or platform cannot be moved away from the landing until the gate is closed.[203] However, in the case of a hoist or lift not connected with mechanical power, it is sufficient if the gate is kept closed and fastened except when the cage or platform is at rest at the landing.[204] Every hoist or lift and every enclosure must be so constructed as to prevent any part of any person or any goods carried in the hoist or lift from being trapped between any part of the hoist or lift and any fixed structure or between the counter-balance weight and any other moving part of the hoist or lift.[205]

The following additional requirements apply to all hoists and lifts used for carrying persons, whether together with goods or otherwise, except a hoist or lift which is not connected with mechanical power.[206] Efficient automatic devices must be provided and maintained to prevent the cage or platform over-running. Every cage must, on each side from which access is afforded to landing, be fitted with a gate, and in connection with every such gate efficient devices must be provided to secure that, when persons or goods are in the cage, the cage cannot be raised or lowered unless the cage is closed, and will come to rest when the gate is opened. When the platform or cage is suspended by rope or chain, there must be at least two ropes or chains separately connected with the platform or cage, each rope or chain and its attachments being capable of carrying the whole

---

[201] S.24(2).

[202] S.24(3); this requirement is absolute - see *Blackeley* v. *C & H Clothing Co* [1958] 1 ALL ER 297.

[203] S.24(4).

[204] S.24(4) proviso.

[205] S.24(5).

[206] S.24(7), (8).

weight of the platform or cage and its maximum working load, and efficient devices must be provided and maintained which will support the platform or cage with its maximum working load in the event of a breakage of the ropes or chains or any other attachments.

If it is shown to the satisfaction of the Director of Factories that it would be unreasonable in the special circumstances of the case to enforce any of the provisions on hoists and lifts in respect of any class or description of hoist, lift, hoistway or liftway, he may, by notice published in the Gazette, except from such requirement hoists, lifts, hoistways or liftways of that class or description and any such exception may be unqualified or may be subject to such conditions as may be contained in the notice.[207]

Chains, ropes and lifting tackle

The following provisions must be complied with as respects every chain, rope or lifting tackle used for the purpose of raising or lowering persons, goods or materials.[208] No chain, rope or lifting tackle must be used unless it is of good construction, sound material, adequate strength and free from patent defect.[209] A table showing the safe working loads of every kind and size of chain, ropes or lifting tackle in use, and, in the case of a multiple sling, the safe working load at different angles of the legs, must be prominently displayed on the premises but, however, where in relation to any lifting tackle the safe working load, or, in the case of a multiple sling, the safe working load at different angles of the legs, is plainly marked upon it, this provision does not apply.[210] No chain, rope or lifting tackle must be used for any load exceeding the safe working load as shown by the table or marked upon it.[211] All chains, ropes and lifting tackle in use must be thoroughly examined at least once in every period of six months, or, at such greater intervals as the Director of Factories may permit in any particular case, by a person approved for that purpose by the Director of Factories by certificate in writing.[212] No chain, rope or lifting tackle must be taken into use in any factory for the first time in that factory unless it has been tested and thoroughly examined by a person approved by the Director of Factories for that purpose and

[207] S.24(10).
[208] S.25(l); lifting tackle means chain slings, rope slings, rings, hooks, shackles and swivels; s.25(2).
[209] S.25(l)(a).
[210] S.25(l)(b).
[211] S.25(l)(c).
[212] S.25(l)(d).

a certificate of such a test and examination has been obtained and a report for each chain, rope, or lifting tackle in the prescribed form must be filed with the Director of Factories and the certificate must be kept available for inspection.[213] Every chain and lifting tackle, except a rope sling, must, unless of a class or description exempted by the Director of Factories by notice published in the Gazette, be annealed at least once in every fourteen months, or, in the case of chains or slings of half-inch bar or smaller, or chains used in connection with molten metal or molten slag, in every six months but chains and lifting tackles not in regular use need be annealed only when necessary.[214]

Cranes and other lifting machines

All parts and working gear, whether fixed or movable, including the anchorage and fixing appliances of every lifting machine, must be of good construction, sound material, adequate strength and free from patent defect, and must be properly maintained.[215] All such parts and gear must be thoroughly examined at least once in every period of fourteen months and also, after every substantial alteration or repair, by a person approved for that purpose by the Director of Factories by certificate in writing.[216] No lifting machine must be taken into use in any factory for the first time in that factory unless it has been tested and all parts and working gear of the machine, whether fixed or movable, including the anchorage and fixing appliances, have been thoroughly examined by a person approved by the Director of Factories for that purpose. And the certificate of such a test and examination specifying the safe working load or loads of the machines and signed by the person making the test and examination, has been obtained and a report for each crane or lifting machine in the prescribed form had been filed with the Director of Factories and the certificate kept available for inspection.[217]

All rails on which a travelling crane moves and every track on which the carriage of a transporter or runway moves, must be of proper size and adequate

---

[213] S.25(l)(e).
[214] S.25(l)(f).
[215] S.26(l); lifting machine means a crane, crab, winch, teagle, pulley block, gin wheel, transporter or runway; S.26(9); maintained means maintained in an efficient state, in efficient working order, and in good repair; S.88(l).
[216] S.26(2).
[217] S.26(3).

strength, and have an even running surface, and such rails or track must be properly laid, adequately supported or suspended and properly maintained.[218]

The safe working load or loads of every lifting machine must be plainly marked on it except that in the case of a jib crane so constructed that the safe working load may be varied by the raising or lowering of the jib, there must be attached either an automatic indicator of safe working loads or a table indicating the safe working loads at corresponding inclinations of the jib or corresponding radii of the load.[219] No lifting machine must, except for the purpose of a test, be loaded beyond the safe working load as marked or indicated on it.[220]

If any person is employed or working on or near the wheel track of a self-propelled overhead crane, in any place where he would be liable to be struck by the crane, effective measures must be taken to ensure that the crane does not approach within four metres of that place.[221] A lifting machine must not be operated except by a person trained and competent to operate that machine, except that it is permissible for such machine to be operated by a person who is under the direct supervision of a qualified person for the purpose of training; and no person under eighteen years of age must be employed to operate any lifting machine driven by mechanical power to give signals to the operator of any such machine.[222]

A register must be kept in every factory with respect to all chains, ropes or lifting tackle and with respect to all lifting machines.[223] The register must set out the following particulars which are contained in schedule 3 to the Act - the name and occupier of the factory, the address and location of the factory, the distinguishing number or mark and description sufficient to identity the chain, rope, or lifting tackle, or the lifting machine, and the date when the chain, rope or lifting tackle or the lifting machine was taken into use in the factory. Other particulars include the date of each examination required to be made with respect to the chain, rope or lifting tackle or the lifting machine and the name of the person by whom it was carried out, particulars of any defect found at any such examination and affecting the safe working load, and of the steps taken to remedy such defect, the date and number of the certificate relating to any examination together with the name and address of the person who issued the

---

[218] S.26(4).
[219] S.26(5).
[220] S.26(6).
[221] S.26(7).
[222] S.26(8).
[223] S.27.

certificate and, in the case of chains and lifting tackle, the dates of annealing or other treatment.

We have seen that the House of Lords held in *British Railway Board* v. *Liptrot*[224] that sections 24 to 26 inclusive are not necessarily complete codes in themselves. The court thought, for example, that the fencing provision in section 17 with respect to dangerous parts of machinery applies to hoist, lifts, chains, ropes, lifting tackle and cranes dealt with in these sections.

Safe means of access and safe place of employment

All floors, steps, stairs, passages, gangways and other parts of a structure or building used as a factory must be of sound construction and properly maintained and kept safe at all times, and before the construction of any factory the building plans and such other documents as the Director of Factories may require, must be submitted to him for approval not less than six months before the commencement of such construction.[225] Maintained means maintained in efficient state, efficient working order and in good repair.[226] It has been held that the test of sound construction is not that it should be so constructed as to be sufficient to withstand some stress which would not occur during normal use but that sound construction means that the floor must be of such sound construction and so maintained as to be fit to be used for the purpose for which the factory is intended to be used.[227] In *Latimer* v. *A.E.C. Ltd*,[228] the House of Lords held that the requirement of the definition of maintained, that is, that the floor be maintained in good repair and in an efficient state, does not include the elimination of some matter which is temporarily superimposed on the floor and that such maintenance is confined to the floor itself.[229] Lord Reid said:[230] "It would be going a long way to say that a floor, perfectly good in itself, ceases to be in an efficient state whenever there is something on it which gives rise to danger."

---

[224] [1967] 2 All ER 1072.
[225] S.28(l).
[226] S.88(l).
[227] *Mayne* v. *Johnstone & Cumbers Ltd*, [1947] 2 ALL ER 159.
[228] [1953] AC 643.
[229] The House felt that the requirement to maintain in efficient working order is inapplicable to a floor.
[230] Ibid., 657.

All openings in floors must be securely fenced, except in so far as the nature of the work renders such fencing impracticable.[231] In *Sanders* v. *F.H. Lloyd & Co Ltd*[232] the court said although there is no doubt that there is some point at which a hole or depression in the floor becomes so small that it cannot, in ordinary language, be called an opening, it held that an opening need not be a hole of sufficient size and depth for someone to fall into or something that could be protected by fencing in the nature of railings. The court also held that fencing includes covering. "I hold that the word fenced...includes, *inter alia*, railing off, covering, or otherwise protecting the opening against the possibility of someone falling into it."[233] The onus is on the employer to show that the nature of the work carried on renders fencing impracticable.[234] And Lord Parker C.J. has said[235] that impracticable is a strong word and that it means not possible or not feasible:

> At any rate, it means something very much more than not reasonably practicable...It seems to me that practicable must impose a stricter standard than reasonably practicable. It may be that certain matters one would take into consideration if the words were reasonably practicable such matters as the cost and the like have to be eliminated.[236]

There must, so far as is reasonably practicable, be provided and maintained in every factory safe means of access to every place at which any person has to be or work.[237] In *Levesley* v. *Thomas Firth and John Brown Ltd*,[238] the English Court of Appeal, applying Latimer's case, held that a temporary and transient obstruction of a passage way was not failure to maintain a safe means of access provided by the employer. In *McCarthy* v. *Coldair Ltd*,[239] the same court held that a ladder is a means of access and also that since the duty to provide is qualified by the words "so far as is reasonably practicable," it is not an absolute duty. The "words show that the duty is not absolute but depends on what is reasonably practicable having regard to the degree of risk and the steps necessary to eliminate the risk."[240] In this case an electrician was going up a

---

231 S.28(2).
232 [1982] 1 ICR 360.
233 Ibid., 364 per Drake J.
234 *Nimmo* v. *Alexander Cowan & Sons Ltd* [1968] AC 107.
235 *Moorcroft* v. *Thomas Powles & Son Ltd* [1962] 1 WLR 1447, 1454.
236 Ibid.,
237 S.28(3).
238 [1953] 2 ALL ER 866.
239 (1951) 2 TLR 1226.
240 Per Denning L.J. Ibid., 1228.

ladder to effect some repair when the ladder slipped and he fell and sustained injury. The floor on which the ladder was standing was smooth and no one was put or anything done to steady it. The court held the employer liable for failure to take the reasonably practicable step of steadying the ladder. But in *Farquhar* v. *Chance Brothers Ltd*,[241] where a mill-wright who was trying to get to the top of a platform otherwise than by obtaining a ladder from a nearby store fell and died it was held that the employers had provided a reasonably safe means of access.

For every staircase in a building or which affords a means of exit from a building, a substantial hand-rail must be provided and maintained. If the staircase has an open side it must be provided on that side and where it has two open sides such hand-rail must be provided and maintained on both sides. Any open side of a staircase must also be guarded by the provision and maintenance of a lower rail or other effective means.[242]

All ladders must be soundly constructed and properly maintained.[243] The duty to properly maintain, is to keep all ladders in an efficient state, efficient working order and in good repair and it is an absolute one.[244]

Sufficient clear and unobstructed space must be maintained at every machine while in motion to enable the work to be carried on without unnecessary risk.[245]

Where any person is to work at a place from where he will be liable to fall a distance of more than two metres, then, unless the place is one which affords secure foothold and, where necessary, secure hand-hold, means must be provided, so far as is reasonably practicable, by fencing or otherwise for ensuring his safety.[246] In *Wigley* v. *British Vinegars Ltd*,[247] the House of Lords held that the sub-section involves two separate questions; first, does the place afford secure foothold, and, where necessary, secure handhold and secondly, if it does not, is it reasonably practicable to provide means, fencing or other means, for ensuring safety? A ladder is a place within the sub-section[248] and provision of safety belt is means of ensuring safety within the sub-section.[249] Such means can, of course, also be fencing.

---

241 (1951) 2 TLR 666.
242 S.28(4).
243 S.28(5).
244 *Cole* v. *Blackstone & Co Ltd*, (1943) 59 TLR 374.
245 S.28(6).
246 S.28(7).
247 [1964] AC 307.
248 *Wigley* v. *British Vinegars Ltd* [1964] AC 307.
249 *McWilliams* v. *Sir William Arrol & Co Ltd*, (1961) SLT 265.

Every single opening or similar doorway used for hoisting or lowering goods or materials, whether by mechanical power or otherwise, must be securely fenced and must be provided with a secure hand-hold on each side and be properly maintained and must, except when the hoisting or lowering of goods or materials is being carried on at the opening or doorway, be kept in position.[250]

Dangerous fumes

Where work has to be done inside any chamber, tank, vat, pit or other confined place in which dangerous fumes[251] are likely to be present, the Director of Factories must be notified in writing, in the prescribed form, before the commencement of work and the following requirements must be met:[252]

1. the confined space must be provided with adequate means of egress for persons entering or working there; [253]
2. suitable breathing apparatus and suitable reviving apparatus and suitable belts and ropes must be provided and maintained so as to be readily accessible and a sufficient number of the persons employed in the factory must be trained and practised in the use of such apparatus and in the method of restoring respiration;[254]
3. no person must enter the confined space for any purpose unless (i) all practicable steps have been taken to remove any fumes which may be present and to prevent any ingress of fumes but, unless it has been ascertained by a suitable test that the space is free from dangerous fumes, the person entering must wear a belt to which there is securely attached a rope of which the free end is held by a person outside; or (ii) the person entering has worn a suitable breathing apparatus.[255]

Without prejudice to these requirements, a person must not enter or remain in any chamber, tank, vat, pit, pipe, flue or similar space for any purpose until it has been sufficiently cooled by ventilation or otherwise to make work safe and either

---

[250] S.28(8).
[251] Fume includes gas or vapour s.88(l)
[252] S.29(l)(a).
[253] S. 29 (1) (b) .
[254] S.29(1)(d) and (e).
[255] S. 29 (1) (c) .

he is ensured of a supply of air adequate for respiration and to render harmless any fumes or he is wearing suitable breathing apparatus.[256]

Explosive or inflammable dust, gas, vapour or substance

Where, in connection with any grinding, sieving or other process giving rise to dust, gas or vapour there may escape into any workroom dust, gas or vapour of such a character and to such an extent as to be liable to explode on ignition, all practicable steps must be taken to prevent such an explosion by enclosure of any plant used in the process, and by removal or prevention of accumulation of the dust, gas or vapour and by exclusion or effective enclosure of possible sources of ignition.[257]

Where there is present in any plant used in any such process as grinding, sieving or other process giving rise to dust, gas or vapour, of such a character and to such an extent as to be liable to explode on ignition, then, unless the plant is so constructed as to withstand the pressure likely to be produced by any such explosion, all practicable steps must be taken to restrict the spread and effects of such an explosion by the provision, in connection with the plant, of chokes, baffles and vents or other equally effective appliances.[258] No plant, tank or vessel which contains or has contained any explosive or inflammable substance must be subjected to any welding, brazing or soldering operation or to any cutting operation which involves the application of heat, until all practicable steps have been taken to remove the substance and any fumes arising there from or to render them non-explosive or non-inflammable. And if any plant, tank or vessel has been subjected to any of the above operation no explosive or inflammable substance must be allowed to enter the plant, tank or vessel until the metal has cooled sufficiently to prevent any risk of igniting the substance.[259]

In *Haigh* v. *Charles W. Ireland Ltd,*[260] the House of Lords had opportunity to construe the word plant in this sub-section. The employers, who carried on business as engineers and metal merchants, bought some scrap metal which contained an old safe. The safe was locked and its key missing. The plaintiff employee was asked to cut the safe open with an oxyacetylene cutter. While doing so there was an explosion which caused the loss of the employee's left leg

---

256 S.29(2).
257 S.30(l).
258 S.30(2).
259 S.30(3).
260 [1973] 3 All ER 1137.

and part of his left hand. Unknown to everyone the safe contained gelignite. In an action for breach of s. 31(4) Factories Act 1961 that is s.30(3) Factories Act it was held by the House that the safe was not a plant within the sub-section or even within the section. Plant, said the House, means plant which is in the factory as part of the apparatus for use in carrying on the industrial process undertaken on the premises. It is not plant if it is there for the purpose of being subjected to an industrial process - if it is there for the purpose of being subjected to an industrial process, as was the safe, it is an article.

The Director of Factories may by certificate in writing, grant, subject to any conditions specified in the certificate, exemption from compliance with any of the requirements of sub-section (3) where he is satisfied that compliance is unnecessary or impracticable.[261]

Steam boilers

A steam boiler means any closed vessel in which, for any purpose, steam is generated under pressure greater than atmospheric pressure and includes any economizer used to heat water being fed to any such vessel, and any superheater used for heating steam.[262]

Every steam boiler and all its fittings and attachments must be of good construction, sound material, adequate strength and free from patent defect and must be properly maintained.[263] By definition maintained means maintained in an efficient state, in efficient working order, and in good repair.[264]

Every steam boiler, whether separate or one of a range, must have attached to it: (i) a suitable safety valve,[265] separate from and incapable of being isolated by any stop-valve, which must be so adjusted as to prevent the boiler being worked at a pressure greater than the maximum permissible working pressure[266] and must be fixed directly to, or as close as practicable to, the boiler; (ii) a suitable stop-

---

[261] S. 30(4).

[262] S. 88(1); the provisions on steam boilers in s.31 do not apply to the boiler of any locomotive used on any railway or the boiler of a ship; s. 31(18).

[263] S.31(l).

[264] S.88(l).

[265] A lever valve is not a suitable safety valve unless the weight is secured on the lever in the correct position; s.31(3).

[266] By s.31(17) maximum permissible working pressure means, in the case of a new steam boiler, that specified in the certificate obtained from an authorized boiler inspector under s.31(13) and, in the case of a steam boiler which has been examined as provided by this section, that specified in the report of the last examination under s.31(11).

valve, connecting the boiler to the steam pipe which must be suitably lagged at all times; (iii) a correct steam pressure gauge, connected to the steam space and easily visible to the boiler attendant,[267] which must indicate the pressure of steam in the boiler in kilograms per square centimetre and have marked upon it, in a distinctive colour, the maximum permissible working pressure;[268] (iv) at least one water gauge of transparent material or other type approved by the Director of Factories, to show the water level in the boiler, and, if the gauge is of the glass tubular type and the working pressure in the boiler normally exceeds three kilograms per square centimetre, the gauge must be provided with an efficient guard but not so as to obstruct the reading of the gauge; and (v) where it is one or two or more boilers, a plate bearing distinctive number which must be easily visible.[269] However, the attachments in (ii) do not apply with respect to economizer and attachments in (iii) and (iv) do not apply to superheaters.[270] Every steam boiler whether separate or one of a range must also be provided with means for attaching a test pressure gauge and a suitable fusible plug or an efficient low-water alarm device but these do not apply with respect to either economizers or superheaters.[271]

No person must enter or be in any steam boiler which is one of a range of two or more steam boilers unless either all inlets through which steam or hot water might otherwise enter the boiler from any other part of the range are disconnected from that part or all valves or taps controlling such entry are closed and securely locked and, where the boiler has a blow-off pipe in connection with one or more other boilers or delivering into a common blow-off vessel or sump, the blow-off valve or tap on each such boiler is so constructed that it can only be opened by a key which cannot be removed until the valve or tap is closed and is the only key in use for that set of blow-off valves or taps.[272] No work must be permitted in any boiler-furnace until it has been sufficiently cooled by ventilation or otherwise to make work safe for the person employed and the Director of Factories has been notified.[273]

Every steam boiler and all its fittings and attachments must be thoroughly examined by an authorized boiler inspector at least once in every period of

---

[267] Every steam boiler attendant must be properly instructed as to his duties; s.31(4).
[268] See note 266.
[269] S.31(2)(a).
[270] S.31(2) proviso.
[271] S.31(2)(b) and (c).
[272] S.31(5).
[273] S.31(6).

fourteen months and also after any extensive repairs.[274] However, the person making an examination may specify in writing a period exceeding fourteen months but not exceeding eighteen months within which the next examination is to be made.[275] Any examination must consist, in the first place, of an examination of the boiler when it is cold and the interior and exterior have been prepared in the prescribed manner and, secondly, except in the case of an economizer or superheater, of an examination when it is under normal steam pressure.[276] The examination under steam pressure must be made as soon as possible after the examination when the boiler was cold and the person making the examination must ensure that the safety valve is so adjusted as to prevent the boiler being worked at a pressure greater than the maximum permissible working pressure.[277] A report of the result of every such examination, in the prescribed form and containing the prescribed particulars, including particulars of the maximum permissible working pressure, and signed by the person making the examination must, as soon as practicable and in any case, within twenty-eight days of the completion of the examination, be entered in or attached to the general register and a certified true copy of the report must be filed with the Director of Factories.[278]

No steam boiler which has previously been used must be taken into use in any factory for the first time in that factory until it has been examined and reported on in accordance with all the provisions on examination of boilers.[279] Similarly, no new steam boiler must be taken into use in any factory unless there has been obtained from an authorized boiler inspector a certificate specifying the maximum permissible working pressure of the steam boiler, stating the nature of the tests to which the steam boiler and fitting have been submitted, and the steam boiler is so marked as to enable it to be identified as the boiler to which the certificate so obtained relates and the certificate is kept available for inspection and a certified true copy is forthwith sent to the Director of Factories.[280]

Where the report of any examination specifies conditions for securing the safe working of a steam boiler, the boiler must not be used except in accordance

---

[274] S.31(17); authorized boiler inspector means any person, whether or not in the civil service of the Federation or of a State, who is authorized by the Director of Factories, by certificate in writing, to carry out examination of steam boilers in accordance with and for the purposes of the section and to issue the certificate referred to in sub-section 13 of this section; s.31(17).

[275] S.31(8).

[276] S.31(9).

[277] S.31(10).

[278] S.31(11).

[279] S.31(12).

[280] S.31(13).

with those conditions.[281] The person making the report of any examination must, within twenty-eight days of the completion of the examination, send to the inspector of the district, a certified true copy of the report in every case where the maximum permissible working pressure is reduced or the examination shows that the boiler cannot continue to be used with safety unless certain repairs are carried out immediately or within a specified time.[282] For the purposes of reports of examinations, the examination of a boiler when it is cold and its examination when it is under steam pressure must be treated as separate cases.[283]

Steam receivers and steam containers

A steam receiver is any vessel or apparatus used for containing steam under pressure greater than atmospheric pressure other than a steam boiler, steam container, a steam pipe or coil or a part of a prime mover.[284] Every steam receiver and all its fittings must be of good construction, sound material, adequate strength and free from patent defect and must be properly maintained.[285] Every steam receiver which is not so constructed and maintained as to withstand with safety the maximum permissible working pressure[286] of the boiler or the maximum pressure which can be obtained in the pipe connecting the receiver with any other source of supply must be fitted with:

i) a suitable reducing valve or other suitable automatic appliance to prevent the safe working pressure of the receiver being exceeded;
ii) a suitable safety valve so adjusted as to permit the steam to escape as soon as the working pressure is exceeded or a suitable appliance for cutting off automatically the supply of steam as soon as the safe working pressure is exceeded;
iii) a correct steam pressure gauge which must indicate the pressure of steam in the receiver in kilogram per square centimetre;
iv) a suitable stop-valve; and

---

281 S.31(14).
282 S.31(15).
283 S.31(16).
284 S.32(10); see above for meaning of prime mover and steam boiler and below for meaning of steam container; steam pipe or coil is not defined.
285 S.32(l).
286 For meaning of maximum permissible working pressure see note 266; s.32(10).

v) except where only one steam receiver is in use, a plate bearing a distinctive number which must be easily visible.[287]

The safety valve and pressure gauge must be fitted either on the steam receiver or on the supply pipe between the receiver and the reducing valve or other appliance to prevent the safe working pressure being exceeded.[288]

Every steam receiver and all its fittings must be thoroughly examined by an authorized boiler inspector,[289] so far as the construction of the receiver permits, at least once in every period of twenty six months.[290] A report of the result of every such examination in the prescribed form and containing the prescribed particulars, including particulars of the safe working pressure, and signed by the person making the examination, must be entered in or attached to the general register and a certified true copy of the report must be filed with the Director of Factories.[291]

No steam receiver which has previously been used must be taken into use in any factory for the first time in that factory until it has been examined and reported upon in accordance with the above provisions.[292] No new steam receiver must be taken into use in any factory unless (i) there has been obtained from the manufacturer of the steam receiver or from an authorized boiler inspector, a certificate specifying the maximum permissible working pressure[293] of the steam receiver and stating the nature of the tests to which the steam receiver and fittings have been subjected; (ii) the steam receiver is so marked as to enable it to be identified as the steam receiver to which the certificate relates;

---

[287] S. 32(2).

[288] S.32(3); for the purposes of this sub-section and sub-section two except paragraph (v) of sub-section two any set of receivers supplied with steam through a single pipe and forming part of a single machine may be treated as one receiver, and except for paragraph (iv) and (v) of sub-section 2 any other set of receivers supplied with steam through a single pipe may be treated as one receiver provided that in either case this does not apply unless the reducing valve or other appliance to prevent the safe working pressure being exceeded is fitted on the single pipe; s.32(4). Safe working pressure means, in the case of a new steam receiver, that specified in the certificate obtained from the manufacturer or an authorized boiler inspector and, in the case of a steam receiver which has been examined in accordance with the statutory provisions, that specified in the report of the last examination; s.32(10).

[289] Authorized boiler inspector means any person, whether or not in the civil service of the Federation or of a State, who is authorized by the Director of Factories by certificate in writing to carry out examination of steam receivers and issue a certificate; s.32(10).

[290] S.32(5).

[291] S.32(6).

[292] S.32(7).

[293] For meaning of maximum permissible working pressure see note 266.

and (iii) the certificate is kept available for inspection and a certified true copy is sent forthwith to the Director of Factories.[294]

Every steam container must be so maintained as to secure that the outlet is at all times kept open and free from obstruction.[295] A steam container is any vessel, other than a steam pipe or coil, constructed with a permanent outlet into the atmosphere or into a space where the pressure does not exceed atmospheric pressure and through which steam is passed at atmospheric pressure or at approximately that pressure, for the purpose of heating, boiling, drying, evaporating or other similar purpose.[296]

Air receivers

An air receiver means any vessel, other than a pipe or coil or an accessory, fitting or part of a compressor, for containing compressed air and connected with an air compressing plant or any fixed vessel for containing compressed air or compressed exhaust gases and used for the purpose of starting an internal combustion engine.[297]

Every air receiver must have marked upon it, so as to be plainly visible, the safe working pressure[298] and, in the case of a receiver connected with an air compressing plant, either be so constructed as to withstand, with safety, the maximum pressure which can be obtained in the compressor, or be fitted with a suitable reducing valve or other suitable appliance to prevent the safe working pressure of the receiver being exceeded.[299] Every air receiver must be fitted with a suitable safety valve so adjusted as to permit the air to escape as soon as the safe working pressure is exceeded and with a correct pressure gauge indicating the pressure in the receiver in kilogrammes per square centimetre.[300] However, for this purpose, any set of air receivers supplied with air through a single pipe may be treated as one receiver but, where it is required that a suitable reducing valve or other suitable appliance to prevent the safe working pressure[301] being

---

[294] S.32(8).
[295] S.32(9).
[296] S.32(10).
[297] S.33(6).
[298] Safe working pressure means the pressure specified in the report of the last examination carried out; s.33(6).
[299] S.33(1)(a) and (b).
[300] S.33(1)(c) and (d).
[301] See note 298.

exceeded be fitted, such set of air receivers cannot be treated as one receiver unless the valve or appliance is fitted on the single pipe.[302]

Every air receiver must also be fitted with a suitable appliance for draining the receiver and be provided with a suitable manhole, handhole or other means which will allow the interior to be thoroughly cleaned and, in case where more than one receiver is in use in the factory, bear a distinguishing mark which must be easily visible.[303]

Every air receiver and its fittings must be of sound construction and properly maintained.[304] Every air receiver must be thoroughly cleaned and examined at least once in every period of twenty six months provided that, in the case of a receiver of solid drawn construction, the person making any such examination may specify in writing a period exceeding twenty six months but not exceeding four years within which the next examination is to be made and, if it is so constructed that the internal surface cannot be thoroughly examined a suitable hydraulic test of the receiver must be carried out in lieu of internal examination.[305] Every examination and test must be carried out by an approved person[306] and a report signed by the person making the examination or test, of the result of every such examination and test, in the prescribed form and containing the prescribed particulars, including particulars of the safe working pressure, must be entered in or attached to the general register and certified true copies of the report and certificate must be filed with the Director of Factories.[307]

The Director of Factories may, by notice published in the Gazette, except from any of the provision of sections 31, 32 and 33 any class or type of steam boiler, steam receiver, steam container or air receiver to which he is satisfied that such provisions cannot reasonably be applied and any such exception may be unqualified or may be subject to such conditions as may be contained in the notice.[308]

---

[302] S.33(2).

[303] S.33(l)(e), (f) and (g).

[304] S.33(3); maintained, of course, means maintained in an efficient state, in efficient working order and in good repair; s.88.(l).

[305] S.33(4).

[306] Approved person means any person, whether or not in the civil service of the Federation or of a State, who is approved by the Director of Factories by certificate in writing for the purpose of carrying out examinations and tests of air receivers; s.33(6).

[307] S.33(5); the provisions of s.33 do not apply to any air receiver forming part of the plant, machinery or equipment of any ship or to any air receiver on any locomotive, carriage, wagon or other rolling stock used on any railway for the haulage of goods or passengers; s.33(7).

[308] S.34.

Prevention of fire

In every factory, there must be correctly installed in appropriate places, effective means of detecting fire, and such means must be provided and maintained so as to be readily accessible, in the case of a manual device, for alerting occupants therein of the occurrence of a fire, and for extinguishing the same, which means must be adequate, suitable and approved by the Director of Factories having regard to the circumstances of each factory.[309]

All stocks of highly inflammable substances must be kept either in a fire-resisting store or in a safe place outside any building provided that no such store must be so situated as to endanger the means of escape from the factory or from any part of it in the event of a fire occurring in the store.[310] Every owner or occupier of a factory must ensure that persons employed in the factory are adequately trained to enable them operate the extinguishing apparatus provided in the factory.[311]

The Director of Factories may impose such conditions as he may choose in connection with any store or place used for the storage of highly inflammable substances and the training of persons employed in the factory in the operation of any extinguishing apparatus in the factory.[312]

Safety in case of fire

Every factory must be provided with adequate means of escape in case of fire for the persons employed in the factory having regard to the circumstances of each case.[313] All such means of escape must be properly maintained and kept free from obstruction.[314]

The contents of any room in which persons are employed must be so arranged or disposed that there is a free passage for all persons in the room to escape in case of fire.[315] While any person is within a factory for the purpose of employment or meals, the doors of the factory and of any room therein in which the person is and any doors which afford a means of exit for persons employed

309 S.35(l).
310 S.35(2).
311 S.35(3).
312 S.35(4).
313 S.36(1).
314 S.36(2).
315 S.36(3).

in the factory from any building or from any enclosure in which the factory is situated, must not be locked or fastened in such manner that they cannot be easily and immediately opened from the inside.[316] All doors affording a means of exit from a factory for the persons in the factory must, except in the case of sliding doors, open outwards.[317]

Every hoistway or liftway inside a building must be completely enclosed with fire-resisting materials and all means of access to the hoist or lift must be fitted with doors of fire-resisting materials but such hoistway or liftway must be enclosed at the top only by some materials easily broken by fire or be provided with a vent at the top.[318] Every window, door or exit affording means of escape in case of fire or giving access thereto, other than the means of exit in ordinary use, must be distinctively and conspicuously marked by a notice printed in red letters of an adequate size and all such notices must be in such form and in English and in such Nigerian languages as an inspector may direct.[319] Effective steps must be taken in every factory to ensure that all the persons employed are familiar with the means of escape in case of fire and the routine to be followed in such a case.[320]

Improvement and prohibition notices

If any inspector is satisfied that any part of the way, work, machinery or plant used in a factory is in such a condition or is so constructed or placed that it is likely to cause bodily injury[321] or that any process or work is carried on or any thing is or has been done in any factory in such a manner as to constitute a risk of bodily injury he must issue an improvement notice stating clearly the danger complained of and requiring the occupier of the factory to take such steps as may be specified in the notice to remedy the danger.[322]

Where an inspector is satisfied that any factory or part of a factory, is in such a condition or is so constructed or placed that any process or work carried on therein cannot be so carried on without undue risk to the safety and health of persons employed there, the inspector must, by notice, prohibit the use for the purpose of that process or work.[323] The notice may prohibit the carrying on of

[316] S.36(4).
[317] S.36(5).
[318] S.36(6).
[319] S. 36(7)
[320] S. 36(8)
[321] Bodily injury includes injury to health; s. 88(1).
[322] S. 37
[323] S.38(l)

any process or work whether indefinitely or until such steps as may be specified in the notice have been taken to enable the process or work concerned to be carried on with due regard to the safety and health of persons employed there and the notice may be revoked on the application of the occupier or owner of the factory after rectifying all the defects contained in the notice to enable the process or work to be carried on with due regard to the safety and health of persons employed there.[324]

Any person aggrieved by any notice - either of improvement or prohibition may appeal against such notice, at first instance, to the minister and from his decision to the Federal High Court.[325]

General provisions on welfare

The general provisions on welfare are contained in Part Four of the Act.[326]

Drinking water

An adequate supply of drinking water must be provided and maintained at suitable points conveniently accessible to all persons employed.[327] A supply of drinking water which is not laid on must be contained in suitable vessel and must be renewed at least daily and all practicable steps must be taken to preserve the water and vessels from contamination; and a drinking water supply, whether laid or not, must, in such cases as an inspector may direct, be clearly indicated by a notice in English and in such Nigerian languages as the inspector may require.[328] A supply of drinking water must not be used for the purpose of washing up and a supply of water for washing up must not be used as drinking water.[329] The location of drinking water must be set apart from the location of water for washing up.[330] There must be provided and maintained for the use of all persons employed adequate and suitable facilities for washing, which must be conveniently accessible and must be kept in clean and orderly condition.[331] However, the Director of Factories may, by certificate in writing, except from any of the requirements for washing facilities where, by reason of the difficulty

---

[324] S. 38(2).
[325] S. 39.
[326] See chapter 4 for possibility of civil action.
[327] S. 40(1)
[328] S. 40(2)
[329] S. 40(3)
[330] S. 40(4)
[331] S. 41(1)

of obtaining an adequate supply of water or the fact that accommodation is restricted and adequate and suitable washing facilities are otherwise conveniently available or such other special circumstances as may be specified in the certificate, the application of the requirement would in his opinion be unreasonable.[332]

The minister may by regulations specify either generally or as respects any class or description of factory[333] or as respects the persons employed in any process, a standard of adequate and suitable washing facilities.[334]

Accommodation for clothing

There must be provided and maintained for the use of all persons employed adequate and suitable accommodation for clothing not worn during working hours.[335]

First-Aid

There must be provided and maintained so as to be readily accessible a first-aid box or cupboard of the prescribed standard and, where more than one hundred and fifty persons are employed, an additional box or cupboard for every additional one hundred and fifty persons.[336] For this purpose the number of persons employed in a factory must be taken to be the largest number of persons employed at any one time and any faction of one hundred and fifty must be reckoned as one hundred and fifty. However, where the persons employed are employed in shifts the calculation of the number employed should be according to the largest number at work at any given shift.[337] Nothing, except appliances or requisites for first-aid, must be kept in a first-aid box or cupboard.[338]

Eaoh first-aid box or cupboard must be placed under the charge of a responsible person who must always be readily available during working hours,

---

[332] S. 41(2).

[333] Class or description includes a group of factories described by reference to locality s. 88(1).

[334] S. 41(3).

[335] S.42; in deciding whether accommodation which is provided is adequate regard must be had to the risk of theft; see *McCarthy* v. *Daily Mirror Newspapers Ltd*, [1949] 1 All ER 801; and see above.

[336] S. 43(1)

[337] S. 43(2)

[338] S. 43(3)

and a notice must be fixed in every work-room stating the name of the person in charge of the first-aid box or cupboard provided in respect of the room.[339] If an ambulance room is provided at the factory and such arrangements are made to ensure the immediate treatment there of all injuries occurring in the factory, the Director of Factories may by certificate in writing exempt the factory from the requirements as to first-aid to such extent and subject to such conditions as he may specify in the certificate.[340]

Special provisions and regulations on health, safety and welfare

In part five of the Act special provisions are made with respect to health, safety and welfare in a factory.

Removal of dust or fumes

In every factory in which, in connection with any process carried on, there is given off any dust or fumes[341] or other impurity of such a character and to such extent as to be likely to be injurious or offensive to the persons employed, or any substantial quantity of dust of any kind, all practicable measures must be taken to protect the persons employed against inhalation of dust or fume or other impurity and to prevent its accumulation in any workroom, and, in particular, where the nature of the process makes it practicable, exhaust appliances must be provided and maintained as near as possible to the point of origin of the dust or fume or other impurity so as to prevent it from polluting the air of any workroom.[342]

It has been held that the provisions of this section are directed towards protecting persons employed against inhalation of dust or fume or other impurities by providing methods of prevention or stopping the impurities from ever getting into circulation and is unlike section 9(1) which is concerned solely with ventilation.[343]

---

[339] S. 43(4)
[340] S. 44
[341] Fume includes gas or vapour; s. 88(1)
[342] S. 45(1)
[343] *Ebbs* v. *John Whitson & Co Ltd* [1952] 2 QB 877; *Graham* v. *Cooperative Wholesale Society Ltd*, [1957] 1 All ER 654.

It is well established that in determining both the possibility or likelihood of dust being injurious and the practicability of remedial or preventive measures, that regard must be had to what the employer knew or ought to have known in the sense that he ought to know what a reasonably prudent and careful employer in the same industry would know.[344] As the English Court of Appeal held in *Cartwright* v. *G.K.N. Sankey Ltd,*[345] the sub-section must be read as referring to fumes likely to be injurious according to the estimation of a reasonably well informed factory occupier or which the actual occupier knew or ought to have known to be likely to be injurious to health and it must be considered in the light of knowledge current during the period of the work. Similarly, Singleton L.J. said that in deciding whether all practicable measures were taken one must have regard to the state of knowledge at the material time, and, particularly, to the knowledge of scientific experts.[346] Furthermore, it seems that in deciding whether all practicable measures have been taken by the employer, and the section twice enjoins him to do this, questions of cost of doing so may be ignored.[347] As Lord Parker C.J. said in *Moorcroft* v. *Thomas Powles & Son Ltd,*[348] it seems that practicable must impose a stricter standard that is reasonably practicable. "It may be that certain matters one would take into consideration if the words were 'reasonably practicable', such matters as the cost and the like, have to be eliminated."[349] The measures which may be taken to prevent inhalation of impurities are not confined to the provision of adequate ventilation but include the provision of masks and the taking of steps to induce those employed to wear them.[350]

No stationary internal combustion engine must be used unless provision is made for conducting the exhaust gases from the engine into the open air.[351]

---

[344] *Adsett* v. *K and L Steelfounders & Engineers Ltd,* [1953] WLR 137 affirmed Court of Appeal [1953] 2 All ER 320; *Cartwright* v. *G.K.N. Sankey Ltd* [1973] 14 KLR 349; *Richards* v. *Highway Ironfounders Ltd,* (1957) 2 All ER 162; *Wallhead* v. *Ruston & Hornsby Ltd* (1973) 14 KIR 285.

[345] *Supra.*

[346] *Adsett* v. *K.&L. Steelfounders and Engineers Ltd,* [1953] 2 All ER 320, 322.

[347] *Cartwright* v. *G.K.N. Sankey Ltd, supra*; *Wallhead* v. *Ruston & Hornsby Ltd, supra.*

[348] [1962] 1 WLR 1447, 1454.

[349] Ibid.

[350] *Crookall* v. *Vickers Armstrong Ltd,* [1955] 2 All ER 12.

[351] S. 45(2).

Meals in certain rooms

Where, in any room any poisonous or otherwise injurious substance is so used as to give rise to any dust or fume, no person must bc permitted to eat food or take drink in that room.[352]

Protective clothing and appliances

Where in any factory workers are employed in any process involving excessive exposure to wet or to injurious or offensive substance, suitable protective clothing and appliances, including where necessary, suitable gloves, footwear, goggles and head coverings, must be provided and maintained for the use of such workers.[353] Similarly, suitable goggles or effective screens must be provided to protect the eyes of the persons employed in the following processes:

(i) dry grinding of metals or articles of metal, applied by hand to a revolving wheel or disc driven by mechanical power;
(ii) turning, external or internal, of non-ferrous metals or cast iron or of articles of such metals or such iron, where the work is done dry, other than precision turning where the use of goggles or a screen would seriously interfere with the work, or turning by means of hand tools;
(iii) welding or cutting of metals by means of an electrical, oxyacetylene or similar process, and
(iv) where the following processes are carried on by means of hand tools or other portable tools;
(a) fettling of metal castings involving the removal of metal;
(b) cutting out or cutting off, not including drilling or punching back, of cold rivets or bolts from boilers or other plant or from ships;
(c) chipping or scaling of boilers or ship's plates; and
(d) breaking or dressing of stone, concrete or slag.[354]

The processes in respect of which goggles must be provided must be the processes of the occupier of the factory and the words "Persons employed in the process" refer to employees of the occupier.[355] Thus an action for damages is not

---

[352] S. 46.
[353] S. 47.
[354] S. 48(1) and schedule 4.
[355] *Whalley* v.*Briggs Motor Bodies Ltd* [1954] 2 All ER 193

available to an employee of an independent contractor who is injured as a result of non-provision of goggles while carrying out his duties under the contract his employer has with the occupier of the factory premises. Also an accident which occurs after the specified process had been completed does not come within s. 48.[356]

The duty to provide suitable goggles is an absolute one but whether goggles have been provided or not is a question of fact.[357] The court had to deal with the issue in *Finch* v. *Telegraph Construction and Maintenance Co Ltd.*[358] The plaintiff was engaged in the process of dry grinding a metal cylinder on a double machine grinder when, either a piece of the material he was grinding or of the grinder itself, got into his eye. In an action for failure to provide goggles the employers contended that they provided goggles because a pair of goggles was kept hanging on a nail in the office of the foreman some 30 feet away from the grinding machine and the men generally knew where the goggles were and could get one if they so desired. The court held that this was not a providing within the sub-section. Devlin J. said, succinctly:[359]

> Of course, goggles would be 'provided' if they were given to each man individually. I do not think that is the only way in which they could be 'provided' but, in my view, in order to 'provide' them within the meaning of the Act it would be necessary either that they should be put in a place where they come easily and obviously to the hand of the workman who is about to grind, or, at the very least, that he should be given clear instruction where he is to get them.[360]

However, the sub-section does not merely require that goggles be provided but that suitable goggles be provided to protect the eyes of the person employed in the process. Whether the goggles provided are suitable to protect the eyes is a question of fact and degree; suitable does not mean that the goggles provided must ensure protection.[361] In *Rogers* v. *George Blair & Co Ltd,*[362] the plaintiff employee was engaged in a process which involved grinding cast iron components on a carborundum wheel. The process involved very large quantities

---

356 *Hay* v. *Dorty Mining Equipment,* [1971] 3 All ER 1136.
357 *Daniels* v. *Ford Mortor Co Ltd* [1955] 1 All ER 218
358 [1949] 1 All ER 452.
359 Ibid. 455
360 See also *Norris* v. *Syndic Manufacturing Co. Ltd* [1952] 1 All ER 935; *Ginty* v. *Belmont Building Supply Ltd,* [1959] All ER 414.
361 *Daniels* v. *Ford Motor Co Ltd* [1955] 1 All ER 218.
362 (1971) 11 KIR 391

of small particles of carborundum, steel and sparks flying off at some velocity in the direction of the eyes. The employer supplied goggles but there was evidence that in the past five years there had been eighteen cases where similar goggles were worn but particles had entered the eyes of the users. While working with goggles a particle of steel or carborundum stuck the plaintiff's left eye and he lost the sight of that eye. It was found that the goggles were the best that could be devised but also that they could have been made suitable if there were an individual fitting for each workman. The English Court of Appeal unanimously held that the employers had not provided suitable goggles. Salmon L.J. said that the protection, to be suitable, need not make it impossible for the accident to happen, but it must make it highly unlikely.[363]

Where in any factory electric welding is carried on effective provisions must be made by screening or otherwise to prevent persons other than persons employed in the welding process, being exposed to the electric arc flash.[364]

Powers of minister to make regulations for health, safety and welfare

Where the minister is satisfied that, owing to the conditions and circumstances of employment or of the nature of the processes carried on in a factory, provision required to be made for securing the health, safety, and welfare of persons employed or any class of them or that any manufacture, machinery, plant, equipment or process used in factories is of such nature as to cause risk of bodily injury or be offensive to persons employed or any class of them, he may, subject to the provisions of the Act and the Labour Act, make such regulations as appear to him to be reasonably practicable and to meet the necessity of the case.[365]

The regulations may apply to all such factories or to any specified class or description[366] of such factories and may provide for the exemption of any specified class or description of factory either absolutely or subject to conditions.[367] The regulations may, without prejudice to the generality of the powers conferred by sub-section (1), (a) prohibit the employment of or modify or limit the hours of employment of all persons or any class of persons in

[363] Ibid., 395.

[364] S. 48(2).

[365] S. 49(1).

[366] Class of description, in relation to factories, includes a group of factories described by reference to locality; S. 88(1).

[367] S. 49(2).

connection with any manufacture, machinery, plant, equipment, appliance, process or description of manual labour or (b) prohibit, limit or control the use of any material or process, or (c) modify or extend with respect to any class or description[368] of factory any provisions of Parts II, III, IV or Part V of the Act being provisions imposing requirements as to health, safety or welfare or (d) make provision for arrangements for preparing or heating and taking meals, for ambulance and first-aid arrangements, for rest rooms, the supply and use of seats in workrooms, the supply of protective clothing and for the supervision of persons employed and may impose duties on owners, employed persons and other persons, as well as on occupiers.[369] The minister may make regulations in connection with the fees to be paid in respect of any matter or thing done under the Act.[370]

Notification and investigation of accidents and industrial diseases

Part six of the Act provides for the notification and investigation of accidents and industrial diseases in factories. Where any accident occurs in a factory which either causes loss of life to a person employed in that factory or disabled any such person for more than three days from performing the duties for which he was employed, written notice of the accident in the prescribed form and accompanied by the prescribed particulars must forthwith be sent to the inspector of the district by the occupier of the factory.[371] Where any accident causing disablement is notified but after which the accident results in the death of the disabled person, notice in writing of the death must be sent to the inspector of

[368] See footnote 366.

[369] S. 49(3); the courts, in England, have had the opportunity to construe s.49. Where Regulations are made compliance with the regulation will absolve the occupier from his corresponding duty under the *Act; Miller* v. *William Boothman & Son Ltd*, [1944] 1 All ER 333; *Automatic Woodturning Co. Ltd* v. *Stringer*, [1957] AC 544. But where the Regulations leave a duty under the Act untouched compliance with the Act is required; *Benn* v. *Kamm & Co Ltd*, [1952] 1 All ER 833. Similarly, compliance with Regulations does not necessarily absolve the employer from his common law duty; *Franklin* v. *Gramophone Co Ltd*, [1948] 1 KB 542

[370] S.49(4); all regulations made by the minister under the Act must be laid before the National Council of Ministers as soon as may be after the date of their making and the Council may, by resolution, approve or reject any such regulations and no such regulations comes into force until 30 days after they have been so approved or such later date as may be specified in the regulations; s.67.

[371] S.51(l); inspector of the district means the inspector specified in the notice required by s.60(l) to be kept posted in a prominent position in every factory; s.88(l).

the district by the occupier of the factory as soon as the death comes to his knowledge.[372]

Where any accident occurs to a person employed, but the occupier of the factory is not the actual employer of the person killed or injured, the actual employer is, if he fails to report the accident to the occupier immediately, guilty of an offence.[373] Any employer or occupier of a factory who fails to report an accident is guilty of an offence and, on conviction, liable to a fine not exceeding ₦1,000.[374]

The minister may, if he considers it expedient, institute a commission of inquiry into frequent or large scale accidents in factories or work-houses[375] in order to recommend such action as would prevent any such accident in the future.[376] If the minister considers that, by reason of the risk of serious bodily injury to persons employed, it is expedient that notice should also be given in every case of any special class of explosion, fire, collapse of buildings, accident to machinery or plant, or other occurrences in a factory, he may by regulations, extend the provisions of section 51 to any such class of occurrences, whether death or disablement is caused or not, and may allow the required notice of any occurrence to which the regulations relate, instead of being sent forthwith, to be sent within the time stipulated by the regulations.[377] The minister may, if he considers it expedient, institute an inquiry into any frequent or large scale dangerous occurrence of the class specified above in order to recommend such action as would prevent any such occurrence in future.[378]

The occupier of any factory who believes, suspects or has reasonable ground for believing or suspecting that a case of occupational disease has occurred in the factory must forthwith send written notice of such case in the prescribed form and accompanied by the prescribed particulars, to the nearest inspector; and the provisions of the Act with respect to the notification of accidents shall apply to any such case in like manner as to any such accident as is mentioned in those provisions.[379] For this purpose, occupational disease means any disease or illness

---

[372] S.51(2).
[373] S.51(3).
[374] S.51(4).
[375] It is not clear what are work-houses.
[376] S.51(5).
[377] S.52(l); See the Factories (Notification of Dangerous Occurrences) Regulations, 1961, LN 105 of 1961 which are continued in force.
[378] S.52(2).
[379] S.53(l); see the Prescribed Forms & Particulars order L.N. 113 of 1956 which are continued in force.

which, in the opinion of the minister, may be contracted by an employed person by reason of the nature of his employment in a factory.[380]

Miscellaneous provisions

In Part Eight, the Act deals with a miscellany of matters.

General register

There must be kept in every factory a register, in the prescribed form, called the general register and there must be entered in or attached to the register:

(i) the certificate of registration of the factory;
(ii) every other certificate issued in respect of the factory by the Director of Factories under the provisions of the Act;
(iii) the prescribed particulars as to the washing, white-washing or colour washing, painting or varnishing of the factory;
(iv) the prescribed particulars as to every accident and case of occupational disease occurring in the factory of which notice is required to be sent to an inspector under the provisions of the Act;
(v) all reports and particulars required by any other provisions of the Act to be entered in or attached to the general register; and
(vi) such other matters as may be prescribed by regulations.[381]

The occupier of a factory must send to an inspector such extracts from the general register as the inspector may from time to time require for the purpose of the execution of his duties under the Act.[382] The general register and every other register or record kept in pursuance of the Act must be preserved and must be kept available for inspection by any inspector for seven years or such shorter period if any as may be prescribed for any class or description of register or record, after the date of the last entry in the register or record.[383]

---

[380] S.53(2); the Declaration of Occupational Diseases Notice, L.N.114 of 1956 are continued in force.
[381] S.58(l).
[382] S.58(2).
[383] S.59.

Posting of abstract of Act

There must be kept posted in a prominent position in every factory,

(i) the prescribed abstract of the Act;[384]
(ii) a notice of the address of the Director of Factories and of the nearest inspector;
(iii) printed copies of any regulations made under part five of the Act[385] which are for the time being in force in the factory or the prescribed abstracts of such regulations, and
(iv) every other notice and document required by the Act to be posted in the factory.[386]

All such documents must be in English and in such Nigerian languages as an inspector may direct and, if a form has been prescribed for any document, it must be posted in that form.[387]

Duties of employed persons

No person employed in a factory or in any other place to which any provision of the Act applies must wilfully interfere with or misuse any means, appliance, convenience or other thing provided in pursuance of the Act for securing the health, safety or welfare of the persons employed in the factory or place.[388] It has been held that the words wilfully interfere with or misuse mean something more than merely touch or misplace and that they mean something in the nature of a perverse intermeddling with the thing provided.[389] Where any means or appliance for securing health or safety is provided for the use of any such person he must use the means or appliance.[390] As we have seen whether there is provision is a question of fact;[391] where the employer has provided a means or appliance for safety the person is under a duty to use it even though he has not

[384] Prescribed means prescribed by order of the minister; s.88(l).
[385] See ante.
[386] S.60(l).
[387] S.60(2).
[388] S.61(l).
[389] *Charles* v. *S. Smith & Sons Ltd*, [1954] 1 All ER 499.
[390] S.61(l).
[391] Ante.

been ordered to use it by the employer unless there is a prohibition by the employer on its use.[392]

No person employed in a factory or in any other place to which any provisions of the Act apply must wilfully and without reasonable cause do anything likely to endanger himself or any other person.[393]

Deduction from wages

The occupier of a factory must not, in respect of anything to be done or provided by him in pursuance of the Act, make any deduction from the sum contracted to be paid by him to any person employed or receive or allow any person in his employment to receive any payment from any such person.[394]

Administration of the Act

The Act provides two principal methods of compelling compliance with its provisions - administrative enforcement by means of factory inspectors and criminal sanctions for breach of the duties laid down. The provisions on the administration of the Act are contained in Part Nine.

The word minister in the Act means the minister charged with responsibility for labour matters.[395] As at the time of this publication he is the Minister of Labour and Productivity. The minister must, within thirty days after the end of each financial year, submit a report on his activities under the Act to the National Council of Ministers.[396]

Then section 64 creates the offices of a Director of Factories of the Federation and such inspectors of factories and other officers by whatever name called, for the purpose of executing the Act.[397] Notice of the appointment of the Director of Factories and inspectors of factories and other officers must be published in the Gazette.[398] The minister must issue to every appointed person a

---

[392] *Norris v. Syndic Manufacturing Co Ltd*, [1952] 1 All ER 935.

[393] S.61(2).

[394] S.62.

[395] S.88(l).

[396] S.63.

[397] S.64(l).

[398] S.64(2); a person who is the occupier of a factory or who is directly interested in the factory or in any process or business carried on in the factory or in a patent connected therewith or is employed

certificate of appointment and when visiting a factory or place to which any of the provisions of the Act applies such person must, if required to do so, produce the certificate to the occupier or other person holding a responsible position of management at the factory.[399]

An inspector must not publish or disclose to any person the details of any manufacturing or commercial or working process which may come to his knowledge in the course of his duties except in so far as is necessary for the purposes of a prosecution for an offence or a coroner's inquest or for the purpose of an inquiry under any (sic) in connection with the safety of any premises or in connection with an accident happening there or in connection with an occupational disease.[400] Any contravention of this provision is an offence.[401] Similarly, an inspector must treat as absolutely confidential the source of any complaint which brings to his notice a contravention of the provisions of the Act and must give no intimation to the occupier or his representative that a visit of inspection was made in consequence of such complaint.[402] Again, any contravention of his provision is an offence.

Powers of inspectors

An inspector has power to do the following things for the purpose of the execution of the Act:

(i) to enter, inspect, and examine, by day or by night, a factory, and every part of the factory, when he has reasonable cause to believe that any person is employed there, and to enter, inspect and examine by day any place which he has reasonable cause to believe to be a factory and any part of any building of which a factory forms part and in which he has reasonable cause to believe that explosive or highly inflammable materials are stored or used;

(ii) to take with him a police officer if he has reasonable cause to apprehend any serious obstruction in the execution of his duty;

---

in or about a factory must not act as an inspector; s.64(4); a contravention is an offence, s.64(7); for penalty see footnote 416.

399 S.64(3).

400 S. 64(5)

401 S. 64(7); the offender is liable to a fine not exceeding ₦500 or to imprisonment for a term not exceeding three months or to both and if the contravention continues to a fine not exceeding ₦100 for each day of contravention; s.70

402 S. 64(6)

(iii) to require the production of the register, certificates, notices and documents kept in pursuance of the Act and to inspect, examine and copy any of them;
(iv) to make such examination and inquiry as may be necessary to ascertain whether the provisions of the Act are complied with;
(v) to require any person whom he finds in a factory to give such information as it is in his power to give as to who is the occupier of the factory;
(vi) to examine any person, either alone or in the presence of any other person, as he thinks fit, with respect to matters under the Act and to require every such person to sign a declaration of the truth of the matters respecting which he is so examined so however that no one must be required to answer any question or to give any evidence tending to incriminate himself;
(vii) in the case of an inspector who is a registered medical practitioner, to carry out such medical examinations as may be necessary for the purposes of his duties under the provisions of the Act;
(viii) to carry out such examination, test and analysis in order to give effect to the Act and take instant photographs in any factory; and
(ix) to exercise such other powers as may be necessary for giving full effect to the provisions of the Act.[403]

The owner or occupier or agent of the owner or occupier must certify or endorse any instant photograph at the time it is taken but refusal to do so does not invalidate the authenticity of the photograph.[404]

The occupier of every factory, his agents and servants, must furnish the means required by an inspector as necessary for any entry, inspection, examination, inquiry or the taking of samples or otherwise for the exercise of his powers in relation to that factory.[405] If any person wilfully delays an inspector in the exercise of any of these powers or fails to comply with the requisition of an inspector in pursuance of the powers or to produce any register, certificate, notice or document which he is required by or in pursuance of the Act to produce, or wilfully withholds any information as to who is the occupier of any factory, or conceals or prevents or attempts to conceal or prevent, a person from appearing before or being examined by an inspector, that person is deemed to obstruct the inspector in the execution of his duties under the Act.[406] Where an inspector is obstructed in the execution of his duties, the person obstructing him is guilty of an offence and liable on conviction to a fine not exceeding ₦1,000 or

---

[403] S. 65(1)
[404] S. 65(2)
[405] S. 65(3)
[406] S. 65(4)

to imprisonment for a term not exceeding six months or to both such fine and imprisonment and where the inspector is so obstructed in a factory the occupier of the factory is also guilty of an offence.[407]

Power to conduct proceedings

Any inspector may, although he is not a legal practitioner, prosecute, conduct or defend before a court any charge, information, complaint or other proceeding arising under the Act or in the discharge of his duty as an inspector.[408] An inspector is competent to give evidence as a witness in any prosecution for an offence against the Act even though the prosecution is brought at his instance or conducted by him.[409]

Power to take samples

An inspector may, at any time after informing the occupier or, if the occupier is not readily available, a manager or other responsible officer in the factory, take for analysis sufficient samples of any substance used or intended to be used in a factory, being a substance in respect of which he suspects a contravention of any regulation made under part five of the Act or which he thinks may prove on analysis to be likely to cause bodily injury to the persons employed.[410]

The occupier or the manager or other responsible person may, at the time when the sample is taken and on providing the necessary appliances, require the inspector to divide the sample into three parts and to mark or seal or fasten up each in such manner as its nature permits and to deliver one part to the occupier or the manager or other responsible person, retain one part for future comparison, and submit one part to the analyst; any analysis must, if so required, be carried out by a government chemist in the public service of the Federation or of a State.[411] A certificate purporting to be a certificate by a government chemist as to the result of an analysis of the sample taken must, in any proceedings, be

[407] S. 65(5); for the penalty as to the offence by an occupier see footnote 401.
[408] S. 66(1).
[409] S. 66(2)
[410] S.50(l); bodily injury includes injury to health; s.88(l)
[411] S.50(2).

admissible as evidence of the matters stated in it but any party to the proceedings may require the person by whom the analysis is made to be called as a witness.[412]

It is unlawful for any person, except in so far as is necessary for the purposes of a prosecution for an offence under the Act, to publish or disclose to any person the results of an analysis and if any person acts in contravention he is guilty of an offence and liable on conviction to a fine not exceeding ₦1,000.[413]

Notice or certificate issued by Director of Factories

Any notice or certificate issued by the Director of Factories may be issued for a limited period or without limitation of period and may be varied or revoked by him but this provision does not apply to a certificate of registration of a factory issued by the Director under the provisions of part one of the Act.[414]

Whenever the Director of Factories issues under the provisions of the Act any certificate approving or authorizing any person for the purpose of any of those provisions, or excepting any factory from the requirements of any of those provisions, or revokes any such certificate, he must notify the issue or revocation of the certificate in the *Gazette*.[415]

Offences, penalties and legal proceedings

These are dealt with in Part ten of the Act. The primary responsibility for contravention of the provisions of the Act is put on the person who is the occupier of the factory.[416] Section 69(1) provides that, in the event of any contravention in or in connection with or in relation to a factory of the provisions of the Act or of any regulation or order made under it, the occupier or, if the contravention is one in respect of which the owner is by or under the Act made responsible, the owner, of the factory is subject as is hereafter provided, guilty of an offence under the Act.

The reason for placing primary responsibility on the occupier, as Lord Atkin has explained, is because it is the occupier who has complete control of the premises and can therefore control its use. As his Lordship said:

---

[412] S.50(3).
[413] S.50(4).
[414] S.65(6).
[415] S.68.
[416] See *Turner v. Courtaulds Ltd* [937]1 All ER 467; *Rippon v. Port of London Authority* [1940] 1 All ER 637.

> the occupiers...have complete control...and can impose their own conditions upon those who enter (the premises) and use either their own plant or the plant of the occupier's. They can insist upon the plant being constantly maintained in a safe condition, can terminate the licence to enter the premises or use the plant in case of breach, and can take any indemnities they think fit.[417]

But the Act does not define the word occupier. In the Scottish case of *Ramsay* v. *Mackie,*[418] Lord MacLaren gave a definition of that term which has often been applied.[419] As he said the occupier is "the person who runs the factory...who regulates and controls the work that is done there, and who is responsible for the fulfilment of the provisions of the Factory Act within it."[420] In the great majority of cases the occupier would be the employer but it would seem that essentially it is a question of the facts in each case who the occupier is.

Where, however, the contravention is by an employed person of the duty placed upon him[421] or by any person of any regulation or order made under the Act which expressly imposes any duty upon him, the employed person or such other person is guilty of an offence and the occupier or owner, as the case may be, will not be guilty of an offence by reason only of such contravention unless, it is proved that he failed to take all reasonable steps to prevent the contravention but any liability of the occupier or owner in respect of the same matter by virtue of some other provisions other than those imposing the duties on the employed person or other person is not affected.[422] In a prosecution under this sub-section the onus is on the prosecution to prove that the occupier or owner failed to take reasonable steps to prevent the contravention.[423]

If the occupier of a factory avails himself of any special exception allowed by or under the Act and fails to comply with any of the conditions attached to the exception, he must be deemed to have contravened the provision of the Act.[424] If any persons are employed in a factory otherwise than in accordance with the provisions of the Act or of any regulation or order made under it any contravention in respect of each such person must be deemed to be a separate contravention.[425]

---

[417] *Smith* v. *Cammell Laird & Co Ltd* [1940] AC 242, 258-259.
[418] 7F (Ct. of Sess) 106.
[419] E.g. in *Cox* v. *Cutler & Sons Ltd*, [1948] 2 All ER 665.
[420] *Ramsay* v. *Mackie* (1904) 7 F (Ct.of Sess) 106, 109.
[421] Under Part VIII of the Act, i.e. s. 61 as to which see above.
[422] S.69(2).
[423] *Carr* v. *Decca Gramophone Co Ltd*, [1947] 2 All ER 20.
[424] S.69(3).
[425] S.69(4).

Where an offence under the Act is committed by a corporate body, firm, co-operative society or other association of individuals every director, manager, secretary or other similar officers of the body, every partner or officer of the firm, every person concerned in the management of the affairs of the co-operative society or association, or every person who was purporting to act in any such capacity is severally guilty of the offence and liable to be proceeded against as if he committed the offence unless he proves that the act or omission constituting the offence took place without his knowledge, connivance or neglect.[426]

Where an act or default for which an occupier or owner of a factory is liable under the Act is in fact the act or default of some agent, servant, worker or other person that agent, servant, worker or other person is guilty of an offence and liable to the penalty as if he were the occupier or owner as the case may be.[427]

Where the occupier or owner of a factory is charged with an offence under the provisions of the Act he is entitled, upon a charge duly made by him and on giving to the prosecution not less than three days notice in writing of his intention, to have any other person whom he charges as the actual offender, whether or not that person is his agent or servant, brought before the court at the time appointed for hearing the charge and, if, after the commission of the offence has been proved, the occupier or owner of the factory proves to the satisfaction of the court that he used all due diligence to enforce the execution of the provisions of the Act and of any relevant regulations or order under it and that the other person so brought to the court committed the offence in question without his consent, connivance or wilful default, that other person must be convicted of the offence and the occupier or owner is not guilty of the offence and the person so convicted must, in the discretion of the court, be also liable to pay costs incidental to the proceedings.[428] Indeed, when it is made to appear to the satisfaction of an inspector at the time of discovering an offence that the occupier or owner, as the case may be, of the factory has used all due diligence to enforce the execution of the Act and of any relevant regulation or order made under it, and by what person the offençe has been committed and that it has been committed without the consent, connivance or wilful default of the occupier or owner and in contravention of his order, the inspector must proceed against the

---

[426] S.69(5).

[427] S.73.

[428] S.74(l); in *Potts or Riddell* v. *Reid* [1943] ACl the House of Lords held that any possible civil liability of an occupier for breach of his statutory duty is not affected by the fact that he is held not to have committed an offence under s.74(l). In a proceedings the prosecution and other person brought to the court each has a right to cross-examine the occupier if he gives evidence and any witnesses called by him in support of his charge, and to call rebutting evidence, s.74(2).

person whom he believes to be the actual offender without first proceeding against the occupier or owner of the factory.[429]

Where any person is substituted for the occupier or owner of a factory under any provision of the Act any order, summons, notice or proceeding which, for the purpose of that provision, is by or under the Act required or authorised to be served on or taken in relation to the occupier or owner is authorized or required, as the case may be, to be served on or taken in relation to that person.[430]

Liability of owner of machine

Where, in a factory, the owner or hirer of a machine or implement moved by mechanical power is some person other than the occupier of the factory, the owner or hirer must, so far as respects any offence under the Act committed in relation to a person who is employed in or about or in connection with that machine or implement and is in the employment or pay of the owner or hirer, be deemed to be the occupier of the factory.[431]

Penalty in case of death or injury

Where any person is killed or dies or suffers any bodily injury,[432] in consequence of the occupier or owner of a factory having contravened any provision of the Act or of any regulation or order made under it, such occupier or owner is liable, without prejudice to any other penalty, to a fine not exceeding ₦5,000 or imprisonment for a term not exceeding 2 years or to both such fine and imprisonment.[433] The whole or any part of the fine may be applied for the benefit of the injured person or his family or otherwise as the court may order.[434] However, where the injury is to health the occupier or owner is not liable unless the injury was caused directly by his contravention and he is also not liable if the charge against him in respect of the act or default by which the death or injury was caused had been heard and dismissed before the death or injury occurred.[435]

---

[429] S.74(3).
[430] S.75
[431] S.76; for application of this section see *Whalley* v. *Briggs Motor Bodies Ltd*, [1954] 2 All ER 193.
[432] Bodily injury includes injury to health; s.88(1).
[433] S.71.
[434] Ibid.
[435] Ibid.

Forgery of certificates and false entries and declarations

Section 72 creates ten offences. If any person:

(i) forges or counterfeits any certificate required by, under or for the purposes of the Act or any order or regulation made under it; or
(ii) gives or signs any such certificate knowing it to be false in any material particular; or
(iii) knowingly utters or makes use of any such certificate; or
(iv) knowingly utters or makes use of as applying to any person, any such certificate which does not so apply; or
(v) impersonates any person named in any such certificate; or
(vi) falsely pretends to be an inspector; or
(vii) wilfully connives at any such forging, counterfeiting, giving, signing, uttering, making use, impersonating or pretending, or
(viii) wilfully makes a false entry in any register, notice, certificate or documents required by, under or for the purposes of the Act or any order or regulation made under it, to be kept or served or sent, or
(ix) wilfully makes or signs a false declaration required by, under or for the purposes of the Act or any order or regulation made under it; or
(x) knowingly makes use of any such false entry or declarations, without prejudice to any other penalty,[436] guilty of an offence and liable on conviction to a fine not exceeding ₦2,000 or to imprisonment for a term not exceeding 12 months or to both such fine and imprisonment.[437]

Prosecution of offences

All offences under the Act must be prosecuted, and all fines recovered, in a magistrate's court.[438] In any proceedings it is sufficient to allege in the charge that the factory is a factory within the meaning given to it in the Act and to state the name of the ostensible occupier of the factory or, where the occupier is a firm, the title of the firm; and the burden of proving that the premises are not a factory or that the occupier named in the charge or information is not the occupier of the factory, lies upon the person alleging such fact.[439] Where any

---

[436] E.g. under the Criminal or Penal Code.
[437] S.72.
[438] S. 77(1).
[439] S. 77(2)

offence is committed by reason of a failure to make an examination, enter a report or do any other thing at or within a time specified by the Act or any regulation or order made under it, the offence must be deemed to continue until the examination is made, or the report entered or the other thing done as the case may be.[440]

If a person is found in a factory at any time at which work is going on or the machinery is in motion except during the intervals for meals or rest, he must[441] until the contrary is proved, be deemed to have been then employed in the factory. Where any entry is required by the Act or any order or regulation made under it to be made in the general register or in any other register or record, the entry made by the occupier of a factory or on his behalf is, as against him, admissible as evidence of the facts stated in it, and the fact that any entry so required with respect to the observance of any provision of the Act or of any order or regulation made under the Act, has not been made must be admissible as evidence that provision has not been observed.[442]

Any document, including any summons or order, required or authorized to be served under the Act may be served on any person by delivering it to him or by leaving it at or sending it by post to his residence or place of business, and, on any firm by delivering it to any partner of the firm or by leaving it at, or sending it by post to, the office of the firm and on the owner or occupier of a factory, including any owner or occupier which is a company or a co-operative society, in any manner as for any person or firm or by delivering it or a true copy of it, to any responsible person apparently not under the age of 16 years at the factory.[443] Any such document may be addressed, for the purpose of service on the occupier, to the occupier at the proper postal address of the factory without further name or description.[444] All of these provisions apply, with necessary modifications, to documents required or authorized under the Act to be sent to any person, firm, owner or occupier, and to the sending, addressing and delivery of such documents.[445]

---

[440] S. 77(3)
[441] S. 78(1)
[442] S. 78(2).
[443] S.79(1).
[444] S.79(2).
[445] S.79(3).

Expenses between owner and occupier

If, by reason of an agreement between the owner and the occupier of premises the whole or any part of which has been let as a factory, the owner or occupier is prevented from carrying out any structural or other alterations in the premises which are necessary to enable him to comply with the provisions of the Act, or in order to conform with any standard or requirement imposed by or under the Act, he may apply to a judge of the Federal High Court in chambers for the terms of the agreement to be set aside or modified.[446] The judge, after hearing the parties and any witnesses whom they may desire to call, may make such an order setting aside or modifying the terms of the agreement as he considers just and equitable in the circumstances of the case.[447]

Where, in any premises the whole or any part of which has been let as a factory, any structural or other alterations are required in order to comply with the provisions of the Act or of any regulation or order made under it, or in order to conform with any standard or requirement imposed by or under the Act, and the owner or occupier as the case may be, alleges that the whole or part of the expenses of the alterations ought to be borne by the occupier or owner, the owner or occupier may apply to a judge of the Federal High Court in chambers for the expenses of the alterations to be apportioned between them.[448] The judge, after hearing the parties and any witnesses whom they may desire to call, may make such an order concerning the expenses or their apportionment as he considers just and equitable in the circumstances of the case, regard being had to the terms of any contract between the parties, or, in the alternative he may, at the request of the owner or occupier, determine the lease.[449]

---

[446] S.80(1).
[447] S.80(2).
[448] S.81(l).
[449] S.81(2).

Chapter 6

Workmen's compensation

Introduction

The common law action for negligence, that is, for breach of an employer's duty to take reasonable care for the safety of his employee has always been fraught with difficulties. As we have seen the defences of common employment, voluntary assumption of risk, expressed in the Latin *volenti non fit injuria*, and contributory negligence rendered the outcome of any such action extremely uncertain. Even today that these defences have either been abolished or considerably modified either by statute or the common law in favour of the injured employee the common law action still retains much of its uncertainty. The injured employee still has to prove fault either in the employer or in any one for whose negligence the employer will be vicariously held liable. In addition the expense of litigation coupled with delay constitute formidable obstacles in a common law action.

Early statutory intervention aimed at reducing the harshness of the common law rules did not prove that satisfactory.[1] A workmen's compensation scheme was, therefore, devised, not as a substitute for a common law action but as an alternative system for compensating injury suffered at work,[2] The fault principle, crucial in a common law action, is absent in the scheme but the injured employee suffers a deliberate cut in the amount of compensation he may receive under the scheme in comparison with the damages he may be entitled to at common law for the same injury.

Lord James of Hereford explains the nature of workmen's compensation briefly as follows:[3]

---

[1] See the Employers' Liability Act 1880.

[2] The first statute on workmen's compensation in Nigeria was enacted in 1941 based on the English Act of 1925. The first statute in England was enacted in 1897.

[3] *Johnson* v. *Marshall, Sons & Co Ltd* [1906] AC 409, 412.

> The main object was to entitle a workman who sustained injury whilst engaged in certain[4] employments to recover compensation from the employer, although he (the employer) was guilty of no fault. The intention was to make "the business" bear the burden of the accidents that arose in course of employment, and relief from this liability is not found even if the injured workman be guilty of negligence.

This basic structure is retained in the Workmen's Compensation Act which has repealed and replaced the Act of 1941. The employer remains the insurer. The amount of compensation must be in accordance with its provisions.[5] The basis for a claim has nothing to do with the negligence or otherwise of the employer nor is the negligence of the employee himself or of a fellow employee relevant consideration. As Lord Atkin said:[6] "Once you have found the work which he is seeking to do to be within his employment the question of negligence, great or small, is irrelevant."

Basis of claim

The basis for a claim of workmen's compensation is contained in section 3(1)[7] which reads, in part, as follows: "if in an employment personal injury by accident arising out of and in the course of the employment is caused to a workman, his employer shall, subject as hereinafter mentioned, be liable to pay compensation in accordance with the provisions of this Act."

However there are four other requirements which may affect an employer's liability to pay compensation. (1) An employer is not liable to pay compensation in respect of any injury which does not incapacitate the workman for a period of at least three consecutive days from earning full wages at the work at which he was engaged.[8] (2) If it is proved that the injury to a workman is attributable to the serious and wilful misconduct of the workman any compensation claimed in respect of that injury must be disallowed but where the injury results in death or serious and permanent incapacity the court, on a consideration of all the circumstances, may award the compensation provided by the Act or such part of

[4] The Workmen's Compensation Act 1897 under which the case was decided applied only to workmen in certain employments.

[5] *Caxton Press (Nig.) Ltd* v. *Adeshina* (1969) 1NMLR 224.

[6] *Harris v. Associated Portland Cement Manufacturers Ltd* [1939] AC 71, 76.

[7] Workmen's Compensation Act, No.17 of 1987 now cap. 470 Laws of the Federation of Nigeria, 1990; all references in this chapter are to Cap. 470 unless otherwise stated.

[8] S.3 (2)(a).

it as it thinks fit.[9] Thus where a workman's injury is attributable to his misconduct, which is serious and wilful, compensation is completely disallowed where the injury does not result in death or serious and permanent incapacity. This will include temporary incapacity, whether total or partial, and any permanent incapacity which is not serious. The burden of proving serious and wilful misconduct is on the employer.[10] The presence of the word serious means that wilfulness alone will not suffice to deprive a workman of compensation.[11] However not every misconduct of a workman is regarded as serious. Whether misconduct amounts to serious misconduct in any given case is a question of fact to be determined on the facts of that case.[12] Whether misconduct is serious is not to be judged from hindsight - that is, from the consequences of the misconduct. In *Johnson* v. *Marshall, Sons & Co Ltd*[13] Lord James thought that seriousness represents a higher standard of misconduct than is required to justify summary dismissal and he gave instances of serious misconduct which he described as "illustrating conditions of absolute disregard of the lives and safety of many."[14] Similarly, in *George* v. *Glasgow Coal Company Ltd*,[15] where misconduct was held to be serious, Lord Robertson said one of the reasons for so holding was that it could have been seen that the order which was disobeyed, when disobeyed, would touch life and limb. However, the House of Lords held in the case that breach of a rule, whether statutory or otherwise, is not, *prima facie*, evidence of serious and wilful misconduct. As to wilfulness it is clear that carelessness or negligence is not wilfulness. The word wilful imports more than negligence, it imports that the misconduct must be deliberate.[16] In *Lewis* v. *Great Western Railway Co*[17] Bramwell LJ said wilful misconduct means misconduct to which the will is a party; something opposed to accident or negligence.

3). No compensation is payable in respect of any incapacity or death resulting from a deliberate self-injury.[18]

4.) No compensation is payable in respect of any incapacity or death resulting from personal injury if the workman has, at any time, represented to the

---

[9] S.3 (2)(b).
[10] *Johnson* v. *Marshall Sons &Co Ltd* [1906] AC 409.
[11] Per Lord James, ibid., 412.
[12] Ibid.
[13] *Supra.*
[14] Ibid. 412 - 413.
[15] [1909] AC 123.
[16] *Johnson* v. *Marshall, Sons & Co Ltd* supra.
[17] (1877) 3 QBD 195.
[18] S. 3(4).

employer that he was not suffering or had not previously suffered from that or a similar injury knowing that the representation was false.[19]

It has already been stated that an injured workman is entitled to compensation under the Act only where his injury is caused by accident which arises out of and in the course of his employment. The burden of proving that the personal injury was caused by accident arising out of and in the course of employment lies upon the injured workman and if he has died as a result of the accident the rule applies to his dependants, if any.[20]

Personal injury

Compensation is payable only in respect of personal injury. Compensation is not payable in respect of damage to or loss of property. However personal injury is not limited to wounds, cuts or bruises which are visible to the eye but includes any other trauma such as nervous shock which produces a physiological injury.[21] For example, a man may suffer injury from strain or exposure.

Accident

Compensation is payable only where the personal injury is caused by an accident. Hence a disease or injury which is the result of a process is not compensable as personal injury but as occupational disease.[22] Accident is distinguishable from process. There must be an element of the fortuitous and unexpected in an accident. Where an injury comes on gradually over time it is process.

In *Roberts* v. *Dorothea Slate Quarries Co Ltd*,[23] a workman, who had worked in a slate works for twenty years, was certified to be disabled by silicosis. Lord Porter agreed that there was no doubt that accident would include a wide range of incidents but that it did not include the growth of incapacity by a continuous process, "The difference between injury by accident and disease had always been recognised and some one incident or definite and distinct series of incidents had been recognised..." There must come a time when the indefinite number of so-called accidents and the length of time over which they occurred

[19] S. 3(5).
[20] *Bender* v. *Owners of Steamship ZENT* [1909] 2 KB 41.
[21] *Yates* v. *South Kirkby, etc. Collieries, Ltd* [1910] 2 KB 538.
[22] For occupational diseases see below.
[23] 1948 WN 246.

took away the element of accident and substituted that of process."[24] In *Steel v. Cammell Laird & Co Ltd*[25] the hands of a workman, who had worked for two years using red and white lead, were seized with cramp while working. He was later found to be suffering from paralysis from lead poisoning. The court held that the injury was not caused by accident. The Master of the Rolls, Collins said the poisoning came on gradually, not suddenly, "and it is impossible to say at what particular time the accident in this case can be said to have happened."[26] In *Brintons Ltd* v. *Turvey*[27] a workman who was sorting wool was infected with anthrax when a bacillus from the wool entered into his eye. A majority of the House of Lords held that the *bacillus* entering the eye was an accident. But Lord Robertson, who dissented, said the "catching of infectious disease" is not within personal injury by accident. It would seem, however, that what the majority regarded as an accident was the striking of the workman by the *bacillus*. As Lord Lindley said, the "fact that an accident causes injury in the shape of disease does not render the cause not an accident."[28]

In *Hensey* v *White*, [29] although the English Court of Appeal said that, for there to be an accident, there must be an element of the fortuitous and unexpected it held, in the case, that there was no accident as the occurrence was brought about by an existing disease. In the case, the workman was endeavouring, with others, to set a wheel in motion in order to start a gas-engine which had become stiff owing to disuse. The workman suddenly put his hand to his stomach and immediately began to vomit. He died vomiting. Post-mortem examination showed that his internal organs were not in the natural state in which the organs of a healthy man should be in. The court held that death resulted from disease and not accident. Collins LJ said: "In the present case there is an entire lack of the fortuitous element."[30] However, the House of Lords decision in *Fenton* v *Thorley & Co Ltd*[31] three years later, makes it clear that there can be an accident by the concurrence of an existing abnormal condition or disease and a sudden occurrence. In the case a workman ruptured himself while exerting himself in turning the wheel of a machine which had got stuck. The question was, had he suffered personal injury by accident? The House of Lords said yes. The word "accident", said the House, must be taken or used in its

---

[24] Ibid., 247.
[25] (1905) 93 LT 357; see also *Broderick* v. *LCC* [1908] 2 KB 807.
[26] Ibid., 359.
[27] [1905] AC 230.
[28] Ibid., 238.
[29] [1900] 1 QB 481
[30] Ibid., 485.
[31] [1903] AC 443

popular and ordinary sense. In that sense Lord Macnghten said the word denotes "an unlooked for mishap or an untoward event which is not expected or designed."[32] Lord Shand said the word "denotes or includes any unexpected personal injury resulting to the workman from any unlooked for mishap or occurrence."[33] Hence a workman who, in the process of lifting a beam, gave it a heave so as to get it on his shoulder, and as a result lacerated the muscle on the right side of his back, was held to have suffered injury caused by accident.[34] Similarly, *in Clover, Clayton & Co Ltd* v *Hughes*,[35] Lord Loreburn said:

> No doubt the ordinary accident is associated with something external; the bursting of a boiler, or an explosion in a mine, for example. But it may be merely from the man's own miscalculation, such as tripping and falling. Or it may be due both to internal and external conditions, as if a seaman were to faint in the rigging and tumble into the sea. I think it may also be something going wrong within the human frame itself, such as the straining of a muscle or the breaking of a blood vessel.[36]

Accidents may, of course, arise from the dangerous nature of the work or machinery or from malfunctioning of machinery or from the negligence of the workman or fellow workman in the course of carrying out duties. In determining whether an occurrence is an accident it is essential to view the occurrence from the standpoint of the injured workman. The deliberate act of another can be an accident when looked at from the viewpoint of the victim of the occurrence.[37] In *Trim Joint District School Board of Management* v *Kelly*,[38] the argument that an act which was designed would not be described as an accident was rejected. There, an assistant teacher in a school was attacked by some of the school boys. He was struck with heavy wooden mallets and he died as a result of his injuries. It was held that the injuries were caused by accident.

Arising out of employment

As we have seen, the basic statutory requirement which an injured workman must satisfy in order to receive compensation, is that his injury was caused by

---

[32] Ibid., 448
[33] Ibid., 451
[34] *Boardman* v *Scott & Whitworth* [1902] 1 KB 46
[35] [1910] AC 242
[36] Ibid., 246
[37] *Challis* v *London & South Western Railway* [1905] 2 KB 154.
[38] [1914] AC 667

accident arising out of and in the course of his employment. There is greater acceptance of the view that the phrase "arising out of and in the course of employment" has two arms and that both arms must be satisfied for a claim to succeed. An accident must not only occur "in the course of, that is to say during actual employment, but in addition must arise, "out of it."[39] Buckley LJ put it this way:[40]

> The words "out of and in the course of the employment" are used conjunctively, not disjunctively. Upon ordinary principles of construction they are not to be read as meaning "out of" that is to say, "in the course of." The former words must mean something different to the latter words. The workman must satisfy both the one and the other.

And the words "out of" have been held to necessitate proof of a causal link or connection between an accident and the employment. In other words the employment must be the cause of the accident. As Lord Haldane said "there is required to be shown something in the nature of a causal relation between the accident and an order, expressed or implied, given by the employer.[41] Similarly the court said in *UAC* v. *Orekyan*[42] that "for an accident to arise out of the employment there must be some causal relations between the accident and the employment other than the mere coincidence of the accident with the currency of the employment."[43] It would appear, therefore, at least in practical terms, that an accident which arises out of must necessarily arise in the course of employment. How can there be a causal relation between accident and employment if an injured workman was not engaged in performing the work he is engaged to do? It is suggested that an accident which arises out of would normally also arise in the course of employment. But the converse may not be true. An accident may arise in the course of employment but may have no causal relation with the employment. In practical terms, therefore, an injured workman may succeed or fail in his claim for compensation depending upon whether the court holds that what he was doing was or was not his employment. The scope given to employment becomes crucial.

The term "employment" includes, of course, the work which a workman is employed to do. That must be what he was engaged upon doing at the time of the

---

[39] Per Viscount Haldane in *Davidson & Co* v. *M'Robb* [1918] AC 304, 317; see also Lord Sumner in *J & P Hutchinson* v. *M'Kinnon* [1916] 1 AC 471, 485.
[40] *Fitzgerald* v. *W.G. Clarke & Son* [1908] 2 KB 796, 799.
[41] *Davidson & Co* v. *M'Robb* [1918] AC 304, 317.
[42] (1961) LLR 144.
[43] Ibid., 145.

accident. So that where a workman is carrying out his duty under his contract of employment any accident which occurs, such as, for example, from an explosion from or of the machinery upon which he is working, or from broken bits of machinery, tool or material with which he is working, or from a malfunctioning of machinery, such an accident would obviously arise out of his employment. The causal relation there is clear. He would also, clearly, be in the course of his employment.

However it is well established that "employment" is not to be confined to the actual work for which a workman is employed. As Lord Shaw has said the expression "arising out of employment" is not confined to the mere "nature of the employment." The expression applies to the employment as such - to its nature, its conditions, its obligations, and its incidents.[44] Lord Finlay said the expression "obviously means arising out of the work which the man is employed to do and what is incident to it in other words, out of his service."[45]

In *Thom (or Simpson)* v. *Sinclair*[46] a woman employed as a fishcurer was engaged in packing kippered herrings into boxes in her employer's shed when a brick wall which was under construction on an adjoining property not belonging to her employer, collapsed on the shed bringing down its roof and part of its wall on the woman. The House of Lords held that the accident arose out of employment. The following is from Lord Parmoor's judgement:[47]

> My Lords, apart from authority it appears to me to be reasonably clear, and in accordance with the ordinary natural meaning of the language of the statute to hold, that if the conditions of his employment oblige a workman to work in a particular building or position which exposes him at the time and on the occasion of the accident to the injury for which compensation is claimed, then, although the accident is not consequent on and has no causal relation to the work on which the workman is employed, such accident arises out of his employment, as incident, not to the character of the work, but to the dangers and risks of the particular building or position in which by the conditions of his employment he is obliged to work. The Workmen's Compensation Act connotes no distinction between such dangers and risks and dangers and risks incident to the plant required in the employment, or to the particular machine at which the workman

[44] *Thom or Simpson* v. *Sinclair* [1917] AC 127, 142.
[45] *Davidson & Co* v. *M'Robb* [1918] AC 304, 314.
[46] [1917] AC 127.
[47] Ibid., 144-145.

> may be engaged at the time of the accident. In either case the workman is subjected to an accident which arises out of his employment.

In *Brooker* v. *Thomas Borthwick & Sons (Australasia) Ltd*[48] the Privy Council said:[49]

> If a workman is injured by some natural force such as lightning, the heat of the sun, or extreme cold, which in itself has no kind of connection with employment, he cannot recover unless he can sufficiently associate such injury with his employment. This he can do if he can show that the employment exposed him in a special degree to suffering such an injury.

In *Challis* v. *London & South Western Railway*[50] the engine driver of a train was injured when a boy wilfully dropped a stone on the train while the driver was driving the train and passing under a bridge. It was held by the English Court of Appeal that the risk of such an occurrence, that is, of mischievous boys throwing missiles at a train in motion, was reasonably incidental to the employment of an engine driver. In *Nisbet* v. *Bayne & Burn*[51] a cashier who was travelling in a train with a large sum of money for the payment of his employer's workmen was shot at and killed and the money stolen. The same court held that the risk of robbery and murder were incidental to his employment as a cashier. An attack on an assistant teacher by school boys was an accident which arose out of the teacher's employment.[52] In *UAC* v. *Orekyan*[53] a workman was employed and put in charge of a petrol station. One morning while the workman was checking the overnight sales in the sales room of the station, a stranger entered the sales room to ask for change. When one of the attendants under the workman told the stranger there was no change the stranger threatened the attendant with a fight. Whereupon the workman took a position between them in order to prevent a fight. The stranger then hit the workman in the eye as a result of which he lost the eye. De Lestang CJ held that there was a clear relation between the accident and employment. He said it seems to me beyond argument that it was the duty of respondent to

[48] [1933] AC 669.
[49] Ibid., 677.
[50] [1905] 2 KB 154.
[51] [1910] 2 KB 689.
[52] *Trim Joint District School Board of Management* v. *Kelly*, Supra.
[53] (1961) LLR 144.

maintain order at the petrol station and to protect his subordinate co-employee from being molested by a stranger.[54]

The so-called locality cases also come under the same principle. If a workman's duty occasions his being at the place where the accident occurs then the accident arises out of employment. *Thom (or Simpson)* v. *Sinclair*,[55] as we have seen, is a good example. Also where a workman who was riding a bicycle through the public streets having been directed by his employer to go on the bicycle to get some plaster and came into collision with a motor car and his leg broken was held to have suffered personal injury by accident arising out of his employment.[56] Lord Finlay said: "The use of the streets by the workman merely to get to or from his work of course stands on a different footing altogether, but as soon as it is established that the work itself involves exposure to the perils of the streets the workman can recover for any injury so occasioned."[57] Where a commercial traveller who was travelling home after business was struck on the road by a falling tree which was blown down by a severe gale the court held that the accident arose out of employment.[58] In *Tanko Maikujeri* v. *Provincial Engineer*[59] a workman was killed by a lorry belonging to a third party while he was working on the side of the road. It was held that the accident arose out of the employment.

In the course of

We have seen that an injured workman must not only show that his injury was caused by accident which arose out of but also that it arose in the course of his employment. As Lord Wright said:[60]

> It is clear that there are two conditions to be fulfilled. What arises "in the course" of the employment is to be distinguished from what arises "out of the employment." The former words relate to time conditioned by reference to the man's service, the later to causality. Not every accident which occurs to a man during the time when he is on his employment - that is, directly or indirectly engaged on what he is employed to do- gives claim to compensation, unless it also arises out of the employment.

---

[54] Ibid., 145.
[55] *Supra*.
[56] *Dennis* v. *A. J. White & Co* [1917] AC 479.
[57] Ibid., 482.
[58] *Lawrence v. George Matthews* [1929] 1 KB 1.
[59] [1981] 2 PLR 587.
[60] *Dover Navigation Co* v. *Craig* [1939] 4 All ER 558, 563.

It is established that the words "in the course of" do not mean merely that the workman is still in employment when the accident happened although, no doubt, his contract of employment must still be subsisting when the accident occurred. "In the course of the employment" does not mean during the currency of the time of the engagement."[61] "In my view," said Lord Dunedin,[62] 'in the course of employment' is a different thing from 'during the period of employment.' It connotes to my mind, the idea that the workman or servant is doing something which is part of his service to his employer or master." In the course of employment, therefore, means that a workman must be engaged in carrying out his duty under his contract of employment. A "workman is acting in the course of his employment when he is engaged 'in doing something he was employed to do.' Or what is, in other and I think better words, in effect the same thing namely, when he is doing something in discharge of a duty to his employer, directly or indirectly, imposed upon him by his contract of service."[63]

However it is also well settled that a workman may be in the course of his employment even where he is engaged in doing something which is not in discharge of a duty to his employer imposed upon him by his contract of employment. In *St. Helens Colliery Co Ltd* v. *Hewitson*[64] Lord Wrenbury said:[65]

> The words "and in the course of" are not equivalent to "during." The accident must occur during the employment, but more than that, it must occur "in the course of the employment." The employment may be by the year. The accident must, of course, be one which happens during the year, but more than that, it must be in the course of employment during the year. The employment may be to do some defined manual work, say, hewing coal, but the accident need not arise when the man is actually using his pick. He may be going down in the cage. He may be resting between shifts. He may be taking a meal. He may be merely standing by, waiting for the next job. All these, and such as these, are not "the employment" but are incidental to the employment. The man is in the course of his employment is engaged in his employment in all such cases.

The same point has been stressed in the more recent decision in *R. V. Industrial Injuries Commissioner.*[66] Salmon, LJ, said I assume that in law a man is working

---

[61] Lord Finlay in *Davidson & Co* v. *M'Robb* [1918] AC 304, 315.
[62] *Davidson & Co* v. *M'Robb*, ibid., 321.
[63] Lord Atkinson in *St. Helens Coliery Co Ltd* v. *Hewitsón* [1924] AC 59, 71.
[64] [1924] AC 59.
[65] Ibid., 91.
[66] [1966] 2 QB 31.

in the course of his employment not only when he is doing what he is employed to do but also when he is doing something for purposes of his own which is reasonably incidental to his employment.[67] And Lord Denning, MR, described it as a "very sensible rule that even though a person is not obliged to be in a particular place, but goes there for something incidental to his employment, such as for a meal to a canteen, he is acting in the course of his employment.[68] In a much earlier case in the House of Lords Lord Loreburn LC said:[69]

> When we speak of a workman being employed it means that he is engaged to do certain things at certain times and in certain places. If the question be whether an accident befell him "in the course" of that employment, the first inquiry is, was he doing any of the things which he might reasonably do while so employed?. The next inquiry is, Did the accident occur within the time covered by the employment?...The last inquiry is, Did the accident occur at a place where he may reasonably be while in the employment?
> And so, to sum it up, I think an accident befalls a man "in the course of" his employment if it occurs while he is doing what a man so employed may reasonably do within a time during which he is employed, and at a place where he may reasonably be during that time to do that thing.

It follows, clearly, that whether anything done by a workman during his hours of work is in discharge of his contractual duty or is reasonably incidental to such a duty is a question of fact. In *Lowry* v. *The Sheffield Coal Co Ltd*,[70] where a workman who was not actually on duty but was going to collect his wages when he was knocked down on the employer's premises by an engine, it was held that the accident arose in the course of his employment. In *Slavin* v. *A.M. Carmichael & Co Ltd.*[71] a workman was employed to drive a tractor to which was attached a scraper for removing top soil. While driving the tractor the scraper jammed so the workman got down to release it with an iron bar. On releasing it a spring sprang into operation and the workman's leg was caught by a rope connected to the spring. He was held to be doing work incidental to his employment as the tractor driver. Lord Macmillan said:[72]

> It is no doubt most relevant in such cases as the present to ascertain the ordinary scope of the workman's employment, in the sense of the job which he was employed to perform. But in the case of many forms of employment uncontemplated vicissitudes may arise with which the employee must cope as

---

[67] Ibid., 51.
[68] Ibid., 47.
[69] *Moore* v. *Manchester Liners Ltd* [1910] AC 498, 500-501.
[70] (1907) 24 TLR 142.
[71] [1945] 1 ALL ER 292.
[72] Ibid., 297.

> best he can, although in so doing he may not strictly be doing the job he was employed to perform.

In *R* v. *Industrial Injuries Commissioner*[73] the workman, a fitter, could smoke only in specially provided booths. When he went to have a smoke during a ten minutes tea break he found all the booths occupied so he squatted beside a booth and was rolling a cigarette and chatting to a colleague when he was struck by a fork-lift driven negligently across the floor. At the time he was struck by the fork-lift he had overstayed the break by five minutes. The Court of Appeal upheld a finding that what he was doing was not incidental to his employment as he had overstayed the tea break. It would appear that the court was reluctant to differ from a finding of fact having agreed that the proper principles of the law had been applied. In deciding in which way the balance should be tilted in such cases it is well to always remember the words of Matthew LJ in *Benson* v. *Lancashire & Yorkshire Railway Company:*[74]

> I wish to say that I do not think that the protection given by the Act can be confined to the time during which a workman is actually engaged in manual labour, and that he would not be protected during the intervals of leisure which may occur in the course of his daily employment. A workman is not a machine, and must be treated as likely to act as workmen ordinarily would during such intervals: and, as regards any reasonable use which, while on the employer's premises, he may make of moments when he is not actually working, I must not be supposed to say that he would be thereby deprived of the protection of the Act.

The problem may arise of when employment begins or ends. A workman is in employment from the time when he commences work to when he closes from his work unless, of course, he interrupts the employment by the doing of something which he is not employed to do or which is not reasonably incidental to his employment. As Collins MR said:

> it would appear *prima facie*...that the man was in his master's employment during the whole of each day, from the time at which he went to his work to the time when he came away, and equally during the dinner hour, if he stayed, as during any other part of the time. He would be there on the contract with his master during all those hours, either directly in order to do that for which he was employed as for some purpose ancillary thereto. That

[73] [1966] 2 QB 31.
[74] [1904] 1 KB 242, 251.

> would embrace all his movements within the ambit of the factory, going or coming or stopping there for any purpose ancillary to his work.[75]

However the course of employment is not limited to the time or place of the specific work which a workman is employed to do. It does not necessarily end when the down tools signal is given, or when the actual workshop where he is working is left. In other words the employment may run on its course by its own momentum beyond the actual stopping place.[76] The leading authority is *John Stewart & Son Ltd* v. *Longhurst.*[77] A carpenter was employed in repairing a barge lying in a dock not open to the public and not belonging to his employer although the employer and his workmen had the permission of the dock owners to pass through the dock on their way to and from the barge upon which repair was being carried out. While on his way home after his day's work but while still on the dock premises the carpenter fell into the water and was drowned. The House of Lords held he was in the course of his employment. The point had been made earlier by the House in *Northumbrian Shipping Co Ltd* v. *McCullum*[78] where Lord Macmillan said:[79]

> It has been recognised time and again that the sphere of a workman's employment is not necessarily limited to the actual place where he does his work. If in going to or coming from his work he has to use an access which is part of his employer's premises or which he is only entitled to traverse because he is going to or coming from his work, he is held to be on his master's business while he is using that access.

Where a workman is already on his employer's premises but he has not reached his actual place of work he may yet be held to be in the course of his employment. A reasonable margin must be allowed to the workman for the purpose of getting to the part of the premises where his actual work is to be carried on.[80] Similarly, a workman who gets to the employer's premises earlier than the time of commencement of work may be in the course of his employment. In *Sharp* v. *Johnson & Co Ltd*[81] a workman had to travel to his work place where work commenced at 6:30 a.m. In order not to get to work late

---

[75] *Blovelt* v. *Sawyer* [1904] 1 KB 271, 273-274.
[76] Per Lord Atkin in *Weaver* v. *Tredegar Iron & Co Ltd* [1940] AC 955, 966.
[77] [1917] AC 249.
[78] (1932) 48 TLR 568.
[79] Ibid., 572.
[80] Per Collins, MR, in *Sharp* v. *Johnson & Co Ltd* [1905] 2 KB 139, 145.
[81] *Supra.*

he had to take a train which enabled him to get to work 20 minutes earlier than 6:30 a.m. When he arrived work that early one morning he was proceeding to take refreshment at a place provided by the employer for that purpose when he fell into an excavation and suffered injury. The English Court of Appeal held that the accident arose in the course of employment.

The terms of a contract of employment may bring travel period within the course of employment. In *Blee* v. *London & North Eastern Railway Co*[82] the terms of the workman's contract provided that he might be called out on emergency work outside his normal working hours and that if he was so called he would be paid overtime pay as from the time he left his home. When he was so called and he was knocked down in the street by a car on his way to the place of work, it was held the accident arose in the course of the employment.

However where a workman is merely on his way to or from his place of work it is well established that he is not in the course of his employment.[83] And this is so even where a workman is travelling in a vehicle provided by the employer either voluntarily or in discharge of a statutory obligation.[84] In *Smith* v. *Elder Dempster Lines Ltd*[85] the court said the general rule is that a man's employment does not begin until he has reached the place where he has to work or the ambit, scope or scene of his duty and it does not continue after he has left it and the periods of going and returning are generally excluded. The facts of the case were these - the workman had the permission of his employer to use a motor tug provided by the employer to ferry their workmen from Lagos to Apapa and back to Lagos at the close of work. The workman finished work at Apapa at 9:45 p.m. on a moonless night and was trying to get into the motor tug by jumping into another motor tug which was between him and the employer's tug when he fell into the lagoon. He suffered a dislocated shoulder. The court said he had left the place where he was employed to work and held that the accident did not arise in the course of employment. But the court admitted two exceptions to the rule. Where a workman is under a contractual obligation to use the means of transport provided and where the transport provided or the access used to get to or from work affords the only reasonable means of doing so any accident occurring may be in the course of employment. In *Scandinavian Shipping Agencies* v. *Ajide*[86] the workman was already in a launch - the Mahogany which was to ferry him and

---

[82] [1938] AC 126; applied in *Dunn* v. *Lockwood & Co* [1947] 1 All ER 446.

[83] *Smith* v. *Elder Dempster Lines Ltd* (1944) 17 NLR 145; *Ngankan* v. *Strabag (Nig) Ltd.* Unreported FSC Suit No.130/60.

[84] *Pascal & Ludwig Inc.* v. *Gabriel Bello,* unreported Suit No.1/42A/68 High Court, Ibadan.

[85] *Supra.*

[86] [1965] 2 All NLR 228.

his co-workmen to Lagos from Apapa and the launch had just moved about 46 centimetres when another workman, in trying to jump into the Mahogany, held the clothes of the workman and both of them fell into the lagoon and drowned. The court held that the deceased workmen were not in the course of employment. In *Pascal & Ludwig Inc.* v. *Gabriel Bello*[87] the deceased workman was employed as a mechanic at the Asejire dam site some kilometres away from Ibadan where he lived. The employer, who was under a statutory duty to provide transportation or pay an allowance in lieu, provided a lorry transport to convey the deceased and other workmen to and from the dam site. On one of its trips to the site from Ibadan the lorry collided with another vehicle and the deceased died on the spot. It was held that the deceased was not in the course of employment.

It seems well settled that when a workman is taking his meal during a meal break on the employer's premises he is in the course of his employment whether or not he is obliged to use the meal facility provided by the employer.[88] The same is true of a workman who uses the toilet facilities. In *Weaver* v. *Tredegar Iron & Coal Co*[89] Lord Atkin said it is well settled that a man injured while taking refreshment on the premises at a permitted hour or otherwise relieving necessities of nature is in the course of his employment. In *Armstrong, Whitworth & Co Ltd* v. *Redford*,[90] a female machinist, during dinner hour, went to a canteen provided by her employer but which she need not use, to have a meal. After the meal she was hurrying down a flight of stairs leading from the canteen to the street in order to get back to her place of work when she slipped and broke her ankle. By a majority of three to two the House of Lords held that the accident arose in the course of employment.[91] Similarly the English Court of Appeal held in *Knight* v. *Howard Wall Ltd*[92] that an accident which happened in a canteen on the employer's premises which the workman was free to use or not as he wished arose in the course of employment.

Forbidden acts of workmen

Sub-section 3(3) reads as follows:

---

[87] *Supra*.
[88] *Blovelt* v. *Sawyer* [1904] 1 KB 271.
[89] [1940] AC 955
[90] Ibid., 966
[91] [1920] AC 757.
[92] [1938] 4 All ER 667.

> For the purpose of this Act, an accident resulting in the death or serious and permanent incapacity of a workman shall be deemed to arise out of and in the course of his employment, notwithstanding that the workman was at the time when the accident happened acting in contravention:
> (a) of any statutory or other regulation applicable to his employment; or
> (b) of any orders given by or on behalf of his employer; or
> (c) that he was acting without instructions from his employer, if such act was done by the workman for the purpose of and in connection with his employer's trade or business.

This sub-section is meant to expand the area of claim for compensation by an injured workman. Before its introduction a workman could not claim where he had disobeyed an order or statutory prohibition although but for such order or prohibition he would have been in the course of his employment. In *Moore & Co* v. *Donnelly*,[93] by statute, where a shot by a miner misses fire the miner must not approach the hole within an hour of the shot. The workman here returned to the place of a shot within ten minutes of the shot and it blew into his face. Clearly he would have been in the course of his employment but for the prohibition but he was unable to recover. The sub-section now permits recovery in that type of case. But a claim may be recovered only in respect of death or serious and permanent incapacity. Therefore it may be necessary at times to distinguish this situation from the case where a prohibition does not limit the scope of employment but merely prescribes a manner of conduct. Where a workman does an act within his employment he can always recover although he may have done it wrongly in the sense of disobeying an order as to how to do it. Lord Dunedin explains the difference thus - there are prohibitions which limit the sphere of employment, and prohibitions which only deal with conduct within the sphere of employment. A transgression of the former class carries with it the result that the man has gone outside the sphere.[94]

It is, of course, a question of fact, which may be a difficult one, whether a prohibition is of one class or the other. The question to ask is, Did the order which was disobeyed limit the sphere of employment, or was it merely a direction not to do certain things, or to do them in a certain way within the sphere of employment?[95] In *Whitehead* v. *Reader*[96] a workman who was employed as a carpenter was entitled to sharpen his tools on a grindstone rotated by machinery but he had orders not to touch the machinery. When, however, the

---

[93] [1921] 1 AC 329; see also *Bourton* v. *Beauchamp* [1920] AC 1001.
[94] *Plumb* v. *Cobden Flour Mills Company Ltd* [1914] AC 62, 67.
[95] Ibid., 66.
[96] [1901] 2 KB 48.

band which rotated the machinery slipped he tried to replace it on the machinery and he was injured. The court held that the order was not of the type that limited the employment. Collins L. J. said:[97]

> I agree in what has already been pointed out, that it is not every breach of a master's orders that would have the effect of terminating the servant's employment so as to excuse the master from the consequences of the breach of his orders. We have to get back to the orders emanating from the master to see what is the sphere of employment of the workman, and it must be competent to the master to limit the sphere. If the servant acting within the sphere of his employment violates the order of his master, the latter is responsible.

It must be noted, however, that the sub-section has no application at all where, in the first place, the workman's act had nothing to do with his duties or anything necessarily ancillary or incidental to his employment. In order words if a workman is not acting in the course of his employment, apart from any prohibition, the sub-section has no application and a claim will not succeed. In *The Queen* v. *d'Albuquerque, Ex parte Bresnahen*,[98] a dock labourer, engaged in loading a ship attempted to use a fork-lift truck left unattended by its driver to remove some boards which were in the way of loading the ship when he and the truck fell into the water and he drowned. It was held he was doing something different from what he was employed to do and so could not rely on the sub-section.[99]

Liability to pay compensation

The liability to pay compensation is, as we have seen, placed on the employer of an injured workman.[100] Although there is no real definition of employer the interpretation section of the Act[101] provides that employer includes:

(i) the government of the Federation of Nigeria and of any State;

---

[97] Ibid., 51.

[98] [1966] 1 Lloyd's Rep.69; see also *Wilson & Clyde Coal Co Ltd* v. *M'Ferrin* and *Kerr* v. *James Dunlop & Co* [1926] AC 377.

[99] In *Kay* v. *ITW Ltd* [1968] 1 QB 140 Sellers LJ thought that had the case been by appeal rather than by the limited procedure of certiorari the Divisional Court might have decided differently; ibid., 151.

[100] S. 3(1).

[101] S.41.

(ii) any body of persons corporate or unincorporate and the legal personal representative of a deceased employer; and,

(iii) where the services of a workman are temporarily lent or let on hire to another person by the person with whom the workman has entered into a contract of service or apprenticeship, the latter shall, for the purposes of the Act, be deemed to continue to be the employer of the workman whilst he is working for that other person; and

(iv) in relation to a person employed for the purposes of any game or recreation and engaged or paid through a club, the manager, or members of the managing committee of the club, shall, for the purposes of this Act, be deemed to be the employer.

An employer may, therefore, be an individual, a firm or partnership, a company or a government. As will be seen a person who is deemed to be a workman who can therefore claim compensation is a person who has entered into or is working under a contract of service or apprenticeship with an employer.

It is suggested that the government of the Federation of Nigeria or of any State will include any unit of such government with which a workman has entered into a contract of employment. The provisions of the Act apply to a workman employed in the public service of the Federation or of any State in the same way and to the same extent as if the employer were a private person.[102] Public service of the Federation or of a State means service of the federation or of a state in any capacity in respect of the government of the federation or of a state. It also includes service as clerk or staff of a legislature, member or staff of any court established by the Constitution or statute, member or staff of any commission or authority established by the Constitution or statute, staff of any statutory corporation or of a local government established by statute, staff of any educational institution established or financed principally by the government of the federation or of a state, staff of any company or enterprise in which the government of the Federation or of a State or their agency owns controlling shares or interest and members or officers of the armed forces of the federation or the Nigeria Police Force.[103]

---

[102] S.2 (1)(a); sub-section 2 (1)(b) appears superfluous as the Nigeria Police Force is already taken care of within the public service.

[103] S. 2(2) and s.318 Constitution of the Federal Republic of Nigeria, 1979. By S.2(2), however, the Act does not apply to any member of the Nigeria Army, the Nigerian Navy or the Nigerian Air Force except a person employed in a civilian capacity or to any workman employed in the public service who has been first engaged outside Nigeria and is not a citizen of Nigeria.

By definition a body of persons unincorporate is an employer. In relation to a person employed for the purposes of any game or recreation and engaged or paid through a club the employer is the manager or members of the managing committee of the club. The legal personal representative of a deceased employer becomes the employer.

Employer also includes any body of persons corporate. Where such an employer is a company within the meaning of a company under the Companies and Allied Matters Act and there is a winding up, unless where it is a winding up voluntarily merely for the purpose of reconstruction or of amalgamation with another company, all amounts due in respect of any compensation are part of the preferential payments which must be paid in priority to all other debts. Where, however, such a company has, at the commencement of the winding up, a policy of insurance in respect of any liability for workmen's compensation to any workman, the above provision is inapplicable and s.26 becomes applicable.[104] By s.26 where such a company has entered into a contract with any insurers in respect of any liability under the Act to any workman, then, in the event of the company having commenced to be wound up or a receiver or manager of the company's business or undertaking business or undertaking having been duly appointed, or possession having been taken by or on behalf of the holders of debentures secured by a floating charge of any property comprised in or subject to the charge, the rights of the company against the insurers as respects that liability are transferred to and vest in the workman. Upon such a transfer the insurers have the same rights and remedies and are subject to the same liabilities as if they were the company. However the insurers are not under any greater liability to the workman than they would have been to the company. If the liability of the insurers to the workman is found to be less than the liability of the company to the workman the workman may claim for the balance in the liquidation or recover the balance from the receiver or manager. Except in such a case the workman cannot prove in the liquidation of the company not even where the insurers have also gone into liquidation.[105] The workman's claim is a direct claim against the insurers.

Where the services of a workman are temporarily lent or let on hire to another person by the person with whom the workman entered into a contract of service or apprenticeship the person with whom he entered into a contract of service or apprenticeship is deemed to continue to be the employer of the workman whilst the workman is working for that other person. Thus the person who lent or gave the workman on hire temporarily remains responsible for all the

---

[104] S. 494 (1)(f) Companies and Allied Matters Act.

[105] In *re Pethick, Dix & Co* [1915] 1 Ch.26; In *re Renishaw Iron Company Ltd* [1917]1 Ch 199.

liabilities and duties including payment of compensation where the workman suffers injury or death. However it is the workman's employment with the borrower or hirer which must be regarded for the purpose of determining whether the injury was caused by accident arising out of or in the cause of employment. It has been said that lending does not involve payment by the borrower to the lender employer and that, unless the lender is prepared to bear the cost of the work, it may mean a direct payment of wages by the borrower to the workman but that in contrast, to let on hire will usually involve payment to the employer who gave the workman on hire.[106] The contract of service between the lender or the person who gave the workman on hire and the workman must be subsisting during the loan or hire period for the original employer to remain liable. Whether there is a lending or hiring would appear to be a question of fact. In *Huscroft* v. *Bennet*[107] the Court held that the evidence showed that the workman's injury was received when he was doing work under a separate and independent contract which he himself had made with another person. Similarly in *Oates* v. *Thomas Turner & Co*[108] where the workman obtained permission from his employer to take in work for other persons provided it did not interfere with the work which the employer required to be done, it was held by the English Court of Appeal that there was no evidence of lending. Only where there is a lending or letting on hire does the original employer remain liable to pay compensation to his workman who suffers injury whilst working for another.

Employment by contractors

Section 23 deals with a situation where a person employs a contractor to carry out work for him. That person is made liable to pay compensation to the workmen of the contractor for injury suffered while carrying out the work. It is provided that where any person-the principal-in the course of or for the purposes of his trade or business, contracts with any other person - the contractor-for the execution by or under the contractor of the whole or any part of any work undertaken by the principal, the principal is liable to pay to any workman employed in the execution of the work any compensation under the Act which he would have been liable to pay if that workman had been immediately employed

[106] Majority judgement of the High Court of Australia in *Fogarty* v. *Dowerin Road Board* (1935) 53 CLR 510, 515.
[107] (1914) 110 LT 494.
[108] (1916) 32 TLR 659.

by him.[109] However this provision does not apply in any case where the accident occurred elsewhere than on, or in, or about premises on which the principal has undertaken to execute the work or which are otherwise under his control or management.[110]

It has been held that the provision is not limited to a case where there are only two parties - a principal and contractor - but that it also applies where there are a principal, a contractor and a sub-contractor.[111] The purpose of the provision, it seems, is to prevent an employer who wants to execute some work in the course of or for the purpose of his business, from avoiding payment of compensation by bringing in an impecunious contractor between himself and workmen engaged in executing the work. As Collins L. J. said:[112]

> The reason of such a provision obviously is that, if a person substitutes another for himself to do that which is his own business, he ought not to escape the liability which would have been imposed upon him, if he had done it himself, towards the workmen employed in that business.

The work undertaken by the principal must be in the course of or for the purpose of the trade or business which he carries on. The word "undertaken" does not mean that the principal executes the work himself but that the work being in the course of or for the purpose of his trade or business he contracts it or any part of it for execution by another. In *Dittmar* v. *Owners of Ship V 593*[113] a company carried on business as coal merchants and lightermen in England and elsewhere including Cape Verde. The company purchased a lighter in England for use in Cape Verde. They entered into a contract with someone to take the lighter to Cape Verde and there deliver it to them. The contractor was to provide efficient crew and pay their wages. One of the crew who was injured on the way was held to come within the provision. In *Hockley* v. *West London Timber & Joinery Company*[114] the workman was not so fortunate. A company carried on the business of manufacturing mouldings. The company usually got timber, which was the raw material it used, from abroad and these were usually carried by contractors to the company's yard where they were then stacked by another contractor. A workman of a stacking contractor fell and was injured while piling

---

[109] S. 23(1).

[110] S. 23(5).

[111] *Dittmar* v. *Owners of Ship* v *593* [1909] 1 KB 389; *Skates* v. *Jones & Co* [1910] 2 KB 903; *Hockley* v. *West London Timber and Joinery Company* [1914] 3 KB 1013.

[112] *Wrigley* v. *Bagley & Wright* [1901] 1 QB 780, 783.

[113] [1909] 1 KB 389; see also *Heywood & Bryett Ltd* v. *Heywood & Son* [1940] 2 KB 145.

[114] *Supra.*

timber in the company's yard. The English Court of Appeal held the workman did not come within the provision. The stacking of timber which was undertaken or contracted out was not part of the business of the manufacturing of mouldings which was the sole business of the principal. It was not enough that the work was incidental to or reasonably necessary for the business of the company.

In *Dittmar* v. *Owners of Ship V593*[115] it was held that premises within the section included a vessel. However whether an accident has occurred on, or in, or about the premises on which the work is being executed is a question of fact. The word "about" is clearly an enlarging word to the words "on, in," and it is a geographical expression and not about the business of the employer.[116] In the many cases in which the courts have had to answer the question whether the accident occurred on, or in or about premises under the control of the principal the courts seemed to have decided the issue on the facts of each case.[117] But in some of them it was thought that "about" meant physical proximity[118] or, as Lord Atkinson said "in close proximity to."[119]

Where a claim or application for compensation is made against a principal he must give notice of it to the contractor who would then be entitled to intervene in any application made against the principal.[120] However, nothing prevents a workman from directly recovering compensation from the contractor- i.e. his employer rather than from the principal.[121] Where no claim can be made against the employer on the ground that the injured employee is not a workman within the Act such a person cannot also claim from the principal.[122]

---

115 *Supra.*

116 Collins LJ in *Fenn* v. *Miller* [1900] 1 QB 788, 792.

117 Workman and cart some 11/2 miles away from factory held not about the factory *Lowth* v. *Ibbotson* [1899] 1 QB 1003; workman and cart in the street close to factory entrance held about the factory *Powell* v. *Brown* [1899] 1 QB 157; a place about 110 to 160 yards away held not about *Fenn* v. *Miller* [1900] 1 QB 788; workman in another's premises held not about principal's premises *Wrigley* v. *Whittaker & Sons* [1902] AC 299; workman who fell into the sea $1^1/_2$ miles away at sea from the point being dredged held not about the dredging premises *Chambers* v. *Whitehaven Harbour Commissioners* [1899] 2 QB 132; a place 1/4 mile away from premises held not about premises *Spacey* v. *Dowlais Gas & Coke Co Ltd* [1905] 2 KB 879; a place two miles away from premises held not about the premises *Andrews* v. *Andrews & Mears* [1908] 2 KB 567; but see *Atkinson* v. *Lumb* [1903] 1 KB 861 where accident occurred on the premises of the principal.

118 *Powell* v. *Brown*; *Fenn* v. *Miller*; supra.

119 *Back* v. *Dick Kerr & Co Ltd* [1906] AC 325, 334.

120 S.23 (3)

121 S. 23(4).

122 *Marks v. Carne* [1909] 2 KB 516.

Where the principal is liable to pay compensation he is entitled to be indemnified by any person who would have been liable to pay compensation to the workman.[123] This person is of course, the contractor who was the employer of the workman. However under section 24(b) the employer would himself be entitled to be indemnified where the injury was caused in circumstances creating a legal liability in some other person by that person.[124]

Persons entitled to compensation

Compensation is payable to or for the benefit of a workman or, where death results from the injury, to or for the benefit of the dependants of the workman.[125] Where a dependant dies before a claim is made or, if a claim has been made, before an order for payment of compensation has been made, the claim for compensation must be dealt with as if the dependant had died before the workman; the deceased dependants legal personal representation has no right to payment of compensation.[126] The right of a dependant to compensation is a direct one against the employer and it is separate and distinct from that of the deceased workman.[127]

Meaning of workman

The word workman has now been given a greatly expanded meaning.[128] A person is deemed to be a workman if either before or after the commencement of the Act he has entered into or is working under a contract of service or apprenticeship with an employer by way of manual labour, clerical work or otherwise, and whether the contract is expressed or implied, is oral or in

---

[123] S. 23(2)

[124] See below.

[125] S.11(l); where death results a medical certificate as to the cause of death must be produced by the dependants of the deceased workman to the employer, s. 11(1) proviso; where there are both total and partial dependants the compensation may be allotted partly to the total and partly to the partial dependants, s. 11(2).

[126] S. 11(3); this provision reverses the decision of the House of Lords in *United Collieries Ltd* v. *Simpson or Hendry* [1909] A.C. 383 that the right of a dependant passed to his executor when the dependant dies without having made a claim.

[127] *Tucker* v. *Oldbury Urban District Council* [1912] 2 KB 317.

[128] Under the old legislation it meant only employees who did manual labour and non-manual employees who earned not more than ₦1,600 per annum.

writing.[129] This definition is familiar[130] and is similar to that which was the subject matter for interpretation by the House of Lords in *National Association of Local Government Officers* v. *Bolton Corporation.*[131] In that case it was held that the words "or otherwise" covered employment which was neither for manual labour nor clerical work. Thus the definition is extended by the words "or otherwise" to cover also any person employed under a contract of service for any type of work other than by way of manual labour or clerical work. As Lord Wright said, the definition was intended to embrace the entire range of wage earning or salaried employment.[132] In other words every employee at common law is also a workman under the Act.[133] It follows therefore that, apart from those employees who are expressly excluded, every employee can claim compensation under the Act provided he meets the conditions laid down for a claim and, as we will be seen, he is not allowed to obtain both common law damages and compensation for the same injury.[134]

By section 1(5) a contract of service also includes service as a tributer. Thus tributers also come within the definition of workman and are able to claim workmen's compensation. A tributer is a person who is employed to win minerals by the holder of a mining right, the grantee of a temporary mining right or temporary mining lease, or the lessee of a mining lease, being a person who may choose his own working place and who receives in return remuneration in accordance with the quality and quantity of the minerals so won paid directly by the person employing him or by his accredited agent.[135]

There are six categories of persons excluded from the definition of workman. Section 1(2) provides that a person shall not be deemed to be a workman if:

---

[129] S.1(1); if, in any proceedings for compensation, it appears that an injured workman was working under an illegal contract of service or apprenticeship the court may, if, having regard to all the circumstances of the case, it thinks proper to do so, deal with it as if the contract was valid s.1(3); also by s.1(4) any reference to a workman who is injured includes, where the workman is dead, a reference to his legal personal representatives or his dependants or any of them or the Federal Attorney-General or such other officer as the Minister may appoint on behalf of the dependants of the workman; such reference is however not for the purpose of entering into an agreement for compensation under s. 16.

[130] There are similar definitions in other labour statutes.

[131] [1943] A.C. 166.

[132] [1943] A.C. 166, 186.

[133] Certain employees are excluded; see text.

[134] Some workmen cannot claim compensation; see text.

[135] s. 259 Minerals & Mining Act 1999, and see s.41

(a) he is a person employed under a contract of service or collective agreement approved for exemption by the Minister charged with responsibility for matters relating to labour;[136] or
(b) a person who is employed otherwise than for the purposes of his employer's trade or business, not being a person employed for the purposes of any game or recreation and engaged or paid through a club; or
(c) an outworker; or
(d) a member of the employer's family dwelling in his house; or
(e) a person employed in agricultural or handicraft work by an employer who normally employs less than ten workmen; or
(f) any class of person whom the Minister may by order published in the Gazette declare not to be workmen for the purposes of this Act.

A person employed for the purposes of any game or recreation and engaged or paid through a club is a workman although he is not employed for the purposes of the employer's trade or business. Any other person who is not employed for the purposes of his employer's trade or business is not a workman; he cannot claim workmen's compensation. Trade and business are not synonymous. Trade involves commerce in goods - the exchange of goods for money or other goods. Business is less precise. Lindley LJ said the word means almost anything which is an occupation as distinguished from a pleasure; any thing which is an occupation or duty which requires attention is a business.[137] In the same case Cotton LJ said business need not be a means of getting payment with a view to profit but that payment is certainly material in considering whether what is being done is, or is not, a business.[137a] It is a question of fact whether a person is employed for the purposes of the employer's trade or business and it depends on the facts of each case.[138] An outworker is defined as a person to whom articles or materials are given out to be made up, cleaned, washed, altered, ornamented, finished or repaired or adapted for sale in his own home or on other premises not under the control or management of the person who gave out the materials or articles.[139] Also a member of the employer's family dwelling in his house is excluded from the term workman.[140] A member of the family of an employer

[136] The meaning of this paragraph, especially the phrase "a person employed under...collective agreement" is obscure; the power to exempt has not been exercised.
[137] *Rolls* v. *Miller* (1884) 27 Ch. D. 71; see also In *re Duty on Estate of Incorporated Council of Law Reporting for England and Wales* (1889) 22 Q.B.D. 279.
[137a] (1884) 27 Ch. D 71, 85.
[138] *Manton* v. *Cantwell* [1920] AC 781.
[139] S. 41.
[140] For its application see *Marks* v. *Carne* [1909] 2 KB 516.

who is not dwelling in the employer's house would, however, be a workman. A member of the family means in respect of a family based on the paternal system, a mother, father, wife, son, daughter, brother, sister, father's father and father's brother and in respect to a family based on the maternal system, mother, father, wife, son, daughter, brother, sister, mother's mother, mother's brother, mother's sister, sister's son, sister's daughter, mother's sister's son and mother's sister's daughter. However in relation to a person who is not a Nigerian member of the family means wife, husband, father, mother, grandfather, grandmother, stepfather, stepmother, son, daughter, grandson, grand-daughter, stepson, step daughter, brother, sister, half-brother or half-sister.[141] A person employed in agricultural or handicraft work is or is not a workman depending on whether or not his employer normally employs less than ten workmen. If an employer normally employs less than ten workmen a person in that employment is not a workman. The crucial word seems to be the word "normally." The question should be whether the employer normally employs less or ten or more workmen and not whether at the time of accident the employer was employing less or ten or more workmen. It is obviously a question of fact.

By section 2(2) two classes of workmen cannot claim workmen's compensation. The Act does not apply to any member of the Nigerian Army, the Nigerian Navy, or the Nigerian Air Force except a workman employed in a civilian capacity. Similarly the Act does not apply to any workman engaged in a place outside Nigeria who is not a Nigerian citizen.

When compensation is payable

Compensation is payable by an employer in three cases - where the injury by accident results in death, where it results in permanent incapacity for work, total or partial and where it results in temporary incapacity for work, total or partial. Compensation is payable by the employer only where the death or incapacity for work "results" from the injury caused by the accident which arose out of and in the course of the employment. It is a question of causation. What caused the death or incapacity of the workman - is it the injury or some other factor such as the setting in of some disease[142] or negligence by a medical doctor?[143] In

[141] S. 41.

[142] See e.g. *Doolan* v. *Henry Hope & Sons Ltd* (1918) 119 LT 14, *Laverick* v. *William Gray & Co Ltd* (1919) 121 LT 289.

[143] See *Rothwell* v. *Caverswall Stone Co Ltd* [1944] 2 All ER 350; the position where the intervening event is a refusal of the workman to undergo medical treatment is dealt with by the Act and is considered below.

Dunham v. *Clare*[144] the deceased met with an accident which caused a wound to his toes. He was treated for the wound as an out-patient at a hospital but after some days erysipelas set in. The English Court of Appeal held that the proper test whether death resulted from the injury was not whether death was the natural or probable consequence of the injury but rather the question was, Did the death or incapacity in fact result from the injury? Or, as Cozens- Hardy L.J. put it, "The question is, from what in fact has death resulted?"[145] Collins M.R. said:[146]

> The question whether death resulted from the injury resolves itself into an inquiry into the chain of causation. If the chain of causation is broken by a *novus actus interveniens* so that the old cause goes and a new one is substituted for it, that is a new act which gives a fresh origin to the after consequences.

In *Rothwell* v. *Caverswall Stone Co Ltd*[147] a workman met with an accident but owing to the negligent diagnosis of a doctor who attended him it was not discovered in time that the injury he sustained was a fractured dislocation of the shoulder. When it was discovered it was too late for treatment to be successful - the arm had become fixed, and the dislocation irreducible. The issue for decision was whether the negligent diagnosis was the intervention of *novus actus*. The Court of Appeal was divided as to whether the principle in *Dunham* v. *Clare*[148] was the correct one to apply or whether principles in some other subsequent decisions of the court were to be applied.[149] Du Parq LJ however thought there was no conflict and his formulation of the applicable principle was later approved by the House of Lords in *Hogan* v. *Bentinck West Hartley Collieries (Owners) Ltd*[150] Du Parq LJ had said:[151]

> In my opinion, the following propositions may be formulated upon the authorities as they stand: first, an existing incapacity "results from" the

---

[144] [1902] 2 KB 292.
[145] [1902] 2 KB 292, 297.
[146] Ibid., 296; see also *Ystradowen Colliery* v. *Griffiths* [1902] 2 KB 533.
[147] [1944] 2 All ER 350.
[148] [1902] 2 KB 292.
[149] The most important of these decisions are *Humber Towing Co Ltd* v. *Barclay*; *Rocca* v. *Stanley Jones & Co Ltd* and *Lakey* v. *Blair & Co Ltd* (1911) 5 BWCC 142; (1914) 7 BWCC 101; and (1916) 10 BWCC 58 respectively.
[150] [1949] 1 All ER 588.
[151] [1902] 2 KB 292, 365.

> original injury if it follows, and is caused by, that injury, and may properly be held so to result even if some supervening cause has aggravated the effects of the original injury and prolonged the period of incapacity. If, however, the existing incapacity ought not fairly to be attributed to the original injury, it may properly be held to result from the new cause and not from the original injury, there would have been no incapacity. Secondly, negligent or inefficient treatment by a doctor or other person may amount to a new cause and the circumstances may justify a finding of fact that the existing incapacity results from the new cause, and does not result from the original injury.

In approving these propositions the House of Lords added that the question whether a present state of incapacity is substantially the result of an accident or of the latter negligent act of a doctor is to ask, in other words, whether the present incapacity is due to the original accident or to the intervention of a *novus actus* which breaks "the chain of causation" and the question can only be answered on a consideration of all the circumstances and, in particular, of the quality of that latter act or event.

Death

Where death results from the injury and the workman leaves any dependant wholly dependent on his earnings the amount of compensation is 42 months' earnings.[152] Where the deceased workman does not leave any dependant wholly dependent on his earnings but leaves any dependant in part so dependent the amount of compensation is such sum as may be determined by the court to be reasonable and proportionate to the injury to the dependant but it must not exceed 42 months' earnings.[153] Where the workman leaves no dependant the employer is only required to pay the reasonable expenses commensurate with the last position the workman held in the employment.[154] Dependants are those members of the family of the deceased workman who were wholly or in part dependent upon his earnings at the time of his death.[155] A member of the family

[152] S. 4(a); where the deceased, before his death, had been paid compensation for either permanent, total or partial, or temporary, total or partial, incapacity the sum so paid is deductible from the sum payable; the meaning of earnings is given below.

[153] S. 4 (b) .

[154] S. 4(c); it does not say to whom it is payable; the English Act of 1925 made provision for payment to the executor or administrator of the deceased or if there was none, to the person to whom the expenses of medical attendance and burial are due.

[155] An illegitimate child as well as his parent or grand parent can be a dependant, s.41; in *Orrell Colliery Co* v. *Schofield* [1909] AC 433 a child was held to be a dependant although he was born

is not to be deemed to be a partial dependant unless he was dependent partially on contributions from the workman for the provision of the ordinary necessaries of life suitable for persons in his class and position.[156] In order to show dependency two facts have to be established; first, that the person is a member of the family[157] and secondly, that there is dependency on the earnings of the deceased workman. Whether a person is dependent on the earnings of a deceased workman is a question of fact in each case.[158] There must be evidence of maintenance and support and of reliance on his earnings for these. An obligation to maintain, such as that of a husband to maintain his wife, is not enough. There must be evidence of actual support and reliance.[159] In *New Monckton Collieries Ltd* v. *Keeling*[160] a husband and wife lived apart for over 20 years during which period the husband did not contribute a kobo of his earnings to the support or maintenance of the wife. It was held the wife was not a dependant. To establish partial depenaency it is not enough to show pecuniary loss as a result of the death of the workman; it must be shown that there was reliance on his contribution in order for the person to provide himself with the ordinary necessaries of life suitable to his class and position. These necessaries include food, clothing and shelter and "the necessary concomitants thereto."[161] In *Simmons* v. *White Brothers*[162] the English Court of Appeal held that to be partially dependent it is not sufficient that the person merely derives benefit from the earnings of the deceased but that "he must be to some extent dependent on him for the ordinary necessaries of life, having regard to his class and position."[163]

It has been held that the maximum compensation which can be awarded for partial dependency is the same as the maximum stipulated for total dependency.[164] As Lord Shaw said:[165]

---

some months after the death of his father and although the mother was not married to the father; the father had however admitted paternity and there was evidence of promise to marry.

[156] S. 41.

[157] For family see above.

[158] *Main Colliery Co* v. *Davies* [1900] AC 358; *New Monckton Collieries Ltd* v. *Keeling* [1911] AC 648; for the manner of proof of dependency and degree of dependency see below.

[159] *New Monckton Collieries Ltd* v. *Keeling* [1911] AC 648.

[160] *Supra*; see also *Hodgson* v. *West Stanley Colliery* [1910] AC 229.

[161] Per Lord Carson in *Welsh Navigation Steam Co Ltd* v. *Evans* [1927] AC 834, 842 - 843.

[162] [1899] 1 QB 1005.

[163] Ibid., 1008, per Romer LJ

[164] *Hodgson* v. *West Stanley Colliery* [1910] AC 229.

[165] Ibid., 238.

> Indications not infrequently appear of an opinion that the maximum awards apply only to cases of total dependency and not to partial dependency. The latter, however, is not so. The statute merely provides that in the case of partial dependency the maxima for total dependency shall not be exceeded. Within that limit the arbitrator is free to do his best to make the compensation meet the loss, according to the circumstances of the case.

Duty to report death

Where the death of a workman, from any cause whatsoever, is brought to the notice of his employer or it comes to his knowledge, the employer must give notice of it to a labour officer within seven days of such knowledge. The notice must state the circumstances of the death if these are known to the employer.[166] The labour officer who receives the notice must make such inquiries as he thinks fit and if it appears to him that a claim for compensation may lie he must ascertain from the employer or such other source as he may determine whether there are any dependants of the deceased workman. He must inform such dependants, if any, of the reported cause and circumstances of the death and ascertain whether the dependants wish to make a claim for compensation and, if necessary, explain how the claim should be made.[167] However this does not prevent any person from making a claim for compensation.[168]

Incapacity to earn

Incapacity to earn must result from the injury for compensation to be payable. Incapacity is either total or partial and total or partial incapacity, whether of a temporary or permanent nature, as incapacitates a workman for any employment which he was capable of undertaking at the time of the accident resulting in such incapacity.[169] Partial incapacity means, where the incapacity is of a temporary nature, such incapacity as reduces the earning capacity of a workman in any employment in which he was engaged at the time of the accident resulting in the incapacity and, where the incapacity is of a permanent nature such incapacity as

---

166 S. 14(1); failure to give such a notice is an offence punishable, on conviction, with a fine not exceeding ₦500; S. 14(3).

167 S. 14(2).

168 S. 14(4).

169 S. 41 ; where the percentage of the loss of earning capacity specified in the 2nd schedule to the Act against any injury or injuries amount to one hundred per cent or more permanent total incapacity is deemed to result from the injury or injuries.

reduces his earning capacity in every employment which he was capable of undertaking at that time.[170]

In *Metal Containers (W.A) Ltd* v. *Iyomifokhai*[171] the workman, a machine operator, met with an accident as a result of which two teeth of his upper jaw were extracted. He was on sick leave for two weeks at the end of which he resumed his work. The employer paid his full wages for the two weeks as well as the cost of a denture. His claim for compensation failed on the ground that there was no evidence to show that the injury resulted in incapacity to earn in his employment or in any other employment which he was capable of undertaking at that time. In *Brian Munro Ltd* v. *Oji*[172] it was held that the fact that a workman is earning less in an employment than he earned in a previous employment in which the accident which caused his injury occurred is not conclusive of incapacity. On the other hand it would seem that the fact that an injured workman is paid his full wages or salary is not conclusive of an absence of incapacity to earn. Where the incapacity is total permanent incapacity the point will not arise and where it is temporary incapacity whether total or partial again the point does not arise-the workman's compensation, as will be seen, is his full pay. But there could be a problem where the incapacity is partial permanent incapacity. In *Bewac Ltd* v. *Alimi Akanbi*[173] the workman suffered permanent partial incapacity. He had been instructed to drive a tractor from Lagos to Benin and thereafter to find his way back to Lagos. While coming back to Lagos the vehicle he was travelling in was involved in an accident and he sustained injuries. Taylor CJ said:[174]

> Having found that the applicant did suffer permanent partial incapacity, does the fact that he was subsequently paid an increase in salary mean that his 'earning capacity' was not reduced by such incapacity? I think the position is that once you have found that permanent partial incapacity is proved then you proceed as in S.9[175] to assess compensation regardless of whether or not in fact the workman is still on the same salary or a higher salary. The point being that employers could easily evade the provisions of the Act by paying a partially incapacitated workman a higher salary than he was earning before

---

[170] S. 41; Every injury specified in the 2nd schedule to the Act except any injury or injuries whose percentage add up to one hundred per cent or more which are deemed to be permanent total incapacity is deemed to result in permanent partial incapacity.

[171] (1959) LLR 130.

[172] 1968 (1) ALR Comm 208.

[173] (1972)2 UILR 297.

[174] Ibid., 301 - 302.

[175] Now S. 7.

> the injury only to dismiss him or reduce the salary long after the statutory period has elapsed.

The Australian High Court is of the same view. In *Thompson* v. *Armstrong & Royse Proprietary Ltd*[176] one of the judges put the matter clearly:[177]

> An injury results in incapacity for work, according to the intention of the Act, when it takes away or diminishes the power of the worker to earn wages in some suitable employment. The phrase does not merely mean inability to work for the employer in whose service the worker was injured. The test is whether he was physically able to earn wages. It is not whether he received wages.

Where there is, in fact, incapacity, the workman would, of course, be entitled to compensation but certainly the employer should be entitled to deduct the wages or salary already paid for the period of the incapacity where such wages or salary are lower than the amount of compensation.

Permanent total incapacity

The amount of compensation for permanent total incapacity is 54 months' earnings.[178] However, where the incapacity is of such a nature that the injured workman must have the constant help of another person an amount of one quarter of that sum is payable as additional compensation.[179]

Permanent partial incapacity

The amount of compensation where permanent partial incapacity results from the injury is determined by the percentage of disability or incapacity resulting from the injury.[180] The second schedule to the Act, contains a list of injuries and the percentage of disability which results from them, Thus, for example, the loss of an arm at wrist is 70%. The amount of compensation for such an injury would be 70% of the amount the workman would have been entitled to if it had been permanent total incapacity - i.e. 54 months earning; the amount is therefore 70% of 54 month's earnings.

---

[176] (1950) 81 CLR 585.

[177] Ibid., 603 per McTierman J.

[178] S. 5.

[179] S. 6.

[180] S. 7(l)(a).

However, as we have seen where an injury results in one hundred per cent loss of earning capacity or more or where the injuries are more than one and the aggregate disability is one hundred per cent or more the injury or injuries are deemed to result in permanent total incapacity.[181] In such cases the amount of compensation is 54 months' earnings. In the case of an injury which is not contained in the second schedule the amount of compensation is "such percentage of the compensation which would have been payable in the case of permanent total incapacity as is not inconsistent with the provisions of the said schedule."[182] Whether or not the injury is specified in the second schedule, where the injury has particular consequences having regard to the special nature of the workman's occupation and provided the court, upon application by the workman, considers that the percentage of the loss of earning capacity as provided above is clearly inadequate, the court may declare such workman to have incurred such higher degree of incapacity as it deems equitable.[183]

Temporary incapacity

Where temporary incapacity, whether total or partial, results from the injury the workman is entitled to be paid his basic wages or salary for six months and if he has not resumed work by the end of that period he becomes entitled only to half his basic pay for a further period of three months.[184] If, at the end of the nine months, he has still not resumed work "and compensation due to him has not been determined" he is entitled to be paid one-quarter of his wages or salary for the following fifteen months.[185]

---

[181] S. 41; where more injuries than one are caused by the same accident the amount of compensation is the total sum of the amount in respect of all the injuries but the amount payable must not exceed the amount payable for permanent total incapacity, i.e., 54 months' earnings; S.7 (3).

[182] S. 7(1)(b); the court may, if it so desires, have the assistance of any medical assessor in such a case; however an assessor acts only in an advisory capacity and must not be an employee of or associated in any pecuniary way with the employer by whom the workman is employed; s.8 (2). A medical assessor may examine the workman in private and must, in such an examination, also examine any allegations made to him in writing either by the workman or the employer with respect to the condition of the workman; the conclusions reached by him may be taken into consideration in deciding the questions in dispute; s.8 (3). The Minister may, on the recommendation of the Minister responsible for health, compile a list of medical practitioner, to act as medical assessors; s.8 (1).

[183] s.7(2).

[184] s. 9 (1) (a) .

[185] s. 9 (1) (b) .

The intended effect of sub-section 9(1)(b) is rather obscure. Presumably it refers to a situation where, during the nine months under sub-section 9(1)(a), permanent partial incapacity has resulted from the injury and the workman has resumed duty and his claim for compensation has been met. If that is so sub-section 9(1)(b) will not apply and the employer is entitled to deduct all the payments made under sub-section 9(1)(a) from the amount of compensation payable to the workman. If however the workman has not resumed the duties of his office (i.e. temporary total incapacity), or where he has resumed those duties but compensation is not due to him because the incapacity remains temporary though partial he is entitled to one quarter of his wages or salary for the next fifteen months. If, at the end of this period, he has still not resumed duty, presumably the incapacity will be regarded as permanent total incapacity. In such a case it may mean that the employer can deduct all the payments under sub-section 9(1)(b) from the compensation payable for permanent total incapacity.

The payments for temporary incapacity may be converted into a lump sum in certain circumstances but again sub-section 9(2) which makes provision for this does not appear to be well drafted. The sub-section provides that where a workman in receipt of any payments for temporary incapacity "intends to leave the neighbourhood in which he was employed, for the purpose of residing elsewheré" he must give notice of this intention to the employer. Both of them may then agree either to convert the payments into a lump sum or continue the payments but where they are unable to come to an agreement either party may apply to the court which has power to order payment of a lump sum and the amount to be so paid or to order the continuance of the monthly payments.[186] A workman who fails to give notice to his employer of his intention to leave the neighbourhood in which he was employed for the purpose of residing elsewhere, or, having given such notice. leaves the neighbourhood without reaching an agreement with his employer regarding the payments or where there is no agreement, leaves without making an application to the court "shall not be entitled to any benefits under the Act during or in respect of the period of his absence: and if the periods of such absence shall exceed six months, the workman shall cease to be entitled to any benefits under the Act."[187] The sanction appears very severe although the condition required to be satisfied is

[186] The court has no power to order payment of a lump sum which, added to any payments of wages or salary already paid, will exceed the amount payable if the incapacity were permanent: S.9 (2)(c).

[187] S 9(3).

uncertain. What is the meaning of "neighbourhood in which he was employed?" Presumably it means the town in which he is employed.

Medical examination and treatment

The provisions for medical examination and treatment of an injured workman are meant to assist the parties in realistically assessing the extent and nature of the injury and thus facilitate the settlement of claims for compensation by agreement which is one of the objects of the statute.

Where a workman has given notice of an accident the employer must, as soon as reasonably possible, arrange to have him medically examined at the employer's expense, either by a medical practitioner named by the employer or by one named by the workman with the employer's approval, which approval must not be unreasonably withheld.[188] However the workman is entitled, at his own expense, to have his own medical practitioner present at an examination whether conducted by a medical practitioner named or approved by the employer.[189] It has been held that this examination is not a once and for all one but that the employer may call on a workman to undergo a further examination provided the request is a proper and reasonable one which is a question of fact.[190] Lord Atkinson said, in justifying the decision, that one of the objects of the statute clearly is that settlements of claims for compensation should, if possible, be arranged by agreement between the employer and the workman and: "Nothing, I think, could be more calculated to defeat that object, and nothing could be more opposed to common sense and reason, than to require that an employer should make up his mind, in all cases, definitely on the result of one examination, whether he would or would not resist the workman's claim."[191]

A workman who is in receipt of any payments for temporary incapacity, whether total or partial, must submit himself for such medical examination from time to time as may be required by the employer.[192]

When an examination is to be carried out by a medical practitioner named by the employer the workman must, when required, attend upon the medical practitioner at the time and place notified to him by either the employer or the

---

[188] S. 15(1).
[189] S. 15(5).
[190] *Smith* v. *D. Davis & Sons Ltd* [1915] AC 528.
[191] Ibid, 536.
[192] S. 15(1).

medical practitioner, provided such time and place are reasonable.[193] If, however, the workman is unable[194] or is not in a fit state to so attend he must notify the employer who must then arrange with the medical practitioner to fix a reasonable time and place for a personal examination of the workman and the employer must send the workman notice accordingly.[195] If a workman fails to submit himself for any examination his right to compensation is suspended until such examination has taken place but if the failure extends for a period of fifteen days from the date on which he was required to submit to examination no compensation is payable unless the court is satisfied that there was reasonable course for such failure.[196] Where a right to compensation is suspended no compensation is payable in respect of the period of suspension.[197]

During a period of temporary total incapacity of a workman the employer must arrange to submit the workman for normal medical treatment by either the employer's medical practitioner or the workman's medical practitioner approved by the employer. The treatment must be at the expense of the employer and includes any specialist treatment which the employer may require the workman to undergo.[198] If a workman fails to submit himself for treatment or, having submitted for treatment, disregards the instructions of the medical practitioner, and it is proved that such failure or disregard was unreasonable in the circumstances of the case, and that the injury has been aggravated as a result, the injury and the resulting incapacity must be deemed to be of the same nature and duration as they might reasonably have been expected to be if the workman had submitted himself for treatment and duly carried out the instructions of the medical practitioner and compensation, if any, is payable accordingly.[199]

Where a claim for compensation is made in respect of the death of a workman but the workman (i) failed to submit himself for examination, or (ii) failed to submit himself for treatment, or (iii) having submitted for treatment disregarded the instructions of the medical practitioner, and if it is proved that such failure or disregard was unreasonable in the circumstances of the case and that the death was caused thereby, the death is deemed not to have resulted from the injury and no compensation is payable in respect of the injury.[200] For the sub-

---

[193] S. 15(2).

[194] Being unable may arise, it seems, from factors other than not being in a fit state and presumably it has to be reasonable.

[195] S. 15(3).

[196] S. 15(4).

[197] S. 15(8).

[198] S. 15(6).

[199] S. 15(7).

[200] S. 15(9).

section to apply it must not only be shown that there was a refusal to submit to examination or treatment or a failure to follow medical instruction given but also that the failure or disregard was unreasonable and that the death was caused not by the injury but by the unreasonable refusal or disregard. Whether a refusal is unreasonable or not is a question of fact.[201] In *Tutton* v. *Owners of Steamship Majestic*[202] the English Court of Appeal held that the question is not whether on a balance of medical evidence the treatment might have been a reasonable one to undergo but whether the workman acted unreasonably in refusing to undergo the treatment. In *Richardson* v. *Redpath, Brown & Co Ltd*[203] the House of Lords said that the material question is not whether the medical advice given to the workman against an operation is more soundly based than advice in favour of it, but whether the workman who refuses to be operated upon is acting reasonably in view of the advice he has received. Viscount Simon said:[204]

> As I have already pointed out in this opinion, and as has been laid down in this House before, the question whether a workman is unreasonable in refusing to undergo a surgical operation is not to be determined by considering whether the best medical opinion would think such an operation advisable or safe, but by judging whether it is proved that the workman, having regard to all the circumstances (including medical advice offered to him against the operation) was unreasonable in so refusing."

Similarly in a recent decision of the Privy Council in *Selvanayagam* v. *University of West Indies*[205] Lord Scarman who delivered the judgement of the Board said "the true question is whether in all the circumstances, including particularly the medical advice received, the plaintiff[206] acted reasonably in refusing surgery.[207] The onus of showing unreasonableness lies on the employer.[208]

---

[201] *Steele* v. *Robert George & Co Ltd* [1943] AC 497; *Tutton* v. *Owners of Steamship Majestic* [1909] 2 KB 54; *Marshall* v. *Orient Steam Navigation Co Ltd* [1910] 1 KB 79.

[202] *Supra.*

[203] [1944] AC 62.

[204] Ibid, 72.

[205] [1983] 1 All E.R. 824.

[206] This was a common law action in which a professor sued for damages for personal injury.

[207] [1983]1 All E.R. 824, 827.

[208] *Richardson* v. *Redpath, Brown & Co Ltd, supra; Steele* v. *Robert George & Co Ltd* [1942] AC 497; in *Warncken* v. *R. Moreland & Son Ltd* [1909]1 KB 184 a workman who refused an operation which all medical witnesses thought was in his own interest and which was of a simple character involving a risk which is hardly appreciable to a man of 30 years old, which the workman was, was held to have been unreasonable; in *Tutton* v. *Owners of Steamship Majestic, supra*, the refusal was not unreasonable as the workman acted on the advice of his own doctor

The refusal to undergo treatment must not only be unreasonable but it must also be proved that it was the cause of the death of the workman. Thus it is not enough to show that the refusal is unreasonable the employer must go further to prove that the death was due to the workman's unreasonableness in refusing to submit to treatment. This is an issue of causation which, it is suggested, is best approached in the spirit which Lord Wright indicated in his decision in *Steele* v. *Robert George & Co Ltd.*[209] As he said, the provision is not easy to understand or apply. It is rather a penalty provision than anything else. I find it not very logical to say that the workman's refusal breaks the chain of causality between the accident and the incapacity. On the contrary, effects of the accident still remain. The operation, furthermore, may not be successful, even if it is not refused. Quite apart from the surgical evidence in the particular case, which may be conflicting, the workman's own physical or mental idiosyncrasy cannot in general be excluded. I believe that arbitrators have approached these questions in a humane and liberal spirit, realising that the question cannot be decided save on sympathetic estimate of the workman's personality and the special circumstances of the particular case.[210]

Calculation of earnings

We have seen that the amount of compensation for death and permanent incapacity are expressed in terms of monthly earnings.[211] Earnings are defined to include the wages paid to the workman by the employer and the value of any food, fuel or quarters supplied to the workman by the employer if, as a result of the accident, the workman is deprived of such food, fuel or quarters. Earnings also include any overtime payments or other special remuneration for work done, whether by way of bonus or otherwise, if of constant character or for work habitually performed. However, earnings do not include remuneration for intermittent overtime or casual payments of a non-recurrent nature or any *ex*

---

who stated to him that the administration of anaesthetics would be dangerous to his life given the condition of his kidney.

209 [1942] AC 497.

210 Ibid, 503 - 504.

211 Compensation for temporary incapacity is, expressed in terms of the workman's "basic pay" although the section also talks of "monthly salary;" neither is defined although it would seem they are intended to mean the same thing; both, in any case, do not mean 'earnings" which is a much wider term. Basic pay, in ordinary language, would not include allowances, overtime pay or bonuses but only the wages or salary contracted to be paid as consideration for work to be done by the workman.

gratia payment whether given by the employer or other person, or the value of a travelling allowance or any travelling concession or a contribution paid by the employer towards any pension or provident fund or a sum paid to a workman to cover any special expenses entailed on him by the nature of his employment.[212]

In calculating monthly earnings section 10(1) enjoins that it must "be computed in such manner as is best calculated to give the rate per month at which the workman was being remunerated during the previous twelve months if he has been so long employed by the same employer, but, if not, then for any less period during which he has been in the employment of the same employer." The object of this provision is to enable the court, or the employer or indeed the workman himself,[213] to arrive at a fair estimate of what the workman was earning at the date of the accident. As has been said, to regard monthly earnings "as rigidly determined by the rate at which the workman was earning remuneration at the precise moment of the accident would be to adopt a principle which would often lead to unfair results. The remuneration which the workman was earning at that particular moment might be abnormally exaggerated or diminished by reason of temporary and exceptional causes which would make it an inaccurate measure of the workman's normal earnings."[214] Of course in a large number of cases, where earnings are expressed as per annum and spread equally over the twelve months of the year there will be no problem. This will be so even where the workman has worked for less than twelve months. The problem arises in those employments in which there are variations from one period of the year to another. In such cases average monthly earnings over twelve months or such less period of actual employment with the same employer will-best give the rate per month.[215]

However, where, because of the shortness of the time during which the workman has been in the employment of his employer or owing to the casual nature of the employment or by the terms of the employment, it is impracticable at the date of the accident to compute the rate of remuneration, regard may be had to the average monthly amount which during the twelve months previous to the accident, was being earned by a person of similar earning capacity in the

---

[212] S. 41(1).

[213] Where a workman so requests the employer must give him a list in writing of the earnings which have been earned by the workman upon which the amount of the monthly earnings may be calculated; s. 10(5).

[214] Per Fletcher Moulton LJ in *Perry* v. *Wright* [1908]1 KB 441, 455 - 456.

[215] In *Perry* v. *Wright* [1908]1 KB 441 Fletcher Moulton LJ held, that average monthly earnings must be calculated by dividing the total earnings during the appropriate period by the number of months the workman actually worked during that period; this computation is best calculated to arrive at a fair monthly earnings.

same grade employed at the same work by the same employer, or, if there is no person so employed, by a person of similar earning capacity in the same grade employed in the same class of employment and in the same local government area where he resides.[216] Thus there are three ways of computing monthly earnings of a workman. First, the workman's own earnings with the same employer are used but where this is impracticable for any of three reasons the earnings of a workman employed in the same grade and in the same work by the same employer must be resorted to and where there is no such workman the earnings of a workman who is not employed by the same employer in whose employment the injured workman is becomes the relevant factor. In the case of either of the two latter methods "regard may be had to the average monthly amount" over the twelve months previous to the accident in determining the monthly earnings of the workman. But it has been held by the English Court of Appeal that regard[217] should also be had to the individual merit or demerit of the workman. Some workmen are better than others, and, if, the man in question was a superior workman evidence may be given of that fact with a view of increasing the compensation that should be paid.[218]

In method two the workman to whose average monthly amount regard may be had must be a person of similar earning capacity in the same grade employed at the same work by the same employer as the injured workman. Employment by the same employer means employed by the same employer in the grade in which the workman injured was employed at the time of the accident "uninterrupted by absence from work due to illness or any other unavoidable cause."[219] In *Greenwood* v. *Joseph Nall & Co Ltd*[220] the House of Lords held that where there is interruption from either of these causes there is no longer employment by the same employer.

Concurrent employment

Where a workman has entered into concurrent contracts of service with two or more employers under which he works at one time for one such employer and at another time for another such employer his monthly earnings must be computed as if his earnings under all such contracts were earnings in the employment of the

[216] S. 10(2).
[217] *Cue* v. *Port of London Authority* [1914] 3 KB 892.
[218] Per Swinten Eady LJ ibid, 902.
[219] S. 10(3).
[220] [1917] AC 1.

employer for whom he was working at the time of the accident.[221] However the earnings under a concurrent contract are to be taken into account only so far as the workman is incapacitated from performing the concurrent contract.[222] Concurrent contracts are contracts running concurrently in respect to employments or services which are separate.[223] In *Lloyd* v. *Midland Railway Company*[224] the workman, a platelayer in the service of a railway company, also worked in a theatre as a check-taker with another employer. His hours of work with the railway company were 6 am to 5:30 p.m. and at the theatre 7 p.m to 10:30 p.m. He was paid weekly in both places. Held - he was under concurrent contracts of service. As Swinten-Eady LJ succinctly put it,[225]

> concurrent contracts of service, [are] where a workman may have contracts at the same time running with two or more employers during the week or month or whatever the period may be. During part of the day or part of the week he would work for one employer, and during another part of the day or another part of the week, as the case may be, he would work for another employer. In that case the weekly earnings under the two are added so as to ascertain what his earnings were, and they are to be treated as if those were the earnings earned in the employment of the employer for whom he was working at the time of the accident."

Distribution of compensation

The provisions of section 12 are to ensure that compensation payable by an employer does not get into wrong hands or get frittered away. The compensation payable in respect of the death of a workman or in respect of permanent incapacity, total or partial, or in respect of temporary incapacity, total or partial, where the monthly payments have been converted into a lump sum, must be paid into court by the employer.[226]

Where the payment is in respect of death the court may order any sum so paid to be apportioned among the dependants of the deceased workman or any of them in such proportion as the court thinks fit, or, in the discretion of the court,

---

[221] S. 10(4).
[222] S. 10(4) proviso.
[223] Per Lord Shaw in *Owners of S.S. Raphael* v. *Brandy* [1911] AC 413, 415.
[224] [1914] 2 KB 53.
[225] *Cue* v. *Port of London Authority* [1914]3 KB 892, 900 - 901
[226] S. 12(1),(3); the receipt of the registrar or other officer of the court is a sufficient discharge in respect of any such payment; s. 12(6)

to be allotted to any one such dependant. Where allotment is ordered the court must pay the sum so allotted to the dependant to whom it is allotted or be invested, applied or otherwise dealt with for his benefit as the court thinks fit.[227] However, where, on application it appears to the court that, on account of the variation of the circumstances of the various dependants or for any other sufficient cause, an order ought to be varied the court may make such order for the variation of the former order as in the circumstances of the case as the court may think just.[228]

The compensation paid to court in respect of permanent incapacity or the lump sum in any case in which payments for temporary incapacity have been so converted, must be paid to the person entitled to it or be invested, applied or otherwise dealt with for his benefit as the court thinks fit.[229]

Any other compensation payable by an employer may be paid to the workman or to the court and when paid to the court must be paid by the court to the person entitled to it.[230]

An employer may, however, make any payment to a workman pending the settlement or determination of the claim.[231] This does not apply to dependants and there is no reason why the employer may not pay the total sum of compensation to the workman. Where payment has been made the court may order that the whole or any part of such payment be deducted from the amount of compensation payable to the workman.[232]

Sub-section 12(7) provides that any order or directions of the court given under section 12 is final.[233]

Agreement as to compensation

The employer and an injured workman may agree the amount of compensation to be paid by the employer but this must not be less than the amount of compensation payable under the Act. An agreement must be in writing and in triplicate. One copy must be kept by the employer, another by the workman and the third sent to the nearest authorised labour officer.[234] Where a workman is unable to read and understand the language in which an agreement is made the

---

[227] S. 12(1).
[228] S. 12(2).
[229] S. 12(3).
[230] S. 12(5).
[231] S. 12(4).
[232] Ibid.
[233] But see footnote 276.
[234] S. 16(1)(a).

agreement will not be binding on him unless it is endorsed by a certificate of an authorised labour officer to the effect that he read over and explained it to the workman and, where necessary, that he interpreted it to him in a language which he understood and that the workman appeared fully to understand and approve the agreement.[235] Where the above requirements are not complied with receipt of compensation will not prevent proceedings being taken by the workman to recover damages at common law as would otherwise be the case.[236]

An agreement may, on application to the court, be made an order of the court.[237] An agreement, whether made an order of the court or not, may on application by any party within three months of the making of the agreement, be cancelled by the court. However, the court may cancel an agreement only if it is proved that the sum paid to the workman is less than the statutory amount for the type of incapacity or that the agreement was entered into in ignorance or under a mistake as to the true nature of the injury or that the agreement was obtained by fraud, undue influence, misrepresentation or other improper means as would, in law, be sufficient ground for avoiding it. Upon cancellation the court may make such order, including an order as to any sum already paid under the agreement, as in the circumstances the court may think just.[238]

Where there is a dispute as to the percentage or degree of the disability of the injured workman or as to the amount of compensation payable the Minister must refer it to a medical board to be constituted by him.[239]

Procedure for claim

It is necessary for the procedure laid down in section 13 for application for compensation to be followed if an otherwise meritorious claim is not to be lost. The section is set out in full:

> 13 - (1) Proceedings for the recovery under this Act of compensation for an injury shall not be maintainable unless (a) notice of the accident has been given by or on behalf of the workman as soon as practicable after the happening thereof and before the workman has voluntarily left the employment in which he was injured; and (b) the application for

[235] S. 16(1)(b).
[236] *Western Nigeria Trading Co Ltd* v. *Ajao* [1965] 2 All NLR.
[237] S. 16(2).
[238] S. 16(3).
[239] S. 16(4); presumably the board has to determine the dispute; for medical boards and their constitution see below.

> compensation with respect to such accident has been made within six months from the occurrence of the accident causing the injury or, in the case of death, within six months from the time of death. (2) The want of, or any defect or inaccuracy in any notice given under sub-section (1) of this section shall not be a bar to the maintenance of such proceedings if the employer is proved to have had knowledge of the accident from any other source at or about the time of the accident, or if it is found in the proceedings for settling the claim that the employer is not, or would not, if a notice or an amended notice were then given and the hearing postponed, be prejudiced in his defence by the want, defect or inaccuracy, or that such want, defect or inaccuracy was occasioned by mistake or other reasonable cause. (3) The failure to make an application within the period specified in subsection (1) of this section shall not be a bar to the maintenance of such proceedings if it is found that the failure was occasioned by mistake or other reasonable cause. (4) Notice in respect of an injury under this Act shall be given as prescribed.

A number of difficulties inherent in the provision have been largely cleared in court decisions. It has been held that the "proceedings" referred to in sub-section 13(1) are not judicial proceedings.[240] What is required is that an application for compensation, which is different from initiation of judicial proceedings, must be made within six months of the accident causing the injury or, in the case of death, six months from the time of death. As Sowemimo J said in *Obi Osu* v. *Cappa & D'Alberto*[241] "the contention of the appellant that notice of claim need not be the initiation of proceedings...is correct."[242] The proper procedure for a claim is that notice of the accident causing the injury must be given by the injured workman or by someone on his behalf as soon as practicable after the accident and an application for compensation must be made within six months either of the accident or death. Where notice has been given and an application made within the stipulated time judicial proceedings may be taken if necessary, even after six months of the accident or death but subject to the general law on limitation of actions.[243] In making a claim it is not necessary to state any sum.[244] Subsection (4) provides that notice must be given as prescribed. Rule 2(1) of the Workmen's Compensation Rules prescribed that notice in respect of an injury must be given in writing in Form A in the first schedule to

---

240 *Powell* v. *Main Colliery Company* [1900] AC 366.

241 (1964) LLR 138.

242 Ibid., 142.

243 By s. 20 (1) this would appear to be as provided in the statute of limitation of the State whose High Court has jurisdiction in the matter.

244 *Thompson* v. *Goold & Co* [1910] AC 409.

the Rules. It is doubtful whether the decision in *Stevens* v. *Insoles, Ltd*[245] where the particulars of the accident were given to the employer's manager who then wrote them down in a company book and the court held notice had been given would be correct under these provisions. In *Isaiah Joseph* v. *Mutiu & Muyide Building Contractor Furniture Company Ltd,*[246] the court held, under the same rule, that the sub-section did not make the giving of notice in writing mandatory. That cannot be correct. Of course, want of notice is not a bar to proceedings for recovery of compensation where the employer is proved to have had knowledge of the accident from any other source as was the case in both proceedings.

The want of notice or any defect or inaccuracy in a given notice is not a bar to the maintenance of proceedings where (i) the employer is proved to have had knowledge of the accident from any other source at or about the time of the accident or, (ii) it is found that the employer is not or would not be prejudiced in his defence by the want, defect or inaccuracy if a notice or an amended notice is given him at the proceedings and the hearing postponed, or (iii) that such want, defect or inaccuracy was occasioned by mistake or other reasonable cause.

Where, as in *Istah Joseph* v. *Mutiu & Muyide Building Contractor Furnishing Co Ltd*[247] the employer was informed of the accident by the workman and he then conveyed the workman to the hospital it is clear that any want of notice or any defect or inaccuracy in any notice given cannot be a bar to the maintenance of proceeding. The employer has knowledge of the accident.

As to prejudice arising from want of notice the onus is on the workman to show that the employer will not be prejudiced in his defence if notice is given at the proceedings and the hearing postponed.[248] In *Hayward* v. *Westleigh Colliery Co Ltd* [249] the House of Lords held that the burden of proof of absence of prejudice lies on the workman and that the court, if not satisfied upon all the facts before it that there is no prejudice, then the workman fails. Whether there is or would be prejudice to the employer by the want of notice is a question of fact and it is for the court to consider all the facts before it. It would seem that where notice of an accident is given at such a time after the accident that the employer would not have the means of proper investigation of the accident or of being able to determine whether the injury resulted from any of a variety of other possible causes rather than from the accident that the employer may be prejudiced in his

---

[245] [1912] 1 KB 36.
[246] (1977) 11 CCHCJ 2657.
[247] *Supra.*
[248] *Hughes* v. *The Coed Talon Colliery Co Ltd* [1909]1 KB 957; *Egerton* v. *Moore* [1912] 2 KB 308.
[249] [1915] AC 540.

defence.[250] Even where an employer would be prejudiced by want of or a defect or inaccuracy in a given notice a workman will still be able to maintain proceedings where he is able to show that the want of notice or any defect or inaccuracy in it is occasioned by mistake or other reasonable cause. The want of notice occasioned by mistake or other reasonable cause is a separate and distinct head upon which want of notice may be excused.[251] As Swinten-Eady LJ said in *Potter* v. *John Welch & Sons*[252] where the court found as a fact that the employers were prejudiced by want of notice "that fact in itself is not sufficient to bar the claim if the want of notice was occasioned by mistake or other reasonable cause."[253] The burden is on the workman to show mistake or other reasonable cause.[254] In *Roles* v. *Pascall & Sons*[255] Cozens - Hardy MR. suggested a definition of mistake as follows - A mistake means that a man takes a wrong view as to the construction or effect of an Act of Parliament, if it is a mistake of law. A mistake of fact may be that the notice is given to some person whom the workman believed to be an agent or a person entitled to receive the notice when he was not. Many instances of that kind may be given. But mistake is not identical with ignorance.[256] In this case the reason given by the workman for failure to give notice of the accident or to make a claim within the stipulated time was that he did not know of the existence of the workman's compensation Act or that he was entitled to compensation for injury by accident arising out of and in the course of his employment. The English Court of Appeal held that ignorance of the existence of the Act and of a any right to claim compensation was not a mistake or reasonable cause. Ignorance may not be a mistake but it is suggested that it might give rise to reasonable cause since reasonable cause should be considered in the circumstances of each case including the level of understanding of the workman.[257] There is reasonable cause where an injuiy is latent and the workman is unaware of its true nature and degree. In *Fenton* v. *Owners of Ship Kelvin*[258] Pollock, Master of the Rolls, said:

---

[250] Ibid.
[251] *Eke* v. *Hart- Dyke* [1910] 2 KB 677.
[252] (1914) 83 LJKB 1852.
[253] Ibid, 1859; see also Lord Cozens-Hardy MR at 1857.
[254] *Egerton* v. *Moore* [1912] 2 KB 308.
[255] [1911] 1 KB 982.
[256] Ibid; 985.
[257] It is suggested that the courts should be guided by the fact that workmen are predominantly illiterate persons. Ignorance was introduced in New South Wales legislation in 1951.
[258] [1925] 2 KB 473.

> I think it is plain there may be a number of gradations, questions of degree. as to whether or not the workman was apprised so clearly of his condition, its origin and its future, as to compel him or throw upon him the duty of giving notice. When, however, the true measure of the situation is only arrived at by lapse of time and by the confidence in the diagnosis which arises from the progress of the disease, particularly where the injury is what may be called latent, then I think that the workman is more readily excused.[259]

In *Shotts Iron & Co* v. *Fordyce*[260] the House of Lords was of the view that where the workman thinks that his injury is a trivial one and that nothing serious has happened to him that that constitutes reasonable cause.

Similarly the failure to make an application for compensation within six months is not a bar to the maintenance of proceedings if it is found that the failure was occasioned by mistake or other reasonable cause. Mistake may be a mistake of law, mixed law and fact or of fact only. The onus is on the workman to show mistake or other reasonable cause.[261] Thus the workman must give an explanation for the failure to make the application within six months and in the absence of such an explanation the claim becomes statute barred.[262] In *Bewac Ltd* v. *Alimi Akanbi*[263] where the employer led the workman to believe that he had accepted liability the court held that that was reasonable cause. However, ignorance of his rights or where the workman knows of his injury but thinks he will recover and so does not bother to make a claim is not reasonable cause.[264] Where reasonable cause is established for failure to make a claim within six months of the accident the bar to the maintenance of proceedings is removed and, subject to the general statute of limitations, proceedings can be taken at any time after the six months.[265]

Where an employer on whom notice of the accident has been served does not, within twenty-one days of the receipt of the notice, agree in writing with the workman as to the amount of compensation to be paid, the workman may, in the prescribed form and manner,[266] make an application for enforcing his claim to compensation to the court.[267] Court means, in any case where a cause of action is

---

[259] Ibid., 483.
[260] [1930] 1 AC 503.
[261] *Egerton* v. *Moore* [1912] 2 KB 308.
[262] *Dunlop Nigeria Industries Ltd* v. *Aladeyelu* CCHCH/3/73 P. 135.
[263] (1972) 2 UILR 297.
[264] *Lingley* v. *Thomas Firth & Sons* [1921] 1 KB 655.
[265] Ibid.
[266] See the Workmen's Compensation (Rules of Court) Rules.
[267] S. 17(1).

within its competence or jurisdiction, a High Court.[268] The court is the court having jurisdiction in the area in which the accident giving rise to the claim occurred.[269] All claims for compensation, unless determined by agreement, and any matter arising out of the proceedings, must be determined by the court no matter the amount involved. The court may call upon any public officer or "any intending medical practitioner" to give evidence if the court is of opinion that such officer or practitioner, is, by virtue of his expert knowledge, able to assist the court.[270]

Where, in any proceedings on a claim for compensation in respect of the death of a workman, the court is satisfied that sufficient evidence as to the dependency on the deceased workman of a person claiming to be a dependant who is residing outside the local government area in which the proceedings are being taken, or as to the degree of such dependency, cannot be procured or cannot be procured without undue hardship to the claimant or other party to the proceedings, a statement as to the dependency and as to the degree of dependency of the claimant signed by the chairman of the Local Government Council in the area in which the claimant resides is *prima facie* proof of the facts therein.[271]

The signature of the chairman must be admitted without proof unless the court has reason to doubt its genuineness.[272] If any evidence is adduced which, in the opinion of the court, traverses the facts in the statement or if for any other reason the court thinks fit, the court may request a magistrate's court having jurisdiction in the local government area in which a person claiming to be a dependant resides, to investigate the fact of the dependency and degree of the dependency of such person.[273] The record of any investigation including the findings of the magistrate's court must be received as evidence in the proceedings and a certificate signed by a magistrate or an officer of the magistrate's court which has conducted the investigation is sufficient proof of

[268] S. 41(1); the court has, save as provided in the Act and any rules made under it, all the powers and jurisdiction exercisable by a High Court in or in connection with civil actions in such court and the law, rules and practice relating to such civil actions and to the enforcement of judgements and orders as the court shall, *mutatis mutandis*, apply; s. 20(1).

[269] S. 17(1).

[270] S. 17(2).

[271] S. 20(2).

[272] S. 20(3).

[273] S. 20(4).

such record and such signature must be admitted without proof unless the court sees reason to doubt its genuineness.[274]

The court may, if it thinks fit, submit any question of law for the decision of a judge of the Court of Appeal and such submission must be in the form of a special case in accordance with rules of court made under the Act.[275] An appeal lies from any order of the court to the Court of Appeal.[276] However an appeal does not lie after thirty days from the date of the order of the court but the Court of Appeal may, if it thinks fit, extend the time for an appeal notwithstanding that the time for appealing has lapsed.[277]

Review of payments

Section 18 provides for the review by the court of any payments payable either by agreement of the parties or under an order of the court upon the application either of the employer or of the workman. Where the application for review is based on a change in the condition of the workman it must be supported by a certificate of a medical practitioner if the services of one are available.[278] Upon review, but subject to the provisions of the Act, any payment may be continued, increased, diminished, converted to a lump sum or ended.[279] Where the accident is found to have resulted in permanent incapacity the compensation must be converted to a lump sum which must then be paid to the court and the court must either pay it to the person entitled or have it invested, applied or otherwise dealt with for his benefit in such manner as the court thinks fit.[280] Where an

---

[274] S. 20(5); sub-section (6) confers jurisdiction in a magistrate's court in a different local government area from that in which the court requesting investigation is.

[275] S. 21; under s. 241(1)(b), Constitution of the Federal Republic of Nigeria, 1999, an appeal lies as of right from decisions of a High Court to the Court of Appeal where the ground of appeal involves a question of law alone.

[276] S. 22(1); the sub-section opens with the words "Subject to the provisions of this section and of section 14 of this Act,"; the reference to section 14 is, presumably, to section 12 which in sub-section (7) curtails a right of appeal; that sub-section as well as sub-section 21(2) which curtails a right of appeal unless with leave, where the amount in dispute is less than eighty naira and sub-section 21(3) which also curtails a right of appeal where the parties have agreed to abide by the decision of the court or where an order of the court gives effect to an agreement made by the parties must be viewed against sections 241 and 242 of the Constitution of the Federal Republic of Nigeria, 1999; see also s. 30(2) below.

[277] S. 22(4) and see s. 243 of the Constitution.

[278] S. 18(1).

[279] S. 18(2).

[280] S. 18(3).

application is made by an employer for any payment to be ended or diminished and the application is supported by the certificate of a medical practitioner, the employer may pay into court "the payment or so much thereof as is equal to the amount by which he contends that the payment should be diminished" and he must undertake to abide with the decision of the court made on a review.[281]

However, the whole of section 18 on review will appear not to be in consonance with some of the changes made by the Act. The purpose for a review provision is that if "the injured workman gets better in health and earns better wages, the employer may apply for a review; on the other hand, the man might get worse and might be able to earn less wages, and he might in such a case take proceedings for a review."[282] This was possible under the repealed statute where the payment which was subject to review was not only periodical but was also subject to changes consequent upon any changes in the incapacity of the workman. Where the injured workman's incapacity for work got worse he could ask for a review upwards but where he got better the employer could apply for a review of compensation payable downwards since the amount payable was necessarily affected by changes in the incapacity of the workman to earn. The formula was $^{2}/_{3}$ (X-Y) where X was the monthly earning of the workman at the time of the accident and Y represented earnings which the workman was earning or capable of earning after the accident.

The repealed statute provided for review only of "periodic payment" which meant payments for temporary incapacity, total or partial. Section 18(1) provides for a review of "Any payment" which could include payment either for death or for permanent incapacity, total or partial both of which are lump sum payments. Although payment for temporary incapacity is periodical under s.9 the periodic payment is fixed and cannot be affected by s.18(5) which provides that in making a review the court must have regard only to the capacity for work of the workman as affected by the accident. In *Crossfield & Sons Ltd* v. *Tanian*[283] the English Court of Appeal held that an application for review cannot be entertained where there has been no change in the circumstances of the case. In *Sharman* v. *Holliday & Greenwood, Ltd*[284] a workman applied for a review on the ground that several employers had refused him employment on the ground that he would be unable to do work on account of his leg which suffered the injury and that on one occasion on which he had been able to obtain work he was subsequently discharged as being incapable of doing it on account of his

[281] S. 18(4).
[282] Per A.L. Smith LJ in *Crossfield & Sons Ltd* v. *Tanian* [1900] 2 QB 629,631.
[283] *Supra.*
[284] [1904] 1 KB 235.

condition. The court held there was evidence of change of circumstances. Mathew LJ said: "I can see nothing in the Act itself which forbids further inquiry if, after the original inquiry, fresh symptoms develop or further incapacity for work is shown to have arisen."[285] In section 9 no account is taken of an injured workman's incapacity to earn full wages or salary in the first six months of temporary incapacity, total or partial or of his capacity to earn more or less than half or one quarter of his salary as the case may be. The fault probably lies in making payment for either total or partial temporary incapacity the same.

The same criticism may be made with respect to section 19 which seeks to limit the power of an employer to end or decrease the amount of compensation being paid. The payments for temporary incapacity are fixed both as to the amount payable monthly and as to the period of payment. The employer is thus obliged to pay the stipulated monthly wages or salary and for the stipulated period unless, of course, the workman dies or suffers permanent incapacity in which case the appropriate compensation becomes payable, less any sum already paid for temporary incapacity.

Preservation of common law action

An injured workman, being also an employee at common law, may be entitled to maintain both a common law action for damages and a claim for workman's compensation where his injury gives rise to an action for negligence and has also arisen out of and in the course of his employment. Whilst the claim for compensation is always against the employer[286] a common law action is brought against the tortfeasor who may be the employer[287] or a third party. Where a common law action lies against someone other than the employer the provisions of section 24 are applicable.

Section 24(a) provides as follows:

> Where the injury in respect of which compensation is payable under this Act was caused in circumstances creating a legal liability in some person other than the employer to pay damages in respect thereof, (a) the workman may take proceedings both against that person to recover damages and against any person liable to pay compensation under this Act for such compensation, but shall not be entitled to recover both damages and compensation.

---

[285] Ibid., 241.

[286] Except possibly under s. 23 as to which see above.

[287] Including vicarious liability of an employer.

In *Page* v. *Burtwell*[288] the English Court of Appeal held first, that the words "creating a legal liability" do not require that liability of the third party has first to be determined but rather that they meant whether a *prima facie* case of liability exists, and secondly that to "recover" did not mean recovery by proceedings but rather whether workman had applied for and received compensation. Thirdly, said the court, the sub-section gave the workman ` right both to take an action for damages against the third party and to claim compensation from his employer subject to the limitation that he could not recover both damages and compensation. In *Aguyala Ekannah* v. *Osakwe*[289] the deceased workman, who was employed as a labourer by Messrs Dorman Long Ltd, was working at the foot of Carter Bridge at Iddo on the Lagos mainland when he was run down and killed by a lorry owned by the first defendant and driven by the second defendant. In an action for damages Dickson J. said that the actual taking of proceedings by a workman is not a *sine qua non* in bringing a case within the sub-section and that a workman is entitled to take proceedings against both parties concurrently "but shall not be entitled to recover both damages and compensation." As there was evidence, including the deceased's dependant's own admission, that he had received compensation he was held not entitled to damages from the defendants. It is submitted, with respect, that that was the correct decision. The sub-section speaks of "recover"- shall not be entitled to recover both damages and compensation. It is suggested that once it is shown that the workman or his dependant has recovered compensation then he cannot recover damages and vice versa. To decide other wise will be to read into the sub-section words that are not there or to give it an unduly strained interpretation.

In *Famuyiwa* v. *Folawiyo*,[290] although the workman admitted under cross-examination that he had been paid compensation under the Workmen Compensation Act, the Supreme Court held, notwithstanding, "that the acceptance of compensation by a workman under our Act[291] is a bar only if the workman knows or is deemed to know that he has an option as to whether to accept compensation under the Act or to claim damages from the stranger at common law."[292] With respect that decision cannot be right. In the judgement of

---

[288] (1908] 2 KB 758.
[289] (1959) LL R 147.
[290] [1972] 1 ALL NLR (pt.2) 11.
[291] Section 26 (1) of the repealed statute which is identical with the present s. 24(a).
[292] Ibid. 21.

Morris J in *Elligott* v. *Nebbett*,[293] upon which the court relied, the word option was never mentioned nor was any reference made to a requirement or need for the workman to exercise an option. In fact the question of knowledge of a right of option did not arise. Neither the provision there under consideration[294] nor any of our provisions has used the word option.[295] The question before the court was simply whether the workman had received compensation. Morris J answered that question in this way: "In my view, the plaintiff has not recovered compensation in such circumstances as to make the bar imposed by s. 30(1) of the Workmen's Compensation Act available to the defendant in the present case.[296] Even in *Oliver* v. *Nautilus Steam Shipping Company*[297] decided under s. 6 of the Workmen's Compensation Act 1897 which provided that the workman may, "at his option" proceed either at common law to recover damages or against his employer for compensation Vaughan-Williams L.J said: "it is perfectly plain, in my judgement, whichever view one may take of the 6th section, that a workman who has received compensation from his employer under the Act cannot afterwards sue the other person. Therefore, the sole question in this case really is, Has Mr Oliver received compensation from his employer under the Act?"[298] The court held, in effect, that as Mr Oliver had received the money he received "without prejudice" he had not received compensation. It is submitted that in all such cases the sole question to which an answer should be sought is whether workmen's compensation has been received? If money has, in fact, been received it has to be determined whether it was received as workmen's compensation. In *Famuyiwa* v. *Folawiyo*[299] that question was answered in the affirmative and the bar ought to have been imposed.

Where the provisions of section 16 on agreement as to compensation are not complied with the workman cannot be held to have recovered compensation.[300]

It is doubted whether a workman who is ignorant of a right at common law for damages but has received compensation in full compliance with section 16 can be said not to have recovered compensation.

An employer who has paid compensation is entitled to be indemnified by the person liable to pay damages in respect of the amount of the compensation and the costs of the proceedings, if any, leading to the payment of the

---

[293] [1948] 1 ALL ER 514.
[294] S. 30 Workmen's Compensation Act 1925.
[295] Ss. 26(1) or 24(a) 1941 or 1987 statute respectively.
[296] Ibid., 515.
[297] [1903] 2 KB 639.
[298] Ibid., 645- 646.
[299] *Supra.*
[300] *Western Nigeria Trading Co Ltd* v. *Ajao* [1965] 2 All NLR 100.

compensation.[301] Also, as we have seen, a contractor who has indemnified his principal is himself entitled to be indemnified by such a person liable to pay damages to the workman. Any question as to the right to and the amount of any such indemnity, if not settled by agreement, must be settled by civil suit, or, by consent of the parties, by arbitration under the Arbitration and Conciliation Act.[302] There is a right of indemnity where compensation has been paid by agreement between the employer and the injured workman.[303] Where the employer who is claiming indemnity contributed by his negligence to the workman's injury it seems that such contributory negligence would be taken into account in determining the amount of indemnity.[304] As Kennedy J. said, "some defences must be open to the party from whom indemnity is claimed."[305]

Where an employer is liable to pay damages to his workman at common law either on account of his personal negligence or on account of the negligence of another employee and also liable to pay compensation because the same injury arose out of and in the course of employment section 25 of the Act becomes applicable. Sub-section 25(1) provides that where the injury was caused by the personal negligence or wilful act of the employer or of some other person for whose act or default the employer is responsible nothing in this Act shall prevent proceedings to recover damages being instituted against the employer in a civil court independently of this Act. But the sub-section has three provisos - (i) a judgement in such proceedings whether for or against the employer is a bar to any claim for compensation; (ii) a judgement in proceedings for compensation, again, whether for or against the employer is a bar to a common law action in respect of the same injury and (iii) an agreement for compensation between the employer and the workman is also a bar to a common law action. It is to be noted that in the first two provisos it is the judgement of the court and not necessarily receipt of damages or compensation which constitutes the bar. Thus there may be a bar even before damages or compensation has been paid by the employer. It is suggested that the question whether there is a bar or not depends entirely on

---

301 S. 24(b); see also *Great Northern Railway* v. *Whitehead & Co Ltd* (1902) 18 TLR 816; in *Lees* v. *Dunkerlay Brothers* [1911] AC 5 it was held that the person liable to pay damages may be a fellow workman whose negligence resulted in the injury.

302 S. 24(b); the arbitration statute is Cap.19 Laws of the Federation of Nigeria 1990; the author has argued elsewhere that the sub-section unduly favours the third party who, if found liable, would have had to pay damages far in excess of the amount of indemnity; why should not the interest of the workman be taken account of in the settling of liability for indemnity between the employer and the stranger? See fn. 319 below.

303 *Thompson & Sons* v. *North Eastern Marine Engineering Co* [903] 1 KB 428.

304 *R & W Paul Ltd* v. *Great Eastern Railway Co* (1920)36 TLR 344.

305 *Thompson & Sons* v. *North Eastern Marine Engineering Co, supra*, 436.

whether in fact there has been a judgement either for damages or compensation or an agreement for compensation and that the ignorance of a workman as to a common law action is irrelevant.[306] In *Segun* v. *West African Airways Corporation*[307] the deceased workman's dependants having obtained compensation brought an action against the workman's employer for damages and the court held that the action could not be maintained.

If, in an action for damages against an employer, it is determined by the court or on appeal that the employer is not liable, but that he would have been liable to pay compensation the action must be dismissed but the court, or where the determination was on appeal, the appellate court, may assess the amount of compensation payable to the workman.[308] However all or part of the costs which in the court's judgement, have been caused by the action being brought instead of claiming compensation may be deducted from the compensation.[309] An appellate court may, instead of assessing the compensation itself, remit the case to the court of first instance for the assessment of the compensation and in such a case may order the court to deduct all or part of the costs of the action for damages from the amount of compensation.[310] The court which assesses the compensation must give a certificate of the compensation it has awarded and the directions it has given as to the deduction of costs and such a certificate has the force and effect of an award by a court.[311]

Medical expenses

An employer is required to defray any reasonable expenses incurred by a workman as a result of an accident arising out of and in the course of his employment in respect of medical, surgical and hospital treatment, skilled nursing services, supply of medicines and surgical dressings, the supply, maintenance, repair and renewal of non-articulated artificial limbs and apparatus and travelling expenses incurred in the course of receiving medical treatment.[312]

---

[306] The equivalent section in the English Workman's Compensation Act 1925 required the workman to opt for damages or compensation and the cases decided on it proceeded on that basis; see e.g. *Young* v. *Bristol Aeroplane Co* [1946] 1 All ER 98

[307] (1957) WRNLR 29.

[308] S. 25(2).

[309] Ibid.

[310] S. 25(4).

[311] S. 25(3).

[312] S. 29(1); expenses to be incurred outside Nigeria must be with the approval of the Federal or State Chief Medical Officer.

The court may order the payment of any of these expenses directly to the persons entitled to it when determining any dispute in respect of compensation or it may do so on the application of any interested person.[313] In *Cappa and D'Alberto Co Ltd* v. *Dr. A. A. Labinjo*[314] the court held that a doctor who had treated a workman could apply to the court for the payment of his charges and that he would be entitled to such payment if they were reasonably incurred by the workman. All disputes as to the necessity for or the character or sufficiency of any medical aid is to be determined by the court.[315] But section 31 provides that the fees and charges for medical aid to workmen within Nigeria must be in accordance with such scale as may be prescribed and no claim for an amount in excess of the scale lies against any workman or his employer in respect of any such medical aid.[316]

Contracting out and assignment of compensation

Any contract or agreement under which a workman relinquishes any right of compensation from an employer is null and void but only in so far as it purports to remove or reduce the liability of any person to pay compensation under the Act.[317] No compensation payable under the Act can be assigned, charged or attached and cannot pass to any other person by operation of law nor can any claim be set off against it.[318]

Compulsory insurance

There had been a long felt need for the compulsory insurance of employers in order to protect workman against impecunious employers.[319] It is unfortunate that the new provision on compulsory insurance cannot take effect until the Minister makes regulations "prescribing anything failing (sic) to be prescribed" for the due enforcement of the provision including, significantly, the categories

---

313 S. 29(2).

314 (1959) LLR 112.

315 S. 30(1); by s.30(2) any decision of the court is final but see footnote 276 ante.

316 See the Workmen's Compensation (Medical Aid Fees And charges) Rules which provide that the fees and charges must be in accordance with the provisions of the Hospital Fees Regulations.

317 S. 27(1).

318 S. 28.

319 See E. E., Uvieghara, 'Injuries At Work - Workmen's Compensation Act,' *The Journal of Business & Social Studies*, Vol. 2. No. 1 Sept., 1969 p.33.

of employers to whom the provision is to apply.[320] When the regulations are made every employer to whom they relate must insure every workman employed[321] by him against injury or death arising out of and in the course of his employment. Any such employer who fails, omits or neglects to do so or fails to comply with any provision of the Regulations will be guilty of an offence and liable on conviction, for a first offence, to a fine equivalent to the premium for the year in question in respect of the number of workmen in his employment and on conviction for a second or subsequent offence to a fine equivalent to double the premium payable for the year in question in respect of the number of workmen employed by him or the sum of two thousand naira whichever is greater.[322]

The minister may also make regulations prescribing such returns, as he thinks fit, to be made by employers and by insurers carrying on the business of insuring employers against their liabilities for compensation under the Act.[323] Any person who is required to make returns who fails to do so within the time within which he is required to do so or who makes or causes to be made a return which is false in any material particular or, on being so required fails to give any information or explanation respecting the return which it is in his power to give, will be guilty of an offence and on conviction liable to a fine of ten naira for every day during which the default continues.[324]

Occupational diseases

As we have seen the courts have insisted that the expression "injury by accident" does not include or extend to cover the growth of incapacity by a continuous process extending over a period of time. As a result diseases which manifest themselves over a period of time as a result of a workman's work have had to be dealt with separately.

---

[320] S. 40(2); failing is probably falling.

[321] S. 40(1).

[322] S. 40(3).

[323] S. 36(1).

[324] S. 36(2). By S. 37 where an offence under the Act is committed by a body corporate or firm or other association of individuals every director, manager, secretary or other similar officer of the body corporate or every partner or officer of firm or every person concerned in the management of the affairs of the association or every person purporting to act in any of these capacities is severally guilty of the offence and liable to be prosecuted and punished as if he had himself committed the offence in an individual capacity unless he proves that the act or omission constituting the offence took place without his knowledge, consent or connivance.

The provisions for compensating an occupational disease were first introduced in 1950.[325] It will be seen that they contain what may be regarded as a flaw. Only a disease already known to medical science as associated with a particular occupation or any of a number of occupations may receive compensation. Indeed a disease which has not been so specified by the Minister cannot receive compensation.[325a]

The main provision is section 32. The section and its first two provisos should, probably, read as follows:

> The minister may by order extend the provisions of this Act to incapacity or death caused by any disease specified in such order, and [where a medical practitioner grants a certificate that a workman is suffering from any disease so specified and a court, on the hearing of an application, is satisfied on the evidence as to the matters stated in the certificate compensation shall be payable as if the disease] was a personal injury by accident arising out of and in the course of employment:
>
> Provided that:
> (a) the disease is due to the nature of the employment as certified by the appropriate medical board;
>
> (b) the Minister may specify in any order made under this section any disease, which, unless otherwise certified by a medical practitioner or the employer can prove to the contrary, shall be deemed to be due to the nature of his employment, if the workman who contracts any such disease was at, [or at any time within one month immediately preceding] the date of disablement aforesaid employed in any occupation specified in the order in relation to the disease.

The words in brackets, which were substituted for similar words in the original provisions, are, in fact, not contained in S. 32.[326] It is not clear whether this is by design or whether it is due to inadvertence. Two other amendments made by the same statute are reflected in section 32. However s.33 and, indeed, s.35, as will be seen, will seem to have meaning only with the inclusion of the words in bracket in the main body of section 32.[327]

---

[325] See the Workmen's Compensation (Amendment) Ordinance No. 23 of 1950.

[325a] See *Okore* v. *Elder Engineering & Airways Co Ltd* Unreported Suit No. WC 27/63, 1964.

[326] Except that for the last eight words in the bracket in the main body of the section the section has the words - compensation shall be payable as if any disease-and they are followed by the words "so specified."

[327] It is also significant that the words are contained in the workmen's Compensation (Specified Diseases) Order.

The Workmen's Compensation (Specified Diseases) order, made under the repealed statute and which took effect on 1st October 1966, is continued in force, apparently, by virtue of section 32. Article 2(1) of the order extends the provisions of the Act to incapacity or death caused by any of 33 diseases specified in the schedule of the order. So that if the words in bracket in the main provision were contained in the section an employee will be able to obtain compensation only where a medical practitioner gives a certificate to the effect that the workman is suffering from any of the specified diseases. But as S.32 stands no such certification is required. In any event the two provisos have, also apparently, to be met. Since an order has in fact been made by virtue of proviso (b) its requirement has to be satisfied. Article 3 of the order provides- that where a workman has contracted any specified disease, that disease must, unless the contrary is specified by a qualified medical practitioner or proved by the employer, be deemed to be due to the nature of his employment if the workman was at, or at any time within one month immediately preceding, the date of his disablement employed in any occupation specified in relation to that disease in the second column of the schedule to the order.[328] If proviso (a) also has to be satisfied there could be conflict between the two provisos. It would seem that proviso (a) is anomalous within s.32. Section 35 seems to suggest that proviso (a) is meant to confer power on the minister to make an order requiring certification by a medical board in certain circumstances or for certain purposes. It is certainly more appropriate for application with respect to s.33. Clearly the whole position is unclear and needs an urgent re-examination.

For the purpose of calculating a workman's earnings, where the workman was, at the date of his incapacity or death, employed in employment to the nature of which the disease is due, the date of commencement of the incapacity or the date of death if there was no previous incapacity, must be treated as the date of the happening of the accident but where the workman was not so employed at the date of his incapacity or death, the last day on which he was so employed must be treated as the date of the accident.[329] But for all other purposes the commencement of the incapacity of the workman or the date of his death, if there was no previous incapacity, must be treated as the date of the happening of the accident.[330]

If the disease has been contracted by a gradual process so that two or more employers are severally liable to pay compensation in respect of it the aggregate amount of compensation recoverable from the employers must not exceed the

[328] This article does not apply to two of the specified diseases.

[329] S. 32 proviso (c).

[330] Ibid.

amount that would be payable by a single employer.[331] In any such case, where the employers are unable to come to an agreement, they are entitled, as between themselves, to such rights of contribution as the court thinks just, having regard to the circumstances of the case, in any action brought or application made by any of them for that purpose.[332]

Section 34 provides that an order made under section 32 in relation to byssinosis, which is one of the specified diseases, may include provision for securing that no compensation is payable in respect of incapacity or death of a workman caused by that disease unless, whether immediately or not, before the date of his disablement, he has been employed in any occupation specified in the order in relation to the disease for a length of time, whether continuous or not, so specified. Article 4 of the Order now provides that compensation is payable in respect of incapacity or death of a workman caused by byssinosis unless, whether immediately or not, before the date of his disablement he has been employed in any of three specified occupations for a period or periods, whether continuous or not, amounting in the aggregate to five years.

Section 33 is as follows:

> An order under section 32 of this Act, may provide that, in relation to any particular specified in any such order, that section shall have effect subject to the modification that for the words "where a medical practitioner grants a certificate that a workman is suffering from any disease so specified" there shall be substituted the words "where a medical board appointed under section 35 of this Act determines that a workman is suffering from any disease so specified and grants a certificate to that effect."

This section seems, clearly, to confirm that for a claim for compensation to succeed under section 32 a medical practitioner has to grant a certificate that the employee is suffering from a specified disease. However the section empowers the minister to require such certification to be done by a medical board rather than a medical practitioner in respect of any specified disease. This has been done in respect of four of the specified diseases. Article 2(2) of the Order provides that in relation to byssinosis, bagassosis, tabacosis or pneumoconiosis section 33[333] is to apply with the modification that the words "where a medical board appointed under section 35 determines that a workman is suffering from any disease so specified and grants a certificate to that effect" are substituted for the words "where a medical practitioner grants a certificate that a workman is

---

331 S. 32 proviso (d).

332 Ibid.

333 Quaere whether not s.32.

suffering from any disease so specified." Thus compensation is payable in respect of any one of the four specified diseases only where an appointed medical board, rather than a medical practitioner, certifies that a workman is suffering from that disease.

The appointment of medical boards is dealt with in section 35. Medical boards may be appointed "for the purposes of section 32 of this Act where it has effect subject to the modification specified in section 34[334] of this Act and for the purposes of any provision in any order under section 32 of this Act where by any matter is authorised or required to be certified by a medical board."[335] The power to appoint a medical board is vested in the minister although he can do so only on the recommendation of the minister responsible for matters relating to health. A board must consist of at least two medical practitioners one of whom must be appointed chairman. A board must not determine the question whether or not an employee is suffering from a specified disease or any other medical question if any member of the board is unable to be present at the consideration of that question, or, in the case of a board consisting of two members, if the board is unable to reach a unanimous decision on that question. In any case where a board is unable to determine any medical question the question must, as soon as possible, be referred to another board appointed by the minister on the recommendation of the minister responsible for matters relating to health. However where the initial board consisted of two members and the reason it was unable to determine the medical question was that it could not reach a unanimous decision, the reference must be to a board consisting of three members whose decision, if not unanimous, must be that of the majority of the members.

Members of a board may be paid such fees or other remuneration and such travelling and other allowances as may be approved by the minister responsible for finance.

Rules of court and regulations

The Chief Justice of Nigeria may make rules of court for regulating proceedings before a High Court.[336] The Rules may prescribe the procedure, forms and fees

---

[334] Surely this should be s. 33.

[335] The second purpose or arm can only be a reference to s.32 proviso (a) but, as we have seen, the proviso is inappropriate. It may also be noted that the purposes do not seem to be able to accommodate S. 16(4) which requires the minister to constitute a medical board "under the provisions of this Act" to determine a dispute as to the percentage or degree of an injured employee's disability or the amount of compensation payable; see ante.

[336] S. 38(1); see the Workmen's Compensation (Rules of Court) Rules which continue to apply and footnote 268 *ante*; Rule 24 and perhaps Rule 26 do not appear to be in consonance with the new statute.

payable in respect of proceedings for compensation.[337] The minister may make regulations, not inconsistent with the provisions of the Act or rules made by the Chief Justice, generally for the purposes of giving effect to the Act.[338]

---

[337] S. 38(2)

[338] S. 38(3); see the Workmen's Compensation Rules which continue in force.

Part Two

Collective labour relations

Chapter 7

Trade union law

Introduction

Collective labour relations find practical expression primarily through the well-known phenomenon of voluntary collective bargaining. And collective bargaining itself, for it to be meaningful, is, in turn, dependent not only on the existence of trade unions, especially trade unions of employees, but also upon the vigour and independence of the unions. Therefore, there can be no doubt that the extent to which the law gives support to the formation and existence of strong and vigorous trade unions, to that extent does it give effect and meaning to collective bargaining.

Definition of trade union

There is often a misconception of the real nature of a trade union. There are persons who regard, for example, students' unions or associations of market women, or even any militant association as a trade union. An understanding of the statutory definition of a trade union will help to dispel such grave misconceptions. Furthermore any association which is a trade union must not perform any act in furtherance of the purposes for which it has been formed, except any steps, including the collection of dues or subscriptions, which may be necessary for getting it registered, unless it has been registered with the Registrar of Trade Unions.[1] Where this provision is contravened the union itself, every official of the union and any member who took any active part in the performance of the contravening act is guilty of an offence punishable with a fine of ₦50.[2]

---

[1] S. 2(1) Trade Unions Act, Cap. 437 Laws of the Federation of Nigeria, 1990. Cap. 437 was first enacted as Decree No.31 of 1973. It repealed and replaced the first statute on trade unions, the Trade Unions Ordinance No.44 of 1938, later cap.200 Laws of the Federation of Nigeria and Lagos, 1958. All section references in this chapter are to Cap.437 unless otherwise stated.

[2] Ss. 2(3) and 49.

A trade union means any combination of workers or employers, whether temporary or permanent, the purpose of which is to regulate the terms and conditions of employment of workers, whether the combination in question would or would not, apart from this Act, be an unlawful combination by reason of any of its purposes being in restraint of trade and whether its purposes do or do not include the provision of benefits for its members.[3]

This definition has only two significant criteria for determining whether an association is a trade union; (i) the combination must be of workers or employers and (ii) it must have the proper purpose; that is, that of regulating the terms and conditions of employment of workers. The rest of the definition has been included in response to the effect of the common law doctrine of restraint of trade on trade unions.[4]

The combination

The combination may be of *workers* or *employers*. Thus both workers and employers can form trade unions. The conception of trade unions as an exclusive workers association is, though popular, however, erroneous. But workers and employers cannot come together in one trade union. A worker is any employee, that is to say any member of the Public Service of the Federation or of a State or any individual (other than a member of any such Public Service) who has entered into or works under a contract with an employer whether the contract is for manual labour, clerical work or otherwise, expressed or implied, oral or in writing, and whether it is a contract personally to execute any work or labour or a contract of apprenticeship.[5]

The definition not only provides clearly that a worker is any employee but also goes on to support that position. In *National Association of Local Government Officers* v *Bolton Corporation*,[6] the House of Lords held that, the words "or otherwise", extend such a definition to include also those employed neither for manual labour nor clerical work. Lord Wright said: "in my opinion or otherwise was intended to embrace the entire range of wage earning or salaried employment."[7]

---

[3] S 1(1).

[4] As to which see below.

[5] S. 52.

[6] [1943] AC 166.

[7] Ibid., 186; strictly there was or there is no need to divide the main part of the definition into two arms: the second arm is wide enough to embrace all employees whether in the public or private

Any employee at common law is, therefore, a worker for the purposes of trade unions.[8] However, the phrase "whether it is a contract personally to execute any work or labour" seems to extend the definition beyond common law employees. As we have seen this phrase refers to self-employed persons usually referred to also as independent contractors.

The purpose

The main purpose for which an association is formed is the distinguishing characteristic of a trade union from other associations. In the case of a trade union the principal purpose must be to regulate the terms and conditions of employment of workers. It is suggested that the omission of the word "principal" which was contained in the old definition[9] is inadvertent. Support is given to this suggestion by section 7(1)(d) which provides that the Registrar of Trade Unions must cancel the registration of any trade union if it is proved to his satisfaction that the principal purpose for which the union is in practice being carried on is a purpose other than that of regulating the terms and conditions of employment of workers.

Similarly, section 28(2)(b) which empowers the Registrar to refuse an alteration of the rules of a trade union if, as a result of the alteration, the principal purpose of the union would cease to be that of regulating the terms and conditions of employment of workers, seems to confirm that the union rules must provide that its principal purpose is the regulation of the terms and conditions of employment of workers. A trade union may, however, have other purposes in addition to the principal purpose. Section 1(2) provides that the fact that a combination has purposes or powers other than the purpose of regulating the terms and conditions of employment of workers cannot prevent its registration as a trade union. But, as already stated, any other object or purpose must be merely ancillary to the purpose of regulating the terms and conditions of employment of workers, i.e., engaging in collective bargaining.

It is suggested that the approach of the court in *Re Union of Ifelodun Timber Dealers and Allied Workers*[10] is the correct one for determining whether an

---

sector. However, the definition covers both sectors; the split may have been influenced by the common law rule that a public servant has no contract with the State; see *Rodwell* v *Thomas* [1944] KB 596. But see now *Shitta-Bey* v *Federal Public Service Commission* (1981) 1 SC 40.

[8] There are, however, exceptions; see below.

[9] S.2 Trade Union Acts Cap,20; Laws of the Federation of Nigeria and Lagos 1958.

[10] [1964] 2 All NLR 63.

association is a trade union or not. A combination applied for registration as a trade union but was refused registration by the Registrar. On appeal, de Lestang C.J. said "...there is nothing in the present case to show that the Association has any rules as yet. Its objects are, however, set out in its constitution and it is necessary to examine these objects as a whole in order to decide whether it is a trade union or not."[11] After examining the objects he concluded: "I can see nothing in these objects which, to use the words of the definition, regulates the relation between workmen and masters or between workmen and workmen or between masters and masters.[12] It seems to me that the main purpose of the association in so far as they may be extracted from the published objects are the protection and expansion of the timber trade and the welfare of all persons, whether they be workmen or employers engaged in that trade. The association does not, therefore, come within the definition of trade union."[13]

The Registrar, similarly refused to register the Motor Collectors' Union of Nigeria and the Cameroons in 1954. The union applied for registration of the union as stated in the "Constitution, Rules and By-Laws." The objects of the union as stated in the Constitution were:

a) it shall be the aim of the union to secure the complete organization in the union of all workers employed in the motor transport workers trade;
b) to collect passengers for motor or transport owners;
c) safe keep the properties of passengers, settle matters and make peace between member and member, members and drivers, member and/or drivers and passengers and generally protect the interests of members;
d) to keep proper watch or account of the driver's paid by the passengers;
e) to cater for the welfare of the passengers or lorry owners financially or otherwise.[14]

The Registrar gave as his ground for refusing to register the union the reason that "the main object of the union seemed to him to be touting for passengers."

A trade union is not necessarily formed by reason only of any agreement between an employer and persons employed by him as to the terms and conditions of the employment or any agreement for the instruction of any person in a profession, trade or handicraft or any agreement between partners as to their

---

[11] Ibid., 64.

[12] This was the required principal purpose under the earlier statute; the approach remains the same however.

[13] Ibid., 64-66.

[14] Letter N. TU 593/6 of November 1954.

own business or any trading agreement between employers or, lastly, any agreement imposing restrictions in connection with the sale of the goodwill of a business.[15]

Freedom to form trade unions

Trade union freedom has, at least, two sides. First, it involves absence of compulsion. There is no statutory provision which compels anyone to join or be a member of a trade union. There is, however, recognition at common law, of the right of unions to establish and maintain a closed shop. As Sargent J. said in *Reynolds* v *Shipping Federation Ltd*,[16] "for many years past no one has questioned the right of a trade union to insist, if they are strong enough to do so, under penalty of a strike that an employer or a group of employers shall employ none but members of the trade union."[17]

Secondly, trade union freedom demands a positive guarantee of a right to form or join a trade union of one's choice. The International Labour Organization Convention No. 87[18] envisages such a guarantee. Part 1 of the Convention, on freedom of association, requires the following protections - employees and employers must have the right to establish and join organizations of their own choosing without previous authorization; they must have the right to draw up their constitutions and rules, elect their representatives in full election, organize their administration and activities and to formulate their programmes and public authorities must refrain from any interference which would restrict these rights or impede their lawful exercise; their organizations must not be made liable to be dissolved or suspended by administrative authority and their organizations must have the right to establish and join federations and confederations and to affiliate with international organizations of employees and employers.[19] Since the attainment of independence in 1960 the Constitution has always guaranteed freedom of association. Section 40 of the Constitution of the Federal Republic of Nigeria, 1999, provides as follows:

---

[15] S. 1(3).

[16] [1924] 1 Ch. 28.

[17] Ibid., 39-40.

[18] Convention Concerning Freedom of Association and Protection of the Right to Organize, 1948. It came into force on July 1950 and Nigeria has ratified it.

[19] In *Collymore* v *Attorney General* [1970] AC 538 the Privy Council held that the abridgment of the rights of free collective bargaining and of the freedom to strike are not abridgments of the right of freedom of association.

> Every person shall be entitled to assemble freely and associate with other persons, and in particular he may form or belong to any political party, trade union or any other association for the protection of his interests:[20]

There is no doubt that this is a guarantee of a fundamental right to form or belong to a trade union of one's choice. In *Basorun* v *Industrial Arbitration Tribunal*[21] the plaintiff, who was a deputy manager in the Central Bank of Nigeria, was also the president of the Central Bank of Nigeria Employees' Union, a duly registered trade union of junior employees of the bank. A trade dispute arose between the Bank and the union and it was referred for arbitration. In its award the arbitration tribunal recommended, *inter alia*, that "no member of the staff above the rank of supervisor may join a trade union of any of the junior staff or participate either directly or indirectly in the activities of such union. The senior staff in their own right may form an association or a trade union of their own to protect their rights." This award was confirmed by an order of the Commissioner for Labour under his statutory powers and it, therefore, became legally binding. The plaintiff, whose rank was above that of a supervisor, brought an action for a declaration that his constitutional right to remain in his chosen union was infringed by the order.[22] Ọdesanya J held that the terms of the confirmed award were wide enough to invite the intervention of the court.

Any person who alleges that his right to form, join or belong to a trade union of his choice has been, is being or likely to be infringed may apply to a High Court in the State in which the infringement is threatened or has occurred for redress.[23] However, as will be seen, the right is not an absolute one. However there are other statutory protections which would be mentioned before considering the derogatory provisions. Any one who is otherwise eligible for membership of a particular trade union cannot be refused admission to membership of that union by reason only that he is of a particular community, tribe, place of origin, religion or political opinion. Any inconsistent provision in the rules of a trade union is, to the existent of the inconsistency, void and if any person is refused admission in contravention of the provision the union itself and every official of the union is guilty of an offence and liable, on summary conviction, to a fine of ₦50.[24]

---

[20] The proviso to the section does not affect trade unions.

[21] Unreported Suit No. LD/105/71, High Court of Lagos State.

[22] S. 26 1963 Constitution identical with S. 40.

[23] S. 46 Constitution

[24] SS 12 & 49.

Under the Labour Act the membership of trade unions of employees who are workers under the Act and their union activities are protected. Section 9(6) of the Act provides that -

No contract shall

(a) make it a condition of employment that a worker shall or shall not join a trade union or shall or shall not relinquish membership of a trade union, or

(b) cause the dismissal of, or otherwise prejudice, a worker-

(i) by reason of trade union membership, or

(ii) because of trade union activities outside working hours, or with the consent of the employer, within working hours, or

(iii) by reason of the fact that he has lost or been deprived of membership of a trade union or has refused or been unable to become, or for any other reason is not, a member of a trade union.

Apparently, this subsection is meant to give statutory force to Article 1 of ILO Convention 98 - the Convention concerning the Application of the Principles of the Right to Organize and to Bargain Collectively, 1949, which Nigeria has ratified. It would seem, however, that the subsection has not captured the essence of that article, which is to ensure adequate protection against anti union discrimination with respect to employment. Its coverage does not extend to employees who are not workers within that term under the Labour Act. As for the extent of the protection offered such workers it would seem limited by the fact that it is tied to the contract of employment. Many rights of an employer or benefits to a worker do not necessarily arise from a contract. There is, for example, no contractual right to promotion. As Brett JSC once said, in a contract of service, there may be many benefits, of which promotion is the most obvious one which the employer is not obliged to grant in the first place.[25] Also, the right to terminate a worker's employment by notice derives, not from contract, but from section 11 of the Act. And, neither the section nor the common law, demands that any reason be given for a termination by notice and, in any event, the motive for the giving of requisite notice is irrelevant to the lawfulness or otherwise of a termination by notice.

A further protection for a class of employees in respect of union membership is given under the Fair Wages clause. Any contractor or sub-contractor who enters into a contract with a government department which contract will receive assistance from the government by way of a grant, loan, subsidy, license,

---

[25] *Morakinyo* v *Ibadan City Council* [1964] 1 AIINLR 219, 222.

guarantee or any other form of assistance must recognize the freedom of his employees to be members of registered trade unions. Breach of this obligation may lead to the offender being struck off the list of approved government contractors.

As has been said, the constitutional right to form or belong to a union of one's choice is not an absolute one. The Constitution provides for derogation, Section 45[26] provides that nothing in section 40 "shall invalidate any law that is reasonably justifiable in a democratic society - (a) in the interest of defence, public safety, public order, public morality or public health; or (b) for the purpose of protecting the rights and freedom of other persons. It must be noted that the derogation thus permitted is by law[27] only and that such law must meet the criterion stipulated, that is, being reasonably justifiable in a democratic society for any one of the stipulated interests or purpose. Thus, clearly, an attempt by an employer to prevent or prohibit an employee from joining a trade union not based on any law will be an infringement of the employee's right. This will include requiring an employee to sign a contract not to be a member of a trade union or, where by his contract of employment, he is made to forgo his right to belong to a trade union.

There are a number of statutory provisions which derogate from the constitutional guarantee of freedom of association. Section 11 of the Trade Unions Act provides that it is not lawful for persons employed in certain establishments to combine, organize themselves or be members of a trade union for purposes of employment but that they may set up joint consultative committees in their establishments. These establishments are the Nigerian Army, Navy or Air Force; the Nigeria Police Force; the Custom and Excise Department, the Immigration Department and the Prison Services; the Customs Preventive Service; the Nigerian Security, Printing and Minting Company Ltd.; the Central Bank of Nigeria; the Nigerian External Telecommunications Ltd.; every Federal or State government establishment the employees of which are authorised to bear arms; and such other establishments as the Minister may from time to time by order specify. The Federal Fire Service has been so specified.[28] In 1978 a number of amendments were made to the Trade Unions Act. One such amendment provided that no executive or senior staff could be a member of or hold office in a trade union whose members were employees of a rank junior to his own but that such staff could form and be members of or hold office in a

[26] S. 41 Constitution, 1979

[27] For the meaning of law see below.

[28] Trade Unions (Prohibition)(Federal Fire Service) Order 1976.

trade union of employees of equal or higher rank than his own.[29] In 1979 this provision was, in turn, amended[30] and section 3 subsections (3) and (4l on membership of trade unions of senior staff now reads as follows-

(3) No staff recognized as a projection of management within the management structure of any organization shall be a member of or hold office in a trade union (whether or not the members of that trade union are workers of a rank junior, equal or higher than his own) if such membership of or the holding of such office in the trade union will lead to a conflict of his loyalties to either the union or to the management. (4) For the purposes of subsection (3) of this section, a person may be recognized as a projection of management within a management structure if his status, authority, powers, duties and accountability which are reflected in his conditions of service are such as normally inhere in a person exercising executive authority (whether or not delegated) within the organization concerned. The effect of these provisions would seem to be that a management staff is totally prohibited from being a member of any trade union only where such membership will lead to a conflict of his loyalty either to the union or his employer. It is clear that there is no blanket prohibition of membership of trade unions of all management staff. As Ayorinde J. held in *National Union of Petroleum and Natural Gas Workers* v *NNPC*[31] the position of each management staff must be considered in the light of his status, authority, powers, duties and accountability and each case must be treated separately. He said: "on the whole I conclude that the best approach to the matter will be to take the case of a staff and to test it as a separate claim. It is impossible to make a blanket ruling that the position held by certain staff will not lead to a conflict of loyalty. Management staff is determined, not by the whim of an employer, but by considering whether the status, authority, duties and accountability of an individual employee are such as are the normal attributes of an employee who exercises executive authority."

A person under the age of sixteen years is prohibited from being a member of a trade union but a person sixteen years old or above but below twenty one years may be a member of a trade union unless the rules of the union provide otherwise. An infant member of a union cannot, however, be an official of a trade union but he may otherwise, subject to the rules of the union, enjoy all the rights of a member and may effectually sign any agreement or other document

---

[29] See s. 1 (1) (a) Trade Unions (Amendment) Decree No.22 of 1978.
[30] See S. 1 Trade Unions (Amendment) Decree No. 86 of 1979.
[31] Unreported Suit No. LD/13/83 High Court of Lagos State.

and give any receipt which may be required to be signed or given by the rules of the union for the purposes of the Act or Regulations made under the Act.[32]

In some cases it is only the capacity of a person to hold office in a union and not membership of the union that is restricted. A person who has been convicted of any of certain offences is disqualified from holding office as an official of a trade union from the date of his conviction up to the end of five years after the date on which he is discharged from prison but where he is not sentenced to a term of imprisonment then up to the end of five years from the date of his conviction.[33] The offences which may so disqualify a person from holding office are the offences created under sections 47 and 48 and the offences under the criminal or penal code which may lead to the disqualification of membership of either the National Assembly or a House of Assembly.[34] Under the Constitution a person is disqualified for election to either National or a House of Assembly if he is under a sentence of death imposed by any court of law or a sentence of imprisonment for an offence involving dishonesty, by whatever name called, exceeding six months imposed on him by any court or where, within a period of less than ten years before an election to any Assembly he has been convicted and sentenced for an offence involving dishonesty or he has been found guilty of a contravention of the code of conduct.[35] Where a person is convicted of any of these offences and an appeal lies against the conviction the person must not be treated as having been convicted unless and until the time for bringing an appeal has expired without an appeal being brought or such an appeal has been brought and abandoned or has been finally determined by the upholding of the conviction.[36] Where any person holding office as an official of a trade union becomes disqualified he must vacate that office forthwith and if he purports to act as an official of a trade union at any time while he is so disqualified he is guilty of an offence and liable, on summary conviction, to a fine of ₦100.[37]

No person must hold office in any capacity in more than one trade union at the same time nor must a person who is a full time official of a central labour organization hold office at the same time in any trade union.[38] Any person who

---

[32] S. 19.

[33] S. 13(1) and (4); where a free pardon is granted the conviction no longer disqualifies; S. 13(1) proviso.

[34] S. 13(3).

[35] Ss 66 (1)(c) and (d) and 107 (1)c) and (d) 1999 Constitution;

[36] S. 13(5).

[37] S. 13(6).

[38] S. 14(1) and (2)

contravenes this provision is guilty of an offence and liable, on summary conviction, to a fine of ₦50.[39]

The question has also arisen whether the requirement of compulsory registration of trade unions offends against the constitutional guarantee of freedom of association. Before 1978 it was clear that the Registrar of Trade Unions had no power to refuse to register any union which applied for registration having satisfied the statutory requirements for registration.

But since that year the law has provided that no combination of employees or employers must be registered as a trade union save with the approval of the Minister of Labour and Productivity on his being satisfied that it is expedient to register the union either by regrouping existing trade unions, registering a new trade union or otherwise howsoever; but no trade union must be registered to represent employees or employers in a place where there already exists a trade union.[40] In *Osawe* v *Registrar of Trade Unions*[41] this provision was challenged on the ground that it infringed section 37 of the Constitution.[42] The High Court held that it was, indeed, an infringement. But both the Court of Appeal and the Supreme Court held otherwise on the ground that the power conferred was necessary to maintain public order.[43] In the Supreme Court Aniagolu JSC said- The proliferation of trade union clearly lends itself to chaos in labour circles - a fact which has the tendency of de-stabilising society by its tendency to wild-cat strikes and work- stoppages called by all sorts of disparate and unviable trade unions. It is, therefore, in the interest of public order that systematic, cohesive and responsible trade unions be established for the good of society.[44] The Supreme Court also held that where the Registrar is satisfied that a registered trade union will adequately cater for the interest of applicants who desire to register a new trade union the Registrar need not proceed with the application for registration. In the words of Kazeem JSC, "this new provision makes it mandatory for the Registrar of Trade Unions, on receiving an application to register any trade union, to ensure that there is no other registered trade union in existence which caters for the same interest as the one applying for registration. If there is, it becomes incumbent in my view, for the Registrar, as the custodian

[39] Ss. 14(3) and 49.

[40] S. 3(2); see s.1(1)(a) Trade Unions (Amendment) Act 1978.

[41] [1985] 1 NWLR 755.

[42] 1979 Constitution, now S. 40

[43] This decision will seem to underscore the point that trade union formation in Nigeria, or, certainly, trade union functioning, is not without previous authorization as required by ILO Convention No. 87.

[44] Ibid., 766.

of such information, to decline to proceed to put into effect the machinery for the registration of the new trade union as set out under section 5(2) of the Trade Unions Act 1973."[45]

Procedure for registration

A trade union is prohibited from performing any act in furtherance of its purposes unless it has been registered with the Registrar of Trade Unions.[46] However, an unregistered trade union may take any steps, including the collection of subscriptions or dues, which may be necessary for the purpose of getting the union registered.[47] An application for the registration of a trade union must be made to the Registrar in the prescribed form and signed, in the case of a trade union of employees, by at least fifty members of the union and, in the case of a trade union of employers, by at least two members of the union.[48] Every application must state the name under which it is proposed that the trade union be registered and the address of the office which, if the union is registered, is to be the registered office of the union.[49] Every application must be accompanied by two copies of the rules of the union and by a list showing the name, address, age and occupation of each of the persons by whom the application is signed and the official title, name, address, age and occupation of each official of the union.[50] Where the Registrar receives an application for the registration of a trade union he must cause a notice of the application to be published in the Gazette, stating that objections to the registration of the trade union may be submitted to him in writing within three months of the publication of the notice.[51] If, however, the application appears to him to be defective in any respect he must notify the applicants accordingly and must take no further action in relation to the application until it has been amended to his satisfaction or a fresh, it is submitted, non-defective, application is made.[52] The Registrar must, within three months after the end of the period for objections, consider any objections submitted to him during the period. If he is satisfied (a) that no proper objection has been raised; (b) that none of the purposes of the trade union is

---

[45] Ibid., 763
[46] S. 2(1).
[47] Ibid., proviso.
[48] S. 3(1)
[49] S. 3(5)
[50] S. 3(6)
[51] S. 5(1) and (2).
[52] S . 5 (1) proviso.

unlawful, and (c) that the requirements of the Act[53] and of the regulations[54] with respect to the registration of trade unions have been complied with, must, subject to an acceptable name,[55] register the union and its rules.[56] On registering a union, the Registrar must issue a certificate of registration which, unless it is proved that the registration of the Union has been cancelled, is conclusive evidence, except in any proceedings for the cancellation of the registration of the union on the ground that its registration was obtained by fraud or as a result of a mistake, that (i) the requirements of the Act and the Regulations with respect to registration have been complied with; (ii) the trade union is authorised to be registered; and (iii) the trade union is a trade union for the purposes of the Act.[57]

If the Registrar refuses to register the union he must, forthwith, send to the applicants a notice in the prescribed form to that effect and stating the grounds of the refusal and specifying the date from which the time for appealing against the refusal is to run, and he must publish a notice to the like effect in the *Gazette*.[58] Any official or member of the union may, within the period of thirty days beginning with the date so specified, appeal to the appropriate court against such refusal.[59] On an appeal the court may make such order as it thinks proper and, without prejudice to the generality of this power, in any proceedings on such an appeal, the court has all the powers vested by the Act in the Registrar and may make any order which might or ought to have been made by the Registrar and the costs of and incident to the appeal including the costs of and incident to any proceedings before the Registrar are in the discretion of the Court.[60]

Before the amendments made in 1996 an appeal against refusal to register a trade union lay to the High Court of the State in which the registered office of the union was situated[61] and a further appeal lay from an order of that court to the Court of Appeal.[62] By the amendments this jurisdiction of a High Court as

---

[53] These include S.4 which provides that every trade union must have registered rules which must contain provisions with respect to the matters listed in schedule to the Act, as to which see below, and S.6 as regards the names of trade union as to which see below also.

[54] See the Trade Unions Regulations which prescribe various forms including the fee and form for application for registration.

[55] See below.

[56] S.5(2).

[57] S.5(6)

[58] S.5(5) (a)

[59] S.5(5)(b); see S.2 Trade Unions (Amendment) (No.2) Act No.26 of 1996, and S. 2(a) Trade Unions (Amendment) Act No 1 of 1999

[60] S.8(1) (a) and (b); see S. 4(a) and S. 4 No 26 of 1996 and No. 1 of 1999 respectively.

[61] S.5(5)(b) before amendment and S. 52; but an unregistered union could not have had a *registered* office.

[62] S. 8(2) now repealed.

well as its powers, including the discretionary power as to costs of and incidental to an appeal, was transferred to the Minister of Labour and the right of appeal to the Court of Appeal was curtailed.[63] But it was obvious that it would have been difficult in practice to fit the Minister into the legal system. In any event the Supreme Court has held that section 6(6)(b) of the constitution gives an unfettered access to the courts for the determination of any civil right or obligation.[64] Furthermore, natural justice at common law and fair hearing under the constitution may well have been trampled upon since it is the Minister who would have refused the registration in the first place.[65]

However, as we have seen, an appeal from refusal to register a trade union now lies, not to a High Court or the Minister, but to the "appropriate court" which is defined to mean "the Industrial Arbitration Panel and the National Industrial Court as the case may be."[66] Presumably this means that an appeal must first be referred to the IAP, presumably by the Minister, and thereafter, if necessary, by the trade union to the NIC. But there is grave doubt as to whether both the IAP and the NIC have jurisdiction in such a matter. Although jurisdiction may be conferred on the NIC by "any other Act" this must be with respect to the settlement of trade disputes, the interpretation of collective agreements and matters connected therewith.[67] It seems obvious that a refusal to register a trade union is not a matter with respect to any of these matters. Even if it is conceded that additional jurisdiction may be conferred by statute, as seems to have been done earlier in 1988,[68] it is submitted that to do so with respect to a fundamental right would be unconstitutional. The right to form or belong to a trade union of one's choice is a fundamental right within section 40 of the constitution and so also, it is submitted, is a right to have a union registered since, without registration a union, its officials and members commit an offence if they carry out any act in furtherance of the purposes of the union. Section 46(2) of the constitution, with the marginal note – Special Jurisdiction of High Court – vests *original* jurisdiction in fundamental rights issues in a High Court. Although section 46(2) opens with the words – Subject to the provisions of this constitution – which may include, among others, section 6 by virtue of which other courts may be authorised to exercise jurisdiction on matters with respect to which the National Assembly may make laws, the IAP and NIC on which jurisdiction have

---

[63] Sc. 5(5)(b) and 8(1)(a); see Ss. 2 and 4 Trade Unions (Amendment) (No. 2) Act 1996 No. 26.

[64] *Adediran* v *Interland Transport Ltd* [1991] 9 NWLR 155.

[65] *Bakare* v *Lagos State Civil Service Commission* [1992] 8 NWLR 641

[66] Ss. 5(5)(b), 8(1) and 52; see Ss. 2, 4 and 8 Trade Unions (Amendment) Act 1999 No. 1.

[67] S. 19(1) Trade Disputes Act, Cap. 432

[68] By S. 1(c) Trade Disputes (Amendment) (No. 2) Decree 1988 No. 57; see now S. 24 Cap 432

been conferred can only owe their existence to section 6(4)(a) which empowers the National Assembly to establish courts other than those established by the Constitution, but their jurisdiction must be subordinate to that of a High Court.

There is also some doubt as to whether there is a right of appeal from a decision of the NIC. The only provision on a right of appeal from the NIC is section 20(3) of the Trade Disputes Act which provision is that an appeal from the decisions of the Court lies as of right to the Court of Appeal on questions of fundamental rights.[69] If the contention that the NIC has no jurisdiction in questions of fundamental right is correct, then it is doubtful if s. 20(3) would be of any avail. It is suggested that it is necessary to give jurisdiction back to the High Courts and restore the right of appeal to the Court of Appeal where registration of a trade union is refused.

Where an application for the registration of a trade union is finally refused the union must be dissolved in accordance with its rules within the period of three months beginning with the date of the final refusal.[70] An application for the registration of a trade union must be taken to be finally refused (a) at the end of the thirty days allowed for appeal where no appeal from the Registrar's refusal is brought within those days; or (b) where an appeal was brought and the Registrar's refusal is confirmed on a final determination, on the date of the final determination; or (c) if the refusal by the Registrar to register was on the ground of its name being objectionable and the matter had been referred to the Minister for his decision, on the date on which the Minister confirms the refusal.[71] If a trade union whose application for registration has been finally refused fails to dissolve accordingly, the union and every official of the union is liable, on summary conviction, to a fine of ₦10 for each day on which the union remains undissolved.[72]

A trade union cannot be registered under a name identical with that of any existing trade union or which so nearly resembles the name of any existing trade union as to be likely to deceive the members of the public.[73] In *Ojo and 4 Ors* (trading under the name and style of Ibadan Cornmillers' Association) v *Registrar of Trade Unions and 5 Ors* (being officers of the Ibadan and District Cornmillers' Association),[74] the High Court rejected an application by the plaintiffs for an injunction to restrain the Registrar from registering the

---

[69] See S. 6(a) Trade Disputes (Amendment) Act 1992 No. 47

[70] S. 9(1) (a) .

[71] S. 9(2); see also s. 6(3) and p. 330.

[72] S. 9(3).

[73] S. 6(1).

[74] Unreported Suit No. LD/521/68 High Court of Lagos State.

defendant trade union in that its name, the Ibadan and District Cornmillers' Association so nearly resembled the plaintiffs registered business name as to be likely to mislead the public. The court held that the plaintiffs, not being a trade union, could not object to the registration of the defendant trade union.

Also, a trade union must not be registered under a name containing any words which, in the opinion of the Registrar, are deceptive or objectionable in that they contain a reference, direct or indirect, to any personage, practice or institution, or are otherwise unsuitable as a name for a trade union.[75] However, if the Registrar refuses to register a trade union on this ground, any official or member of the union may require the matter to be referred to the Minister whose decision on the matter is final.[76] Where, however, on such reference, the Minister decides that a particular trade union may be registered under a certain name the union may be registered under that name.[77]

Cancellation of registration

Section 7 provides that if any of the following six grounds is proved to the satisfaction of the Registrar of Trade Unions, he must cancel the registration of the trade union:

a) that the registration of the trade union was obtained by fraud or as the result of a mistake; or
b) that any of the purposes of the union is unlawful; or
c) that, after receipt of a warning in writing from the Registrar, the union has deliberately contravened or continued to contravene any provision of the Act or the regulations;[78] or
d) that the principal purpose for which the union is in practice being carried on is a purpose other than that of regulating the terms and conditions of employment of workers; or
e) that the union though still in existence, has ceased to function; or f) that the union has ceased to exist.[79]

---

[75] S. 6(2).

[76] S. 6(3); but quaere whether not unconstitutional in view of s.6(6) (b) of the 1979 Constitution. See *Government of Imo State* v *Greeco Construction and Engineering Associates Ltd.* [1985] 3 NWLR 71.

[77] S. 6(4).

[78] One provision of the Act, which is constantly violated by the unions, is the duty to make an annual return contained in S.36; see further below.

Where the Registrar proposes to cancel the registration of a trade union he must send a notice in the prescribed form to the trade union at its registered office, stating that he proposes to cancel the union's registration and specifying briefly, the ground or grounds on which he proposes to do so.[80] It must also specify a date, not less than two months after the date of the notice, and stating that unless before that date, he is satisfied that the registration ought not to be cancelled, he will proceed to cancel the registration on the expiration of a period of thirty days beginning from that date unless an appeal against the proposed cancellation is taken within that period.[81]

Where the Registrar has sent a notice, and the trade union is still in existence on the date specified in the notice, and the Registrar has not withdrawn the notice before that date, any official or member of the trade union may, within the period of thirty days beginning with that date, appeal to the appropriate court against the proposed cancellation.[82] On an appeal the court may make such order as it thinks proper; and without prejudice to the generality of this power, in any proceedings on such an appeal, the court has all the powers vested by the Act in the Registrar, and may make any order which might or ought to have been made by the Registrar.[83] The costs of and incidental to the appeal including the costs of

---

[79] This provision is, perhaps, unlikely to be operative since the 1976-78 reorganization of the unions into much larger and virile ones. In 1976, the Federal Military Government promulgated the Trade Unions (Central Labour Organizations) (Special Provisions) Decree 1976 under which an administrator was appointed with responsibility, *inter alia,* "for taking all steps as the Administrator may consider necessary to encourage and effect the formation, whether by amalgamation or federation of existing trade unions or otherwise, of strong and effective trade unions. " The result was that the 983, mainly "house" unions then on the register and some others were re-grouped on industrial basis into 70 unions. 42 of these were unions of junior employees, 18 unions of Senior staff, 9 of employers and the Nigerian Union of Pensioners. The Registrar was enjoined to register all the 70 unions: see s.5 (b) (iii)Trade Unions (Amendment) Decree No.22 of 1978 which gave effect to the restructuring exercise; in *Nigerian Nurses' Association* v *A.G. of the Federation* (1981) 1 FNR 55; (1981)11-12 SC1 the Supreme Court held that the Act terminated the existence of all the trade unions then on the register with effect from the date on which it came into effect. A further restructuring, initiated by the Nigerian Labour Congress to which the 42 unions were, by statute, deemed affiliated, but assisted by government, has reduced the number of these unions to 29. Only 19 of these unions remained untouched; see Trade Unions (Amendment) Act No.4 of 1996.

[80] S. 7(2) (a)

[81] S. 7(2) (b)

[82] S. 7(3); see S.3 Trade Unions (Amendment)(No.2) Act No.26 of 1996, and S. 3 1999 No. 1

[83] S. 8(1) (a); see S.4(a) ibid.

and incidental to any proceedings before the Registrar, are in the discretion of the court.[84]

The amendments of 1999 affect the right of appeal against a proposal to cancel the registration of a trade union in the same way as they affect the right of appeal from a refusal to register a trade union.[85] Thus the same comments and arguments apply, *mutatis mutandis*, with respect to the jurisdiction of the IAP and the NIC in an appeal against a proposal to cancel the registration of a registered trade union as they apply to the right of appeal against a refusal to register a trade union.[86]

The Registrar must not cancel the registration of a trade union before the expiration of the period of thirty days beginning with the date specified in the notice of a proposed cancellation and, also where an appeal against the proposed cancellation is taken within that period, he must not cancel the registration unless the appeal is abandoned or the proposed cancellation is confirmed on the final determination of the appeal.[87]

A trade union whose registration is cancelled ceases to enjoy the privileges conferred by the Act on trade unions but any liabilities incurred by the union before the date of cancellation is not affected by the cancellation and may be enforced against the union on or after that date as if the cancellation had not taken place.[88] A trade union whose registration is cancelled must be dissolved in accordance with its rules within the period of three months beginning with the date of the cancellation.[89] If the union fails to do so the union and every official of the union will be liable, on summary conviction, to a fine of ₦10 for each day on which the union remains undissolved after the end of the three months.[90]

Where a trade union is voluntarily dissolved in accordance with its rules, a notice in the prescribed form signed by a person who immediately before the dissolution was an official of the union., stating that the union has been dissolved, and the original certificate of registration of the union must be delivered to the Registrar not more than thirty days after the date on which the union ceases to exist.[91] Where such a notice is received by the Registrar, the provisions of section 7 are not applicable, but the Registrar, when satisfied that

[84] S. 8(1) (b)
[85] See f.n. 56, 57, 74 and 85.
[86] See above at p. 326 et Seq.
[87] S. 7(4).
[88] S. 7(5).
[89] S. 9(1)(b)
[90] S. 9(3)
[91] S. 18(1).

the trade union has been duly dissolved, must cancel the registration of the union and notify the person by who the notice was signed that the registration has been cancelled.[92] Where either the notice of voluntary dissolution or the original certificate of registration of the dissolved union is not delivered to the Registrar every person who immediately before the dissolution, was an official of the union, is guilty of an offence and liable, on summary conviction, to a fine of ₦50.[93]

Where a trade union registered under the Act ceases to be so registered it must not, thereafter, perform any act in furtherance of its purposes but it may take any steps which may be necessary for the purpose of dissolving the union.[94]

Where there is a violation of this prohibition, the union and every official of the union and any member who, not being an official, but took any active part in the performance of that act will be guilty of any offence and liable, on summary conviction, to a fine of ₦50.[95]

Obligations of registration

Registered office

Every trade union must have a registered office to which all communications and notices may be addressed.[96] On registering a trade union the Registrar must record as its registered office the office whose address is stated in the application for registration.[97] Any change in the situation of the registered office of trade union must be notified to the Registrar within thirty days after the date of the change and the change must be recorded by the Registrar.[98] If any union continues for more than thirty days without having a registered office the trade union and every official of the union will be liable, on summary conviction, to a fine of ₦10 for every day during which, after the end of the thirty days, it continues without a registered office.[99]

---

[92] S. 10(2).
[93] Ss. 10(3) and 49.
[94] S. 2(2).
[95] Ss. 2(3) and 49.
[96] S. 20(1)
[97] S. 20(2).
[98] S. 20(3)
[99] S. 20(4)

Annual return

Every registered trade union must send to the Registrar before 1st June in each year, an annual return in the prescribed form and must be made out to such date as may be prescribed and must be certified as correct by the duly appointed auditor.[100] An annual return must include:

a) full particulars of the assets and liabilities of the union at the date to which the return is made out;
b) full particulars of the receipts and expenditure during the year ending on that date;
c) the prescribed particulars of the membership of the union at the date, and of any changes which occurred therein during the year ending with that date; and
d) evidence that the amount due to the Nigerian Labour Congress from the check-off contribution of its members has be paid to it;[101]
e) such other particulars as may be prescribed and must show separately the amount expended by the union during the year on each of its various purposes.[102]

An annual return must be accompanied by (a) a copy of the rules of the union as in force on the date to which the return is made out; (b) a copy of all alterations of the rules of the union and all new rules adopted during the year ending with that date, showing in respect of each alteration or new rule the date on which it was adopted whether or not it has been registered and, if so, the date on which it came or will come into force; and (c) a complete list of the officials of the union at the date to which the return is made out, and a list of all changes in the officials which occurred during the year ending on that date, showing the date of each such change.[103] Upon request by any member of the union the union must deliver or send to the member a copy, free of charge, of the latest annual return sent to the Registrar.[104]

---

[100] S. 36(1)
[101] S. 36(2)(d)
[102] S. 36(2)
[103] S. 36(3); upon contravention of any of the requirements of subsection (1) to (3) of S. 36 the Union and every official of the union will be guilty of an offence and liable, on summary conviction, to a fine of ₦50; Ss.36(5) and 49
[104] S 36(4); upon a contravention of this sub-section the union and every official of the union who knowingly caused or permitted it will be liable, on summary conviction to a fine of N10 for each offence; S. 36(6).

Duty of treasurer to render accounts

The treasurer of a trade union, whenever he is required to do so by the rules of the union, or when specially directed to do so by the committee of management, must prepare a full and accurate account showing (a) all sums received or paid by him since the date to which the last account submitted by him was made out; and (b) the balance remaining in his hands at that date and must cause the account, when prepared, to be audited by the duly appointed auditor.[105] Every such account, after being audited, must be submitted by the treasurer to the members of the union in accordance with its rules, or if the account was prepared on the special directions of the committee of management, in accordance with those directions.[106] Where the treasurer is required to do so by a resolution passed at a meeting of the union or is directed to do so by the committee of management, he must, as soon as possible, hand over to the union the balance due from him to the union as certified by the duly appointed auditor, and, must also, if required, hand over all bounds, securities, books, papers and other property of the union in his possession or custody.[107] In determining the balance due from the treasurer the auditor must add to the balance shown as due from the treasurer in the latest account submitted by him any sums received by the treasurer on account of the union since the date to which the account was made up but must also deduct any sums paid by the treasurer on account of the union since that date.[108]

If the treasurer fails to hand over in full to the union the balance due from him, the union or any person capable of suing as a representative of the union, may institute civil proceedings against the treasurer for the balance due and for all sums received by him on account of the union since the date to which the account was made up but he may, in the proceedings, set off any sums which may have been paid by him to or on account of the union since that date.[109] Similarly, if the treasurer fails to hand over any of the other union property which he is required to hand over, the union or any person capable of suing as a representative of the union may initiate civil proceedings against the treasurer for

---

[105] S. 37(1).
[106] S. 37(2).
[107] S. 37(3).
[108] S. 37(4).
[109] S. 37(5).

its delivery to the union.[110] In any of such proceedings the court must order the defendant to pay the plaintiff's costs.[111]

Where an audited account is submitted to the members of a trade union or to the committee of management, the union must also send a copy of the account to the Registrar within one month after the date on which it is so submitted.[112] If the union fails to do so the union and every official of the union who knowingly caused or permitted the failure will be guilty of an offence and liable on summary conviction, to a fine of ₦50.[113]

Powers of the Registrar

The Registrar may, at any time, and notwithstanding the above provisions, call upon the treasurer, the committee of management or any other official of a registered trade union to prepare and submit to him within a period of thirty days from the date of the call letter detailed accounts of the funds of the union in respect of any particular period.[114] Any accounts submitted must show in detail such information as the Registrar may direct and must, if the Registrar so directs, be audited, by the duly appointed auditor before being submitted to the Registrar.[115] If any person whose duty it is to prepare or assist to prepare the accounts called for by the Registrar, or to audit or submit such accounts, fails to do so without reasonable excuse, proof of which lies on him, he is guilty of an offence and liable, on summary conviction, to a fine of ₦50.[116]

If these accounts or the audited accounts sent to the Registrar having either been submitted to the members of the union or to the committee of management as required in section 38 are, in the opinion of the Registrar, unsatisfactory in that he is unable to satisfy himself as regards any question which affects or is likely to affect the accuracy of the account and, in particular any question as to:

a) the manner in which the account has been kept and prepared; or
b) the sufficiency or otherwise of existing checks against irregularity or fraud; or

---

[110] S. 37(6).
[111] S. 37(7); the duty of the treasurer to render accounts apply, so far as they are capable of applying, to every other official of a trade union and, accordingly, references to the treasurer must be so construed- S. 37(8).
[112] S. 38(1)
[113] Ss. 38 (2) and 49
[114] S. 39(1)
[115] Ibid.
[116] Ss. 39 (2) and 49

c) the authority for any departure from the rules of the union; or
d) the existence or otherwise of authority for all expenditure shown in the accounts; or
e) the amount of any sums due to the union, other than subscriptions and other sums due from members of the union under its rules, and the reasons for any failure to collect any such sums so due: or
f) the existence of any outstanding advances by or deposits with the union which are of an unusual character; or
g) the verification of any material assets of the union which are shown in the account;

the Registrar may, in his discretion either (a) direct all or any of the books, records or other documents of the union to be delivered to him for examination by himself or by an auditor appointed by him or (b) direct that the account be audited by an auditor designated by him for the purpose.[117] A designated auditor has power to require all or any of the books, records or other documents of the union to be produced to him, and to inspect and, if he thinks fit, take copies of or extracts from any such document so far as it appears to him necessary to do so for the purpose of auditing the account to which it relates and, for the purpose of auditing the account, to enter any premises of the union at all reasonable times.[118] Any person who fails to deliver to the Registrar any document which the Registrar has directed should be delivered to him or fails to produce to a designated auditor any document which he requires to be produced to him or who obstructs, molests or hinders a designated auditor in the exercise of the powers conferred on him will be guilty of an offence and liable, on summary conviction, to a fine of ₦50.[119] The cost of either an examination by an auditor or audit by an auditor, as certified by the Registrar, must be paid by the trade union and, if not so paid, may be recovered from the union as if it were a simple contract debt due to the Registrar.[120]

Where, as a result of an examination by the Registrar or an auditor or an audit by an auditor of the accounts, it appears to the Registrar that any offence, whether under the Act or the regulations or any other enactment,[121] has been committed by the union or by any other person, and that it is expedient to do so by reason of the refusal or neglect of the union or its members to take legal

[117] S. 40(1) and (2).
[118] S. 40(3)
[119] Ss. 40(4) and 49
[120] S. 40(5)
[121] E.g. the Criminal and Penal Codes.

proceedings, the Registrar may, on behalf, of the union institute criminal proceedings for the offence.[122] Similarly, if it appears to the Registrar from such examination or audit that any sum due to the union, other than subscriptions and other sums due from members of the union under its rules, has not been collected, the Registrar may, by reason of the same expediency, on behalf of the union and in its name, institute civil proceedings for the recovery of the sum due.[123] In any such civil proceedings the court has the power to make an order for the payment of costs to or by the Registrar as if he were a party to the proceedings.[124]

Registrar of trade unions

Section 48 of the Act provides for the appointment of a Registrar of Trade Unions for the purposes of the Act and "there may be appointed for those purposes one or more Assistant Registrars of Trade Unions..." The office of the Registrar or of any assistant is an office in the Federal Ministry responsible for labour, but no appointment takes effect unless notice of it has been published in the Gazette. Anything which is required or authorized to be done by or to the Registrar under the Act or regulations may be done by or to any Assistant Registrar whom he may authorize, either specifically or generally, for the purpose.

It is the duty of the Registrar to cause notice of the following matters to be published in the Gazette:

a) the registration of a trade union under the Act;
b) the cancellation of the registration of any registered trade union;
c) the registration of any change of name or of any alteration of the rules of any registered trade union;
d) the merger[116a] of any two or more trade unions;
e) any change in the situation of the registered office of a registered trade union; and
f) the dissolution of a trade union which is or has been registered.[125]

---

[122] S. 41(1).
[123] Ibid.
[124] S. 41 (2)
[116a] Substituted for amalgamation as required by the new provisions on mergers; see s.7 Trade Unions (Amendment) Decree 1996.
[125] S. 46, this is without prejudice to any of the requirements of the Act or the regulations.

If any person in any application, return, notice, certificate, statutory declaration or other document required to be made, sent or given to the Registrar under or for the purposes of the Act or the regulations, makes any statement which he knows to be false in a material particular, or recklessly makes any statement which is false in a material particular, he is guilty of an offence and liable, on summary conviction, to a fine of ₦200 or to imprisonment for a term of six months.[126]

Benefits of registration

A registered trade union enjoys a number of benefits which registration confers. Any profits of a registered trade union which are not derived from a trade or business carried on by the union are exempt from any tax.[127] Another advantage is that any member of a trade union, including an infant member, is empowered to nominate any person to whom any sum, not exceeding ₦100,[128] which is payable by the union on his death, as the person to whom such sum is to be paid on his death.[129] On receiving satisfactory proof of the death of the nominator, the trade union must pay to the nominee so much of the amount due by reason of the death of the nominator as is covered by the nomination.[130] A nomination must be in writing and signed by the nominator but may be partly printed and it must be delivered by hand or through the post at the registered office of the trade union. A nomination may be revoked or varied from time to time. Any revocation or variation must be in writing and signed by the nominator but may also be partly printed and must also be delivered by hand or through the post at the registered office of the trade union.[131]

---

[126] S. 48; a conviction for this offence disqualifies a person from holding an office in a trade union for a term of years.

[127] S. 19(1)(e) Companies Income Tax Act Cap.60 Laws of the Federation of Nigeria, 1990, for exemption from companies income tax, S. 27 (1)(d) Capital Gains Tax Act, Cap. 42, for exemption from capital gains tax and S. 19(1) and schedule 3 item 15 of the Personal Income Tax Act, No. 104 of 1993 for exemption from personal income tax.

[128] S. 2 5 (3).

[129] S. 25(1)

[130] Ibid.

[131] S. 25(2); a person who is an official of the same union as the nominator is disqualified from being nominated unless he or she is the husband, wife, father, mother, child, brother, sister, nephew, or niece of the nominator; S. 25(4).

Recognition of trade union

The provision for the compulsory recognition of trade unions by employers, first introduced by the Trade Unions Act in 1973 has now been modified.[132] Section 24 of the Act now provides that "where there is a trade union of which persons in the employment of an employer are members, that trade union, shall, without further assurance, on registration in accordance with the provisions of this Act, be entitled to recognition by the employer.[133] If an employer deliberately fails to recognize any such registered trade union to which his employees belong as members, he is guilty of an offence and liable, on summary conviction, to a fine of to ₦1,000[134] Presumably the offence continues until recognition is granted.

Legal status of registered union

We have seen that a trade union which is not registered is prohibited from performing any act in furtherance of the purposes for which it was formed except, such steps which are necessary for the purpose of registration. A registered trade union is thus able to perform any act in furtherance of its objects. It is also established beyond doubt that a registered trade union can sue and be sued in its registered name.[135] What is not so clear is whether by registration a trade union acquires legal personality of its own. In the case of *Nigerian Civil Service Union (WS)* v *Allen*[136] the court held that a registered trade union is not a legal entity. In an earlier decision in *Nigerian Stevedores and Dockworkers Union* v *Opara,*[137] Betuel J. observed "that the union is either a quasi juristic person by virtue of the operation of the provision of our Trade Union Act or it is not. " But more recently, however, Obaseki J.S.C. said, *obiter*, in *Nigeria Nurses' Association* v *Attorney General of the Federation,*[138] that a

---

[132] S 1 (e) Trade Unions (Amendment) Act 1978.

[133] S. 24(1).

[134] S. 24(2).

[135] *Taff Vale Railway Co.* v *Amalgamated Society of Railway Servants* [1901] AC 426; *Nigerian Stevedores and Dockworkers' Union* v *Opara* Unreported Suit No. P/111/1963, *High Court, Port Harcourt; Okongwu* v *Anunobi* (1966) LLR 49; *Nigeria Union of Registered Draughtsmen* v *Architect Registration Council of Nigeria* 1974(1) NMLR 108.

[136] (1972) 2 UILR 316.

[137] *Supra*

[138] (1981) 11 -12 SC 1, 11 and 12; the other members of the Supreme Court did not mention the point.

trade union has legal personality. It is suggested, with respect, that the view of Obaseki J.S.C. is the correct one.

Corporate personality may be conferred by statute either by express provision or by implication.[139] The Trade Unions Act does not expressly incorporate registered trade unions so that if a registered trade union is a legal entity, it can only be by inference from the meaning and effect of the provisions of the Act. The Act places a duty on a registered trade union to have a registered office,[140] to render an annual return,[141] and to submit an audited account of its funds to the Registrar,[142] and it may be convicted and liable to a penalty for failure to carry out these and other duties.[143] The provisions of two other sections of the Act are significant in this respect.

While the Act which in sub-section 22(4)(a)(ii) prohibits the courts from entertaining any action instituted for the purpose of directly enforcing, in relation to an unregistered trade union, "any trust on which funds of the union are to be held" would seem to indicate that unregistered trade unions must appoint trustees to hold such funds, the Act is silent in relation to registered trade unions with respect to their legal capacity to hold their property. Secondly, sub-section 27(4) which provides that the property of each of the merging unions become "vested in the merged union" also seems to imply that a registered trade union can hold its property, real or personal, in its name.[144]

As we have seen, upon registration, a trade union acquires a major attribute of corporate personality. A registered trade union is able to sue and it can be sued in its registered name. Indeed, it acquires a sort of proprietary right to the registered name. It is freed from the vagaries of a representative action which constitutes a major obstacle to actions by unincorporated associations. Thus two important attributes of corporate personality which a registered trade union enjoys may be noted. As Lord Keith said in *Bonsor* v *Musicians' Union*[145] a registered trade union:

> differs from an unincorporated association in that it is unnecessary to consider who were the members at any particular time. For instance, it is

---

139 *Tone River Conservators* v *Ash* (1829) 10 B s C 349. S.44 provides that the Companies & Allied Matters Act does not apply to trade unions and that the registration of a trade union under that Act is void.

140 S. 20(1).

141 S. 36 (1)

142 S. 38(1)

143 See Ss. 9(3), 20(4), 21 (3), 36(5) and 38(2).

144 For S. 27(4) see S. 5(c) Trade Unions (Amendment) Acts No.4 of 1996.

145 [1956] AC 104.

> immaterial who were the members at the time that any cause of action arose, or what members have joined the union since the cause of action arose. The registered trade union may be said to assume a collective responsibility for all members past, present and future, in respect of any cause of action for which it may be made liable... irrespective of the date of action. On the other hand, the judgment creditor can look only to the funds of such a trade union to satisfy his debt, and to the extent to which these may be augmented from time to time by contributions of members, whether new or old, they will still be available for the unsatisfied judgment creditor.[146]

It is also pertinent to compare the provisions of the Trade Unions Act with those of the now repealed English Trade Unions Act 1871 upon which the Act was modelled.[147] In *Bonsor* v *Musicians' Union*,[148] the question arose for the first time before the House of Lords whether a trade union registered under the 1871 Act was a juridical person. Of the five law lords, two, Lords Somerset and McDermott, held it was not, but two others, i.e. Lords Morton and Potter, or perhaps two and half as will be seen, held that it was. Lord Keith appeared to seat on the fence; he said - in a sense, a registered trade union is a legal entity but not that it is a legal entity distinguishable at any moment of time from the members of which it is at that time composed.[149]

Lord MacDermott reached his conclusions only after a careful consideration of the provisions of the Act. He referred to Sections 7 and 8 of the 1871 Act which made provision for the holding of union property by trustees and which were "relied upon by the union as a clear indication that Parliament did not intend to make the registered trade union a judicial person, and as such capable of holding its own assets in its own name."[150] There are no equivalents of those sections in our Act. His Lordship also referred to section 9 of the Act which provided that the trustees of a registered trade union or any other officer who may be so authorized by the union rules, may "bring or defend, or cause to be brought or defended, any action, touching or concerning the property, right, or claim to property of the trade union,," and continued, "...if, as the appellant claims, this Act made the registered union a juridical person there seems no very convincing reason why it should not have been left to sue and be sued respecting

[146] Ibid., 149-150.
[147] Via the Trade Unions Ordinance enacted in 1938.
[148] *Supra*
[149] [1956] AC 104, 149.
[150] Ibid., 137.

its property without conferring these special powers upon its officers and trustees."[151]

An equivalent of section 9 is, similarly, omitted from the Act of 1973. And these missions do not appear to be an oversight. Indeed, there is no requirement in the first schedule to our Act as there was in the first schedule to the 1871 Act that the Union rules must provide, among other matters, for the appointment and removal of a trustee or trustees. Instead it is expressly provided in our Act that the registered union may sue respecting its property. Thus, Section 37(5) of our Act provides that the union or any person capable of suing as a representative may sue and section 41 (1) provides that in certain circumstances the Registrar may, if, it is expedient to do so by reason of the refusal or neglect of the union or the members to take legal proceedings, to take the action on behalf of the union and in the union's name.

It is submitted that these provisions and omission, if taken together, evince a sufficient intention to make a registered trade union a judicial person. If the corporateness of a registered trade is accepted it becomes easy to hold that the union rules constitute contractual terms between the union and its members. However, it may be argued that this result will be in conflict with the provision of sub-section 22(2) (a) which prohibits any court from entertaining any legal proceedings instituted with the object of directly enforcing or recovering damages for the breach of "any agreement between the members of a trade union as such relating to the terms and conditions on which members of the union shall or shall not employ person or be employed." It is suggested, however, that nothing precludes the courts from holding that the rules of registered trade unions constitute terms of contract both between the union and each member and between the members *inter se*.[152] If this is done it becomes easy to accommodate sub-section 22(2) (a).

The union rules

Every trade union must have registered rules.[153] Where the Registrar registers a union he must, at the same time, register its rules.[154] A trade union must, on

[151] [1956] AC 104, 137

[152] Although there is no direct authority for this suggestion, company law offers a useful analogy: see *Rayfield* v *Hands* [1960] Ch.1; also per Lord Keith in *Bonsor* v *Musicians' Union* [1956] AC 104, 152; Gower, Modern Company Law 3rd ed. p. 262. It is also noteworthy that although, S.14 of the Ghanaian Trade Union Ordinance expressly incorporates registered trade unions its section 5 is identical with our section 22(2) (a); see below.

[153] S. 4(1) and (2) (a)

[154] S. 5(3)

being requested by any person, deliver or send to him a copy of the rules of the union on payment of a sum not exceeding fifty kobo.[155] Where, however, the rules book is sent by post the cost of the postage may be charged in addition to the price.[156] If any person, with intent to mislead or defraud, supplies or lends to any member or prospective member of a registered trade union a copy of any rules or of any alteration or amendment of any rules other than those actually in force at the time, on the false pretence that what was supplied or lent represents the rules of the unions then in force or that there are no other rules of the union, he is guilty of an offence.[157] Similarly, if any person with intent to mislead or defraud, supplies or lends a copy of any rules to any person on the false pretence that they are the rules of the union he is guilty of an offence.[158] Either of these offences is punishable with a fine, on summary conviction, of ₦200 or imprisonment for a term of six months.[159]

A trade union may alter its rules by the method of doing so provided in its rules but an alteration cannot take effect until the alteration is registered. But the Registrar must not register an alteration of the rules of a trade union if, as a result of the alteration the rules of the union would cease to contain provisions with respect to the various matters mentioned in schedule 1 of the Act or the principal purpose of the trade union would cease to be that of regulating the terms and conditions of employment of workers.[160]

An alteration of the rules of a trade union comes into effect, if the rules so provide, on a date later than the date of the registration of the alteration but otherwise it comes into effect on the date on which it is registered.[161] The difficulty with this provision is that it has not spelt out what it means by registration. The Court of Appeal had to contend with this problem in *Nigeria Civil Service Union* v *Essien.*[162] The union carried out an alteration of some of the rules of the union and sent it to the Registrar. The Registrar subsequently wrote to the union requesting the union to print the rules and thereafter inform him of having done so. The rules were not printed but it was contended that they

---

[155] S. 21(1); if a trade union contravenes this sub-section the trade union and every official of the union who knowingly caused or permitted the contravention will be liable, on summary conviction, to a fine of ₦10 for each of offence; s. 21(3).

[156] S. 21(2).

[157] S. 47(1).

[158] S. 47(3).

[159] S. 47(4)

[160] S. 28(2).

[161] S. 28(3)

[162] [1985] 3 NWLR 306

had been registered. The Court of Appeal held that the rules had been registered. Nnaemeka-Agu J.C.A. whose judgment all the other members of the court agreed with, said registration means no more than that the alteration or amendment after being passed by the union in accordance with their constitution is communicated to the Registrar in the usual manner and he, having satisfied himself that the alteration or amendment does not contravene sub-section (2) of section 27[163] records or takes note of the amendment or alteration in official record kept for the purpose.[164] He continued- if the legislators intended that the amended constitution incorporating the amendment or alteration should first be printed they would have said so expressly. Indeed once the proposed amendment does not fall foul of sub-section 2 of the section, the Registrar has no alternative but to register it.[165] Yet, the problem remains as to when and, indeed, whether he has registered the alteration by making a note or otherwise recording it in the official record kept for that purpose. It is suggested that it is reasonable to require the Registrar to inform the union in writing of the registration of an alteration of its rules. The duty of the Registrar to cause the registration of any alteration of the rules of a registered trade union to be published in the Gazette presupposes that the registration precedes such publication.

The rules of a trade union play an important role in the management and control of the trade union. They are regarded as contractually binding as between the union and its members, and between the members *inter se*. As Lord MacDermott said in *Bonsor* v *Musicians' Union*,[166] the contract, which is formed on admission by an acceptance of the union rules, has long been the generally accepted view of the bond by which the members of a trade union are held in association.[167] In an earlier House of Lords decision Lord Davey had said[168] the rules in fact, form the social contract between the members, and every person on becoming a member accedes to them and is bound by them. Lord Atkinson also made the same point when he said: "of course when a workman becomes a member of a trade union, he contracts to be bound by the rules of that union, and the contracts which he enters into with the union or with each of his fellow-

[163] Now 28
[164] Ibid., 320
[165] Ibid., 320
[166] [1956] AC 104 see also *Yorkshire Miners Association* v *Howden* [1905] AC 256 *Kelly* v *NATSOPA* (1915) 31 TLR 632; *Abbot* v *Sullivan* [1925] 1 KB 189; *Faramus* v *Film Artistes* [1964] AC 925.
[167] [1905] AC 104, 135-136.
[168] *Yorkshire Miners' Association* v *Howden* [1905] AC 256, 268.

workmen are to be found, if found at all, in those rules."[169] Similarly, in more recent times, Nnaemeka-Agu J . C.A. in the Court of Appeal said a trade union's constitution "is a contract between the members *inter se*.[170]

Although, trade unions are at liberty, in almost the same terms as individuals, to enter into whatever terms of contract they choose, in so far as their rules are concerned they are subject to a fair amount of control by both statute and the common law. By section 4, every trade union must have registered rules which must be registered at the same time with the union itself. Furthermore the rules must contain provisions with respect to the various matters mentioned in the first schedule of the Act and the Registrar must not register a trade union whose rules do not contain these matters. The schedule lists fifteen matters which are as follows:

1. The name of the trade union: The name which the union proposes as its name must not only be stated in union rules but, as we have seen, must also be stated in the application for the registration of the union. We have also seen that the Registrar is empowered to refuse to register a trade union whose name is objectionable and that the name with which a trade union is registered can only be changed in accordance with the provisions of the Act. A trade union may change its name if, but only if, not less than two-thirds of all its members have, in secret ballot, voted in favour of the proposed change; but even then, a change of name does not take effect until it is registered with the Registrar.[171] Where a union proposes to change its name and it has obtained the necessary majority vote in favour of the change the union must then send to the Registrar a notice in the prescribed form of the proposed change of name signed by seven members of the union and counter-signed by the secretary of the union and a statutory declaration by the secretary that the requirements as to the necessary vote in favour have been complied with.[172] On receipt of the notice and the statutory declaration and if satisfied that the requirements of the Act and the regulations have been complied with the Registrar must register the change of name.[173] However, the provisions regarding objectionable names apply also to a change of name.[174] The Registrar is empowered to refuse to register a name which is

[169] *Amalgamated Society of Carpenters, Cabinet Makers & Joiners* v *Braithwaite* [1922] 2 AC 440, 455.

[170] *Nigeria Civil Service Union* v *Essien* (1985) 3 NWLR 306, 315.

[171] S. 26(1)

[172] S.26(2)

[173] S. 26(3)

[174] S. 6(5) (a)

identical with that of any existing trade union or which so nearly resembles the name of any existing trade union as to be likely to deceive the members or the public.[175] Similarly, a name which contains any words which, in the Registrar's opinion, are deceptive or objectionable in that they contain a reference, direct or indirect, to any patronage, practice or institution, or are otherwise unsuitable as a name for a trade union will not be registered.[176] However, in the latter case any official or member of the union may require the matter to be referred to the Minister.[177] The Minister's decision on it is final and if he decides that a particular trade union may be registered under a certain name the union may be registered under that name.[178] Where a trade union changes its name, the change of name does not affect any right or obligation of the union or of any of its members, and any pending legal proceedings may be continued by or against the trade union or any person as a representative of the union, notwithstanding its change of name.[179]

2. The whole of the purposes of the trade union, and the purposes for which its funds may be applied must be stated. It may be reiterated that although the principal purpose of a trade union must be to regulate the terms and conditions of employment of employees but this need not be the only purpose of the union. Indeed, Section 1(2) provides that the fact that a trade union either of workers or of employers has purposes or powers other than the purpose of regulating the terms and conditions of employment of employees should not prevent it from being registered under the Act. A trade union may have as many purposes or objects as its members desire. What is required is that the rules must contain the whole of the purposes of the union. In addition to this statutory requirement it is also wise to state all the purposes of the union in its rules book because it has been held that the *ultra vires* doctrine also applies to trade unions.[180] In other words a trade union can only pursue those objects or purposes

---

[175] S. 6 (1).

[176] S. 6(2).

[177] S. 6 (3)

[178] S. 6 (3). And (4); quaere whether not unconstitutional the apparent effect being a denial of access to the court which is guaranteed under S.6(6)(b) Constitution, see *Government of Imo State* v *Greeco Construction & Engineering Associates Ltd.* [1985] 3 NWLR 71.

[179] S. 26(4)

[180] *Re Durham Miners' Association* v *Cann* (1900) 17 TLR 39; *Bennet* v *National Amalgamated Society of Operative House and Ship Painters and Decorators* (1915) 31 TLR 203; *Thomas* v *National Union of Mineworkers* [1986] 1 Ch.20; the doctrine has now been modified with respect to companies registered under the Companies and Allied Matters Act; see s. 39(3); however since by s. 44 of the Trade Unions Act CAMA does not apply to trade unions and any registration of a trade union under it is void s. 39(3) CAMA cannot of its own apply to trade unions.

for which provision are made in its rules. Any act which is *ultra vires* is null and void.

A trade union must also provide for the purposes for which its funds may be applied. The funds of a union may be expended in carrying out any of the purposes of the union. This is made clear in section 1(2) which provides that a trade union may apply its funds for any lawful purpose for the time being authorized by its rules, including in particular, if so authorized, that of providing benefits for its members. But where a trade union intends to apply its funds towards an object which is not one of its purposes, it is necessary to so provide in the rules. For example a trade union cannot apply its funds towards a political object unless the rules of the union so provide.

In addition section 15(1) provides specifically that, unless the rules of a trade union otherwise provide, in so far as the funds of a trade union represent payments which the members are required to make under the rules, whether by way of subscriptions, dues or otherwise, these funds must not be applied, whether directly, or through any other union, association or body, or in any other indirect manner, to the furtherance of any political objective. For this purpose section 15(3) defines political objectives as the following, and no others - (a) the making of contributions towards the fund of any political party; (b) the payment of any expenses incurred, whether directly or indirectly by a candidate or prospective candidate for election to any political office in Nigeria or any part of Nigeria and whether incurred before, during or after the election in connection with his candidature or election; (c) the holding of any meeting or the distribution of any literature or documents in support of any such candidate or prospective candidate; (d) the maintenance of any person while he holds in Nigeria or any part of Nigeria political office to which he has been elected; (e) the registration of electors in Nigeria or any part of Nigeria; and (f) the holding of a political meeting of any kind or the distribution of political literature or political documents of any kind, unless the main purpose of the meeting or distribution is to further the regulation of the terms and conditions of employment of workers.

The statutory prohibition is narrower both in terms of funds and objects. A breach of the statutory provision is an offence. If the funds, as defined, are applied to the furtherance of any of the enumerated political objectives the trade union and every official of the union will be guilty of an offence and on summary conviction liable to a fine of N50.[181] An individual member of the union should be able to take an action for an injunction to stop such application

[181] Ss. 15(2) and 49.

of the funds since it would be an *ultra vires* act. At common law, as has been already stated, the expenditure of any funds of the union for any purpose not contained in the union rules will be *ultra vires* the union and any member of the union can ask for an injunction in the courts to stop it.[182] The Act preserves this right as well as provide its own remedy. Section 18(1) provides that, without prejudice to the right of any person having a sufficient interest in the relief sought to apply for an injunction to restrain any unauthorized or unlawful application of the funds of a trade union, an injunction restraining any such application of the funds of a trade union may be granted by the High Court of the State in which the registered office of the union is situated upon the application of the Attorney-General of the Federation or of the Registrar or of any five or more members of the union. The High Court may, in addition to or instead of granting an injunction, order that the whole or any part of the funds of the trade union be paid over to the Public Trustee to be administered, or disposed of in accordance with the rules of the union.[183]

No person must apply the funds of a trade union, whether directly or through any other trade union, association or body, for the purpose of any legal proceedings relating to his election or appointment into any office in the trade union.[184] Any person who does so apply such funds is guilty of an offence and liable, on conviction, to a fine of ₦5,000.[185]

2a. Subscriptions and dues: The subscriptions and dues, if any, which members of the trade union are required to pay must be stipulated in the rules book. As will be seen, it is provided that any agreement for the payment by any person of any subscription or penalty to a trade union cannot be directly enforced by the courts.[186] And under the general contractual principles an employer would be in breach of contract to unilaterally deduct union subscription from the wages or salary of an employee. However, check-off of members contribution to their union is made compulsory with respect to certain trade unions. Section 16A provides that, where an employer has recognised[187] any of the registered trade unions specified in the third schedule to the Act, the

[182] *Yorkshire Miners Association* v *Howden* [1905] AC 256; *Thomas* v *National Union of Mineworkers, supra.*

[183] S. 18(2)

[184] S. 16(1)

[185] S. 16(2).

[186] S. 22(1) and (2) (b); for the constitutionality or otherwise of this provision see below.

[187] For recognition of trade unions by employers see s.24 and below.

employer must make deduction from the wages of every worker[188] who is eligible to be a member of the union for the purpose of paying contributions to the trade union so registered (SIC, recognised) and pay any sum so deducted directly to the registered office of the trade union.[189] Section 16A will seem to have impliedly repealed section 5(3) Labour Act which makes similar provisions for compulsory check-off of union contributions.[190] If this is so then the statutory right to contract out of the check-off system has been taken away.[191]

However, it is now provided that compliance with section 16A, i.e. operating the check-off by an employer, is "subject to the insertion of a "No Strike" and "No lock-out" clauses in the relevant collective bargaining agreements between the workers and their employers.[192] The purpose or effect of this provision is not readily apparent especially as strikes and lock-outs are, in effect, banned. However it will appear that some meaning is intended to be given to the provision by section 17(4) (d) which provides that the system of automatic check-off must, in respect of any particular union, cease to operate forthwith upon "a strike action embarked upon by a union in breach of the collective Bargaining Agreement between the workers and the employer."[193] Automatic check-off also ceases to operate forthwith upon the dissolution of a recognised union, the revocation of the certificate of registration of a union or the cancellation of the registration of a union by the Registrar.[194]

Section 5(4) of the Labour Act which provides that no deductions may be made from the wages and salaries of persons who are eligible members of any of the trade unions specified in Part B of schedule 3 to the Act except the person has accepted, in writing, to make voluntary contributions to the trade union, would appear to have been rendered otiose by the amendment of part B schedule

---

[188] This term is, under the Act, more or less, synonymous with the common law concept of employee and so much wider in scope than under the Labour Act from which the provision is derived.

[189] S.16A; see S.3 Trade Unions (Amendment) Act, 1996 No. 4 and S. 5 Trade Unions (Amendment) Act 1999 No 1.

[190] While S. 5(3) Labour Act applies to workers as defined in the Labour Act S. 1 6A applies, it seems intended, to workers as defined in the Trade Unions Act where it is more embracing; see note 188.

[191] However this right was or is available only to workers under the Labour Act; in any event its removal will be commendable since, in practice, both the union members and non-members usually enjoy the benefits of collective bargaining.

[192] S. 16A proviso; see S. 5 Trade Unions (Amendment) (No.2) Act 1996; "no lock-out" added by S.5 No. 1 of 1999.

[193] See S. 6 No. 26 of 1996.

[194] S. 17(4)(a)-(c); see S. 6 ibid.

3 of the Act.[195] Part B contained the names of the registered trade unions of Senior employees and of employers. The new part B lists what is called the jurisdictional scope of each of the re-structured trade unions contained in part A and none of which was contained in the old part B. However it is doubted whether, in fact, such a statutory provision is necessary. An employer would normally be in breach of contract where he makes a deduction from the salary or wages of his employee which deduction is not authorised by law or made with the consent of the employee.

Section 5(6) of the Labour Act which requires that an employer send a list of the names of the employees from whose wages deductions are made along with the total sum so deducted would appear to remain in full force.

3. Union benefits: If the trade union is to provide benefits for its members the conditions under which any member will become entitled to any benefit. We have seen that section 1 provides that for a combination to be a trade union it must have the principal purpose of regulating the terms and conditions of employment of workers and whether its purposes do or do include the provision of benefits for its members. And also that a trade union may apply its funds for any lawful purpose for the time being authorized by its rules, including in particular, if so authorized, that of providing benefits for its member. But, as will be seen, even where the rules of a union make provision for benefits for its members, a member may be unable to enforce by a court action non-payment of a benefit to which he has become entitled.[196]

4. Disciplinary rules: The fines and forfeitures which may be imposed on members of the Union must be stipulated in the rules. This provision should include all disciplinary measures such as the grounds for suspension of or expulsion from membership in addition to fines which may be imposed and for what conduct or misconduct. There is no common law power in a trade union to suspend or expel a member.

5. The procedure for making, altering or revoking the rules: There is no implied power in a trade union to amend its rules; it can acquire such a power by

---

[195] See s. 10 Trade Unions (Amendment) Act 1996 and s. 9 Trade Unions (Amendment)(No.2) Act 1996.

[196] See below.

its rules[197] and, as we have seen, section 28 provides that a trade union may alter its rules by any method provided by its rules.

6. **Management committee**: There must be a provision for the appointment and removal of appointed and elected officers.[198]

7. **Qualification for membership**: The qualifications for membership of the trade union which must include a provision to the effect that such a person must be normally engaged in the trade or industry or elected or appointed to represent workers' interest in the said trade or industry.[199] However, in view of the constitutional guarantee of a right or freedom to belong to a union of one's choice, the extent, if at all, to which a trade union can, by its rules, exclude persons from its membership is called into question. It is interesting to note that the International Labour Organisation Convention No.87 provides for accommodating both freedom of association and the right of a union to exclude membership of the union. Article 2 of the convention provides that workers and employers shall have the right to establish and, subject only to the rules of the organisation concerned, to join organisations of their own choosing without previous authorization. The problem then is, can a union, by its rules, preclude a person from exercising his constitutional right to be a member of the union if that union is the union of his own choosing?

The constitutional right, though fundamental, is not absolute. Derogation by law is allowed. There are, at least, two grounds upon which it may be held that trade union rules fall within "law" in the constitutional provision under consideration. The first is that, since the rules are required by the Trade Unions Act to contain provisions with respect to the matters enumerated in the first schedule to the Act and that a union must not be registered unless it has rules which contain such provision and, further, that if a union is registered its rules must, at the same time, be registered, it is arguable that registered trade union rules have statutory flavour even if they cannot properly be regarded as subsidiary legislation.

This point was made in *John Enas Dubre* v *National Union of Petroleum and Natural Gas Worker*[200] but, regrettably, the Court of Appeal said it was off the mark because it was not an issue submitted for determination in the court

---

[197] *Harrington* v *Sendall* (1903) Ch. 921.

[198] S. 4(1) and para. 7 1st schedule; see S.8 Trade Unions (Amendment) (No.2) Act No.26 of 1996 and S.9 No. 1 of 1999.

[199] S. 4(1) and para. 8 1st schedule; see ibid.

[200] Judgments of the Court of Appeal, part 2, April-July 1984 p.341.

below. In *Elufioye* v *Halilu*[201] the Supreme Court appears to approve the rejection, by the Court of Appeal, of a similar point raised in that case. But the point was, clearly, an obiter. However the second ground upon which union rules may be held to be "law" under the constitutional provision would appear to be more unassailable. Under both the Independence and Republican Constitutions law, for this purpose, was defined to include "an unwritten rule of law."[202] In *Serikin Pawa* v *Raji Akengbe*[203] it was held that customary law came within this definition. If that decision is correct and, it is humbly submitted that it is, then the common law must equally fall within "law", under any such constitutional provision.[204] The rules of a union are, at common law, regarded as contractually binding.[205]

8. **Membership of management committee**: Before 1996 what was required was that a trade union must provide in its rules book that the general committee of management of the union, by whatever name called, must consist only of persons who were members of the union.[206] The only exceptions made were with respect to the President or Secretary of the union, in order, perhaps, to allow for the appointment of suitable and proper persons to those positions from outside the union membership if it was found necessary to do so.[207] That policy position was dramatically changed in 1996 and the rules were then required to contain a provision which protected the exclusive rights of members of a union to the membership of all policy-making organs of the union.[208] In 1999 policy again changed. Now the rules book is required to contain a provision that the general committee of management, by whatever name called, must consist of all persons all of whom are members of the trade union.[209] This probably means that only members of the union can be members of the general committee of management of the union. And this would have restored the pre-1996 position except that no exception is made with respect to a President or Secretary. But the definition of member of trade

[201] [1993] 6 NWLR 570.
[202] S. 32, S. 33 1960, 1963 Constitution respectively.
[203] (1961) WRLR 268.
[204] Including the 1979 Constitution and the draft Constitution which, regrettably, omit to define "law" in s.41 and s.48 respectively. It is significant that "law" is spelt with a small letter "l"
[205] See *supra*.
[206] S. 4 and paragraph 9 1st Schedule.
[207] S. 4 and paragraph 9 proviso 1st Schedule
[208] S. 4 and para. 9 1st Schedule as amended by S.8 Trade Unions (Amendment) (No. 2) Act 1996 No. 26.
[209] S. 4 and para. 9 1st Schedule as amended by S.9 Trade Unions (Amendment) Act 1999 No. 1

union now provided would appear to change the position completely. Member of a trade union means a person normally engaged in a trade or industry which the trade union represents and a person either elected or appointed by a trade union to represent workers interest.[210] It follows from this unorthodox definition that any person who is employed in any trade or industry for which a union caters may be a member of the committee of management of the union as well as any person who is even not so employed but is either elected or appointed by the union to represent workers' interest, whatever that may mean. Thus any or all of the members of a management committee need not be actual members of the union within the popular meaning of that term, i.e. that they applied for and were admitted into membership in accordance with the union rules.[211] The same definition should also affect the application of the statutory provision[212] which stipulates that no person is eligible to contest any elective post under any registered trade union, unless he is a member of any of those unions.[213] Again, it means that actual membership of the union is not a requirement for eligibility to stand election for office in any of those unions.

It seems clear that these results are not intended. If they are it is suggested that they cannot be conducive to the effective and proper management of the unions. The whole of the definition of member of a trade union needs to be repealed and the pre-1996 paragraph 9 of the first schedule restored.[214]

9 A provision for the keeping of a nominal roll of members showing the trade, calling or usual occupation of each member and, where possible, in the case of a trade union of employees, the name of his employer.

10. A provision for the investment of the funds of the trade union or their deposit in a bank.

11. A provision for the keeping of full and accurate accounts by the treasurer, for the annual or more frequent periodical audit, by a person to be appointed by the

---

[210] S.52 as amended by S.8(b) 1999 No. 1

[211] Para 7 above shows clearly that engagement in the relevant trade or industry is only required to be made one of the qualifications for membership of a trade union.

[212] It seems this should be S. 33(7) and not S.33(5) as the renumbering prescribed in S. 6 (c) of the Trade Unions (Amendment) Act 1999 No. 1 would indicate; the subsections are confusing

[213] S. 33(6); see S.6(b) 1996 No. 4, S. 6(c) No. 1 and f.n. 204 *supra*.

[214] The definition also applies to eligibility to contest elective post under the Nigerian Labour Congress; see below at p. 386.

trade union with the approval of the Registrar, of the accounts so kept and for their submission, when audited, to the members.

12. Inspection of books: A provision for the inspection of the books, accounts and nominal roll of members of the trade union by a person who has an interest in the funds of the union. In *Norey* v *Keep,*[215] a member applied to inspect the union accounts by means of an accountant. The court held that a member or members not only have a personal right to inspect but were also entitled to exercise the right through an agent.

13. Strikes: A provision that no member of the union can take part in a strike unless a majority of the members have, in secret ballot, voted in favour of the strike. In view of s. 17 of the Trade Disputes Act which should be regarded as making all strike actions illegal such a provision has, perhaps, been rendered otiose. In any event both the implementation and enforcement of such a rule are fraught with enormous problems. Since the rule applies to the union itself and not to any branch of the union it will seem that a union must obtain a majority vote of all its members even in respect of a matter affecting only a local group of its members or a branch of the union. Indeed it appears that a branch of a union cannot lawfully call a strike independently of the parent body. Furthermore the rule is impracticable of implementation. Of this Mr. Umoh has written that:[216]

> Since virtually every company has branches all over the country, so also are union members scattered in the various states. It is doubtful whether any company will give its employees time off to assemble at one place for the purpose of voting by a secret ballot to embark on a strike action.
>
> The alternative is to post ballot papers to various branches of the union for secret voting. But how efficient is our postal system? By the time the ballot papers are returned to the headquarters of the union, the purpose for which the strike was to be organized may have been overtaken by events. And for unions with branches in all the[217] states, it may take up to six months or more to get back ballot papers.

The rule will also be difficult to enforce. There may be a breach of such a rule either by the union in calling a strike without the necessary majority or ballot or by a member or members by refusing to go on strike assuming a strike

---

[215] [1909] 1 Ch. 561.

[216] *The Daily Times*, 13th August 1973. Mr. Umoh James Umoh was the Labour Correspondent.

[217] Now 36 States.

is lawfully embarked upon by the union. It is suggested that an action in court to enforce either breach will be caught by sub-section 22(2) (a) which prohibits a court from entertaining:

> any legal proceedings instituted for the purpose of directly enforcing....or of recovering damages for any agreement between the members of a trade union as such relating to the terms and conditions on which members of the union shall or shall not employ persons or be employed.[218]

When a trade union calls a strike there is little doubt that it is over terms and conditions upon which its members shall or shall not be employed. In *Baker* v *Ingall,*[219] Phillimore J. said:

> It seems that the agreements contemplated by that sub-section are agreements between members of a trade union as to the conditions of employment, and not as to whether a member shall or shall not be employed. That is to say, the conditions referred to in the subsection are conditions of employment in regard to such things as wages, hours and bonds of arrangements between the employer and employee. They are not conditions upon which a man shall seek employment or return to his trade but are the conditions of his employment when he is actually employed.[220]

This view will appear to be too narrow. There is no reason to doubt that a strike over the terms and conditions on which a union member would continue or return to his work or seek employment falls within the sub-section.

14. Dissolution of a union: The procedure for dissolving the trade union and for the distribution of its assets, if any, must be provided for in the rules. We have seen that the Registrar has power to refuse to register any union whose rules do not conform with Schedule 1. Observance of that duty will ensure the avoidance of the difficulty which the court faced as a result of the omission of a rule on dissolution in *Ubiku* v *Registrar of Trade Unions.*[221] Where, however, the rules do not contain a rule on distribution on dissolution assets of the union become divisible on common law principles.[222]

---

[218] Section 22 is discussed fully below.
[219] [1911] 2 KB 132.
[220] Ibid., 139.
[221] (1966) LLR 236.
[222] *Re Printers & Transferors Amalgamated Trades Protection Society* [1899] 2 Ch. 184.

Rules of natural justice

It is well established that the rules of natural justice will be read into the union rules in all situations where the union rules empower the union or its officials to exercise judicial or quasi-judicial functions. "It is clear," said Cussack J., "that a committee fails at its peril to observe the rules of natural justice if it is exercising a judicial or quasi-judicial function."[223] The exercise of a power which postulates an enquiry, such as expulsion or other disciplinary measure against a member of the union, is a judicial or quasi-judicial function.

Before 1971, the weight of authority seemed to have been that where a union was performing an administrative function as distinct from a judicial or quasi-judicial function it was not obliged to observe the rules of natural justice. The courts, in particular Lord Denning, now insist that the rules must be implied in all cases. In *Breen* v *Amalgamated Engineering Union*,[224] rule 3 (12) of the union empowered the District Committee of the union to give approval to the election of a shop steward in order for him to be able to act.

The District Committee rejected the election of the plaintiff as a shop steward in his place of work. He was given no reason for the refusal. The plaintiff requested that the matter be reconsidered and asked for reasons. At a subsequent meeting, at which the plaintiff was also absent, the Committee adhered to its earlier decision but this time directed its secretary to inform the plaintiff of the reasons for the refusal. The plaintiff, in an action, claimed, *inter alia*, a declaration that the decision of the Committee was *ultra vires*, invalid and void, being contrary to natural justice. It was held by Cussack J., that there was no duty to observe natural justice because neither when the Committee first considered the matter, nor at the second meeting was it acting or exercising a judicial or quasi-judicial function. "It was entirely a matter for discretion whether the plaintiff was approved or not."[225] On appeal the English Court of Appeal,[226] on this point, unanimously held, and it may be summarized in the words of Lord Denning, that

> It is now well settled that a statutory body, which is entrusted by statute with a discretion, must act fairly. It does not matter whether its functions are described as judicial or quasi-judicial on the one hand, or what you will, still

---

[223] *Breen* v *Amalgamated Engineering Union* [1970] 2 All ER 179, 182.
[224] [1970] 2 All ER 179.
[225] Ibid., 182.
[226] [1971]1 All ER 1148.

> it must act fairly. It must in a proper case, give a party a chance to be heard.[227]

The principle applies not only to statutory bodies but also to all domestic bodies, including trade unions. If the rules set up a domestic body, said Lord Denning, and give it a discretion, it is to be implied that that body must exercise its discretion fairly. Even though its functions are not judicial or quasi-judicial, but only administrative, still it must act fairly.[228]

Can, however, the rules of natural justice be excluded by express provision to that effect in the union rules? Since the rule of the law of contract is that an express provision prevails over an implied term,[229] can the rules of natural justice be excluded by a term of the rules or constitution which simply declares that the rules of natural justice are excluded or by the inclusion in the rules of terms inconsistent with the rules of natural justice? Does an unfettered discretionary power automatically exclude the rules of natural justice?

In *Russell* v *Duke of Norfolk*,[230] a majority of the English Court of Appeal held that natural justice could not be implied into a contract the terms of which conferred an unrestricted discretion in the stewards of a jockey club in withdrawing trainers' licences. But in *Breen* v *Amalgamated Engineering Union*,[231] the same court unanimously held that a discretionary power does not exclude the application of the rules of natural justice. Where the rules, by express provision, exclude the rules of natural justice, Maugham, J., felt no doubt that the matter must be decided by the terms of the rules.[232]

> In such a case... where the tribunal is the result of rules adopted by persons who have formed the association known as a trade union, it seems reasonably clear that the rights of the plaintiff against the defendants must depend simply on the contract, and that the material terms of the contract must be found in the rules.[233]

The learned judge added, "if, for instance, there was a clearly expressed rule stating that a member might be expelled by a defined body without calling upon the member in question to explain his conduct, (there is) no reason for supposing

---

[227] Ibid., 1153.
[228] Ibid., 1154.
[229] But see *Johnstone* v *Bloomsbury Health Authority* (1991) 2 All ER 292.
[230] [1949] 1 All ER 109
[231] Above...
[232] *Maclean v Workers' Union* [1929] 1 Ch. 602.
[233] Ibid., 623

that the courts would interfere with such a rule on the ground of public policy.[234] Yet, the courts have, in a number of decisions, said they will interfere with such a rule on that very ground.[235] Thus, in *Dawkins* v *Antrobus*,[236] Brett L.J. said that the court can properly entertain the question whether "anything has been done which is contrary to natural justice, although it is within the rules of a club-in other words, whether the rules of the club are contrary to natural justice.[237]

Similarly, in *Faramus* v *Film Artistes' Association,*[238] although both the English Court of Appeal and the House of Lords affirmed the doctrine of freedom or sanctity of contract, both courts made it clear that a contractual term which deals with enquiry, such as in expulsion cases, may be held to be void if it is contrary to natural justice.

In general terms natural justice comprises two main rules - (i) that both sides must be heard - *audi alteram partem* - and (ii) that the person or body deciding comes to its decision without bias. The rule that both sides must be heard requires that the party alleged to have committed some misconduct must be given a timely notice of the full charge against him and an opportunity for him to answer the charge. In *Annamunthodo* v *Oilfield Workers' Trade Union,*[239] the appellant, a member of the defendant union, was charged before the general council of the union with offences against certain rules of the union. The appellant attended a meeting of the council to answer to the charges and evidence was taken, but, owing to some other engagement, he failed to attend the adjourned sitting of the council a week later, at which the charges were held proved against him. He was expelled, not by virtue of the rules under which he was charged, but under a different rule the breach of which he had not been charged with. The Judicial Committee of the Privy Council held that there was an infringement of natural justice. It also has been held that failure to give notice to any member of the body vested with the power of expulsion of the meeting of that body at which an expulsion was pronounced invalidated the decision.[240]

---

[234] Ibid., 623-4

[235] *Abbot* v *Sullivan* [1952]1 KB 189, 198; *Lee* v *Showmen's Guild of Great Britain* [1952] 2 QB 329, 341; *Bonsor* v *Musicians' Union* [1954] Ch 479, 485; *Hiles* v *Amalgamated Society of Woodworkers* [1968] 1 Ch . 440, 452.

[236] (1881) 17 Ch. D. 615

[237] Ibid., 630

[238] [1963] 2 QB 527; [1964] AC 925

[239] [1961] AC 945.

[240] *Lane* v *Norman* (1891) 66 LT 83; *Young* v *Ladies Imperial Club Ltd.* [1920] 2 KB 523; *Leary* v *National Union of Vehicle Builders* [1971] Ch. 34.

Secondly, natural justice requires that the body reach its decision without bias. As Viscount Simon said in *White* v *Kuzych*[241]-What those who considered the charges ought to bring to their task was a will to reach an honest conclusion after hearing what was urged on either side, and a resolve not to make up their minds beforehand on his personal guilt, however firmly they held their conviction as to union policy, and however strong they shared in previous adverse criticism of the respondent's conduct. It is not required of members of the tribunal to bring to the inquiry the strict impartiality of mind with which a judge should approach and decide between two litigants - that 'icy impartiality of a Rhadamanthus' which Bowen L.J., in *Jackson* v *Barry Railway Co.*[242] thought could not be expected of the engineer-arbitrator.[243] Thus, in *Maclean* v *The Workers' Union,*[244] it was held that there was no breach of natural justice although two members of the committee which took the decision had earlier manifested a hostile attitude towards the plaintiff.

Enforceability of union rules

Trade Unions were, in the early decided cases, almost entirely excluded from the area of the law of contract. First, the unions were severely affected by the common law doctrine of restraint of trade. Where union's rules were designed to regulate the terms upon which the union members could dispose of their labour the union was stigmatised as being in restraint of trade and its rules unenforceable.[245] Second, the courts declined jurisdiction to interfere to enforce the rules of voluntary societies unless a proprietary right was shown to exist. The intervention of the courts was based on a right to property in the society of which a member had been improperly deprived. Sir George Jessel's judgment in *Rigby* v *Connol*[246] contains a clear statement of this principle. There, the plaintiff sought the court's aid to restrain the defendants from excluding him from the membership and benefits of the trade union of which he was a member. Sir George, the Master of the Rolls, said:

---

[241] [1951] AC 585.
[242] [1893] 1 Ch . 238, 248.
[243] [1951] AC 585, 595.
[244] [1929]1Ch. 602.
[245] *Hilton* v *Eckersley* 6 E & B 47; *Hornby* v *Close* (1867) LR2 QB 153.
[246] (1880) 14 Ch .D . 482

> The first question that I will consider is, what is the jurisdiction of a Court of Equity as regards interfering at the instance of a member of a society to prevent his being improperly expelled there-from? I have no doubt whatever that the foundation of the jurisdiction is the right of property vested in the member of the society, and of which he is unjustly deprived by such unlawful expulsion. There is no such jurisdiction that I am aware of reposed,..in any of the...Courts to decide upon the rights of persons to associate together when the association possesses no property...That is to say, the Courts, as such, have never dreamt of enforcing agreements strictly personal in their nature...in such cases no Court of Justice can interfere so long as there is no property the right to which is taken way from the person complaining.[247]

But, as we have seen, this principle later gave way to the principles of the law of contract as the basis for the jurisdiction of the courts. As for the doctrine of restraint of trade it was left to statute to modify it with respect to trade union. A trade union may not necessarily be in restraint of trade. Whether or not it is depends on its purposes or objects as manifested by its rules. As Lord Shaw put it in *Russell* v *Amalgamated Society of Carpenters & Joiners*[248] the issue is one determinable by a survey and construction of the rules of the union. He explained the approach thus:

> The last-mentioned rule itself provides in most comprehensive terms for fine, suspension, or expulsion of any member upon satisfactory proof being given that such member has refused to comply with the decision of a managing committee, branch committee or branch. Under the organization, accordingly, it is apparent that the workman, considered as a free disposer of his own labour, is thus confronted with a situation of great seriousness should his freedom conflict with the decisions of any of the committee referred to.... So far as the individual liberty of the worker is concerned, it is accordingly fairly plain that trade in respect of him is restrained, but that would not be sufficient to satisfy the conditions of unlawfulness unless these were also such as to affect trade in general or the public at large. Upon this subject it, however, appears that provisions are made for granting assistance to other trades and for levies of three pence per week per member "in the event of any great struggle between capital and labour in our own or any other trade. " My Lords, I have only indicated these points from the rules for the purpose of saying that the course adopted by the counsel for the association was the perfectly natural and proper course of a frank admission that these rules are, in fact, in restraint of trade. They mean, and appear, to provide the materials and machinery under which, according to the decision and at the discretion of

[247] Ibid., 487

[248] [1912] AC 421

> the officials of the association, a particular trade may not merely be restrained, but by concerted action with other branches of industry, that trade and the trade of the country at large may be actually paralysed.[249]

However, where the rules of a union can be construed as serving benevolent purposes and not purely to regulate the disposal of the labour of its members, such rules are enforceable within the general rules of the law of contract. In *Swaine* v *Wilson*[250] where the general object of the union was the giving of relief to members when disabled by age or accident or when unemployed, it was held that the union was not in restraint of trade. In *Gozney* v *Bristol Trade and Provident Society*,[251] the rules of the union provided for raising funds to secure to the members certain benefits including superanuation, sickness, funeral, travelling and trade benefits. Rule 40(2) provided strike pay will only be paid in support of members endeavouring to secure an advance of wages or resisting a reduction of same, resisting an increase of the hours of labour, and, when desirable, endeavouring to secure a reduction of same. This rule, said Channel J. in the Divisional Court, rendered the union unlawful as being in restraint of trade, although, as he also said, the great majority of the rules and many of the objects of the union were not only not objectionable, but even laudable. The rule, he said, suggested strongly that the real object of the union was to provide funds "for a fight, and further, for a fight which is to be conducted subject to the approval of the executive. The freedom of action of members appears, therefore, to be fettered by their joining this society."[252] The Court of Appeal however held the union was "just inside the limits of legality"[253] In *Osborne* v *Amalgamated Society of Railway Servants*,[254] the same court, that is the English Court of Appeal, also held, upon the construction of the rules of the union, that it was not in restraint of trade.

However, there is no doubt that the vast majority of trade unions will, at common law, be in restraint of trade. The onus of proving that a trade union is unlawful in that its purpose or purposes are in restraint of trade lies upon the person who alleges the unlawfulness.[255] It has been said that this is a "difficult

---

[249] Ibid., 434-5

[250] (1889) 24 QBD 252.

[251] [1909] 1 KB 901.

[252] Ibid., 911.

[253] Ibid., 917.

[254] [1911] 1 Ch. 540.

[255] *Mason* v *Provident Clothings Supply Co. Ltd.* [1913] AC 724,733; *Morris* v *Saxelby* [1916] 1 AC 688, 700.

task"[256] but the better opinion would appear to be the contrary in view of the nature of and usual purposes of trade unions. However, any trade union which would have been unlawful at common law for this reason is now legalized by statute. Section 22(1) provides that the:

> purposes of a trade union shall not, by reason only that they are in restraint of trade, be unlawful so as to render void or voidable any agreement or trust relating to the union...

This subsection validates not only the purposes or object rules, but also all the other rules, of the union. In *Faramus* v *Film Artistes Association*[257] it was argued that the subsection validates only the purposes or object clauses of the union rules and that a rule of the union which is not an object rule, but a "mere incidental piece of its internal organization"[258] is still void irrespective of the subsection. The majority of the English Court of Appeal[259] however, rejected that view and were upheld by the House of Lords[260] where Lord Evershed said:

> according to the language of the section the effect is to give validity to any agreement which may be made as appurtenant to or in pursuance of the purposes of the union where the purposes themselves are in restraint of trade.[261]

Thus, any rule of a union which would have been void and unenforceable because the purposes of the union are in restraint of trade is protected by the subsection . In other words, the subsection gives a trade union carte blanche to make any rule it likes, however unreasonable it may be in restraint of trade, provided that there is no other ground of illegality.[262]

However, it was not intended to open the whole range of trade union activities to the control of the courts. Accordingly, the subsection excludes certain agreements of a trade union from enforcement in the courts. The rest of subsection 22(1) reads:

> ...but nothing in this subsection shall enable any court to entertain any legal proceedings instituted for the purpose of directly enforcing any agreement

---

256 *Ubiku* v *Registrar of Trade Unions* (1966) LLR 96, 100:
257 [1963] 2 QB 527.
258 Ibid., 541.
259 Ibid.
260 [1964] 2 AC 925.
261 Ibid., 842-3
262 Per Diplock L.J. in *Faramus* v *Film Artists' Association* [1963] QB 527, 559

> mentioned in subsection (2) below, or of recovering damages for any breach of any agreement so mentioned.

It is clear, therefore, that unlike in the case of a trade union which is lawful at common law in that its purposes are not in restraint of trade and whose agreements are therefore enforceable within the general law of contract, not all the rules of trade unions which are unlawful at common law but are validated by subsection 22(1) are enforceable by the courts. In the words of Lord Robson:

> It is to be observed that the Act did not go the length of abrogating or altering the general law against restraint of trade. It grafted an exception on it in favour of certain classes of persons, but by s.4 (s.22) it maintained the principle of the old law even against those persons, to the extent of refusing the assistance of the courts in the direct enforcement of contracts between members of a trade union. Had it gone further and altogether excluded the application of the common law doctrine in this connection, the courts would have been compelled to give full effect by decree, or by injunction, to contracts whereby workmen had bound themselves not to undertake certain legitimate kinds of work, and to refrain, under certain circumstances, from working at their trade at all, except by leave of their union, no matter what their immediate necessities might be.[263]

It has, however, been argued that when a registered union which, at Common law, is lawful sues or is sued in its registered name, that it is something in the Act which enables the action to be entertained by the court; that, therefore, the enforcement of the agreements of such a union is equally similarly limited.[264] In other words, where a lawful union sues or is sued in it registered name, it is exactly in the same position as a union which is unlawful at common law but validated by the Act. But, as Professor Grunfeld has said, with respect, quite rightly, in the case of a registered lawful union, that it can sue or be sued in its registered name is only a procedural matter; "it is the lawfulness of the rule book at common law that 'enables' the court to entertain the action"[265] A trade union whose purposes are not in restraint of trade can enforce all its rules independently of the Act. However, unlike the repealed Trade Union Act[266] which provided that "nothing in this Act shall enable," the present Act avoids all doubts by providing that "nothing in this subsection shall enable the matters

263 *Russell* v *Amalgamated Society of Carpenters and Joiners* [1912] AC 421.

264 Wedderburn, *The Worker and the Law*, Macgibbon & Kee, 1966 p.298, 440-1

265 Grunfeld, *Modern Trade Union Law*, p.71.

266 Cap. 200 Laws of the Federation of Nigeria and Lagos, 1958.

listed in subsection 22(2) to be directly enforced. The subsection does not deal with the registration of trade unions. The agreements which are not to be directly enforced by the courts are contained in subsection 22(2) which reads as follows: (2) The said agreements are the following: (a) any agreement between the members of a trade union as such relating to the terms and conditions on which members of the union shall or shall not employ persons or be employed; (b) any agreement for the payment by any person of any subscription or penalty to a trade union; (c) any agreement for the application of the funds of a trade union:

(i) to provide benefits to its members: or
(ii) to make payments to any employer or worker who is not a member of the union in consideration of his acting in conformity with the rules or resolutions of the union; or
(iii) to discharge any fine imposed upon any person by a court;

(d) any agreement such that every party thereto is one or other of the following, that is to say a trade union, a federation of trade union, or a central labour organization; (e) any bond to secure the performance of any agreement mentioned in paragraphs (a) to (d) above.

Subsection (3) then provides *ex abundanti cautela*, that nothing in section 22 shall render unlawful any of these agreements. Thus, the section only renders the agreements unenforceable in the courts but not unlawful. Although the intention of the section seems clear enough it has not been easy to determine how to give effect to it. What is the meaning of directly? At first the courts took an attitude which gave maximum application to the section. Thus, in *Rigby* v *Connol*[267] the rules of the union provided for the subscriptions of its members to be applied to provide benefits for its members but that any member who apprenticed his son in a shop employing non-union men would be fined and would be disentitled from receiving benefit until such fine was paid. The plaintiff, a member of the union, apprenticed his son in a foul shop and was fined. He refused to pay the fine and was expelled from the union. He brought an action claiming to be entitled to participate in the union benefits and also an order restraining his expulsion. It was held that the action would directly enforce an agreement to provide benefits to members and was therefore barred. In the same year this decision was followed in *Duke* v *Littleboy*,[268] but two years later Fry J., took a contrary view

[267] (1880) 14 Ch. D.482.
[268] (1880) 49 LJ Ch . 802.

in *Wolfe* v *Mathews*.[269] The plaintiff sought an injunction to restrain the defendants from applying money from the funds of the union in carrying out an amalgamation of the union with another union. The defendants objected to the action on the ground that it was an attempt to enforce an agreement for the application of the funds of the union. Fry J. held that the action was maintainable and granted an injunction. It was not an action directly to enforce the application of the funds of the union. He said:

> Now it is plain that this is not an action to recover damages for the breach of an agreement, neither is it...an action to directly enforce an agreement.... An order that the defendants should pay money to the plaintiffs would be a direct enforcement of an agreement for the application of the funds but all that is sought here is to prevent the payment of the monies to somebody else. Either that is no enforcement of an agreement at all, or it is an indirect enforcement.[270]

Which probably means that a negative or restraining order will not be a direct enforcement. Apart from *Chamberlains Wharf Ltd.* v *Smith*,[271] where *Rigby* v *Connol*[272] was once more followed, this view seems to have prevailed in subsequent cases. In Chamberlain's case, the committee of the union passed a resolution to expel the plaintiffs for alleged breaches of the union rules. The plaintiffs brought an action to restrain the committee members from acting on the resolution. The English Court of Appeal held that it had no jurisdiction to entertain the action. But this decision is effectively countered by the decision of the House of Lords in *Yorkshire Miner's Association* v *Howden*.[273] The objects for which the union was established included payment of benefits to members on a strike or lockout. The plaintiff, a member of the union, sought an injunction to prevent the union paying out strike money in support of a strike he alleged was called not in accordance with the union rules. It was pleaded that this was an action directly to enforce provision of benefits to members. By a majority, the House held that this was not so. The object of the litigation, said Lord Macnaghten, was simply to prevent misapplication of the funds of the union, not to administer those funds, or to apply them for the purpose of providing benefits to members.[274]

---

[269] (1882) 21 Ch . D . 194.
[270] Ibid., 196.
[271] [1900] 2 Ch . 605.
[272] Above
[273] [1905] AC 256
[274] Ibid., A65

Similarly, Buckley L.J. in his judgment in *Osborne* v *Amalgamated Society of Railway Servants*[275] said:

> But it is said that an order to declare his expulsion *ultra vires* and a proper consequential injunction will be an enforcement of the agreement in the rules to apply the funds to provide him with benefits. I cannot follow the contention. The plaintiff was a member of a society with (amongst others) rights as regard those benefits which were unenforceable. How can an order to restore him to membership do more than make him what he was before, namely, a member with the same unenforceable rights? How does such an order enforce those rights? What benefit in the application of the funds is it that the order compels the society to give him. Obviously none. If he succeeds in the action he merely resumes the position in which he stood before. His rights by way of benefit are neither greater nor less than before his expulsion.[276]

In *Amalgamated Society of Carpenters and Joiners* v *Braithwaite,*[277] *Lord Atkinson* described this reasoning of Buckley L.J. as "thoroughly sound.[278] In this case the defendant union threatened to expel the plaintiff under a rule which provided for expelling any member "working on a co-partnership system when such system makes provisions for the operatives holding only a minority of the shares." The plaintiff claimed an injunction to restrain the expulsion. The union objected to the grant of an injunction on the ground that it was instituted with the object of directly enforcing either an agreement between members of the union concerning the conditions on which they may or may not be employed or an agreement for the application of the funds of the union to provide benefits to members. The House held that the jurisdiction of the court was not ousted by section 22. The two grounds of objection were countered as follows: that such an action is no attempt to interfere with the application of the funds at all. "It is nothing," said Lord Buckmaster, "but a declaration as to membership with an injunction in its support. It is therefore a totally different proposition to say that a man claims to possess rights and that he seeks to enforce the obligations they create. The latter may be prevented by the section, the former is not." He continued, "nor is he seeking to enforce an agreement with regard to the terms upon which workmen are to be employed. He says that the conditions imposed do not apply to the conditions of his labour, which is the exact opposite of any

---

275 [1911] 1 Ch 540

276 Ibid., 567.

277 [1922] 2 AC 440.

278 Ibid., 465

attempt to enforce such conditions."[279] In the words of Coleridge J. in *Blackall* v *National Union of Foundry Workers of Great Britain & Ireland:*[280]

> Not to construe the word directly in its strict sense would be to expunge the word from the statute. The reinstatement by the court of a member of a trade union alleged to have been rejected for non-compliance with a rule embodying an agreement within Section 4 (s.22) of the Act... is not prohibited, because it does not directly enforce the agreement.[281]

It is thus established that an injunction will be granted where it will not have the effect of directly enforcing a subsection 22(2) agreement. But an injunction will be refused where it will directly enforce such an agreement. Nor will damages be granted in respect of a breach of an agreement within the subsection. There have been divergent views with respect to a declaratory judgment. In *Gozney* v *Bristol Trade and Provident Society,*[282] Fletcher Moulton L.J. expressed the view that the courts have jurisdiction to give a declaratory judgment in respect of a subsection 22(2) agreement. He said:

> But I am not prepared to say that the courts may not properly be asked to make declarations as to the meaning and effect of rules of trade unions, even though it cannot enforce claims under them.[283]

Similarly, Lord Buckmaster said, *obiter*, in *Amalgamated Society of Carpenters and Joiners* v *Braithwaite,*[284] that to construe a rule is not directly to enforce an agreement. But in *McLuskey* v *Cole,*[285] the English Court of Appeal declined jurisdiction on the ground that the agreement came within subsection 22(3). It is suggested that a declaratory judgement cannot be said to be a direct enforcement of subsection 22(2) agreements since such a judgment has only a moral sanction. It will be different of course when there is an attempt to couple it with an injunctive order. It will conduce to the proper running of trade unions if the courts are able to declare the legal rights and duties of the members and officials without necessarily having the power to enforce the observance of the

---

279 Ibid., 567

280 (1923) 39 TLR 431.

281 Ibid., 432

282 [1909] KB 901

283 Ibid., 918

284 [1922] 2 AC 440, 451

285 [1922] 1 Ch. 7.

rights. Subsection 22(2) agreements are not necessarily unlawful agreements as we have seen.

Declaration was made in *Ibadan Newsvendors Association* v *Dyke*,[286] and *Madu* v *Nigeria Coal Miners' Union*[287] both expulsion cases and claimed in *Sowunmi* v *Nigerian Union of Seamen*,[288] an election case. In these cases it was not doubted that the agreements fell outside subsection 22(2). In *Nigeria Civil Service Union* v *Ikyaagba*,[289] the dissolution of the Benue State Council of the Union was declared *ultra vires*, null and void not having been carried out in accordance with the constitution of the union . In addition, the Court of Appeal agreed with the trial judge that to prove that an official of the union has been removed from office, the minutes of the meeting at which the removal was carried out must be produced from the proper custody. A letter merely announcing the removal from office of an official cannot constitute a removal within the constitution.

In *Ubiku* v *Registrar of Trade Unions*,[290] the court ran into some problem. Initially there existed four unions representing petroleum workers throughout the country. By an agreement, duly registered with the Registrar of Trade Unions, the unions amalgamated and became known as the Nigerian Oil, Chemical and Allied Workers' Union (NOCAWU). Two years later, some members of NOCAWU who had belonged to one of the four original unions, the Shell B. P. and Allied Workers' Union, decided to breakaway and revive their union. The plaintiffs, officials of NOCAWU, sought an injunction to restrain the Union, the third defendants, from representing itself as a trade union. Counsel for the union submitted that the jurisdiction of the court was ousted in that this was an agreement between two registered trade unions. The court, however, held that the action was maintainable on the ground that since the Act in one section contemplated an agreement between the unions before an amalgamation could be effected it could not, in another section, prohibit the enforcement of the agreement. The decision is, of course, erroneous. The section provides clearly and in unambiguous terms that any agreement between a trade union and another trade union cannot be directly enforced nor can damages be recovered for any breach of such an agreement. In the Australian case of *Railway Workers and General Labourers' Association* v *United Labourers' Protective Society*,[291] the

[286] Unreported Suit No. 1/62/63 High Court, Ibadan.
[287] See *Federal Ministry of Labour Quarterly Review*, Dec.1964, paras 244-51
[288] Unreported Suit No. LD/422/65, High Court, Lagos.
[289] Court of Appeal Judgments Jan - May 1985, p. 233.
[290] (1966) LLR 95
[291] (1914) 14 SR (NSW) 1.

plaintiff union sued the defendant union to recover the expenses it had expended in pursuance of an agreement between the two unions to amalgamate, the defendant union having repudiated the agreement. The court declined jurisdiction on the ground that it was an action directly to enforce an agreement between one trade union and another.

The issue may be raised, as it has been raised in respect of sections 23 and 43 which, respectively, confer immunity on trade unions in tort actions and on tort feasors committing certain torts, about the constitutionality of that part of S.22 which provides that nothing in subsection 22(1) "shall enable any court to entertain any legal proceedings instituted for the purpose of directly enforcing any agreement in subsection (2) of this section, or of recovering damages for any breach of any agreement so mentioned." The point is examined in some detail in the discussion of s. 23 one of the sections under which it has been raised. It suffices here to state that, in our opinion, none of the three provisions is, in any way, unconstitutional.

Unregistered trade unions

An unregistered trade union which, at common law, would be unlawful for the reason that it's purposes are in unreasonable restraint of trade, is also legalized by S.22, although, only for a specified period. But, as we have seen, a trade union is prohibited from performing any act in furtherance of the purposes of the union where it has not been registered. Subsection 22(4) provides that subsection (1) to (3) of s.22 apply in relation to an unregistered trade union as they apply to a registered trade union. Thus the purposes, agreements and trusts of an unregistered trade union are enforceable by virtue of s.22(1) even if the union were in unreasonable restraint of trade. But subsection 22 (4) further provides that this is "subject to the following restrictions, that is to say:

a) if the trade union has not been registered, the said provisions shall apply only as regards
i) the agreement whereby the union is formed or any agreement whereby a person joins the union;
ii) Any trust on which any funds of the union are to be held; and
iii)any agreement for the use of any premises as the office of the union;

This drafting does not give any felicity. What it probably means is that the courts are not thereby enabled to entertain any legal proceedings instituted for the purpose of directly enforcing or of recovering damages for any breach of the agreements or trust mentioned in the subsection. If an application for the registration of the union is finally refused the provisions of s.22 (1), (2) and (3) cease to apply to the union at the end of a period of three months beginning with the date of the final refusal. If the registration of a trade union is cancelled the provisions apply only during the period of three months beginning with the date of the cancellation.

Expulsion rules

It has been shown that section 22 renders all contracts and trusts of a registered trade union enforceable except those mentioned in the section itself. The courts have granted relief in many cases including expulsion and election issues. For example, as Buckley L.J. said in *Osborne* v *Amalgamated Society of Railway Servants*,[292] there is nothing in the section to prevent a court from entertaining legal proceedings to enforce a member's right to his vote or his distributive share in winding up. Furthermore, as has been pointed out already, where the union is lawful at common law, the contracts of the union are freely enforceable in the courts.

The union rules book contract has been considered by the courts more, especially in expulsion cases. The requirement that the rules or constitution of a union should provide for expulsion and other disciplinary measures has been mentioned. There is no inherent common law power in a union to expel a member.[293] A power to expel must be exercised in strict compliance with the expulsion rule otherwise the expulsion is wrongful. Expulsion rules are penal rules and are therefore construed strictly.[294] In *Blackall* v *National Union of Foundry Workers of Great Britain and Ireland*,[295] a rule provided for the exclusion of a member for non-payment of contribution for over twenty weeks. The plaintiff's purported exclusion a few days before he would have been in arrears for over twenty weeks was held not to be justified by the rules. Often unions couch some expulsion rules in general terms usually referred to as blanket

---

[292] [1911] 1 Ch. 540.

[293] *Dawkins* v *Antrobus* (1881) 17 Ch. D.615 per Jessel MR at 620; *Luby* v *Warwickshire Miners Association* [1912] 2 Ch. 371; *Kelly* v *NATOSOPA* (1915) 31 TLR 632; *Abbott* v *Sullivan* [1952] 1 KB 189.

[294] *Per Coleridge J. In Blackall* v *National Union of Foundry Workers of Great Britain and Ireland* (1923) 39 TLR 431; 433.

[295] *Supra*

rules. Thus a union rule may provide for expulsion of "any member.... who, in the opinion of the executive committee, injures the reputation of the union or conducts himself in a manner not conducive to the interest of the union."[296] In such cases the courts reserve the right to inquire whether in fact the conduct of the member has injured the reputation of the union. In *Wolstenholme* v *Amalgamated Musicians' Union*,[297] the plaintiff was expelled from the defendant union under a rule authorizing expulsion for conduct which "brought the union into discredit." The court held that his action for wrongful expulsion failed since there were ample materials on which the union could justifiably come to the conclusion that the plaintiff's conduct brought the union into discredit.

In *Evans* v *National Union of Printing, Bookbinding and Paper Workers*[298] rule 24(2) (f) rendered a member liable to expulsion "if he has knowingly acted to the detriment of the interest of the union." The plaintiff was a casual jobbing hand in the employment of a firm of printers. He did not like the work he was offered to do so he absented himself from work. The committee of his branch of the union considered the matter and instructed him to accept the work offered him. He still refused to do so. He was again summoned before the committee and charged with insubordination in refusing to accept the instruction of the committee. His expulsion for conduct detrimental to the interests of the union was upheld by the court. But in *Lee* v *Showmen's Guild of Great Britain*[299] the refusal of a union member to accept the union committee's decision on allocation of sites at a fairground was held not to be "unfair competition with regard to the renting, taking or letting of ground or position.'' In *Silvester* v *National Union of Printing, Bookbinding and Paper Workers*[300] the plaintiff refused to do overtime work with his employers even when ordered by the union to do so. As, however, the union rules did not provide for compulsory overtime the court held that the plaintiff's conduct could not amount to acting "to the detriment of the interests of the union."

In *Santer* v *National Graphical Association*,[301] a rule of the union required that where an allegation of a contravention of the union rules is made, it must be investigated by the committee of the member's branch and "the member concerned shall have the right at any such investigation to answer the charge, either in writing or in person, and call witness." This rule was not followed

[296] See *Edet Ekpo Udokisai* v *Edet Isiah* (1974) 4 UILR 186.
[297] [1920] 2 Ch. 388
[298] [1938] 4 AllER 51
[299] [1952] 2 QB 329
[300] (1967) 1 KIR 679
[301] (1972) 14 KIR 193

Stevenson J. held that the non-observance resulted in a very grave breach of contract on the part of the union. He said:

> It is perfectly obvious to my mind that the rules of the union were not observed, that the expulsion of the plaintiff from the union was a nullity, and in doing what they did the union was committing a very grave breach of the contract between itself and the applicant as a member, the terms of which are to be ascertained from the rules.[302]

Another aspect of strict compliance with an expulsion rule is that only the body in which the power to expel is vested can validly exercise the power. *In Bonsor* v *Musicians Union,*[303] where the power to expel was vested in the branch committee of the union and the purported expulsion was carried out by the secretary of the union, it was held that the expulsion was wrongful. Similarly, an expulsion carried out by the president of the union was held wrongful as the rules of the union vested the power of expulsion in the executive committee of the union.[304] Participation in the deliberation of the body vested with the power of expulsion by someone who is not a member of that body will also invalidate the decision.[305]

Also, as we have seen, an expulsion carried out in breach of the rules of natural justice is wrongful. In *Lawlor* v *Union of Post Office Workers,*[306] the plaintiff and others were expelled under a rule which stated that "any member shall be expelled from the union who in the opinion of the executive council is not a fit and proper person for membership." The notice of expulsion merely stated that they were being expelled for "unconstitutional action in respect of rule 19 of the union rules" but it did not state what the acts were which were unconstitutional. Nor was anyone of them given an opportunity to be heard in his defence. The court held there was breach of natural justice so that the expulsion was wrongful. In *Annamunthodo* v *Oilfields Workers' Trade Union,*[307] as we have seen, failure to give the plaintiff notice of the charge for which he was held guilty was held to be a breach of a natural justice which vitiated the purported expulsion.

---

[302] Ibid., 201

[303] [1954] 1 Ch. 479

[304] *Edet Ekpo Udokisai* v *Edet Isiah* (1974) 4 UILR 186; see also *Leary* v *National Union of Vehicle Builders* [1971] Ch. 34.

[305] *Lane* v *Norman* (1891) 66 LT 83; *Leary* v *National Union of Vehicle Builders, supra.*

[306] [1965] 1 All ER 353.

[307] [1961] AC 945.

It is fairly well established that the jurisdiction of the courts to pronounce upon the decisions of the trade unions cannot be ousted by union rules. This limitation on the powers of the unions is based on public policy which maintains that parties cannot, by contract, oust the ordinary courts from their jurisdiction.[308] Thus, in *Leigh* v *National Union of Railwaymen*,[309] where a rule provided that no order or decision of the expelling body may be questioned, reversed, controlled or suspended safe by way of appeal under the rules of the union, Groff J., held that that rule could not oust the jurisdiction of the court. It seems, however, that resort to the courts may be delayed where the rules provide that a member must first exhaust an internal appeal system or domestic remedies before going to the courts. The courts will normally give effect to such a provision unless the plaintiff is able to show cause why it should interfere with the contractual position. Where the plaintiff is not contractually bound to exhaust an internal system of remedies a right to internal appeal does not preclude resort to the courts before exercising that right. In this case the courts will more readily grant relief although, it may also require the plaintiff to first use the domestic remedy. Resort to the courts before the exhaustion of internal remedy will be granted where it is shown that the internal remedy would be inadequate and that the plaintiff might suffer substantial injustice if he has to wait to pursue the domestic remedy.[310]

However, access to the courts is guaranteed by the Constitution for the determination of any question as to the civil rights and obligations of any person.[311]

Remedies for breach of union rules

It is clear that the remedies of a declaratory judgment, injunction and damages are available in an action for breach of the union constitution which is outside section 22. In a claim for damages for breach of contract the plaintiff must prove special damages; there is, of course, no room for general damages. Where a

[308] *Lee* v *Showmen's Guild of Great Britain* [1952] 2 QB 329; *Baker* v *Jones* [1954] 1 WLR 1005; *Bonsor* v *Musicians Union* [1954] 1 Ch. 479; *Lawlor* v *Union of Post Office Workers* [1965] 1 All ER 353.

[309] [1969] All ER 1249.

[310] *White* v *Kuzych* [1951]AC 585; *Lawlor* v *Union of Post Office Workers* [1965] 2 WLR 579; *Leigh* v *National Union of Railwaymen* [1969] 3 All ER 1249.

[311] S. (6)(6)(b) Constitution; *Attorney General* v *Hassan* [1985] 2 NWLR (pt.8)483; *Government of Imo State* v *Greeco Construction & Engineering Associates Ltd.* [1985] 3 NWLR (pt.II) 71

union member loses his job as a result of the wrongful loss of his union membership there is no doubt that such a plaintiff is entitled to damages.[312] But the closed shop which would normally give rise to that type of situation is largely absent in this country.[313] A plaintiff in the normal type of case will only find some consolation in the words of Ungoed-Thomas J. in *Lawlor* v *Union* of *Post Office Workers*:[314]

> It is rightly pointed out that loss of membership of the union does not mean loss of job, so that the disadvantage to the plaintiff is not of a financial character. But the disadvantage is more than merely social. The expulsion does affect the expelled member in his work. It affects his standing with and relation to other members. The trade union is concerned with members in their capacity as workers in their jobs, and expulsion excludes from the advantages which such membership confers. Trade unions, to their honour also develop strong ties of loyalty amongst their members, and loss of membership strikes deep, and not less so because it may not strike at the pocket.[315]

It appears that additional jurisdiction has now been conferred on the Industrial Arbitration Panel (IAP) with a right of appeal to the National Industrial Court "in the case of intra-union disputes arising from the organization and running of a trade union as laid down in the union constitution or inter-union disputes arising from the restructuring of trade unions established under the Trade Unions Act.[316] Presumably, intra-union disputes include any breach of the union constitution or rules book such as an expulsion or an election carried out in contravention of the rules of the union. The awards of arbitration tribunals, which are appointed by the chairman of the IAP to hear particular trade disputes, have been dictated by the nature of the dispute itself and the remedy sought.[317] The same principles will probably apply to the awards with respect to intra-union disputes. What is not clear is whether the jurisdiction of the ordinary courts in intra- and inter-union disputes has been supplanted.

---

[312] *Akintemi* v *Onwumechili* [1985] 1 NWLR (pt.1) 68.
[313] *Edwards* v *Society of Graphical & Allied Trades*, [1970] 1 All ER 905.
[314] [1965] 2 WLR 579
[315] Ibid.
[316] S. 24 Trade Disputes Act
[317] See below.

The rule in *Foss* v *Harbottle*

The intervention of the courts in the administration of trade unions is also governed by the rule known as the Rule in *Foss* v *Harbottle*.[318] Although the rule was first developed in relation to corporations it has been held to apply to trade unions.[319] The rule has been stated as follows: if an act is *intra vires* the corporation, and therefore one which can be sanctioned by the majority of the corporators properly assembled in general meeting, the court will not entertain any proceedings to restrain the doing of the act resolved upon unless such proceedings are brought by the majority of the corporators and in the name of the corporation itself.[320] This means, in effect, that an individual member or a minority of members of a trade union will not be allowed to maintain an action in respect of an *intra vires* act although it is carried out wrongfully or irregularly where such an act can be ratified by a simple majority of the members of the union. If the court interferes on behalf of a minority nothing stops the majority from carrying out the act again in the same way it had earlier done if it were minded to do so. The court would have acted in futility. If the majority believe that the wrong was done to the union then the union, acting through the majority, can sue. If the majority decide not to sue the wrong lies. *Jenkins L. J.* further explains as follows:

> If a mere majority of the members of the company or association is in favour of what has been done, then *cadit queastio*. No wrong had been done to the company or association and there is nothing in respect of which any one can sue. If, on the other hand, a simple majority of members of the company or association is against what has been done, then there is no valid reason why the company or association itself should not sue.[321]

However, there are exceptions to the rule although it may not be that accurate to refer to them as exceptions. *Sir Robert Megarry* V. C. explains the reason for the exceptions.[322] As he said - if the rule in *Foss* v *Harbottle* had remained unqualified, the way would have been open for the majority to stultify any proceedings which were for the benefit of the minority and to the disadvantage

---

[318] (1843) 2 Hare 461

[319] *Abubakri* v *Smith* (1973) 6 SC 31; *Elufioye* v *Halilu* [1993]6 NWLR 570 *Mbene* v *Ofili* 1968 (1) ALR (Comm) 235; *Cotter* v *National Union of Seamen* [1929] 2 Ch . 58.

[320] *Cotter* v *National Union of Seamen, supra,* 107-8, per *Lawrence L.J*.

[321] *Edwards* v *Halliwell* [1950] 2 All ER 1064, 1066.

[322] *Estmanco (Kilner House) Ltd.* v *Greater London Council* [1982] 1 All ER 437.

of the majority.[323] One exception is that the rule does not apply where what has been done is *ultra vires* the union or is illegal.[324] A second exception is that the rule has no application where what has been done amounts to a fraud on the minority and the persons against whom an action may be brought are themselves in control of the union and refuse to allow an action to be brought in the name of the union.[325] Another exception is that an individual member or minority members can sue where what has been done can be validly done or sanctioned, not by a simple majority of the members of the union, but only by some special majority of the members of the union.[326]

A further exception is the converse of the rule. As the rule applies where the wrong complained of is a wrong done to the union itself, it does not apply where the wrong is a violation of the right of an individual. Where what has been done irregularly invades the personal or individual right of a member of a union that member has a right to sue.[327] As *Jenkins L.J.* said "it is implicit in the rule that the matter relied on as constituting the cause of action should be a cause of action properly belonging to the general body of corporators or members of the company or association as opposed to a cause of action which some individual member can assert in his own right.[328] These four exceptions were discussed fully in the judgment of Jenkins L.J. in *Edwards* v *Halliwell*[329] In that judgment he had said "that the rule is not an inflexible rule and it will be relaxed where necessary in the interests of justice."[330] This statement has been interpreted as establishing a fifth exception.[331] Although this exception or statement has been described by the English Court of Appeal as not a practical test[332] the Supreme Court has not only accepted it but, has in fact, also applied it.[333]

Yet another exception, the sixth, has been established. Where a union's rules book or constitution provides that any member of the union has a right to initiate an action at his own expense in connection with any breach of the

---

[323] Ibid., 443
[324] *Mbene* v *Ofili supra*
[325] Ibid.
[326] *Cotter* v *National Union of Seamen, supra; Edwards* v *Halliwell, supra*; *Mbene* v *Ofili, supra*
[327] *Edwards* v *Halliwell, supra.*
[328] Ibid., 1066-7.
[329] *Supra*; see also *Elufioye* v *Halilu* [1993] 6 NWLR 570
[330] [1950] 2 All ER 1064, 1067.
[331] *Prudential Assurance Co. Ltd.* v *Newman Industries Ltd.* [1980] 2 All ER 841, 877.
[332] *Prudential Assurance Co. Ltd.* v *Newman Industries Ltd.*, [1982] 1 All ER 354, 366; see also *Estmanco (Kilner House) Ltd.* v *Greater London Council* [1982] 1 All ER 437, 444 per Sir Robert Megarry V.C.
[333] *Edokpolo & Co. Ltd.* v *Sem-Edo Wire Industries Ltd.* [1984] NSCC 553.

union constitution then the rule in *Foss* v *Harbottle* does not apply to prevent an action by a member.[334] This exception was confirmed by the *Supreme Court in Elufioye* v *Halilu.*[335] In this case the Supreme Court also considered the relationship between the rule and the constitutional guarantee of access to the courts for the determination of one's civil rights and obligations.[336] According to the court, since the terms of a union's constitution constitute terms of contract between the union and each member and between the members *inter se* a breach of a constitutional provision raises questions as to the civil rights and obligations of the parties to the contract and, as such, a party has a right of access to the court notwithstanding the rule. As Omo JSC put it:[337]

> Once the civil rights and obligations of the plaintiffs as individuals are affected, as I hold they are here the courts in exercise of their judicial power set out above[338] can look into such rights and obligations, and for that purpose the plaintiffs have a *locus standi* before them. Such right guaranteed under the Constitution cannot be in any way detrimentally affected by the common law rule in *Foss* v *Harbottle.*

It is clear, therefore, whether it is regarded as an exception to the rule or not, that an individual union member can sue for breach of the union's constitution where he can show that such a breach affects his individual civil right or obligation even where none of the established exceptions to the rule is applicable. It may well be, however, that whenever the constitutional right can be invoked that, at least, the fourth exception can also apply. For example, the right to vote which may be denied as a consequence of a breach of a union's constitution has been held to be an invasion of an individual's right entitling him to sue.[339] Indeed, Karibi-Whyte, JSC, would appear to agree with this suggestion. As he said - the rule in *Foss* v *Harbottle* (*supra*) will not apply to exclude a person who can establish a personal right as distinct from that of the association. In this sense it is *ad idem* with section 6(6) (b) of the Constitution 1979 where there is *locus standi* if the determination of the civil rights and

---

[334] *Oduduru* v *National Union of Hotel & Personnel Services Workers*, unreported Appeal No. FCA/L/226/83; *Agbonikhena* v *Egbe* [1987] 2 NWLR 494; *Elufioye* v *Halilu* [1993] 6 NWLR 570.

[335] *Supra.*

[336] S. 6(6)(b) Constitution.

[337] [1993] 6 NW LR 570, 595.

[338] Ibid.

[339] *Pender* v *Lushington* (1877) 6 Ch. D. 70, 80.

obligations of the plaintiff is involved.[340] But Omo, JSC, who gave the leading judgement appeared to regard the constitutional provision as wider in scope. His Lordship said:[341] "it is only where the right and obligation of an individual are in issue, and such a case does not fit into the exceptions under the rule in *Foss* v *Harbottle*, that there may be a conflict since *locus standi* is available to the individual in a determination of his right and obligations, whether or not these concern a Trade Union and it is in respect of matters to which the rule in *Foss* v *Harbottle* is normally applicable."

International affiliation

Since 1989, except for a period of just over five years between 1991 and 1996, there has been statutory regulation of affiliation of Nigerian trade unions and central labour organisations to international trade unions bodies or organizations. The first statute, the Trade Unions (International Affiliation) Decree,[342] not only prohibited any registered trade union from affiliating with any international labour organization or trade secretariat except as provided by the Decree but also provided that the central labour organisation[343] and all the registered trade unions must cease to be affiliated with any international labour organisation or trade secretariat except as permitted by the Decree. And the Decree only permitted affiliation by the central labour organisation and only to the Organisation for African Trade Union Unity (OATUU), the Organisation of Trade Union of West Africa and any other international labour organisation specifically approved by the government. The individual trade unions were not permitted to affiliate at all. Thus any affiliation of any of the registered trade unions had to cease as also any affiliation of the Nigeria Labour Congress (NLC) to any other international body other than the ones to which the Decree permitted affiliation. The Decree was repealed in 1991[344] but in 1996[345] the same restrictions were re-imposed although, this time, the Act permitted the affiliation of not only the NLC but also of any registered trade union to the same bodies and under the same conditions. However, in 1999[346] a more liberal approach was

---

340 *Elufioye* v *Halilu* [1993] 6 NWLR 570, 599.
341 Ibid., 595; five members of the court agreed with the leading judgment and one dissented.
342 1989 No. 35.
343 In effect, the Nigeria Labour Congress being the only centre allowed by law.
344 Trade Unions (International Affiliation) (Repeal) Act, 1991 No. 32
345 Trade Unions (International Affiliation) Act, 1996 No. 29.
346 Trade Unions (International Affiliation) (Amendment) Act 1999 No. 2.

adopted owing, no doubt, to the anticipated withdrawal of military rule, which had rendered the country desolate, and the advent of democratic rule.

Thus the NLC or any trade union may now affiliate with any international labour organization or trade secretariat in accordance with the provisions of the Act.[347] These provisions are, however, not too stringent. An application must be made by a trade union or the NLC, which must be submitted with the details for the affiliation, to the Minister[348] for his approval and he is required to give his decision within 30 days of "documented evidence of receipt of such application."[349] Where no decision is received within those 30 days and another 7 days, i.e. 37 consecutive days in all, it is deemed that an approval has been received.[350] Where, however, the Minister, for whatever reason, refuses, objects or withholds his approval, he must cause the reason for such refusal, objection or disapproval, to be communicated to the trade union or centre concerned within the same 30 days of documented evidence of receipt of the application.[351] In such a case any further representation must, in the first instance, be made to the Minister but, on a further refusal, the trade union or centre has a right of appeal to the National Industrial Court.[352] Probably there is a right of appeal from the National Industrial Court (NIC) to the Court of Appeal and thence to the Supreme Court. An appeal is allowed as of right from a decision of the NIC to the Court of Appeal on questions of fundamental rights as contained in Chapter IV of the Constitution.[353] It would seem clear that a right to affiliate with another trade union body or organization is a fundamental right within section 40 of the Constitution which guarantees a right to every person to associate with other persons and form or belong to any trade union or any other association for the protection of his interests.[354]

---

[347] S.1(1) 1996 No. 29; see S.2 1999 No. 2.

[348] By S. 2, ibid.; Minister means the Minister charged with the responsibility for trade unions union matters; this must be the Minister responsible for labour since the Constitution defines labour to include trade unions.

[349] S. 1(2) 1996 No. 29; See S. 2 1999 No. 2.

[350] S. 1(3) ibid.

[351] S. 1(4) ibid.

[352] S. 1(5), ibid.

[353] S. 20(3) Trade Disputes Act, Cap 432; see S.6(a) Trade Disputes (Amendment) Act, 1992 No. 47

[354] Quaere whether the NIC has jurisdiction in issues of fundamental rights since the Constitution vests that jurisdiction in the High Courts; see *supra* p. 329

Chapter 8

Trade unions merger, federations of trade unions and central labour organisations

Trade union merger

The history of the unions has recorded two major restructuring of the unions into larger trade unions along industrial lines. The first exercise was concluded in 1978 and the second in 1996. Both were assisted by the government and in neither exercise were the statutory provisions on amalgamation, now merger, applied. Indeed, there is no available record of the use of the amalgamation provisions which were intended to encourage the formation of large and viable trade unions. Although the newly introduced provisions demand the barest minimum of formalities they are also likely to remain otiose. The newly restructured unions may be reluctant to give up their existence. However this remains to be seen.

Two or more trade unions may merge and become one trade union but cannot do so unless a resolution to that effect, signed by the president or secretary of each of the merging unions,[1] is presented to the Registrar of Trade Unions and the rules proposed for the merging[2] unions and the terms of the merger have both been forwarded to the Registrar.[3] Where these requirements are satisfied the Registrar must, forthwith, register the new union.[4] The new union comes into existence on the date it is registered.[5] The property of each of the merging unions become vested in the new union to the extent provided in the

---

[1] Merging unions mean the unions proposing to merge; s. 27(8) Trade Unions Act; the whole of s.27 derives from the Trade Unions (Amendment) Act 1996. All references to sections in this chapter are to the Trade Unions Act unless otherwise stated.

[2] Quaere whether not merged union; merged union means the trade union which will emerge from the merger; s. 27(8).

[3] S. 27(1).

[4] S. 27(3).

[5] S. 27(4); a merger cannot take effect until it is registered; s.27(2).

terms of the merger forwarded to the Registrar without the requirement of any form of conveyance or transfer other than those contained in the terms of the merger forwarded to the Registrar.[6] Each of the merging unions ceases to exist and its registration must be canceled forthwith.[7]

On cancelling the registration of the merging unions the Registrar must send to the address at which, immediately before the cancellation, the registered office of each of the unions was situated, a notice in the prescribed form, stating the date and the grounds for the cancellation and must cause a similar notice to be published in the Federal Gazette; and the original certificate of registration of the union must be delivered to the Registrar not more than 30 days after the date of the cancellation.[8] Where the certificate is not delivered within the 30 days every person who, on the date of the cancellation, was an official or member of the union is guilty of an offence and liable, on summary conviction, to a fine of to ₦50.[9] However the merger of unions does not prejudice the right of any creditor of a (merging) trade union.[10]

Federations of trade unions

The formation of federations of trade unions is also encouraged. A federation of trade unions means any association or combination of trade unions, whether temporary or permanent, the purposes of which include that of regulating the terms and conditions of employment of workers.[11] However, a federation of trade unions cannot come into existence until it is registered with the Registrar of Trade Unions.[12] Any person who purports to do any act on behalf of a proposed federation of trade unions before it is registered is guilty of an offence and liable, on summary conviction, to a fine of ₦ 50.[13]

A federation of trade unions may be formed by two or more trade unions whose members are employed in the same trade, occupation or industry, or in substantially similar trades, occupations or industries. Any two or more trade unions may form a federation only where, in the case of each of the unions

[6] Ibid.
[7] S. 27(5).
[8] Ss. 27(6); 7(6).
[9] Ss. 27(6); 7(7) and 49.
[10] S. 27(7).
[11] S. 52; presumably the stipulated purpose must be its principal purpose; see ante for a discussion of principal purpose and the meaning of worker.
[12] S. 29(2).
[13] Ss. 29(5) and 52.

concerned, a resolution has, in a secret ballot held at a meeting, whether annual or special, of delegates representing all the members of the union, been passed in circumstances such that the votes cast in favour of the resolution represent a simple majority of the members of the union.[14] And not less than thirty days before the date of the meeting a notice in the prescribed form setting out the resolution must have been given to the Registrar and all reasonable steps taken by the union to secure that, not less than thirty days before the meeting, every member of the union was supplied with a similar notice.[15] Where these requirements have been complied with an application in the prescribed form, signed by seven members of each one of the unions proposing to form the federation and countersigned by the secretary of each one of those unions must then be sent to the Registrar together with a statutory declaration by the Secretary of each of the unions in respect of his union to the effect that the requirements of section 29(1) have been complied with.[16] On receipt of an application, together with the statutory declarations, the Registrar, if satisfied that the requirements of the Act and of the regulations with respect to the registration of federations of trade unions have been complied with, must register the federation.[17] On registering a federation, the Registrar must record the office whose address is stated on the application form for registration as the registered office of the federation. Notice of any change in the situation of the registered office must be given to the Registrar within thirty days after the date of the change and the Registrar must register the change.[18]

A trade union may become a member of a registered federation of trade unions but it cannot do so unless its members are employed in the same trade, occupation or industry or substantially similar trades, occupation or industries as the members of the trade unions which belong to the federation.[19] The joining union must also be eligible for membership of the federation under the rules of the federation and a resolution approving the proposed application for membership of the federation has, in a secret ballot held at an annual or special delegates meeting, been passed by a simple majority of the members of the

---

[14] S. 29(1)(a); it may be very difficult to obtain a majority vote of the members of the union at a delegates' meetings.

[15] S. 29(1)(b) and (c).

[16] S. 29(3).

[17] S. 29(5).

[18] Every federation must have a registered office to which all communications and notices may be addressed; Ss.20(1) and 31; if any federation continues for more than 30 days without having a registered office, the federation and every official is liable, on summary conviction, to a fine of ₦10 for every day, after the 30 days, for which it so continues. Ss.20(4) and 31.

[19] S. 30(1) (a) .

union[20] and all reasonable steps were taken by the union to secure that, not less than thirty days before the date of the meeting, every member of the union was supplied with a notice in the prescribed form setting out the resolution.[21] Where these requirements have been complied with it appears that a joint action by the federations and the union then becomes necessary. Subsection 30(3) provides that where a federation and the union have complied with the above requirements, there must be sent to the Registrar; a) notice in the prescribed form of the proposed admission signed by seven members of the union and countersigned by its secretary; b) a statutory declaration by the secretary of the union that the above requirements have been complied with and c) a certificate in the prescribed form signed by the secretary of the federation that the admission of the union has been approved in accordance with the rules of the federation. On receipt of these documents, the Registrar, if satisfied that the requirements of the Act and the regulations have been complied with, must register the union as a member of the federation.[22]

The grounds on which and the procedure to be followed for the cancellation of the registration of a federation of trade unions are the same as for a trade union.[23]

No person must be an official of more than one federation of trade unions at the same time but a person who is an official of a federation may, at the same time, be an official of a trade union or the Nigeria Labour Congress, which is the only central labour organization, or of all three.[24] Any person who contravenes this provision is guilty of an offence and punishable, on summary conviction with a fine of ₦50.[25]

Section 31 provides that the provisions of Sections 13, 15, 18, 19(1) (in so far as it relates to capacity to be an official), 20 to 23, 26 and 28 apply, *mutatis mutandis*, to federations as they apply to trade unions. These sections are discussed fully in relation to trade unions in various parts of this book. They relate, respectively, to disqualification from holding office, application of dues for political purposes, right to restrain misapplication of funds, capacity of infant, registered office, sale of rules book, validation of unlawfulness at common law, immunity from tort action, change of name and alteration of rules book.

---

[20] See f n 14, for the difficulty inherent in this requirement.
[21] S. 30(1) (b) and (c).
[22] S. 30 (4).
[23] S. 7(8).
[24] S. 32(1).
[25] Ss. 32(2) and 49.

Central labour organizations

On 23 July, 1970, the Commissioner for Labour[26] addressed a meeting of employers and representatives of central labour organizations and stated that he proposed to bring under statutory control the formation, registration and some activities of central labour organizations. This proposal was carried into effect by the Trade Unions Act 1973. The Act made the registration of the then existing four central labour organizations automatic[27] and provided for the procedure for the formation of new centres[28] as well as for the amalgamation of central labour organizations.[29] These provisions were later repealed by the Trade Unions (Amendment) Act 1978 which, however, left intact some other provisions of the Act with respect to a registered central labour organization as well as make its own provisions in the same regard.[30]

The Nigeria Labour Congress is now the only central labour organization in the country. The Registrar of Trade Unions was enjoined to register the Congress as the only central labour organization upon the coming into effect of the Trade Unions (Amendment) Act 1978, on 3rd August 1977.[31] Section 34 provides that the Congress has powers, subject to its rules, a) to represent the general interest of its members on any national advisory body set up by the Government of the Federation; b) to collect and disseminate to its members information and advice on economic and social matters; c) to give advice, encouragement or financial assistance to any of its members in need of it; d) to promote the education of members of trade unions in the field of labour relations and connected field ; and e) to render any other assistance provided for under the articles of affiliation. But the Congress must not engage in collective bargaining on behalf of any trade union or federation of trade unions except where it is

[26] Now the Minister of Labour and Productivity.

[27] S. 37 repealed by S.1(1)(j) of the Trade Unions (Amendment) Act 1978; the existing centres were the Labour Unity Front, the Nigerian Trade Union Congress, the Nigerian Workers' Council and United Labour Congress of Nigeria. For the history of the growth of central labour organizations in Nigeria, see E. E. Uvieghara, *Trade Union Law in Nigeria*, EPH Benin City.

[28] S. 33, however a new S.33 is now substituted by S.1 (1) (i) Trade Unions (Amendment) Act 1978.

[29] S 36 now repealed by S.1(1)(i) Trade Unions (Amendment) Act 1978.

[30] There appeared to have been some conflict between the Trade Unions (Central Labour Organizations (Special Provisions) Act 1976 and the Trade Unions (Amendment) Act 1978. S. 1 of the former cancelled the registration of the four centres registered under S . 37 Trade Unions Act 1973 while S .1 (1) (j) of the later repealed the section. A worse confusion was between S. 9(3) of the former and S.1(1)(j) of the later. While the former provided that Ss.33-38 of the Trade Union Ac, shall cease to have effect" the later repealed Ss. 36-38 of the same Act.

[31] S. 33(1); see S. 1 (1) (I) Trade Unions (Amendment) Act, 1978, s.3 of which gave the Act retrospective effect.

requested to do so by a trade union or federation which is a party to the collective bargaining.[32] If the Congress acts in contravention of this provision, the Congress itself and every one of its officials and every trade union or federation on behalf of which it so acts and every one of its officials is, each, guilty of an offence and liable, on summary conviction, to a fine of ₦50.[33]

Since 1978 affiliation of trade unions to the Nigerian Labour Congress has been governed by statute. The fundamental policy seems to be not only to preclude trade unions of senior employees from being affiliates of the NLC but also from having a central labour organisation of their own. In 1978 it was provided that "all trade unions, other than associations of senior staff or employers are hereby deemed to be affiliated to" the NLC.[34]

Many, including this author, thought this provision did not preclude affiliation of registered trade unions of senior staff to the NLC. Indeed, two senior staff unions, the Shop and Distributive Trade Senior Staff Association and the Academic Staff Union of Universities, were purportedly affiliated to the NLC. However, in 1986, the 70 registered trade unions were divided into two groups in the 3rd schedule to the Act. Part A of the schedule, with the title, Workers' Unions, comprised only the 42 unions of supposedly junior employees and Part B. with the title, Senior Staff Unions, was made up of the unions of senior staff and employers. The unions in Part A were deemed to be affiliated to the NLC and those in Part B were prohibited from such affiliation.[35]

However, in 1996, some of the trade unions listed in Part A were re-structured and the number of unions listed in that Part became reduced to twenty-nine.[36] Part B was also amended by completely omitting the list of trade unions of senior staff and employers and providing instead what was described as the jurisdictional scope of the twenty-nine unions in Part A.[37] In 1999 Parts A and B were again amended and a Part C created.[38] Thus Schedule 3 now contains three Parts. Part A, with the title "List of Restructured Trade Unions Affiliated to the Central Labour Organisation"[39] now has 29 trade unions listed. Part A now also includes "Any other workers' trade union registered under this Act and publish (sic) from time to time, in the Federal *Gazette*".[40] Part B still

---

[32] S. 34(2)
[33] Ss. 34(3) and 49.
[34] See S. 1. Trade unions Amendment Act 1978.
[35] See the Trade Unions (Miscellaneous Provisions) Decree 1986, No. 17
[36] S. 10 Trade Unions (Amendment) Act, 1996 No. 4
[37] S. 33(3); Ss 2, 6(a) and10 ibid.
[38] Trade Unions (Amendment) Act, 1999 No. 1.
[39] The number 29 in the title is deleted; see s.10(a)(i) ibid.
[40] S. 10(a)(ii) ibid.

contains the jurisdictional areas of some of the unions in Part A[41] with some amendments made in the jurisdictional areas of some of the unions,[42] while Part C is a relisting of the unions of senior employees and employers under the heading "Senior Staff and Employers' Associations".[43]

The unions listed in Part A are deemed to be affiliated to the NLC.[44] It is an offence for a trade union not so listed to be affiliated to the NLC.[45] Any person, including any officer or official of a trade union, guilty of this offence is liable, on conviction, to a fine of ₦1,000 or twelve months imprisonment or to both such fine and imprisonment.[46] In addition, if the Minister is satisfied that there has been a violation of the provision concerning affiliation he may cause the name of the trade union concerned to be struck of the register of trade unions.[47]

No person is eligible to contest any elective post in the NLC unless he is a member of any of the unions specified in Part A of the third schedule,[48] i.e. all registered unions other than those of senior staff or employers. However, this requirement could be considerably watered-down by the application of the definition of member of trade union provided. Member of trade union means a person normally engaged in a trade or industry which the trade union represents a person either elected or appointed by a trade union to represent workers' interest.[49]

Every trade union must pay to the Nigeria Labour Congress, out of the contribution received from its members, a sum equal to 10 per cent of the total sum received or such sum as may, from time to time, be specified in the constitution of the NLC.[50] Any trade union which fails to pay its contribution is guilty of an offence and liable, on conviction, to a fine of twice the amount of

---

41 S. 33(3); see s.6(b) ibid

42 S. 10(b)(ii) ibid

43 S. 5(7); see S.2(b) ibid.; but re-enacting S. 5(7) and the relisting would appear superfluous since both serve no useful purpose; the registration of the unions in 1978 by virtue of the Trade Unions (Amendment) Decree 1978 No. 27 remains valid and subsisting by virtue of s. 6(b) of the Interpretation Act. Cap 192 in spite of the repeal of S.5(7) in 1996; the listing has no function whatsoever; the registration of trade unions is with the Registrar of Trade Unions.

44 S. 33(2); see S.6(a) Trade Unions (Amendment) Act 1996 No. 4.

45 S. 33(4); see ibid.

46 S. 33(5); see ibid.; it is not clear what subsections of S.33 are still in force; the confusion arises from the amendments made to the section by S.6(a) of the Trade Unions (Amendment) Act 1996 No. 4.

47 S. 33(6); see ibid.

48 S. 33(7); see s. 6(b) ibid.

49 S. 52; see S.8(b) Trade Unions (Amendment) Act 1999 No. 1; we have suggested the repeal of this definition; see *supra* p. 354.

50 S. 17(1); see S. 4 Trade Unions (Amendment) Act 1996 No.4; this obligation probably applies only with respect to the trade unions affiliated to the NLC and not to "every trade union."

the contribution.[51] And neither the institution of proceedings for the offence nor the imposition of a fine relieves the union from its liability to pay the contribution.[52]

Section 35 contains elaborate provisions for the admission of either a trade union or registered federation of trade unions as a "member" of a central labour organization. The provisions have remained dormant and now seem redundant unless membership of a central labour organisation is meant to be different from affiliation with it. The sections of Part 1 of the Act which are made applicable to federations of trade unions by section 31 are, also, with necessary modifications or exceptions, applicable to the NLC as they apply to trade unions.[53] These sections are 13, 15,. 18, 19(1) as far as it relates to capacity to be an official, 20 to 23, 26 and 28. They relate, respectively, to disqualification from holding office, prohibition of the application of dues for political purposes, right to restrain misapplication of funds, capacity to be a union official, registered office, sale of constitution, common law unlawfulness, immunity from tort action, change of name and alteration of the constitution. These sections have been discussed fully in relation to trade unions. Furthermore, the NLC must make an annual return to the Registrar in the same manner as trade unions.[54] Similarly, the treasurer of NLC is under an obligation to render accounts[55] and the other powers of the Registrar over the funds and accounts of trade unions are also exercisable in the same manner and to the same extent over the funds and accounts of the NLC.[56]

The statutory provisions within which the NLC may affiliate with any international trade union organization or trade secretariat have already been discussed.[57]

---

[51] S. 17(2).
[52] S. 17(3).
[53] S. 34(4).
[54] Ss .36 and 52
[55] Ss 37, 38 and 52.
[56] Ss. 39, 40, 48 and 52; these sections are discussed above with respect to trade unions.
[57] See above p. 378

Chapter 9

Legal framework of collective bargaining

Introduction

The term 'collective bargaining' is applied to those arrangements under which wages and conditions of employment are settled by a bargain, in the form of an agreement made between employers or associations of employers and workers' organizations.[1] The International Labour Organisation Convention No. 98 enjoins members of the Organisation to take measures appropriate to national conditions where necessary, to encourage and promote the full development and utilisation of machinery for voluntary negotiation between employers or employers' organization and workers' organisations, with a view to the regulation of terms and conditions of employment by means of collective agreements.[2]

The concept of voluntary collective bargaining has long been accepted by all sides to the employment relationship. Affirming this policy in 1954 Government said - Government re-affirms its confidence in the effectiveness of voluntary negotiation and collective bargaining for the determination of wages. The long term interest of government, employers and trade unions alike would seem to rest on the process of consultation and discussion which is the foundation of democracy in industry.[3] Again, in the Third National Development Plan for 1975-80, Government reiterated this policy as follows - The Government continues to pursue its policy of industrial self-government, whereby it encourages employers and workers to try to settle questions of wages and conditions of employment by collective bargaining and only intervenes in the last resort or in the public interest as an impartial conciliator or arbiter.[4] The

---

[1] Ministry of Labour (G. B.) *Industrial Relations Handbook*, revised edition, 1961, at p. 18.
[2] Article 4; Nigeria ratified the Convention on 17th October, 1960.
[3] *Annual Report* of the Department of Labour, 1954/55 para. 20.
[4] Third National Development Plan 1975-80, Vol . 283, para. 2 (e) .

Nigeria Employers Consultative Association[5] (NECA) has also proclaimed its commitment to the same policy. Thus, in its memorandum to the Morgan Commission in 1963 it stated as follows The Association wishes to state that since its inception it has subscribed to those policies and as far as it has been possible within the powers of the Association, it has encouraged its members to deal with responsible trade unions and to regulate relations between employers and workers by voluntary collective bargaining.

These avowals must not, however, be taken to indicate the measure of collective bargaining that has taken place in practice. Although there are no available data to show the extent to which collective bargaining is practiced there can, however, be no doubt that there has always been more collective bargaining in the private than in the public sector. In spite of the establishment of, first, Whitley councils, and later, Joint Negotiating Councils, in the public sector, there has not always been meaningful bargaining within the sector. The phenomenon of the appointment, on almost a regular basis, of Commissions to review and recommend wages and other conditions of employment of public servants is a clear manifestation of the absence of collective bargaining in the public sector.[6] Also, although there has been a decline in the appointment of wages commissions in recent years, the introduction, since 1968 of what is, in effect, compulsory arbitration of trade disputes would appear to have had a negative effect on collective bargaining, not only in the public, but also in the private sector.[7]

Nonetheless, the law has always provided a framework to encourage, promote and assist meaningful collective bargaining. It is generally accepted that trade unions, especially trade unions of employees, are a vital, if not an indispensable component, of the collective bargaining machinery. Hence the statutory law has always made provisions to ensure the existence of vigorous trade unions. As we have seen statute has legalized all trade unions which, at common law, would have been illegal. As we would see there are also statutory provisions which neutralise some of the common law wrongs which would otherwise hinder the unions in participating fully and actively in collective bargaining. In 1973 statutory provision was made, for the first time, for the compulsory recognition of registered trade unions by employers, obviously, for

---

[5] NECA is a voluntary non-profit making association of employers formed in 1957. Membership is open to association of employers as well as individual employers. It has hundreds of members including the most "influential" employers in the country.

[6] The Commissions include those headed by Gorsuch (1955); Mbanefo (1959); Morgan (1964); Elwood (1966); Adebo (1971) and Udoji (1975).

[7] See further below.

the purpose of collective bargaining. And as we have seen a major restructuring of the unions was undertaken in 1976-1978 in order to create larger and more viable unions. A further restructuring took place in 1996 resulting in only twenty-nine unions of those employees who would fall within the general description of junior workers.

Also, the first statute on the settlement of trade disputes enacted in 1941, gave maximum support to collective bargaining.[8] Although government was empowered, and it alone was so empowered, to intervene in the settlement of disputes it could appoint a conciliator only upon the application of either party to a dispute and after taking into consideration the existence and adequacy of means available for conciliation and the circumstances of the case. Similarly government could refer a dispute to an arbitration tribunal only where both parties to a dispute gave their consent and, where there was an existing arrangement for conciliation or arbitration, not unless and until there was a failure to obtain a settlement by the existing arrangement. And it appeared that neither the terms of settlement at conciliation nor an award at arbitration was binding on the parties. And there was a right to strike or lock-out in the sense that these activities were not prohibited by law. These positions remained the same until 1968. In 1960 a voluntary check-off system of payment of union dues was introduced with the objective of improving the finances of the unions and generally removing the need to depend on foreign subventions.[9] The check-off system became compulsory in 1978.[10]

However, in 1968, and since that year, there has been increasing statutory intervention in the collective bargaining process. The *coup d'etat* which took place on January 15, 1966, together with the ensuing political instability which culminated in a civil war in 1967 perhaps, brought about this change in policy. An emergency Decree in 1968, in effect, put a ban on strikes and lock-outs. It also introduced a quasi form of compulsory arbitration of trade disputes, which, no doubt, is an abridgment of the freedom to bargain collectively,[11] in place of the hitherto voluntary system.[12] The following year strikes and lock-outs were

[8] Trade Disputes (Arbitration & Inquiry) Ordinance No. 32 of 1941 applied only in Lagos until 1957 when it was made applicable to the whole country by the Trade Disputes (Arbitration and Inquiry) (Federal Application) Ordinance. No. 46 of 1957.

[9] Labour Code (Amendment) Act 1960 which took effect on January 26, 1961.

[10] Labour (Amendment) Act 1978. See now s. 5(3) Labour Act and s. 16A Trade Unions Act by virtue of s. 3 Trade Unions (Amendment) Decree 1996.

[11] See *Collymore* v. *Attorney General* [1970] AC 538, 547 per Lord Donovan in giving the judgment of the Privy Council.

[12] The Trade Disputes (Emergency Provisions) Decree No.21 of 1968. It suspended the Ordinance, later Act, of 1941.

expressly banned with a provision for a sanction of imprisonment for five years without option of a fine for any contravention. Employers were also prohibited from granting any general or percentage wage increase to any group of employees without the approval of the federal government.[13] In 1976 these provisions which were put forward and regarded as temporary war time measures were made permanent.[14] Any employer who grants a general or percentage wage increase to any group of employees without the approval of the Minister of Labour and Productivity will be guilty of an offence and, on conviction, liable, in the case of an individual to imprisonment for three years and in the case of a body corporate to a fine of ₦25,000.[15]

In 1977 a more far reaching enactment was put on the statute book. The Productivity, Prices and Incomes Board Decree, later Act, established the Productivity, Prices and Incomes Board with the functions, *inter alia*, to advise the governments on national incomes policy, inform them of current and incipient trends in wages and advise on guidelines within which increases in wages should be confined. The Board was also empowered to prepare guidelines on any question relating to wages or other forms of income or to prices, charges or other sums payable under transactions of any description. The Board issued annually an Incomes Policy Guidelines. Most of the Guidelines prohibited general increases in wages and salaries and the introduction of new fringe benefits or the upward revision of existing ones.[16] The Incomes Policy Guidelines 1993 was the last issued by the Board. It allowed increases in wages and salaries subject to the approval of government. Any revision of fringe benefits or the introduction of new ones also had to receive the approval of government. An application for approval of any negotiated benefits had to be accompanied by a copy of productivity schemes or evidence of improvement in productivity authenticated by the National Productivity Centre. In 1993 the 1977 statute was repealed and the Board dissolved by the National Salaries, Incomes and Wages Commission Act.[17] The functions of the Commission are similar to those of the dissolved Board although more extensive. They include, to advise the Federal Government on National incomes policy, recommend the proportions of income growth which should be utilised for general wage increase, inform the Federal Government of current and incipient trends in wages

---

[13] Trade Disputes (Emergency Provisions)(Amendment)(No.2) Decree No.53 of 1969.

[14] Trade Disputes Decree No.7 of 1976 as amended in 1977 now Cap .432.

[15] S.18 (1) and (2) Trade Disputes Act.

[16] See, e.g., *Nigerian Petroleum Refining Co. Ltd.* v. *Petroleum and Gas Senior Staff Association* 1982 - 83 NICLR 277.

[17] No. 99 of 1993.

and propose guidelines within which increases in wages should be confined, to examine, streamline and recommend salary scales applicable to each post in the public service, examine areas in which rationalization and harmonisation of wages, salaries and other conditions of employment are desirable and feasible as between the public and private sectors of the economy and recommend guidelines which will ensure sustained harmony in work compensation policies in both the public and private sectors, examine the salary structures in the public and private sectors and recommend a general wages framework with reasonable features of relativity and maximum levels which are in consonance with the national economy and examine the current rate of retirement benefits and recommend appropriate mechanism for periodic review of retirement benefits.[18] The power to issue guidelines is conferred on the Commission in words identical to those used in the earlier statute.[19] Any person who contravenes a guideline or regulation made under it will be guilty of an offence and liable, on conviction to a fine of ₦10,000 or imprisonment for a term of two years or to both.[20]

It is also provided that where a collective agreement between employers and employees involves increases in wages, salaries and fringe benefits three copies of the agreement must be submitted to the Commission for advice.[21] But the purpose for this provision is not clear.

The present position may be stated in the words of government as follows: In recent years government has introduced a system of issuing guidelines which regulate wage increases as a way of moderating inflationary trends in the economy. While it is the intention of government to retain this partial control mechanism, the essence of policy will be to encourage collective bargaining and free negotiation within the limits suggested in the guidelines as a means of democratising industrial relations.[22]

Institutionalised collective bargaining

The main purpose of collective bargaining remains to settle terms and conditions of employment. As Lord Donovan put it for the Privy Council-It is, of course, true that the main purpose of most trade unions of employees is the improvement

---

[18] S. 3 ibid.; altogether the functions number 18.
[19] S. 10 ibid.
[20] S. 11 ibid.
[21] S. 13 ibid.
[22] Fourth National Development Plan 1980-85 Vol. 1 p. 306.

of wages and conditions.[23] However statute has always taken a hand in regulating the employment relationship usually by establishing minimum terms and conditions of employment although statutory regulation has been inadequate not only in respect of the quality and quantity of its provisions but also with respect to the area or subject matter covered. Thus, for example, matters such as job security, redundancy, health, welfare and safety of workers have not received as much statutory intervention as modern employment conditions would appear to demand.

The question of employee participation in decision making at his place of work, often referred to as industrial democracy, has received only rudimentary attention and only in company law. However statute gave rather early attention to the protection of certain categories of employees. As we have seen this began with an Ordinance of 1877 and has culminated in the Labour Act already discussed extensively. The statutory provisions on workmen's compensation and factories have also been similarly discussed. There are also statutory provisions on minimum wages and conditions, pensions and gratuities, training of employees and settlement of industrial disputes .

Wages boards system

Machinery for the fixing of minimum wages has long been institutionalized by law. The first statute was the Labour (Amendment) Ordinance No. 17 of 1932 which amended the Labour Ordinance No.1 of 1929 to confer power on the Governor in Council to fix minimum wages where the Governor found that wages of any class of labourers were unreasonably low. These powers were later enacted as the Labour (Wage Fixing and Registration) Ordinance No.40 of 1943. The Governor in Council was empowered to fix a minimum wage for any occupation in Nigeria or any part of Nigeria in which he was satisfied that the wages were unreasonably low. The order fixing such minimum wage could include the fixing of minimum wages for piece-work, time work or the minimum wages to be paid to any special classes of employees within the occupation. However, the Governor could act only upon the recommendation of a Labour Advisory Board. The provisions of the 1943 Ordinance were later incorporated into the Labour Code Ordinance 1945 but later again became the Wages Board Ordinance 1957. The 1957 Ordinance, later Act,[24] was itself repealed by the

[23] *Collymore* v. *Attorney-General* [1970] AC 538, 547.
[24] Designation of Ordinances Act 1961

Wages Board and Industrial Councils Act No. 1 of 1973. This Act has extended considerably the principles which hitherto underlined our minimum wages policy.

In addition to the powers for the establishment of Industrial Wages Board it provides for the establishment of a National Wages Board and Area Minimum Wages Committees and for some regulation of Joint Industrial Councils. The provisions of the Wages Board and Industrial Councils Act do not apply to all employees but, like the Labour Act, apply only to employees who fall within the definition of the term worker given in the Labour Act.[25]

Industrial wages board

There are two ways in which an industrial wages board may be established. The first is that the Minister of Labour and Productivity may, by order, direct that an industrial wages board be established in relation to the workers described in the order itself and their employers if he is of the opinion that wages are unreasonably low or that no adequate machinery exists for the effective regulation of wages or other conditions of employment of those workers.[26] The Minister must, in the order establishing the Board, determine the area with respect to which it may exercise any of its powers and perform any of its duties.[27] The second procedure is more elaborate and is, perhaps the method that should normally be employed in establishing an industrial wages board.[28] If the Minister is of the opinion that wages are unreasonably low or no adequate machinery exists for the effective regulation of wages or other conditions of employment of any workers, he may refer the question whether an industrial wages board should be established with respect to any of those workers and their employers to a Commission of Inquiry.[29] The Commission must publish its terms

[25] S. 27(2) Wages & Industrial Councils Act, Cap. 466.

[26] S. 1(1). Local Government workers may not be included, proviso s.1 (1); the Governor of a State may also exercise this power to establish a board within his state and may include local government workers, but only after consultation with the Minister. However, a Governor may not exercise this power where the Minister's order has been made; similarly, where a Governor has made an order the Minister cannot make an order establishing a board so long as the Governor's order subsists; s. 2(1) and (2) ibid.

[27] S. 1(2) ibid.

[28] In introducing the Wages Board Bill in the House of Representative in 1957 the then Minister of Labour and Welfare suggested that the use of the first method should generally be exceptional. See House of Representative's Debates 1957 Vol. I, p. 487.

[29] S. 3 Wages Board & Industrial Councils Act; a Commission of Inquiry is appointed by the Minister and consists of three independent persons, one of whom may be appointed chairman and another deputy chairman to act in the absence of the chairman, and not more than two persons

of reference and state a period of not less than forty days within which it will consider written representations. It may hear oral evidence and must make all such investigations as appear to it to be necessary and must consider any written representatives made to it.[30] If the Commission is of opinion, with respect to the workers with whom it is concerned, that wages are not unreasonably low or that there exists adequate machinery for regulating the wages or other conditions of employment of those workers, and that there is no reason to believe that the machinery is likely to cease to exist or cease to be adequate for that purpose, it must report accordingly to the Minister.[31]

It may include in its report any suggestions which it may think fit to make as to the improvement of that machinery and the Minister may take such steps as appear to him to be expedient and practicable to secure the improvements.[32]

If, however, the Commission is of opinion with respect to the workers with whom it is concerned that wages are unreasonably low or that no adequate machinery for regulating the wages or other conditions of employment does exist or that the existing machinery is likely to cease to exist or cease to be adequate for that purpose and that as a result reasonable standards of wages or other conditions of employment are not being or will not be maintained, the Commission may make a report to the Minister accordingly.[33] It may include in its report a recommendation called "an industrial wages board recommendation" for the establishment of an industrial wages board in respect of those workers and their employers.[34] If the Minister thinks fit he may make an industrial wages board order giving effect to the recommendation.[35] However, the Minister may refer the report back to the Commission and the Commission must then reconsider it having regard to any observations made by the Minister and must make a further report which may similarly be referred back to the Commission.[36]

---

representing employers and an equal number representing workers in relation to whom the commission is to operate. Before appointing the employers' and workers' representatives, the Minister must consult with such organizations representing employers and workers respectively as he thinks fit. The representatives must be persons who are not themselves connected with the subject of inquiry. Assessors may be appointed but they can neither vote nor be parties to any report or recommendation of the Commission; independent person means a person who is a retired or self-employed member of the professional classes, or a member of the judiciary, the clergy or the teaching staff of a university; s. 24(7) and Schedule 1 ibid.

[30] S. 7(1) ibid.

[31] S. 4(1) ibid.

[32] S. 4(1) and (2) ibid.

[33] S. 4(3) ibid.

[34] Ibid.

[35] S. 4(4) ibid.

[36] S. 7(3) ibid., this should be subsection (2) since s. 7 has only two subsections.

Before making any industrial wages board order under either procedure, the Minister must publish a notice in the Federal Gazette of his intention to do so.[37] The notice must contain the text of the proposed order and must specify the time, which must not be more than forty days from the date of publication, within which any objection made with respect to the order must be made to the Minister.[38] Every objection must be in writing and must state the specific grounds of the objection and the omission, additions or modifications asked for. The Minister must consider any objection properly made to him but no other.[39] After considering all the objections, he may make the order without amendments or make the order with such amendments as he considers necessary or expedient or refrain from making the order.[40] Where the Minister makes an industrial wages board order he must publish it and the report of a Commission of inquiry where applicable in the Federal Gazette. The order comes into operation on the date on which it is so published or on such later date as the order may specify.[41]

The members of an Industrial Wages Board are appointed by the Minister after consultation with the organization, if any, which appear to him to represent the employers or workers directly concerned.[42] An industrial wages board consists of not more than three independent persons,[43] and such number of persons who in the Minister's opinion, represent employers in relation to whom the board is to operate and an equal number of persons who in his opinion represent workers in relation to whom the board is to operate.[44] The Minister must appoint the chairman from among the independent members and may appoint a deputy chairman, also from among the independent members, to act in the absence of the chairman and must appoint a secretary who must be a labour officer.[45] The members of a board hold office on such conditions as may be determined by the Minister.[46]

An industrial wages board may recommend the wages to be paid by the employers to their workers described in the order establishing the board.[47] A board may also, if the Minister has given his permission for it to consider the

---

[37] S. 5(1) ibid.
[38] S. 5(2) ibid.; quaere whether not "less" is intended.
[39] S. 5(4) ibid.
[40] S. 5(5) ibid.
[41] S. 5(6) ibid.
[42] S. 24(7) and Schedule 1.
[43] See f. n . 29 for meaning of independent member.
[44] Schedule 1 ibid.
[45] Ibid.
[46] Ibid.
[47] S. 8(1) ibid.

making of a recommendation for a condition or conditions of employment other than wages, either generally or for any particular work, make such a recommendation for the workers to whom the board refers.[48] However, before recommending any wages or condition, the board must publish a notice of the wages or condition it proposes to recommend and the manner in which and the time, not being less than forty days from the date of the notice, in which objections to the recommendation may be made and must consider any objections properly lodged.[49]

Where a board has recommended any wages or any other condition of employment it must, forthwith, send notification of it to the Minister and the notification may include a statement of the date from which the board recommends that the wages or condition should become effective.[50] On receipt of a notification the Minister must, by order, fix the wages or condition but he may, if he thinks fit, refer the recommendation back to the Board which must then reconsider it having regard to any observations made by the Minister and may, if it thinks fit, resubmit it to the Minister either without amendment or with such amendments as it thinks fit having regard to the Minister's observations.[51] Where recommendations are so re-submitted it may similarly be referred back and the board may treat it in the same manner.[52] It is clear that the Minister cannot himself amend any recommendation and, on the other hand, the recommendation cannot have force of law without an order of the Minister fixing the recommended wages or conditions.[53]

Wages and conditions fixed by order of the Minister are known as statutory minimum wages and statutory minimum conditions respectively. An employer must pay to the worker wages not less than the statutory minimum wages clear of all deductions except those required by law or in respect of contributions to provident or pension funds or schemes agreed to by the workers and approved by the Governor of the appropriate State.[54] Similarly, an employer must, in cases to which the statutory minimum condition is applicable, apply to the worker a condition not less favourable to the worker than the statutory minimum

[48] S. 9(1) ibid.

[49] Ss. 8(2) and 9(2) Wage; Board s Industrial Councils Act.

[50] S. 10(1) ibid.

[51] S. 10(2)(a) and (b) ibid.

[52] S. 10(2) ibid.

[53] No order can have effect so as to prejudice any rights touching conditions of employment, holidays or wages conferred upon any worker by or under any other enactment or other written law; s.11 ibid.

[54] S.12(1)ibid.

condition.[55] An employer who fails to so pay the statutory minimum wage or apply the statutory minimum condition is guilty of an offence and on conviction liable to a fine not exceeding ₦200 and in the case of a continuing offence to a fine not exceeding ₦50 for each day or period during which the offence continues.[56] The court may by the conviction adjudge the employer convicted to pay in addition to any fine, such sum as appears to the court to be due to the worker on account of wages, the wages being calculated on the basis of the statutory minimum wages, or, in the case of statutory minimum condition, such sum by way of compensation as may appear to the court to be due to the worker by reason of the failure.[57]

However, the power of the court to order such payment is not in derogation of the right of the worker to recover wages or any sum as may be due to him by any other proceedings in a court of competent jurisdiction.[58] Any agreement for the payment of wages or the application of any other condition of employment in contravention of the above provisions is void.[59] However, if the Minister is satisfied that any worker employed or who desires to be employed in any occupation to which statutory minimum wages are applicable is affected by any infirmity or physical injury which renders him incapable of earning the statutory minimum wages, he may if he thinks fit, grant to the worker a permit exempting him from the payment of wages less than the statutory minimum wages.[60] The permit may be made subject to such conditions, if any, as the Minister may impose. While the permit is in force and any conditions imposed are complied with, the employer will not be guilty of an offence if he pays to the workers wages less than the statutory minimum wages. A permit may be so granted as to have effect from the date on which the application for it was made to the Minister and may be suspended or revoked at any time by the Minister.[61]

An industrial wages board must consider, as occasion requires, any matter referred to it by the Minister with reference to the conditions of employment of the workers in respect of whom and in respect of whose employers the board has been appointed and must make a report on it to the Minister.[62]

---

[55] S. 12(3) ibid.
[56] S. 12(1),(3) ibid.
[57] S. 12(2) and (4) ibid.
[58] ibid.
[59] S. 12 (6) ibid.
[60] S. 13(1) ibid.
[61] S. 13(2) ibid.
[62] S. 14, ibid.

Every employer of workers in respect of whom an industrial wages board order has been made or a notice of intention to make an order has been published has a duty to keep such records of wages or conditions of employment as are necessary to show that the provisions of the Act are being complied with as respects persons in his employment. He must retain such records for a period of three years. He must also cause to be kept posted in some conspicuous place in the place of employment in such manner and in such form as may be approved by the Minister a copy of every notice relating to wages or conditions of employment of the workers which is published by an industrial wages board as required by the Act and a copy of every order made by the Minister relating to the wages or conditions of employment of the workers or such abstract from every such notice as the Minister may approve. Failure to do so is an offence and on conviction punishable with a fine not exceeding ₦100 and a daily penalty not exceeding ₦10.[63]

The very significant point must be made that the wages board system has never been intended to be a substitute for primary collective bargaining between management and employees' organization. Indeed, the tripartite nature of the composition of an industrial wages board is intentional and aimed at infusing the spirit and practice of negotiation and bargaining in the members of the board. Thus, the fact that both sides will have to convince the independent members will make for careful and well-reasoned arguments based on relevant facts of the matter at issue. Frequent meeting of both sides in this way should lead to greater respect and understanding of the other side's point of view.[64] Unlike a Labour Advisory Board under the earlier statutes, an industrial wages board once established continues in existence until abolished. It has a duty to keep the wages and conditions of the workers for whom it is established under continuous review. Accordingly, the Act provides that, if at any time, the Minister considers that the wages or other conditions of employment of workers to whom an industrial wages board order relates or the machinery for the regulation of those wages or conditions have been so altered as to render the industrial wages board unnecessary, he may, by order, abolish it.[65] The Act has abolished all the wages boards established under the 1957 Act.[66] However it saves all the Orders under that Act as well as the Orders in Council made under the earlier statutes.[67] While,

---

[63] S. 15 ibid.

[64] See E.E. Uvieghara, "The Wages Board System in Nigeria," *The Nigeria Law Journal* Vol . 8 1974 p. 1

[65] S. 6 ibid.

[66] S. 26(2) and schedule 2(2).

[67] S. 26 and schedule 2(1) (b) and (c) .

clearly, the minimum wages fixed under the Orders in Council or Order have become grossly inadequate and are, in any case, superseded by the national minimum wage fixed by statute, the conditions of employment remain relevant.[68] Some of the matters dealt with include age for employment, maximum working hours, sick leave with pay, holiday with pay, medical attention, intervals for meals and washing facilities. Some have provisions for safety devices and conditions of domestic service. For example, the Retail and Ancillary Trades (Lagos) Minimum Remuneration and Conditions of Employment Order, 1960 in addition to laying down minimum wages in respect of workers engaged in retail sale of goods in Lagos also deals with their conditions of employment. Thus cashiers, sales clerks, shop assistants, store keepers, copy typists, custom clerks, book-keepers who are engaged in retail sale in Lagos seem entitled to two weeks holiday with pay in a year while watchmen, messengers and labourers are entitled to one week holiday with pay in a year. All the workers covered by the order are entitled, it seems, after a period of six months continuous employment, to sick leave with pay of seven days in any period of six months. They are also given a limited right to medical treatment at the expense of their employer. And both the sick leave pay and medical treatment are in addition to any claim under the workmen's compensation scheme.

Although the wages boards established under the Act of 1957 have been dissolved no industrial wages board has been established under the current statute. It will thus appear that the whole system has gone into disuse. The Nigeria Employers' Consultative Association once expressed the view "that any justification for wages board or other similar government legislation will disappear in due course of time as each industry, and every industry, begins to settle its own affairs through the process of collective bargaining." This does not appear to be the case. It appears, instead, that both the wages board system and collective bargaining have not found their feet.

---

[68] See the conditions of Employment (Tailoring, Shirt-making and Ancillary Trades or Occupations) Order in Council; The Conditions of Employment (Printing and Allied Trades or Occupations) Order in Council; The conditions of Employment (Minefield) Order in Council; The conditions of Employment (Motor Industry Trades and Occupations)(Lagos State) Order, in Council; The conditions of Employment (Stevedore and Dock Labour in the Port of Lagos) Order in Council; The conditions of Employment (Catering Trade) (Lagos State) Order in Council; The conditions of Employment (Building and Civil Engineering Industry) (Lagos State) Order in Council; and the Retail and Ancillary Trade (Lagos) Minimum Remuneration and conditions of Employment Order. See Wages Boards and Industrial Councils Act, Cap. 466, List of subsidiary Legislation.

National wages board and Area minimum wages committees

The Wages Board and Industrial Councils Act also makes provision for other machinery for settling of the terms and conditions of employment of workers. The agreement signed between the government of the Federation, the Nigeria Employers' Consultative Association and officials of the Joint Action Committee of Trade Unions on 24 July, 1964, in conclusion of the negotiations which followed the general strike of June 1964 provided, *inter alia*, for the establishment of a National Wages Council and a National Joint Industrial Council for each major industry in the country. These terms of the agreement have been given effect to in the Act.

The Minister may, by order, establish a board to be known as the National Wages Board, for the Federation and may, after consultation with the Governor of a State, set up an Area Minimum Wages Committee for the State.[69] The functions of the Board will be:

i) to examine the application to all unskilled workers of any agreed minimum wage rate in any specified area;
ii) to examine from time to time the adequacy of minimum wage rates for unskilled workers in the light of any recommendations received from area minimum wages committees;
iii) to consider any matter referred to it by the Minister with reference to the minimum rates of unskilled workers in any area for which an area minimum wages committee has been set up; and
iv) to report and make recommendations accordingly to the Minister.[70]

The functions of an Area Minimum Wages Committee are:

i) to make recommendations to the Board on the minimum wages of unskilled workers in the committee's area;
ii) to carry out specific investigations on matters referred to it by the Board;
iii) to submit to the Board reports, minutes and any other information it considers desirable for the effective exercise of the Board's functions and
iv) to determine urban and rural sub-areas in its area.[71]

---

[69] S. 16(1) Wages Board and Industrial Councils Act.
[70] S. 16(2) ibid.

Both the Board and the Committees are therefore, to be concerned primarily with the minimum wages payable to unskilled workers. However in 1981 a national minimum wages was fixed by statute[72] although an earlier recommendation for the enactment of a three zonal minimum wage had been rejected by government.[73]

Joint industrial councils

Employers and workers in an industry may establish a joint industrial council for the purpose of negotiating and reaching agreements relating to such matters as are considered by the parties to be matters for negotiation.[74] Where a council is established it must register its agreed constitution and functions with the Minister and any changes agreed upon from time to time must also be so registered.[75] Where a council has agreed on any matter concerning wages or conditions of employment for any specified workers or group of workers in an industry it must register the agreement with the Minister for his information. However, the Minister may, by order declare that the provisions of the agreement or any part of it "shall be binding on the workers to whom they relate, and that effect shall be given to them accordingly."[76] The effect of this provision is not quite clear. It may mean either that the agreement or part of it so declared is binding only on the workers who must then give effect to it accordingly, or that although, binding only on the workers to whom it relates, effect must be given to it by the employers. The latter interpretation is obviously preferable but it will put undue strain on the words employed by the provision.

A council which reaches an agreement may apply to the Minister to have the terms of such an agreement extended to cover other employers and workers within the industry to which the agreement relates.[77] However, upon receipt of such an application, the Minister must satisfy himself that the organizations of employers and workers concerned represent a sufficient proportion of the employers and workers in the industry in question having regard to its individual circumstances.[78] If the Minister is so satisfied, he must then publish a notice in

---

[72] National Minimum Wage Act; see below.

[73] Salaries and Wages Review Commission 1970-71 headed by Adebo.

[74] S.18(1) ibid.

[75] S.18(2) ibid.

[76] S.18(3) ibid.

[77] S.19(1) ibid.

[78] S.19(2) ibid.

the Federal Gazette specifying the terms of the agreement and indicating his intention to make an order extending all or any of the terms of the agreement to such employers and workers engaged in the industry as are not parties to the agreement and specifying also the time, being not more[79] than forty days from the date of the notice, within which any objection to his intention must be made to him. Every objection must be in writing and must state the specific grounds of the objection and the omissions, additions and modifications asked for and the Minister must consider any objections properly made to him.[80]

After considering all the objections the Minister may make the order without amendments or make the order with such amendments as he considers necessary or expedient or refrain from making the order.[81] Where an order is made it must specify the employers and workers to whom the agreement is to be extended.[82] The order must be published in the Federal Gazette and it comes into operation on the date of publication or on such later date as the order may specify.[83] Any wages or conditions of employment fixed by an order have effect as if they are statutory minimum wages or statutory minimum conditions, as the case may be, fixed upon the recommendation of an industrial wages board.[84] Thus, the same enforcement procedures and sanctions for infringement apply.

There is, however, provision for exempting an employer from an order. An employer affected by an order may appeal in writing to the Minister for a permit of exemption from the order.[85] On receipt of such an appeal, the Minister may reject it off hand or refer it to any person or persons appointed by himself for investigation. Where the appeal is referred, having regard to the grounds of the appeal and the circumstances of the employer, the investigator must submit a report to the Minister within sixty days from the date of appointment.[86] The Minister may either reject the appeal or issue an exemption permit accordingly specifying in the permit the minimum wage and conditions which must apply to the workers engaged by the employer.[87] Such wages and conditions have effect as minimum statutory wages and minimum statutory conditions respectively.[88]

---

[79] Quaere whether not "less."
[80] S. 19(3) ibid.
[81] S. 19(4) ibid.
[82] S. 19(2) (a) ibid.
[83] S. 19(5) ibid.
[84] S. 19(6) ibid.
[85] S. 20.
[86] S. 20(2) ibid.
[87] S. 20(3) ibid.
[88] S.24(4) ibid.

National minimum wage

In 1980, the Nigeria Labour Congress put up a charter of demands which included the fixing of a national minimum wage. This led to the enactment of the National Minimum Wage Act in 1981. The Act lays down a national minimum Wage. Every employer must pay a wage not less than a national minimum wage of ₦5,500 per month to every employee under his establishment.[89] Any agreement for the payment of wages less than the national minimum wage is void and has no effect whatsoever.[90] The employer must pay the wage clear of all deductions except those required by law or deductions in respect of contributions to provident or pension funds or schemes agreed to by the employees and approved by the Minister.[91] If the employer fails to do so he is guilty of an offence and on conviction liable to a fine not exceeding ₦100 and in the case of a continuing offence to a fine not exceeding ₦10 for each day during which the offence continues. On conviction for an offence the court may make an order that the convicted employer must pay, in addition to any fine, such sum as appears to the court to be due to the employee on account of wages, the wages being calculated on the basis of the national minimum wages.[92] However, this power of the court is not in derogation of the right of the employee himself to recover wages due to him by any other proceedings in a court of competent jurisdiction.

The duty to pay the national minimum wage does not apply to an employer in an establishment in which less than fifty employees are employed[93] or in which employees are employed on part-time basis[94] or at which employees are paid on commission or piece-rate basis[95] or in respect of employees in seasonal employment such as agriculture or to any person employed in a vessel or air-craft to which the laws regulating merchant shipping or civil aviation apply.[96] In addition, the Minister may, by order published in the *Gazette*, grant other

[89] S. 1(1) National Minimum Wage Act, cap. 267, as amended by the National Minimum Wage (Amendment) Act, 2000.

[90] S. 1 (2) ibid.

[91] S. 3(1) ibid.

[92] S. 3(2) ibid.

[93] The number of 50 was raised to 500 by the National Minimum Wage (Amendment) Order 1986 but the status quo was restored after protests from the Unions; see the National Minimum Wage (Amendment) (Revocation) Order 1987

[94] Part time work means work of a duration of less than 40 hours per week; S. 9 ibid., what is not clear is whether all the employees must be employed on part time basis or whether if only some are so employed the whole establishment is exempt.

[95] The comment in f. n . 94 above applies *mutatis mutandi.*

[96] S . 2 (1) National Minimum Wage Act.

exemptions as he deems necessary in the interest of the national economy taking into consideration reports from wages boards[97] or such other body as might make representation for exemption.[98]

If the Minister is satisfied that any employee, in employment or desiring to be employed in any occupation to which the national minimum wage is applicable is affected by an infirmity or physical injury which renders him incapable of earning the national minimum wage, the Minister may, if he thinks fit, grant a permit to the employer, subject to such conditions, if any, as he may impose, exempting him from the provision relating to the payment of wages less than the national minimum wage in respect of the employee. While such permit is in force and any conditions imposed are complied with, the employer will not be guilty of an offence if he pays to the employees a lesser wage than the national minimum wage. A permit may be so granted as to have effect from the date on which the application was made to the Minister and may be suspended or revoked at any time by the Minister.[99]

Every employer who is affected by the Act must keep such records of wages or conditions of employment as are necessary to show that the provisions of the Act are being complied with in respect of the employees in his employment.[100] Such records must be retained for a period of three years and if the employer fails to do so, he is guilty of any offence and on conviction liable to a fine not exceeding ₦100 and to a penalty not exceeding ₦10 for each day during which the offence continues.[101]

Administration of the Act

The Minister may authorize any public officer in the civil service of the Federation to act for the purpose of the Act and every authorized labour officer within that term in the Labour Act is deemed to have been so authorized.[102]

Every authorized officer must be furnished with a certificate of his authority and when visiting an employer's premises for the purposes of the Act he must, if so required, produce the certificate to the employer or other person holding a responsible position of management at the premises.[103] An authorized officer

---

[97] They are, since 1973, called Industrial Wages Boards.
[98] S. 2 (2) National Minimum Wage Act.
[99] S. 4(1) ibid.
[100] S. 5 ibid.
[101] S. 5 ibid.
[102] S. 6(1) ibid.
[103] S. 6(2) ibid.

may require the production by an employer of conditions of employment and inspect and examine them and copy any part or order any person found to have contravened any provision of the Act to take remedial action within a specified period of time and, subject generally to the powers of the Attorney-General of the Federation, institute proceedings for any offence under the Act, if he so wishes, appear and have all the necessary powers for the conduct of the proceedings.[104]

An officer who is authorized by general or special directions of the Minister may, if it appears to him that a sum is due from an employer to an employee, on account of the payment of wages less than the national minimum wage, may institute on behalf and in the name of the employee civil proceedings for the recovery of that sum.[105] In any such proceedings the court may make an order for the payment of costs by the authorized officer as if he were a party to the proceedings.[106] However, the power of an authorized officer to take proceedings is not in derogation of any right of the employee himself to recover the sum by civil proceedings.[107]

Any person who refuses or neglects to furnish the means required by an authorized officer as being necessary for any entry in the exercise of his powers or hinders him in the exercise of his powers or refuses or neglects to produce any document or to give any information which an officer in the exercise of his powers requires him to produce or give, is guilty of an offence.[108] Similarly, any person who makes or causes to be made or knowingly allows to be made any wages sheet, record of wages or record of conditions of employment which is false in any material particular or produces or causes to be produced or knowingly allows to be produced any such wages sheet or record to an officer acting in the exercise of his powers knowing the wage sheet or record to be false or furnishes any information to an authorized officer acting in the exercise of his powers knowing the information to be false is guilty of an offence. An offence is punishable, on conviction with a fine not exceeding ₦500 or to imprisonment for a period not exceeding three months or to both such fine and imprisonment.

Where an offence for which an employer is liable to a penalty has in fact been committed by some agent of the employer or by some other person that agent or person is liable to be proceeded against for the offence in the same

[104] S. 6(3) ibid.
[105] S. 6(4) ibid.
[106] S. 6(4) ibid.
[107] S. 6(5) ibid.
[108] S. 8 ibid.

manner as if he were the employer.[109] Where an employer is charged with an offence he is entitled, upon complaint duly made by him and on giving to the prosecution not less than three days' notice in writing of his intention, to have any other person to whose act or default he alleges the offence was due, brought before the court at the time appointed for the hearing of the charge. If, after the commission of the offence have been proved, the employer proves that the offence was due to the act or default of that other person, that person may be charged with the offence or if the employer further proves that he had used all due diligence to secure that the Act is complied with, he must be acquitted of the offence.[110] The prosecution as well as the person whom the employer charges with the offence has the right to cross-examine him if he gives evidence and also any witness called by him in support of his plea and to call rebutting evidence.[111] The court may make such order as it thinks fit for the payment of costs by any party to the proceedings, other than the prosecution, to any other party. Where it appears to an authorized officer than an offence has been committed in respect of which proceedings might be undertaken against an employer under the Act and the officer is reasonably satisfied that the offence was due to the act or default of some other person and that the employer could establish a defence under the above provision the officer may cause proceedings to be taken against that other person. In any such proceedings the person may be charged with the offence and on proof that the offence was due to his act or default be convicted for the offence for which the employer might have been charged.[112]

The Act may be criticized on the ground that it does not offer any protection to those employees who are in greater need of statutory protection. It is the small employer, whose employees are most unlikely to be union members, who is more likely to pay starvation wages. The only justification for excluding employees whose employer employs less than fifty persons is perhaps the need not to create more unemployment. An equally serious defect of the Act is the absence of an indexation provision. Even at the time of the promulgation of the Act, it was not clear that the stipulated wage was adequate. It seemed to have been based solely on the alleged inability of the various governments to pay a higher wage![113]

---

[109] S. 7(1) ibid.

[110] S. 7(2) ibid.

[111] S. 7(3) ibid.

[112] S. 7(4) ibid.

[113] See the Report of the Senate Committee on Labour on the Issue of a National Minimum Wage and Other Labour Matters - the Report contains the views of the various State Governments, the Nigeria Employers' Consultative Association, the Nigeria Labour Congress and others. For a detailed consideration see E.E. Uvieghara, "The Wages Board System in Nigeria," NLJ Vol. 8, 1974, p. 1.

Retirement pensions

The modernisation of society has, no doubt, brought about enormous improvements in our lives. But it has also brought about a number of drawbacks. One such drawback is the collapse or near collapse of the extended family tradition and the consequent eclipse of the succour it used to offer especially to the needy, the young and the aged. Old age care is ceasing to be a matter for the family but instead is becoming more a matter for the individual himself. Increasingly employees are worrying about what would happen to them when they retire; that is, when they can no longer offer their labour for wages. And more and more they are giving greater attention to the provision for pension after retirement, pension itself being a product of modernization.

The payment of pension and gratuity was introduced in the public service within the first three years of the last century.[114] But there was no absolute right to pension[115] and it ceased either upon conviction[116] or bankruptcy.[117] It was, however, made not assignable.[118]

To-day pension in the public service is regulated by the Constitution. The Constitution provides that the right of a person in the public service of the Federation or of a state to receive pension or gratuity shall be regulated by law and that any benefit to which a person is entitled in accordance with or under such law must not be withheld or altered to his disadvantage except to such extent as is permissible under any law.[119] In addition it provides that pensions must be reviewed every five years or together with any civil service salary review, whichever is earlier, and also that pensions in respect of service in the public service of the Federation or a State must not be taxed.[120]

The current law on pensions in the public service is the Pensions Act.[121] It provides that any pension or gratuity granted to any person on his retirement

---

[114] See e. g. Pensions Proclamation No. 14 of 1901 of the Protectorate of Northern Nigeria and Pensions Ordinance No. 4 of 1902 of the Colony of Lagos.

[115] S. 9 Pensions Ordinance No. 4 of 1902.

[116] S. 11 ibid.

[117] S. 12 ibid.

[118] S. 10 ibid.; it is noteworthy that salary, upon which pension was based, was defined to include personal allowance, house allowance or the estimated value of free quarters and any fees paid out by way of salary; schedule to Ord. No. 4 of 1902.

[119] Ss. 173 and 210 Constitution of the Federal Republic of Nigeria, 1999.

[120] Ibid.

[121] Cap . 346 Laws of the Federation of Nigeria, 1990; the States have similar statutes.

from the public service of the Federation must be computed on the final pay of the person entitled to it.[122] Retirement is defined to mean cessation of service after service for a period of not less than fifteen years, that period being the stipulated period which qualifies an officer for a pension and gratuity.[123] But pension or gratuity would be granted to an officer only where he retires in any of the following circumstances:[124] voluntary retirement after fifteen years continuous service, compulsory retirement upon attaining the age of sixty years,[125] compulsory retirement for the purpose of facilitating improvements in an officer's department or ministry for greater efficiency or economy, on certification by a properly constituted medical board that an officer is no longer mentally or physically capable of carrying out the functions of his office, on total or permanent disablement while in service, on abolition of office as a result of a reorganization in a department or ministry and on being giving three months' notice to retire by the Federal Civil Service Commission, requirement by the Federal Civil Service Commission to retire on the ground that the retirement is in the public interest. Pension and or gratuity are also payable where an officer dies in service or in the course of his official duty or is missing and presumed dead.[126]

Pension must be paid for a minimum period of five years after retirement.[127] The amount payable either as gratuity or pension depends on the amount of the final pay and the number of years of service after the qualifying period for the grant of gratuity or pension. However, in the case of pension, the amount must not exceed 70 per cent of the highest pensionable emoluments earned at any time during the course of service.[128]

Pensions and gratuities are not assignable or transferable or liable to be withheld, attached, sequestrated or levied upon for or in respect of any debt or claim except for the purpose of satisfying a debt due to the Federal Government or an order of any court for the payment of periodical sums of money towards the maintenance of the wife or former wife or minor child of the officer to whom

---

[122] S. 1 Pensions Act. Final pay now includes various allowances; see esp. Circular No. 63216/5.1/X/702 of 25th January, 1993.

[123] S. 24 Pensions Act.

[124] S. 3(1) ibid.

[125] S. 4(1) ibid.; by s. 4 (2) the Minister may require an officer to retire at any time after he has attained 45 years merely by giving him three months' notice in writing.

[126] Ss. 5, 6 and 10, ibid., respectively.

[127] S. 11 ibid.

[128] S. 22(1) ibid.; there are a number of statutory exceptions which allow 100% pension, see e.g. for judges Pension Rights of Judges Act, Cap. 347; see now S.291(3) of the Constitution; for the Inspector-General of Police, Police (Pension Rights of Inspect-General of Police) Act No. 66 of 1993 and for University academic staff, s. 9 Universities (Miscellaneous Provisions) Act 1993, No 11.

a pension or gratuity has been granted.[129] Where the minister is satisfied that a sum is due to the Federal Government from an officer to whom a pension or gratuity has been granted or that an overpayment of pension or gratuity has been made to an officer, the minister may authorise the deduction from the pension or gratuity such sum or overpayment at such times as he may think fit.[130]

Private sector

The National Provident Fund Scheme was established in 1961 essentially for the private sector.[131] Contributions to the Fund were made by both employers and employees. The main benefits were retirement, survivorship and invalidity benefits. Criticism of the scheme was rife. The benefits were small in amount. Benefits often took a long time to be paid and sometimes claims were not met at all. The Nigeria Social Insurance Trust Fund was, therefore, established in place of the NPF.[132]

The new Fund covers every person who is employed (i) by a company incorporated under the Companies and Allied Matters Act, or (ii) by a partnership irrespective of the number of persons employed by the company or partnership, or (iii) in any other case, where the number of persons employed is not less than five.[133] All such employees and their employers must register with the Nigeria Social Insurance Trust Fund Management Board which is the body established to manage the Fund.[134] The existence of a private pension scheme in respect of workers[135] in such employment does not exempt such employees or their employer from the provisions of the Act.[136] In other words such employees and their employer must register with the Board although there is a private pension scheme in operation. In effect all employers in the private sector and their employees must register with the Board.[137]

---

[129] S. 18 ibid.

[130] S. 19 ibid.

[131] National Provident Fund Act Cap. 273 Laws of the Federation of Nigeria, 1990 which was enacted in 1961, No. 20 of 1961.

[132] Nigeria Social Insurance Trust Fund Act 1993, No. 73; s. 42 repealed cap. 273.

[133] S. 10 ibid; the drafting seems rather clumsy!

[134] Ss. 2 and 10(2) ibid.

[135] The terms worker, persons employed and employee are used in s. 10 although only employee is defined; they are probably meant to mean the same thing, i.e., employee as defined.

[136] S. 10(3) ibid.

[137] Section 11 exempts only the following - (i) those employed in the public service and are covered by the Pensions Act (or a Law?); (ii) persons entitled to diplomatic or equivalent status; (iii) a

Contributions to the Fund must be paid on a monthly basis at any rate prescribed by regulations and must be computed by reference to the wages of the employee concerned.[138] The current prescribed rate of contribution is 7.5 per cent of an employee's insurable monthly earnings, 2.5 per cent of which is paid by an employee from his earnings and 5 per cent by the employer on the employee's behalf.[139] The insurable monthly earning of an employee must be computed in such a manner as is best calculated to give the rate per month at which an employee is being remunerated by his employer.[140] Any gratuity and annual bonus must be included but any payment by way of a pension or which is derived from shares under a profit sharing scheme must be excluded.[141] And any payment in kind such as provision of board or lodging must be included but its money value must be as specified by the Fund.[142] However an employee's insurable earnings must not be computed such that his annual earnings exceed ₦48,000.[143]

Contributions fall due on the last day of the month.[144] The late payment of any contribution attracts a penalty of 5 per cent of the amount unpaid and this amount must be added for each month or part of a month after the date when payment should have been made.[145] Any added amount is recoverable by the Board as a debt owing to it by the employer but the Board may remit, wholly or partly, any penalty.[146]

Contributions are inalienable and do not constitute assets for the benefit of creditors in the event of the bankruptcy or insolvency of the contributor.[147] Also they are deductible for assessment to tax.[148]

The benefits payable are exempt from taxation and are not liable to attachment for debt under any process of law.[149] There are six categories of benefits - retirement pension benefit, retirement grant, survivors benefit, death

---

non-citizen of Nigeria who is employed for a period of less than 6 years at a time provided he is either covered by a scheme by virtue of his employment or by a scheme in any other country.

[138] S. 13(1) ibid.

[139] See Nigeria Social Insurance Trust Fund (General) Regulations 1994; S. 1, 2 of 1994.

[140] Ibid.

[141] Ibid.

[142] Ibid.

[143] Ibid.

[144] S. 13(2) Nigeria Social Insurance Trust Fund Act 1993.

[145] S. 14(1) ibid., when payment should be made is not clear; could it be a reasonable time after the contribution fell due on the last day of the month?

[146] S. 14 ibid.

[147] S. 34(2) ibid.

[148] S. 35 ibid.

[149] S. 34(1) ibid.

grant, invalidity benefit and invalidity grant. The Board may, however, approve any other benefit from time to time.[150] A contributor may apply to have his contributions (benefits) converted into credits towards the purchase of real property for the use of the contributor or his family for residential purposes or towards the purchase of or acquisition of equity holding in the company which employs him.[151]

The conditions prescribed in the Regulations to be satisfied before benefits become payable are rather complex.[152] To qualify for retirement pension a contributor must attain, at least, the age of 60 years, must have retired from employment or show that any remuneration for any work he is engaged in is not equal to or more than the national minimum wage and that he has been credited with not less than 120 months contributions. In addition he must have made, at least, 75 per cent of the contributions which should have been made between his age at the start of the scheme and at the retirement age, subject to a minimum of 36 months contributions. Retirement pension is 30 per cent of the final average earnings on which contributions were based. It is payable for life. Retirement grant is an additional lump sum equivalent to two years pension for those who qualify for pension. Those who do not qualify for retirement pension but have contributed at least for 12 months retirement grant is the total monthly contribution multiplied by the total number of months for which contribution was made.

Invalidity pension is 30 per cent of final average earnings and is payable for life unless the invalidity ceases earlier. To qualify for invalidity pension at least 36 months contributions should have been made. Invalidity grant is the equivalent of the final monthly contributions immediately prior to the invalidity multiplied by the number of months of paid contributions. A survivor's benefit is payable to the survivor of a deceased contributor. A survivor's pension, which is 100 per cent, of the deceased's retirement pension, is payable for the life of a widow or widower unless she or he remarries or, in the case of a child survivor, until the attainment of age 25 years. A survivor's grant is a lump sum payment of the equivalent of the deceased's invalidity or retirement grant.

---

[150] S. 16 ibid.

[151] S. 17 ibid.

[152] Most of what is written below on the Fund is taken from the Fund's Publication - Questions & Answers on what you need to know About the Nigeria Social Insurance Trust Fund (NSITF).

Training

The law which provides for employee training did not, at the beginning, go as far as providing that employers must actually give training to their employees. It may have been that it was for that reason that many employers regarded the contribution which they were required to make towards training as an imposed tax which they were quite willing to forgo. It took almost two decades for this defect to be repaired.

The Industrial Training Fund - the Fund - was established by statute[153] in 1971 to be used to promote and encourage the acquisition of skills in industry or commerce with a view to generating a pool of indigenous trained manpower sufficient to meet the needs of the economy.[154] The Fund is made up by payment into it of contributions by employers[155] and such sums as may be provided by the Federal Government for that purpose.[156] Any employer who has twenty-five or more employees[157] in his employment must, not later than 1st April in the following year, contribute, for the last calendar year, one per cent of the amount of his annual pay roll to the Fund.[158] Where a contribution is not paid within the time stipulated a sum equal to five per cent of the unpaid amount must be added for each month or part of a month after the date on which payment should have been made but the Governing Council of the Fund may, if it thinks fit, remit in whole or in part any such penalty.[159] Furthermore, a contribution to the Fund, including any interest or penalty payable or imposed for non payment or for late payment, may be recovered by action as a debt owing to the Fund at any time within six years from the date when it became due.[160]

Every contributing employer must, at all times, provide adequate training for his indigenous staff with a view to improving on the skills related to their job and

---

[153] S. 1 Industrial Training Fund Decree No. 47 of 1971 now S. 1. Industrial Training Fund Act, Cap 182 Laws of the Federation of Nigeria, 1990.

[154] S. 2 ibid.

[155] Employer means any person engaged in industry or commerce with whom an employee entered into a contract of service or apprenticeship and who is responsible for the payment of wages or remuneration to the employee; S. 15 ibid.

[156] S. 1 ibid.

[157] Employees means all persons, whether Nigerians or not, employed in return for a salary, wages or other consideration, and whether employed full time or part time, and includes temporary employees who work for periods of not less than three months in a year; S. 6(4) ibid.

[158] S. 6(1) and (2) ibid.

[159] S. 8

[160] S. 10(1) and (3).

evidence of such training must be forwarded to the Fund.[161] Any employer who fails to do so is guilty of an offence and liable, on conviction, in the case of a body corporate, to a fine of ₦5,000 for the first offence and ₦10,000 for each subsequent offence and, in the case of the Chief Executive, Secretary or other principal officer of the company, to a fine of ₦ 1,000 or two years imprisonment for a first offence and two years imprisonment without option of a fine for each subsequent offence.[162]

The administration of the Fund in vested in a Governing Council and a Director General. The Director General is the administrative head of the Fund and, subject to the directions of the Council, is responsible for the assessment of contributions, the collection and payment of moneys into the Fund, and the payment of all disbursements. He also has responsibility to account for all moneys collected, paid or otherwise expended by the Fund and generally for ensuring the achievement of the aims of the Fund.[163] The Director General may require any employer to furnish such returns and other information and to keep such records and produce them for examination by, or on behalf of, the Director General as appears to him to be necessary for carrying out his functions.[164] If any employer fails, neglects or refuses to furnish such returns the Director General or any of his staff authorised by him has power to assess, according to his best of judgement, the appropriate levy or contribution the employer must pay to the Fund. However such assessment does not prevent the Director General or any staff so authorised to assess the actual amount of the employer's liability when the employer subsequently makes his returns.[165] Any person who knowingly or recklessly furnishes any returns or information which is false in a material particular or wilfully makes a false entry in any record required to be produced or, with intent to deceive, makes use of any such entry which he knows to be false is guilty of an offence.[166] Any person who is found guilty of any such

---

[161] S. 7A ibid; see S. 4 Industrial Training Fund (Amendment) Act No.44 of 1990.

[162] S. 7A(2) ibid; this provision is rather confusing; employer as defined, need not be a body corporate or a "company; " also it is not clear whether any failure to train or give evidence of such training automatically renders both "the body corporate" (employer) and the Chief Executive, etc. liable or whether an employer or its chief executive or both have to be shown to have committed the offence.

[163] S.5 ibid.

[164] S. 13 ibid; S. 1(c) (iii) Industrial Training Fund (Amendment) Decree 1976 No. 14 substituted "Director" for "Secretary" and by S. 3 Industrial Training Fund (Amendment) Act 1990 No.44 "Director General" is substituted for "Director".

[165] S. 14(1); it is clear that the substitution made by S.5 Industrial Training Fund (Amendment) Act 1990, No.44, is for S.14 and not S.13.

[166] S. 14(2) ibid; see f.n. 165.

offence is liable, on conviction, in the case of a body corporate, to a fine of ₦5,000 for a first offence and ₦10,000 for each subsequent offence and, in the case of the Chief Executive, Secretary or other Principal Officer of the company (employer), to a fine of ₦1,000 or two years imprisonment for a first offence and three years imprisonment without option of fine for each subsequent offence.[167] If any question of fact arises as to the liability of an employer to pay contributions the question must be determined by the minister whose decision is final.[168]

The Governing Council of the Fund may make a refund of up to sixty per cent of the amount paid by an employer if the Council is satisfied that the training programme of the employer is adequate.[169] The Council has power to, *inter alia*, provide courses and other facilities for the training of persons in employment or to be employed, approve such courses and facilities provided by others and to carry out or assist in carrying out relevant research.[170]

Settlement of disputes

Third party assistance to employers and their employees in the settlement of differences which they cannot by themselves resolve was first provided by the Trade Dispute (Arbitration and Inquiry) Ordinance, later Act, which was enacted in 1941. The underlying principle of this statute was one of voluntariness. It eschewed compulsion completely. The Act was repealed along with two Decrees which were promulgated to deal with the conditions of the civil war.[171]

However, both the Act and the Decrees have greatly influenced the provisions of the existing statute under which services for the settlement of trade disputes are now offered by the Government. A trade dispute means any dispute between employers and employees or between employees and employees which is connected with the employment or non-employment or the teams of employment and physical conditions of work of any person.[172] Where there

---

[167] S. 14(3) ibid.

[168] S. 12; but note s. 6(6) (b) of the Constitution which gives unfettered access to the courts for the determination of one's rights.

[169] S. 7(1) ibid.

[170] S. 4 (1)(a),(b) and (f) ibid.

[171] S. 51 (2) & 2nd Schedule Trade Disputes Decree No. 7 of 1976 now Cap. 432; all section references in the remainder of this chapter are to Cap. 432 unless otherwise stated.

[172] See s. 47(l). The word used in the Act is worker but is defined to embrace employees at common law. However, the Act does not apply to any member of the Nigerian Army, Navy or Air Force or to any member of the Nigerian Police Force or the Customs Preventive Service, or to any officer

exists any collective agreement for the settlement of a trade dispute at least three copies of the agreement must be deposited by the parties to it with the Minister of Labour and Productivity within fourteen days of the execution of the agreement.[173] Any person who fails to do so is guilty of an offence and, on conviction, liable to a fine of ₦100.[174]

A collective agreement means any agreement in writing for the settlement of disputes and relating to terms of employment and physical conditions of work concluded between an employer, a group of employers or one or more organisations representing employers on the one hand and one or more trade unions or organisations representing employees on the other hand.[175] Upon receipt of copies of a collective agreement, the Minister may make an order the terms of which may in respect of the agreement specify that the provisions of the agreement or any part of the agreement be binding on the employers and employees to whom they relate.[176] If any person fails to comply with the term of such an order he is guilty of an offence and liable on conviction to a fine of ₦100 or to imprisonment for six months.[177]

The Act provides the procedures to be followed for the settlement of a trade dispute which exists or is apprehended.[178] The parties to the dispute are enjoined to first attempt to settle it by any existing agreed means for the settlement of disputes.[179] If the attempt fails or if no such agreed means exists, the parties must, within seven days of the failure or within seven days of the date on which the dispute arose or was first apprehended where no means for settlement exists, meet together by themselves or their representatives under the presidency of a mediator mutually agreed upon and appointed by or on behalf of the parties with a view to the amicable settlement of the dispute.[180] However, if, within seven days of the appointment of the mediator the dispute is not settled, it must then be reported to the Minister or his Permanent Secretary by or on behalf of either of the parties within three days of the end of those seven days.[181] A report must be

---

of whatever rank appointed to carry out duties within the meaning of the Customs & Excise Management Act, the Immigration Act and the Prisons Act or to any member of service of the Federal or State Government authorised to bear arms; S. 48(2).

173 S. 2(1).

174 I bid.

175 S. 47(1).

176 S. 2(3).

177 S. 2(4).

178 See below for the Minister's power to apprehend a dispute.

179 S. 3(1).

180 S. 3(2).

181 S. 5(1).

in writing and must record the points on which the parties disagree and describe the steps already taken by them to reach a settlement.[182] If the Minister or the Permanent Secretary is not satisfied that all the above requirements for internal settlement have been substantially complied with, he must issue to the parties a notice in writing specifying the steps which must be taken to satisfy those requirements and may specify in the notice the time within which any particular step must be taken.[183] Where, after the expiration of the period specified in the notice or, if no period is specified, after the expiration of fourteen days following the date the notice is issued, the dispute remains unsettled and the Minister is satisfied that the steps specified in the notice have been taken or that either party is, for its part, refusing to take those steps or any of them, he "may proceed to exercise such of his powers under Sections 7, 8, 16 or 32 as may appear to him appropriate."[184]

These sections respectively empower the Minister to appoint a conciliator, refer a dispute to the Industrial Arbitration Panel (IAP), refer certain types of disputes directly to the National Industrial Court (NIC) and to appoint a board of inquiry. While it appears, therefore, that the Minister may refer a dispute directly to the IAP without first appointing a conciliator it seems, as will be seen, that by virtue of s. 8(1) he may refer a dispute to the IAP only after the receipt by him of a report of a conciliator. However, where a conciliator is appointed and he fails to effect a settlement, the dispute will then normally be referred to the IAP before it goes to the NIC where an award of an arbitration tribunal of the IAP has not been accepted by both parties to the dispute. The Minister may, however, in his discretion, refer a dispute directly to the NIC after receiving a report of a conciliator where employees in an essential service[185] are a party to the dispute and must do so where it appears to him that, in the circumstances of the dispute reference to the IAP would not be appropriate.[186]

The Minister is empowered to apprehend a trade dispute. Where a trade dispute is apprehended by the Minister, he may in writing inform the parties or their representatives of his apprehension and of steps he proposes to take for the purpose of resolving the dispute.[187] Such steps as he may take include the appointment of a conciliator under s. 7, a reference of the dispute or any matter

---

[182] S. 5(2).
[183] S. 6(1), as modified by the Trade Disputes (Delegation of Certain Statutory Functions) Order 1984.
[184] S. 6(2).
[185] For essential services see below.
[186] S.16.
[187] S. 4.

relating to it for settlement to the IAP under s. 8 and a reference of the dispute to a board of inquiry under s. 32. It appears an apprehended dispute can get to the NIC only via the IAP.

Conciliation

The Minister or his Permanent Secretary may appoint a fit person to act as conciliator for the purpose of effecting a settlement of a dispute.[188] An appointed conciliator must inquire into the causes and circumstances of the dispute and, by negotiation with the parties, endeavour to bring about a settlement.[189] A conciliator has seven days within which to act. If a settlement is reached within that period the conciliator must report the fact to the Minister and must forward to him a memorandum of the terms of the settlement signed by the representatives of the parties.[190] As from the date it is signed or such earlier or later date as specified in it, the terms recorded in the memorandum become binding on the employers and employees to whom the terms relate. The breach by any person of the terms of a binding memorandum is an offence punishable, on conviction, with a fine, in the case of an employee or a trade union, of ₦200 and in the case of an employer or an organization representing employers, of ₦2,000.[191]

Furthermore, the contracts of employment between the employers and the employees in question are deemed to include a provision that the rate of wages to be paid and the conditions of employment to be observed under the contracts must be in accordance with the terms of binding memorandum until varied by a subsequent agreement, settlement or award. Accordingly, the provisions of such contracts must be read subject to the terms of the settlement and any failure to give effect to them constitutes a breach of contract.[192] An action for damages for breach of contract could, therefore, lie. If a settlement is not reached within seven days of the appointment of a conciliator, or, if, after attempting negotiation with the parties he is satisfied that he will not be able to bring about a settlement, the conciliator must forthwith report the fact to the Minister.[193]

---

188 S. 7(1); as modified by the Trade Disputes (Delegation of Certain Statutory Functions) Order 1984.
189 S. 7(2).
190 S. 7(3).
191 S. 7(4)
192 S. 47(2)
193 S. 7(5).

Industrial Arbitration Panel (IAP)

Where the Minister receives a report from a conciliator of his failure or inability to bring about a settlement of the dispute he must refer it to the Industrial Arbitration Panel within fourteen days of receipt of the report.[194] The Chairman of the Panel must then constitute an arbitration tribunal for the dispute. An arbitration tribunal may consist of a sole arbitrator, selected from among the members of the panel by the chairman or of a single arbitrator selected from among the members of the panel by the chairman and assisted by assessors[195] or of one or more arbitrators nominated by or on behalf of the employers concerned and an equal number of arbitrators nominated by or on behalf of the employees concerned, all nominations being made from among the members of the Panel and presided over by the chairman or vice-chairman.[196]

The chairman decides which one of the three types of tribunal to constitute depending on which appears to him to be appropriate having regard to the subject matter of the dispute and the means by which an attempt to settle the dispute had been made earlier.[197] Where there is a vacancy in the number of assessors, the chairman may either direct the tribunal to act notwithstanding the vacancy or fill the vacancy from the appropriate panel of assessors.[198] Similarly, where a vacancy occurs in an arbitration tribunal consisting of more than one arbitrator the tribunal may, with the consent of the party which nominated him, act notwithstanding the vacancy.[199] However any act, proceeding or determination of an arbitration tribunal cannot be questioned on the ground that

---

[194] S. 8(1). The IAP is supposed to consist of a Chairman, a vice-chairman and not less than ten other members two of whom must be nominated by organizations appearing to the Minister as representing the interests of employers and two nominated by organizations appearing to the Minister as representing the interests of employees. All appointments are by the Minister; S.8(2). Every member of the Panel holds office for four years in the first instance unless he resigns or is removed earlier but is eligible for re-appointment for one more term of four years; S.9 A member must vacate office when he attains the age of 65 years; S. 10.

[195] Assessors are appointed by the Chairman from the panels of employers' and employees' representatives drawn up from time to time by the Minister on the recommendation of employers or organisations representing the interest of employers and by organizations representing the interests of employees respectively. The assessors to be appointed must be one or more equal members of the panels of assessors nominated by or on behalf of the employers and employees concerned, Ss. 8(5) and 26.

[196] S. 8(4).

[197] S. 8(3).

[198] S. 11(2).

[199] S. 11(3).

a member or assessor was not validly appointed or on the ground of an unfilled vacancy.[200]

Awards

Two rules which govern awards of an arbitration tribunal must be noted. The first provision is that an arbitration tribunal has no power either to grant any general or percentage wage increase or to approve any such grant by an employer unless with the approval of the Minister of Labour and Productivity.[201] A second provision is that where an arbitration tribunal is of the view, at arbitration, that a case has been made for an increase in salaries, the tribunal must then refer the decision as to the level of increase to the National Salaries, Incomes and Wages Commission for advice.[202]

The award of an arbitration tribunal consisting of a single arbitrator assisted by assessors must be made by the arbitrator only and where a tribunal consists of more than one arbitrator, their award may be unanimous or by majority.[203] An arbitration tribunal must make its award within twenty one days of its constitution or such longer period as the Minister may in any particular case allow and must send a copy forthwith to the Minister, and must not be communicated to the parties affected.[204] On receipt of an award if the Minister considers it desirable he may refer the award back to the tribunal for reconsideration.[205] If the Minister does not consider it desirable to refer the award back to the tribunal or on receipt of the award after the tribunal has reconsidered it, he must immediately cause a notice to be given to the parties or their representatives and to be published in such other manner, if any, as he thinks fit. The notice must set out the award and specify the time, which must not be more than seven days from the publication of the notice,[206] within which and the manner in which notice of objection to the award may be given to the Minister by or on behalf of either party to the dispute and state that unless notice

[200] S. 11 (4).
[201] S. 18(3).
[202] S . 12 National Salaries, Incomes and Wages Commission Act 1993, No. 99
[203] S. 8(6).
[204] S. 12(1).
[205] S. 12(3).
[206] In *Federal Ministry of Health* v. *Nation Association of Nigerian Nurses and Midwives* [1980-81], NICLR 18 after an award had been notified to the parties the chairman of the IAP amended the award and the amended award was subsequently notified by the Minister to the parties. The court held that time of publication of notice was the subsequent date; therefore the period for objection began to run from that date.

of objection to the award is given by one or both of the parties within the time and in the manner specified the award will be confirmed by the Minister.[207] If no notice of objection is given within the time and in the manner specified, the Minister must publish in the Gazette a notice confirming the award and the award becomes binding on the employers and employees to whom it relates as from the date of the award, or such earlier or later date as may be specified in the award.[208]

Any person who fails to comply with a binding award is guilty of an offence and liable on conviction in the case of an individual to a fine of ₦200 or imprisonment for six months and in the case of a body corporate to a fine of ₦2,000.[209] If after conviction for such an offence, there is continued failure to comply with the award there is further offence punishable on conviction with a fine of ₦200 in the case of an individual and ₦2,000 in the case of a body corporate for each day on which the offence continues.[210] Where an offence committed by a body corporate is found to have been committed with the consent or connivance of or attributable to any act or default on the part of any person in apparent control of the body corporate the person or persons and the body are deemed to have committed the offence.[211] As from the date on which an award becomes binding the contracts between the employers and employees concerned must be deemed to include a provision that the rate of wages to be paid and the conditions of employment to be observed under the contract must be in accordance with the award. Accordingly, the provisions of the contract must be read subject to the award and any failure to give effect to the award constitutes a breach of contract.[212]

Where a trade dispute referred to arbitration involves questions as to wages, hours of work or any other terms or conditions of or affecting employment which are regulated by any statutory provisions the tribunal must not make any award that are less favourable to the employees.[213]

As to what happens where objection is made to an award of a tribunal there are two seemingly conflicting provisions. The earlier of the two is that if notice of objection is given to the Minister the Minister must, forthwith, refer the

---

[207] S. 12(2).
[208] S. 12(4).
[209] S. 12(5).
[210] S. 12(6).
[211] S. 12(7).
[212] S. 47(2).
[213] S. 11 (5).

dispute to the National Industrial Court.[214] But another and subsequent provision is that an appeal lies from the decisions (awards?) of the Industrial Arbitration Panel to the NIC as of right in matters of disputes conferred on it; and this includes, primarily, trade disputes.[215] It seems clear that the effect of the latter provision is to dispense with the reference function of the Minister. Nothing much would be gained if an appeal has to be routed through the Minister. The problem which may arise as to how the Minister would know whether an objection (appeal) has not been made so as to be able to confirm an award can be solved merely by communicating notice of an appeal to him. The Minister has no power to refer a dispute to the NIC where there has been no objection to an award of an arbitration tribunal.[216]

However, as we have seen, the Minister has power to refer a dispute directly to the NIC where the dispute is one to which employees in any essential service are a party or where in the circumstances of the case reference of the dispute to an arbitration tribunal would not be appropriate. This power apparently still subsists in the Minister.

Also additional jurisdiction would appear to have been conferred on the IAP. Section 24 provides as follows:[217]

> A right of appeal shall lie to the court from the awards of the Industrial Arbitration Panel which shall be execrable in the case of intra-union disputes arising from the organization and running of a trade union as laid down in the union constitution or inter-union disputes arising from the restructuring of trade unions established under the Trade Unions Act.

Although, the drafting may be said to be ambiguous and inelegant, it is suggested that the section confers additional jurisdiction in the IAP to make awards in (i) intra-union disputes which may arise from a breach of the union rules book or constitution and ii) inter-union disputes arising from the restructuring of the unions as sanctioned by the Trade Unions (Amendment) Act 1978. Both types of disputes would seem not to be trade disputes as, although they are obviously disputes between workers and workers, they may lack the necessary subject matter of a statutory trade dispute. Nonetheless, it is perhaps the Minister alone who can refer such a dispute to the IAP. An appeal lies to the

---

214 S. 13(1);

215 S. 21; see S. 1(c) Trade Disputes (Amendment)(No.2) Decree 1988 No.57.

216 *National Union of Textile, Garment & Tailoring Workers of Nigeria* v. *Atlantic Textile Manufacturing C. Ltd.*, 1980-81 NICLR 81.

217 See S. 1 Trade Disputes (Amendment) (No. 2) Decree 1988, No. 57.

NIC from an award of an arbitration tribunal in either type of dispute. And the jurisdiction of the ordinary courts has been removed in trade and such inter or intra-union disputes. No person must commence an action, the subject matter of a trade dispute or any inter or intra-union dispute in a court of law.[218] A contravention of this provision is an offence which is punishable, on conviction, with a fine of ₦10,000 or imprisonment for a term of one year or both such fine and imprisonment.[219]

Enforcement of award

The IAP is now empowered to enforce its awards. As we have seen failure to comply with a binding award of the IAP is punishable with a fine or imprisonment. It may also amount to breach of contract.[220] Now the IAP "may commit for contempt any person or a representative of a trade union or association who does any act or commits an omission which in the opinion of the Panel constitutes contempt of the Panel."[221]

If the chairman of the IAP "considers the evidence sufficient to commit for contempt a person or body of persons, he shall commit such a person or persons for trial in the High Court and shall, until the trial, either admit him to bail or send him to prison for safe keeping."[222] The warrant of the IAP is sufficient authority to the person in charge of any prison for the custody of prisoners committed for trial.[223]

Before this provision it had been held by the Court of Appeal that IAP has no criminal jurisdiction and that failure to comply with an award of the IAP could properly be prosecuted in the Magistrates' courts.[224] Prosecution in the Magistrates' courts may now be unnecessary although the failure to comply with an award remains an offence with the stipulated penalty. The new powers of the IAP seem certain to ensure compliance with its awards. However, it is clear that the IAP is still not vested with criminal jurisdiction. It must also be noted that an arbitration tribunal can still not try for contempt. Section 35(4) which provides

---

[218] S.1A(1); see s. 2 Trade Disputes (Amendment) Decree 1992, No. 47; see further below as to the difficulty inherent in this provision.

[219] S.1A(3); see ibid.

[220] S. 47 (2); *Rufai* v. *Dorman Long Amalgamated Engineering Ltd.* (1978) 5/CCHCJ.

[221] S. 22.

[222] S. 23(1)

[223] S. 23(2).

[224] *Ekene-dili Chukwu Ltd.* v. *Mrs. G. I. Akinboboye, Chief Magistrate Court* No. 1, Lagos (1987) NWLR 306; (1987) 2 QLRN 44.

that any person who commits an act of contempt whether the act is or is not committed in the presence of the members sitting in the exercise of its functions is liable on summary conviction before a High Court, to a fine of ₦200 or to imprisonment for three months, has not been repealed.

The IAP has power to make orders, when necessary, for the appointment of a public trustee for the management of the affairs and finances of a trade union involved in an intra-union dispute.[225]

National Industrial Court

This court was established for the first time by the Trade Dispute Act 1976 and began sitting in June 1978. It consists of a President and four ordinary members all of whom must be persons of good standing being, to the knowledge of the Minister, well acquainted with the employment conditions in Nigeria, and, at least, one of whom must, to his satisfaction, have a competent knowledge of economics, industry or trade.[226] In dealing with any matter the court may be constituted, at the discretion of the President, either by all five members or by the President and two ordinary members.[227] It may be assisted by assessors at the discretion of the President.[228] A decision of the court may be taken by a majority vote.[229] The normal seat of the court is Lagos but it may and has in fact sat outside Lagos for the purpose of dealing with a trade dispute.[230]

All appointments to the court are made by the Head of State but, in the case of the President of the Court, after consultation with the Federal Judicial Service Commission.[231] A person is not qualified to hold the office of President of the Court unless he has been a judge of a court of unlimited jurisdiction in civil and criminal matters in some part of the Commonwealth or a court having jurisdiction in appeals from any such court or he is qualified for admission as an advocate in Nigeria and has been so qualified for not less than ten years.[232] The president or any other member of the court must vacate office when he attains the age of sixty-five years.[233] The President of the Court or any other member of the court may be removed from office by the President acting, in the case of an

---

[225] S. 50.
[226] S. 19(2).
[227] S. 19(3).
[228] S. 19(4).
[229] S. 19(5).
[230] S. 19(6).
[231] S. 25(1).
[232] S. 25(2).
[233] S. 28(1) and (2).

ordinary member, after consultation with the Federal Judicial Service Commission.[234] A member may resign his office by notice in writing addressed to the President.[235] However, the President or any other member of the court holds office, unless he has previously resigned or been removed, for four years in the first instance and it may be renewed only for one more term of four years.[236]

Where the court has begun to consider any matter and the President becomes incapable of continuing to take part in the proceedings on account of sickness or for any other reason, the President must, after consultation with the Chief Justice of Nigeria, appoint, as soon as possible, a person qualified to hold the office to act for the purposes of the proceedings.[237] Where it is an ordinary member who becomes similarly incapable of continuing to take part in a proceedings, the President of the court must re-constitute the court. The court may be so reconstituted by removing the member who has become incapable of continuing and another member where the court consists of all five members but where it is constituted by the President and only two ordinary members by substituting another member for the one who has become incapable of continuing.[238]

The Court must determine an appeal made to it or any trade dispute referred to it not later than thirty working days from the day it begins to consider the matter.[239] An award of the court is binding on the employers and employees to whom it relates as from the date of the award or such earlier or later date as may be specified in the award.[240] Where the terms of an award are more favourable than any statutory provisions affecting the terms and conditions of employment of the employees concerned, the award prevails.[241] Any person who fails to comply with an award of the court is guilty of an offence and liable, on conviction, in the case of an individual, to a fine of ₦200 or imprisonment for six months and in the case of a body corporate to a fine of ₦2,000.[242] If, after conviction, a person continues to fail to comply with the award he is guilty of a further offence and liable on conviction to a fine of ₦200 in the case of an

---

[234] S. 28(4).
[235] S. 28(5).
[236] S. 29.
[237] S. 27(1).
[238] S. 27(2).
[239] S. 20(2).
[240] S. 13(2)(a); see s. 3 Trade Disputes (Amendment) Act 1992, No. 47.
[241] S. 13(3).
[242] S.13(4)

individual or ₦2,000 in the case of a body corporate for each day on which the offence continues.[243]

Where an offence by a body corporate is found to have been committed with the consent or connivance of or attributable to any act or default on the part of any person in apparent control of the body corporate both that person and the body are deemed to have committed the offence.[244] Also, breach of the terms of an award amounts to breach of contract. This is dealt with in s. 47(2) which provides that as from the date on which the award becomes binding the contract between the employers and employees in question must be deemed to include a provision that the rate of wages to be paid and the conditions of employment to be observed under the contract must be in accordance with the award until varied by a subsequent agreement, settlement or award and accordingly the provisions of that contract must be read subject to the award and any failure to give effect to award constitutes a breach of contract. In 1992 the statutory provisions that an award of the NIC was final and that no appeal lay to any other body or person from any determination of the court were substituted for. The substitute provision is that an appeal from the decision of the court shall lie as of right to the Court of Appeal on questions of fundamental rights as contained in Chapter IV of the Constitution of the Federal Republic of Nigeria 1979.[245] This provision does not appear to alter the pre-1992 position. There is neither a constitutional nor other statutory provision conferring a right of appeal from decisions of the NIC to any court. Even the above express provision will appear inapplicable since the NIC is not vested with jurisdiction in questions of fundamental right. Indeed, the provision would appear unconstitutional since the constitution vests jurisdiction for fundamental rights infringement in a High Court in the State in which contravention takes place.[246]

The awards which the court has made have been as diverse and novel as those made by arbitration tribunals. This is understandable in view of the rather general way in which the jurisdiction of the court is expressed, that is "to make awards for the purpose of settling trade disputes." Naturally, the type of award

---

[243] S. 13(5).

[244] S. 13(6); in *Nigeria Union of Civil Service Typists, Stenographers and Allied Staff* v. *Attorney-General and Government of Ogun State*, 1982-83 NICLR 190 Counsel's contention that the Government of Ogun State was a body corporate and the Governor a person in apparent control of it was left undecided by the NIC.

[245] S. 20(3); see s. 6(a) Trade Disputes (Amendment) Decree 1992, No.47.

[246] S. 46(1) 1999 Constitution; The same argument renders the new s.13(2)(b) otiose; for a fuller consideration of the Trade Disputes (Amendment) Decree 1992, No.47, see E. E. Uvieghara, 'Review of Cases and Statutes on Labour Law,' (1993) JNL Vol. 2 No. p . 35.

has been determined by the nature of the dispute. In so far as the common law[247] remedies of specific performance and damages are concerned the court appears to be completely oblivious of them or, at least, of the principles which govern them. Arbitration tribunals have made a number of reinstatement orders which have been put into effect. It appears that the court is not necessarily adverse to making such an order although, as it would seem, it will do so only where there are no practical difficulties in the way of its implementation. In *Metal Products Workers' Union of Nigeria* v. *Alzico Ltd*,[248] the court simply declined to make an order for reinstatement without stating any reason. In *Nigerian Sugar Company Ltd*. v. *National Union of Food Beverages and Tobacco Employees*,[249] the court said: I n view of the time lag (a period of over three years) and as it is obvious that the company must have filled all the posts of the dismissed workers by now, the court does not consider that any useful purpose will be served by enforcing the reinstatement of these workers, most of whom might themselves have secured other jobs elsewhere.[250]

In *Industrial Cartons Ltd*. v. *National Union of Paper and Paper Products Workers*,[251] Mr. Faneye who was alleged to be a negligent employee was given a letter of termination. On receiving the letter, he was alleged to have called out all employees and cause a disruption of work. He plucked off the glasses of the Chief Engineer from his face and chased him and the engineer ran for his dear life. At the IAP, the reinstatement of Mr. Faneye was ordered and the court agreed that the termination was not for the reason of negligent work but on account of union activities. The court said this conclusion should logically have led to a decision to uphold the IAP award for the re-instatement of Mr. Faneye in his former employment but it declined to do so on account of the incidents in which he had been involved. The court said it was "under no illusions that the forcible reinstatement of Mr. Faneye in these circumstances, will be in the interest of either Mr. Faneye or of discipline and industrial peace within the organisation. These should be the overriding considerations in any decision this court takes in this matter.[252]

In the *Austrian-Nigeria Lace Manufacturing Co. Ltd.* v. *National Union of Textile, Garment and Tailoring Workers of Nigeria*,[253] the court also agreed with

[247] Used to include doctrines of equity.

[248] 1978-79 NICLR 61.

[249] 1978-79 N I CLR 69.

[250] Ibid. 75.

[251] 1980-81 NICLR 54.

[252] Ibid . 64

[253] 1982-83 NICLR 59.

the IAP that the purported termination of the employment of sixteen employees of the company was wrongful. The court said it found "that the Appellants' actions constituted an unwarranted and unnecessary provocation of the workers, who demonstrated all along their willingness to comply with the provisions of the relevant laws in their dealings with the Appellants"[254] but overruled the IAP's award of reinstatement. It said that it "does not consider, for reasons of practicality and enforcement, that an order for the reinstatement of the sixteen workers would serve the purpose of effective and satisfactory settlement of this matter.[255]

In *Nigerian Tobacco Co. Ltd.* v. *National Union of Food, Beverages and Tobacco Employees,*[256] the court refused reinstatement. "In the peculiar circumstances of the determination of the appointment of...the court considers that his reinstatement will not serve a useful purpose."[257] Similarly, in *Nigerian Asbestos Industries Ltd.* v. *National Union of Chemical and Non-Metallic Products Workers,*[258] the IAP awarded reinstatement to the employee who had been wrongfully removed on account of his trade union activities, but the court refused reinstatement having "regard to all the circumstances of this case and, in particular, considering the undesirability of making an order for the reinstatement of...in his former employment,"[259] but the court gave no indication of the grounds which rendered it undesirable to reinstate the employee. Again, in *Management of Express Insurance Company Ltd.* v. *National Union of Banks, Insurance and Financial Institutions Employees,*[260] the IAP ordered reinstatement but the court said - Having regard to the circumstances of this particular case, the court is not disposed to order the reinstatement of the dismissed workers as requested by the Respondent.[261] With respect to compensation for loss of employment the court's attitude has equally been ambivalent. In some of the decisions the court has awarded what it calls severance pay,[262] and in others redundancy benefit.[263] The reason for the

[254] Ibid . 90.
[255] Ibid . 92.
[256] 1982-83 NICLR 164.
[257] Ibid . 182.
[258] 1986 NICLR 83.
[259] Ibid. 121.
[260] 1986 NICLR 230.
[261] Ibid. 253.
[262] *Metal Products Workers of Nigeria* v. *Alzico Ltd., Nigerian Sugar Co. Ltd.* v. *National Union of Food Beverages and Tobacco Employees; Nigerian Sewing Machine Manufacturing Co. Ltd.,* v. *National Union of Shop and Distributive Employees; Stadium Hotel* v. *National Union of Hotels and Personal Services Workers*; 1978-79 N I CLR 61, 69, 77 and 921 respectively. *NTC* v.

introduction of severance pay is not articulated nor has its application been uniform. In some decisions it might well be that the result would be the same as a claim for damages at common law.[264] It would appear however that in most of the cases the wrongfully removed employee got more compensation than he would have got at common law as damages for wrongful termination of employment. For example, in *Industrial Cartons Ltd.* v. *National Union of Paper and Paper Products Workers*,[265] the court simply ordered that six months' salary was adequate compensation in addition to various other items of claim in spite of the fact that the contract provided for termination by either side by one month's notice or a month's salary in lieu of such notice.

Issue of jurisdiction

The NIC is conferred with jurisdiction "to the exclusion of any other court" to (a) make awards for the purpose of settling trade disputes and (b) determine questions as to the interpretation of (i) any collective agreement (ii) any award by the court or an arbitration tribunal and (iii) the terms of settlement of any trade dispute as recorded in the memorandum of settlement signed by the parties.[266] And, in a round about manner, the court is also conferred with jurisdiction, on appeal, which is as of right, from awards of the IAP in intra-union disputes arising from the organization and running of any trade union as laid down in its constitution and in inter-union disputes arising from the (any?) restructuring of trade unions.[267]

But, in spite of the expressed exclusiveness of the court's jurisdiction in the settling of trade disputes, such disputes continued to be taken to the regular

National Union of Food, beverages and Tobacco Employees, 1982-83 NICLR 163; *Austrian-Nigeria Lace Manufacturing Co. Ltd.* v. *National Union of Textile, Garment & Tailoring Workers of Nigeria*, 1982-83 NICLR 59; *Management of Atlas (Nig.) Ltd.* v. *Shop & Distributive Trade Senior Staff Association*, 1986 NICLR 43; and *Management of Express Insurance Company Ltd.* v. *National Union of Banks, Insurance and Financial Institutions Employees*, 1986 N I CLR 230.

[263] *Grizi (Nig.) Ltd* v. *Grizi (Nig.) Ltd., and Group of Companies Workers' Union*, 1978-79 N I CLR 27.

[264] *Footwear, Leather and Rubber Products Workers Union of Nigeria* v. *Management of Sanusi Rubber Works Ltd.*, 1984-85 NICLR 98; *Nigerian Asbestos Industries Ltd.* v. *National Union of Chemical, & Non-Metallic Products Workers* 1986 NICLR 83.

[265] 1980-81 N I CLR 54.

[266] S. 20(1)

[267] S. 24; see s. 1 Trade Disputes (Amendment)(No.2) Decree 1988, No. 57; the original provision apparently had only the restructuring sanctioned by the Trade Unions (Amendment) Act, 1978, No. 22 in mind.

courts. Hence, by amendment, it is provided that no person may commence an action, the subject matter of a trade dispute or any inter- or intra-union dispute in a court of law.[268] Any person who contravenes this provision commits an offence and is liable, on conviction, to a fine of ₦10,000 or to imprisonment for a term of one year or to both such fine and term of imprisonment.[269] However, there were, at least, two reasons why even the amendment, as was the initial provision, may not have achieved the intended result. One of the two reasons arose from the interpretation of the Supreme Court of section 236 of the 1979 Constitution which conferred unlimited jurisdiction on the High Courts of the States to hear and determine, *inter alia*, any civil proceedings in which the existence or extent of a legal right, power, duty, liability, privilege, interest, obligation or claim was in issue.[270] The effect of the interpretation was that the jurisdiction of a State High Court to hear and determine any civil matter could not be ousted. It meant, therefore, that both a State High Court and the National Industrial Court had concurrent jurisdiction in trade disputes, such disputes being civil in nature.[271] This obstacle has been removed by section 272 of the Constitution which omits the word "unlimited" upon which the interpretation was based. The other reason remains. It stems from the general failure to understand and give the statutory definition of trade dispute its true and correct meaning. It is apparent that the view held generally is that a dispute concerning terms and conditions of employment is a trade dispute only where a trade union is involved. Thus a dispute may fall within the jurisdiction of the NIC or of the regular courts depending upon whether a trade union is involved in the dispute or not. In *Nigerian Tobacco Company* v. *National Union of Food, Beverages & Tobacco Employees*[272] the NIC said as follows - it is indeed clear from the definition that a dispute between an employer and his employee which affects the terms and conditions of such employment constitutes a trade dispute which can be taken up

---

[268] S. 1 A(1); see s. 2 Trade Disputes (Amendment) Act, 1992, No.47.

[269] S. 1A(3); see ibid; we have suggested elsewhere that the imposition of a criminal sanction may be counter productive; we made alternative suggestion; see E . E . Uvieghara; Review of Cases and Statutes Labour Law, (1993) JNL Vol.2, No. 1, pp. 40-41.

[270] *Savannah Bank* v. *Pan Atlantic Shipping & Transport Agencies Ltd.* (1987) I NWLR 212; *Western Steel Works* v. *Iron & Steel Workers* (1987) 1 NNLR 284. For the contention that the interpretation wais wrong see E. E . Uvieghara, *Nigerian Labour Laws. The Past, Present and the Future,* Inaugural Lecture Series, University of Lagos Press, 1987, p. 45. Even if the interpretation was correct it was clear that it would have been against the spirit of s. 6(5((g) of the Constitution and that it would constitute an obstacle to the establishment of courts with specialised jurisdiction.

[271] Section 236 of the of 1979 is now S. 272 of the 1999 Constitution

[272] 1982-83 N I CLR 164.

by a recognised union on behalf of its members. The court does not accept the submission that a dispute between an employer and his employee regarding the termination of the employee's appointment can only fall within the provisions of the Act if it has some connections with trade union activities of the employee.[273] There is no doubt that what the court has just said is the correct interpretation of the definition of a trade dispute. But the question is, why must such a dispute be taken up on an employee's behalf by a trade union? A trade dispute remains a trade dispute whether or not an employee is represented by a trade union. As the court itself has rightly said the "primary right, however, to be a party to a trade dispute belongs to the workers on the one hand and the employers on the other hand. Contrary to the argument that has been canvassed for the trade union, the right of appearance before this court belongs to the workers. The trade unions are only the representatives of the workers.[274] And, by the definition of a trade dispute, it need not be a dispute connected with the employment or non-employment or the terms of employment or physical conditions of work of more than one employee. It must also be noted that, although the terms employers and workers are used in the definition, that, in the interpretation of enactments words in the singular include the plural and words in the plural include the singular.[275]

It is unfortunate that the court of Appeal failed to avail itself of the opportunity presented to it in the case of *Akinade* v *Non-Academic Staff Union of Educational & Associated Institutions*[275a] to give an authoritative interpretation. In that case, the Oyo State High Court, in Ibadan, held that an action for wrongful termination of the employment of the plaintiff could not be tried in the High Court as it was a trade dispute.

The NIC has dealt with many cases which it would otherwise not have dealt with only because the wrongfully removed employees were, at one time or the other, union officials.[276] It cannot be right that the court's jurisdiction has to depend upon whether or not an employee is a union member or official and that

---

[273] Ibid. 178.

[274] *Western Textile Industries Co. Ltd.* v. *Ado-Ekiti Westexinco Workers Union* 1978-79 N I CLR 107, 111.

[275] S. 14(b) Interpretation Act, Cap. 192.

[275a] *The Guardian*, Lagos, Tuesday February 9, 1999

[276] In *Nigerian Tobacco Company Ltd.* v. *National Union of Food, Beverages and Tobacco Employees* 1982-83 N I CLR 164 one of the two employees wrongfully removed had been the National Vice President of the union; in *National Union of Paper and Paper Products Workers* v. *The Management of Wahum Packages Nigeria Ltd.*, 1982-83 NICLR 202 the employee who alleged wrongful termination was a branch chairman of the union; and in *Nigerian Asbestos Industries Ltd.* v. *National Union of Chemical & Non-Metallic Products Workers* 1986 N I CLR 83 the wrongfully removed employee was also a branch chairman of his union.

the union is willing or able to represent him. Whether an employee is a member of a trade union or not may be purely fortuitous. The same fallacy would appear to underlie the provisions on the settlement of disputes under the Labour Act. It is provided that where an employer or worker neglects or refuses to fulfil a contract or any question, difference or dispute arises as to the rights or liabilities of a party to a contract or touching any misconduct, neglect, ill-treatment or injury to the person or property of a party to a contract any party to the contract feeling himself aggrieved may make complaint to a court having jurisdiction.[277] The court having jurisdiction is a magistrate or district court.[278] But these provisions are not to apply to a trade dispute, that is to say, any dispute or difference between employers and workers or between workers and other workers connected with the employment or non-employment or the terms of the employment or the conditions of labour or any person.[279] The distinction sought to be made is untenable at least in so far as it is based on the definition of a trade dispute. A complaint or dispute within the provision is a trade dispute. Indeed the NIC has decided disputes arising out of the provisions of the Labour Act. For example in *Vicenti Engineering Ltd.* v. *Civil Service Technical Workers' Union*[280] one of the grounds of the award of the IAP related to the Labour Act provision on annual leave with full pay and the NIC held that it was "bound to enforce the Labour Decree 1974 and all arguments to the contrary are rejected."[281] It is believed that the distinction which is sought to be made or which can be more usefully made is between legal rights, i.e., claims of a legal nature or alleged to arise from a breach of a legal right and future rights or interests not yet vested as a legal right.[282] In other words a claim or claims by one or more employees arising out of a contract of employment, a binding settlement or award, a judgment or a statute are best suited for adjudication in the regular courts while claims or demands by way of collective bargaining via employees trade unions for improved or other terms and conditions of employment are eminently suitable for arbitral processes. While claims within the former category usually involve issues of law issues within the latter class are usually more of facts.

---

[277] S. 81 (1) Labour Act, Cap. 198.

[278] S. 80(1) ibid.

[279] S. 81 (6) ibid.

[280] 1978-79 N I CLR 57.

[281] Ibid., 60.

[282] This suggestion was first made in my inaugural lecture cited in footnote 270 ante; for its criticism see Ogunniyi, *Nigerian Labour and Employment Law in Perspective*, 1991, Folio Publishers , p. 301; and for my response see my review cited at footnote 269 at p. 43.

As we have seen the NIC also has jurisdiction, to the exclusion of any other court, to determine questions as to the interpretation of (i) any award either of the court itself or of any arbitration tribunal which is binding, (ii) any collective agreement and (iii) the terms of settlement of any trade dispute as recorded by the conciliator in the memorandum signed by the representatives of the parties to the dispute.[283] Where any question arises as to the interpretation of a binding award the Minister or any party to the award may make an application to the court for a decision on the question.[284] On an application the court may decide the matter after hearing the parties to the award or, with the prior consent of the parties, without hearing them. The decision of the court is final and is deemed to form part of the original award and must be given effect accordingly.[285] However an appeal from the decision of the court lies, as of right, to the Court of Appeal on questions of fundamental rights under the Constitution.[286] In the case of a collective agreement the Minister or any party to a collective agreement may make an application to the court for a decision of the court as to the interpretation of any term or provision of the collective agreement.[287] Upon such an application the court may decide the matter after hearing the Minister or the parties to the agreement or, with the consent of the Minister or the parties, without hearing them. The decision of the court is final and conclusive with respect to the interpretation of the term or provision of the collective agreement concerned.[288]

Nothing is said as to how a binding settlement may be taken to the court for interpretation, although jurisdiction is conferred on the court for that purpose. Since a settlement has similar features with an award including their bindingness and statutory incorporation into contracts of employment it is suggested that they are treated alike. Thus an application for the interpretation of a binding

---

[283] Some such applications have been made; in *Nigeria Union of Construction and Civil Engineering Workers* v. *Construction & Civil Engineering Employers' Association of Nigeria* 1982-83 NICLR 94 and *National Union of Furniture, Fixtures and Wood Workers* v. *Management of General Enterprises Ltd. Kano* 1986 NICLR 207 an application for the interpretation of a collective agreement was made by a party to the agreement; an application for the interpretation of an award of the IAP was made in *Printing & Publishing Workers Union* v. *Caxton Press (W.A.) Ltd.* and *Lagos State Transport Corporation* v. *National Union of Road Transport Workers* 1982-83 NICLR 11 and 126 respectively.

[284] S. 14(1).

[285] S. 14 (1).

[286] S. 14(2) as amended by s. 4 Trade Disputes (Amendment) Act 1992; but quaere whether the NIC has jurisdiction in questions of fundamental rights under the Constitution; see pp 427-428 above.

[287] S. 15(1).

[288] S. 15(2).

settlement may be made by the Minister or any party to the settlement and the court may decided the matter after hearing the parties or with their prior consent, without hearing them and the decision of the court should be final and form part of the original settlement and have effect accordingly.

The deletion (repeal!) of subsection 20(4)[289] which provided that the jurisdiction conferred on the NIC was not to prejudice any jurisdiction of the Supreme Court conferred by either section 213(2) (c) or section 259 of the Constitution or any jurisdiction of a High Court conferred by section 42 of the Constitution will seem not to have resulted in any change in the jurisdiction of any of those courts, i.e., the NIC, a High Court or the Supreme Court.[290] It is, indeed, doubtful whether section 20(4) was ever needed. Since the NIC has never been vested with jurisdiction in questions of fundamental rights under the Constitution there can be no question that its jurisdiction is prejudicial to the special jurisdiction of a High Court in fundamental rights conferred by section 42 or of the Supreme Court conferred by section 213(2)(c). Similarly section 259 continues to apply to the NIC in spite of the repeal of subsection 20(4). By subsection 259(1) where any question arises in any proceedings in any court of law in any part of Nigeria, other than in the Supreme Court, the Court of Appeal or a High Court, and the court is of the opinion that the question involves a substantial question of law, the court may, but, must if any of the parties to the proceedings so requests, refer the question to a High Court having jurisdiction in that part of Nigeria. If the High Court is of opinion that the question involves a substantial question of law it must refer the question to the Court of Appeal but if it is of opinion that it does not involve a substantial question of law it must remit it to the court which made the reference for that court to dispose of in accordance with such directions as the High Court may think fit to give.

Enforcement of awards

The court may enforce any of its awards, including decisions given on an interpretation of an award, by committal proceedings.[291] It may commit for contempt any person whose act or omission, in the opinion of the court,

---

[289] S. 20(4) was originally s. 15(3); for its repeal see s. 6(b) Trade Disputes (Amendment) Act 1992, No. 47.

[290] Ss. 213(2) (c) and 259 of 1979 Constitution are now respectively, ss. 233(2) (b) and 295 of the 1999 Constitution; S. 42 is now S. 46.

[291] Failure to comply with an award of the court remains an offence which, on conviction, is punishable with a fine or imprisonment. See ante.

constitutes contempt of the court.[292] If the President of the court considers the evidence sufficient to commit for contempt any person, he must commit such a person for trial in the High Court and must, until the trial, either admit the person to bail or send him to prison for safe keeping.[293] The warrant of the court is sufficient authority to the person in charge of any prison appointed for the custody of prisoners committed for trial to take such a person into custody for safe keeping.[294] Any person who commits an act of contempt, whether the act is or is not committed in the presence of the members of the court sitting in the exercise of its functions, is liable, on summary conviction before a High Court, to a fine of ₦200 or to imprisonment for three months.[295] Under the 1979 Constitution the NIC was not a superior court of record.[296] But by an amendment in 1992 it became a superior court of record.[297] Thus it could have been argued that the court was empowered to punish for contempt of itself, at least, any contempt committed in *facie curiae*. It was, however, doubtful whether it could do so in the face of Section 35(4). However, now that the court has resumed its constitutional status any such power is lost[297a]. It would also mean that *certiorari* can issue from the High Court to it for excess of jurisdiction or for an error of law in the face of its award. There is no doubt that certiorari lies from the High Court to an arbitration tribunal. In *National Union of Textile, Garment and Tailoring Workers of Nigeria* v. *Atlantic Textile Manufacturing Co. Ltd.*, the NIC felt bond to take judicial notice of the issuance of an order of *certiorari* by the High Court of Lagos State and held that the interim order made by the arbitration tribunal was null and void.

Board of inquiry

Where any trade dispute exists or is apprehended, the Minister may cause inquiry to be made into the causes and circumstances of the dispute and, if he thinks fit, may refer any matter appearing to him to be connected with or relevant

---

292 S. 22

293 S. 23(1)

294 S. 23(2).

295 S. 35 (4).

296 S. 6(3) 1979 Constitution.

297 S. 1(3) Constitution (Suspension & Modification) Decree 1993, No.107 subjected the Constitution to any Decree. For the amendment see s. 5 Trades Disputes (Amendment) Act 1992, No. 47 which inserts a new subsection (2) in s. 19 as follows: (2) The Court shall be a superior court of record.

297a S. 6(3) 1999 Constitution; this constitutional provision overrides the amendment.

to the dispute to a board of inquiry appointed for the purpose by him.[298] The board must inquire into the matter referred to it and report to the Minister.[299] The Minister may also refer any other matter connected with industrial conditions in Nigeria to a board of inquiry appointed for the purpose by him and the board must inquire into the matter referred to it and report on it to the Minister.[300] A board of inquiry may consist of a chairman and such other persons as the Minister thinks fit to appoint or it may consist of one person only.[301] A board which consists of more than one person may act notwithstanding any vacancy in its membership.[302] A board, may, if it thinks fit, make interim reports.[303] Every report of a board, whether interim or minority or any other, must be submitted to the Minister.[304] The Minister may cause to be published, at such time or times and in such manner as he thinks fit, any information obtained or conclusions reached by a board of inquiry.[305]

However, any information obtained by the board in the course of its inquiry with respect to any trade union or any business or undertaking being an information which is not available otherwise through evidence given at the inquiry must not be included in any report of any board or in any publication authorised by the Minister.[306] This may only be done where consent is given on behalf of the union or business as the case may be.[307] A breach of this provision is an offence punishable on conviction with a fine of ₦200.[308]

Powers, practice and procedure

An arbitration tribunal, the National Industrial Court or a board of inquiry has the following powers set out in s. 35(1) of the Act. It may:

(i) require any person to furnish, in writing or otherwise, such particulars relating to the matter before it as it may require;

---

[298] S. 32 (1).
[299] Ibid.
[300] S. 32(2).
[301] S. 32(3).
[302] S. 32(4).
[303] S. 33(1).
[304] S. 33(2).
[305] S. 33(3).
[306] S. 33(4).
[307] S. 33(5).
[308] S. 33(6).

(ii) require any person to attend before it and give evidence on oath or affirmation or otherwise with respect to any matter relevant to the matter before it;
(iii) compel the production before it of books, papers, documents and other things for the purpose of enabling them to be examined or referred to so far as may be necessary in order to obtain information relevant to the matter before it;
(iv) consider and deal with the matter before it in the absence of any party who has been duly summoned or served with a notice to appear;
(v) admit or exclude the public or the press, or both, from any of its sitting;
(vi) adjourn from time to time; and
(vii) generally give all such directions and do all such things as are necessary or expedient for dealing speedily and justly with the matter before it.

For the purpose of enforcing any summon, direction or order issued, given or made by virtue of the above powers, it has the like powers as are exercisable by the Supreme Court.[309] However, if any person, on being required under these powers to furnish any particulars, answer any question or produce any book, paper, document or other things, objects to doing so on the ground that, to do so would tend to incriminate him or on any other lawful ground, he is not bound to comply with the requirement and is not liable to any punishment for refusing to do so.[310]

In any proceedings before the court or an arbitration tribunal either party may appear by a legal practitioner and in any proceedings before a board of inquiry the board may, at its discretion, permit any interested person to appear before it by a legal practitioner.[311]

The Chief Justice of Nigeria may make rules as to the practice and procedure to be followed by the NIC and the Minister may make regulations with respect to the exercise of the functions of an arbitration tribunal or a board of inquiry.[312] Subject to such rules or regulations the NIC or an arbitration tribunal or board of inquiry may regulate its procedure and proceedings as it thinks fit and is not bound to act in any formal manner.[313] The court, an arbitration tribunal or a board of inquiry is not bound by any rules of evidence but may inform itself on

[309] S. 35(2).
[310] S. 35(3).
[311] S. 37.
[312] S. 36(1) and (2).
[313] S. 36(3) (a).

any matter in such manner as it thinks just.[314] In *Persons Running the Defunct Western Textile Industries Co. Ltd.* v. *National Union of Textile, Garment and Tailoring Workers of Nigeria*,[315] the NIC held that it could allow additional facts or evidence to be produced even after an adjournment for judgment but before judgment was given. Similarly, in *National Union of Chemical and Non-Metallic Products Workers* v. *Management of Metal Box Toyo Glass Ltd.*,[316] the NIC held that, not being bound by strict rules of evidence, it could, either on the motion of the parties before it or on its own motion, admit further evidence if it is demonstrably clear that the ends of justice can be better served by allowing such additional evidence.

Where the press have been admitted to any sitting of an arbitration tribunal, the NIC or a board of inquiry, and not otherwise, a fair and accurate report of summary of the proceedings, including any evidence heard in the course of the proceedings, may be published but until the award of the court or tribunal or the result of the inquiry has been officially published, no comment must be published in respect of the proceedings or the evidence.[317] A contravention of this provision is an offence punishable on conviction with a fine of ₦200.[318]

The powers of the National Industrial Court under the National Industrial Court Rules 1979 include, *inter alia*, power to join a party not already a party to the proceedings, to entertain and consider interlocutory applications, to make interim awards or encourage the parties to reach mutual settlement between themselves and to make such order as seem just where such mutual settlement is reached.[319]

A party may discontinue or withdraw his claim and the court must then make such order as may seem just. Where a party has been duly served the court may deal with the matter in his absence and the court may encourage parties, in respect of a case coming before it in the first instance, to reach mutual settlement between themselves.[320] The court may review any order made by it where application is made within fourteen days of the date of the order. Where it appears to the court that any person has been guilty of unreasonable delay, or of taking improper, vexatious or unnecessary steps in any proceedings or of other unreasonable conduct, the court may make an order for costs or expenses against

---

314 S. 36(3)(b).
315 1980-81 NICLR 86.
316 1984-85 NICLR 39.
317 S. 38(1).
318 S.38(2).
319 Rules 14, 15 and 17 respectively.
320 Rules 21, 22 and 23

him.[321] Any notice or other document required to be served or delivered to any person may be sent by registered post or left at his address for service or, where no address for service has been given, at his registered office, principal place of business or last known address. A document served by post is assumed, in the absence of evidence to the contrary, to have been delivered in the normal course of post. The court may direct that service of any document be dispensed with or be effected otherwise than in the manner prescribed above. The court may inform itself on any matter relating to the rules of evidence but is not bound by them.

Protection of essential services

Industrial action by employees engaged in the provision of essential services to the community may disrupt such services and consequently inconvenience the community. The Criminal Code and Penal Code made provisions for the protection of water and electricity supply by requiring employees engaged in those undertakings to give a stipulated period of notice before going on strike. These provisions were repealed by the Trade Disputes Act in 1976 which, however, made similar provisions in sections 40 and 41. The new provisions apply not only to electricity and water but to essential services which is defined very widely.[321a] However, s.10(2) of the Trade Disputes (Essential Service) Act[322] provides that while the Act is in force sections 40 and 41 stand suspended. Thus it is the Trade Disputes (Essential Services) Act which now has provisions for the protection of essential services.

Definition of essential service

Essential service means:[322a]

(a) the public service of the Federation or of a State which shall for the purposes of this Act include service, in a civil capacity, of persons employed in the armed forces of the Federation or any part thereof and also, of persons, employed in an industry or undertaking (corporate or unincorporate) which deals or is connected with the manufacture or

---

[321] Rules 26 and 27
[321a] S.47 and 1st Schedule; the definition is exactly the same as the one given in the Trade Dispute (Essential Services) Act.
[322] Cap. 433; all references in the remainder of this Chapter are to Cap. 433 unless otherwise stated.
[322a] S. 9(1)

production of materials for use in the armed forces of the Federation or any part thereof;

(b) any service established, provided or maintained by the government of the Federation or of a State, by a local government council, a town council or any municipal or statutory authority, or by private enterprise -

(i) for, or in connection with, the supply of electricity, power or water, or fuel of any kind;

(ii) for or in connection with, sound broadcasting or postal, telegraphic, cable, wireless or telephonic communications;

(iii) for maintaining ports, harbours, docks or aerodromes, or in connection with, transportation of persons, goods or livestock by road, rail, sea, river or air;

(iv) for, or in connection with, the burial of the dead, hospitals, the treatment of the sick, the prevention of disease, or any of the following public health matters, namely, sanitation, road-cleansing and the disposal of night-soil and rubbish;

(v) for dealing with outbreaks of fire;

(vi) for or in connection with teaching or the provision of educational services at primary, secondary or tertiary institutions.[322b]

(c) service in any capacity in any of the following organizations -

(i) the Central Bank of Nigeria;

(ii) the Nigerian Security, Printing and Minting Company Limited;

(iii) any body corporate licensed to carry on banking business under the Banking Act.

The main aim of the law is to ensure that all those who are engaged in essential services follow the procedure laid down by law for the settlement of any differences. Where a particular group of such employees fails to do so the group may be proscribed. Such a group may also be proscribed where it intentionally disrupts the essential service within which it operates or the national economy.

If the President is satisfied that any trade union or association any of the members of which are employed in any essential service is or has been engaged in acts calculated to disrupt the economy or to obstruct or disrupt the smooth

[322b] See S. 1 Teaching, Etc. (Essential Services) Act 1993 No. 30.

running of any essential service or has wilfully failed to comply with the procedure laid down in the Trade Disputes Act for the settlement of trade disputes, he may by order published in the Gazette proscribed the union or association.[323]

A proscribed union or association ceases to exist as from the date of the order of proscription. A proscribed trade union must, not later than fourteen days from the date of proscription, surrender its certificate of registration to the Registrar of Trade Unions who must forthwith cancel such registration.[324] As from the commencement of the proscription order all properties, whether movable or immovable, of the union or association, whether held in its name or held by any person for or in trust for it, is forfeited to the Federal Government and vests in the Government free of encumbrances without any further assurance.[325] Any person who holds any such property must, within fourteen days of the making of the order, or, where the property comes into his possession after the making of the order, within fourteen days of its coming into his possession, deliver such property to the Secretary to the Federal Government or notify him in writing of the place where the property may be recovered. In the latter case, the person must take all other steps as the Secretary may require in the recovery of such property.[326] Any person who contravenes or fails to comply with the above provisions with respect to the property of a union or association is guilty of an offence and on summary conviction liable to imprisonment for a term not exceeding five years.[327]

Any employer or any official of an association of employers or any official of a trade union or any person, not being an official of a trade union, who in any way performs or assumes a leadership role in a trade union or faction of a trade union and either is or has been engaged in acts calculated to disrupt the economy or obstruct or disrupt the smooth running of any essential service or has willfully failed to comply with the procedure for settling trade disputes laid out in the Trade Disputes Act is guilty of an offence.[328] Where a person who is guilty of

---

[323] S. 1(1); association means any body of persons, by whatever name called, associated for a common purpose, but does not include a trade union, s. 9(1).

[324] S. 1(2).

[325] S. 1(3).

[326] S. 1(4)

[327] S. 1(5).

[328] S. 2(1); employer includes reference to any director, manager, secretary or other similar official or any person purporting to act in any such capacity and references to trade union or faction of trade union includes reference to any group of workers associated for a common purpose; s. 2(4); person is taken as performing or assuming a leadership role if it is proved that, at the material

the offence is an employer or official of an employer or an official of any association of employers he is liable, on conviction, to a fine of ₦10,000 and where such a person is an official of a trade union or is a person who, not being an official of a trade union, in any way performs or assumes a leadership role in any such trade union or faction of a trade union, he is liable, on conviction, to a fine of ₦200 or imprisonment for six months or to both such fine and imprisonment. In addition, any such person must not, at any time after conviction, continue to be or become an official of any trade union, including any faction of a trade union, or association any of the members of which are employed in essential services.[329]

Where a trade union or association has been proscribed, no other trade union consisting of the same or substantially the same members as those of the proscribed union must be registered until a period of not less than six months has elapsed, from the date of the proscription order and no association having the same or similar objectives and consisting of the same or substantially the same members as those of the proscribed association must be formed within the same period of time.[330] Any official of a trade union or association immediately before its proscription must not, at any time after the proscription, be an official of a union or association any of the members of which are employed in any essential service.[331] Any such official who contravenes this provision is guilty of an offence and, on conviction, liable to imprisonment for a term not exceeding five years.[332]

It has also been thought necessary to include a power of detention in addition to these powers which appear formidable enough. The Inspector General of Police or Chief of General Staff, if satisfied that any person who was an official or member of a proscribed trade union or association has, subsequent to the proscription, been concerned in acts prejudicial to industrial peace or in acts calculated to obstruct or disrupt the smooth running of any essential services and that it is therefore necessary to exercise control over him, he may by order in writing direct that the person be detained in a civil prison or a police station. It is then the duty of the superintendent or other person in charge of any prison or the police officer in charge of any police station to whom the order is delivered to

---

time or during the material period, he had performed functions or assumed duties which are normally within the competence of an official of a trade union or purported so to do; S. 2(3).

329 S 2(2).

330 S. 3.

331 S. 4(1).

332 S. 4(2).

keep the person in custody until the order is revoked.[333] Any order is also full authority for any police officer or member of the armed forces to arrest the person to whom the order relates and to remove him to a civil prison or police station.[334]

Section 8 suspends the constitutional provisions on fundamental human rights for the purposes of the Act. Accordingly, an application for a writ of *habeas corpus ad subjiciendum* does not lie at the instance of any one detained under the Act nor does a suit or other legal proceedings lie against any person for anything done or intended to be done in pursuance of the Act. There is no doubt that sections 5 and 8 must now be regarded as unconstitutional under democratic governance.

Military governments had always subjected constitutional provisions to Decrees by which they legislated. The military even often resorted to the promulgation of special Decrees. For example, rather than proscribe the Academic Staff Union of Universities under the Trade Disputes (Essential Services) Act which allows a proscribed union to re-register after six months, it was twice proscribed under a special Decree.[335] Similarly a dissension within the Nigerian Labour Congress was dealt with under the National Economic Emergency Powers Decree 1985.[336]

In addition to the above provisions which apply to all essential services, including the teaching and other educational services, there are provisions which apply especially to teaching and other educational services.

A member of staff, whether teaching or non-teaching, employed in any primary, secondary or tertiary educational institution is prohibited from embarking on an industrial action in the form of a strike, sit-down strike, work-to-rule or any other kind of industrial action which is calculated to disrupt the smooth running of teaching or educational services in any of those institutions.[337] Where such a member of staff continues or persists in any such industrial action for more than one week, he is deemed to have resigned his appointment but

---

333 S. 5(1).

334 S. 5(3).

335 Academic Staff Union of Universities (Proscription) and Prohibition From Participation in Trade Union Activities) Decree 1988; the latest is the Trade Disputes, (Essential Services Deregulation, Proscription and Prohibition from Participation in trade Union Activities) Decree 1996, No. 24 promulgated on the same day as the Trade Disputes (Essential Services) (Proscription) Order 1996 was made proscribing the same three trade unions; the purport of the Decree is obscure.

336 See National Economic Emergency Powers (Nigerian Labour Congress) (Amendment) Order 1988 and National Economic Emergency Powers (Extension, Etc.) Decree 1986.

337 S. 2(1) Teaching, Etc. (Essential Services) Act 1993 No. 30.

without prejudice to any accrued rights.[338] Also such a member of staff is liable to vacate such accommodation as would have been provided by the institution for him in any part of Nigeria.[339] And every person who is either an ordinary or executive committee member of the trade union or association which embarked on the industrial action is guilty of an offence and liable, on conviction, to imprisonment for a term not exceeding two years.[340] Such an offence is triable in the Federal High Court.[341]

Section 3 which provides that, notwithstanding anything contained in the Constitution, the African Charter on Human and Peoples' Rights (Ratification & Enforcement) Act or any other enactment, no proceedings shall lie or be instituted in any court for or on account of any act, matter or thing done or purported to be done in respect of the Act and that if any proceeding had been instituted such proceeding shall abate, be discharged and made void, would appear clearly, to offend against the Constitution.[342]

---

[338] S. 2(2) ibid.

[339] S. 2(3) ibid.; see s. 2 Teaching, Etc. (Essential Services)(Amendment) Act 1993 No 44.

[340] S. 2(4) ibid.

[341] S. 2(5) ibid.

[342] S. 1 Constitution of the Federal Republic of Nigeria, 1999

Chapter 10

Industrial conflict and the Law

The "freedom in conducting a trade is not absolute or unconditional. It is only a particular aspect of the citizen's right to personal freedom and, like other aspects of that right, is qualified by various legal limitations either by statute or by common law."[1] This is true of trade unions as it is of any other institution or an individual. In common with all citizens, a union, its officials and members are obliged to carry out the purposes of the union within the law. In this chapter the manner in which and the extent to which the criminal law and the law of tort affect the activities of trade unions will be discussed.

The right to strike, that is, the right of employees collectively to withdraw their labour, is regarded by many as an integral part of collective bargaining. As Lord Wright has said: "Where the rights of labour are concerned, the rights of the employer are conditioned by the rights of the men to give or withhold their services. The right to strike is an essential element in the principle of collective bargaining."[2] Professor Wedderburn adds that, "to protect such a right is to recognize the fact that the limits set to the right to strike and to lock-out are one measure of the strength which each party can in the last resort bring to bear at the bargaining table...the strength of a union's position is bound to be related to its power and its right to call out its members, so long as any semblance of collective bargaining survives."[3]

We have seen however that both collective bargaining and the right to strike have been emasculated.

A strike is defined as the cessation of work by a body of persons employed acting in combination or a concerted refusal or a refusal under a common understanding of any number of persons employed to continue to work for an employer in consequence of a dispute, done as a means of compelling their employer or any person or body of persons employed, or to aid other workers in compelling their employer or any person or body of persons employed, to accept or not to accept terms of employment and physical conditions of work.[4] Thus, a

---

[1] *Crofter Hand Woven Harris Tweed* v *Veitch* [1942] AC 435, 463, per Lord Wright.

[2] Ibid.

[3] *Op. cit.*, 236.

[4] S. 47 Trade Disputes Act, Cap. 432, Laws of the Federation of Nigeria, 1990.

strike includes a sympathetic strike. It also includes the so-called work-to-rule or go-slow as cessation of work is defined to include deliberately working at less than usual speed or with less than usual efficiency and refusal to continue to work to include a refusal to work at usual speed or with usual efficiency. Section 17(1) Trade Disputes Act[5] provides that an employer must not declare or take part in a lock-out[6] and an employee must not take part in a strike in connection with any trade dispute where (a) the procedure specified in section 3 or 5 of the Act has not been complied with in relation to the dispute; or (b) a conciliator has been appointed under section 7 of the Act for the purpose of effecting a settlement of the dispute; or (c) the dispute has been referred for settlement to the Industrial Arbitration Panel under section 8 of the Act; or (d) an award by an arbitration tribunal had become binding under section 12 (3) of the Act; or (e) the dispute has subsequently been referred to the National Industrial Court under section 13(1) or 16 of this Act; or (f) the National Industrial Court has issued an award on the reference. The purpose of setting out s. 17(1) in full is to show that it does not leave any room for a lawful strike. Its effect, it is submitted, is to prohibit strikes completely.[6a] Any person who contravenes the provision is guilty of an offence and is liable, on conviction, in the case of an individual, to a fine of ₦100 or to imprisonment for six months and in the case of a body corporate, to a fine of ₦1,000.[7]

Furthermore, any employee who takes part in a strike is not entitled to any wages or other remuneration for the period of the strike and any such period does not count for the purpose of reckoning the period of continuous employment and all rights dependent on continuity are prejudicially affected accordingly.[8] It is believed that the second arm of this provision only permits the deduction of the period of a strike in the reckoning of a period of continuous

---

[5] Cap. 432 ibid.

[6] A lockout is defined as the closing of a place of employment, or the suspension of work, or the refusal by an employer to continue to employ any number of persons employed by him in consequence of a dispute, done with a view to compelling those persons, or to aid another employer in compelling persons employed by him, to accept terms of employment and physical conditions of work. S. 47, ibid. The prohibition of lockouts can hardly be regarded as limiting the rights and powers of employers in the same way and to the extent to which a ban on strikes affects the rights and powers of employees.

[6a] See *Eche* v *State Education Commission*; *Chigbo* v *Local Government Service Commission* (1983)1 FNR 386 where the court held that a strike in such circumstances would be illegal, although it also held, inconsistently, it is submitted, that where there is compliance with only one of the subsections of section 13 (now 17) a strike thereafter cannot be said to be an illegal strike.

[7] S. 17(2) ibid.

[8] S. 42(1) ibid.

employment; it is intended to overlook the breach of the contract of employment which a strike constitutes.[9] This interpretation seems clear enough and is, in practical terms, to be preferred. Where an employer locks out his employees, the employees are entitled to wages and any other applicable remuneration for the period of the lockout and this period must not prejudicially affect any rights of the employees being rights dependent on the continuity of period of employment.[10] If any question arises as to whether there has been a lockout it must, on application to the Minister by the employees or their representatives, be determined by him and his decision is final.[11]

Criminal conspiracy

Notwithstanding the prohibition of strikes, they continue to occur. Indeed, strikes have always been on the increase. Although, by taking part in a strike, an employee commits an offence, there are, in addition, a number of other criminal offences which such employees may commit either by agreeing to take a strike action or by actually taking a strike action. One such criminal offence is criminal conspiracy. Both the Criminal and Penal Codes[12] contain provisions on criminal conspiracy.

The provisions on criminal conspiracy in the Criminal Code which are particularly related to industrial conflict are contained in chapter fifty four i.e. Ss. 516 to 518. Sections 516 and 517 provide that any person who conspires with another to commit an offence commits criminal conspiracy. An offence is an act or omission which renders the person doing the act or making the omission liable to punishment under the criminal code or any statute. It is clear therefore, that when employees go on strike they can be prosecuted not only for going on strike but also for criminal conspiracy; as we have seen anyone who goes on strike is liable to punishment. The offence of criminal conspiracy may also be committed even where the conspiracy is not necessarily to commit an offence. S. 518 Criminal Code provides as follows:

Any person who conspires with another to effect any of the following purposes:

---

[9] See below.

[10] S. 42(2) cap. 432.

[11] Ibid.; but see s. 6(6)(b) of the Constitution for a right of access to the courts.

[12] The Criminal Code is the schedule to the Criminal Code Act, Cap.77; it applies in the States in the South. The Penal Code which is the schedule to the Penal Code Law, Cap.89 of the Laws of Northern Nigeria, 1963, is applied in the States in the North.

(1) to prevent or defeat the execution or enforcement of any Act, Law, Statute, or Order in Council; or
(2) to cause any injury to the person or reputation of any person, or to depreciate the value of any property of any person; or
(3) to prevent or obstruct the free and lawful disposition of any property by the owner thereof for its fair value; or
(4) to injure any person in his trade or profession; or
(5) to prevent or obstruct, by means of any act or acts which if done by an individual person would constitute an offence on his part, the free and lawful exercise by any person of his trade, profession, or occupation; or
(6) to effect any unlawful purpose; or
(7) to effect any lawful purpose by any unlawful means; is guilty of a misdemeanor, and is liable to imprisonment for two years.

There are no cases to show that this section has ever been applied to employees on industrial action. This may be proof enough that the section has no immediate relevance to industrial disputes. However, in the Australian case of *Brisbane Shipwrights' Provident Union* v *Heggie*,[13] the equivalent of subsection 4 was applied although, the case went to trial as civil rather than criminal conspiracy. The respondent was employed as a shipwright in the service of the Queensland Government at one of the government docks. When called upon to join the union and pay the admission fee he refused whereupon the union informed the Government that unless the respondent was dismissed the union would call out its men employed at the dock and would stay out so long as the respondent's employment continued. It was held that this was conspiracy to injure the respondent in his trade or profession.

Subsections (6) and (7) are also very wide in scope as the word unlawful appears to have been given the meaning which it seems to have at common law.[14] It seems that at common law, unlawful would include not only criminal offences but also torts and even acts which are not breaches of the law but are either immoral or injurious to the public.[15] The gist of the offence of criminal conspiracy lies, not in doing the act or effecting the purpose for which the conspiracy is formed, but in the forming of the scheme or the agreement between the parties.[16] Thus, employees who merely agree to take a strike action can be

---

[13] (1906) 3 CLR 686.

[14] See *Majekodunmi* v *R.* (1952) 14 WACA 64; also the Ugandan case of *R.* v *Jamnades* 13 WACA 147.

[15] Turner, *Kenny's Outlines of Criminal Law*; *Shaw* v *DPP* [1961] 2 WLR 897.

[16] *Majekodunmi* v *R.*, *supra.*

prosecuted for the offence of criminal conspiracy. It will be an agreement to effect an unlawful purpose. Where employees actually go on strike the difficulty in proving the agreement to effect the unlawful purpose to go on strike, would have been removed.

Section 96(1) and (2) of the Penal Code provides as follows:

(1) when two or more persons agree to do or cause to be done (a) an illegal act; or (b) an act which is not illegal by illegal means, such an agreement is called a criminal conspiracy.

(2) Notwithstanding the provisions of Subsection (1), no agreement except an agreement to commit an offence shall amount to a criminal conspiracy unless some act besides the agreement is done by one or more parties to such agreement in pursuance thereof.

There is therefore no criminal conspiracy under the Penal Code unless one or more of the conspirators have carried the illegal act into effect. Illegal is everything which is prohibited by law and which is an offence or which furnishes ground for a civil action.[17] However, both codes remove the offence of criminal conspiracy from the area of trade dispute. The Criminal Code provides that the provisions of Section 516 to 518 do not apply to an agreement or combination of two or more persons to do or procure to be done any act in contemplation or furtherance of a trade dispute if such act committed by one person would not be punishable as an offence.[18] Therefore, where employees engage in industrial action in contemplation or furtherance of a trade dispute they can be charged for criminal conspiracy only where they carry out an act which if done by one employee would be punishable as an offence. However, under the Criminal Code there is no defence if the offence by an individual would be punishable only by a fine.[19] It is not clear whether employees who have taken part in strike in furtherance of a trade dispute can avail themselves of the protection of S. 51 8A Criminal Code or S. 96 Explanation 2 of the Penal Code. Although, it is true that s. 13 Trade Disputes Act provides that an employee who takes part in a strike is guilty of an offence, but strike itself is defined by the same statute as a concerted action by more than one employee. An individual employee who withdraws his labour is not guilty of an offence; he cannot in fact be said to be engaged in a

[17] S . 2 9 Penal Code.

[18] S. 51 8A Criminal Code. See s. 96 Explanation 2 Penal Code; the phrase "in contemplation or furtherance of a trade dispute" upon which protection depends is discussed below.

[19] S. 518A(1) Criminal Code.

strike. The better view would seem to be that criminal conspiracy cannot arise where employees in contemplation or furtherance of a trade dispute take a strike action.

It seems that trade unions or their officials may also be prosecuted under S. 422 of the Criminal Code which provides that - any person who conspires with another by deceit or any fraudulent means to effect the market price of anything publicly sold, or to defraud the public, or any person, whether a particular person or not, or to extort any property[20] from any person, is guilty of a felony, and is liable to imprisonment for seven years. In *Ogundipe* v *R*,[21] the appellants, officials of a union of labourers, who demanded higher rates of pay from contractors who required the services of the labourers were charged under the section with conspiracy to extort. Although, they were held not liable this was only because, as Verity C.J. said, the court was unable to find that the appellants conspired to achieve their aim by any deceit or fraudulent means.

Picketing

Picketing is that aspect of industrial action which consists of placing a "picket", which may comprise of a single individual or more persons, at or near the place where employees are employed for the purpose of communicating with persons on the subject matter of the action. The law provides for picketing and this may not necessarily be affected by the prohibition of strikes. The basic law is in S. 42(1) Trade Unions Act which reads as follows:

> It shall be lawful for one or more persons, acting on their own behalf or on behalf of a trade union or registered federation of trade unions or of an individual employer or firm in contemplation or furtherance of a trade dispute, to attend at or near a house or place where a person resides or works or carries on business or happens to be, if they so attend merely for the purpose of peacefully obtaining or communicating information or of peacefully persuading any person to work or abstain from working.

The right to picket is however a precarious one. A number of offences may easily be committed while picketing. First, picketing is allowed only in contemplation or furtherance of a trade dispute. This phrase is discussed later. Second, pickets may only attend at or near a house or place where a person

[20] Property includes everything, animate or inanimate, capable of being the subject of ownership; S. 1 ibid.

[21] (1954) 14 WACA 465.

resides or works or carries on business or happens to be. However, a place where a person happens to be is not limited to a place where the person habitually frequents. It includes any place where an employee or other person is found however casually.[22] However, pickets cannot go into or stay in any such place. As Lord O'Brien C.J. said in *Larkin* v *Belfast Harbour Commissioners*,[23] the words in the section

> are...intended to enlarge the field of operations - the physical area of the operations of representatives of trade unions or of others...it was never intended to authorize as a matter of right an invasion into a man's house, or entry against the will of the owner into a place of business.[24]

But there is no reason why pickets may not use the highway for the purpose of picketing. Everyone has a right to the use of the highway. As the Irish Supreme Court pointed out in *Ferguson* v *O'Gorman*,[25] when the legislature declared it lawful for persons to attend at or near a house or place it cannot reasonably have contemplated that such a house or place would be situated in a waste or no-man's land. The usual approach to a residence or place of business is a public highway, and, unless the right to attend is a right to attend on a public highway, it is difficult to see how the right to picket can be exercised at all.[26] In fact, the courts have said that the right to attend is, perhaps, the only privilege conferred by the section.[27] The effect of the section is that an attendance which comes within the section is lawful; it does not, by itself, constituted an offence or a tort. As Viscount Dilhorne said, "it is only the attendance which of itself is not to be criminal or a tort if in contemplation or furtherance of a trade dispute and if only for a specified period."[28]

However, pickets may quite easily commit offences and even torts while using the highway. Under the Criminal Code any person who prevents the public from having access to any part of a highway by an excessive and unreasonable temporary use of it commits an offence.[29] It is a question of fact whether use of the highway is excessive and unreasonable. The facts of the English case of

---

[22] *Charnock* v *Court* [1899] 2 Ch.35.
[23] (1908) 2 I R 214.
[24] Ibid.
[25] (1937) IR 620.
[26] Ibid.
[27] *Broom* v *DPP* [1974] 1 All ER 314; *Kavanagh* v *Hiscock* [1974] 2 All ER 177.
[28] *Broom* v *DPP* [l974] 1 All ER 314, 322.
[29] S. 234; see also S. 194 Penal Code.

Tynan v *Balmar*,[30] appear to be an excellent example of such a user. About forty pickets formed and moved around in a circle on the highway in front of the main entrance to the picketed factory. The court held that the section "clearly did not authorize this conduct."[31] In *Queen* v *Imoudu & Ors*,[32] Imoudu, (now known as "Labour Leader No. 1") as a result of his fearless leadership of the militant Nigerian Union of Railwaymen, was convicted along with five others on a charge of taking part in a riot. The riotous behaviour was said to have arisen out of the determination of the men to compel all railway workers to join in the demonstration intended to draw the attention of the employer to certain demands made by the union.

Under the Criminal Code provision on breach of the peace,[33] it has been held that the test is not whether a breach of the peace has actually occurred but rather whether the conduct complained of is likely to lead to a breach of the peace.[34] In dealing with the same problem in English law Lord Parker C.J., said that the law on breach of the peace is reasonably plain.[35] "First, the mere statement by a Constable that he did anticipate that there might be a breach of the peace is clearly not enough. There must exist proved facts from which a Constable could reasonably have anticipated such a breach. Second, it is not enough that his contemplation is that there is a remote possibility but there must be a real possibility of a breach of the peace."[36] And as May J. has added: "where, however, a police officer reasonably anticipates that in the circumstances obtaining in the particular case, the consequence of any peaceful picketing may well be a breach of the peace, either by the pickets or by spectators, whether supporters of the pickets or not, then it is the duty of that police officer to take such steps as are reasonably necessary to prevent that anticipated breach of the peace."[37]

It is not only through the manner of attendance that pickets may commit an offence. As we have seen, the purposes of the attendance must not be otherwise than peacefully to obtain or communicate information or peacefully to persuade any person to work or abstain from working. Persuasion is limited to persuasion either to work or to abstain from working. Thus, only employees may be

---

[30] [1966] 2 All ER 133.
[31] Ibid., pp. 136-7.
[32] [1961] 1 All NLR13.
[33] S. 249(d); see also S. 133 Penal Code.
[34] *Uke* v *Ogie* (1955) 15 WACA 15.
[35] *Piddington* v *Bates* [1960] 3 All ER 660.
[36] Ibid.
[37] *Kavanagh* v *Hiscock* [1974] 2 All ER 177, 185.

persuaded not to join a strike or break a strike. Non-employees such as suppliers, shoppers, clients or other customers may not be persuaded but may only be communicated with.

The line between communication and persuasion, although, obviously a fine one, must be drawn by the courts based on the facts of each case. A communication which is accompanied by defamatory matter or a falsehood ceases to be peaceful communication.[38] The section does not confer a right, in the sense of a right to compel anyone to stop or stop and listen to a communication or to be persuaded.[39] In *Kavanagh* v *Hiscock*,[40] Lord Widgery C.J., said it is inapt to describe the right given by the section as a right. He agreed with Lord Salmon in *Broom* v *DPP*[41] that the word "immunity" is a much better word.[42] Therefore, pickets have no right to stop anyone or stop any vehicle in order to try to persuade persons not to work or to work or to communicate, at all, with persons.

There are many other offences which pickets may commit. These include assault, battery or even arson. Section 366 and 367 of the Criminal Code and 396 of the Penal Code also create a number of offences. Sections 366 and 367 are reproduced below: S. 366. Subject to the provisions of the Trade Unions Act, any person, who, with intent to prevent or hinder any other person from doing any act which he is lawfully entitled to do, or with intent to compel him to do any act which he is lawfully entitled to abstain from doing, or to abstain from doing any act which he is lawfully entitled to do:

(a) threatens such other person with injury to his person, reputation, or property, or property of anyone in whom he is interested;
(b) or persistently follows such other person about from place to place; or
(c) hides any tools, clothes or other property owned or used by such other person or deprives him of or hinders him in the use thereof; or
(d) watches or besets the house or other place where such other person resides or works or carries on business or happens to be, or the approach to such house or place; or

[38] *Pink* v *Federation of Trades and Labour Unions* (1892) 8 TLR 216; *Ratcliffe* v *Evans* (1892) 2 QB 524; *Ryan* v *Cooke & Quinn* (1938) IR 512.

[39] *Tynan* v *Balmar* [1966] 2 All ER 133; *Broom* v *DPP* [1974] 1 All ER 314; *Kavanagh* v *Hiscock* [1974] 2 All ER 177.

[40] *Supra.*

[41] *Supra.*

[42] [1974] 2 All ER 177, 183

(e) follows such other person with two or more other persons in a disorderly manner in or through any street or road; or

(f) induces or attempts to induce that person to believe that he or any person in whom he is interested, will become an object of displeasure to the Government of Nigeria or to any person employed in the public service of Nigeria; is guilty of an offence and is liable on conviction to imprisonment for one year.

S. 367 Any person who, with any of the intents in the proceeding section mentioned, assaults any other person or anyone in whom he is interest, is guilty of a felony, and liable to imprisonment for five years.

While S. 366 is stipulated to be subject to the provisions of the Trade Union Act - including, certainly, S. 42 of the Act - section 367 is not so protected; in any event picketing accompanied by assault, which is the use of force of any kind,[43] is clearly not protected by section 42. There is only one offence created by S. 366 and the subsections merely stipulated the different modes of committing the offence.[44] Of the six ways in which the offence may be committed, it seems clear that only the mode prescribed in subsection (d) may be protected by S. 42 of the Trade Unions Act. Section 42(2) provides that anything declared by subsection (1) to be lawful cannot constitute an offence under any law in force in Nigeria and in particular does not constitute an offence under section 366 of the Criminal Code or any corresponding enactment in force in any part of Nigeria. Although, it is arguable that to watch or beset is not quite the same thing as attend at or near, it is suggested that no offence will be committed where, in contemplation or furtherance of a trade dispute, pickets watch or beset a place for the purpose of either peacefully obtaining or communicating information or of peacefully persuading any person to work or abstain from working. Where there is no trade dispute or where no attempt to obtain or communicate information or persuade workers is made watching or besetting will, however, be an offence.[45]

To persistently follow a person from place to place will seem to always be an offence.[46] In *Smith* v *Thomasson*,[47] the court held that one person following

---

[43] See 252 Criminal Code

[44] *Wilson* v *Renton* (1910) 1 SLT 30

[45] Ibid.

[46] *Smith* v *Thomason* (1890) 62 LT 68

[47] *Supra.*

another persistently was sufficient to constitute the offence. Similarly, the same offense will be committed where pickets follow a person in a disorderly manner in or through any street or road.[48] In *R* v *Mckenzie*,[49] the court said that the "gist and pith" of the offence is not the following in a disorderly manner but the doing so with a view to compel the person followed to abstain from doing some act he had a legal right to do.[50] Indeed, the court held that the acts which the person followed had a legal right to do and which the defendant by his conduct intended to compel him to abstain from doing ought to be specified. It is suggested that this view is to be preferred to that of Pollock B in *Smith* v *Thomasson*[51] where he said that it is clear that the legislature intended to prevent mere acts though done without any expressed intention.

Trade unions and the Law of Torts

Apart from criminal offences the activities of pickets and also in particular of trade union officials while carrying out industrial action, are also affected by the law of torts. *In Ojo* v *Balogun & Ors*,[52] the defendant barricaded the only entrance to the premises of the employer and made threatening and abusive noise and in particular threatened that no member of the senior staff of the company would be allowed to pass or drive through the gate. The plaintiff, a senior employee of the company brought an action for an injunction to restrain the defendants from continuing their conduct. Although, the court did not find that the defendant committed any tort it granted the injunction. The court said:

> I certainly do not think that any law, either here in Nigeria or in England or in any civilized country for that matter would give its blessings to any act or acts which would amount to threats or violence, or which would precipitate violence leading to a breach of the peace simply because the act or acts is or are in contemplation or furtherance of a trade dispute.[53]

In *Thomas* v *National Union of Mineworkers*[54] Scott J. said that in order to

---

[48] *Wilson* v *Renton, supra.*
[49] [1892] 2 QB 519
[50] Ibid. 522.
[51] (1890) 62 LT 68
[52] (1980) 7-9 CCHCJ 261
[53] Ibid. 265
[54] [1985] 2 All ER 1

decide to what extent picketing that falls outside the section is tortuous, recourse must be had to the general law of tort. The court held it was tortuous to carry out picketing in a manner that was an unreasonable harassment of the men, who decided to work. In this case, some of the miners who were on strike decided to return to work. A daily congregation of an average of 50 to 70 men attended the colliery gates to picket. They hurled abuses at the men who had to be conveyed in vehicles to and from work and in police presence. The court said the men had a right to work and that they should not be required, in order to exercise that right, to tolerate the situation created by the pickets. An injunction was granted.

However, the well known torts associated with industrial actions, are the so-called economic torts of conspiracy, inducing breach of contract and intimidation. In 1901 the House of Lords handed down two decisions which severely enlarged the common law liabilities of trade unions in torts. *Taff Vale Railway Co.* v *Amalgamated Society of Railway Servants,*[55] laid it down that a registered trade union could be sued in its registered name and its funds used to satisfy any damages while *Quinn* v *Leathem,*[56] created the tort of conspiracy. These decisions caused not a little stir within and even outside the trade union movement in England. Professor Wedderburn writes of the Taff Vale decision that it "became part of working-class culture, part of the way "they will treat trade unions if they can."[57]

In 1903, a Royal Commission was appointed under the chairmanship of Lord Dunedin to report on any necessary reform. The commission's reports formed the basis of the Trade Disputes Act 1906. Three out of the four principal sections of the Act, have direct relevance in the law of tort. Section 1 removed liability for conspiracy, the *Quinn* v *Leathem* tort. This section is however not contained in the Trade Unions Act nor in any other legislation, the reason being, probably, that by 1938 when the first trade union legislation was enacted in Nigeria, changed judicial attitude towards the unions had rendered statutory protection largely unnecessary.[58] Section 3 of the 1906 Act which is reproduced in S. 43 of the Trade Unions Act, protects the tort of inducing breach of contract and similar torts while the effect of the Taff Vale decision was met in S. 4 which, with important additions, forms S. 23 of the Trade unions Act which confers almost total immunity in tort actions on trade unions.

---

[55] [1901] AC 426
[56] [1901] AC 495
[57] *The Worker and the Law* (Pelican), p. 227
[58] See especially *Sorrel* v *Smith* [1925] AC 700

Immunity in tort action

Section 23 reads:

> 1) An action against a trade union (whether of workers or employers) in respect of any tortuous act alleged to have been committed by or on behalf of the trade union in contemplation of or in furtherance of a trade dispute shall not be entertained by any court in Nigeria.
> 2) Subsection (1) above applies both to an action against a trade union in its registered name and to an action against one or more persons as representatives of a trade union.

The section protects the union itself alone and not an official or member of the union who committed the tort.[59] In other words, a trade union cannot be made liable vicariously for a tort committed by its servant in the course of carrying out union activities. An action cannot be brought against the union either in the union's registered name or by a representative action.[60] However, a trade union is protected only where the tort is committed in contemplation of furtherance of a trade dispute. This phrase is examined below. However, given a trade dispute, a trade union is protected from all torts including not only the well known economic torts of conspiracy, inducing breach of contract or intimidation, but also other torts such as the tort of negligence or defamation. Thus, in *Momodu* v *Municipal and Local Authority Workers' Union* and *Ohikhena*,[61] the plaintiff's action for libel against the defendant union and its general secretary was struck out when, as the judge held, the publication of the alleged libel in the newspaper was done in contemplation or furtherance of a trade dispute.[62]

While it is clear that the section protects a trade union from an action for damages for a tort that has been committed there has been doubt as to whether it also prevents an action for an injunction to stop a threatened tort. In *Ware de*

[59] *Bussy* v *Amalgamated Society of Railway Servants & Bell* (1908) 24 TLR 437; *Vatcher & Sons Ltd.* v *London Society of Compositors* [1913] AC 107; *Adebola* v *Babayemi* (Unreported) Suit No. JD/12/63 High Court, Jos; *Boulting* v *Association of Cinematography, Television & Allied Technicians* [1963] 2 QB 606; *Ojo* v *Balogun & Ors.* (1980) 7-9 CCHCJ 261

[60] The decision of the Court of Appeal in *Jeje* v *Kadiri* [1987] 4 NWLR 460 that "both the union and its members were protected under section 21 of the Trade Union Act, 1973" is wrong.

[61] Unreported Suit No. B/57/68 High Court Benin City.

[62] The judge was, however, in error in holding that there was a trade dispute; see below; the judge was also in error in striking out the action as against the general secretary of the union; as we have seen the section protects the union itself and not individuals.

Freville v *Motor Transport Association*,[63] Scrutton L.J. thought that the unions are also protected from an action for an injunction to stop a union committing a tort although he felt he was straining the language of the Act in reaching that conclusion. The learned judge emphasized the word "action" which he held embraced an action for damages or an injunction and said that in any case the legislature could not have intended that action can be taken to stop a threatened tort for which no damages could be claimed if committed. And in *Boulting* v *Association of Cinematograph, Television & Allied Technicians*,[64] Lord Denning M.R. said that in deference to the great authority of Scrutton L.J. he would not, in such cases, grant an injunction but added that "Strictly speaking, those words do not forbid an action for an injunction in respect of a tortuous act which is about to be committed."[65] Upjohn and Diplock L.J. in the same case, agreed that Scrutton L.J's construction was not only a strained interpretation of the section as he himself admitted, but also that it entirely gave the "go-by" to the words "alleged to have been committed" in the section. Upjohn L.J. added: "I think the court it entitled to grant an injunction to prevent an apprehended injury, as it would in the ordinary case, and all the more so if the statute has provided that if in fact the tort is committed, he shall be left without remedy."[66] In *Bowles* v *Lindley*,[67] Atkinson J. said, *obiter*, that he would prefer to follow Upjohn L.J. rather than Scrutton L.J. However, in *Torquay Hotel Co. Ltd.* v *Cousins*[68] the English Court of Appeal upheld the view of Scrutton L.J. on the ground that that interpretation is in accord with the intention in enacting the section, to protect the funds of trade unions from being depleted by the payment of damages. This is because where an injunction is granted against a trade union and the injunction is disobeyed the only processes of enforcement would be monetary, that is, sequestration of the assets of the union or a fine.[69]

Section 23 does not, however, preclude the union itself suing for damages for any tort committed against itself.[70]

On the other hand, where there is no trade dispute or where a tort is committed but not in contemplation or furtherance of a trade dispute[71] section 23

[63] [(1921] 3 K.B 40, 78; see also the same view of Atkin L.J. at 92
[64] [1963] 2 Q.B 606
[65] Ibid. 629
[66] Ibid. 644
[67] [1965] 1 Lloyd's Rep 207
[68] [1969] 1 All ER 522.
[69] See Per Russell and Winn L.J.J. at 533 and 536 respectively, ibid.
[70] See *National Union of General & Municipal Workers* v *Gillian* [1946] KB 81
[71] See below for "in contemplation or furtherance of a trade dispute".

does not preclude an action against a trade union for damages.

Liability in tort

The liability of a union in tort is founded on the general principle of vicarious liability. Farewell J. said, at first instance, in *Taff Vale Rly Co.* v *Amalgamated Society of Railway Servants*[72] that:

> The acts complained of are the acts of the association. They are acts done by their agents in the course of the management and direction of a strike; the undertaking such management and direction is one of the main objects of the defendant society, and it is perfectly lawful; but the society in undertaking such management, undertook also the responsibility for the manner in which the strike is carried out.[73]

It is suggested that these words do not imply liability other than a vicarious one.[74] Thus, as we have seen, a trade union would be vicariously liable, only where it is shown both that i) the person who committed the tort was a servant or an agent of the union and ii) he was acting in the course of his union duties. The union constitution or rules book would assist in determining both issues.

In *Heatons Transport* v *Transport & General Workers' Union,*[75] the House of Lords had to decide whether the union was vicariously liable for the consequences of industrial action carried out by shop stewards. The House said no new development was involved in the laws relating to the responsibility of master or principal for the act of a servant or agent. In each case the test is the same, was the servant or agent acting on behalf of and within the scope of the authority conferred by the master or principal?[76] On the question of the authority of the servant or agent, Lord Wilberforce who delivered the judgment of the House said:

> The authority any be conferred 1) by the rules expressly or by implication 2) under the rules presumably by express or implied delegation 3) by virtue of

---

[72] [1901] AC 426

[73] Ibid. 431

[74] See also Romer & Stirling L.J.J. in *Giblan* v *National Amalgamated Labourers' Union of Great Britain & Ireland* [1903] 2 K.B 620, 623 respectively.

[75] [1973] AC 15

[76] Ibid., 99

> the office held…4) "or otherwise," which must include custom and practice, the course of dealing and the series of events which have happened in the particular case.[77]

In *Denaby and Cadeby Main Collieres Ltd.* v *Yorkshire Miners' Association,*[78] the supreme government of the union was vested in a council which consisted of the union officials and one delegate from each branch of the union. Each branch could call a strike. However, where a branch has called a strike, strike pay from union funds would be paid only "if the employers refuse to remedy their grievances and after all proper and peaceful means have been tried to effect a settlement by deputations from members with the advice and assistance of the council, and such member or members be permitted to cease work by the sanction of the association in accordance with the rules." The rules required sanction of a strike for strike pay by a plebiscite of the entire union.

At the *Denaby and Cabeby* collieries certain of those branches summoned a meeting at which it was decided to go on strike. When the union council learnt of the strike the next day it refused to give strike pay and advised the men to go back to work. In an action against the union the House of Lords held that no liability attached to the union. Lord Loreburn L.C. asked,

> can it be said in the face of these rules that the association is liable in damages for the action of delegates or branch officials or committees in procuring a strike (whether accompanied or not by breach of contract) without a ballot, without the sanction of the council and without a registered vote of the entire association?[79]

He answered that question in the negative. Lord James agreed with the Court of Appeal that no liability attached to the union central body because "…there is nothing to be found in the rules that makes the officers of the branches the agents of the central body, and also because (there is) no evidence from which it can be shown that authority was given to the branches to act…as such agents."[80]

---

[77] Ibid. 100
[78] [1906] AC 384.
[79] Ibid., 391
[80] Ibid., 405

Is section 23 constitutional?

In *Idowu* v *Dalamal Textile Mills Ltd. & 2 Ors*[81] the constitutionality of sections 21 and 46 (now 23 and 43 respectively) was raised, apparently, for the first time. The facts of the case are as follows. The plaintiff, Mr. A. F. Idowu and the 2nd and 3rd defendants, Messrs Olusegun Adebanyi and Sylvester Adeghibe, respectively were all three employees of the 1st defendant, *Dalamal Textile Mills Ltd.* All three were members of the Textile Garment and Tailoring senior staff Association, a registered trade union. The 2nd and 3rd defendants were respectively chairman and secretary of the local branch of the union and the plaintiff had once been its chairman. Members of the union at the 1st defendants place accused the plaintiff of anti-union activities and would not allow him to attend work without molestation. The plaintiff stopped going to work alleging suspension from work by the 1st defendant which evidence the court accepted. The plaintiff's employment was eventually terminated. He brought an action claiming a number of declarations, an order restraining the 2nd and 3rd defendant from preventing him from performing his duties and an order directing the 1st defendant to pay all the arrears of salary, which had accrued to him. The 2nd and 3rd defendants contended that the court could not entertain the action because of sections 21 and 46 of the Trade Unions Act. But the plaintiff argued that the two sections were inconsistent with sections 236, 42, 6, 33, 251 and 274 of the constitution and were, therefore, unconstitutional and void. The court said it was in agreement with this submission. It said "any law inconsistent with any provision of the constitution must be declared invalid by the Court. It is my view therefore that sections 21 and 46 of the Trade union Act 1973 are invalid, null and void." Unfortunately the court failed to either consider or show the inconsistency between either of the two sections and any or all of the constitutional provisions mentioned.[81a]

The view of the Court may be regarded as a mere *obiter dictum* especially with respect to section 21. There was no allegation that any tort was committed by or on behalf of the union and, indeed, the union was not a party to the action. So section 21 could not have been invoked. The action was primarily for breach of contract.[82] It was, therefore, clear that the Court had jurisdiction. However the decision raised a serious and, perhaps, a fundamental issue. If the opinion of the court is upheld it may undermine the basis of some aspects of our industrial

---

[81] Unreported Suit No. LD/500/89 High Court of Lagos State

[81a] Sections 236, 42, 6, 33, 251 and 274 of the 1979 Constitution are now sections 272, 46, 6, 36, 287 and 315 respectively of the 1999 Constitution.

[82] Only s.46 could possibly have been in issue as it could be argued that some of the claims made in the action were with respect to terminating (inducing) the contract of employment of the plaintiff.

relations unwittingly. It would become possible for trade unions and or their officials or members to be held liable for torts committed even in contemplation or furtherance of a trade dispute and their funds used to pay damages.[83]

In *Jeje* v *Kadiri*[84] in applying section 21 the Court of Appeal said that, having regard to the wording of the section, "it is a matter of ouster of jurisdiction of the court, not merely a statutory defence."[85] Whether or not it is correct to describe the section as a statutory defence, it seems clear that it is not an ouster of jurisdiction. Both the High Court and the Court of Appeal had and assumed jurisdiction in the case. Black's *Law Dictionary* gives a number of definitions of jurisdiction as follows: a term of comprehensive import embracing every kind of judicial action. It is the power of the court to decide a matter in controversy and presupposes the existence of a duly constituted court with control over the subject matter and the parties. Jurisdiction defines the powers of courts to inquire into facts, apply the law, make decisions, and declare judgment. The legal right by which judges exercise their authority. It exists when court has cognizance of class of cases involved, proper parties are present, and point to be decided is within powers of court. Power and authority of a court to hear and determine a judicial proceeding; and power to render particular judgment in question. The right and power of a court to adjudicate concerning the subject matter in a given case.

Neither section 23 nor section 43 would appear to be inconsistent with any of the provisions of the constitution mentioned above within the meaning of any of the above definitions of jurisdiction. In *Adediran* v *Interland Transport Ltd.*[86] the Supreme Court held that what section 6 (6) (b) of the constitution has done is to give unrestricted access to the court. As Karibi-Whyte, JSC, said: "The constitution of this country has vested in every person the right to bring actions before the courts for the determination of his civil rights and obligations. No other law can that away the exercise of such right."[87]

Clearly any statutory provision which seeks to bar access to the courts to have civil rights and obligations of persons determined would be unconstitutional. It does not seem, however, that either section 23 or 43 has that effect. The sections do not bar access to the courts. They grant immunity to trade

---

[83] Although, even now, the defences under sections 23 and 43 may not be allowed by the courts where a tort is committed in carrying out a strike action since strikes have been made unlawful; however, torts may be committed outside strike actions but within trade dispute.

[84] [1987] 4 NWLR 460.

[85] Ibid., 469

[86] [1991] 9 NWLR 155

[87] Ibid., 181

unions or their officers in certain circumstances. These circumstances have to be established in the courts. A plaintiff who alleges he has suffered damages as a result of a tort committed by a trade union or a union official is not precluded by either section from going to court to have his rights determined. And for the defendant to avail himself of the protection offered by either section he has to prove that the tort was committed in contemplation or furtherance of a trade dispute. In considering all of these the court would be determining the civil rights and obligations of the parties. The court will not only decide on the facts but must also rely on the relevant statutory provisions and courts decisions. If the court finds that there is no trade dispute or that, there being a trade dispute, but the tort was not committed either in contemplation or furtherance of it the court is at liberty to award the appropriate remedy. But where a tort is shown to have been committed in contemplation or furtherance of a trade dispute there is no liability. This reasoning has the support of the Supreme Court. In *Adediran* v *Interland Transport Ltd*[88] one of the issues before the court was whether the requirement at common law that, unlike in private nuisance a private plaintiff in public nuisance can only take an action as a relator survives section 6 (6) (b) of the constitution. Although the court held that the common law distinction between public and private nuisance with respect to the institution of actions does not survival the constitutional provision it said the common law distinction otherwise remains in determining the rights of the parties in such cases. In the words of Karibi-Whyte JSC, "The common law distinction between public and private nuisance is therefore not here applicable, in the institution of actions. It is however still essential in the determination of the right and the injury complained of."[89] In other words the constitutional provision has not altered the common law of nuisance.

The constitutionality of section 22 may, similarly, be upheld. On the surface value of the words of the section it could be interpreted to actually deny access to the court to enforce any of the matters mentioned in subsection (2) of the section. It is suggested, however, that this is not so. Before the court may decline to entertain any proceedings it has to decide whether such proceedings is instituted for the purpose of directly enforcing any of the stipulated agreements or for recovering damages for any breach of such an agreement.[90]

---

[88] Ibid., 469.

[89] Ibid., 181; emphasis is supplied.

[90] For cases on the scope of "directly" see *ante* Chapter 7

Civil conspiracy

There are two forms of the tort of conspiracy. Conspiracy as defined in *Mulcahy* v *R.*[91] and *Majekodunmi* v *R.*[92] is both a crime and a tort at common law but with the single and important difference that while the crime is complete in the agreement, civil conspiracy lies, in addition to the agreement, in doing the act agreed upon to the damage of the plaintiff. In this form, therefore, the tort is committed where two or more agree to do an unlawful act or to do a lawful act by unlawful means and the act is actually done to the injury or damage of the plaintiff. This is because civil conspiracy demands that there must be proof of damage to the plaintiff. As Lord Diplock said in *Lonrho* v *Shell Petroleum*,[93] "The gist of the cause of action is damage to the plaintiff; so long as it remains unexecuted, the agreement, which alone constitutes the crime of conspiracy, causes no damage; it is only acts done in execution of the agreement that are capable of doing that. So the tort, unlike the crime, consists not of agreement but of concerted action taken pursuant to agreement."[94]

In its second and general form, the tort resides not in any unlawfulness but in the purpose of the conspiracy. The decision in *Quinn* v *Leathem*[95] in 1901 is the earliest decision in which the fully developed tort in its general form was applied; or more accurately, it was in that decision by the House of Lords that the tort was finally established, although it was left to later decisions of the House to explain and clarify the real nature and, to a large extent, the boundaries of the tort in this general form. But the legal history of the tort may be said to have really begun about the middle of the nineteenth century. With the repeal in 1825 of the various Combination Acts, the English unions were supposed to have obtained freedom to carry on with labour matters with a minimum of statutory restrictions.[96] But, as it turned out, statutory restrictions only gave way

---

[91] (1868) LR 3HL 306
[92] (1952) 14 WACA 64.
[93] [1981] 2 All ER 456
[94] Ibid., 463
[95] [1901] AC 495
[96] Before 1824 workmen were subject to a number of statutory restrictions. They hardly had any say in the fixing of their wages. An Act of 1562, An Act containing divers Orders for artificers, labourers, servants in husbandry and apprentices, 5 Eliz C.4 repealed previous laws touching or concerning their hiring, working and wage but still provided for the fixing of wages by justices of the peace. An Act of 1799, an Act to prevent unlawful combinations of Workmen, 39 Geo 3 C106 provided that all contracts, covenant and agreements made or entered into by or between workmen concerning conditions of employment was to be illegal null and void. This Act was repealed in the following year by an Act of a similar name and purpose - 39 and 4(1 Geo 3 C106. It prohibited combinations of workmen. In 1824 an Act was passed to repeal the law which

to common law interference, and between 1825 and 1871 when the first trade union statute was enacted, "the tender mercies of the common law were (equally) cruel towards the union."[97]

In particular criminal conspiracy was used through the courts to hamper the activities of the trade unions. Thus, in 1851 S. 3 of the Act of 1825 was used to sustain a charge of criminal conspiracy against workmen who merely asked for increase in wages an exercise allowed by S. 4 of the Act.[98] In the Court of Queen's Bench[99] Lord Campbell said: "Here the offence consists in a conspiracy (which is a common law offence) to violate an act of Parliament."[100] Therefore when the Trade Union Act 1871 was passed S. 2 removed liability for criminal conspiracy. But that section was ignored in the following year in *R.* v *Bunn*,[101] when workers in a gas company who agreed to withdraw their labour unless a dismissed fellow employee was reinstated, were found guilty of common law criminal conspiracy. That decision led to the inclusion of S. 3 in the Conspiracy and Protection of Property Act 1875 reproduced verbatim in an amendment of our Criminal Code in S. 518A, with the object, once more of removing liability for criminal conspiracy, but this time from the area of trade dispute only. "At that time," said Lord Loreburn in 1906 "no one took any interest in the question of civil liability, and...there never had been any attempt to make out any civil liability. It was only criminal liability that was thought of when an amendment was being contemplated in the law of conspiracy."[102] When conspiracy resurrected it appeared in the form of civil conspiracy.

The English Court of Appeal decision in *Gregory* v *Duke of Brunswick*[103] where there was an agreement to hiss an actor has been much relied upon as authority for the tort of conspiracy.[104] But we must turn to the decision of the

---

prohibited the combination of workmen. The Act, 5 Geo 4 C95. provided, *inter alia*, that certain combinations of master and workmen should be exempt from punishment. S. 2 provided that workmen who entered into combinations to obtain better conditions of employment were not to be subject nor liable to prosecution for conspiracy. S. 5 however prohibited the use of violence. threats and intimidation in achieving those goals. The real liberty allowed by this Act was abused and in the following year the Act and many others were repealed. The freedom conferred under the 1825 Act, 6 Geo C129 was somewhat narrower.

[97] 116 Parl. Deb. 689.

[98] *R.* v *Rowlands* (1851) 5 Cox CC436

[99] (1851) Cox CC466

[100] Ibid., 489

[101] (1872) 12 Cox CC316

[102] 116 Parl Deb 689

[103] (1844) 8 M & G 953

[104] See per *Lord Esher and Lopes L.J. in Temperton* v *Rusell* (1893) 1 Q.B.D. 715 at 728-9 and 731 respectively and Lord Macnaghten in *Quinn* v *Leathem* [1901] AC 495, 510.

House of Lords in *Mogul Steamship Co.* v *McGregor, Gow & Co.*,[105] for *dicta* which foreshadowed the modern tort as finally established in *Quinn* v *Leathem*.[106] Although, the Mogul decision confirmed the right of everyone, whether as an individual or in combination with others, to pursue his business in the manner of his choosing, even with injurious consequences to others, so long as unlawful means are not employed, there were clear statements contained in some of the judgment which foreshadowed a *Quinn* v *Leathem* conspiracy. Indeed, in *Temperton* v *Russell*[107] the following year, one of the grounds of liability was conspiracy to injure, and the Court of Appeal relied heavily on the Mogul decision.[108] In *Allen* v *Flood*,[109] five years later, Lord Shand drew the important distinction that a combination of different persons in pursuit of a legitimate trade object occurred in the case of the Mogul Steamship Company, and was there held to be lawful. Combination for no such object but in pursuit really of a malicious purpose to ruin or injure another would, I should say, be clearly unlawful.[110]

It was left to the House of Lords to provide an authoritative decision in *Quinn* v *Leathem*.[111] The plaintiff, a butcher named Leathem, employed non-unionists. He was requested by the defendants, who were officials of a butchers' assistants union, to dismiss the men but he refused, although, he agreed to allow them into the union and promised to pay their admission fees and any fines. The defendants insisted that the men would not be admitted into the union and that they must "walk the streets for twelve months." Leathem still refused to discharge the employees. Whereupon, in order to put pressure upon him, the defendants approached one Munce, another butcher who for many years had been buying meat from Leathem, and warned him that unless he ceased buying from Leathem, his own men, who were union members would be called out. Munce consequently stopped dealing with the plaintiff who, as a result, suffered loss. He sued for conspiracy to injure him in his business. The House of Lords unanimously held the defendants liable but their Lordships differed a great deal in their reason for decision. Their rationes ranged from the very wide and vague ground given by Lord Lindley that a "threat to call men out given by a trade official to an employer of men belonging to the union and willing to work with

---

105 [1892] AC 25

106 [1901] AC 495

107 *Supra*

108 See per Lords Macnaghten and Lindley in *Quinn* v *Leathem*, ibid., at 509 and 535 respectively

109 [1898] AC1

110 Ibid., 168-9

111 [1901] AC 495

him is a form of coercion, intimidation, molestation or annoyance to them and to him very difficult to resist, and, to say the least, requiring justification,[112] to the more definite and modest one of Lord Shand. Lord Shand said: "...their acts were wrongful and malicious in the sense found by the jury - that is to say, they acted by conspiracy, not for the sole purpose of advancing their own interest as workmen, but for the sole purpose of injuring the plaintiff in his trade."[113] While it is unlikely that a jury or the court will to-day come to the same conclusion on the same facts it is clear that Lord Shand was here reiterating his view in *Allen* v *Flood,*[114] that a combination in pursuit of a trade object is lawful although resulting in injury to others, but a combination for no such object, but in pursuit of a malicious purpose to injure another, is unlawful. The other four law lords in essence based their judgments on a conspiracy to injure.

A quarter of a century later, the House of Lords had another opportunity to examine the matter. In *Sorrell* v *Smith,*[115] a union of newspaper retailers in enforcing a policy of limiting the number of retail newspaper shops in an area, procured the plaintiff, a member of the union, to withdraw his patronage from one Richie who was supplying papers to some newcomer retailers and from whom the plaintiff normally obtained his papers, and to transfer to another wholesale agent, Watson. Richie struck back by persuading the defendants, a committee known as Circulating Managers' Committee, to threaten to cut off supply of newspapers to Watson unless he stopped supplies to the plaintiff. Watson terminated supplies to the plaintiff. In an action for injunction to restrain the defendants from interfering with the right of the plaintiff to continue or enter into contractual relations with Watson and with his right generally to carry on business as he wished, Russell J. at first instance, expressed the view that *Quinn* v *Leathem*[116] decided that a combination to induce by threats a man's customer not to deal with him was, if damage results, actionable, unless there was justification and also that the decision did not turn upon the existence in the combination of an intention to injure the plaintiff. On appeal, the Court of Appeal, following its decision in *Ware de Freville* v *Motor Transport Association,*[117] held that an intention to injure was an essential element of the *Quinn* v *Leathem* decision. The House of Lords unanimously upheld the Court of Appeal although it held that the real purpose of the defendants was to promote

---

[112] Ibid., 538
[113] Ibid., 515
[114] Ibid. [1898] AC 1
[115] [1925] AC 700
[116] [1901] AC 495
[117] [1921] 3 KB 40

their business interests and not to injure the plaintiff. However, in what should clearly be regarded as an *obiter dictum,* Viscount Cave, in whose judgment Lord Atkinson concurred, seemed to favour a view of a general tort of wrongful interference. He postulated the following two propositions which he said are deducible from the House of Lords decisions in *Mogul Steamship Co.* v *McGregor; Gow & Co.,*[118] *Allen* v *Flood*[119]and *Quinn* v *Leathem*:[120]

> I deduce as materials for the decision of the present case two propositions of law, which may be stated as follows:
>
> 1) A combination of two or more persons willfully to injure a man in his trade is unlawful and, if it results in damage to him, is actionable.
> 2) If the real purpose of the combination is, not to injure another, but to forward or defend the trade of those who enter into it, then no wrong is committed and no action will lie, although damage to another ensures...[121]

Those propositions could be said to represent the law of civil conspiracy but his lordship added that:

> although, the proposition is confined to a combination of two or more, it does not necessarily follow that the existence of a combination is essential to the commission of the tort. There is some authority for the view that what is unlawful in two is not lawful in one, and that the circumstance that two or more persons combine to cause the injury, while it may be very relevant as evidence of the purpose and as an aggravation of the damage, is not itself an essential element in the cause of action.[122]

Lords Denedin and Buckmaster took the opposite view. Lord Dunedin branded as heresy opinions that the element of a combination was merely an incidental feature of *Quinn* v *Leathem.*[123] In 1942, in *Crofter Hand-Woven Harris Tweed* v *Veitch,*[124] the House decidedly came down on the side of Lord Dunedin. As Lord Wright said there: that the decision is *Quinn* v *Leathem* turned on conspiracy cannot now be doubted and must be accepted as the law.[125]

---

[118] [1892] AC 25
[119] [1898] AC 1
[120] [1901] AC 495
[121] [1925] AC 700, 712
[122] Ibid., 713
[123] [1901] AC 495
[124] [1942] AC 435.
[125] Ibid.

Apart, therefore, from damage which must be proved in order to sustain the action, the tort of conspiracy lies in the nature of the conspiracy itself. The test is to ask, what is the real object or purpose of the combination? If the real object of the persons who have agreed to carry out the act is to inflict damage on the plaintiff then the conspiracy is an actionable conspiracy if damage does in fact result.

> ....If there is more than one purpose actuating a combination, liability must depend on ascertaining the predominant purpose. If that predominant purpose is to damage another person and damage results, that is a tortious conspiracy. If the predominant purpose is the lawful protection or promotion of any lawful interest of the combiners (no illegal means being employed), it is not a tortious conspiracy, even though it causes damages to another person.[126]

The crucial issue upon which liability turns is, therefore, the true purpose, or if there are more than one purpose, the predominant purpose, of the combiners. If it is to promote or advance the lawful or legitimate interest of the combiners no ability lies, even though injury is caused to the plaintiff; but if the true or predominant purpose of the combination is to inflict injury on the plaintiff, and damage results, the tort is committed. In *Lonrho* v *Shell Petroleum,*[127] Lord Diplock stated, in a judgment with which' all the members of the House of Lords agreed, that:

> The civil tort of conspiracy to injure the plaintiff's commercial interest where that is the predominant purpose of the agreement between the defendant and the acts done in execution of it which caused damage to the plaintiff must I think be accepted by this House as too well-established to be discarded, however anomalous it may seem today. It was applied by this House eighty years ago in *Quinn* v *Leathem* (1901) A.C. 495 and accepted as good law in the Crofter case in 1942, where it was made clear that injury to the plaintiff and not the self-interest of the defendants must be the predominant purpose of the agreement in execution of which the damage-causing act were done[128]

The concept of legitimate interest is a dynamic one. It covers any "lawful interests"[129] including, of course, trade competition[130] and labour disputes.[131] It

---

[126] *Crofter Hand Woven Harris Tweed* v *Veitch* [1942] AC 435, 455 per Viscount Simon LC
[127] [1981] 2 All ER 456
[128] Ibid., 464
[129] *Crofter Hand Woven Harris Tweed* v *Veitch supra,* per Viscount Simon LC
[130] *Sorrell* v *Smith* [1925] AC 700; *Crofter Hand Woven Harris Tweed* v *Veitch, supra*

includes interests which may not necessarily be quantifiable in financial or other tangible form. Interest is not to be equated with material interests. In *Scala (Wolverhampton) Ltd.* v *Ratcliffe,*[132] the plaintiff, proprietor of the Scala Ballroom, maintained a colour bar policy which excluded black persons from the dance floor. The Musicians Union, of which the defendants were officials, and which included many black musicians in its membership, gave notice to the plaintiff that its members would not be permitted to perform at the ballroom so long as the obnoxious policy obtained. In an action for conspiracy it was held that the combination was to advance the legitimate interests of the musicians. It is most likely that the same view will now be taken of the facts in *Quinn* v *Leathem.*[133] The intention of the unionist to advance their interest is even more evident.

But, where, taking the examples given by Viscount Maugham, the object of the combination is a dislike of the religious views or the politics or the race or colour of the plaintiff, or a mere demonstration of power by busybodies, it is more likely that the true or predominant purpose is to injure the plaintiff.[134] As Lord Wright said, proof of malevolent feelings, coupled with proof that the combiners had in view no tangible benefit to themselves would clearly be enough to show that the combination was wrongful.[135] The facts in *Huntley* v *Thornton*[136] illustrate such a case. The plaintiff was a member of the union and was employed at Hartlepool. On the rejection of a wage claim the union called a strike which the plaintiff refused to join. He was summoned to attend before the Hartlepool District Committee of the union to defend himself. At this meeting, the Committee resolved and recommended expulsion of the plaintiff from the union to the Executive Council of the union for "refusing to carry out the instruction of the Executive Council and desire to place on record their disgust at the arrogant attitude adopted by him at the meeting." A second recommendation for expulsion was similarly rejected. The Committee then met and purported to expel the plaintiff for his disrespectful attitude towards the Committee. This was communicated to the executive council which, again, rejected it.

Meanwhile, the plaintiff, who had been ostracized, resigned his job and left Hartlepool to work at Bradford. Not being content with that arrangement he came back to seek employment at Hartlepool. Following his return, the secretary

---

[132] [1958] 3 All ER 220.

[133] [1901] AC 495

[134] *Crofter Hand Woven Harris Tweed* v *Veitch* [1942] AC 435, 451

[135] Ibid., 495

[136] [1951] 1 WLR 321

of the district committee, on the instruction of that committee, circulated among all shop stewards in the district a letter urging them to make efforts "in all factories where we have official shop stewards," to ensure that the plaintiff did not obtain employment and expressed their intention to withdraw labour from wherever he was given a job. The Secretary also wrote to one Thornton, the Secretary of the neighbouring district, Tees-Side, soliciting his help in preventing the plaintiff from obtaining employment in that district. The plaintiff managed to secure a job at a power station, in the Tees-Side district. Thornton then asked Langford, a shop steward at the power station, to oppose the employment and as a result of pressure from both Thornton and Langford the plaintiff was paid off. He then endeavoured to make peace with the Hartlepool district committee but his efforts were rejected. Instead he was informed that he had been expelled for arrears of contribution.

The plaintiff brought an action for conspiracy against Thornton, Langford and the Secretary and members of the Hartlepool District Committee. The court held that the conspiracy was to injure the plaintiff in his trade; it was not to promote any legitimate interest of the defendants. Harman J. agreed that it was arguable that in the early days of the dispute the members of the Committee honestly took the view that nothing but the expulsion of the plaintiff would uphold the prestige of the union. At that stage it may well have been that they were acting to advance their legitimate interests. But at the stage when it had become clear that the Executive Council would not countenance the expulsion "the District Committee had entirely lost sight of what the interests of the union demanded, and thought only of their own ruffled dignity. It had become a question of the District Committee's prestige; they were determined to use any weapon ready to hand to vindicate their authority, and grossly abused the quite frightening powers at their command.[137]

Inducing breach of contract

The decision of the House of Lords in *Merkur Island Shipping Corporation* v *Laughton*,[138] has established a third form, in addition to the two well known forms, of the tort of inducing breach of contract. Indeed, it may not be proper to call this third form a tort of inducing breach of contract since, as will be seen, unlike the two other types, it does not involve an actual breach of contract. The

[137] Ibid., 341.
[138] [1983] 2 AC 570

three forms may be stated as follows:

1. Knowingly and intentionally and without justification, to induce or procure one party to a contract to break the contract to the damage of the other party to the contract. In this form the tort may be referred to as the primary or *Lumley* v *Gye*[139] form. Here the interference with the contract is direct in the sense that it is directed to one party to the contract. In this primary form the tort has its origin in the old action which a master had against a defendant for enticing his servant away. In *Lumley* v *Gye*, in 1853, counsel for the defendant denied that an action for breach of contract extended beyond a master's right to bring an action for enticing away his servant. Even actions for enticing, he said, "are anomalies, having their origin in times when slavery existed; they are intelligible on the assumption that the servant is the property of his master; and although they have been continued long after all but free service has ceased, they are still confined to cases where the relation of master and servant in the strict sense exists."[140]

Colegridge J. agreed with that argument but the majority of the court, *Cromption and Eve J.J.*, rejected it. In *Randle* v *Nottidge*,[141] the *Federal Supreme Court* emphasized the difference between an action for inducing breach of contract and an action for enticing away a servant. Hubbard. Ag. F.J. said: "The two causes of action are not precisely the same, and the point is not merely academic…it should be remembered that the basis of the action for enticing away is the injury to the plaintiff's right to services and this right need not necessarily arise from a contract."[142] *Lumley* v *Gye*,[143] was applied in *Bowen* v *Hall*,[144] in 1881 and in *Temperton* v *Russell*,[145] in 1893. In the latter decision the principle of *Lumley* v *Gye* was held not to be confined to a breach of a contract of service but that it applies to a breach of any type of contract.

2. Knowingly and intentionally to procure the breach of a contract by one party to the contract to the damage of the other not by inducing that party directly

[139] (1853) 2 E & B 216.
[140] Ibid.
[141] (1956) 1 FSC 96
[142] Ibid., 97
[143] *Supra*
[144] (1881) 6 QBD 333
[145] [1893] 1 QB 715

but by employing some unlawful means whereby he is prevented or rendered unable to perform the contract.

In this form, the tort differs from its *Lumley* v *Gye* or primary form only in the manner of bringing about the breach of contract. It owes its origin to the Court of Appeal decision in *Thomson* v *Deakin.*[146] In that case the suggestion of counsel that the tort should be strictly limited to a *Lumley* v *Gye* situation was rejected. The court held that the tort could also take the form of or be extended to include, "indirect" interference whereby pressure is brought to bear, not directly on one of the contracting parties as in its primary form, but indirectly by means of an unlawful act as a result of which one of the contracting parties breaks the contract to the damage of the other.[147] "It seems to me" said Evershed, MR, in *Thomson* v *Deakin,*[148] "that the intervener, assuming in all cases that he knows of the contract and he acts with the aim and object of procuring its breach to the damage of B, one of the contracting parties, will be liable not only i) if he directly intervenes by persuading A to break it, but also ii) if he intervenes by the commission of some act wrongful in itself so as to prevent A from in fact performing his contract and also iii) if he persuades a third party, for example, a servant of A, to do an act in itself wrongful or not legitimate (as committing a breach of a contract of service with A) so as to render, as intended, impossible, A's performance of his contract with B." It will be seen that the Master of the Rolls' categories ii) and iii) come within unlawful means but it is category iii), breach of the contract of employment of the employees of one of the contracting parties, that is more commonly employed in industrial actions in procuring the breach of contract. This happens when union officials call their men out on strike and the pressure thus put on their employer induces him to break contract with the plaintiff. Jenkins L.J. explains this further:

> I would hold this form of actionable interference strictly confined to cases where it is clearly shown, first, that the person charged with actionable interference knew of the existence of the contract and intended to procure its breach; second, that the person so charged did definitely and unequivocally persuade, induce or procure the employees concerned to break their contracts of employment with the intent I have mentioned; third, that the employees so persuaded, induced or procured did in fact break their contract, of employment; and fourth, that breach of contract forming the alleged subject

[146] [1952] 1 Ch 646

[147] For the degree or extent of "indirectness" see below.

[148] *Supra*, 681

> of interference ensued as a necessary consequence of the breaches by the employees concerned of their contracts of employment.[149]

The learned Lord Justice added that the expression *necessary consequence* means that it must be shown that by reason of the withdrawal of the services of the employees concerned, the contract breaker was rendered unable, as a matter of practical possibility, to perform his side of the contract. In other words, by the use of the unlawful means, the defendant has produced a situation within which it is practically impossible for the party to the contract to carry out his part of the contract. This was what happened in *Stratford* v *Lindley.*[150] The plaintiff company carried on business by hiring out and repairing barges. Hirers or owners of barges send their own employees to take or deliver barges to the company and these employees belonged to the same union. Because a sister company of the plaintiff company refused to recognize the union, the union struck at the plaintiff company by instructing its members not to man, service or tow barges owned by the *plaintiff* company. It's business came to a standstill. The House of Lords held that the defendants, officials of the union, had procured branches of the hiring contracts between the plaintiff company and its customers by the use of unlawful means, that is by inducing the union members to break their contracts of employment with the company's customers.

3. It is possible to construct a new form of the tort from *dicta* of Lords Reid and Denning, the decision of the Court of Appeal in *Torquay Hotel Co. Ltd.* v *Cousins,*[151] and of both the Court of Appeal and the House of Lords in *Merkur Island Shipping Corporation* v *Laughton.*[152] As we have seen in either of the two forms of the tort already discussed, there must be actual breach of contract either by direct or indirect inducement. In *Stratford* v *Lindley,*[153] however, Lord Reid said: "I need not consider whether or how far the principle of *Lumley* v *Gye*[154] covers deliberate and direct interference with the execution of a contract without that causing any breach."[155] But Lord Donovan in the same case rejected the argument that there was a tort

---

[149] Ibid., 696-7
[150] [1964] 3 All ER 102
[151] [1969] 1 All ER 522
[152] [1983] 2 AC 570
[153] *Supra*
[154] (1853) 2 E & B 216
[155] [1964] 3 All ER 102, 106

consisting of some undefinable interference which fell short of inducing breach of contract. Such an argument, he said, was "novel and surprising."[156]

In *Daily Mirror Newspapers Ltd.* v *Gardner,*[157] Lord Denning M.R. said, "I have always understood that if one person interferes with the trade or business of another, and does so by unlawful means, then he is acting unlawfully, even though he does not procure or induce any actual breach of contract. Interference by unlawful means is enough."[158] In *Torquay Hotel Co. Ltd.* v *Cousins*[159] the Court of Appeal dealt with the matter further. The plaintiff company, a hotel, brought an action for an injunction to restrain the defendants, union officials, from causing a breach of a contract of supply of fuel by Esso. The contract contained an exception clause with respect, *inter alia,* to a labour dispute which prevented supply. This being so, could it be said that the union had threatened to cause a breach of contract? The majority of the court, Russell and Winn L.J.J. held that the exception clause did not prevent a breach of contract, it only provided a defence for the breach. "It is an exception from liability for non-performance rather than an exception from obligation to perform."[160] The Master of the Rolls, Lord Denning, however, sustained the action for injunction on a different basis. He said the exception clause would prevent the oil company from being in breach of contract but that the principle of *Lumley* v *Gye* extends not only to inducing breach of contract but also to preventing the performance of it. The new tort, he said, comprised three elements:

> First, there must be *interference* in the execution of a contract. The interference is not confined to the procurement of a *breach* of contract. It extends to a case where a third person *prevents* or *hinders* one party from performing his contract, even, though it be not a breach. Second, the interference must be *deliberate.* The person must know of the contract or, at any rate, turn a blind eye to it and intend to interfere with it.
> ...Third, the interference must be *direct.* Indirect interference will not do ... indirect interference is only unlawful if unlawful means are used.[161]

In *Merkur Island Shipping Corporation* v *Laughton,*[162] the House of Lords

---

[156] Ibid., 117
[157] [1968] 2 QB 768; see also *Emerald Construction Co Ltd* v *Lowthian* [1966] 1 WLR 691, 701.
[158] Ibid., 783
[159] [1969] 1 All ER 522
[160] Ibid., 534 per Russell L.J.
[161] Ibid., 530
[162] [1983] 2 AC 570.

unanimously upheld the existence of a tort of actionable interference with contractual rights without there being a breach of contract. Lord Diplock who delivered a judgment with which all the other members of the House agreed, quoted Lord Denning's first element of the tort with approval and said:

> that Jenkins L.J.[163] though using the expression *breach,* was not intending to confine the tort of actionable interference with contractual rights to the procuring of such non-performance of primary obligations under a contract as would necessarily give rise to secondary obligations to make monetary compensation by way of damages. All prevention of due performance of a primary obligation under a contract was intended to be included even though no secondary obligation to make monetary compensation thereupon came into existence, because the second obligation was excluded by some *force majeure* clause.[164]

It would seem that both direct and indirect interference with the performance of a contract is actionable where damage results. The various *dicta* of Lord Denning M.R. and that of Lord Reid, support direct interference being actionable. In the Merkur Shipping case the interference was indirect and by unlawful means that is breach of contract of employment of workmen. Indeed, the unlawful means employed there was some two remove from the commercial contract whose performance was interfered with but the Court of Appeal held that it made no difference. Dillon L.J. said, "I cannot for my part see any distinction in principle between indirect interference at the first stage and indirect interference at a second or remoter stage." The logic which led Jenkins L.J. to conclude that the tort, which had started in its primary form with direct interference, extended to indirect interference leads equally to the conclusion that an action lies for interference at a second or more remote stages, provided that Jenkins L.J.'s four conditions are satisfied.[165]

The elements which are common to all three forms of the tort are *knowledge, intention* and *damage.* It must be shown that the defendant knew of the existence of the contract and that he intended to induce or procure its breach or to interfere with its performance as the case may be. However, knowledge of the exact terms of the contract is not required. It is enough knowledge if the defendant has sufficient knowledge of the terms so as to know that he is inducing a breach of

---

163 In *Thomson* v *Deakin* [1952] Ch 646
164 [1983] 2 AC 570, 608.
165 Ibid., 588

contract.[166] Even constructive knowledge is enough.[167] In the words of Lord Denning: "*Even if they did not know of the actual terms of the contract, but had the means of knowledge which they deliberately disregarded - that would be enough.* Like the man who turns blind eye, so here, if the officers deliberately sought to get this contract terminated, needless of its terms... they would do wrong."[168] Where the contract is usual in a trade or business and the defendant in that trade or business would normally be conversant with it, he would be deemed to have knowledge of it. In the Merkur Island Shipping case the defendants who were senior officials of the International Transport Worker's Federation ITF were "deemed to have known of the almost certain existence of contracts of carriage to which the shipowners were parties."[169] In the House of Lords, Lord Diplock said there can hardly be any one better informed than ITF as to the terms of the sort of contracts under which ships are employed.[170] There must also be an intention to bring about a breach or to interfere with the contract. The absence of an intention to induce a breach was fatal to the plaintiff's claim in *White* v *Riley.*[171] *H*owever, a reckless disregard whether or not a breach will occur will suffice. As Diplock L.J. said in *Emerald, Construction Co.* v *Lowthian,*[172] The element of intent needed to constitute the tort is sufficiently established if it be proved that the defendants intended the party procured or induced to bring the contract to an end by breach of it if there were no way of bringing it to an end lawfully.[173] Lastly, there must be damage.[174]

The element of inducement or procurement of breach of contract is not free from difficulty. The difficulty is in determining what act amounts to inducing, procuring or persuading. As the Master of the Rolls, Evershed, said in *Thomson* v *Deakin,*[175] it is not always easy to distinguish what might be called persuasion, from what might be called advice, meaning by the later term, a mere statement of, or drawing of the attention of the party addressed to the state of facts as they

---

[166] *Stratford* v *Lindley* [1965] AC 269, 332 per Lord Pearce.

[167] *Emerald Construction Co. Ltd.* v *Lowthian,* [1966] 1 WLR 619; *Daily Mirror Newspaper Ltd* v *Gardner* [1968] 2 QB 762

[168] [1966] 1 WLR 691, 700-1

[169] [1983] 2 AC 570, 591 and approved by Lord Diplock at 608

[170] Ibid., 608

[171] Ibid. [1921] 1 Ch 1

[172] *Supra*

[173] Ibid., 704

[174] *Exchange Telegraph Co* v *Gregory & Co* [1896] 1 QB 147; *Bents Brewery Co Ltd* v *Hogan* [1945] 2 All ER 570.

[175] [1952] 1 Ch 646, 686

are. In *Thomson* v *Deakin*[176] itself, one ground for the decision was that, the breach of contract which occurred was not attributable to any act of the defendant which induced it. But where union officials resolve to call a strike and ask the union members to come out on strike, it seems clear that there is inducement. In *South Wales Miners' Federation* v *Glarmorgan Coal Co,*[177] resolutions by union officials as a result of which union members stopped work were held to be more than mere advice. Lord Lindley said:

> That there are cases in which it is not actionable to exhort a person to break a contract may be admitted and it is very difficult to draw a sharp line separating all such eases from all others. Bur the so-called advice here was much more than counsel; it was accompanied by orders to stop '(work),' which could not be disobeyed with impunity.[178]

There are two defences to the tort of inducing breach of contract, one being at *common* law and the other *statutory.* The common law defence of justification however seems available only against the tort in its primary or *Lumley* v *Gye* form.[179] Even then it is not very clear what will amount to justification for inducing a breach of contract. Absence of ill-will or the presence of good faith is not necessarily enough. In *Read* v *Friendly Society of Operative Stone Masons of England,*[180] Darling J. said it was not justification that those who induced the breach of a contract of apprenticeship acted in *bona fide* in their best interest nor was it enough that they were not actuated by improper motives. I think their sufficient justification for interference with plaintiffs' right must be an equal or superior right in themselves, and that not one can !egally excuse himself to a man, of whose contract he has procured the breach, on the ground that he acted on a wrong understanding of his own rights, or without malice, or *bona fide,* or in the best interest of himself, nor even that he acted as an altruist, seeking only the good of another and careless of his own advantage.[181]

Similarly, in *South Wales Miners' Federation* v *Glarmorgan Coal Company,*[182] where union officials acted in the honest belief that a stoppage of

---

176 *Supra*

177 [1905] AC 239

178 Ibid., 254

179 *Mogul Steamship Co* v *McGregor, Gow & Co* (1889) QBD, 613 per Bowen LJ; *Quinn* v *Leathem* [1901] AC 495, 510 per Lord Macnaghten,; *South Wales Miners Federation* v *Glarmorgan Coal Co* [1905] AC 239, 246.

180 [1902] 2 KB 88

181 Ibid., 96-7.

182 [1905] AC 239

work would benefit both the workmen and the employers, the court held there was no justification. The only one case in which the defence of justification has succeeded is *Brimlow* v *Casson,*[183] where the defendants acted not only in their own interest but also to protect public morality. The contract broken there was a contract under which a theatre manager paid his chorus girls such low wages that the girls had to resort to prostitution to supplement their wages. However, Russell J. pointed out that the courts cannot lay down a general rule as a general guide in such cases. Each case must therefore depend on its own facts.

The statutory defence is contained in S. 43 Trade Unions Act which also provides defences to the tort of intimidation. This tort will now be considered before S. 43

Intimidation

Where, by threats of an unlawful act, damage is caused to the plaintiff, an action for intimidation will lie at the instance of such plaintiff. *Garret* v *Taylor,*[184] is one authority of *respectable antiquity*[185] for the tort of intimidation. There the plaintiff had a lease of a stone quarry and the defendants, by threats of mayhem and vexatious suits against the plaintiff's customers and workmen, caused the customers to desist from going to buy and the workmen from going to work. Similarly, in *Tarleton* v *M'Gawley,*[186] the plaintiff's ship was lying off the Cameroon and after some Cameroonians had gone to the ship in a canoe for the purpose of trading and were returning, the master of another vessel fired cannon at the canoe killing one of the persons in it and thereby prevented further trading with the plaintiff.

A more modern authority is *Rookes* v *Barnard.*[187] The facts of the case are, briefly, as follows. The plaintiff was employed by the British Overseas Airways Corporation (BOAC) as a draughtsman as its London airport. The plaintiff and all the draughtsmen at BOAC belonged to the Association of Engineering and Ship-Building (AESB) union which maintained a one hundred per cent closed shop. There was an agreement between the union and BOAC a term of which was a "no-strike" clause. The plaintiff became dissatisfied with the union and

---

[183] [1924] Ch 302
[184] (1920) Cr. Jac. 567
[185] *Rookes* v *Barnard* [1964] 1 All ER 367, 384 per Lord Evershed
[186] 1793 Peake 270
[187] *Supra*

resigned from it. The airport branch of the union then passed a resolution that unless BOAC removed the plaintiff if he continued to refuse to re-join the union, the union will call out its members on strike. BOAC succumbed to the threat and first suspend the plaintiff on full pay and later terminated his employment by proper notice. The plaintiff brought an action against the union officials in that they had used unlawful means to threaten his employer as a result of which he had suffered damage. The unlawful means urged by the plaintiff was the threat of the officials, who were also employees of BOAC, to break their contract of employment.

Counsel for the defendants argued that the tort of intimidation comprehended only threats of criminal or tortuous acts and excluded a threat to break a contract. At first instance Sach J. agreed with the plaintiff and an appeal was taken to the Court of Appeal. There Pearson L.J. asked:[188] "Should this obscure, unfamiliar and peculiar cause of action which has its roots in cases of physical violence and threats of violence, be extended to cover a case in which there is only a threat to break a contract?" The court refused to so extend it. On appeal the House of Lords held that a threat that a contract will be broken fell within unlawful means for the purpose of the tort of intimidation.[189] Lords Evershed and Devlin relied on the no-strike clause which had been conceded to have become implied in the contracts of employment of the draughtmen including two of the defendants but the majority spoke in general terms which, it would seem, does not confine the decision to the no-strike clause. Lord Reid said:[190]

> Intimidation of any kind appears to me to be highly objectionable. The law was not slow to prevent it when violence or threats of violence were the most effective means. Now that subtler means are at least equally effective I see no reason why the law should have to turn a blind eye to them. We have to tolerate intimidation by means which have been held to be lawful, but there I would stop.

The Court of Appeal was once again faced with the same problem in *Morgan* v *Fry.*[191] The plaintiff and others broke away from the Transport and General Workers' Union and formed the Union of Port Workers. The defendant Fry, an official of the Transport Union, gave notice to the employers that after a certain date all the members of the union would be instructed not to work with those

---

[188] [1962] 2 All E.R. 579, 608.
[189] [1964] AC 1129
[190] Ibid., 1169
[191] [1968] 2 QB 710

who formed the Port Workers union and other non-unionists. The employers then gave proper notice to the plaintiff to terminate his employment. He brought an action for damages for the tort of intimidation. The full implication of the *Rookes* v *Barnard* decision had to be faced by the court. The issue turned on the nature and effect of a strike notice. Was the notice given by the defendant Fry a threat of breach of contract by the employees who were members of the union of which Fry was an official? The orthodox view is that a strike notice of proper length takes effect so as to terminate the contract of employment.[192] A strike would therefore not involve breach of contract. It follows that a notice of sufficient length cannot be a threat of breach of contract.

But more recent views are that a strike notice is in fact always an indication of an intention to breach the contract of employment. In *Stratford* v *Lindley,*[193] Lord Denning M.R. stated this argument in this way:

> Suppose that a trade union officer gives 'strike notice.' He says to an employer: 'We are going to call a strike on Monday week unless you... dismiss yonder man who is not a member of the union...' Such a notice is not to be construed as if it were a week's notice on behalf of the men to terminate their employment, for that is the last thing any of the men would desire. They do not want to lose their pension rights and so forth by giving up their jobs. The 'strike notice' is nothing more or less than a notice that the men will not come to work. In short, that they will break their contracts... In these circumstances, the trade union officer, by giving the 'strike notice,' issues a threat to the employer. He threatens to induce the men to break their contracts of employment unless the employer complies with their demand. That is a threat to commit a tort. It is clear intimidation.[194]

Was there, therefore, intimidation in *Morgan* v *Fry*[195] The court said No. Lord Denning recoiled from his stand in *Stratford* v *Lindley*[196] for if that argument were correct, it would do away with the right to strike.[197] He and Davies, L.J. held that a "strike notice" of proper length does not amount to a threat of unlawful action nor does it terminate the contract. In the words of Lord Denning:

---

[192] *Allen* v *Flood* [1898] AC 1; *Santen* v *Busnach* (1913) 29 TLR 214; *White* v *Riley* [1921] 1 Ch 1
[193] [1965] AC 269
[194] Ibid., 285
[195] [1968] 2 QB 710
[196] [1965] AC 269
[197] [1968] 2 QB 710, 728

> The truth is that neither employer nor workmen wish to take the drastic action of termination if it can be avoided The men do not wish to leave their work for ever. The employers do not wish to scatter their labour force to the four Winds. Each side, is, therefore, content to accept a 'strike notice' of proper length as lawful. It is an implication read into the contract by the modern law as to trade disputes. If a strike takes place, the contract of employment is not terminated. It is suspended during the strike and revives again when the strike is over.[198]

Davies L.J. also accepted the suspension theory as the basis of the explanation of a strike notice.[199] Russell, L.J. felt that such a notification involves a breach of contract but that it ought not to be regarded, for the purposes of the tort of intimidation as constituting unlawful means. Russell L.J.'s view is, of course, not supportable in view of the decision in *Rookes* v *Barnard,* but, it is not clear that even the majority view can stand against that decision. In *Cummings* v *Charles Connell & Co. (Shipbuilding) Ltd.,*[200] the argument that a lockout, like a strike, merely suspends a contract of employment was rejected. The court held that a lockout, like a strike, amounts to a breach of contract.

Defences in Common Law

In *Morgan* v *Fry,*[201] Lord Denning M.R. said the courts have not yet been called upon to consider what part, if any, the common law defence of justification plays in the tort of intimidation. He suggested the possibility of such a defence when he said that if the plaintiff, Mr. Morgan, and others who shared his views and acted with him, "were really trouble makers who fomented discord in the docks, without lawful cause or excuse, then Mr. Fry (the defendant) and his colleagues might well be justified in saying the men could not work with them any longer."[202] But the other members of the court declined to express any opinion on a possible common law defence of justification.

---

198 Ibid.

199 For difficulties in the suspension theory, see Ken Foster, Strikes and Employment Contracts, 34 MLR 275.

200 1969 SLT 25

201 *Supra*

202 Ibid., 729

Statutory

Section 43 of the Trade Unions Act provides defences to both the torts of inducing breach of contract and intimidation. The section is as follows:

1) An act done by a person in contemplation or furtherance of a trade dispute shall not be actionable in tort on any one or more of the following grounds only, that is to say,

a) that it induces some other person to break a contract of employment; or

b) that it is an interference with the trade, business or employment of some other person or with the right of some other person to dispose of his capital or labour as he wishes; or

c) that it consists in his threatening that a contract of employment (whether one to which he is a party or not) will be broken; or

d) that it consists in his threatening that he will induce some other person to break a contract of employment to which that other person is a party

2) Nothing in subsection (1) above shall prevent an act done in contemplation or furtherance of a trade dispute from being actionable in tort on any ground not mentioned in that subsection.

Subsections 43(1)(a) and (b) are defences to the tort of inducing breach of contract and the tort of interference with a contract respectively while subsections 43 (1)(c) and (d) afford protection against the tort of intimidation. All the defences are available only when the tort is committed in *contemplation or furtherance of a trade dispute.* This formula is considered below:

Furthermore, the defences are limited in other respects. The courts have put such a construction on the words *ground only* that S. 43 may not afford a defence where any of the torts is committed by the use of unlawful means. In *Conway* v *Wade,*[203] Lord Loreburn indicated, *obiter*, "that if inducing is accompanied by threats or violence, the section does not give protection" for then there is some other ground of action besides the ground that it induces some other person to break a contract.[204] In *Rookes* v *Barnard,* the House of Lords unanimously affirmed that interpretation of the words on the ground only. The section does not countenance the use of tortuous means.[205] In the words of Lord

[203] [1909] AC 506
[204] Ibid.
[205] *Rookes* v *Barnard* [1964] 1 All ER 367, 405 per Lord Devlin.

Devlin[206]

> if the means of inducement are honestly persuasive and nothing more, the inducer commits the tort of inducing a breach of contract and nothing more. But if the means are slanderous or deceitful, he may commit also the tort of defamation or of deceit. Then if an action is brought, it will not be only on the ground of inducing a breach of contract but also on the ground of slander or deceit, and the section will not prevent it.

Going by that interpretation it means that S. 43 offers no defence where breach of a contract of employment is induced indirectly by the breach of employees of their contracts of employment or where a contract of employment is interfered with by the same means or in the case of indirect intimidation as in *Rookes* v *Barnard*[207] itself.

As we have seen, employees who go on strike commit a crime. Also, there is no doubt that a strike will also amount to civil conspiracy in its narrow form. It follows that, an indirect conduct will always be accompanied by both a crime and at least one tort. Section 43 (1) (a) will, therefore, offer a defence only where the tort is in primary or *Lumley* v *Gye*[208] form, that is direct interference as happened in *Camden Exhibition and Display Ltd.* v *Lynott.*[209] The defence is also confined to directly inducing only a breach of a contract of employment. It offers no protection against directly inducing breach of a commercial contract.

Now that a tort of unlawful interference with the performance of a contract seems established it may be that the defence provided in S. 43 (1) (b) will be called into action. As Lord Reid explained in *Rookes* v *Barnard*[210]

> Parliament had...to provide for the possibility that mere interference, if no justification were proved, would be held to a tort, and I think that what Parliament did in enacting the second part of S. 3 [(i.e. S. 43) (1) (b)] was to put in a provision which would be necessary to achieve their object if the law should go one way, but unnecessary if it went the other way.

The full potential of this defence has not yet been worked out by the courts. But we have seen that the subsection offers no protection where the interfering conduct is accompanied by any criminal, tortuous or other wrong. It could not,

---

206 Ibid., 403
207 [1964] 1 All ER 367
208 (1853) 2 E & B 216
209 [1966] 1 QB 555
210 *Supra*, 379-80

for example, avail the defendants in *Merkur Island Shipping Corporation* v *Laughton*,[211] where the interference with the contract was by unlawful means.

Subsection 43(1)(c) and (d) was intended specifically to reverse the decision in *Rookes* v *Barnard*[212] although, only to the extent that the contract threatened to be broken, that is the means employed in the intimidation, is a contract of employment. Thus, to threaten to break or to induce another to break a commercial contract is not protected. The defence is supposed to be available to unionists who threaten to break their own contracts of employment or union official who threaten to call their men out on a strike. However, it is not clear that the defence will succeed since a strike is unlawful.

In contemplation or furtherance of trade dispute

We have seen that the statutory immunities and defences provided by the Trade Unions Act and the Criminal and Penal Codes depend for their success, on showing that the conduct complaint of was committed in contemplation or furtherance of a trade dispute. It is vital, therefore, to determine the scope of this phrase which has been aptly described as the "golden formula". A trade dispute is defined as any dispute between employers and workers, or between workers and worker, which is connected with the employment or non-employment, or the terms of employment or conditions of work of any person.[213] Thus a trade dispute must have employees, at least, on one side of the dispute; a dispute between employer and employer is not a statutory trade dispute.[214] Worker, as has been discussed, means any employee. The definition of workmen under the repealed Trade union Act extended, expressly, to all employees "whether or not in the employment of the employer with whom a trade dispute arises." That clearly, covered employees who took sympathetic action.[215] It is believed that the present definition also covers employees who take sympathetic action since an employee is any person who had entered into or works under a contract with an employer. Where a trade union acts in behalf of its members with an employer or another trade union there may, nonetheless, be a trade dispute between workers and employers or between workers and workers. "It would be strangely out of

---

211 [1983] 2 AC 570

212 *Supra*

213 S 52 Trade Unions Act; S. 518 A(A) Criminal Code; S.96 Expl. 2 Penal Code

214 *Larkin* v *Long* [1915] AC 814; *Conway* v *Wade* [1909] AC 506, 517 per Lord Atkinson

215 *Conway* v *Wade*, *supra*, per Lord Loreburn

date to hold," said Lord Wright, "that a trade union cannot act on behalf of its members in a trade dispute, or that a difference between a trade union acting for its members and their employers cannot be a trade dispute."[216]

Also an employee does not cease to be so merely because he has been dismissed and is out of work or that he has been forced to take up other work.[217]

In addition, the dispute must have the required subject matter. It must be connected with one or more of the following subject matters: the employment or non-employment, terms of employment or conditions of work of any person. In *NWL Ltd.* v *Woods,*[218] the House of Lords held that all that is required is that the dispute be connected with one or more of the permitted subject matters. "If it be connected, it is a trade dispute, and it is immaterial whether the dispute also relates to other matters or has an extraneous, e.g. political or personal, motive. The connection is all that has to be shown."[219] Thus a dispute may be political or personal in character and yet be connected with, for example, the terms and conditions of employment. But the connection to the permitted subject matter must be a genuine one and not merely a sham. Where the alleged connection is a mere pretext or cover for another dispute which is in no way connected with any of the subject of a trade dispute there is no trade dispute. Thus the fact that a dispute has more than one connection does not necessarily rule out the existence of a trade dispute. As Lord Diplock has even said it does not "matter that the demand is made and the dispute pursued with more than one object in mind and that of those objects the predominant one is not the improvement of the terms and conditions of employment of those workers to whom the demand relates."[220]

This liberal approach to the question of connection casts some doubt on the correctness of some earlier decisions. Indeed, in *NWL Ltd.* v *Woods*[221] the House expressed some doubt about that aspect of its decision in *Conway* v *Wade*[222] to the effect that there was no trade dispute. Lord Scarman went as far as saying that - on the face of it, the dispute in the case was so connected.[223]

Huntley v *Thornton,*[224] the facts of which have been given, is more difficult

[216] *NALGO* v *Bolton Corporation* [1943] AC 166, 169; *Bird* v *O'Neal* [1960] AC 907; *Beetham* v *Trinidad Cement Ltd* [1969] AC 132
[217] *Ferguson* v *O'Gorman* (1937) IR 620 per Meredith J
[218] [1979] 1 WLR 1294
[219] Ibid.
[220] Ibid., 1304
[221] *Supra*
[222] [1909] AC 506
[223] [1979] 1 WLR 1294, 1313
[224] [1957] 1 WLR 321

to evaluate in the light of this new approach. Perhaps, the court was right in holding that the trade dispute which existed in the early stages of the dispute soon lost the necessary connection. As Harman J. said: "The dispute, if it could be so called, had become an internecine struggle between members of the union and no interests of the trade were involved. It was a personal matter."[225] Cases in which an employee has been dismissed by the employer as a result of union pressure because the employee refused to join the union have been held to involve trade dispute.[226]

Recognition disputes have also been held to be trade disputes.[227] As Lord Denning said in delivering the judgement of the Board in *Beetham* v *Trinidad Cement Ltd.*,[228] if the union were able to obtain bargaining status it would be able to promote the interests of its members far better than if it were unrecognized. Although, the recognition of trade unions by employers is compulsory, the only sanction provided for non recognition is a fine on conviction. Recognition disputes can, therefore, still arise. Lord Pearce said in *Stratford* v *Lindley,*[229] that "when a union makes a genuine claim on the employers for bargaining status with a view to regulating or improving the conditions or pay of their workmen and the employers reject the claim, a trade dispute is in contemplation even though no active dispute has yet arisen."

In *Stratford* v *Lindley,*[230] two unions acting jointly on behalf of their respective members, tried for some years to open negotiations as bargaining partners with the employer of their members. The employer refused on all occasions to negotiate. When later one of the two unions which had about ninety per cent of the employees in its membership made a unilateral approach to the employer it was granted bargaining status. The other union, without making its own approach for recognition struck at the employer. The House of Lords held there was no trade dispute. The reason for this seemed to be that the union did not ask the employer whether it had changed its mind as it had done with the other union.

In *Momodu* v *Municipal and Local Authority Workers' Union & Ohikhena,*[231] the dispute was, clearly, union rivalry and did not appear connected with any of the permitted subject matters as the judge held. The judge found

---

[225] Ibid., 350.
[226] *Hodges* v *Webb* [1920] 2 Ch 70; *White* v *Riley* [1921] 1 Ch 1.
[227] *Beetham* v *Trinidad Cement Ltd* [1960] AC 135
[228] Ibid.
[229] [1964] 3 All ER 102, 113.
[230] *Supra*
[231] Unreported Suit No B/57/68 High Court Benin.

"that there was great rivalry and dispute between the two unions, NULAS[232] and MULAWU[233] who were catering for the same class of persons and therefore fighting over membership, in which NULAS was being worsted." Paragraph 9 of the statement of claim in the libel suit brought by the plaintiff, who was the principal Secretary of the state branch of the NULAS, read in part as follows:

> plaintiff will lead both oral and documentary evidence to show i) that consequent upon the said publication the NULAS Midwest has, between said publication and December 1968 lost many members some of whom have since joined the 1st defendant; ii) that the 2nd defendant formed or was a party to the formation about 1964 of the now defunct Midwest NULAS, a trade union whose sole aim was to send the plaintiff and his trade union out of trade union business in Midwest by any means, fair or foul.

The absence of a necessary subject matter seemed clear.

Similarly, in *British Broadcasting Corporation* v *Hearn,*[234] the English Court of Appeal held there was no trade dispute. On account of South Africa's obnoxious apartheid policy a trade union asked the BBC to stop an intended live television broadcast via satellite of a football match which would be received in South African. Although the BBC refused to comply it was held there was no trade dispute. One of the judges said it was "a coercive action unconnected with a trade dispute. It is a self-created power of censorship."[235]

There must not only be a trade dispute but also the act complained of must have been done either in contemplation or in furtherance of such trade dispute. The test whether there is a trade dispute is an objective one. It is a question of the facts of each case. To act in contemplation of a dispute, the dispute must be imminent. As Lord Shaw said in *Conway* v *Wade*[236] the argument was well founded that the contemplation of such a dispute must be the contemplation of something impending or likely to occur, and that the words do not cover the case of coercive interference in which the intervener may have in his own mind that if he does not get his own way he will thereupon take ways and means to bring a trade dispute into existence. To contemplate a trade dispute is to have before the mind some objective event or situation, with those elements of fact or probability to which I have adverted, but does not mean a contemplation, mediation or

---

[232] Nigerian Union of Local Authority Staff.
[233] Municipal & Local Authority Workers Union of Nigeria
[234] [1978] 1 All ER 111
[235] Ibid., per Lord Denning MR
[236] [1909] AC 506, 522

resolve in regard to something as yet wholly within the mind and of a subjective character. Similarly, a dispute must be in existence for it to be furthered. A dispute exists whenever a difference exists and a difference can exist long before the parties become locked in combat.[237] But the test whether in fact the act was done in contemplation or furtherance of a trade dispute is a subjective one. Two recent decisions of the House of Lords make his abundantly clear. In *Express Newspapers Ltd.* v *Macshane*[238] Lord Scarman said:

> To contemplate a trade dispute is to have before the mind some objective event or situation ... but does not mean...something as yet wholly within the mind and of a subjective character" per Lord Shaw of Dunfermline in *Conway* v *Wade*. Likewise to further a trade dispute presupposes that a dispute exists. In either case, the court must ask itself whether a trade dispute as defined... is either imminent or actual, and unless it is, it cannot be said that the defendant acted in contemplation or furtherance of it. A fanciful suggestion of a dispute will not do: the defendant must have in mind an objective event or situation. It follows therefore that, once it is shown that a trade dispute exists, the person who acts, but not the court, is the judge of whether his acts will further the dispute. If he is acting honestly the law leaves to him the choice of what to do.

Duport Steels Ltd v *Sirs*[239] soon came up on appeal from the Court of Appeal. The House affirmed its decision in the *Macshane Case* and upbraided the Court of Appeal for its attempt to evade that decision. Lord Diplock said:[240]

> The test whether an act was done by a person in contemplation or furtherance of a trade dispute and so entitled him to immunity from a part of the common law of tort, is purely objective i.e., provided that the doer of the act honestly thinks at the time he does it that it may help one of the parties to a dispute to achieve their objectives and does it for that purpose, he is protected by the section.

---

[237] *Beetham* v *Trinidad Cement Ltd* [1960] AC 132
[238] [1980] 1 All ER 65, 78
[239] [1980] 1 All ER 529
[240] Ibid., 541

Index

www.ingramcontent.com/pod-product-compliance
Lightning Source LLC
Chambersburg PA
CBHW031318230926
51848CB00001B/6
9789782601162